Diabetic Cookbook for Beginners

1000+ Easy, Delicious and Healthy Recipes for the Newly Diagnosed | Includes 28-Day of Natural Meal Plan to Manage Type 2 Diabetes and Prediabetes Effortlessy

Judy Gambino

Copyright

All right reserved

The content contained within this book may not be reproduced, duplicated or transmitted without direct written permission from the author or the publisher.

Under no circumstances will any blame or legal responsibility be held against the publisher, or author, for any damages, reparation, or monetary loss due to the information contained within this book, either directly or indirectly.

Legal Notice:

This book is copyright protected. It is only for personal use. You cannot amend, distribute, sell, use, quote or paraphrase any part, or the content within this book, without the consent of the author or publisher.

Disclaimer Notice:

Please note the information contained within this document is for educational and entertainment purposes only. All effort has been executed to present accurate, up to date, reliable, complete information. No warranties of any kind are declared or implied. Readers acknowledge that the author is not engaging in the rendering of legal, financial, medical or professional advice. The content within this book has been derived from various sources. Please consult a licensed professional before attempting any techniques outlined in this book.

TABLE OF CONTENTS

Introduction 20
BREAKFAST RECIPES 29
1. TASTY BREAKFAST OATS.............................29
2. BASIL AND SAUSAGE FRITTATA 29
3. EGGS FLORENTINE WITH YOGURT SALSA 29
4. CRUSTLESS CAPRESE QUICHE......................29
5. EGGS A LA SHRIMP 30
6. CHEESE BREAD CUPS 30
7. CREAMY QUINOA WITH PEACHES................30
8. BERRY FRENCH TOAST STRATAS..................30
9. CREAMY APPLE CINNAMON STEAL-CUT OATMEAL 31
10. CHOCOLATE PANCAKE WITH STRAWBERRIES.............31
11. SHAKSHOUKA MEDITERRANEAN BREAKFAST 31
12. BREAKFAST CASSEROLE WITH SAUSAGE AND CHEESE 31
13. PANCAKES 32
14. MEDITERRANEAN TOAST 32
15. MEDITERRANEAN BREAKFAST EGG MUFFINS.............32
16. MEDITERRANEAN OMELETTE.....................32
17. ZUCCHINI AND TOMATO FRITTATA............32
18. BLACKBERRY GINGER OVERNIGHT BULGAR................33
19. MEDITERRANEAN BREAKFAST SANDWICH 33
20. EGGS WITH TOMATOES, OLIVES AND FETA 33
21. BREAKFAST BURRITO 33
22. MEDITERRANEAN BREAKFAST QUINOA 34
23. PANCAKES WITH BERRIES AND WHIPPED CREAM 34
24. MEDITERRANEAN FRITTATA.......................34
25. TASTY SOUFFLE' 34
26. HEALTHY SHAKSHUKA 34
COD NUGGETS 35
27. BAKED OATMEAL 35
28. CORN EGGS AND POPATO BAKE 35
29. PARMESAN AND ASPARAGUS FRITTATA.....35
30. CHEESE SOUFFLE' CASSEROLE 36
31. FRUIT CAKE OATMEAL................................36
32. DEVILED EGGS..36
33. SPINACH & BACON EGG CUPS....................36
34. 15 MINUTE LOW-CARB OATMEAL 37
35. BACON & EGG MUFFINS 37
36. BREAKFAST QUESADILLA............................37
37. ACORN SQUASH NESTS 38
38. JOHNNYCAKES AND PUMPKIN BUTTER 38
39. OVERNIGHT OATS 38
40. LOW-CARB STEAK BREAKFAST HASH 38
41. BACON BREAKFAST ENCHILADAS................39
42. BREAKFAST CUP OMELETTES 39
43. DIABETES-FRIENDLY SOURDOUGH FRENCH TOAST 39
44. OATMEAL RECIPE FOR DIABETIC CHILDREN................40
45. HEALTHY BREAKFAST SKILLET 40
46. COTTAGE CHEESE BREAKFAST BOWL (KETO, LOW CARB, DIABETIC FRIENDLY)......................................40
47. LOW CARB BREAKFAST BURRITOS 40
48. VEGETABLE PANCAKE | HEALTHY BREAKFAST | DIABETIC DIET 41
49. BUCKWHEAT APPLE MUFFINS....................41
50. HEALTHY SUGAR-FREE GRANOLA 41
51. EASY DIABETIC BREAKFAST: MIXED BERRY PARFAIT....42
52. HAM AND BROCCOLI FRITTATA 42
53. OAT RISOTTO WITH CHORIZO 42
54. SUGAR-FREE FRENCH TOAST......................43
55. UPMA 43
56. MUSHROOM SURPRISE 43
57. HIPPIE BREAKFAST PORRIDGE....................43
58. PANCAKES – DIABETIC FRIENDLY 44

59. MEXICAN-STYLE STEAK AND EGGS BREAKFAST 44
60. BREAKFAST BURRITO CASSEROLE 44
61. EASY SUGAR-FREE BREAKFAST SAUSAGE 45
62. LOW-CARB BREAKFAST SCRAMBLE 45
63. SWEET AND SMOKY BAKED EGGS 45
64. SMOOTHIE BREAKFAST BOWL 45
65. SOUTHWEST BREAKFAST QUICHE 46
66. POWER GRANOLA 46
67. SUMMER FRUIT SMOOTHIE 46
68. PUMPKIN APPLE PROTEIN BARS 46
69. GLUTEN-FREE BANANA BREAD 47
70. EGG AND AVOCADO TOASTS 47
71. DIABETIC BREAKFAST EGG CUPS 47
72. AVOCADO AND GOAT CHEESE TOAST 47
73. SLOW COOKER BREAKFAST CASSEROLE 48
74. ASPARAGUS FRITTATA 48
75. SPANISH POTATO OMELET 48
76. CHILAQUILES CASSEROLE 48
77. MUSHROOM SCRAMBLED EGGS 49
78. CRUSTLESS SPINACH QUICHE 49
79. MIXED GREENS WITH CRANBERRIES, BACON, AND WALNUTS 49
80. SPINACH AND PARMESAN EGG BITES 50
81. CRUSTLESS ASPARAGUS AND TOMATO QUICHE 50

SOUPS AND STEW 50

82. SLOW COOKER CHICKEN NOODLE SOUP 50
83. 3-ALARM CHILI 51

Vegetable Soup 51

84. ASIAN SOUP WITH SHREDDED CHICKEN AND RICE 52
85. STEAK AND MUSHROOM SOUP 52
86. SPICY TORTILLA SOUP 52
87. TURKEY MINESTRONE 53
88. EASY CREAM OF TOMATO SOUP 53
89. MOM'S CHICKEN SOUP WITH EGG WHITE MATZO BALLS 53
90. SPRING VEGETABLE SOUP WITH SCALLION AND DILL-FLECKED MATZO BALLS 54
91. HEARTY BUTTERNUT SQUASH SOUP 54
92. PASTA E FAGIOLI (PASTA AND BEAN SOUP) 55
93. FRUIT SOUP 55
94. MISO SOUP 55
95. COLD HERB SOUP 55
96. RED PEPPER SOUP 56
97. COLD PEACH SOUP 56
98. TOMATO-BASIL SOUP 56
99. BUTTERNUT SQUASH SOUP 56
100. 5-WAY CHILI 57
101. WHITE CHILI 57
102. SQUASH AND APPLE SOUP 58
103. WATERCRESS SOUP 58
104. MUSHROOM BARLEY SOUP 58
105. CUCUMBER BUTTERMILK SOUP 59
106. ARTICHOKE AND LEEK SOUP 59
107. CURRIED LIMA BEAN APERITIF SOUP 59
108. GREEK NAVY BEAN AND VEGETABLE SOUP 60
109. MEDITERRANEAN CHICKEN STEW 60
110. BEEF STEW (LOW-CARB) 60
111. CAJUN STEW 61
112. CHICKEN BARLEY SOUP 61
113. ALL-IN-ONE BURGER STEW 61
114. CAULIFLOWER ALMOND SOUP 61
115. SOUTHWEST WHITE BEAN STEW 62
116. NEW ENGLAND CLAM CHOWDER 62
117. ZESTY VEGETARIAN CHILI 62
118. BUTTERNUT SQUASH AND MILLET SOUP 63
119. CREAMY YELLOW SQUASH SOUP 63
120. SWEET POTATO MINESTRONE 63
121. ITALIAN PASTA SOUP WITH FENNEL 63
122. MOROCCAN LENTIL & VEGETABLE SOUP FOR DIABETICS 64

123. EASY-AS-PIE HOLIDAY SOUP 64
124. BROCCOLI & POTATO CHOWDER 64
125. VEGETARIAN CHILI WITH BROWN RICE 65
126. BUTTERNUT BISQUE 65
127. MUSHROOM & CHICKEN SKILLET 65
128. QUICK BROCCOLI SOUP 65

SALAD RECIPES 66

129. TOMATO CAPRESE SALAD 66
130. EGG SALAD 66
131. LETTUCE SALAD WITH HOT BACON DRESSING 66
132. ASPARAGUS-BERRY SALAD 66
133. POTATO SALAD 66
134. GRILLED ROMAINE AND ASPARAGUS SALAD 67
135. PARSLEY, PEAR, AND WALNUT SALAD 67
136. FALL HARVEST COLESLAW 67
137. CRUNCHY VEGETABLE SALAD 67
138. CREAMY CHOPPED CAULIFLOWER SALAD 68
139. SPINACH & WARM MUSHROOM SALAD 68
140. MIXED GREEN SALAD WITH GRAPEFRUIT & CRANBERRIES 68
141. MELON, TOMATO & ONION SALAD WITH GOAT CHEESE 68
142. THE ULTIMATE WEDGE SALAD RECIPE 69
143. CRISPY BRUSSEL SPROUTS QUINOA SALAD RECIPE ... 69
144. HARVEST SALAD 69
145. GREEK ORZO PASTA SALAD WITH LEMON VINAIGRETTE 70
146. CHUNKY STRAWBERRY SALAD WITH POPPYSEED DRESSING 70
147. WILD RICE SALAD WITH BLUEBERRIES AND HERBS ... 70
148. BUBBLY TACO SALAD BOWLS RECIPE 71
149. CHICKEN SALAD 72
150. AMBROSIA SALAD RECIPE 72
151. THE BEST MACARONI SALAD RECIPE 72
152. FRESH PEACH SALAD RECIPE WITH BASIL 72
153. SPICY SALAD RECIPE 73
154. CUCUMBER SALAD 73
155. MESSICAN SALAD 73
156. COBB SALAD 73
157. MORROCCAN CARROT SALAD 74
158. 5 LAYER SALAD 74
159. CUCUMBER MANGO SALAD 74
160. TUNA MACARONI SALAD 74
161. LAYERED MEXICAN SALAD 75
162. ARUGULA SALAD WITH SUN-DRIED TOMATO VINAIGRETTE 75
163. QUICK' ' N HEALTHY TACO SALAD 75
164. SANTA FE GRILLED VEGETABLE SALAD 75
165. AVOCADO AND BLUEBERRY FRUIT SALAD 76
166. CAPRESE SALAD 76
167. GINGER, ORANGE, AND SESAME DRESSING 76
168. GREENS AND BROCCOLI SALAD WITH POPPY VINAIGRETTE 76
169. BOUNTIFUL HARVEST VEGETABLE SALAD 77
170. ZUCCHINI RIBBON SALAD 77
171. GRAPE TOMATO SALAD WITH WHITE BEANS AND CUCUMBER 77
172. SPRINGTIME PANZANELLA 77
173. SIRLOIN STEAK ANTIPASTO SALAD 78
174. PEAR AND CRANBERRY SALAD 78
175. GREENS AND PEAR WITH MAPLE-MUSTARD DRESSING 78
176. CHICKEN AND SPINACH SALAD 78
177. CHICKEN AND CANTALOUPE SALAD WITH TOASTED PECANS 79
178. FRUIT SALAD WITH CREAMY BANANA DRESSING 79
179. MAIN-DISH MEDITERRANEAN SALAD 79
180. FENNEL WHEAT BERRY SALAD 79
181. APPLE-WALNUT SALAD WITH BLUE CHEESE-HONEY VINAIGRETTE 80
182. SPINACH SALAD WITH POMEGRANATE VINAIGRETTE 80
183. GARDEN PASTA SALAD 80

184. BROWN RICE, ASPARAGUS, AND TOMATO SALAD.... 80
185. SPINACH SALAD WITH BEETS.................................. 81
186. GREEN BEAN, WALNUT, AND BLUE CHEESE PASTA SALAD 81
187. HAM AND PINEAPPLE SALAD FOR ONE 81
188. WINTER FRUIT AND SPINACH SALAD..................... 81
189. COOL WHEAT BERRY SALAD 81
190. CUCUMBER YOGURT DRESSING 82
191. ASIAN VEGETABLE AND SOBA NOODLE SALAD 82
192. QUICK RAINBOW TORTELLINI VEGETABLE SALAD 82
193. LUSCIOUS LOBSTER SALAD 83
194. HOLD-THE-MAYO COLESLAW 83
195. GERMAN-STYLE POTATO SALAD 83
196. GRILLED ROMAINE AND ASPARAGUS SALAD 83
197. PARSLEY, PEAR, AND WALNUT SALAD 83
198. FALL HARVEST COLESLAW 84
199. CRUNCHY VEGETABLE SALAD WITH CHIPOTLE-RANCH DRESSING 84

DESSERT RECIPES 84
200. LEMON CHIFFON TOPPED WITH BERRIES............... 84
201. COCONUT PIE 84
202. TANGERINE PANNA COTTA 85
203. CINNEMON APPLE SAUTE' 85
204. MIXED BERRY SNACK CAKE 85
205. FUDGY BROWNIES 85
206. MAPLE AND CINNAMON PEACHES 86
207. GINGERBREAD BISCUITS 86
208. SESAME DATE AND ALMOND BALLS 86
209. FRUITY OAT BARS 86
210. BANANA SPLIT ICE CREAM PIE 87
211. FRUIT & NUT QUINOA 87
212. BEETS WITH HORSERADISH CREAM 87
213. BLUEBERRY CUPCAKES WITH CREAM CHEESE FROSTING 87
214. CHOCOLATE MINT SANDWICH COOKIES 88
215. PUMPKIN SPICE MINI DONUTS 88

216. MOCHA CRINKLE COOKIES..................................... 89
217. CHOCOLATE CINNAMON CAKE 89
218. EGGNOG SANDWICH COOKIES 89
219. CHOCOLATE-BAKED GRAPEFRUIT.......................... 90
220. BLUEBERRY BLISS... 90
221. PUMPKIN CUSTARD 90
222. CHOCOLATE CLUSTERS 90
223. SPLENDA FOUR INGREDIENT PEANUT BUTTER COOKIES... 90
224. SUMMER STRAWBERRY ORANGE CUPS 91
225. CAULIFLOWER PILAF 91
226. ANGELIC MACAROONS 91
227. APPLE CINNAMON GRILL 91
228. ANGELIC CUPCAKES 92
229. CHOCOLATE CHIP FROZEN YOGURT 92
230. ICE CREAM CAKE 92
231. FROZEN BERRY ICE CREAM 92
232. APPLE BUTTER ROLLS.. 92
233. APPLE PECAN SPICE SQUARES 93
234. APPLE-CHEDDAR SCONES 93
235. APPLE AND OATMEAL COOKIE CRUMBLE............. 93
236. GLAZED PLUM PASTRY 94
237. CHOCOLATE MOCHA PUDDING 94
238. RAISIN-APRICOT LOAF CAKE MIX 94
239. ORANGE AND APRICOT CHIFFON CAKE 94
240. ORANGE CUPCAKES WITH ORANGE-GINGER FROSTING 95
241. YOGURT LIME TARTLETS 95
242. BROWNED BUTTER SPRITZ COOKIES 96
243. DIABETIC SPICED BAKED APPLES RECIPE 96
244. DIABETIC MACAROON 96
245. AVOCADO ICE CREAM... 96
246. FLOURLESS CHOCOLATE CAKE 97
247. KETO CHERRY CHOCOLATE BROWNIES 97

AIR FRYER RECIPES..97

#	Entry	Page
248.	AIR-FRYER ROASTED VEGGIES	97
249.	MARINATED AIR FRYER VEGETABLES	98
250.	AIR FRYER VEGETABLES	98
251.	AIRFRIED VEGETABLES	98
252.	AIR FRYER VEGETABLES	99
253.	ROASTED AIR FRYER VEGETABLES	99
254.	AIR FRYER ROAST VEGETABLES	99
255.	AIR FRYER VEGGIES	99
256.	AIR FRYER "ROASTED" ASPARAGUS	99
257.	AIR FRYER VEGETABLES	100
258.	AIR FRYER CHIMICHANGAS	100
259.	AIR-FRIED SHRIMP	100
260.	AIR FRYER POTSTICKERS	101
261.	LUMPIA IN THE AIR FRYER	101
262.	CAJUN AIR FRYER SALMON	101
263.	AIR FRYER LEMON PEPPER SHRIMP	102
264.	AIR FRYER MEATLOAF	102
265.	AIR FRYER BAKED POTATOES	102
266.	AIR FRYER RIB-EYE STEAK	102
267.	AIR FRYER COCONUT SHRIMP	102
	SIDE DISH RECIPES	103
268.	BAKED PLANTAIN FOR DIABETICS	103
269.	MICROWAVE LIMA BEAN CASSEROLE	103
270.	POLISH CHILLED FISH IN HORSERADISH SAUCE	103
271.	COLORFUL VEGETABLE CASSEROLE	103
272.	SPINACH ALMOND CASSEROLE	104
273.	GREEK CHRISTMAS BREAD	104
274.	FRIED BROWN RICE FOR DIABETICS	104
275.	RICH-TASTING RED CLAM SAUCE	105
276.	BASMATI RICE PILAF	105
277.	MAKE-AHEAD MASHED POTATOES	105
278.	SAVORY BREAD DRESSING	105
279.	TURKEY GRAVY FOR DIABETICS	106
280.	DIABETIC STUFFED PEPPERS RECIPE	106
281.	ORZO STUFFED PEPPERS	106
282.	LEMON-PEPPER-GLAZED VEGGIE TOSS	106
283.	BLACK BEAN AND VEGETABLE ENCHILADAS	107
284.	ZESTY BROCCOLI SALAD	107
285.	EXOTIC AMARETTO MAROON CARROTS	107
286.	COUNTRY-STYLE COLLARD GREENS	107
287.	LUSCIOUS LENTILS	107
288.	DILL GREEN BEANS	108
289.	WHERE'S-THE-BEEF BEAN BURGERS	108
290.	INSTANT REFRIED BEANS RECIPE FOR DIABETICS	108
291.	SPICY BLACK BEAN BURRITOS	109
292.	DIABETIC SUMMER SQUASH SIDE DISH RECIPE	109
293.	ASPARAGUS WITH MUSTARD VINAIGRETTE	109
294.	BLACK BEANS AND RICE	109
295.	GINGER-CARAWAY CARROTS	110
296.	STIR-FRIED SNOW PEAS	110
297.	CORNY ZUCCHINI MEDLEY	110
298.	ARTICHOKE SANDWICH SPREAD	110
299.	SEASONED BRUSSELS SPROUTS	110
300.	GREEN BEAN AND RED PEPPER SAUTÉ	111
301.	BALSAMIC-BASIL SLICED TOMATOES	111
302.	TANGY STEAMED GREEN BEAN SALAD	111
303.	SQUASH AND CORN	111
304.	BLACK BEAN AND RICE RECIPE FOR DIABETICS	112
305.	GINGERED SNOW PEAS	112
306.	ROASTED WINTER VEGETABLE BLEND	112
	BEEF PORK AND LAMB	112
307.	ITALIAN STYLE PORK CHOPS	112
308.	PORK LOIN CHOPSTOPPED WITH PEACH SALSA	113
309.	MARVELOUS MEATBALLS	113
310.	MEATBALL SOUP	113
311.	TACO MEAT	113
312.	ORANGE CINNAMON BEEF STEW	114
313.	BEEF & PUMPKIN STEW	114
314.	PIE WITH MUSHROOMS, SMOKED CHEDDAR, BACON, AND SOUR CREAM	114

315. SLIGHTLY ITALIANO MEAT LOAF 115
316. STUFFED CABBAGE ROLLS 115
317. CHEESESTEAK LETTUCE CUPS 115
318. SLOW COOKER CORNED BEEF AND CABBAGE 115
319. SIRLOIN STEAK STRIPS.. 116
320. SPICY BEEF ROAST 116
321. CHIPOTLE CHEESEBURGERS 116
322. SIMPLE GRILLED LAMB CHOPS 116
323. ROAST LEG OF LAMB 117
324. ROASTED LAMB BREAST 117
325. MOROCCAN LAMB STEW WITH APRICOTS 117
326. SLOW COOKER LAMB CHOPS 118
327. GRILLED LEG OF LAMB STEAKS 118
328. EASY MEATLOAF 118
329. CLASSIC MEATLOAF 118
330. SALISBURY STEAK 119
331. LEEK AND PORK STIR FRY....................................... 119
332. HEARTY MEATBALL SOUP 119
333. ITALIAN PORK CHOPS 120
334. PORK CHOPS WITH ONION GRAVY 120
335. BLACKBERRY PULLED PORK SHOULDER 120
336. SLOW COOKER PORK TENDERLOIN 121
337. SMOPKY PORK CHOPS AND TOMATOES.................. 121
338. PORK CHOPS WITH APPLE STUFFING 121
339. INDONESIAN PORK TENDERLOIN............................ 121
340. ROASTED LEG LAMB 122
341. LAMB CHOPS CURRY... 122
342. GRILLED LAMB CHOPS 122
343. PORK AND CABBAGE 122
344. GLAZED HAM BALLS 123
345. CORNED BEEF BRISKET 123
346. STIR-FRYED BEEF & ZUCCHINI WITH PESTO 123
347. HEARTY POT ROAST 123
348. MUSHROOM AND WALNUT MEAT LOAF................. 124
349. GREEK STEAK WRAPS.. 124

350. BEEF STROGANOFF 124
351. GARLIC ROASTED RIB 125
352. BEEF STEW 125
353. MERLOT MARINATED BEEF KEBEB 125
354. BEEF AND BROCCOLI STIR-FRY............................... 126
355. GRILLED STEAK WITH SWEET PEPPER SALSA 126
356. SHREDDED BEEF FOR TACOS 126
357. SLOW COOKER CHIPOTLE BEEF STEW 126
358. BLACK PEPPER AND COFFEE STEAK 127
359. GARLIC AND LIME BEEF ROAST WITH CILANTRO PESTO
.... 127
360. SESAME BEEF STIR-FRY 127
361. BROILED DIJON BURGERS 127
362. BEEF GRAVY SUPREME 128
363. SMOTHERED BURGERS 128
364. LOW CARB CABBAGE ROLLS 128
365. BEEF & BROCCOLI 128
366. BEEF PECAN 129
367. BEEF STEW WITH PUMPKIN 129
368. CHEESEBURGER CASSEROLE 129
369. CHEESE CASSEROLE 130
370. CHILI BEEF 130
371. FILLET STEAK WITH DEEP-FRIED ONIONS 130
372. RIB OF BEEF 131
373. STEAK WITH MUSTARD SAUCE 131
374. BEEF FILLET WITH PORT 132
375. GRILLED FLANK STEAK WITH CUMIN AIOLI 132
376. ROAST BEEF MELT... 132
377. RED HOT SIRLOIN 133
378. HAMBURGERS... 133
379. KEEMA 133
380. LOW-CARB STROGANOFF STEW 133
381. MANDARIN BEEF SAUTE 133
382. MARVELOUS MEATBALLS 134
383. MEATBALL SOUP... 134

#	Recipe	Page
384.	NIGHTSHADE-FREE TACO MEAT	134
385.	BREAKFAST CASSEROLE	134
386.	BEEF TIPS IN CROCKPOT	135
387.	ORANGE CINNAMON BEEF STEW	135
388.	BEEF & PUMPKIN STEW	135
389.	PIE WITH MUSHROOMS, SMOKED CHEDDAR, BACON, AND SOUR CREAM	135
390.	SLIGHTLY ITALIANO MEAT LOAF	136
391.	STUFFED CABBAGE ROLLS	136
392.	TANGERINE-BEEF STIR-FRY	136
393.	PHILLY CHEESESTEAK LETTUCE CUPS	137
394.	LOW-CARB BEEF STROGANOFF	137
395.	INDIAN RED CURRY	137
396.	SLOW COOKER CORNED BEEF AND CABBAGE	137
397.	SIRLOIN STEAK STRIPS	137
398.	SPICY BEEF ROAST	138
399.	TERIYAKI KABOBS	138
400.	MEATLOAF	138
401.	BLEU BURGER	139
402.	CHIPOTLE CHEESEBURGERS	139
403.	GRILLED LAMB CHOPS WITH GARLIC AND HERBS	139
404.	GRILLED LAMB LOIN CHOPS WITH CORN ON THE COB AND GRILLED ROMAINE	139
405.	MOUSSAKA	140
406.	LOW CARB HAMBURGER HELPER	140
407.	SLOW-COOKED ROAST LEG OF LAMB	141
408.	LAMB SHANKS WITH BARLEY, GARDEN PEAS, AND MINT	141
409.	LIGHTER LAMB HOTPOT	141
410.	LAMB GYROS	142
411.	TURMERIC LAMB CHOPS WITH CRISPY POTATOES AND BROCCOLI	142
412.	ROASTED EGGPLANT WITH SPICED LAMB	142
413.	HONEY SPICED LAMB CASSEROLE	143
414.	JUICY LAMB BURGERS	143
415.	SHEPHERD'S PIE – DIABETIC FRIENDLY	143
416.	LAMB, SWEET POTATO, AND ALMOND SLOW-COOKED CURRY	144
417.	MOROCCAN LAMB STEW	144
418.	HERB-CRUSTED RACK OF LAMB	144
419.	DIABETIC BRAISED LAMB WITH CARROTS	144
420.	LAMB KEBABS WITH VERDANT SALSA	145
421.	GARLICKY MUSTARD LAMB CHOPS	145
422.	LAMB AND VEGETABLE STEW	145
423.	MAPLE AND SAGE PORK CHOPS	146
424.	STUFFED PORK TENDERLOIN	146
425.	MAPLE AND APPLE PORK CHOPS	146
426.	GRILLED PORK CHOPS WITH CHERRY SAUCE	146
427.	STUFFED PORK TENDERLOIN WITH COLLARD GREENS	146
428.	GRILLADES OF PORK	147
429.	CROCK-POT VEGETABLE SOUP	147
430.	JUMBLETTI	147
431.	BALSAMIC BEEF, MUSHROOMS, AND ONIONS	148
432.	KOREAN-STYLE BEEF AND PASTA	148
433.	STUFFED EGGPLANT	148
434.	CHEDDAR STUFFED BEEF BURGER	149
435.	GRILLED STEAK AND BLACK BEAN TACOS	149
436.	BEEF WITH CABBAGE AND CARROTS	149
437.	DIABETIC BEEF AND ARTICHOKE CASSEROLE RECIPE	149
438.	HOLIDAY STUFFED BEEF TENDERLOIN	150
439.	CALDO DE RES	150
440.	CHEF LALA'S GOODNESS PLATTER	150
441.	CRANBERRY-GLAZED PORK CHOPS	151
442.	SMOKED SAUSAGE PITA POCKETS	151
443.	FETTUCCINE AND VEGETABLE SALAD	152
444.	STIR-FRY BEEF AND SPAGHETTI	152
445.	BEEF AND BROCCOLI STROGANOFF	152
446.	CLASSIC BEEF STEW	153
447.	JALAPEÑO CHEESEBURGERS	153
448.	MINI MARINATED BEEF SKEWERS	153

- 449. APRICOT BRISKET 153
- 450. PORK STIR-FRY 154
- 451. DIRTY RICE 154
- 452. BEEFY BARLEY MUSHROOM SOUP 154
- 453. CHEESEBURGERS 155
- 454. GARLIC GRILLED BEEF BROCHETTES 155
- 455. SPICY PORK CHOP SUPPER 155
- 456. HASH BROWN BREAKFAST CASSEROLE FOR DIABETICS 155
- 457. BEEF MEATBALLS ON BOK CHOY NESTS ... 156
- 458. ESTOFADO DE BISTEC CON PAPAS 156

SMOOTHIES RECIPES 156

- 459. KIWI VANILLA YOGURT SMOOTHIE 156
- 460. DRAGON FRUIT SMOOTHIE BOWL 157
- 461. THE ULTIMATE GREEN SMOOTHIE RECIPE 157
- 462. PEACH SMOOTHIE (DIABETIC) 157
- 463. DIABETES-FRIENDLY CHOCOLATE CHIA SMOOTHIE RECIPE 157
- 464. LOWER CARB STRAWBERRY SMOOTHIE 157
- 465. BALANCED BLOOD SUGAR SMOOTHIE 157
- 466. SPINACH SMOOTHIE (LOW-CARB & GLUTEN-FREE) 158
- 467. PINEAPPLE KALE SMOOTHIE 158
- 468. BERRY DELICIOUS SMOOTHIE PACK 158
- 469. TROPICAL PARADISE GREEN SMOOTHIE PACK 158
- 470. CHOCOLATE PEANUT BUTTER & BANANA SMOOTHIE PACK 158
- 471. LOW CARB DIABETIC BREAKFAST SMOOTHIE 158
- 472. GREEN SMOOTHIE 159
- 473. AYURVEDIC DIGESTIVE TEA 159
- 474. SPICED CITRUS TEA 159
- 475. TROPICAL GREEN SHAKE 159
- 476. HONEYDEW AGUA FRESCA 159
- 477. MINT-GREEN TEA COOLERS 159
- 478. BANANA-BERRY SMOOTHIE RECIPE FOR DIABETICS 160
- 479. SIMPLE SPICED TEA MIX FOR DIABETICS 160
- 480. BLACKBERRY LEMONADE 160
- 481. BANANA RASPBERRY REFRESHER 160
- 482. CHOCOLATE HAZELNUT COFFEE 160
- 483. CANTALOUPE COOLER 160
- 484. TOFU BERRY SMOOTHIE 160
- 485. ORANGE SPICE COFFEE MIX 161
- 486. CHOCOLATE AVOCADO SMOOTHIE 161

DIABETIC SAUCES, DIPS, AND DRESSING 161

- 487. KETO RANCH DRESSING 161
- 488. CHEESY ARTICHOKE DIP 161
- 489. LOW CARB BBQ SAUCE 161
- 490. FAT-FREE HONEY MUSTARD SAUCE 162
- 491. CHICKEN MARINADE FOR GRILLING 162
- 492. HOMEMADE PESTO SAUCE: NUT FREE 162
- 493. SPICY GUACAMOLE 162
- 494. CHOPPED CHICKEN SALAD 162
- 495. MEDITERRANEAN ROASTED PEPPER DIP 163
- 496. TANGY SPINACH DIP 163
- 497. SOUTH-OF-THE-BORDER BEAN DIP 163
- 498. PARMESAN SPINACH DIP 163
- 499. ITALIAN-STYLE CAPONATA 164
- 500. SPRINGTIME DIP 164
- 501. CHEESY PARTY BAKE 164
- 502. CRANBERRY-NUT SPREAD 164
- 503. IN-A-WINK GUACAMOLE DIP 164
- 504. BOO-TIFUL BEAN DIP 164
- 505. SUN-DRIED TOMATO PESTO DIP 165
- 506. TANGY ONION DIP 165

DIABETIC FISH AND SEAFOOD RECIPES 165

- 507. CRUSTED SALMON 165
- 508. CLAM SPAGHETTI 165
- 509. COD GRATIN 166
- 510. FISH FILLET CRUSTED WITH CUMIN 166
- 511. HERB AND PARMESAN CRUSTED FISH 166
- 512. HALIBUT WITH VEGETABLES 166
- 513. CHIPOTLE SPICY FISH TACOS 167

514. ASPARAGUS WITH SCALLOPS 167
515. SESAME TUNA STEAK 167
516. SHRIMP CREOLE 167
517. TUNA BAKE WITH CHEESE SWIRLS 168
518. TILAPIA FILLET WITH FRUITY SALSA 168
519. MEDITERRANEAN TUNA CUPS 168
520. ROASTED SEA BASS 168
521. SHRIMP STEWED IN CURRY BUTTER 169
522. SAIGON SHRIMP 169
523. BASIL-LIME SHRIMP 169
524. SHRIMP IN BRANDY CREAM 169
525. SHRIMP IN CURRIED COCONUT MILK 170
526. SALMON IN GINGER CREAM 170
527. BUTTERED SALMON WITH CREOLE SEASONINGS 170
528. GLAZED, GRILLED SALMON 170
529. SALMON IN CITRUS VINAIGRETTE 171
530. MAKES 8 CAKES 171
531. EXTRA-CRISPY FISH WITH LEMON-DILL DIP 171
532. SALMON TERIYAKI 171
533. TUNA CASSEROLE 171
534. DILLY TUNA SALAD 172
535. GRILLED HADDOCK WITH PEACH-MANGO SALSA 172
536. SESAME SHRIMP AND ASPARAGUS 172
537. PARMESAN CRUSTED CATFISH 172
538. SPICY "FRIED" FISH FILLET 172
539. FRESH TOMATO AND CLAM SAUCE WITH WHOLE-GRAIN LINGUINE 173
540. HONEY-SOY BROILED SALMON 173
541. FETA-SPINACH SALMON ROAST 173
542. BARBECUED SEA-BASS 173
543. EASY TUNA CASSEROLE 174
544. DEVILED CRAB 174
545. FISH CAKES 174
546. SLOW-ROASTED SALMON 174
547. SALMON PATTIES 175
548. TRADITIONAL STOVETOP TUNA-NOODLE CASSEROLE 175
549. CRAB CAKES WITH SESAME CRUST 175
550. SMOKED SHRIMP AND CHEESE QUESADILLAS 175
551. CREAMY SHRIMP PIE WITH RICE CRUST 175
552. BARLEY-SPINACH-FISH BAKE 176
553. GRILLED SALMON WITH ROASTED PEPPERS 176
554. BAKED BREAD CRUMB–CRUSTED FISH WITH LEMON 176
555. BAKED RED SNAPPER ALMANDINE 176
556. A-TASTE-OF-ITALY BAKED FISH 177
557. SALMON CASSEROLE 177
558. SALMON HASH 177
559. BAKED SNAPPER WITH ORANGE-RICE DRESSING 177
560. SHRIMP MICROWAVE CASSEROLE 178
561. CRUNCHY "FRIED" CATFISH FILLETS 178
562. BAKED ORANGE ROUGHY WITH SPICY PLUM SAUCE 178
563. GRILLED TUNA WITH HONEY MUSTARD 179
564. SWEET ONION–BAKED YELLOWTAIL SNAPPER 179
565. STIR-FRIED GINGER SCALLOPS WITH VEGETABLES ..179
566. SCALLOPS AND SHRIMP WITH WHITE BEAN SAUCE 180
567. SMOKED MUSSELS AND PASTA 180
568. TUNA STEAKS 180
569. SALMON PINWHEELS 180
570. FISH AMANDINE 181
571. SALMON & ASPARAGUS WITH LEMON-GARLIC BUTTER SAUCE 181
572. CHINESE STEAMED FISH 181
573. SWORDFISH VERACRUZ 181
574. DIJON SALMON WITH GREEN BEAN PILAF 182
575. FISH PIE 182
576. TILAPIA 182
577. TROUT AND SPECIAL SAUCE 183
578. PEACH SALMON 183
579. SKILLET BARBECUED SALMON 183

580. BACON AND SALMON BAKE 183
581. CHEESY SALMON CASSEROLE 184
582. TUNA AND SPINACH BAKE 184
583. EASY SALMON OR TUNA PATTIES 184
584. SALMON CAKES 184
585. SALMON WITH LEMON LIME BUTTER 185
586. GRILLED GLAZED SALMON 185
587. GINGER MUSTARD FISH 185
588. AIOLI FISH BAKE 185
589. FISH AND ASPARAGUS WITH TARRAGON MUSTARD SAUCE 186
590. TRUITE AU BLEU 186
591. SEA BASS WITH TAPENADE CREAM SAUCE 186
592. CHILI-BACON SCALLOPS 187
593. GREEK ROASTED FISH WITH VEGETABLES 187
594. MOqUECA 187
595. HERBY MEDITERRANEAN FISH WITH WILTED GREENS & MUSHROOMS 187
596. GARLICY PEPPERED CREOLE SALMON FILLETS 188
597. LOW-CARB PARSLEY MASHED CAULIFLOWER WITH FISH CUTLETS 188
598. FISH PIE 188
599. BAKED FISH 189
600. TROUT AND GHEE SAUCE 189
601. CHAR-GRILLED FISH KEBABS WITH PESTO POTATOES 189
602. GRILLED SALMON 190
603. EASY LOW CARB BAKED FISH 190
604. SALMON & SHRIMP PASTA 190
605. SEAFOOD SAUSAGE GUMBO 190
606. CUMIN-CRUSTED FISH FILLETS 191
607. SALMON WITH CILANTRO-LIME SALSA 191
608. TARRAGON SEAFOOD PASTA SALAD 191
609. DILLED SALMON PASTA WITH ASPARAGUS 192
610. SUN-DRIED TOMATO SEASONED SALMON 192
611. GIRL CHEF'S GRILLED LOBSTER 192

612. GRILLED SEA SCALLOPS WITH A WATERMELON THREE-WAY & DANDELION GREENS 193
613. BLACKENED SHRIMP WITH TOMATOES AND RED ONION 193
614. SPINACH, CRAB, AND ARTICHOKE DIP 193
615. SOUTHERN CRAB CAKES WITH RÉMOULADE DIPPING SAUCE 193
616. SHRIMP CAPRESE PASTA 194
617. SCALLOP AND ARTICHOKE HEART CASSEROLE 194
618. BARBECUED SHRIMP OVER TROPICAL RICE 194
619. SHRIMP & CAPER VERMICELLI 195
620. SHRIMP AND WATERMELON CEVICHE 195
621. PESTO PASTA WITH SCALLOPS 195
622. HOT SHRIMP WITH COOL SALSA 195
623. FRESH GARLIC SHRIMP LINGUINE 196
624. WARM SHRIMP, ARTICHOKE, AND PARMESAN SALAD 196
625. SPICY FISH TACOS 196
626. GREEK FESTIVAL FISH 196
627. ALMOND CRUSTED FISH FILLETS 197
628. FLORENTINE FISH ROLL-UPS 197
629. FIESTA FISH TACOS 197
630. PEPPERED SHRIMP SKEWERS 197
631. SAUTÉED SHRIMP RECIPE FOR DIABETICS 198
632. SPICY SHRIMP APPETIZERS 198
633. TRIPLE-QUICK SHRIMP AND PASTA 198
634. CRAB SOUP 198
635. GREEK SHRIMP 199
636. CLASSIC GUMBO 199
637. SHRIMP AND BEET SMÖRGÅSOR 199
638. SHRIMP PO'BOY 199
639. FISH CREOLE 200
640. SEAFOOD KABOBS 200
641. PRIMAVERA FISH FILLETS 200
642. FISH WITH CHINESE GINGER SCALLION SAUCE 201
643. SEAFOOD KABOBS HAWAIIAN 201

644. SIZZLIN' CATFISH 201
645. FAST 'N' FIERY GRILLED CATFISH 201
646. SESAME-CRUSTED SWORDFISH 201
647. LOUISIANA BROILED CATFISH 202
648. ASIAN FISH 202
649. ENSENADA SHRIMP TOSTADAS..........................202

DIABETIC VEGETARIAN AND VEGAN RECIPES......202

650. STUFFED EGGPLANT..202
651. CREAMED SPINACH 203
652. SOUR CREAM MASHED POTATOES 203
653. ASPARAGUS BAKE 203
654. GLAZED CARROTS 203
655. BROCCOLI AND SQUASH MEDLEY 204
656. CREAMED PEAS AND MUSHROOMS 204
657. ASPARAGUS PEPPER STIR-FRY..........................204
658. SWEET POTATO CASSEROLE..............................204
659. TOMATO AND VEGGIE GAZPACHO 205
660. BULGUR, GRAPE, AND KALE SALAD..................205
661. ASPARAGUS AND EDAMAME SALAD 205
662. FRESH PEAS WITH MINT....................................206
663. VEGETABLE SOUP WITH SHIRATAKI AND EDAMAME 206
664. PORTABELLO MUSHROOM STROGANOFF 206
665. FRESH ASPARAGUS TOPPED WITH SUNNY-SIDE-UP EGGS...206
666. POTATO, BROCCOLI, AND FENNEL SALAD................207
667. SPINACH WITH GARLIC, RAISINS, AND PEANUTS.....207
668. SESAME SUGAR SNAP PEAS 207
669. BROCCOLI RABE SAUTE 208
670. BALSAMIC BRUSSELS SPROUTS 208
671. PARMESAN-CRUSTED HALIBUT WITH SPICY BRUSSELS SPROUTS 208
672. SPINACH SALAD WITH SEARED BOK CHOY, GINGER, AND CILANTRO 208
673. ROASTED BEET AND CARROT SALAD...............209
674. SPINACH, FETA, AND GRAPE TOMATO OMELET 209
675. VIETNAMESE PHO 209
676. CHICKEN SALAD STUFFED AVOCADO 210
677. GARLIC SNOW PEAS WITH CILANTRO 210
678. SPINACH VEGETABLE KUGEL 210
679. SAUTEED SPINACH WITH GARLIC............................210
680. LEMON ASPARAGUS AND CARROTS 211
681. GREEN BEANS WITH MUSHROOMS 211
682. BAKED STUFFED ONIONS WITH SPINACH FETA 211
683. SUGAR SNAP PEAS AND CARROTS 211
684. SPINACH SAUTE WITH MUSHROOMS 211
685. MARINATED ASPARAGUS, TOMATO, AND HEARTS OF PALM 212
686. ROASTED STUFFED PORTOBELLO MUSHROOMS WITH SPINACH-CILANTRO PESTO 212
687. GREEN BEANS AND RED ONION SALAD 212
688. ASPARAGUS WITH PINE NUTS AND PIMENTO 212
689. CORN AND TOMATO POLENTA 212
690. ROASTED ASPARAGUS..213
691. ASPARAGUS CHEF SALAD 213
692. COUSCOUS WITH VEGETABLES 213
693. ROMAINE, RED ONION, AND FENNEL SALAD WITH TART LIME DRESSING 213
694. SOOTHING CUCUMBER MINT SOUP 213
695. SAUTEED SPINACH 214
696. BROCCOLI WITH ASIAN TOFU 214

DIABETIC POULTRY (CHICKEN) RECIPES 214

697. CHICKEN MARSALA 214
698. BRAISE CHICKEN WITH WILD MUSHROOM.............214
699. CHICKEN STIR-FRY 215
700. HERB ROASTED CHICKEN 215
701. MANDARIN CHICKEN SALAD 215
702. TURKEY ENCHILADA 215
703. TASTY FIESTA TURKEY 216
704. ZETSY LIME TURKEY..216
705. WALNUT TURKEY MEATBALL IN TOMATO SAUCE ...216
706. BALSAMIC AND GARLIC CHICKEN THIGHS................217

707. SAUTEES CHICKEN WITH TEXAS SPICE RUB 217
708. SPICY CACTUS TURKEY 217
709. CHICKEN WITH GREEN CURRY SAUCE 217
710. BRAISED CHICKEN WITH ORANGE 218
711. BALSAMIC CHICJEN AND MUSHROOMS 218
712. LOW CARB TURKEY MEATLOAF 218
713. MARINATED CHICKEN 219
714. OVEN FRIED CHICKEN LEGS 219
715. OVEN BARBECUED CHICKEN 219
716. CHICKEN WITH FRESH HERBS 219
717. CHICKEN WITH MUSHROOMS IN A CHAMPAGNE CREAM SAUCE 219
718. HOT ITALIAN CHICKEN 220
719. TURKEY ROAST 220
720. TURKEY'N'EGGS 220
721. FRIED CHICKEN 221
722. FREACH CHICKEN 221
723. POULTRY TASTE-OF SUMMER CHICKEN 221
724. POULTRY SKINLESS ROAST CHICKEN WITH HERBS AND SPICES 221
725. PEPPER-LIME CHICKEN 222
726. TURKEY BURGER 222
727. CURRY CHICKEN 222
728. BLACK PEPPER CITRUS CHICKEN 222
729. LEMON SAGE TURKEY 223
730. ASIAN GRILLED CHICKEN BREASTS 223
731. BEER CHICKEN 223
732. INJECTOR CHICKEN BREASTS 223
733. CHICKEN KABOBS 223
734. SPANISH CHICKEN KABOBS 224
735. CHICKEN FINGERS 224
736. JALAPENO AND BACON CHICKEN BREASTS 224
737. GRILLED CHICKEN SALAD 224
738. GREEK CHICKEN 225
739. LEMON MUSTARD HERB CHICKEN 225

740. PINEAPPLE-ORANGE GRILLED CHICKEN BREASTS 225
741. HERBED CHICKEN AND BROWN RICE DINNER 225
742. WALNUT CHICKEN 226
743. CHICKEN AND MUSHROOM RICE CASSEROLE 226
744. EASY CHICKEN PAPRIKASH 226
745. CHICKEN AND BROCCOLI CASSEROLE 226
746. CHICKEN AND GREEN BEAN STOVETOP CASSEROLE 226
747. CHICKEN PASTA WITH HERB SAUCE 227
748. CHICKEN AND ASPARAGUS IN WHITE WINE SAUCE 227
749. CHICKEN KALAMATA 227
750. ROTISSERIE CHICKEN 227
751. GRILLED ROASTING CHICKEN 228
752. OVEN BARBECUED CHICKEN 228
753. OVEN FRIED CHICKEN 228
754. CHICKEN AND GARLIC 228
755. CHICKEN AND VERMICELLI, LOW-CARBED 229
756. CHICKEN WINGS IN PEANUT SAUCE 229
757. LEMON BAKED CHICKEN 229
758. DELICIOUS CHICKEN NUGGETS 229
759. CHICKEN WINGS AND TASTY MINT CHUTNEY 230
760. CHICKEN CHOWDER WITH YOGURT AND TOMATO 230
761. COUNTRY ROOT VEGETABLE AND CHICKEN 230
762. ZESTY CAULIFLOWER SALAD WITH CHICKEN DRUMSTICKS 230
763. CHICKEN BREASTS WITH PARMESAN AND PEPPERS 231
764. SPAGHETTI SQUASH AND CHICKEN SAUSAGE 231
765. CASHEW-BASIL PESTO COVERED CHICKEN WINGS .. 231
766. CHICKEN BREASTS FROM THE MEDITERRANEAN 231
767. ROAST TURKEY AND AN AVOCADO SAUCE 232
768. GORGONZOLA PANNA COTTA WITH CHICKEN 232
769. MEDITERRANEAN CHICKEN IN A HERB SAUCE 232
770. CHICKEN MEATBALLS 232
771. TASTY GRILLED CHICKEN WINGS 233
772. BAKED CHICKEN 233
773. TASTE-OF SUMMER CHICKEN 233

- 774. PARMESAN CHICKEN STRIPS 233
- 775. ITALIAN GRILLED CHICKEN 233
- 776. GRILLED TURKEY BREAST WITH BASIL & MOZZARELLA 234
- 777. CHICKEN SHAWARMA 234
- 778. CHICKEN LAAL MIRCH 234
- 779. GHEE ROASTED CHICKEN 234
- 780. CHICKEN SHEEKH KABAB 234
- 781. GRILLED CHICKEN & GARLIC PARSLEY LEMON SAUCE 235
- 782. SLOW COOKER BALSAMIC CHICKEN 235
- 783. CHICKEN SOUP 235
- 784. CHICKEN & KALE SOUP 235
- 785. DRUNKEN CHICKEN WINGS 236
- 786. ROAST CHICKEN WITH BALSAMIC VINEGAR 236
- 787. ORANGE-FIVE-SPICE ROASTED CHICKEN 236
- 788. GREEK ROASTED CHICKEN 236
- 789. CLASSIC BARBECUED CHICKEN 237
- 790. KOREAN BARBECUED CHICKEN 237
- 791. CHICKEN WITH BACON, CREAM, AND THYME 237
- 792. CINNAMON-SPICED LEMON CHICKEN 238
- 793. CHUNKY CHICKEN STEW 238
- 794. SKINLESS ROAST CHICKEN WITH HERBS AND SPICES 238
- 795. PEPPER-LIME CHICKEN 238
- 796. ORANGE-TANGERINE CHICKEN 238
- 797. CHICKEN PHILLY CHEESE STEAK SANDWICH 239
- 798. CHICKEN WITH LEMON GARLIC SAUCE 239
- 799. GREEK MARINATED CHICKEN 240
- 800. CHICKEN PICCATA 240
- 801. BAKED CHICKEN CORDON BLEU 240
- 802. PERFECT GRILLED CHICKEN BREASTS 241
- 803. HEALTHY CHICKEN PICCATA 241
- 804. CHICKEN, SHRIMP AND STEAK SKEWERS WITH SOFRITO 241
- 805. CHICKEN JAMBALAYA 242
- 806. CHICKEN WITH BEAN THREAD AND RICE NOODLES 242
- 807. CHICKEN FLORENTINE PIZZA FOR DIABETICS 242
- 808. CILANTRO POLLO ENCHILADAS 243
- 809. INDIAN BROILED CHICKEN....................................243
- 810. PENNY-WISE CHICKEN POT PIE 243
- 811. EASY CHEESY VEGETABLE CASSEROLE...................243
- 812. QUICK CHICKEN NOODLE SOUP 244
- 813. DIABETIC CHICKEN NOODLE SOUP RECIPE.............244
- 814. OVEN "FRIED" CHICKEN FOR DIABETICS 244
- 815. ALOHA CHICKEN 245
- 816. TWO-MINUTE TURKEY WRAP 245
- 817. DIABETIC CHICKEN, BROCCOLI, AND RICE BAKE RECIPE 245
- 818. BOW TIES WITH CHICKEN AND MUSHROOM SAUCE 245
- 819. CURRIED CHICKEN SALAD....................................246
- 820. ROSEMARY CHICKEN ORZO..................................246
- 821. SKILLET CHICKEN PICCATA 246
- 822. PESTO CHICKEN SALAD 246
- 823. HOISIN CHICKEN WITH ORANGE SAUCE 247
- 824. SPICY APRICOT GLAZED CHICKEN..........................247
- 825. "THINK THIN" CHICKEN GRAVY 248
- 826. CHICKEN DINNER SALAD WITH GREEN ONION DRESSING 248
- 827. CARIBBEAN CHICKEN SALAD 248
- 828. LIME GRILLED CHICKEN RECIPE FOR DIABETICS.......248
- 829. TERIYAKI CHICKEN DRUMMIES 249
- 830. SPAGHETTI SQUASH WITH CHUNKY TOMATO SAUCE 249
- 831. DIABETIC LEMON CHICKEN RECIPE 249
- 832. BASIL CHICKEN BITES...249
- 833. LOW-SODIUM HERB ROASTED CHICKEN RECIPE......250
- 834. EASY SOUTH-OF-THE-BORDER GRILLED CHICKEN FOR DIABETICS..250
- 835. SLOW-COOKED SOUTHWESTERN CHICKEN CHILI 250
- 836. ASIAN RAINBOW CHICKEN SALAD.........................250

837. MOROCCAN LEMON CHICKEN WITH OLIVES 251
838. WHOLE-GRAIN ROTINI WITH ASPARAGUS AND CHICKEN 251
839. CHICKEN WITH SPINACH AND ARTICHOKES 251
840. GRILLED BUFFALO CHICKEN TENDERS 252
841. CHOPPED ROASTED CHICKEN SALAD 252
842. PROVENÇAL LEMON AND OLIVE CHICKEN 252
843. CHICKEN AND SWEET POTATO CHILI FOR DIABETICS 252
844. EASY CHICKEN, SPINACH, AND WILD RICE SOUP 253
845. VEGETABLE-CHICKEN NOODLE SOUP 253
846. CHICKEN NUGGETS WITH BARBECUE DIPPING SAUCE 253
847. PROSCIUTTO, ASPARAGUS, AND CHICKEN PIZZA 253
848. ASPARAGUS AND CHEDDAR STUFFED CHICKEN BREASTS FOR DIABETICS 254
849. CREAMY BAKED CHICKEN WITH ARTICHOKES AND MUSHROOMS 254
850. GRILLED CHICKEN ADOBO 254
851. QUICK ORANGE CHICKEN 255
852. FAJITA-SEASONED GRILLED CHICKEN 255
853. GRILLED CHICKEN WITH CORN AND BLACK BEAN SALSA 255
854. ASIAN CHICKEN 255
855. LEMON PEPPER CHICKEN WINGS 255
856. GRILLED MARINATED CHICKEN 256
857. BARLEY AND SAUSAGE GUMBO 256
858. "PAPPARDELLE" OF CHICKEN WITH WINTER PESTO 256
PLANT BASET DIABETIC RECIPES 257
859. BANANA LOTION PIE CHIA PUDDING 257
860. CHICKPEA FLOUR SCRAMBLE 257
861. CARROT CAKE OVERNIGHT OATS 257
862. FRUIT-FILLED PROTEIN-PACKED OVER NIGHT QUINOA & OATS 257
863. COCONUT RICE PUDDING 258
864. SUPER GREEN AVOCADO SMOOTHIE 258
865. SUNBUTTER BAKED OATMEAL CUPS 258

866. AVOCADO EGG SALAD 258
867. BLUEBERRY FRENCH TOAST WITH BANANA MOUSSE 258
868. BLUEBERRY PANCAKES 259
869. BURRITO WITH SWEET POTATO 259
870. APPLE CINNAMON BAKED OATMEAL 259
871. CHAI SMOOTHIE BOWL 260
872. TEMPEH AVOCADO SANDWICH WITH HUMMUS.... 260
873. BANANA PROTEINS SMOOTHIE BOWL WITH HEMP AND CACAO 260
874. BLUEBERRY HEMP PEAR PORRIDGE 260
875. VANILLA BREAKFAST MILLET WITH APPLE 260
876. MATCHA SMOOTHIE BOWL WITH BANANA MILK ... 261
877. TACOS 261
878. CONGEE WITH SMOKED VEGETABLES AND TOFU ... 261
879. SCRAMBLED EGGS 261
880. AMARANTH POWER PUBS WITH HEMP SEEDS 262
881. OMELETTE WITH MUSHROOM 262
882. AQUAFABA GRANOLA WITH DATES (OIL-FREE) 262
883. PROTEIN MUFFINS 262
884. SPICY BUFFALO CHICKPEA WRAPS 263
885. CHICKPEA SUNFLOWER SANDWICH 263
886. RAINBOW "RAW-MAINE" TACO BOATS 263
887. QUINOA GADO-GADO BOWL 264
888. VEGAN "BLT" SANDWICH 264
889. GREEK GODDESS BOWL 264
890. CURRIED CAULIFLOWER, GRAPE, AND LENTIL SALAD 265
891. ABUNDANCE KALE SALAD WITH SAVORY TAHINI DRESSING 265
892. LOADED KALE SALAD 266
893. PORTOBELLO POT ROAST 266
894. TUNA SALAD 266
895. NO-BAKE CINNAMON APPLE POWER BARS 267
896. BLUEBERRY BRAN MUFFINS 267

897. WHITE BEAN AND ARTICHOKE VEGAN SANDWICH FILLING 267
898. CHEESE AND ONION CRISPY ROASTED CHICKPEAS ..268
899. SEEDY POWER COOKIES 268
900. MINT CHOCOLATE TRUFFLE LARABAR BITES 268
901. TRI COLORED BACKYARD PASTA SALAD 268
902. CHIPOTLE TOMATO RICE ENERGY BOWL 269
903. GREEN GODDESS BUDDHA BOWL 269
904. PISTACHIO TURMERIC RICE ENERGY BOW 269
905. MEDITERRANEAN EDAMAME QUINOA BOWL 270
906. NOURISH LENTIL BOWL 270
907. EDAMAME MASALA DARK BROWN BASMATI RICE BOWL 270
908. EGG SALAD SANDWICH 271
909. EASY GRILLABLE VEGGIE BURGERS 271
910. MAC 'N' CHEESE 271
911. MOROCCAN LENTIL-STUFFED EGGPLANT 272
912. GARLIC AND WHITE WINE PASTA WITH BRUSSELS SPROUTS 272
913. KALE SALAD WITH SAVORY TAHINI DRESSING 273
914. BUTTERNUT SQUASH VEGGIE PIZZA 273
915. YELLOW COCONUT CURRY WITH MANGO 274
916. BAKED QUINOA DARK BEAN FALAFEL 274
917. KALE SALAD WITH CRISPY CHICKPEAS 275
918. LENTIL SALAD WITH CURD CHEESE 275
919. BULGUR HACK CHILI 275
920. LIME PRAWNS ON WILD RICE 275
921. SWEET POTATO CURRY WITH PUMPKIN 276
922. PASTA WITH CHICKPEA SAUCE 276
923. SPICY TOFU WITH QUINOA AND AVOCADO SALAD .276
924. CHILI WITHOUT CARNE 276
925. TEXMEX SALAD 277
926. POBLANO AND PORTOBELLO FAJITAS 277
927. STUFFED PEPPERS WITH QUINOA 277
928. COLORFUL QUINOA SALAD WITH POMEGRANATE ..278
929. SALAD WITH SMOKED TOFU 278

930. EGGPLANT CAVIAR WITH BASIL PISTOU 278
931. POTATO CURRY WITH PUMPKIN 278
932. TOASTED CHARD WITH MACADAMIA CHEESE 279
933. COUSCOUS SALAD WITH SOY DIP 279
934. SWEET DESSERT TARTE FLAMBÉE 279
935. NO BAKE PROTEIN ENERGY BALL 279
936. FUDGE BROWNIES 280
937. POMEGRANATE MASGHATI DESSERT 280
938. VANILLA CUPCAKES 280
939. CHOCOLATE FUDGE TRUFFLES 281
940. CHOCOLATE AVOCADO COOKIES 281
941. AVOCADO CHOCOLATE MOUSSE 281
942. GOLDEN MYLK CHEESECAK 281
943. PEANUT BUTTER MUDSLIDE ICE CREAM 282
944. LEMON CAKE 282
945. BROWNIES 282
946. SEA SALT BUTTERSCOTCH TART 283
947. SIMPLE BECHAMEL SAUCE 283
948. MOZZARELLA AND CASHEW CHEESE SAUCE 283
949. SPICY CHEESE SAUCE 283
950. GREEN CHEESE SAUCE AND NACHO CHILE 283
951. HOMEMADE WORCESTERSHIRE SAUCE 284
952. TZATZIKI 284
953. SPICY MUSTARD 284
954. FISH SAUCE 284
955. CREAMY CUCUMBER HERB 284
956. HARISSA 285
957. CHEESE PASTE 285
958. TOASTED BANANA CARAMEL SAUCE 285
959. ROASTED RED PEPPER HUMMUS 285
960. QUESO 285
961. SUN-DRENCHED TOMATO SPREAD 286
962. MIXED HERBS WITH ALMONDS AND PEPITA PESTO 286
963. SPICY MARINARA SAUCE 286
964. DILUTED BANANA CARAMEL SAUCE 286

- 965. MAPLE WALNUT VEGAN CREAM CHEESE ... 286
- SNACKS ... 287
- 966. CUCUMBER SANDWICH BITES ... 287
- 967. SUMMER SQUASH RIBBONS WITH LEMON AND RICOTTA ... 287
- 968. GREEN BEANS WITH PINE NUTS AND GARLIC ... 287
- 969. CUCUMBERS WITH FETA, MINT, AND SUMAC ... 287
- 970. CHERRY TOMATO BRUSCHETTA ... 287
- 971. ROASTED ROSEMARY OLIVES ... 288
- 972. SPICED MAPLE NUTS ... 288
- 973. FIGS WITH MASCARPONE AND HONEY ... 288
- 974. PISTACHIO-STUFFED DATES ... 288
- 975. PORTABLE PACKED PICNIC PIECES ... 288
- 976. MEDITERRANEAN PICNIC SNACK ... 289
- 977. TOMATO AND BASIL FINGER SANDWICHES ... 289
- 978. GREEK YOGHURT WITH STRAWBERRIES ... 289
- 979. HERBED OLIVES ... 289
- 980. BACON-WRAPPED CHICKEN TENDERS ... 289
- 981. SWEET AND SPICY MEAT BALLS ... 289
- 982. GARLIC BREAD ... 289
- 983. CHOCOLATE BISCUITS ... 290
- 984. WHIPPED COCONUT CREAM WITH BERRIES ... 290
- 985. SOUS VIDE EGG BITES ... 290
- 986. PEPPERONI CHIPS ... 290
- 987. CHEDDAR BASIL BITES ... 290
- 988. ZUCCHINI CHIPS ... 291
- 989. EASY ALMOND BUTTER FAT BOMBS ... 291
- 990. GREEK ORANGE HONEY CAKE WITH PISTACHIOS ... 291
- 991. AVOCADO CHIPS ... 291
- 992. PEPPERONI PIZZA MOZZARELLA CRISPS ... 292
- 993. PARMESAN CRISPS ... 292
- 994. TOASTED SPICY ALMONDS ... 292
- 995. TOMATO BASIL SKEWERS ... 292
- 996. COLD FETA OLIVE SPREAD ... 292
- 997. FUN PICNIC SNACK ... 292
- 998. CREAMY BLUEBERRY ... 292
- 999. CHERRIES IN RICOTTA ... 293
- MEDITERRANEAN SPINACH CAKES ... 293
- 1000. CREAMY LENTIL CAKES ... 293
- 1001. ROASTED SQUASH WRAP ... 293
- 1002. OLIVE FETA-HONEY CAKES ... 293
- 1003. HAZELNUT COOKIES ... 294
- 1004. FETA-OLIVE CAKES ... 294
- 1005. ROOT VEGETABLE PAVE ... 294
- 1006. SPINACH AND ARTICHOKE PIZZA ... 294
- 1007. BREADSTICK PIZZA ... 295
- 1008. SUMMER DESSERT PIZZA ... 295
- 1009. PATRIOTIC TACO SALAD ... 295
- 1010. KALE BRUSCHETTA ... 296
- 1011. CARAMELIZED ONION & PEPPER VEGAN QUESADILLAS ... 296
- 1012. WAFFLED FALAFEL ... 296
- 1013. ARTICHOKES ALLA ROMANA (SERVES 8) ... 296
- 1014. MEDITERRANEAN WRAP ... 297
- 1015. SNACK CRACKERS ... 297
- 1016. FURIKAKE SNACK MIX ... 297
- 1017. APPLE CHEESECAKE SNACK BARS ... 298
- 1018. FRESH PARFAIT ... 298
- 1019. SPICED CARROT RAISIN BREAD ... 298
- 1020. PUMPKIN BARS ... 298
- 1021. EASY PEAR CRISP ... 299
- 1022. ROASTED PINEAPPLE WITH MAPLE GLAZE ... 299
- 1023. CARAMELIZED ONIONS AND BELL PEPPERS ... 299
- 1024. SWEET POTATO CASSEROLE ... 299
- 1025. KALE CHIPS ... 300
- 1026. MICROWAVE-BAKED STUFFED APPLES ... 300
- 1027. CARROT AND VANILLA CAKE COOKIES ... 300
- 1028. OATMEAL WALNUT CHOCOLATE CHIP COOKIES ... 300
- 1029. AVOCADO DETOX SMOOTHIE ... 300
- 1030. SWEET PUMPKIN PUDDING ... 301

1031. BEET SPINACH SALAD 301

1032. GRILLED AVOCADO IN CURRY SAUCE 301

1033. BROCCOLI CAULIFLOWER PUREE 301

1034. CAPRESE SNACK 302

    RECIPES A TO Z 303

Introduction

What Is Diabetes?

Diabetes is a disease that affects your body's ability to produce or use insulin. Insulin is a hormone. When your body turns the food you eat into energy (also called sugar or glucose), insulin is released to help transport this energy to the cells. Insulin acts as a "key." Its chemical message tells the cell to open and receive glucose. If you produce little or no insulin or are insulin resistant, too much sugar remains in your blood. Blood glucose levels are higher than average for individuals with diabetes.

There are two main types of diabetes: Type 1 and Type 2.

Diabetes is a disease that occurs when your blood glucose, also called blood sugar, is too high. Blood glucose is your primary source of energy and comes from the food you eat. Insulin, a hormone made by the pancreas, helps glucose from food get into your cells to be used for energy. Sometimes your body doesn't make enough or any insulin or doesn't use insulin well. Glucose then stays in your blood and doesn't reach your cells.

What Is Type 1 Diabetes?

When you are affected with Type 1 diabetes, your pancreas does not produce insulin. Type 1 diabetes, once called juvenile diabetes, is often diagnosed in children or teens. However, it can also occur in adults. This type accounts for 5-10 percent of people with diabetes.

What Is Type 2 Diabetes?

Type 2 diabetes occurs when the body does not produce enough insulin or when the cells cannot use insulin properly, which is called insulin resistance. Type 2 diabetes is commonly called "adult-onset diabetes" since it is diagnosed later in life, generally after 45. It accounts for 90-95 percent of people with diabetes. In recent years, Type 2 diabetes has been diagnosed in younger people, including children, more frequently than in the past.

Gestational Diabetes

Gestational diabetes develops in some women when they are pregnant. Most of the time, this type of diabetes goes away after the baby is born. However, if you've had gestational diabetes, you have a greater chance of developing type 2 diabetes later in life. Sometimes diabetes diagnosed during pregnancy is type 2 diabetes.

Pre-diabetes

This is a condition in which the blood contains high amounts of sugar, but the amount of sugar is not high enough to result in diabetes mellitus type 2.

Who's at Greater Risk?

As the incidence of diabetes grows, more is understood about the disease and who is at risk. Regular testing is recommended for anyone who:

- Has a family member with diabetes, especially type 2 diabetes.
- Is of African American, Hispanic American, Native American, Southeast Asian or Pacific Islander heritage.
- Has had gestational diabetes or a baby weighing more than nine pounds at birth.
- Leads a sedentary or inactive lifestyle.
- Has components of the "metabolic syndrome," which in- cludes abnormal blood lipids (high triglycerides and low HDL—or "good"—cholesterol), high blood pressure, obe- sity, insulin resistance and polycystic ovary syndrome in women.

Healthy Food Options

If you have diabetes or pre-diabetes, every calorie consumed on the diabetic diet is a crucial factor to the improvement of your health. The following are nutritious foods you can choose from:

Dietary Fiber:

You should eat foods rich in dietary fiber, such as wheat bran, whole-wheat flour, legumes (lentils, peas, beans, etc.), nuts, fruits and veggies.

Healthy Carbs:

Consume only the healthiest carbs, like low-fat dairy products, legumes (lentils, peas and beans), whole grains, veggies and fruits.

Healthy Fats:

These foods will support lowered cholesterol levels, such as peanut oil, olive oil, canola oil, olives, walnuts, pecans, almonds, and avocados.

Healthy Protein:

Fishes such as bluefish, sardines, tuna, mackerel and salmon are very rich in omega-3 fatty acids. Omega-3 fatty acids lower triglycerides (blood fats) which in turn keeps the heart healthy.

FOOD TO EAT

For type 1 diabetes:

- Nutritious foods with a high percentage of vitamins and minerals
- Healthy fats and proteins: beans, avocado, egg, meat
- Carbohydrates (after being cleared by the doctor)
- Fruits: Dry fruits, fresh grapes, berries, fresh juice, melons
- Vegetables: boiled potato, asparagus, corn, beetroot, carrot, cucumber, onion, tomatoes, celery, sprouts
- Whole grains: Brown rice, bran cereal

For type 2 diabetes:

- Complex carbs: Brown rice, whole wheat, oatmeal
- Fish: Salmon, herring, and mackerel are great sources for fatty fish
- Leafy green vegetables such as spinach, kale, carrots, cucumbers, onions, and tomatoes
- Cinnamon: a great way to improve insulin sensitivity
- Eggs: increases good HDL cholesterol
- Chia seeds: digestible carbs, also help in weight loss

Besides these, turmeric, Greek yogurt, nuts, extra-virgin olive oil, flaxseeds, apple cider vinegar, strawberries, garlic, and squash are great food items to prevent or check diabetes.

FOOD TO AVOID

- Sugary and aerated drinks
- Processed food laden with trans-fat
- White bread
- Pasta and Rice
- Artificial sweet cereals
- Flavored coffee
- Honey and Maple syrup
- Factory-packaged fruit juice

Signs and Symptoms of Type 2 Diabetes

Signs and symptoms of type 2 diabetes typically strengthen slowly. In fact, you may have type 2 Diabetes for years and not knowing it.

The symptoms are:

Frequent infections	Fatigue	Increased thirst
Slow-healing sores	Consistent urination	Increased in hunger
Unintended weight loss	Blurred Sight	Darkened skin, in the neck & armpits

Causes of Type 2 Diabetes

According to research type 2 diabetes forms when the physique becomes resis- tance to insulin or when the pancreas is unable to supply adequate insulin. Exactly why this happens is unknown, even though genetics and environmental motives, similar to overweight and inactive, seem to be contributing reasons.

How insulin works

Insulin is a hormone that comes from the gland established at the back of and under the belly (pancreas).

1. The pancreas secretes insulin into the bloodstream.
2. The insulin courses, empowering sugar to enter your bloodstream.
3. Insulin lowers the quantity of sugar on your bloodstream.
4. As your blood sugar level drops, so does the secretion of insulin out of your pancreas.

The position of glucose

Glucose — a sugar — is a foremost source of power for the cells that make up muscle mass and other tissues.

1. Glucose comes from two primary sources: meals and your liver.
2. Sugar is absorbed into the bloodstream, the place it enters cells with the aid of insulin.
3. Your liver stores and makes glucose.

4. When your glucose levels are low, comparable to when you haven't eaten in a even as, the liver breaks down saved glycogen into glucose to keep your glucose level within a usual variety.

In type 2 diabetes, this procedure doesn't work well. As an alternative of relocating into your cells, sugar builds up in your bloodstream. As blood sugar levels broad- en, the insulin-producing beta cells in the pancreas unlock more insulin, but ulti- mately these cells turn out to be impaired and are not able to make enough insulin to fulfill the body's needs. In the so much common type 1 diabetes, the immune system mistakenly destroys the beta cells, leaving the body with practically zero insulin.

Prevention of Type 2 Diabetes

Healthy lifestyle selections can help avoid type 2 diabetes, and that is real even if you could have diabetes in your family. If you happen to've already acquired a prognosis of diabetes, you need to use healthy lifestyle alternatives to help prevent issues. In case you have prediabetes, lifestyle changes can gradual or stop the development to diabetes.

A healthy lifestyle includes:

1. Taking Body Nutrients foods. Select foods slash in fat and calories and greater in fiber. Focus on fruits, vegetables and whole grains.

2. Activity. Aim for a minimum of 30 to 60 minutes of moderate physical activity — or 15 to 30 minutes of vigorous aerobic activity — on most days. Take a brisk everyday walk. Swim laps. If you can't fit in a long workout, spread your activity throughout the day.

3. Slim Down. If you're overweight, losing 5 to 10 percent of your body weight can reduce the risk of diabetes. To maintain your weight in a healthy range, focal point on everlasting changes to your eating and exercise habits. Encourage yourself via remembering the advantages of shedding weight, such as a healthier heart, more power and elevated vanity.

4. Avoiding being sedentary for long periods. Sitting nonetheless for long periods can broaden your chance of variety 2 diabetes. Try to get up every 30 minutes and move around for at least a few minutes.

1 Week

	BREAKFAST	LUNCH	SNACKS	DINNER
MONDAY	Breakfast Casserole with Sausage and Cheese	Asian Soup With Shredded Chicken And Rice	Pistachio-Stuffed Dates	Grilled Turkey Breast With Basil & Mozzarella
TUESDAY	Mediterranean Breakfast Egg Muffins	Squash And Apple Soup	Portable Packed Picnic Pieces	Greek Festival Fish
WEDNESDAY	Zucchini and Tomato Frittata	Chicken Salad	Mediterranean Picnic Snack	Asparagus And Edamame Salad
THURSDSAY	Blackberry Ginger Overnight Bulgar	Italian Style Pork Chops	Greek Yoghurt with Strawberries	Portabello Mushroom Stroganoff
FRIDAY	Breakfast Muffin Crostini	Tuna Pasta Salad	Cheddar Basil Bites	Asparagus With Pine Nuts And Pimento
SATURDAY	Breakfast Burrito	Turkey and Avocado Roll	Zucchini Chips	Apricots and Ice Cream
SUNDAY	Mediterranean Frittata	Broccoli-Cheese Baked Potato	Easy Almond Butter Fat Bombs	Pear, Celery, Latte and Grapes

2 Week

	BREAKFAST	LUNCH	SNACKS	DINNER
MONDAY	Eggs with Tomatoes, Olives and Feta	Asian Soup With Shredded Chicken And Rice	Avocado Chips	Injector Chicken Breasts
TUESDAY	Corn Eggs And Popato Bake	Grilled Romaine And Asparagus Salad	Pepperoni Pizza Mozzarella Crisps	Triple-Quick Shrimp And Pasta
WEDNESDAY	Zucchini and Tomato Frittata	Morroccan Carrot Salad	Parmesan Crisps	Mango, Cottage Cheese and Yogurt
THURSDSAY	Parmesan And Asparagus Frittata	Pork Loin Chopstopped With Peach Salsa	Tomato Basil Skewers	Sweet Potato Casserole
FRIDAY	Cheese Souffle' Casserole	Crusted Salmon	Fun Picnic Snack	Broccoli With Asian Tofu
SATURDAY	Spinach & Bacon Egg Cups	Pie With Mushrooms, Smoked Cheddar, Bacon, And Sour Cream	Mediterranean Spinach Cakes Beet Salad	Apricots and Ice Cream
SUNDAY	15 Minute Low-Carb Oatmeal	Asparagus Chef Salad	Roasted Squash Wrap	Pear, Celery, Latte and Grapes

3 Week

	BREAKFAST	LUNCH	SNACKS	DINNER
MONDAY	Breakfast Quesadilla	Asian Soup With Shredded Chicken And Rice	Hazelnut Cookies	Herbed Chicken And Brown Rice Dinner
TUESDAY	Acorn Squash Nests	Grilled Romaine And Asparagus Salad	Feta-Olive Cakes	Greek Shrimp
WEDNESDAY	Overnight Oats	Hearty Butternut Squash Soup	Spinach And Artichoke Pizza	Creamed Peas And Mushrooms
THURSDSAY	Blackberry Ginger Overnight Bulgar	Tangerine-Beef Stir-Fry	Caramelized Onion & Pepper Vegan Quesadillas	Couscous With Vegetables
FRIDAY	Bacon Breakfast Enchiladas	Cod Gratin	Waffled Falafel	Lemon Pepper Chicken Wings
SATURDAY	Breakfast Cup Omelettes	Chicken Marsala	Mediterranean Wrap	Chicken With Green Curry Sauce
SUNDAY	Diabetes-Friendly Sourdough French Toast	Broccoli-Cheese Baked Potato	Apple Cheesecake Snack Bars	Savory Italian Grilled Chicken

4 Week

	BREAKFAST	LUNCH	SNACKS	DINNER
MONDAY	Healthy Breakfast Skillet	Asian Soup With Shredded Chicken And Rice	Easy Pear Crisp	Chicken And Asparagus In White Wine Sauce
TUESDAY	Cottage Cheese Breakfast Bowl	Grilled Romaine And Asparagus Salad	Caramelized Onions and Bell Peppers	Spinach Salad with Pomegranate Vinaigrette
WEDNESDAY	Low Carb Breakfast Burritos	Tomato-Basil soup	Avocado Detox Smoothie	Primavera Fish Fillets
THURSDSAY	Diabetes-Friendly Chocolate Chia Smoothie	Cheesesteak Lettuce Cups	Beet Spinach Salad	Broccoli And Squash Medley
FRIDAY	Buckwheat Apple Muffins	Fish Fillet Crusted With Cumin	Grilled Avocado in Curry Sauce	Mediterranean Edamame Quinoa Bowl
SATURDAY	Breakfast Burrito	Herb Roasted Chicken	Broccoli Cauliflower Puree	Garlic And White Wine Pasta With Brussels Sprouts
SUNDAY	Mediterranean Frittata	Broccoli-Cheese Baked Potato	Caprese Snack	Baked Quinoa Dark Bean Falafel

BREAKFAST RECIPES

1. TASTY BREAKFAST OATS

Preparation 40 minutes
Serves 2 persons

Ingredients

- Quick-cooking oats – 1 ½ cups
- Brown sugar – ¾ cup
- Flaxseed meal – ¾ cup
- All-purpose baking flour (gluten-free) ½ cup
- Baking powder – 1 teaspoon
- Ground cinnamon – ½ teaspoon
- Salt – ¼ teaspoon
- Banana (mashed) – 1
- Rice milk – ¼ cup
- Egg – 1
- Vanilla extract – 1 teaspoon

Directions

- Begin by preheating the oven by setting the temperature to 360 degrees Fahrenheit.
- Take a baking pan and grease it lightly with butter.
- Take a glass bowl and add the brown sugar, oats, baking powder, salt, and cinnamon. Give it a nice mix.
- Take another bowl and add the rice milk, banana, vanilla extract, and egg.
- Mix well to combine. Transfer this prepared mixture into the sugar and oats mixture and mix well.
- Pour the prepared mixture into the greased baking pan.
- Place the baking pan into the preheated oven and bake for about 20 minutes.
- Cover the baking pan using a towel, as it will help the brownies hold the moisture. Let it sit covered for about 5 minutes.
- Cut it into 12 equal pieces and serve!

Nutrition Facts

Calories per Serving: 130 Cal Fat: 4.1g Protein: 3.3g Carbohydrates: 21g

2. BASIL AND SAUSAGE FRITTATA

Preparation 15 Minutes
Serves 4 Persons

Ingredients

- Fresh basil 0.25 cups Tomatoes 1 cup Green onion 0.5 cups
- Part-skim shredded mozzarella 1 ounce
- Egg substitute 1.5 cups Chicken sausage 8 ounces
- Extra virgin olive oil 2 teaspoons

Directions

- Pour the olive oil into a pan set over medium heat.
- Place the sausage into the pan and cook until it starts to brown, flipping it as needed.
- Pour the egg substitute into the pan, allowing it to evenly spread over the sausage, and cook for approximately 1 minute and then remove from the heat.
- Place the green onions, basil, cheese, and tomatoes on top and
- evenly.
- Cook until cheese melts and egg substitute is thoroughly cooked.

Nutrition Facts

Calories per Serving: 180 cal Fat: 8g Protein: 21g Carbohydrates: 19g

3. EGGS FLORENTINE WITH YOGURT SALSA

Preparation 20 Minutes
Serves 4 Persons

Ingredients

- 1 cup low-fat Greek yogurt Pinch of ground turmeric
- Juice of ½ lemon Pinch of cayenne pepper (optional) Fine-grained kosher salt, to taste
- 2 teaspoons white vinegar
- 4 eggs
- 2 whole-wheat english muffins
- 1 tablespoon unsalted butter

Directions

- Wilt the spinach by adding the entire bag and ¼ cup of water to a sauté pan. Cook over medium-low heat, covered, to steam for about 5 minutes. Press with the back of a spoon through a strainer to remove any excess water, and put spinach on a covered plate.
- In a medium bowl, whisk together the yogurt and turmeric until well combined, and then add in the lemon juice and stir. Stir in cayenne pepper, if desired. Season with salt. To poach the eggs, fill a medium sauté pan two-thirds full with water and add the vinegar.
- Over medium-high heat, bring the water to a low simmer, and then crack one egg at a time, add it to a small cup, and then slide it onto the surface of the water.
- Nudge the egg white with a spoon to keep it close to the yolk and prevent it from spreading out in the water. When one egg begins to firm slightly, slip in the next egg, until all the eggs are in the pan.
- Gently remove from the heat, cover the pan, and allow the eggs to sit for 3 to 4 minutes or so, until they're done. Then remove them carefully with a slotted spoon. Toast and butter the English muffin halves. Top each one with the spinach and then a poached egg, and pour some yogurt hollandaise over the top.

Nutrition Facts

Calories per Serving: 155 cal Fat: 8g Protein: 10g Carbohydrates: 10g

4. CRUSTLESS CAPRESE QUICHE

Preparation 60 Minutes
Serves 6 Persons

Ingredients

- Grape tomatoes - 1 ½ cup (cut in half)
- Fresh basil (chopped) - ½ cup
- Garlic (minced) - 4 cloves
- Eggs - 10 large
- Almond milk (unsweetened) - ½ cup
- Sea salt - 3/4 teaspoon
- Black pepper - 1/4 teaspoon
- Mozzarella cheese (fresh) - 6 oz

Directions

- Start by preheating the oven by setting the temperature to 350 degrees
- Fahrenheit.
- Cut the mozzarella cheese into small cubes and place 2/3 of the cubed cheese into a large mixing bowl. Keep the rest of the cheese aside.
- Now add in the basil, halved tomatoes and garlic to the mozzarella cheese.
- Mix well to combine. Transfer the mozzarella cheese mix into a 9-inch round glass baking dish and spread it evenly at the bottom.
- Take another bowl and add in the milk, eggs, black pepper and sea salt.

- Whisk until all **Ingredients:** are well incorporated.
- Pour the prepared egg mixture over the tomatoes and cheese mix.
- Place the baking dish into the preheated oven and bake for around 45 minutes.
- Top the baked quiche with the remaining mozzarella cheese and place the baking dish back into the oven and bake for another 20 minutes.
- The top should be golden brown and the inside of the quiche should be nicely cooked.
- Remove the quiche from the oven and finish by topping with freshly chopped basil.

Nutrition Facts

Calories per Serving: 180 cal Fat: 8g Protein: 21g Carbohydrates: 19g

5. EGGS A LA SHRIMP

Preparation 30 Minutes
Serves 6 Persons
Ingredients

- 1 Tbsp. canola oil
- 3 green onions with tops, sliced, onion
- ¼ cup finely chopped celery
- 4 oz. shrimp, frozen or canned
- 3 Tbsp. plus ¼ cup white wine
- 4 large eggs 1 cup egg substitute
- 4 oz. frozen peas, or fresh
- ¼ tsp. salt
- ¼ tsp. pepper fresh parsley

Directions

- Preheat electric skillet to 375°F, or cast-iron skillet to medium high.
- Heat oil in skillet. Sauté onions, until limp.
- Add celery and sauté until softened.
- Add shrimp and 3 Tbsp. white wine. Cover and steam over low heat for 3 minutes.
- In a medium-sized mixing bowl, toss eggs and egg substitute with
- ¼ cup white wine. Pour into skillet.
- Stir in peas and seasonings.
- Turn skillet to 300°F, or medium low. Stir gently as mixture cooks. Cook just until mixture sets according to your liking.
- Serve on warm platter surrounded with fresh parsley.

Nutrition Facts

Calories per Serving: 135 cal Fat: 6g Protein: 14g Carbohydrates: 9g

6. CHEESE BREAD CUPS

Preparation 25 Minutes
Serves 2 Persons
Ingredients:

- 2 eggs
- 2 tablespoons cheddar cheese grated
- Salt and pepper to taste
- 1 ham slice, cut into
- 2 pieces
- 4 bread slices, flatten with rolling pin

Directions

- Spray the inside of 2 ramekins with cooking spray.
- Place 2 flat pieces of bread into each ramekin.
- Add the ham slice pieces into each ramekin.
- Crack an egg in each ramekin, then sprinkle with cheese.
- Season with salt and pepper.
- Place the ramekins into air fryer at 300 Fahrenheit for 15- minutes.
- Serve warm.

Nutrition Facts

Calories per Serving: 162 cal Fat: 8g Protein: 11g Carbohydrates: 8g

7. CREAMY QUINOA WITH PEACHS

Preparation 30 Minutes
Serves 4 Persons
Ingredients

- 2 cups water 1 cup (rinsed) quinoa
- 1 tsp ground nutmeg
- 1 tsp ground cinnamon
- 1/2 cup Greek yogurt, fat-free
- 1 chopped large fresh peach
- 1 pinch ground nutmeg
- 2 tbsps honey 1 tbsp lemon juice

Directions

- Add 2 cups water into a saucepan over med-heat and bring to boiling.
- Add quinoa into the boiling water and stir.
- Adjust to low heat and simmer quinoa for 15-20 minutes until softened.
- Drain water and stir in 1 tsp nutmeg and cinnamon.
- Add yogurt and chopped peach into a bowl and stir to combine.
- Add quinoa into a bowl and top with 2 tbsps of the yogurt mixture.
- Dribble 1 tsp lime juice and 1 tsp honey over quinoa and sprinkle with nutmeg.

Nutrition Facts

Calories per Serving: 219 cal Fat: 3g Protein: 9g Carbohydrates: 40g

8. BERRY FRENCH TOAST STRATAS

Preparation 65 Minutes
Serves 6 Persons
Ingredients

- 3 cups assorted fresh berries
- 1 tablespoon granulated sugar
- 4 cups cubes whole wheat bread
- 1½ cups fat-free egg product or 6 eggs
- ½ cup fat-free (skim) milk
- ½ cup fat-free half-and-half 2 tablespoons honey 1½ teaspoons vanilla
- 1 teaspoon ground cinnamon
- ¼ teaspoon ground nutmeg
- ½ teaspoon powdered suga

Directions

- In medium bowl, mix fruit and granulated sugar; set aside.
- Heat oven to 350°F. Spray 12 regular-size muffin cups generously with cooking spray.
- Divide bread cubes evenly among muffin cups.
- 3 In large bowl, beat remaining **Ingredients:**, except powdered sugar, with fork or whisk until well mixed.
- Pour egg mixture over bread cubes, pushing down lightly with spoon to soak bread cubes.
- Bake 20 to 25 minutes or until centers are set.
- Cool 5 minutes.
- Remove from muffin cups, placing 2 stratas on each of 6 plates.
- Divide fruit mixture evenly over stratas; sprinkle with powdered sugar.

Nutrition Facts

Calories per Serving: 195 cal Fat: 1,5g Protein: 11g Carbohydrates: 31g

9. CREAMY APPLE CINNAMON STEAL-CUT OATMEAL

Preparation 30 Minutes
Serves 6 Persons

Ingredients

- 1 cup steel-cut oats
- 2 cups 1 percent milk
- 2 cups nonfat half-and-half
- 2 cinnamon sticks
- 1 Mcintosh, Granny Smith, or Golden Delicious apple, peeled, cored, and diced
- ⅛ teaspoon fine-grained kosher salt
- 1 teaspoon pure vanilla extract
- ¼ cup dried cranberries divided
- 3 tablespoons sucralose–brown sugar
- ½ cup chopped walnuts

Directions

- In a medium bowl, combine the oats, milk, and half-and-half, and cover. Soak in the refrigerator overnight.
- Remove the oats from the refrigerator, and place into a heavy-bottomed saucepan. Add the cinnamon, diced apples, and salt, and bring to a boil over high heat.
- Stir and reduce the heat to medium-low. Simmer, stirring often, until the oatmeal is soft, for about 10 minutes.
- Stir in the vanilla, half the cranberries or raisins, and the sweetener, if using. Simmer for 5 minutes more, stirring continuously. Remove the cinnamon sticks, if using.
- Meanwhile, in a separate sauté pan, toast the chopped walnuts over medium heat for 6 minutes, stirring, until golden and fragrant.
- Spoon the oatmeal into bowls. Sprinkle with the remaining cranberries or raisins and with the toasted walnuts.

Nutrition Facts

Calories per Serving: 135 cal Fat: 6g Protein: 14g Carbohydrates: 9g

10. CHOCOLATE PANCAKE WITH STRAWBERRIES

Preparation 25 Minutes
Serves 4 Persons

Ingredients

- ¾ cup light chocolate soymilk
- ¼ cup fat-free egg product
- 1 tablespoon canola oil
- ¾ cup all-purpose flour
- 2 tablespoons sugar
- 2 tbls unsweetened baking cocoa
- 1 teaspoon baking powder
- ⅛ teaspoon salt
- 1 cup sliced fresh strawberries Sliced banana, if desired
- French vanilla fat-free yogurt, if desired

Directions

- In medium bowl, beat soymilk, egg product and oil with whisk until smooth.
- Stir in remaining **Ingredients:** except strawberries, banana and yogurt.
- Spray griddle or 10-inch skillet with cooking spray;
- Heat griddle to 375°F or heat skillet over medium heat.
- For each pancake, pour slightly less than ¼ cup batter onto hot riddle.
- Cook pancakes until puffed and dry around edges.
- Turn and cook other sides until golden brown.
- Serve with strawberries, banana and yogurt.

Nutrition Facts

Calories per Serving: 210 cal Fat: 4,5g Protein: 6g Carbohydrates: 36g

11. SHAKSHOUKA MEDITERRANEAN BREAKFAST

Total Time: 30 min
Servings: 4

Ingredients

- Finely sliced onion – 1
- Garlic cloves chopped – 1
- Chopped tomatoes -1 15 oz
- Red bell peppers – 2
- Spicy harissa – 1 teaspoon
- Sugar – 1 teaspoon
- Olive oil – 2 tablespoons
- Chopped parsley – 1 tablespoon
- Eggs – 4
- Salt and pepper to taste

Directions:

- Place a skillet over medium heat and then add olive oil. After that, add onions and peppers. Cook for about 5 minutes as you stir occasionally.
- Add garlic and then cook for one more minute. Add tomatoes, harissa and sugar, and cook for 7 minutes. Season with salt and pepper. Next, use a wooden spoon to make about 4 indentations in the mixture and then add an egg to each of the holes.
- Cover the pot and allow to cook until the egg whites are set. Sprinkle the mixture with fresh parsley.
- Serve and enjoy with some crusty bread.

Nutrition Facts:

Calories per serving: 455; Carbohydrates: 3g; Protein: 25g; Fat: 38g; Sugar: 0g; Sodium: 350mg; Fiber: 0g

12. BREAKFAST CASSEROLE WITH SAUSAGE AND CHEESE

Total Time: 45 min
Servings: 5

Ingredients

- Breakfast sausage – 1 pound
- Eggs – 10 large
- Heavy cream
- Cheddar cheese
- Fresh parsley
- Ground dry mustard – 1 teaspoon
- Salt and black pepper ¼ teaspoon

Directions:

- Have the oven preheated to 370F.
- Place a greased skillet over medium heat and then cook minced garlic for a minute or until fragrant.
- Add sausage and then allow to cook for about 10 minutes or until no longer pink.
- In a bowl, whisk together the eggs, half of cheddar cheese, parsley, heavy cream, sea salt and black pepper.
- Have the casserole dish and then arrange the crumbled sausage at the bottom of the dish.

- Pour the egg mixture over the cooked sausages and then sprinkle with the remaining cheddar cheese.
- Place in the oven and then bake for 30 minutes or until the cheese is melted and eggs set.

Nutrition Facts:

Calories per serving: 281; Carbohydrates: 1g; Protein: 17g; Fat: 23g; Sugar: 0g.

13. PANCAKES

Total Time: 20 min

Servings: 2

Ingredients

- Eggs – 2
- Vanilla protein powder – 2 scoops
- Baking Powder – 2 teaspoon
- Liquid stevia – 5 drops
- Pastured butter
- Heavy cream

Directions:

- Place all the Ingredients apart from butter into a blender. Blend until smooth and well mixed.
- Place frying pan over medium heat and then grease with butter.
- Add the blended mixture into the frying pan and then allow to cook as you flip once the bubbles appear over the pancake.
- Turn the other side and cook as well.
- Remove from heat once cooked and then serve in a plate.
- Top it up with butter or ghee and then enjoy!

Nutrition Facts:

Calories per serving: 400; Carbohydrates: 1g; Protein: 28g; Fat: 37g; Sugar: 1g; Sodium: 340mg; Fiber: 0g

14. MEDITERRANEAN TOAST

Total Time: 20 min

Servings: 1

Ingredients

- Whole-wheat or multigrain bread – 1 slice
- Roasted red pepper hummus – 1 tablespoon
- Mashed avocado – 1/3

- Sliced cherry tomatoes – 3
- Sliced Greek olives – 3
- Hard-boiled egg sliced – 1
- Reduced fat crumbled feta – 1 ½ teaspoon

Directions:

- Toast the slice of bread and then top with mashed avocado and hummus.
- Add the cherry tomatoes and olives. Top with the sliced hard-boiled egg and feta.
- Season with salt and pepper and then enjoy!

Nutrition Facts:

Calories per serving: 333; Carbohydrates: 33g; Protein: 16g; Fat: 17g; Sugar: 3g; Sodium: 730mg; Fiber: 8g

15. MEDITERRANEAN BREAKFAST EGG MUFFINS

Total Time: 40 min

Servings: 2

Ingredients

- Cooking oil spray
- Eggs – 3
- Skimmed milk – 2 tablespoons
- Grated parmesan cheese – 4 tablespoons
- Red pepper finely chopped – ¼
- Chopped tomatoes
- Grated cheddar cheese – 25g
- Leek finely chopped – 35g
- Baby spinach finely chopped – 25g

Directions:

- Get the oven preheated to 400F. Spray silicon muffin tin with the cooking spray.
- Whisk eggs, parmesan cheese and milk together in a pouring jug and then season.
- Mix all of the finely chopped vegetables into a bowl and then portion into 6 muffin cups.
- Pour the egg mixture over each of the muffin cups and then mix with the chopped vegetables.
- Divide grated cheddar cheese and use to top each of the muffin cups.

- Place in the oven and bake in the center of the oven for about 20 minutes or until the egg is set.

Nutrition Facts:

Calories per serving: 308; Carbohydrates: 9g; Protein: 24g; Fat: 19g; Sugar: 4g; Sodium: 0mg; Fiber: 1g

16. MEDITERRANEAN OMELETTE

Total Time: 15 min

Servings: 1

Ingredients

- Oil or butter – 1 teaspoon
- Milk or cream – 1 tablespoon
- Diced tomato – 2 tablespoons
- Sliced kalamata olives – 2 tablespoons
- Artichoke heart quartered – 1
- Crumbled feta cheese – 1 tablespoon
- Romesco sauce – 1 tablespoon

Directions:

- Place a skillet over medium heat. Pour a mixture of milk, egg, oregano salt and pepper and then add to the skillet and cover.
- Cook the egg mixture until the eggs begin to set. Sprinkle with artichoke, olive, and feta on the half part of the egg and then fold the remaining part of the egg over.
- Cook the folded egg for about a minute then remove from the heat and top with romesco sauce.
- Serve and enjoy!

Nutrition Facts:

Calories per serving: 303; Carbohydrates: 21g; Protein: 18g; Fat: 17g; Sugar: 4g; Sodium: 630mg; Fiber: 5g

17. ZUCCHINI AND TOMATO FRITTATA

Total Time: 15 min

Servings: 8

Ingredients

- Eggs – 8
- Crushed red pepper – ¼ teaspoon
- Olive oil – 1 tablespoon
- Thinly sliced zucchini – 1
- Cherry tomatoes – ½ cup halved
- Fresh mozzarella balls – 2 ounces
- Coarsely Chopped walnuts – 1/3 cup

Directions:

- Get the skillet preheated. In a medium bowl, whisk the eggs together and then add salt and crushed red pepper.
- Heat olive oil in a skillet over medium heat. Add zucchini slices at the bottom of the skillet and cook for about 3 minutes as you turn once.
- Top zucchini with cherry tomatoes and then pour egg mixture into the skillet. Top with mozzarella balls and walnuts. Cook for about 5 minutes or until the sides begin to set.
- Broil it 4 inches from the heat for about minutes or until set.
- Cut into wedges and then serve with slices of tomatoes and basil leaves with additional olive oil.

Nutrition Facts:

Calories per serving: 281; Carbohydrates: 4g; Protein: 18g; Fat: 22g; Sugar: 4g; Sodium: 334mg; Fiber: 1g

18. BLACKBERRY GINGER OVERNIGHT BULGAR

Total Time: 10 min
Servings: 2

Ingredients

- Plain low-fat yoghurt – 2/3 cup
- Bulgar – ¼ cup
- Refrigerated coconut milk – 3 tablespoons
- Honey – 2 tablespoons
- Crystallized ginger – ¼ teaspoon
- Blackberries – ¼ cup

Directions:

- In a bowl, stir the Ingredients all together apart from the blackberries.
- Divide the mixture into two half jars and then top with blackberries.
- Stir and then serve.

Nutrition Facts:

Calories per serving: 215; Carbohydrates: 4g; Protein: 8g; Fat: 2g; Sugar: 8g; Sodium: 74mg; Fiber: 1g

19. MEDITERRANEAN BREAKFAST SANDWICH

Total Time: 20 min

Ingredients

- Multigrain sandwich thins – 4
- Olive oil – 4 teaspoons
- Fresh rosemary – 1 tablespoon
- Eggs – 4
- Fresh baby spinach leaves – 2 cups
- Medium tomato – cut into thin slices
- Reduced feta cheese – 4 tablespoons
- Kosher salt – 1/8 teaspoon
- Freshly ground black pepper

Directions:

- Get the oven preheated to 375F.
- Split the sandwich thins and then brush the cut sides with 2 teaspoons of olive oil. Place the sandwich on a baking sheet and then toast in the oven for about 5 minutes or until the edges are crisp and light brown.
- Place a large skillet over medium heat and then add the remaining 2 teaspoons of olive oil. Add rosemary into the skillet and then cook.
- Break eggs into the skillet one at a time. Cook for a minute or until the whites are set and the yolks runny.
- Break the yolks with spatula and then flip the eggs and cook on one side until well done. After which, remove it from the heat.
- Place the bottom halves of toasted sandwich thins onto four serving plates and then top with tomato slices, an egg and a teaspoon of feta cheese.
- Sprinkle again with the remaining sandwich thin halves and enjoy.

Nutrition Facts:

Calories per serving: 242; Carbohydrates: 6g; Protein: 8g; Fat: 2g; Sugar: 8g; Sodium: 74mg; Fiber: 1g

20. EGGS WITH TOMATOES, OLIVES AND FETA

Total Time: 15 min
Servings: 4

Ingredients

- Ripe diced tomatoes – 3
- Olive oil – 2 tablespoons
- Pitted and sliced Greek olives – 10
- Eggs – 4
- Grated feta cheese – 1 cup
- Salt and pepper to taste

Directions:

- Sauté tomatoes in olive oil for about 10 minutes and then fry in a large pan.
- Add olives into the pan and then cook for 5 minutes. In a bowl, whisk the eggs and then add to the frying pan. Cook the eggs over medium heat or until they begin to set. Add feta cheese and cook to the desired consistency.
- Add salt and pepper to taste and then serve and enjoy.

Nutrition Facts:

Calories per serving: 230; Carbohydrates: 4g; Protein: 7g; Fat: 4g; Sugar: 5g; Sodium: 87mg; Fiber: 1g

21. BREAKFAST BURRITO

Total Time: 20 min
Servings: 1

Ingredients

- Tortillas – 6
- Eggs – 9
- Baby spinach – 2 cups
- Black Olives – 3 tablespoons
- Sun-dried tomatoes – 3 tablespoons chopped
- Feta cheese – ½ cup
- Canned refried beans – ¾ cup
- Salsa for garnish

Directions:

- Use non-stick spray to spray a medium pan and then place over medium heat. Scramble eggs and toss for about 5 minutes.
- Add spinach, the sundried tomatoes and black olives. Continue to stir until no longer wet. Add feta cheese and then cover and allow to cook until the cheese is melted.
- Add 2 tablespoons of the refried beans on each tortilla and then top with the egg mixture. Divide equally between all the burritos and then wrap.
- Grill the burritos in a frying pan until lightly browned and then serve hot with salsa and fruit.

Nutrition Facts:

Calories per serving: 252; Carbohydrates: 21g; Protein: 14g; Fat: 11g; Sugar: 3g; Sodium: 687mg; Fiber: 2g

22. MEDITERRANEAN BREAKFAST QUINOA

Total Time: 25 min

Ingredients

- Ground Cinnamon- 1 teaspoon
- Raw almonds chopped – ¼ cup
- Quinoa – 1 cup
- Vanilla extract – 1 teaspoon
- Honey – 2 tablespoons
- Pitted dates – 2 dried and chopped
- Finely chopped dried apricots – 5

Directions:

- Place a skillet over medium heat and then toast the almonds for 5 minutes and set aside.
- Place a saucepan over medium heat and then cook quinoa and cinnamon together until warmed through.
- 3.Add milk and sea salt to the saucepan and then stir and bring to a boil. Reduce the heat to low and then cover the saucepan and allow to cook for 15 minutes.
- 4.Stir in vanilla, dates, honey, apricots and about half of the almonds into the saucepan.
- 5.Top quinoa mixtures with remaining almonds and then serve and enjoy.

Nutrition Facts:

Calories per serving: 330; Carbohydrates: 15g; Protein: 14g; Fat: 10g; Sugar: 3g; Sodium:680mg; Fiber: 4g

23. PANCAKES WITH BERRIES AND WHIPPED CREAM

Total Time: 20 min

Servings: 4

Ingredients

- Cottage cheese - 200g
- Eggs - 4
- Psyllium husk powder - 1 tbsp
- Coconut oil or butter - 50g
- Toppings
- Fresh raspberries/ blueberries
- Or strawberries - 120g
- Whipping cream - 225mls

Instructions

- Put all the ingredients in a bowl and blend to form batter using a wide fork and then leave to expand for 5 minutes to 10 minutes.
- Let the butter or oil heat in the frying pan and then fry the pancakes on medium heat for about 4 minutes, flipping carefully. Ensure that the cheese lumps do not stick on to the pan.
- Serve with blueberries or the other berries as convenient.

Nutritional Information:

Calories per serving: 80; Carbohydrates: 4g; Protein: 12g; Fat: 36g; Sugar: 1g; Sodium:210mg; Fiber: 0g

24. MEDITERRANEAN FRITTATA

Total Time: 40 min

Servings: 6

Ingredients

- Eggs – 12
- Goat cheese – 6 ounces
- Grated parmesan cheese – 1/ cup
- Cremini mushrooms – 4 ounces
- Deli ham – ¼ pound
- Pinch of salt – 1
- Roasted red peppers – 1 jar
- Olive oil

Directions:

- Get the oven preheated to 350°F. In a mixing bowl, add eggs, roasted red peppers parmesan, goat cheese and salt. Whisk thoroughly together.
- Coat an iron skillet with olive oil and then place over medium heat and add the mushrooms and cook for a minute or until soft.
- Add diced ham and then allow it to fry for one more minute. Pour in the egg mixture. Ensure it's well mixed and even.
- Transfer carefully to the oven and then let the frittata bake for 30 minutes or until puffy and golden.
- Remove from the pan and then allow to stay for a few minutes. After that, cut into wedges and enjoy.

Nutrition Facts:

Calories per serving: 530; Carbohydrates: 5g; Protein: 41g; Fat: 40g; Sugar: 3g; Sodium: 900mg; Fiber: 1g

25. TASTY SOUFFLE'

Preparation 80 Minutes

Serves 12 Persons

Ingredients

- ½ lb. reduced-fat pork sausage
- 2¼ cups egg substitute
- 3 cups fat-free milk
- 1½ tsp. dry mustard
- ¾ tsp. salt
- 3 slices bread, cubed
- ¾ cup grated 75%-less-fat cheddar

Directions

- Brown pork sausage and drain excess fat.
- Set aside.
- Combine egg substitute, milk, mustard, and salt.
- Add sausage, bread, and cheese.
- Spoon into greased 9x13-Inch pan.
- Cover and refrigerate overnight.
- Bake, uncovered, at 350°F for 1 hour.

Nutrition Facts

Calories per Serving: 115 cal Fat: 4g Protein: 12g Carbohydrates: 7g

26. HEALTHY SHAKSHUKA

Preparation 30 Minutes

Serves 4 Persons

Ingredients

- Olive oil - 2 tablespoons
- Onion 1 medium
- Garlic (minced) 1 clove
- Cumin (ground)
- 1 teaspoon Pepper 1 teaspoon
- Chili powder
- 1 teaspoon Salt
- 1/2 teaspoon Sriracha chili sauce
- 1 teaspoon Tomatoes (chopped)
- 2 medium Eggs
- 4 large Fresh cilantro (chopped)
- 2 teaspoons Whole pita bread, toasted

Directions

- Take a large cast-iron pan and place it on medium flame. Pour in the oil and let it heat through.
- Toss in the onion and sauté for about 5 minutes.

- Now add in the garlic, cumin, pepper, chili powder, salt and chili sauce. Stir well and cook for another 30 seconds.
- Add in the chopped tomatoes and stir well.
- Cook for about 5 minutes or until the tomatoes have broken down and the sauce has thickened.
- Keep stirring to prevent it from sticking to the bottom.
- Use the back of the spoon to make 4 wells in the tomato mixture. Crack 1 egg into each of the wells.
- Cover the pan with a lid and cook for about 5-6 minutes.
- Finish by sprinkling with freshly chopped cilantro and serve with toasted pita bread.

Nutrition Facts
Calories per Serving: 159 cal Fat: 12g Protein: 7g Carbohydrates: 6g

COD NUGGETS

Preparation 20 Minutes
Serves 4 Persons

Ingredients
- 1 lb. Of cod For breading
- 2 eggs, beaten
- 2 tablespoons olive oil
- 1 cup almond flour
- ¾ cup breadcrumbs
- 1 teaspoon dried parsley Pinch of sea salt
- ½ teaspoon black pepper

Directions
- Preheat the air fryer to 390 Fahrenheit.
- Cut the cod into strips about 1-inch by 2-inches.
- Blend breadcrumbs, olive oil, salt, parsley and pepper in a food
- processor.
- In three separate bowls, add breadcrumbs, eggs, and flour.
- Place each piece of fish into flour, then the eggs, and the breadcrumbs.
- Add pieces of cod to air fryer basket and cook for 10 minutes.
- Serve warm.

Nutrition Facts
Calories per Serving: 213 cal Fat: 12g Protein: 13g Carbohydrates: 9g

27. BAKED OATMEAL

Preparation 25 Minutes
Serves 4 Persons

Ingredients
- Rolled oats – 6 cups
- Eggs (beaten) 4
- Frozen blueberries 2 cups
- Applesauce 1 cup
- Brown sugar 1 cup
- Skim milk 2 cups
- Flaxseed meal ¼ cup
- Wheat germ 3 tablespoons
- Baking powder 1 tablespoon Cinnamon (ground) 1 tablespoon
- Vanilla extract 2 teaspoons
- Salt ½ teaspoon

Directions
- Start by preheating the oven by setting the temperature to 350 degrees Fahrenheit.
- Take a large glass mixing bowl and add the eggs, oats, applesauce, blueberries, skim milk, wheat germ, brown sugar, flaxseed meal, cinnamon, salt, baking powder, and vanilla.
- Mix until well combined.
- Take a baking dish measuring 9 x 13 inches.
- Grease it with cooking spray.
- Pour the prepared oats mixture into the greased baking dish.
- Place the baking dish into the preheated oven and bake for about 30 minutes. The oats will be tender by now.
- Once done, take out the baking dish and cut it into 15 equal pieces.
- Serve right away!

Nutrition Facts
Calories per Serving: 223 cal Fat: 4g Protein: 8g Carbohydrates: 40g

28. CORN EGGS AND POPATO BAKE

Preparation 90 Minutes
Serves 8 Persons

Ingredients
- 4 cups frozen diced hash brown potatoes (from 2-lb bag), thawed
- ½ cup frozen whole-kernel corn thawed
- ¼ cup chopped roasted red bell
- 1½ cups shredded reduced-fat cheese
- 10 eggs or 2½ cups fat-free egg product
- ½ cup fat-free small-curd cottage cheese
- ½ teaspoon dried oregano leaves
- ¼ teaspoon garlic powder 4 medium green onions, chopped

Directions
- Heat oven to 350°F.
- Spray 11x7-inch glass baking dish with cooking spray.
- In baking dish, layer potatoes, corn, bell peppers and 1 cup of the shredded cheese.
- In medium bowl, beat eggs, cottage cheese, oregano and garlic powder with whisk until well blended.
- Slowly pour over potato mixture.
- Sprinkle with onions and remaining ½ cup shredded cheese.
- Cover and bake 30 minutes.
- Uncover and bake about 30 minutes longer or until knife inserted in center comes out clean.
- Let stand 5 to 10 minutes before cutting

Nutrition Facts
Calories per Serving: 240 cal Fat: 11g Protein: 16g Carbohydrates: 18g

29. PARMESAN AND ASPARAGUS FRITTATA

Preparation 30 Minutes
Serves 6 Persons

Ingredients
- 2 lean turkey or chicken sausages 1 tablespoon extra-virgin olive oil
- ¼ cup chopped roasted asparagus

- ¼ cup chopped red bell pepper 1 chopped plum tomato 6 eggs, scrambled
- 2 tablespoons nonfat half-and-half
- ½ cup grated Parmesan, divided
- ⅛ teaspoon fine-grained kosher salt
- ⅛ teaspoon freshly ground black pepper

Directions

- Preheat the oven to broil setting.
- Remove the casings from the turkey or chicken sausage, and crumble the meat in a medium sauté pan. Cook thoroughly over medium-high heat. Set aside.
- Heat a nonstick, oven-safe sauté pan, skillet, or griddle pan over medium-high heat. Add the olive oil to the pan. Add the asparagus, bell pepper, and tomato, and cook for about 3 to 5 minutes.
- Meanwhile, whisk the eggs, half-and-half, ¼ cup of the Parmesan, salt, and pepper in a medium bowl.
- Add the egg mixture and sausage crumbles to the pan with the vegetables. Cook for 5 minutes, or until the egg mixture has set on the bottom and begins to firm up on top.
- Top with the remaining Parmesan. Place pan in the oven, and broil for 3 to 4 minutes, until golden and firm. Remove the frittata from the oven, cut it into 6 slices, and serve hot.

Nutrition Facts

Calories per Serving: 255 cal Fat: 15g Protein: 27g Carbohydrates: 2g

30. CHEESE SOUFFLE' CASSEROLE

Preparation 20 Minutes

Serves 6 Persons

Ingredients

- 8 slices bread cubed
- 2 cups grated fat-free cheddar cheese
- 1 cup cooked, chopped extra-lean,
- lower-sodium ham
- 4 eggs 1 cup fat-free half-and-half
- 1 cup fat-free evaporated milk
- 1 Tbsp. parsley paprika

Directions

- Lightly grease slow cooker.
- Alternate layers of bread and cheese and ham.
- Beat together eggs, half-and-half, milk, and parsley.
- Pour over bread in slow cooker.
- Sprinkle with paprika.
- Cover and cook on Low 3– hours.
- The longer cooking time yields a firmer, dryer dish.
- About 30 minutes before finish, increase temperature to High and remove lid.

Nutrition Facts

Calories per Serving: 233 cal Fat: 5g Protein: 23g Carbohydrates: 22g

31. FRUIT CAKE OATMEAL

Preparation 370 Minutes

Serves 16 Persons

Ingredients

- 23 oz. applesauce, unsweetened
- 10 cups water
- 1 (10 oz.) bag carrots, shredded
- 2 cups steel cut oats
- 1 cup raisins 1 (8 oz.) can (drained) crushed pineapple
- 2 tbsps ground cinnamon
- 1/3 cup granular splenda, if desired
- 1 tsp salt, if desired
- 1 tbsp pumpkin pie spice

Directions

- Add salt, pumpkin pie spice, cinnamon, sweetener, raisins, pineapple, car- rots, oats, applesauce and water into big slow cooker pot and combine.
- Seal the lid and cook for 6 hours on low.

Nutrition Facts

Calories per Serving: 139 cal Fat: 1g Protein: 3g Carbohydrates: 30g

32. DEVILED EGGS

Preparation 20 Minutes

Serves 6 Persons

Ingredients

- 6 eggs 1 teaspoon fine-grained kosher salt
- 1 tablespoon plus
- 1 teaspoon white vinegar, divided
- ¼ cup low-fat or nonfat mayonnaise
- 1 teaspoon yellow mustard Freshly ground black pepper, to taste
- ½ teaspoon ground paprika for garnish
- ¼ cup minced chives for garnish

Directions

- Put the eggs in an even layer in a pot, covered by 2 inches of cold water, 1 teaspoon of the salt, and 1 tablespoon of the white vinegar.
- Cook on high heat until the water is just about to boil; then remove them from the heat, cover, and let sit for 12 minutes in the hot water.
- Remove the eggs with a slotted spoon, and place them in a bowl of ice water.
- Carefully crack the eggs to remove the shells and peels.
- Halve the eggs lengthwise, spooning out the yolks and placing them in a bowl. Place the whites on a plate or your serving tray.
- Mash the yolks with a potato mash- er or a fork. Add the remaining vinegar, the mayonnaise, and the mustard, and stir to combine. Season with salt and pepper.
- Fill the egg whites with 1 tablespoon of the deviled yolks. Garnish with a sprinkle of paprika and with chives, if desired.

Nutrition Facts

Calories per Serving: 168 cal Fat: 14g Protein: 6g Carbohydrates: 1g

33. SPINACH & BACON EGG CUPS

Prep Time: 5 minutes

Cook Time: 15 – 18 minutes

Total Time: 20 – 23 minutes

Ingredients

- Six eggs
- Three tablespoons milk
- ¾ cup finely chopped spinach
- 1 cup shredded Cheddar cheese
- Four strips bacon, cooked and chopped
- ¼ teaspoon black pepper

Directions

- Preheat oven to 350F and grease a 24-count mini muffin pan.

- In a large bowl, whisk the eggs and milk. Add the chopped spinach, shredded Cheddar cheese, chopped bacon, and black pepper. Stir to combine.
- Distribute the egg mixture evenly into the muffin cups.
- Bake in the preheated oven for 15-18 minutes.
- Once cooked, allow mini quiches to cool in the pan before carefully removing them with a small knife or spatula.

Nutrition Facts

Serving Size: 4 mini egg cups| Calories: 188| Sugar: 0.7g| Sodium: 329.7mg| Fat: 13.9g| Saturated Fat: 6.1g| Carbohydrates: 1.6g| Fiber: 0.1g| Protein: 13.6g| Cholesterol: 212.8mg

34. 15 MINUTE LOW-CARB OATMEAL

Prep Time: 5 minutes
Cook Time: 10 minutes
Total Time: 15 minutes

Ingredients

- 1/2 cup almond flour
- 4 tbsp. coconut flour
- 2 tbsp. flax meal
- 2 tbsp. chia seeds
- 1 tsp. ground cinnamon
- 10 – 15 drops liquid Stevia
- 1 1/2 cup unsweetened almond milk
- 1 tsp. vanilla extract
- Salt to taste

Directions

- Add the almond flour, coconut flour, flax seed powder, chia seeds, and ground cinnamon to a mixing bowl. Whisk together until well-combined.
- Transfer the dry ingredients to a pot over medium heat. Add the stevia drops, almond milk, and vanilla extract, then stir well.
- Cook the oatmeal for 3 – 5 minutes until it's warmed through and starting to thicken. Remove from the heat and taste, adding salt if desired.
- Serve the oatmeal warm with your desired low-carb toppings.

Nutrition Facts

Fat 24.3g| Saturated Fat 2.4g| Trans Fat 0g| Polyunsaturated Fat 2.7g| Monounsaturated Fat 0.6g| Sodium 159mg| Potassium 164mg| Carbohydrates 16.7g| Fiber 11g| Sugar 2.1g| Protein 11.7g

35. BACON & EGG MUFFINS

Prep Time: 10 Minutes
Cook Time: 30 Minutes
Total Time: 40 minutes

Ingredients

- Eight slices of turkey bacon
- One small green pepper (minced)
- One banana pepper (minced)
- ¼ large onion (minced)
- Four eggs
- ¼ cup nonfat milk
- ⅔ cup shredded cheddar cheese

Directions

- Slice the bacon in half lengthwise, then crosswise into thin strips.
- In a pan over medium-high heat, cook the bacon and the minced green pepper, banana pepper, and onion.
- Once the bacon is crisp and the vegetables are soft, remove from heat and cool slightly.
- Preheat the oven to 350°F and spray a 6-cup muffin pan with nonstick spray.
- Whisk the eggs together with the milk.
- Pour the egg mixture into six muffin cups, then evenly distribute the bacon mixture into each one. Divide the cheese between each cup.
- Place in the oven and bake for about 20 minutes or until the egg is set.

Nutrition Facts

Fat 9.3g| Saturated fat 3.8g| Polyunsaturated Fat 0.2g| Monounsaturated Fat 1.4g| Cholesterol 151.4mg| Sodium 282.3mg| Potassium 100mg| Carbohydrates 3g| Fiber 0.5g| Sugar 1.2g| Protein 12g

36. BREAKFAST QUESADILLA

Prep Time: 15 Min
Cook Time: 16 Min
Servings: 6Servings
Serving Size: 1 Wedge

Ingredients

- One nonstick cooking spray
- 1/4 cup canned green chiles
- Four eggs (beaten)
- 1/4 tsp black pepper
- Two 10-inch whole wheat flour tortillas
- 1 1/2 cup reduced-fat cheddar cheese, or use Mexican blend, Monterey Jack, or pepper jack (reduced fat)
- Four slice turkey bacon (cooked crisp and crumbled)

Directions

- Coat a small skillet lightly with cooking spray.
- Saute green chiles over medium-low heat for 1-2 minutes. Add beaten eggs and cook, stirring, until scrambled and set. Season with pepper.
- Coat a second, large skillet lightly with cooking spray. Place one tortilla in the skillet and cook over medium heat until air bubbles form about 1 minute. Flip the tortilla over and cook for 1 minute more (do not let tortilla get crispy).
- Spread half the cheese evenly over the tortilla, covering the edges.
- Reduce heat to low. Quickly arrange half the cooked bacon and half the egg mixture over the cheese. Cook until the cheese starts to melt, about 1 minute.
- Fold tortillas in half to create a half-moon shape. Flip folded tortilla over and cook until it is lightly toasted and the cheese filling is wholly melted 1-2 minutes.
- Transfer quesadilla to a cutting board. Recoat the skillet with cooking spray, and repeat with the second tortilla and remaining cheese, bacon, and egg mixture.
- Cut each quesadilla into three wedges and serve immediately with fresh salsa.

Nutrition Facts

Total Fat: 10g| Saturated Fat: 4g| Cholesterol: 140mg| Sodium: 460mg| Total Carbohydrate: 8g| Dietary Fiber:

5g| Total Sugars: 1g| Protein: 14g| Potassium: 135mg| Phosphorus: 260mg

37. ACORN SQUASH NESTS

Total Time: 30 minutes

Ingredients

- One acorn squash
- 2 tbsp vegetable broth
- 1 tbsp olive oil
- 1/2 tsp Red pepper flakes
- 1/2 tsp black pepper
- Four egg

Directions

- Preheat oven to 425°F.
- Cut the acorn squash in half and clean out the inside.
- Cut the squash into slices (about 1/2 inch or however thick you'd like) so that there is a "hole" in the center of each piece where the seeds used to be. Place these slices onto a baking sheet.
- Mix broth, oil, and spices in a bowl.
- Brush squash slices with mixture.
- Cook at 425°F for 15 minutes.
- Add one egg to each squash hole.
- Heat at 350°F for 12 minutes.
- Once out of the oven, let it cool slightly, serve, and enjoy!

Nutrition Facts

Carbohydrates: 12g | Protein: 6g | Fat: 8g | Saturated Fat: 2g | Sodium: 100mg | Fiber: 2g

38. JOHNNYCAKES AND PUMPKIN BUTTER

Prep Time: 20 Mins
Cook Time: 25 Mins
Total Time: 45 Mins

Ingredients

- Johnnycakes
- 1/2 cup cornmeal white or yellow
- 1/2 cup Flaxseed meal
- One teaspoon salt
- One tablespoon Granular Stevia
- 3/4 cup Boiling Water
- Two tablespoons butter unsalted
- 1/3 cup Almond milk plain, no added flavor or sugar

Pumpkin Butter

- 1 15 ounces can Pumpkin puree
- 3/4 cup Granular Stevia
- One teaspoon Maple extract
- 1/4 cup Water
- One teaspoon Lemon juice
- 1/2 Peeled and pureed, medium Apple or 1/3 cup unsweetened applesauce
- 1 1/4 Teaspoon Pumpkin Spice Mix
- Homemade Pumpkin spice mix
- 1/2 teaspoon vanilla powder
- 1/2 teaspoon Ground Cinnamon
- 1/4 teaspoon Ground Ginger
- 1/8 teaspoon Ground Clove
- Pinch Ground Allspice
- Pinch Ground Nutmeg

Directions

- Recipe for Johnnycakes
- In a bowl, combine Cornmeal, Flaxseed meal, Salt, and Stevia.
- Boil water and butter together to melt butter.
- Add boiling water and melted butter to the dry ingredients and combine.
- Warm the Almond milk and then add to cornmeal and water mixture.
- Using a sizeable oiled skillet or pan over medium-high heat, scoop or spoon out portions of the batter and cook for 2 minutes on each side. Serve immediately or hold warm.

Recipe For No Sugar Added Pumpkin Butter.

- In a small to medium-sized pan, combine the Pumpkin, Stevia, Maple extract, and water. Set aside.
- Peel the half Apple. Using a blender or stick blender, puree the Apple together with the spice mix. If using applesauce, then simply combine with the spice mix.
- Add the pureed Apple mixture or applesauce mixture together with the pumpkin mixture.
- Heat over medium heat for 20 minutes, stirring occasionally. The Pumpkin will darken in color and thicken while cooking.
- Once cooked, serve immediately.

- Pumpkin butter can be stored for up to 7 days in an airtight container in the refrigerator. Enjoy.

Nutrition Facts

Carbohydrates: 13g| Protein: 5g| Fat: 12g| Saturated Fat: 2g| Cholesterol: 2mg| Sodium: 722mg| Fiber: 3g

39. OVERNIGHT OATS

Prep Time: 10 mins

Ingredients

- 1 cup oats rolled
- One tablespoon nut butter
- One teaspoon cinnamon
- One teaspoon chia seeds
- 1 cup milk
- Toppings (add in the morning)
- Fresh fruit
- Nuts and seeds
- Maple syrup or a sweetener of your choice.

Directions

- Mix in a bowl the oats, nut butter, cinnamon, chia seeds and add the milk. With a spoon, mix all the ingredients well.
- Cover the bowl or separate the oats in individual jars and leave it in the fridge overnight or at least two hours before you want to eat it.
- Add toppings of your choice and enjoy.

Nutrition Facts

Fat: 9g| Sodium: 210mg| Protein: 23g| Carbohydrates: 3g

40. LOW-CARB STEAK BREAKFAST HASH

Prep Time: 10 minutes
Cook Time: 10 minutes
Total Time: 20 minutes
Servings: 4

Ingredients

- Two tablespoon butter preferably grass-fed, quantity divided
- 8 ounces steak of choice (ribeye, fillet, sirloin), preferably grass-fed cut into 1-inch squares
- 4 ounces cauliflower florets (about 1/4 medium head) chopped

- 4 ounces yellow onion (about one medium) chopped
- 3 ounces red bell pepper (about 1/2) sliced
- 3 ounces yellow bell pepper (about 1/2) sliced
- 1-ounce jalapeno pepper (about 1/2) finely minced
- One tablespoon fresh parsley chopped

Directions

- Melt one tablespoon butter in a large skillet over medium-high heat.
- When the pan is hot and a drop of water sizzles when added to the pan, add the chunks of steak.
- Season steak cubes with salt and pepper. Sear on each side over medium-high heat, then turn heat to low and cook to desired doneness.
- Remove steak from the pan to a plate. Tent with foil to keep warm.
- Turn heat to medium and add the second tablespoon of butter.
- When the butter stops foaming, add cauliflower and cook for about 2 minutes, stirring occasionally. Add onion to the pan and cook until edges of the onion are just starting to brown, then stir in the peppers. Season with salt and pepper,
- When peppers are crisp-tender and onions and cauliflower are tender and cooked through, stir in steak cubes and any liquid collected. Stir in parsley just before serving.
- Taste and adjust seasoning with salt and freshly ground black pepper, if desired.

Nutrition Facts
Fat: 14g| Carbs: 10g| Fiber: 2g| Protein: 12g| Net carbs: 8g

41. BACON BREAKFAST ENCHILADAS

Prep Time 10 minutes
Cook Time 30 minutes
Total Time 40 minutes

Ingredients

- 1 tbsp coconut oil
- Three eggs
- Seven pieces bacon
- 1/2 cup onion chopped
- 1/2 cup bell pepper chopped
- 2 oz Neufchatel cream cheese
- 1/4 cup water
- 1/4 tsp salt
- 1/2 cup cheddar cheese shredded

Directions

- Heat oil in a nonstick skillet (or a cast-iron skillet on high heat). In a small bowl, beat eggs.
- When the skillet is hot, sprinkle a small pinch of salt in the center, pour about 2 tbsp of egg into the skillet.
- Use the back of a spoon to spread the egg into a square shape approximately the size of a piece of bread.
- When the top is set, flip. Place each completed wrap on a plate.
- Add the sprinkle of salt before each wrap to prevent sticking. Make six wraps.
- Fry bacon until crisp. Set aside. In the same skillet, sauté the onion and pepper mixture until soft.
- In a small saucepan, heat the cream cheese, water, and salt. Whisk to combine into a creamy sauce.
- Divide the onion and pepper mixture into sixths.
- Place a line of onions and peppers into each egg wrap. Top with a tablespoon of shredded cheese.
- Break a piece of bacon in half and place it over the cheese.
- Roll the wrap like an enchilada and place seam down in an 8-inch square casserole dish.
- Repeat with the remaining
- Pour the cream cheese sauce over the top of the enchiladas and smooth with a spoon.
- Sprinkle the remaining cheese over the sauce. Crumble the last slice of bacon over the top.
- Bake the enchiladas for 15 minutes at 350 degrees.

Nutrition Facts
Fat: 32g| Saturated Fat: 16g| Polyunsaturated Fat: 2g| Monounsaturated Fat 9g| Sodium 1109mg| Potassium 321mg| Carbohydrates 5g| Fiber 1g| Sugar 2g| Protein 23g| Calcium 190mg| Iron 1.6mg

42. BREAKFAST CUP OMELETTES

Prep Time: 5 minutes
Cook Time: 12 minutes
Total Time: 17 minutes

Ingredients

- Three large eggs
- 50 ml milk
- 100 grams cheese grated
- 1 tsp butter
- One pinch of salt & ground black pepper to taste
- Fillings to your preference

Directions

- Preheat oven to 180°c (fan)
- Grease 6 holes of a muffin tin with butter
- Whisk up the eggs & milk in a jug
- Chop up your fillings & add some to each hole
- Pour over the egg & milk mixture (to 3/4 full as these will rise when cooking)
- Season to your liking
- Top with grated cheddar
- Cook in the oven at around for 12-15 mins or until golden

Nutrition Facts
Calories: 114kcal | Carbohydrates: 1g | Protein: 8g | Fat: 9g | of which saturates: 5g | of which sugars: 1g

43. DIABETES-FRIENDLY SOURDOUGH FRENCH TOAST

Prep Time: 15 minutes
Cook Time: 20 minutes
Total Time: 35 minutes

Ingredients

- One large egg beaten
- ¼ cup whole milk
- 1 Tbsp Truvia Sweet Complete All-Purpose Sweetener

- 1 tsp vanilla extract
- 1 tsp almond extract
- ½ tsp ground cinnamon
- Four slices sourdough bread using gluten-free sourdough if needed
- 2 tbsp unsweetened peanut butter
- 1 cup frozen berries thawed
- 2 Tbsp Truvia Confectioners Sweetener

Directions

- Have all of your ingredients out and ready to go.
- Combine the egg, milk, Truvia Sweet Complete All-Purpose Sweetener, vanilla extract, almond extract, and cinnamon in a bowl. Carefully whisk the mixture together until thoroughly combined.
- Layer your pieces of bread in a large baking dish or a wide shallow bowl. Pour the egg mixture over the bread slices making sure to cover them evenly. Soak for 5 minutes, rearrange the bread slices to ensure even saturation, and then soak for five more minutes.
- While the bread is soaking, heat a large skillet over medium heat on your stovetop. (Make sure the pan is good and hot and has been warming for at least 5 minutes before moving on to the next step.)
- Spray the pan with your preferred cooking oil spray.
- Remove the bread from the dish, making sure to shake off any excess milk/egg mixture. Place the pieces of bread in the pan and cook for 4-5 minutes with a lid on the pan to help hold the heat in.
- After 4-5 minutes, flip the French toast and cook for another 3-4 minutes with the lid on the pan.
- Remove the French toast from the pan and transfer it to two plates. Top your French toast evenly with the peanut butter, berries, and Truvia Confectioners Sweetener.
- Enjoy!

Nutrition FactsValue

Carbohydrates: 78g | Protein: 19g | Fat: 13g | Saturated Fat: 2.5g | Sodium: 650mg | Fiber: 6g | Sugar: 14g

44. OATMEAL RECIPE FOR DIABETIC CHILDREN

Prep Time: 2 Mins
Cook Time: 5 Mins
Total Time: 7 Mins

Ingredients

- Two packets Instant Oatmeal
- 2/3 cup Fairlife Milk
- 2/3 cup Water
- 1-2 tbsp Brown Sugar to taste
- 1/2 tsp Vanilla Extract
- Cinnamon to taste

Directions

- Place two instant oatmeal packets into a two qt saucepan
- Add every ingredient into the saucepan and mix.
- Cook until done.

45. HEALTHY BREAKFAST SKILLET

Prep Time: 9 minutes
Cook Time: 21 minutes
Total Time: 30 minutes
Servings: 4

Ingredients

- 2 Tbsp olive oil
- 2 cup shredded hash browns, frozen*
- 1 tsp olive oil
- 3 cups diced veggies (peppers, onions, mushrooms, etc.)
- Two eggs
- ½ cup sharp cheese, shredded

Directions

- Heat 2 Tbsp olive oil in a heavy skillet, then add 2 cups shredded hash browns.
- Spread hash browns out in skillet and sprinkle with salt and pepper. Cook over medium to medium-low heat until brown on the bottom about 7 minutes.
- Flip hash browns over sprinkle with salt and pepper, then cook on low for seven more minutes.
- Meanwhile, heat 1 tsp olive oil in a nonstick skillet, then add diced veggies and saute over medium heat for 5 minutes until softened.
- Layer sautéed veggies on top of hash browns. Make two small holes in the mixture, then gently drop eggs in.
- Lightly sprinkle with salt and pepper, and cheese.
- Cover pan and cook over low until eggs are set- about 7 minutes.

Nutrition Facts

Fat: 25g| Saturated Fat: 6g| Cholesterol: 97mg| Sodium: 389mg| Potassium: 689mg| Carbohydrates: 33g| Fiber: 4g| Sugar: 4g| Protein: 10g

46. COTTAGE CHEESE BREAKFAST BOWL (KETO, LOW CARB, DIABETIC FRIENDLY)

Prep Time: 2 mins
Total Time: 2 mins

Ingredients

- ½ - ¾ cup cottage cheese (I use 1%)
- One teaspoon flaxseed oil
- One teaspoon chia seeds
- ¼ cup frozen berries (one small handful)
- Three tablespoons of walnuts - chopped or broken into pieces.

Directions

- Scoop the cottage cheese into a bowl. Drizzle with flaxseed oil.
- Sprinkle on the chia seeds.
- Top with frozen mixed berries and walnuts.
- Serve immediately.

Nutrition Facts

Fat: 1.7g| Saturated Fat: 1.0g| Protein: 1.4g| Cholesterol: 7.1mg| Sodium: 239mg| Total Carbohydrates: 4.5g| Dietary Fiber: 0.2g| Sugars: 1.3g

47. LOW CARB BREAKFAST BURRITOS

Total Time: 30-60 Minutes

Ingredients

- Nonstick cooking spray
- Four eggs
- 1 cup chopped veggies of choice (bell peppers, mushrooms, tomatoes, onions, etc.)
- Cheddar cheese, shredded (optional)

- Eight slices ham

Directions

- In a skillet that has been sprayed with nonstick cooking spray, saute the veggies for a couple of minutes until tender.
- In a small bowl, whisk the eggs and cheese (if using). Add whisked egg to the veggie mixture and scramble until cooked through.
- Place ham slices (2 for each "burrito") on a flat surface and divide egg mixture evenly onto the pieces. Roll up the ham slice around the egg mixture, creating a burrito.
- Return ham rolls to the pan for a quick browning on top and bottom.

Nutrition Facts

Carbohydrates: 9g| Protein: 3g| Fat: 2g| Saturated Fat: 1g| Sodium: 79mg| Fiber: 2g

48. VEGETABLE PANCAKE | HEALTHY BREAKFAST | DIABETIC DIET

Prep Time: 10 mins
Cook Time: 20 mins
Total Time: 30 mins

Ingredients

- ½ cup broccoli florets
- ½ cup onion thinly sliced
- ½ cup white cabbage thinly sliced
- ½ cup purple cabbage thinly sliced
- ½ cup carrot thinly sliced
- ½ cup spring onion roughly chopped
- ½ cup oats flour
- ½ cup barley flour
- ½ tsp salt
- 1 tsp ajwain
- ¼ tsp crushed pepper

Directions

- To begin with vegetable pancake, firstly we need to chop vegetables of your choice & keep them aside.
- Next, take a wide bowl and add the chopped vegetables one by one
- Then add oats flour and barley flour
- Further add salt, ajwain, and crushed pepper

- Mix everything well before adding water
- Now add little water and mix all ingredients so that the batter of the pancake should not be too thin or too thick.
- Once the batter is ready, keep it aside.
- In the meantime, heat a Tawa on moderate flame & apply very little oil
- Once the Tawa is hot enough, pour a ladle full of batter on the tawa & spread evenly
- Again add little oil to the vegetable pancake & cover the lid
- Cook for 2 to 3 mins & then carefully open the lid
- The base of the pancake is cooked well. Now flip over the pancake and cook the other side
- Again flip it and cook for one more minute
- Take out to a plate and turn off the heat
- Now the healthy & tasty vegetable pancake is ready to serve!
- Enjoy this with chutney or tomato ketchup!

Nutrition Facts

Carbohydrates: 37g | Protein: 6g | Fat: 2g | Saturated Fat: 1g | Sodium: 419mg | Potassium: 381mg | Fiber: 7g | Sugar: 4g | Calcium: 58mg | Iron: 2mg

49. BUCKWHEAT APPLE MUFFINS

Total Time: 60 minutes

Ingredients

- Nonstick cooking spray (optional)
- 3/4 cup buckwheat flour
- 1/4 cup flaxseed meal
- One teaspoon baking powder
- 1/4 teaspoon salt
- One large egg
- 1/2 cup unsweetened almond milk
- 1/4 cup coconut oil, melted
- One tablespoon honey
- Two apples, cored, one dice, and one sliced
- 1/2 cup walnut pieces

Directions

- Preheat the oven to 350 degrees F. Line the cups of a muffin tin with paper liners or lightly coat with nonstick cooking spray
- In a large mixing bowl, whisk together the buckwheat flour, flaxseed meal, baking powder, and salt.
- In another bowl, whisk together the egg, almond milk, coconut oil, and honey. Fold the wet mixture into the dry mixture until just mixed. Stir in the diced apple and walnuts.
- Spoon the batter into muffin cups. Top each muffin with one apple slice.
- Bake until browned and a toothpick inserted into the center of a muffin comes out clean, about 25 minutes. Cool for 10 minutes before serving.

Nutritional Details

Total Fat: 10g| Sat Fat: 5g| Cholesterol: 14mg| Sodium: 93mg| Carbs: 13g| Fiber: 3g| Sugars: 5g| Protein: 3g

50. HEALTHY SUGAR-FREE GRANOLA

Prep Time: 5 minutes
Cook Time: 20 minutes
Total Time: 25 minutes

Ingredients

- 1/4 cup coconut oil
- One teaspoon cinnamon
- One teaspoon vanilla extract
- 1/4 cup erythritol or two tablespoons of a Stevia or Monkfruit and Erythritol Blend
- One pinch salt
- 1.5 cups shredded/ flaked coconut sugar-free
- 1 cup slivered/flaked almonds
- 1 cup pepita seeds
- 1 cup sunflower seeds
- 1 cup 'nuts of choice'- pecans, macadamias, hazelnuts, walnuts, etc
- Two tablespoons almond meal/almond flour
- 1/4 cup chia seeds-optional omit for a more traditional granola

Directions

- Preheat your oven to 150 C/ 300 F fan-forced.

- Melt the coconut oil on the stovetop or in the microwave. Mix the erythritol, cinnamon, vanilla extract, and salt in with the coconut oil. Mix all of the dry ingredients in a large bowl. Stir the coconut oil mixture through a dry mix until it is evenly coated.

- Line a large baking tray with a piece of quality baking paper. Evenly spread the granola mix onto the tray. Bake for 20-25 minutes, stirring the granola every 4-5 minutes to prevent browning too much in one place. Remove when granola is a golden color all over.

Nutrition Facts
Calories: 157kcal | Carbohydrates: 3g | Protein: 3g | Fat: 14g | Fiber: 3g

51. EASY DIABETIC BREAKFAST: MIXED BERRY PARFAIT

Prep Time: 5 minutes

Ingredients
- 3.7 oz frozen mixed berries - Equiv. 3/4 cup - defrosted
- 1/2 cup greek yogurt
- 1/4 cup flaked almonds
- 2 Tablespoon desiccated coconut
- 1/4 teaspoon ground cinnamon
- 2 Tablespoon sunflower seeds
- 5-7 drops liquid stevia extract - optional
- Mixed Berry Parfait

Directions
- If you want to parfait a bit sweeter, stir the liquid stevia into the yogurt.
- Layer the ingredients into two glasses starting with the berries, little almonds, sunflower seeds, coconut, a sprinkle of cinnamon, a thin layer of yogurt; then repeat until you use all the ingredients.

Nutrition Facts
Total Fat: 22g| Saturated Fat: 7g| Polyunsaturated Fat: 5g| Monounsaturated Fat: 1g| Cholesterol: 13mg| Sodium: 36mg Potassium: 104mg| Total Carbohydrates: 25g| Dietary Fiber: 7g| Sugars: 13g| Protein: 9g

52. HAM AND BROCCOLI FRITTATA

Prep Time: 10 Min
Cook Time: 25 Min
Servings: 4 Servings
Serving Size: 1/4 frittata

Ingredients
- 1 nonstick cooking spray
- 2 cup packaged hash brown potatoes or freshly grated potato
- 255g small broccoli florets (rinsed and drained, but not dried. Some water droplets should cling to the broccoli)
- Four eggs
- Four egg whites
- 57g lower-sodium, low-fat ham (cut into 1/4-inch cubes)
- 1/4 cup skim milk
- 1/4 tsp black pepper

Directions
- Preheat the oven to 400°F.
- Lightly spray a medium ovenproof skillet with cooking spray. Heat over medium heat. Remove from the heat. Put the potatoes in the skillet. Lightly spray with cooking spray. Cook for 4–5 minutes, or until the potatoes are golden brown, stirring occasionally.
- Put the broccoli in a microwaveable bowl. Microwave, covered, on 100% power (high) for 4 to 5 minutes, or until tender-crisp. Drain in a colander. Stir the broccoli into the potatoes.
- In a medium bowl, whisk together the egg whites and eggs. Whisk in the ham, milk, and pepper. Pour the mixture over the potatoes and broccoli, stirring well.
- Bake for 15–18 minutes, or until the eggs are set (it shouldn't jiggle when the frittata is gently shaken). Let excellent for at least 10 minutes, then cut into four equal slices.

Nutrition Facts
Total Fat: 6g| Saturated Fat: 1.5g| Cholesterol: 195mg| Sodium: 290mg| Total Carbohydrate: 14g| Dietary Fiber: 3g| Total Sugars: 3g| Added Sugars: 1g| Protein: 15g| Potassium: 510mg| Phosphorus: 220mg

53. OAT RISOTTO WITH CHORIZO

Prep Time: 20 minutes
Cook Time: 40 minutes
Total Time: 1 hour
Servings: 4

Ingredients
- 3/4 lb chorizo (340g)
- 2 cups water (500 ml)
- 1/2 teaspoon salt (2.5 ml)
- 1 1/3 cups steel-cut oats (335 ml)
- 1 1/2 cups chicken broth (375 ml)
- 1/2 cup Parmesan cheese finely shredded, divided (125 ml)
- Two teaspoons olive oil (10 ml)
- 2 cups broccoli florets (500 ml)
- 2 cups tomatoes diced (500 ml)
- 1/4 teaspoon black pepper freshly ground (1 ml)
- 1/8 teaspoon sea salt (.5 ml)
- 1/4 cup parsley fresh, to garnish, (60 ml)

Directions
- Slice the chorizo into 1/4" rounds.
- In a large saucepan, bring the water to a boil. Add steel cut oats and salt, constantly stirring until water returns to a spot.
- Reduce heat and simmer, covered, for 25 minutes or until oats are tender, stirring occasionally.
- Stir in chicken broth and simmer, uncovered, for about 5 minutes or until mixture is creamy. Do not overcook.
- Add 6 Tbsp of the parmesan cheese and stir until cheese is melted.
- Meanwhile, in a large nonstick skillet, sauté chorizo and broccoli in olive oil until chorizo is browned. Stir in tomatoes, pepper, and the remaining 1/8 tsp salt.
- Divide risotto between four dishes and top with chorizo and broccoli. Sprinkle with fresh parsley and reserved cheese.

Nutrition Facts:
Calories: 341| Fat: 12g| Saturated Fat: 1g| Fiber: 0.5g| Sodium: 302mg| Cholesterol: 189mg| Protein: 35g| Carbohydrates: 23g

54. SUGAR-FREE FRENCH TOAST

Prep Time: 15 mins
Cook Time: 15 mins
Total Time: 30 mins
Servings: 4

Ingredients

- Eight slices Bread
- ¼ cup Butter
- ½ tsp Ground Cinnamon
- ¼ tsp Nutmeg
- 2 tbsp Splenda
- 2 Eggs ½ cup Milk
- 1 tsp Vanilla Extract

Directions

- Start by melting your butter in a skillet or griddle over medium heat.
- While your butter is melting, combine the sugar alternative (if granular), nutmeg, and cinnamon. Set this bowl aside.
- In another bowl, whisk together the eggs, milk, and vanilla extract. Then, stir in the ingredients from the bowl and the sugar alternative if that alternative is non-granular.
- Lastly, pour this mixture into a shallow bowl or pie plate.
- Dredge or dip each piece of bread through the mixture in the shallow bowl, covering it entirely.
- Then place the bread onto the heated skillet.
- Cook until browned, flipping midway through.
- Your toast should be golden, and the eggs should be cooked.

Nutrition Facts

Carbohydrates: 29g | Protein: 9g | Fat: 15g | Saturated Fat: 8g | Cholesterol: 112mg | Sodium: 436mg | Potassium: 180mg | Fiber: 2g | Sugar: 5g | Calcium: 134mg | Iron: 2.4mg

55. UPMA

Prep Time: 5 Mins
Cook Time: 8 Mins
Total Time: 13 Mins

Ingredients

- 1 cup Rava/ Semolina
- 4 tsp Refined Oil
- 1 tsp Mustard Seeds
- 1/2 inch Ginger finely chopped
- 1 Onion finely chopped
- One small tomato finely chopped
- 6 - 8 Curry Leaves
- 1 Green Chilli chopped
- Salt 1/2 tsp or as per taste
- 1 tsp urad dal

Directions

- Dry roast semolina or sooji in a pan for 2 minutes. Keep stirring continuously else it will burn.
- In 2 minutes, semolina or Rava will be fragrant enough. Remove from pan and keep on a dry plate.
- In the same pan, heat oil. Add some mustard seeds and let them splutter.
- At the same time, add some urad dal also.
- Then add chopped ginger, curry leaves, chopped onions, green chilies, and saute till it's translucent.
- Add chopped tomatoes and cook for another 2 minutes.
- In the meanwhile, heat 2.5 cups of water in a bowl.
- Add boiling hot water to the pan.
- Next, add roasted semolina a little and keep stirring till all rava is added to the water in a pan.
- Let it simmer for some time till all water is absorbed.
- Now turn off the heat and cover the pan with a lid.
- After 2 - 3 minutes, fluff it with a fork.
- Garnish with some fresh coriander leaves or grated coconut and serve with chutney or ketchup.

Nutrition Facts

Calories: 85kcal

56. MUSHROOM SURPRISE

Total Time: 30 mins
Serves: 2

Ingredients

- To make Mushroom Surprise, you'll need:
- 2 Portobello mushrooms
- 1 tsp. garlic, finely chopped
- 1 tbsp. cheddar cheese, finely grated
- 1 tsp. dried thyme or rosemary
- 4 tsp. olive oil
- Two large eggs
- Salt and pepper to taste

Directions

- Preheat the oven to 200°C/Gas Mark
- Place the mushrooms on a baking tray lined with foil.
- Sprinkle the mushrooms with garlic, salt, and pepper to taste.
- Bake for up to 10 minutes or until tender.
- In the meantime, whisk the eggs in a bowl and flavor with salt and pepper to taste.
- Heat the olive oil in a frying pan and over low to medium heat, and cook the egg. Stir gently while cooking until the egg has cooked through and set.
- When the mushrooms are cooked, spoon half of the egg mixture over each mushroom.
- Sprinkle with cheese and the thyme/rosemary.
- Serve immediately.

Nutrition Facts

Calories 184 | Total fat 15.8g | Saturated Fat 3.4g | Carbohydrates 7.4g | Fibre 0.2g | Protein 8.5g

57. HIPPIE BREAKFAST PORRIDGE

Total Time: 30 mins

Ingredients

- 1/4 cup brown rice (50 g)
- 1/4 cup brown lentils (50 g)
- 1/4 cup steel-cut oats (45 g)
- 1/4 cup hulled barley (50 g)
- One cinnamon stick
- 2 cups water
- 1/2 teaspoon vanilla extract

Directions

- Place the brown rice, lentils, oats, and barley in a fine-mesh strainer and rinse well with water. Tap the filter against the sink to remove as much excess water as possible.

- Press the saute setting on your Instant Pot and heat the inner pot for 2 minutes. Transfer the rinsed grain mixture along with the cinnamon stick to the Instant Pot and saute for 2 minutes, stirring frequently.
- Turn off the Instant Pot and add the water. Stir, and then lock the lid into place, making sure the nozzle is in the sealing position.
- Use the Manual (or Pressure Cooking) mode and set the timer for 12 minutes. Use the natural release method when the timer goes off.
- Remove the lid and add the vanilla. Cool to room temperature, then promptly store in your fridge. You can leave the cinnamon stick in for added flavor or take it out before storing it.
- Once you have your grains made, heat up however much you want in a saucepan with some non-dairy milk. Place in a bowl and top with chopped nuts, fruit, non-dairy milk, and a little sweetener of your choice.

Nutrition Facts

Carbohydrates: 21g| Protein: 5g| Fat: 13g| Saturated Fat: 2g|Sodium: 237mg| Fiber: 4g

58. PANCAKES – DIABETIC FRIENDLY

Prep Time: 5 Minutes
Cook Time: 8 Minutes
Yield: 4

Ingredients

- 100g ground rice
- 25g cornflour
- Pinch salt
- Two eggs, beaten
- 300ml milk
- Little sunflower oil for frying

Directions

- Beat together all the ingredients in a bowl.
- Heat a medium nonstick pan and brush with a bit of oil.
- Stir the butter mixture before adding a ladle-full to the pan – tip the pan so the combination covers the base. Cook for 1–2 minutes on each side until golden.
- Repeat until the mixture has been used up (each time, stir the batter before adding it to the pan).
- Serve with berries to make them even more delicious.

Nutrition Facts

Carbohydrates: 19g| Protein: 4g| Fat: 4g| Saturated Fat: 1g| Sodium: 222mg| Fiber: 3g

59. MEXICAN-STYLE STEAK AND EGGS BREAKFAST

Total Time: 20 mins

Ingredients

- One beef Top Sirloin Steak Boneless cut 3/4 inch thick (about 12 ounces)
- Salt
- Two teaspoons vegetable oil
- Six small flour tortillas (6-inch diameter), warmed
- 1-1/2 cups egg substitute
- Six tablespoons reduced-fat shredded Cheddar cheese
- Six tablespoons guacamole
- Six tablespoons salsa
- Six tablespoons reduced-fat sour cream

Directions

- Heat a large, heavy nonstick skillet over medium heat until hot. Season beef steak with salt, as desired. Place beef in skillet.
- Pan-broil 10 to 13 minutes for medium-rare (145F) to medium (160F) doneness, turning occasionally. Remove beef from skillet. Set aside; keep warm.
- Heat oil in the same skillet over medium heat until hot. Add eggs and scramble until set, stirring occasionally; keep warm.
- Carve steak into thin slices. Top each tortilla with equal amounts of eggs, steak, and one tablespoon each of cheese, guacamole, salsa, and sour cream. Serve immediately.

Nutrition Facts

Fat: 10g| Saturated Fat: 4g| Fiber: 2g| Sodium: 553mg| Cholesterol: 45mg| Protein: 24g| Carbohydrates: 20g

60. BREAKFAST BURRITO CASSEROLE

Prep Time: 10 Minutes
Cook Time: 35 Minutes
Total Time: 45 Minutes
Servings: 6

Ingredients

- ½ cup Potato (about half a medium potato)
- ½ cup Green Bell Pepper, chopped
- 1 cup Portabella Mushrooms, chopped
- 2 Garlic Cloves
- 2 Green Onion stalks (sub ¼ cup chopped white or yellow onion)
- 8 oz Ground Breakfast Sausage
- 1 Tbsp Oil
- 4 Large Eggs
- 1 cup Shredded Cheddar Cheese (or Mexican blend)

Directions

Prep

- Peel the potato. Chop the potato into ¼ to ½ pieces. Set aside in a bowl.
- Chop the bell pepper and mushrooms into ¼ to ½ pieces. Set aside in a separate bowl.
- Peel and roughly chop the garlic. Add it to the pepper and mushroom bowl.
- Slice the green onions crosswise. Add the white parts to the mushroom bowl and set the green features aside in a separate bowl for garnish.

Cook

- Heat an oven-safe skillet on the stove on medium-low heat. When hot, add the sausage and break it apart as it cooks. Cook for up to 4 minutes.
- Scoop the sausage into a separate bowl.
- Add the potatoes to the skillet and cook for 4 minutes, stirring once halfway through.

- Add ¼ cup of water to the skillet. Stir the potatoes, scraping the bottom of the pan, and let the water cook-off.
- Preheat the oven to 350°F.
- Add the oil and mushroom mixture to the skillet and stir. Let it cook for 5 minutes, stirring once halfway through.
- If the vegetables stick to the pan, add two tablespoons of water and stir, scraping the bottom of the pan.
- Meanwhile, in a bowl, crack the eggs and add ½ cup of cheese. Stir together well.
- Return the sausage to the pan and stir, evenly distributing everything.
- Pour the egg mixture on top and help spread it across. Sprinkle the remaining ½ cup of cheese on top.
- Bake in the middle of the oven for 10 minutes.
- Remove and garnish with green onions.

Nutrition Facts
Carbohydrates: 9g | Protein: 12g | Fat: 22g | Saturated Fat: 8g | Polyunsaturated Fat: 1g | Monounsaturated Fat: 4g | Cholesterol: 104mg | Sodium: 366mg | Potassium: 331mg | Fiber: 1g | Vitamin C: 21.5mg | Calcium: 90mg | Iron: 1.3mg

61. EASY SUGAR-FREE BREAKFAST SAUSAGE

Prep Time: 15 minutes
Cook Time: 10 minutes

Ingredients
- 2 pounds ground pork
- 2 tsp bell's seasoning or 1/2 tsp each dried sage, rosemary, thyme, pepper
- 2 tsp salt
- 1/2 tsp garlic powder
- 1 tsp ground fennel seeds
- 1 tbsp fresh chopped parsley
- Optional: crushed red pepper flakes
- 1 tbsp avocado oil

Directions
- Mix all the ingredients, except the oil.
- Form 16 balls and flatten by gently pressing in the center of each ball to form an indent. This will help keep their shape.
- Heat the oil in a large skillet over medium-high heat. Once the oil is hot, place eight patties into the skillet. Cook 3-4 minutes on each side until browned and internal temperature reaches 165 degrees F. Remove from the skillet and cook the remaining eight parties in the same manner. Serve with fresh chopped parsley over the tip.

Nutrition Facts
Fat 26g | Saturated Fat 9g | Cholesterol: 82mg | Sodium: 645mg | Potassium: 335mg | Carbohydrates: 1g | Fiber: 1g | Sugar: 1g | Protein: 19g | Vitamin C: 2mg | Calcium: 20mg | Iron: 1mg

62. LOW-CARB BREAKFAST SCRAMBLE

Ready: 20 minutes

Ingredients
- 1/2 cup Egg Substitute
- 1/2 cup Low-fat cottage cheese
- One tablespoon Soy protein powder
- Nonstick spray
- Two strips of Turkey bacon cooked & crumbled
- One teaspoon parsley or cilantro, chopped
- One large Low Carb Tortilla
- 1/4 cup salsa Choose your heat level

Directions
- Place the cottage cheese in a tea strainer and allow it to drain excess liquid.
- Cut a tortilla in half and place each half on a plate.
- Blend the egg substitute with the soy protein, then add in the cottage cheese.
- Scramble this in a sprayed pan until it starts to set. Add in the crumbled bacon and stir in the parsley.
- When the eggs have set, place 1/2 of the mixture on each tortilla. Putting it slightly to one side of the center makes the next step easier.
- Put a spoonful of salsa on top of the eggs, then roll the tortilla into a cone shape. Put the rest of the salsa on the top as a garnish. Sprinkle with more cilantro (or green onion) if you wish.
- Serve immediately.

Nutrients Value
Cals: 190 | Total Fat: 8g | Satfat: 2g | Polyfat: 2g | Monofat: 3g | Chol: 18mg | Na: 827 | K: 417 | Total Carbs: 14g | Fiber: 7g | Net Carbs: 7g

63. SWEET AND SMOKY BAKED EGGS

Prep time: 5 min
Cook time: 25 min
Servings: 4 Servings

Ingredients
- Two sizeable ripe beefsteak or heirloom tomatoes
- 1 tsp ground black pepper
- 1 tsp cumin
- Four eggs (medium)
- 2 tsp Parmesan cheese (grated reduced-fat)

Directions
- Preheat oven to 350°F.
- Wash tomatoes and cut in half. Scoop out the pulp and seeds, leaving about a 1/2-inch rim of tomato.
- Place cut-side up in a greased glass baking dish.
- Sprinkle each tomato half with pepper and cumin. Break an egg into each tomato "shell." Sprinkle each egg with 1/2 tsp of the cheese.
- Bake until the eggs are set, roughly 25 minutes.

Nutrition Facts
Total Fat: 4.5g | Saturated Fat: 1.5g | Cholesterol: 165mg | Sodium: 85mg | Total Carbohydrate: 4g | Dietary Fiber: 1g | Total Sugars: 2g | Protein: 7g | Potassium: 260mg | Phosphorus: 115mg

64. SMOOTHIE BREAKFAST BOWL

Prep Time: 5 Min
Servings: 2 Servings
Serving Size: About 1 Cup

Ingredients
- 3/4 cup unsweetened almond milk
- 1/2 cup nonfat plain Greek yogurt
- 1 cup frozen mixed fruit
- 2 cup baby spinach

- One med frozen banana (sliced)
- 1 bar KIND Maple Glazed Pecan & Sea Salt bar OR 1/2 cup low sugar granola (crumbled)

Directions

- Combine all ingredients except the KIND bar in a blender. Purée until smooth and thick, stopping to stir the mixture in between blending at times.
- Pour smoothie mixture into two bowls. Top each bowl with half of the crumbled KIND bar.

Nutrition Facts

Total Fat: 10g| Saturated Fat: 1g| Cholesterol: 10mg| Sodium: 180mg| Total Carbohydrate: 34g Dietary Fiber: 7g| Total Sugars: 19g| Added Sugars: 2g| Protein: 11g| Potassium: 670mg Phosphorus: 170mg

65. SOUTHWEST BREAKFAST QUICHE

Prep Time: 10 Min
Cook Time: 40 Min
Servings: 6 Servings
Serving Size: 1 Slice

Ingredients

- One nonstick cooking spray
- Three eggs
- 1/4 cup whole wheat flour
- 1/2 tsp baking powder
- 1/2 cup egg whites or egg substitute
- 1/4 cup skim milk
- 1 (7-oz) can green chiles
- 1 cup fat-free cottage cheese (whipped in a food processor until smooth)
- 1 cup reduced-fat shredded cheddar cheese

Directions

- Preheat oven to 400º F. Coat a 9-inch round or square baking dish with canola cooking spray; set aside.
- In the mixer bowl, combine eggs, flour, and baking powder, and beat until blended. Add egg whites and milk and beat until smooth. On low speed, beat in green chilis, cottage cheese, and shredded cheese.
- Pour mixture into prepared dish and bake for 15 minutes. Reduce heat to 350-degrees and bake for about 25 minutes more (until quiche is firm in the center and top is golden brown). Cut into six equal slices and serve as is or top with salsa, avocado, or plain Greek yogurt.

Nutrition Facts

Total Fat: 7g| Saturated Fat: 3.5g| Cholesterol: 110mg| Sodium: 500mg| Total Carbohydrate: 10g| Dietary Fiber: 1g| Total Sugars: 4g| Protein: 16g| Potassium: 230mg| Phosphorus: 300mg

66. POWER GRANOLA

Prep Time: 15 Min
Servings: 22 Servings

Ingredients

- 1 cup unsalted cashews (chopped)
- 1 cup unsalted raw pumpkin seeds (pepitas)
- 1 cup unsalted pecans (chopped)
- 1 cup unsalted sunflower seeds
- 1 cup old-fashioned rolled oats (not quick-cooking)
- 1/4 cup peanut butter
- 1/4 cup olive oil
- 1/4 cup Splenda Brown Sugar blend

Directions

- Preheat an oven to 300 degrees.
- Line a baking sheet with parchment paper or foil. Coat with nonstick cooking spray and set aside.
- In a bowl, combine cashews, pumpkin seeds, pecans, sunflower seeds, and oats. Set aside.
- In the microwave, melt peanut butter, oil, and Splenda Brown Sugar together. Stir to combine.
- Pour peanut butter mixture over oat mixture and stir to coat.
- Spread granola in a packed, single layer onto the prepared baking sheet. Bake for 40-45 minutes, stirring every 10 minutes to ensure even browning.
- Remove from oven and let cool completely. Break up granola and store in an airtight container.

Nutrition Facts

Total Fat: 17g| Saturated Fat: 2g| Total Carbohydrate: 8g| Dietary Fiber: 2g| Total Sugars: 2g| Protein: 5g| Potassium: 190mg| Phosphorus: 210mg

67. SUMMER FRUIT SMOOTHIE

Prep Time: 10 Min
Servings: 4 Servings
Serving Size: 1 Cup

Ingredients

- 1 cup fresh blueberries
- 1 cup chopped fresh strawberries
- Two peaches (peeled, seeded, and chopped)
- peach flavored Greek-style yogurt (nonfat)
- 1 cup almond milk (unsweetened)
- 2 tsp ground flax seed
- 1/2 ice cup

Directions

- Combine all ingredients in a blender and puree until smooth.

Nutrition Facts

Total Fat: 5g| Saturated Fat: 0.5g| Sodium: 50mg| Total Carbohydrate: 22g| Dietary Fiber: 4g| Total Sugars: 14g| Protein: 5g| Potassium: 330mg| Phosphorus: 60mg

68. PUMPKIN APPLE PROTEIN BARS

Prep time: 10 min
Servings: 12 Servings

Ingredients

- One nonstick cooking spray
- One egg
- Two egg whites
- 1 tsp vanilla extract
- 3 tsp Splenda Brown Sugar blend
- 1/3 cup canned Pumpkin
- 1/4 cup unsweetened applesauce
- One apple (peeled and grated)
- 1/2 cup old-fashioned rolled oats
- 1/4 cup almond flour
- One scoop reduced-carb vanilla protein powder (18 g protein per scoop)
- 1 tsp ground cinnamon
- 1/2 tsp baking powder

Directions

1. Preheat oven to 350 degrees F. Coat an 8x8 baking pan with cooking spray.

2. In a medium bowl, whisk together egg, egg whites, vanilla, Splenda Brown Sugar Blend, Pumpkin, applesauce, and grated apple.

3. In another medium bowl, mix oats, almond meal, protein powder, cinnamon, and baking powder.

4. Add wet ingredients to dry ingredients and mix until blended.

5. Pour into prepared baking dish and bake for 25 minutes.

6. Let cool before cutting and serving.

Nutrition Facts

Total Fat: 2g| Cholesterol: 20mg| Sodium: 35mg| Total Carbohydrate: 9g| Dietary Fiber: 1g| Total Sugars: 4g| Protein: 4g| Potassium: 85mg

69. GLUTEN-FREE BANANA BREAD

Prep Time: 15 Min
Cook Time: 35 Min
Servings: 16 Servings

Ingredients

- One nonstick cooking spray
- Four med very ripe bananas (mashed)
- 2 tsp olive oil
- 1 cup low-fat buttermilk (low-fat)
- Two egg whites
- 1 tsp vanilla extract
- 1/4 cup Splenda Sugar Blend
- 2 cup gluten-free baking mix
- 3 tbsp ground flax seed

Directions

1. Preheat oven to 350 degrees. Spray an 8x4-inch loaf pan with cooking spray.

2. In a large bowl, combine bananas, oil, buttermilk, egg whites, vanilla, and Splenda Sugar Blend; mix well.

3. Add gluten-free baking mix and flaxseed and mix until blended. Pour batter into loaf pan. Bake for 30-35 minutes or until a toothpick inserted in the center comes out clean.

Nutrition Facts

Total Fat: 3g| Sodium: 240mg| Total Carbohydrate: 25g| Dietary Fiber: 3g| Total Sugars: 9g| Protein: 4g| Potassium: 280mg| Phosphorus: 70mg

70. EGG AND AVOCADO TOASTS

Prep time: 15 min
Servings: 4 Servings

Ingredients

- Four eggs
- Four slices of hearty whole-grain bread
- One avocado (mashed)
- 1/2 tsp salt
- 1/4 tsp black pepper
- 1/4 cup plain nonfat Greek yogurt

Directions

- To poach each egg, fill a 1-cup microwaveable bowl or teacup with 1/2 cup water. Gently crack an egg into the water, making sure it's completely submerged. Cover with a saucer and microwave on high for about 1 minute, or until the white is set and the yolk is starting to set but still soft (not runny).

- Toast the bread and spread each piece with 1/4 of the mashed avocado.

- Sprinkle avocado with salt (optional) and pepper. Top each piece with a poached egg. Top the egg with 1 Tbsp. Greek yogurt.

Nutrition Facts

Total Fat: 12g| Saturated Fat: 3g| Cholesterol: 185mg| Sodium: 380mg| Total Carbohydrate: 26g| Dietary Fiber: 9g| Total Sugars: 4g| Protein: 12g| Potassium: 330mg| Phosphorus: 240mg

71. DIABETIC BREAKFAST EGG CUPS

Prep Time: 5 minutes
Cook Time: 20 minutes
Servings: 4

Ingredients

- Eight eggs
- Two tbs pesto
- Four tbs sun-dried tomatoes
- 3/4 cup cottage cheese adds creaminess
- 1/2 cup milk
- 2 tsp garlic powder
- Make-Ahead Egg Cups

Directions

- Preheat oven to 350 degrees
- Pesto Egg Cups Diabetes Breakfast
- Add all ingredients to a large bowl, mix all ingredients
- Diabetic breakfast - Make ahead
- spray the muffin tin with cooking spray or use cupcake liners
- Pour egg mixture into muffin tin
- Diabetes Egg Cups - Breakfast
- Bake for 20 minutes or until not jiggly in the middle.

Nutrition Facts

Total Fat: 6g| Saturated Fat: 2g| Cholesterol: 143mg| Sodium: 112mg| Potassium: 59mg| Total Carbohydrates: 1g| Dietary Fiber: 0.04g| Sugars: 1g| Protein 6g

72. AVOCADO AND GOAT CHEESE TOAST

Prep Time: 5 mins
Servings: 2

Ingredients

- Two slices of whole-wheat thin-sliced bread
- (I love Ezekiel sprouted bread and Dave's Killer Bread)
- ½ avocado
- 2 tbsp crumbled goat cheese
- Salt

Directions

- In a toaster or broiler, toast the bread until browned.

- Remove the flesh from the avocado. In a medium bowl, use a fork to mash the avocado flesh. Spread it onto the toast.

- Add any toppings and serve.

Nutritional Value

Fat 24.3g| Saturated Fat 2.4g| Trans Fat 0g| Polyunsaturated Fat 2.7g| Monounsaturated Fat 0.6g| Sodium 159mg| Potassium 164mg| Carbohydrates 16.7g| Fiber 11g| Sugar 2.1g| Protein 11.7g

73. SLOW COOKER BREAKFAST CASSEROLE

Total Time: 5 hours

Ingredients

- Nonstick cooking spray
- 1 pound lean turkey breakfast sausage
- 4 cups frozen shredded hash browns
- Two scallions, white and green parts, minced
- 3/4 cup shredded low-fat cheddar cheese
- One large red or yellow bell pepper, finely diced
- One small onion, finely diced
- Eight eggs
- 1 cup skim milk
- One teaspoon salt-free all-purpose seasoning
- 1/2 teaspoon ground black pepper

Directions

- Cook turkey breakfast sausage. Then set aside to cool slightly.
- Coat the inside of the slow cooker with cook-ing spray. Add hash browns, scallions, cheese, bell pepper, onion, and cooked sausage. Stir to combine.
- In a medium bowl, whisk together eggs, milk, salt-free seasoning, and pepper. Pour over the hash brown mixture and mix again to incorporate.
- Cook on high for 4 hours.

Nutritional Value

Carbohydrates: 20g| Protein: 23g| Fat: 8g| Saturated Fat: 2g| Sodium: 382mg| Fiber: 2g

74. ASPARAGUS FRITTATA

Prep Time: 5 Minutes
Cook Time: 15 Minutes
Total Time: 20 Minutes

Ingredients

- 1-½ cup egg substitute (6 egg equivalents)
- Two scallions, chopped
- 1/3 cup Parmesan cheese
- Two tablespoons olive oil
- 24 asparagus spears, trimmed
- One teaspoon dried mint

Directions

- Slice trimmed asparagus into 1-inch diagonal pieces. Heat oil in a 10-inch nonstick skillet and sauté asparagus and scallions for about five minutes.
- Blend egg substitute, cheese, and mint. Pour over asparagus and scallions in skillet and cook on medium heat, gently pulling sides back from skillet to cook egg substitute throughout. Cover skillet with lid once egg mixture is half-cooked. Use a spatula to divide into fourths and turn once.

Nutrition Facts

Total Fat: 6g| Sodium: 90mg| Total Carbohydrate: 8g| Dietary Fiber: 3g| Total Sugars: 3g| Added Sugars: 1g| Protein: 15g|

75. SPANISH POTATO OMELET

Prep Time: 10 Minutes
Cook Time: 150 Minutes
Total Time: 160 Minutes

Ingredients

- Nonstick cooking spray
- 1 pound russet potatoes, peeled and cut into 3/4-inch pieces
- Two tablespoons olive oil
- 1/2 cup chopped onion (1 medium)
- 3/4 teaspoon salt
- 1/4 teaspoon black pepper
- 12 eggs, lightly beaten
- 1/2 cup shredded reduced-fat cheddar cheese (2 ounces)
- 1/2 cup chopped tomato (1 medium)

Directions

- Line a 3 1/2- or 4-quart round slow cooker with a disposable slow cooker liner.
- Coat the liner with cooking spray. In a large skillet, cook potatoes in hot oil over medium heat for about 5 minutes or until lightly browned, stirring frequently.
- Add onion; cook for 2 to 3 minutes more or until onion is tender, frequently stirring (the potatoes should still be firm).
- Transfer potato mixture to the prepared cooker. Sprinkle with salt and pepper.
- Pour eggs on top of the potato mixture; stir gently to distribute potatoes evenly.
- Cover and cook in a low-heat setting for about 2 1/2 hours or until eggs are set.
- Using a knife, loosen the omelet from the disposable liner; transfer the omelet to a plate.
- Sprinkle with cheese. Cover with foil and let stand for 5 minutes to melt the cheese slightly. Cut omelets into wedges. Top with tomato. Serve warm or at room temperature.

Nutrition Facts

Cal:202| Total Fat: 12g| Sat Fat: 4g| Chol: 284mg| Sodium: 389mg| Carb: 11g| Fiber: 1g| Sugars: 1g| Protein: 12g

76. CHILAQUILES CASSEROLE

Prep Time: 10 Minutes
Cook Time: 45 Minutes
Total Time: 55 Minutes

Ingredients

- One tablespoon vegetable oil
- 1 cup chopped onion (1 large)
- Two cloves garlic, minced
- Nonstick cooking spray
- 12 6-inch corn tortillas, cut into 1-inch pieces
- 2 cups shredded reduced-fat Monterey Jack cheese (8 ounces)
- 2 4 – ounce can diced green chile peppers, undrained
- Four eggs, lightly beaten
- 2 cups low-fat buttermilk
- 1/2 teaspoon salt
- 1/4 teaspoon ground black pepper
- 1/8 teaspoon ground cumin
- 1/8 teaspoon dried oregano, crushed
- Salsa (optional)

Directions

- Preheat oven to 375 degrees F. In a large skillet, heat oil over medium heat. Add onion and garlic; cook until tender.
- Meanwhile, coat a 2-quart rectangular baking dish with cooking spray. Spread half of the tortilla pieces in the bottom of the prepared baking dish. Top with half of the cheese and one can of chile peppers. Sprinkle with

onion mixture. Top with the remaining tortilla pieces, cheese, and chile peppers.

- In a large bowl, combine eggs, buttermilk, salt, black pepper, cumin, and oregano. Pour evenly over ingredients in the baking dish.
- Bake for 35 to 40 minutes or until the center is set and edges are lightly browned. Let stand 15 minutes before serving. If desired, serve with salsa.

Nutrition Facts
15g Total Fat| 6g Satfat| 125mg Chol| 532mg Sodium| 23g Carb| 3g Fiber| 5g Sugars| 14g Protein

77. MUSHROOM SCRAMBLED EGGS

Prep Time: 10 Minutes
Cook Time: 10 Minutes
Total Time: 20 Minutes

Ingredients

- Nonstick cooking spray
- 1/2 cup sliced fresh mushrooms
- 1/4 cup thinly sliced green onions
- One teaspoon cooking oil
- 1 8 – ounce carton refrigerated or frozen egg product, thawed, or four eggs, beaten
- 1/4 cup fat-free milk
- 1/8 teaspoon ground black pepper
- 1/2 cup shredded reduced-fat cheddar cheese (2 ounces) or 1/4 cup crumbled feta or blue cheese (2 ounces)
- One slice turkey bacon or bacon, crisp-cooked and crumbled
- Eight grape or cherry tomatoes halved

Directions

- Coat an unheated large nonstick skillet with nonstick cooking spray— Preheat the skillet over medium heat. Add mushrooms and green onions. Cook and stir for 5 to 7 minutes or until vegetables are tender. Stir in oil.
- In a medium bowl, stir together egg, milk, and pepper. Pour egg mixture into skillet. Cook, without stirring, until mixture begins to set on the bottom and around the edge. Using a large spoon or spatula, lift and fold the partially cooked egg mixture, so the uncooked portion flows underneath.

- Sprinkle with cheese and bacon. Continue cooking over medium heat for 2 to 3 minutes or until the egg mixture is cooked through but is still glossy and moist. Remove from heat immediately.
- To serve, top with tomatoes.

Nutrition Facts
5g total fat| 2g sat fat| 13mg chol| 286mg sodium| 5g carb| 1g fiber| 11g protein

78. CRUSTLESS SPINACH QUICHE

Prep Time: 10 minutes
Cook Time: 50 minutes
Total Time: 1 hour
Servings: 6 slices

Ingredients

- One tablespoon butter
- One small onion (about 1/2 cup) finely diced
- Two cloves garlic minced
- Four large eggs
- One ¼ cups Heavy Cream
- ¼ teaspoon dried oregano
- ⅛ teaspoon dried red pepper flakes
- 1 cup feta cheese (about 4 ounces) crumbled
- One 10-ounce pkg frozen spinach defrosted, water squeezed out.

Directions

- Preheat oven to 325º Fahrenheit. Butter or grease a 9-inch pie dish.
- Heat a medium skillet over medium-low heat. Add Butter. When butter melts, stir in the onions. Cook onions until soft and translucent and just beginning to brown on the edges. Stir in garlic. Cook gently while stirring until garlic is fragrant--about one minute. Remove pan from the heat and set aside.
- I was cooking the onions and garlic for the quiche.
- In a medium mixing bowl, whisk together the eggs, heavy cream, oregano, sea salt, and red pepper flakes. Set aside.
- Wet ingredients in a mixing bowl.
- Transfer the onion and garlic mixture to the pie dish. Spread evenly.

- I am spreading the onions and garlic in the pie dish.
- Sprinkle the feta cheese over the onion and garlic mixture.
- I am adding the feta cheese over the onions.
- Evenly distribute the spinach over the feta cheese, breaking up any clumps.
- I am adding spinach to the quiche.
- Give the egg mixture one more stir, then pour it over the ingredients in the pie dish.
- Crustless Spinach Quiche ready to go in the oven.
- Bake in the preheated oven for 50-55 minutes, or until the quiche is set and starting to brown on top.
- Crustless spinach quiche after it has baked.

Nutrition Facts
Fat: 15g| Saturated Fat: 9g| Monounsaturated Fat: 3g| Cholesterol: 166mg| Sodium: 353mg| Potassium: 87mg| Carbohydrates: 5g| Fiber: 1g| Sugar: 2g| Protein: 10g

79. MIXED GREENS WITH CRANBERRIES, BACON, AND WALNUTS

Prep time: 10 min
Servings: 5 Servings

Ingredients

- Two slice bacon (cut into 1-inch pieces)
- 1/4 walnuts (chopped)
- 1 (10-oz) bag spring lettuce mix
- 170g broccoli slaw mix
- 2 tsp dried cranberries
- 2 tsp balsamic vinegar
- 1/2 tsp Dijon mustard
- 2 1/2 tsp olive oil
- 1 tsp honey or two packets of artificial sweetener

Directions

5. In a medium skillet, cook the bacon over medium-high heat until done. Place the bacon on a paper towel and set it aside.

6. Place the walnuts in a small nonstick skillet on low heat and cook until the walnuts begin to brown, about 4 minutes.

7. In a salad bowl, mix all of the salad ingredients.

8. In a small bowl, whisk together the dressing ingredients. Pour dressing ingredients over the salad and toss to coat.

Nutrition Facts

Total Fat: 13g| Saturated Fat: 2g| Cholesterol: 10mg| Sodium: 150mg| Total Carbohydrate: 12g| Dietary Fiber: 3g| Total Sugars: 8g| Protein: 5g| Potassium: 280mg| Phosphorus: 80mg

80. SPINACH AND PARMESAN EGG BITES

Prep time: 15 min
Cook time: 20 min
Servings: 8 Servings

Ingredients

- One nonstick cooking spray
- frozen spinach (thawed and squeezed dry)
- 1/4 roasted red peppers (drained and chopped)
- Two green onions (thinly sliced)
- 1 tbsp plus 1 tsp grated Parmesan cheese
- 1 cup egg substitute
- 1/2 cup skim milk
- 1 tsp mustard powder
- 1/8 tsp salt
- 1/8 tsp black pepper

Directions

1. Preheat the oven to 350°F. Lightly spray 16 cups of two 12-cup mini muffin pans or 16 cups of a 24-cup mini muffin pan with cooking spray.

2. In a medium bowl, using a fork, separate the spinach into small pieces. Stir in the roasted peppers and green onions. Spoon the spinach mixture into the sprayed muffin cups. Sprinkle the Parmesan over the spinach mixture.

3. In a separate medium bowl, whisk together the remaining ingredients. Pour into the filled muffin cups. Fill the empty muffin cups with water to keep the pan from warping.

4. Bake for 18–20 minutes, or until a wooden toothpick inserted in the center comes out clean. Transfer the pans to a cooling rack. Let cool for 10 minutes. Using a thin spatula or flat knife, loosen the sides of the quiche bites. Serve warm.

5. Refrigerate leftovers in an airtight container for up to 5 days. To reheat, put 4–6 quiche bites on a microwaveable plate. Microwave on 100% power (high) for 45 seconds to 1 minute, or until heated through.

Nutrition Facts

Total Fat: 1.5g| Saturated Fat: 0.5g| Sodium: 190mg| Total Carbohydrate: 3g| Dietary Fiber: 1g| Total Sugars: 1g| Protein: 6g| Potassium: 270mg| Phosphorus: 80mg

81. CRUSTLESS ASPARAGUS AND TOMATO QUICHE

Prep time: 10 mins
Cook time: 40 mins
Servings: 4 Servings

Ingredients

- Nonstick cooking spray
- One asparagus (trimmed and cut diagonally into 2-inch pieces)
- Four green onions (chopped)
- 12 grape or cherry tomatoes (halved)
- 1 cup skim milk
- Four eggs
- Four egg whites
- 2 tsp dijon mustard
- 1 1/2 tsp chopped fresh thyme or 1/2 tsp dried thyme
- 1/4 tsp black pepper
- 1/2 cup shredded low-fat cheddar or Colby cheese

Directions

1. Preheat the oven to 350°F. Lightly spray a 9-inch glass pie pan with cooking spray.

2. In a medium nonstick skillet, heat the oil over medium heat, swirling to coat the bottom. Cook the asparagus and green onions for 4–5 minutes, or until soft. Arrange the asparagus mixture and the tomatoes in the pie pan.

3. In a medium bowl, whisk together the remaining ingredients except for the cheese. Pour the mixture over the vegetables. Sprinkle with the cheese.

4. Bake for 30–35 minutes, or until a knife inserted in the center comes out clean. Let the quiche cool for about 10 minutes before slicing into four equal slices.

Nutrition Facts

Total Fat: 5g| Saturated Fat: 1.5g| Cholesterol: 100mg| Sodium: 280mg| Total Carbohydrate: 10g| Dietary Fiber: 3g| Total Sugars: 7g| Protein: 15g| Potassium: 500mg| Phosphorus: 250mg

SOUPS AND STEW

82. SLOW COOKER CHICKEN NOODLE SOUP

Servings: 6
Prep time: 10 minutes
Cook time: 4 hours
Total: 4 hours 10 minutes

Ingredients

- One 3-pound whole chicken, cut into eight pieces

- Two large onions: one should be peeled and quartered, and one should be small diced
- Three large carrots: one should be peeled and quartered, and two should be small diced
- Three sprigs of flat-leaf parsley
- ½ teaspoon crushed dried thyme
- ½ teaspoon crushed dried marjoram
- ¼ teaspoon freshly ground pepper
- 1-quart canned no-salt, no-fat chicken broth
- 1 quart boiling water
- 6 ounces medium-wide noodles (cooked separately)
- 4 ounces button mushrooms, sliced
- ½ pound fresh spinach, well washed and large stems removed
- Two celery stalks, diced small

Directions

1. Rinse and pat dry chicken—place in a 5-quart or larger crockery slow cooker. Place the peeled and quarter onion peeled and quartered carrot and parsley around chicken pieces. Sprinkle with thyme, marjoram, and pepper.
2. Add chicken broth, cover, and cook on low for 7 to 8 hours or on high for 2 1/2 to 3 hours.
3. When done cooking, remove and discard the onion, carrot, and parsley.
4. Skim off and discard all surface fat from the broth.
5. Remove the chicken from broth and cool for about 10 minutes, until cool enough to handle. Remove and discard the chicken skin and bones. Shred chicken.
6. Add shredded chicken back to the slow cooker and bring to a simmer.
7. Add diced onion, diced carrots, diced celery, mushroom, and spinach. Simmer for 10 minutes.
8. Meanwhile, cook noodles according to package directions.
9. Before serving, add cooked noodles to soup and season with salt and pepper (to taste).

Nutrition Facts

31g Protein| 7g Total Fat| 1.8g Saturated Fat| 24g Carbohydrates| 2g Dietary Fiber| 72mg Cholesterol| 615mg Potassium| 121mg Sodium

83. 3-ALARM CHILI

Prep Time: 15 Minutes
Cook Time: 1 Hour
Total: 1 Hour 15 Minutes

Ingredients

- 1 pound top sirloin, coarsely ground
- One medium white onion, 6 ounces, chopped
- One large clove of garlic, minced
- One medium red bell pepper, 6 ounces, seeded and chopped
- Three tablespoons chili powder
- ½ tablespoon ground cumin
- One teaspoon crushed dried oregano
- 1 14 1/2-ounce no salt added crushed tomatoes
- ½ cup low-sodium canned beef broth
- ½ cup plain nonfat yogurt
- Two tablespoons minced fresh cilantro
- ¼ teaspoon cayenne pepper
- Salt (to taste)
- Freshly ground pepper (to taste)

Directions

1. Put the ground sirloin in a large saucepan over medium heat. Cook, stirring, until beef is no longer pink. Drain off any fat or juices.
2. Measure 2 tablespoons of the onion; set aside.
3. Put remaining onion, garlic, and bell pepper into the pot and cook, stirring, for 5 minutes. Stir in chili powder, cumin, oregano, tomatoes with their liquid, and beef broth.
4. Lower heat to simmer and cook, covered, until meat and vegetables are tender, about 35 to 45 minutes.
5. Meanwhile, finely mince the reserved onion. Place in a small bowl and stir in remaining topping ingredients. Set aside.
6. When the Chili is done, spoon into a bowl and offer to the top to spoon onto each serving.

Nutrition Facts

31g Protein| 8g Total Fat| 3.0g Saturated Fat| 17g Carbohydrate| 4g Dietary Fiber| 75mg Cholesterol| 147mg Sodium

Vegetable Soup

Servings: 6
Prep Time: 20 Minutes
Cook Time: 1 Hour
Total: 1 Hour 20 Minutes

Ingredients

- One tablespoon olive oil
- ½ pound leeks, trimmed, split in half lengthwise, and well rinsed
- One medium white onion, chopped
- ½ pound carrots, peeled and thinly sliced on the diagonal
- Two large celery ribs, thinly sliced on the diagonal
- Two tablespoons dried lentils
- Two tablespoons dried split peas
- Two tablespoons dried small white beans
- One teaspoon crushed dried thyme
- ½ teaspoon freshly ground pepper
- 2 quarts low-sodium canned chicken or vegetable broth
- 1 14 1/2-ounce can no salt added plum tomatoes, drained and coarsely chopped
- 4 ounces fresh spinach, well rinsed and tough stems discarded

Directions

- In a large soup pot, heat oil over medium-low heat.

- Add leeks and onion to the pot. Cook, stirring, until vegetable wilt (about 5 minutes).
- Add remaining ingredients, except tomatoes and spinach. Bring to a boil. Reduce heat and simmer, covered, for 45 minutes, stirring occasionally.
- Add tomatoes and continue to simmer, covered, for another 15 minutes, until white beans are tender.
- Add spinach and simmer, uncovered, until wilted, about 3 minutes, stirring.
- Ladle into soup bowls and serve.

Nutrition Facts

8g Protein| 3g Total Fat| 0.4g Saturated Fat| 23g Carbohydrate| 7g Dietary Fiber, 110mg Sodium

84. ASIAN SOUP WITH SHREDDED CHICKEN AND RICE

Servings: 4
Prep Time: 30 Minutes
Cook Time: 30 Minutes
Total: 1 Hour

Ingredients

- Four dried black mushrooms, rinsed
- One large clove of garlic, minced
- One small Serrano or Thai chile pepper, seeded and minced
- One tablespoon minced fresh ginger
- 6 cups low-sodium canned chicken broth
- Two teaspoons low-sodium soy sauce
- Two 6-ounce chicken breast halves, poached and shredded
- 4 ounces snow peas, trimmed
- One small carrot, 2 ounces, thinly sliced
- Two freshwater chestnuts, peeled and thinly sliced (maybe used canned)
- Four scallions, thinly sliced
- 1 cup hot cooked rice
- Salt (to taste)
- Freshly ground pepper (to taste)

Directions

- In a soup pot, combine mushrooms, garlic, chile pepper, ginger, chicken broth, and soy sauce. Bring to a boil over medium heat. Boil for 2 minutes. Remove from heat, cover, and let stand for 30 minutes.
- Using a slotted spoon, remove black mushrooms and slice. Return to the pot.
- Bring the mixture back to a boil. Add remaining ingredients, except scallions and rice.
- Lower heat and simmer, partially covered, for 10 minutes.
- Stir in scallions and ladle soup into wide soup bowls.
- Place 1/4 cup of the hot rice in the center of each bowl. Serve at once.

Nutrition Facts

26g Protein| 1g Total Fat| 0.4g Saturated Fat| 20g Carbohydrate| 2g Dietary Fiber| 49mg Cholesterol| 216mg Sodium

85. STEAK AND MUSHROOM SOUP

Total Time: 6 hours

Ingredients

- Two medium onions, about 1/2 pound, coarsely chopped
- Three garlic cloves, minced
- Two carrots, peeled and finely chopped
- Two ribs celery, finely chopped
- Three tablespoons unbleached all-purpose flour
- One teaspoon crushed dried thyme
- ½ teaspoon lemon pepper seasoning
- 1 ½ pounds lean beef top round steak, trimmed of all fat and cut into 1-inch cubes
- 1 14 1/2-ounce can low-sodium diced tomatoes
- 1 pound button mushrooms, cleaned and thickly sliced
- 7 cups fat-free low-sodium canned beef broth
- One large bay leaf
- 1 pound Swiss chard, coarsely chopped

Directions

- Put onion, garlic, carrots, and celery in a 5-quart or larger crockery slow cooker.
- In a large self-sealing plastic bag, combine flour, lemon pepper seasoning, and thyme. Add beef cubes and toss to coat evenly—place meat on top of the onion mixture. Cover the heart with the tomatoes and their juice. Top with the mushrooms. Pour beef broth into a slow cooker. Add the bay leaf. Do not stir.
- Cover and cook on LOW for 8 1/2 to 9 1/2 hours or on HIGH for 4 1/4 to 4 3/4 hours.
- Add the chard and stir the soup, removing and discarding the bay leaf—cover and cook on LOW for 15 minutes or on HIGH for 10 minutes.

Nutrition FactsInformation

- 19g Protein| 3g Total Fat|1.0g Saturated Fat| 9g Carbohydrate| 2g Dietary Fiber| 38mg Cholesterol| 158mg Sodium

86. SPICY TORTILLA SOUP

Servings: 4
Prep Time: 30 Minutes
Cook Time: 30 Minutes
Total: 1 Hour

Ingredients

- 6 cups 98% fat-free, no-salt-added canned chicken broth
- Cooking spray
- 1 cup chopped white onion
- Two jalapeño chile peppers, seeded and minced
- Two cloves garlic, minced
- 2 cups chopped plum tomato
- ½ tablespoon crushed dried oregano
- Six fresh corn tortillas, cut into thin strips
- 1 cup shredded cooked chicken breast
- ¾ cup shredded low-fat monterey jack cheese
- One small ripe avocado, pitted, peeled, and cut lengthwise into 12 wedges
- Two scallions, white part, and 2 inches green chopped
- Three tablespoons chopped cilantro
- One fresh lime, cut into six wedges
- Salt and pepper, to taste

Directions

- Preheat oven to 450°F. Lightly coat a baking sheet with cooking spray.

Arrange tortilla strips in a single layer on the baking sheet and bake until crisp, 5 to 7 minutes, tossing strips occasionally. Remove from oven and set aside.

- In a large soup pot, bring chicken broth to a boil; reduce heat, and simmer.
- Lightly coat a large nonstick skillet with cooking spray. Add onion, chile peppers, and garlic. Sauté over medium-low heat for 5 minutes, stirring occasionally.
- Add tomato, oregano, and pepper. Sauté, stirring, for 1 minute.
- Transfer mixture to soup pot and stir into the simmering broth. Cover and simmer for 20 minutes.
- Stir cooked chicken into simmering soup.

To Serve:

- Place two tablespoons of shredded cheese in each of 6 shallow soup bowls.
- Divide the soup equally between the bowls and top each serving with two avocado slices and some scallion and cilantro.
- Float tortilla strips on top and offer a wedge of lime to squeeze over each serving.

Nutrition Facts

17g Protein| 8g Total Fat| 2.7g Saturated Fat| 21g Carbohydrates| 4g Dietary Fiber| 30mg Cholesterol| 221mg Sodium

87. TURKEY MINESTRONE

Servings: 4
Prep Time: 15 Minutes
Cook Time: 50 Minutes
Total: 1 Hour 5 Minutes

Ingredients

- One clove garlic, minced
- 6 cups 98% fat-free, no-salt-added canned chicken broth
- One medium red-skinned potato, scrubbed and diced
- ¼ cup dried split peas
- ½ teaspoon crushed dried basil
- ½ teaspoon crushed dried thyme
- One small bay leaf
- One medium zucchini, cut into 1-inch cubes
- One sizeable ripe plum tomato, seeded and diced
- One 15-ounce cannellini beans, rinsed and drained
- 1 cup chopped cooked turkey meat
- ¼ cup chopped flat-leaf parsley (optional)
- Two tablespoons freshly grated Parmesan cheese (optional)

Directions

- In a large pot, heat oil over medium heat. Add onion and garlic. Sauté until onion is wilted, about 5 minutes. Stir in chicken broth.
- Raise heat and add potato, split peas, basil, thyme, and bay leaf. Bring to a boil, reduce heat, and simmer, uncovered, for 30 minutes.
- Remove bay leaf. Stir in zucchini, tomato, cannellini beans, and turkey. Simmer, uncovered, another 15 minutes, stirring occasionally.
- Ladle into soup bowls. If using, sprinkle each serving with parsley and then some of the grated cheese.

Nutrition Facts

20g Protein| 4g Total Fat| 0.9g Saturated Fat| 26g Carbohydrates| 7g Dietary Fiber| 27mg Cholesterol| 253mg Sodium

88. EASY CREAM OF TOMATO SOUP

Servings: 12
Prep Time: 15 Minutes
Cook Time: 20 Minutes
Total: 35 Minutes

Ingredients

- One tablespoon reduced-fat margarine
- One tablespoon canola oil
- One medium onion, finely chopped
- ½ teaspoon crushed dried thyme
- ¼ teaspoon crushed dried oregano
- Three 14.5-ounce cans of no-salt-added diced tomatoes with the juice
- 5 cups no-salt-added canned chicken broth
- Pinch cayenne pepper (optional)
- Salt (optional)
- Freshly ground pepper (to taste)
- Two 12-ounce cans of evaporated skim milk

Directions

- In a heavy soup pot, heat margarine, and oil over medium-low heat.
- Add onion and cook, frequently stirring, until onion is very limp (about 10 minutes), taking care to not let the onion brown.
- Add thyme, oregano, tomatoes with their juice, and chicken broth. Bring to a boil; reduce heat to low and simmer, partially covered, for 20 minutes.
- Taste soup, adding cayenne and salt (if using), and pepper.
- Stir in evaporated milk and heat through. Do not let the mixture boil.

Nutrition Facts

7g Protein| 2g Total Fat| 0.3g Saturated Fat| 13g Carbohydrate| 1g Dietary Fiber| 2g Cholesterol| 112mg Sodium

89. MOM'S CHICKEN SOUP WITH EGG WHITE MATZO BALLS

Servings: 12
Prep Time: 10 Minutes

Ingredients

- One broiler chicken, about 3 pounds (1440 g), cut into eight pieces, neck included, cleaned, all fat removed
- One large onion
- Three whole cloves
- One sweet potato, scrubbed
- One turnip, peeled and left whole
- 4 cups fat-free, low-sodium kosher for Passover chicken stock or half water/half dry white Passover wine
- Three large sprigs of fresh dill
- Three sprigs parsley
- Two bay leaves
- Freshly ground pepper
- Egg white matzo balls (recipe follows)
- Chopped fresh dill for garnish (optional)

Directions

- Place the chicken and onion in a large soup pot. Stick the cloves into the onion. Place in the pot along with the

sweet potato and turnip. Cover with broth or water/wine mixture. Bring to a simmer and add the herbs. Skim the soup as needed.
- Simmer until the chicken falls off the bone and the vegetables are soft, 2 1/2 to 3 hours. Strain the soup into a pot and refrigerate so that you can remove any fat which congeals as it gets cold.
- Discard the herbs, onion, and turnip. Peel the sweet potato and dice.
- Refrigerate in a small microwave-proof covered container. Cut the chicken into chunks, discarding the bones.
- Pack the chicken into a self-sealing storage bag and refrigerate it to use in another meal, such as for chicken salad.

To Serve:
- Reheat the chicken soup to a lively simmer.
- Reheat the sweet potato in the microwave.
- Ladle the hot soup into 12 heated shallow soup plates, adding one cooked matzo ball to each serving.
- Scatter the sweet potato cubes into the soup and sprinkle with dill (if using).
- Serve hot.
- Refrigerate any leftover soup, sweet potato, and cooked matzo balls separately.

Nutrition Facts

15g Protein| 6g Total Fat| 1.0g Saturated Fat| 8g Carbohydrates| 36mg Cholesterol| 188mg Potassium| 105mg Sodium

90. SPRING VEGETABLE SOUP WITH SCALLION AND DILL-FLECKED MATZO BALLS

Servings: 8
Prep Time: 2 Hours
Cook Time: 55 Minutes
Total: 2 Hours 55 Minutes

Ingredients

- 3 Tbs unsalted pareve kosher-for-Passover margarine
- Three scallions
- Two large eggs
- 1 Tbs fat-free, no-salt-added canned chicken broth
- ½ tsp kosher salt
- ¼ tsp freshly ground pepper
- ½ cup unsalted matzo meal
- 1 Tbs minced fresh dill
- Canola oil cooking spray
- Three medium carrots, diced
- 2 cups small broccoli florets
- Two small zucchini, diced
- Two yellow crookneck squash, diced
- 8 ounces shiitake mushrooms, stems removed, caps sliced
- One small red onion, diced
- Two large cloves of garlic, minced
- 6 cups fat-free, no-salt-added canned chicken broth
- One 28-ounce no-salt-added canned diced tomatoes
- 4 ounces sugar snap peas, trimmed
- 2 Tbs fresh dill, chopped

Directions

For The Matzo Balls:

1. Melt margarine in a heavy small skillet over medium heat. Add scallions and sauté until tender, about 2 minutes. Cool.
2. In a medium bowl, whisk eggs, chicken broth, salt, and pepper. Mix in scallion mixture, matzo meal, and dill. Cover and chill until firm, at least 2 hours.
3. Line a baking sheet with parchment paper or plastic wrap. Using moistened palms, roll rounded teaspoonfuls of matzo mixture into small balls. Place on prepared baking sheet. Chill for 30 minutes.
4. Bring a large pot of lightly salted water to a boil. Drop matzo balls into boiling water. Cover and cook until matzo balls are tender, about 25 minutes.
5. Using a slotted spoon, transfer matzo balls to a large plate.

For The Soup:

6. Lightly coat a large, heavy soup pot with cooking spray. Add carrots, broccoli, zucchini, squash, mushrooms, red onion, and garlic.
7. Sauté until vegetables are almost tender, about 10 minutes.
8. Add broth, tomatoes with their juice, sugar snap peas, and dill. Simmer until vegetables are tender, about 20 minutes.
9. Add matzo balls to the soup and continue to cook until heated through. The soup will be thick.
10. Ladle into soup bowls and serve.

Nutrition Facts

8g Protein| 6g Total Fat| 1.3g Saturated Fat| 22g Carbohydrates| 5g Dietary Fiber| 53mg Cholesterol| 193mg Sodium

91. HEARTY BUTTERNUT SQUASH SOUP

Servings: 6
Prep Time: 30 Minutes
Cook Time: 15 Minutes
Total: 45 Minutes

Ingredients

- 1 1/2 inch piece of ginger, peeled and sliced thin
- ½ cup dry white wine
- 2 cups fat-free, no-salt-added canned chicken broth
- ½ onion, chopped
- One rib celery, chopped
- Two large garlic cloves, minced
- One ¾ lbs butternut squash, peeled and cubed

- 1/3 cup nonfat, plain yogurt, plus additional for garnish
- 1/3 cup skim milk
- 2 Tbs chopped, fresh chives

Directions

- Place the ginger and wine in a small pot. Bring to a simmer. Remove from heat and steep while you prepare the soup.
- In a large pot, cook the onions, celery, and garlic in 1/2 cup of the stock until the onion is wilted.
- Add the remaining stock and squash and bring to a simmer. Continue to simmer until the squash is tender, adding more stock or water as needed.
- Using a food processor or blender, puree squash mixture until smooth. If using a food processor, do this in batches, so the machine does not overflow.
- Whisk in the yogurt and milk.
- Drain the wine and discard the ginger. Add the wine to the soup.
- Reheat (do not boil to avoid curdling) and serve with a dollop of yogurt and a sprinkling of chives.

Nutrition Facts

4g Protein| 18g Carbohydrates| 4g Dietary Fiber| 43mg Sodium

92. PASTA E FAGIOLI (PASTA AND BEAN SOUP)

Total Time: 50-60 minutes

Ingredients

- Olive oil cooking spray
- One small onion, 4 ounces (120 g), chopped
- One carrot, 3 ounces (90 g), chopped
- One zucchini, 4 ounces (120 g), chopped
- 2 ounces (60 g) button mushrooms, cleaned and sliced
- 1 14 1/2-ounce (435 g) no salt added diced tomatoes with juice
- One 16-ounce (480 g) can of cannellini beans, rinsed well
- 3 cups (720 ml) canned fat-free low-sodium beef or vegetable broth
- Freshly ground pepper
- 6 ounces (180 g) dried penne pasta or other pasta
- 2 tablespoons (24 g) grated Parmesan cheese

Direction

- Spray a nonstick-covered pot with cooking spray. Add the onion, carrot, zucchini, and mushrooms; sauté for 5 to 6 minutes until onions wilt.
- Add the tomatoes with their juice and simmer, covered, for 20 minutes. Add the beans and simmer, uncovered, for 5 minutes. Add the broth and cook, uncovered, for 10 minutes. Cool and freeze in an airtight container.
- When ready to serve, reheat in a pot or the microwave. While the soup is reheating, cook the pasta according to package directions to al dente. (Do not overcook the pasta as it will continue to cook in the hot soup). Drain the pasta and combine it with the soup.
- Ladle into soup bowls, topping each serving with a sprinkling of Parmesan cheese.

Nutrition Facts

9g Protein| 2g Total Fat| 0.5g Saturated Fat| 35g Carbohydrate| 4g Dietary Fiber| 2mg Cholesterol| 181mg Sodium

93. FRUIT SOUP

Total Time: 30 minutes

Ingredients

- 1 ½ Cups orange juice
- ½ cup plain nonfat yogurt
- 1 Tbs sugar
- One 10-ounce (300 g) frozen raspberries, thawed
- One medium banana, sliced

Directions

- In a blender, place the orange juice, yogurt, sugar, and thawed raspberries. Blend until smooth.
- Divide the banana slices between 4 soup bowls. Top with equal amounts of the orange juice mixture.
- Serve at once to eat with a spoon.

Nutrition Facts

4g Protein| 1g Total Fat| 30g Carbohydrate| 6g Dietary Fiber| 1g Cholesterol| 25mg Sodium

94. MISO SOUP

Total Time: 30 minutes

Ingredients

- Six dried black mushrooms
- Instant miso soup for 6
- Six carrot flowers
- One scallion, chopped including some green
- 12 1/3-inch squares of firm tofu, about 2 ounces (60 g) total
- Six slices of bamboo shoots

Directions

- Soak the mushrooms in warm water to cover until softened, about 20 minutes. Drain, and discard the stems. Cut the caps into small squares.
- Prepare the instant miso according to directions and keep warm.
- Cut six paper-thin slices of carrot and then fashion into a flower by cutting out notches around the edge. If you wish. Leaving them around also looks fine.
- Place the small cubes of tofu on a paper towel and press lightly to dry and press.
- Place the tofu, sliced scallion, and bamboo shoots in the soup and warm through.
- Spoon into a bowl and decorate with mushrooms and carrot flowers.

Nutrition Facts

5g Protein| 2g Total Fat| 0.4 G Saturated Fat| 9g Carbohydrate| 3g Dietary Fiber| 721mg Sodium

95. COLD HERB SOUP

Total Time: 20 minutes

Ingredients

- Butter-flavored cooking spray
- ¾ lb sweet onion, chopped
- 1 ½ tbs all-purpose flour
- One 16-ounce (454g) canned low-fat, low-salt chicken broth
- ¾ cup water
- 1 cup chopped flat-leaf parsley
- One 2/3-ounce (20g) container frozen chopped chives or 1/2 cup (20g) snipped fresh
- 4 tbs minced fresh tarragon leaves
- Six springs fresh thyme
- 1/3 cup fat-free sour cream
- Fresh lemon slices and fresh herbs for garnish

Directions

- Lightly coat a large saucepan with cooking spray. Add the onion and cook until the onion is soft, stirring occasionally. Add the flour and cook, stirring, for 2 minutes.
- Pour in the broth and water. Bring to a simmer and stir until slightly thickened. Add the herbs and simmer for 3 minutes.
- Remove from heat and allow to cool for 10 minutes. Remove the thyme sprigs.
- Working in batches, transfer mixture to a food processor or blender and process until smooth, adding the sour cream to the last collection. In a large bowl, combine batches and refrigerate, covered, until cold.
- Serve in small soup bowls with lemon slices and herbs for garnish.

Nutrition Facts

6g Protein| 1g Total Fat| 0.1g Saturated Fat| 18g Carbohydrate| 3g Dietary Fiber| 2mg Cholesterol| 257mg Sodium

96. RED PEPPER SOUP

Total Time: 1 hour

Ingredients

- Olive oil cooking spray
- Two large red bell peppers, about 1 pound total
- Two small carrots, 6 ounces (180 g), peeled and quartered lengthwise
- Two shallots, peeled and cut in half
- Two garlic cloves, peeled and cut in half
- 1 tsp olive oil
- One pear, peeled and quartered, core and seeds removed
- 3 cups fat-free low-sodium canned chicken broth
- Salt (optional)
- Freshly ground pepper
- Dash of hot pepper sauce

Directions

- Preheat oven to 400°F (205°C). Lightly spray a roasting pan with cooking spray.
- Place peppers, carrots, shallots, and garlic in a roasting pan. Lightly spray vegetables with cooking spray. Roast for 20 minutes. Using tongs, turn peppers over. Add pears to the roasting pan and continue to bake for another 10 minutes. Remove from oven and immediately place peppers in a paper bag for 10 minutes to sweat. Wash off the blackened skin under cold running water. Remove seeds and core.
- Place peppers, shallots, garlic, and pear in the work bowl of a food processor fitted with a steel blade. Process until smooth.
- Transfer mixture to a heavy saucepan. Blend in chicken broth and hot pepper sauce. Bring to a boil, reduce heat, and simmer for 10 minutes. Taste and add salt (if using) and pepper.
- Ladle into four soup bowls. Serve hot.

Nutrition Facts

3g Protein| 2g Total Fat| 0.2g Saturated Fat| 19g Carbohydrate| 5g Dietary Fiber| 48mg Sodium

97. COLD PEACH SOUP

Total Time: 4 hours

Ingredients

- Four large ripe peaches, about 2 pounds, peeled, pitted, and chopped
- ½ of a 10-ounce cantaloupe, peeled, seeded, and chopped
- ½ Cup fresh orange juice
- ¼ cup dry white wine or unsweetened apple juice
- Dash cayenne pe
- ¼ cup fat-free sour cream
- Snipped fresh chives for garnish

Directions

- In a food processor or blender, puree the peaches and melon until smooth. With the food processor running, add the orange juice, wine, and cayenne pepper through the feed tube. Continue to process until smooth.
- Transfer mixture to a nonreactive bowl. Taste and add a teaspoon or two spoonable sugar substitutes, if needed, to sweeten to taste. Cover and chill for at least 3 hours before serving.
- To serve, stir well and ladle into six small soup bowls. Top each serving with a small dollop of sour cream and a sprinkling of chives.

Nutrition Facts

2g protein| 17g carbohydrate| 2g dietary fiber| 1mg cholesterol 10mg sodium

98. TOMATO-BASIL SOUP

Total Time: 30 minutes

Ingredients

- Two 28-ounce (793 g total) cans of low-sodium crushed tomatoes
- One large onion, about 1/2 pound (225 g), chopped
- Three large garlic cloves, minced
- Two medium celery ribs celery with leaves, chopped
- 1 quart (1 l) low-sodium beef broth, defatted
- Two teaspoons (10 ml) paprika
- One teaspoon (4 g) sugar
- Two tablespoons (18 g) cornstarch
- Two tablespoons (30 ml) dry sherry or additional beef broth
- 1/2 cup (10 g) packed finely chopped fresh basil leaves
- One tablespoon (12.5 g) reduced-fat margarine
- Salt (optional) to taste
- Freshly ground pepper to taste

Direction

- Simmer the tomatoes, onion, garlic, and celery in a covered soup pot for 15 minutes.
- Process the vegetables in a food processor or blender in small batches. Return to the pot.
- Add the beef broth, paprika, and sugar. Combine the cornstarch and dry sherry; stir until well dissolved. Add to the soup and stir. Bring to a simmer again and cook for another 5 minutes.
- Stir in the basil and margarine. Taste for seasoning, adding salt (if using) and pepper to taste.
- Transfer soup to a preheated 2-quart thermos. Serve warm in small cups.

Nutrition Facts

3g Protein| 1g Total Fat| 0.2g Saturated| 12g Carbohydrate| 2g Dietary Fiber| 47mg Sodium

99. BUTTERNUT SQUASH SOUP

Total Time: 2 hour

Ingredients

- Butter-flavored cooking spray
- 1 1/3 pounds (600 g) butternut squash, halved and seeded
- 4 ounces (120 g) minced onion
- One tablespoon (15 ml) minced fresh ginger
- 5 cups (1200 ml) canned low-fat, low-salt chicken broth
- Two tablespoons (30 ml) dry sherry
- 1/2 teaspoon (2.5 ml) kosher salt (optional)
- Freshly ground pepper
- Chopped cilantro for garnish
- Roasted squash seeds for garnish

Direction

- Preheat oven to 400°F (200°C), Gas Mark Lightly coat a heavy baking sheet with cooking spray.
- Place the squash, cut side down, on the sheet, and bake until who can easily pierce it with a sharp knife, about 1 hour. Bake the seeds at the same time. Remove the squash, calm, and remove and coarsely chop the flesh, discarding the skin.
- Coat a large pot with cooking spray. Add the onion and ginger and cook until wilted, about 4 minutes. Stir in 4 cups (960 ml) of the broth and the squash. Bring to a simmer and cook, breaking up the squash pieces with a wooden spoon, for about 30 minutes. Stir in the sherry and last cup of broth. Taste for seasoning and add salt (if using) and pepper.
- Transfer to a preheated thermos. Place cilantro and roasted squash seeds in self-sealing plastic bags. When ready to serve, pour into cups and top each serving with chopped cilantro and a teaspoon of the roasted seeds.

Nutrition Facts

3g Protein| 9g Carbohydrates| 2g Dietary Fiber 91mg Sodium

100. 5-WAY CHILI

Servings: 8
Prep Time: 30 Minutes
Cook Time: 30 Minutes
Total: 1 Hour

Ingredients

- 1 ½ pounds ground sirloin
- Two medium onions, chopped
- One celery rib, chopped
- Four large cloves; garlic, minced
- Two tablespoons of good-quality chili powder
- One tablespoon paprika
- ½ teaspoon crushed dried basil
- ½ teaspoon crushed dried oregano
- ½ teaspoon crushed dried thyme
- One teaspoon ground cinnamon
- ½ teaspoon cayenne pepper
- ½ teaspoon ground cumin
- ½ teaspoon crushed red pepper flakes
- ¼ teaspoon ground allspice
- Salt (optional)
- Freshly ground pepper
- 2 14 1/2--ounce cans no-salt-added diced tomatoes with their juice
- One 8-ounce can of no-salt-added tomato sauce
- 1 cup water
- 12 ounces dried thin spaghetti
- 1 cup chopped onion (for serving)
- ½ cup low-fat shredded cheddar cheese (for serving)
- 1 cup drained dark red kidney beans (for serving)

Directions

- In a large nonstick pot, brown ground sirloin, onion, celery, and garlic over medium heat, occasionally stirring, until beef is browned and vegetables are limp for about 10 minutes. Drain off and discard all fat.
- Stir in chili powder, paprika, basil, oregano, thyme, cinnamon, cayenne pepper, ground cumin, red pepper flakes, and allspice. Season with salt (if using) and pepper to taste.
- Stir in tomatoes and tomato sauce. Add 1/2 cup water, adding additional water as needed to reach desired consistency. Partially cover and simmer for 30 minutes. Cool and then refrigerate overnight (this will intensify the flavor, but you don't have to do it).
- When ready to serve, reheat on the stove for at least 15 minutes while cooking the spaghetti, following package directions, and al dente. Drain the spaghetti and keep warm.
- Place the chopped onion, shredded cheese, and kidney beans in small serving bowls.
- To serve, divide the hot spaghetti between shallow soup bowls. Ladle hot Chili over each serving and pass the condiments separately to spoon onto each serving.

Nutrition Facts

401 calories (22% calories from fat), 29 g protein, 10 g total fat (3.6 g saturated fat), 50 g carbohydrates, 6 g dietary fiber, 32 mg cholesterol, 376 mg sodium

101. WHITE CHILI

Servings: 12
Prep Time: 1 Hour
Cook Time: 8 Hours
Total: 9 Hours

Ingredients

- 1 pound dried Great Northern beans, rinsed and picked over
- 7 cups fat-free low-sodium canned chicken broth
- Two medium onions, about 1/2 pound, chopped
- Three garlic cloves, minced
- Two tablespoons chopped fresh cilantro
- Two tablespoons chopped fresh mint
- Two tablespoons chopped fresh flat-leaf parsley
- One bay leaf (optional)
- One tablespoon ground cumin
- One teaspoon crushed dried oregano
- One teaspoon crushed dried thyme
- One small jalapeño chile pepper, seeded and minced
- 2 pounds boneless, skinless chicken breasts
- Salt and pepper, to taste
- Chopped red onion (optional)

Directions

- Put beans and water in a large pot and bring to a boil on top of the stove. Boil for 2 minutes, turn off the heat, cover, and let stand for 1 hour. Drain beans and place in the slow cooker.

- Add 5 cups of the broth to the slow cooker, along with the onion, garlic, cilantro, mint, parsley, bay leaf (if using), oregano, thyme, and chile peppers. Stir well.
- Cover and cook on LOW for 8 to 10 hours or on HIGH for 4 to 5 hours. Suppose cooking on HIGH, stirring after 2 hours of cooking time.
- About 30 minutes before who will do Chili, in a large skillet, poach a chicken breast in the remaining 2 cups chicken broth until just tender, about 15 minutes. Cool and cut chicken into bite-size pieces. Reserve chicken and broth.
- When beans are tender, remove about 3 cups of the beans and mash with a potato masher or in the food processor. Return mashed beans to the cooker and add the chicken pieces. Stir well.
- If cooking on LOW, change the setting to HIGH. Add some of the reserved broth as needed to thin the Chili to desired consistency (Chili should be thick). Cook, uncovered until chicken is heated through (about 10 to 15 minutes).
- Sprinkle with chopped red onion before serving, if you want.

Nutrition Facts

31g Protein| 4g Total Fat| 0.8g Saturated Fat| 15g Carbohydrate| 4g Dietary Fiber| 72mg Cholesterol| 72mg Sodium

102. SQUASH AND APPLE SOUP

Total Time: 1 hour

Ingredients

- Two medium butternut squash, about 2 pounds (960 g) each
- Three medium Granny Smith apples
- Two large cloves of garlic, peeled
- Salt (optional) and freshly ground pepper
- 4 cups (960 ml) fat-free, no-salt-added canned chicken broth
- Two teaspoons (10 ml) fresh thyme leaves or 1/2 teaspoon (2.5 ml) crushed dried

Direction

- Preheat oven to 425°F (220°C), Gas Mark Line a large baking sheet with parchment paper.
- Cut squash in half lengthwise; scoop out and discard seeds. Peel and core two apples. Cut in half. Place cavity side down on the parchment paper along with the garlic cloves.
- Season the inside of the squash with salt (if using) and pepper. Place cut side down on the baking sheet. Roast until squash is tender when pierced with a fork, about 40 minutes. Remove from oven and allow to cool enough to handle.
- Peel squash and work in batches as needed, puree squash flesh, roasted apples, and roasted garlic. Puree until smooth. Transfer squash mixture to a large, heavy pot. Whisk in chicken broth and thyme. Slowly heat over medium-low heat until steaming and hot, stirring frequently.
- While the soup is heating, cut the remaining apple in half and remove the core. Cut 12 skinny apple slices (you'll have about 1/2 apple left to use as a snack or another meal).
- Ladle hot soup into 12 heated soup tureen or individual bowls. Float apple slices on top and serve.

Nutrition Facts

2g Protein| 19g Carbohydrate| 5g Dietary Fiber| 19mg Sodium

103. WATERCRESS SOUP

Total Time: 30 minutes

Ingredients

- Refrigerated butter-flavored cooking spray
- One tablespoon (12.5 g) reduced-calorie margarine
- 1/2 cup (80 g) chopped onion
- Two bunches watercress
- 8 cups (1.9 l) canned low-fat, low-sodium chicken broth
- Two medium Russet potatoes, peeled and thinly sliced
- Salt (optional) and freshly ground pepper to taste
- 2 cups (480 ml) evaporated skim milk
- Skim milk (optional)
- Lemon slices for garnish (optional)

Direction

- Lightly coat the bottom of a large saucepan with cooking spray. Add margarine and place over medium heat. Add onion and sauté until onion is limp about 4 minutes.
- Meanwhile, rinse the watercress and drain on paper towels. Add the leaves and tender stems to the saucepan and sauté for 2 minutes.
- Add chicken broth and potatoes. Cook, covered, until potatoes are tender, about 20 minutes.
- Transfer mixture to a food processor or blender. Process until smooth. Return the mixture to the saucepan and season with salt (if using) and pepper. Stir in the evaporated milk and reheat, adding a bit of skim milk (if desired) to thin to desired consistency. Serve in wide, shallow soup bowls.
- If desired, float a lemon slice on each serving.

Nutrition Facts

8g Protein| 1g Total Fat| 0.2g Saturated Fat| 15g Carbohydrates| 1g Dietary Fiber| 555mg Potassium

104. MUSHROOM BARLEY SOUP

Total Time: 1 Hour 30 Minutes

Ingredients

- 1/2 ounce (14 g) dried porcini or shiitake mushrooms
- 1 cup (240 ml) boiling water
- Olive oil cooking spray
- Three large cloves of garlic, minced
- Two medium onions chopped
- One rib celery, chopped
- 1 pound (480 g) button mushrooms, sliced thin
- Two teaspoons (10 ml) light soy sauce
- Two tablespoons (30 ml) dry sherry

- 3 cups (720 ml) 98% fat-free, no-salt-added canned beef broth
- 2 cups (480 ml) water
- 1/2 cup (75 g) medium pearl barley
- Three carrots cut into coins
- Two sprigs of fresh thyme
- One sprig of fresh rosemary
- Freshly ground pepper

Direction

- In a small bowl, soak the dried mushrooms in the boiling water for about 20 minutes. Chop the mushrooms on a cutting board and reserve the liquid. Strain the liquid in a sieve lined with a paper towel and set it aside.
- Coat a heavy nonstick soup pot with cooking spray. Add the garlic, onion, and celery.
- Cook, often stirring, until the onion is translucent and soft.
- Add the mushrooms, soaked dried mushrooms, soy sauce, and sherry.
- Sauté until most of the liquid has evaporated.
- Add the broth, water, soaking juice, barley, carrots, thyme, and rosemary.
- Bring to a simmer. Cover and simmer for 1 hour.
- Season with pepper and serve.
- Before serving, remove the herb sprigs. Ladle into warmed bowls. Serve immediately.

Nutrition Facts

7g Protein| 1g Total Fat| 0.1g Saturated Fat| 25g Carbohydrates| 6g Dietary Fiber| 162mg Sodium

105. CUCUMBER BUTTERMILK SOUP

Total Time: 30 minutes

Ingredients

- Medium cucumbers, about 1 pound (480 g) peeled
- Two scallions, white part only, chopped
- 2 cups (472 ml) low-fat buttermilk
- 1 3/4 cups (472 ml) canned low-fat, low-sodium chicken broth
- 1/4 teaspoon (1.25 ml) salt (optional)
- Freshly ground pepper to taste
- One tablespoon (15 ml) fresh lemon juice
- Chopped fresh mint (optional)
- Paper-thin slices of unpeeled cucumber for garnish
- Grated lemon zest for garnish.

Direction

- Cut peeled cucumbers in half lengthwise. Scoop out and discard the seeds. Coarsely grate the cucumber.
- In a large bowl, combine the cucumber, scallion, buttermilk, chicken stock, salt (if using), pepper, and lemon juice. Mix well. Cover and refrigerate for several hours until well chilled.
- To serve, stir the soup and ladle it into small bowls or cups. Sprinkle with chopped mint (if using) and garnish with cucumber slices and lemon zest.

Nutrition Facts

4g Protein| 1g Total Fat| 0.5g Saturated Fat| 7g Carbohydrate| 1g Dietary Fiber| 3g Cholesterol| 219mg Sodium

106. ARTICHOKE AND LEEK SOUP

Total Time: 1 hour 30 minutes

Ingredients

- 14-ounce (390g) can artichoke hearts, drained
- Butter-flavored cooking spray
- 1 cup (160g) sliced leeks, white part only
- 2 1/2 cups (600ml) 98% fat-free, no-salt-added canned chicken broth
- Two tablespoons (29g) light sour cream

Direction

- Finely chop artichoke hearts in a food processor or by hand.
- Lightly coat a sizeable nonstick pot with cooking spray. Add leeks and cook, occasionally stirring, until leeks are tender but not browned, about 10 minutes. Add chopped artichoke hearts and cook for another minute or two.
- Stir in chicken broth, cover, and simmer for 15 minutes. Transfer mixture to a food processor or blender and process until smooth. Place puree in a covered container and chill for several hours.
- When ready to serve, whisk in sour cream and ladle into chilled soup bowls. Serve cold.

Nutrition Facts

4g Protein| 1g Total Fat| 0.4g Saturated Fat| 10g Carbohydrates| 1g Dietary Fiber| 3mg Cholesterol| 277mg Sodium

107. CURRIED LIMA BEAN APERITIF SOUP

Total Time: 20 minutes

Ingredients

- 10 ounce(285 g) package frozen lima beans
- One tablespoon (15 ml) margarine
- One bunch scallions, white and 1-inch green, sliced (about 1/2 cup, 45 g)
- One teaspoon (5 ml) curry powder
- 1/2 teaspoon salt (2.5 ml) (optional)
- 1/8 teaspoon (0.6ml) pepper
- 1/2 teaspoon (2.5 ml) crushed dried tarragon
- Four sprigs of flat-leaf parsley
- 2 cups (480 ml) fat-free low-sodium chicken broth
- 1/2 cup (120 ml) skim milk

Direction

- Thaw the lima beans and place them in the bowl of a food processor or blender. Add the margarine, scallions, curry powder, salt and pepper, tarragon, and parsley. Process until smooth.
- Place the lima bean mixture into a pot. Add the broth and milk. Bring to a simmer, cover, and simmer for 10 minutes. If the soup is too thick, add water to bring it the consistency of a thick cream soup.
- Spoon 1/4 cup soup into espresso cups and serve as an aperitif.

Nutrition Facts

2g Protein| 1g Total Fat| 4g Carbohydrate| 1g Dietary Fiber| 48mg Sodium

108. GREEK NAVY BEAN AND VEGETABLE SOUP

Total Time: 4 hours

Ingredients

- 2 cups (260 g) dried navy beans, washed and picked over
- 2 quarts (2 l) 98% fat-free, no-salt-added canned chicken broth
- Two medium onions, chopped
- One bay leaf
- Two teaspoons (10 ml) crushed dried oregano
- One teaspoon (5 ml) crushed dried thyme
- One teaspoon (5 ml) dried dill weed
- 1/2 teaspoon (2.5 ml) crushed dried rosemary
- 1/8 teaspoon (0.6 ml) cayenne pepper
- Two medium carrots, peeled and sliced
- Two medium thin-skinned potatoes, peeled and diced
- Two ribs celery with leaves, chopped
- Three ripe plum tomatoes, finely chopped
- Salt (optional) and freshly ground pepper
- Olive oil cooking spray
- Two large cloves of garlic, minced
- 1/4 cup (60 ml) fresh lemon juice
- 1/4 cup (15 g) chopped flat-leaf parsley

Direction

- Place beans in a large soup pot. Add chicken broth and place on stove over medium-high heat. Bring to a boil. Reduce heat and simmer for 2 to 3 minutes. Remove from heat, cover, and let stand for 1 hour.
- Return pot to stove, add half of the chopped onion, the bay leaf, oregano, thyme, dill weed, rosemary, and cayenne pepper. Gently simmer, covered, for 1 hour.
- Add the carrots, potatoes, celery, and tomatoes. Simmer, covered, until the beans and vegetables are tender, about 30 to 40 minutes. Season with salt (if using) and pepper to taste. Discard the bay leaf.
- Lightly coat a small nonstick skillet with cooking spray. Add remaining chopped onion and garlic. Sauté over medium-low heat until onion is limp, about 5 minutes.
- Transfer the onion-garlic mixture to a food processor or blender and add lemon juice and parsley. Pulse until mixture forms a thick puree. Stir puree into hot soup and continue to simmer for another 5 minutes.
- Ladle into soup bowls and serve hot.

Nutrition Facts

20g Protein| 1g Total Fat| 0.3g Saturated Fat| 58g Carbohydrates| 20g Dietary Fiber| 91mg Sodium

109. MEDITERRANEAN CHICKEN STEW

Servings: 4
Prep Time: 30 Minutes
Cook Time: 1 Hour 30 Minutes
Total: 2 Hours

Ingredients

- Cooking spray
- Two whole bone-in chicken breasts (2 pounds total), skinned and cut into quarters.
- Two medium onions, sliced
- Two large garlic cloves, minced
- One yellow or red bell pepper, seeded and chopped
- One teaspoon turmeric
- ½ teaspoon ground cinnamon
- ½ teaspoon ground ginger
- 2 pounds sweet potatoes, peel and cut into cubes
- 1 14.5 ounces can no-salt-added diced tomatoes, drained
- Two tablespoons golden raisins
- 2 cups fat-free low-sodium canned chicken broth
- Salt and pepper, to taste

Directions

- Lightly spray a covered nonstick pot with cooking spray. Add the chicken and brown over high heat for 2 minutes, turning the chicken once. Lower the heat and transfer the chicken to a plate. Set aside.
- Add all remaining ingredients to the pot except the reserved chicken pieces. Bring to a simmer and cook for 2 minutes.
- Return the chicken to the pot, cover, and simmer for 30 to 40 minutes until the chicken barely falls off the bones.
- Divide the sweet potatoes and chicken between 4 shallow soup plates. Raise the heat under the pot and reduce the sauce for 2 minutes, constantly stirring (this will thicken it). Pour some of the mixtures over each serving; serve at once.

Nutrition Facts

39g Protein| 5g Total Fat| 1.3g Saturated Fat| 58g Carbohydrate| 8g Dietary Fiber| 90mg Cholesterol| 132mg Sodium

110. BEEF STEW (LOW-CARB)

Prep Time: 10 minutes
Cook Time: 1 hour 15 minutes
Total Time: 1 hour 25 minutes
Servings: 4

Ingredients

- Two tablespoons canola oil
- 1½ pounds beef stewing meat (cubed)
- One teaspoon salt
- ¼ teaspoon black pepper
- 1 cup onion (diced)
- Two carrots (cut into rounds)
- Two cloves garlic (minced)
- Four fresh thyme sprigs
- Two tablespoons red wine vinegar
- 4 cups beef broth
- Two bay leaves
- 1 pound turnips (cubed)

- Two tablespoons butter

Directions

- Heat a cast iron dutch oven over high heat. Add one tablespoon of oil.
- Season the beef with salt and pepper.
- Add the beef to the pan in a single layer and sear for a few minutes until well browned. Remove the meat from the pan and set it aside.
- Add another tablespoon of oil to the pan, then add the onions, carrots, garlic, and fresh thyme. Mix well and cook until the onions are tender.
- Add the vinegar. Scrape any brown bits off the bottom of the dutch oven.
- Add the broth, beef, bay leaves, turnips, and butter. Mix well, then bring everything to a boil.
- Once the mixture is boiling, reduce to a simmer. Cook for 45 – 60 minutes until the turnips and beef are tender.

Nutrition Facts

Fat 20g| Saturated Fat 7.1g| Polyunsaturated Fat 2.3g| Monounsaturated Fat 6.2g| Cholesterol 130.8mg| Sodium 823mg| Potassium 330mg| Carbohydrates 15.1g| Fiber 3.9g| Sugar 7.4g| Protein 44.7g

111. CAJUN STEW

Total Time: 15 minutes

Ingredients

- One teaspoon canola oil
- One onion, chopped
- One stalk celery, chopped
- One clove garlic, minced
- One boneless skinless chicken thigh (about 4 ounces), cut into bite-size pieces
- 2 (2-ounce) turkey or chicken andouille sausage links, sliced into 1/4-inch-thick pieces
- 1 cup low-sodium chicken broth
- One can (about 14 ounces) of no-salt-added diced tomatoes
- 2 cups frozen sliced okra
- 1 cup cooked brown rice
- 1/4 teaspoon red pepper flakes
- 1/4 teaspoon salt
- 1/8 teaspoon black pepper
- 1/8 teaspoon dried thyme

Direction

- Heat oil in a large saucepan over medium-high heat. Add onion, celery, and garlic; cook and stir for 3 minutes. Add chicken and turkey sausage; cook and stir 2 minutes, or until browned on all sides. Pour in broth, stirring to scrape up browned bits.
- Stir tomatoes, okra, rice, red pepper flakes, salt, black pepper, and thyme into a saucepan. Bring to a boil. Reduce heat to low; cover and cook 10 minutes.

Nutrition Facts

Carbohydrates: 24g| Protein: 14g| Fat: 6g| Saturated Fat: 1g| Cholesterol: 47mg| Sodium: 436mg| Fiber: 5g

112. CHICKEN BARLEY SOUP

Total Time: 30 minutes

Ingredients

- One teaspoon olive oil
- 3/4 cup chopped onion
- 3/4 cup chopped carrot
- 3/4 cup chopped celery
- One package (8 ounces) of sliced mushrooms
- Two cloves garlic, minced
- 1/4 teaspoon black pepper
- 1/2 cup uncooked quick-cooking barley
- 1/4 teaspoon dried thyme
- 4 cups fat-free reduced-sodium chicken broth
- 1 cup chopped cooked chicken
- One bay leaf
- Juice of 1 lemon
- Parsley (optional)

Directions

- Place oil in Dutch oven. Add onion, carrot, celery, mushrooms, and garlic. Cook over medium-high heat for 5 minutes.
- Add pepper, barley, thyme, broth, chicken, and bay leaf. Bring to a boil; reduce heat, cover and simmer 25 minutes, or until vegetables are tender.
- Remove and discard bay leaf. Stir in lemon juice and sprinkle with parsley, if desired.

Nutrition Facts

Carbohydrates: 15g| Protein: 9g| Fat: 1g| Saturated Fat: 1g| Cholesterol: 13mg| Sodium: 307mg| Fiber: 2g

113. ALL-IN-ONE BURGER STEW

Total Time: 25 minutes

Ingredients

- 1 pound lean ground beef
- 2 cups frozen Italian-style vegetables
- One can (about 14 ounces) diced tomatoes with basil and garlic
- One can (about 14 ounces) beef broth
- 2 1/2 cups uncooked medium egg noodles
- Salt and black pepper

Directions

- Brown beef 6 to 8 minutes in a Dutch oven or large skillet over medium-high heat, stirring to break up meat. Drain fat.
- Add vegetables, tomatoes, and broth; bring to a boil over high heat.
- Add noodles; reduce heat to medium. Cover; cook 12 to 15 minutes or until vegetables and noodles are tender. Season with salt and pepper.

Nutrition Facts

Carbohydrates: 20g| Protein: 17g| Saturated Fat: 11g| Cholesterol: 62mg| Sodium: 428mg

114. CAULIFLOWER ALMOND SOUP

Total Time: 30 minutes

Ingredients

- Two tablespoons almond oil
- Two stalks of celery, chopped (about 1 cup)
- One leek, white and light green parts, sliced (about 1/2 cup)
- One small head of cauliflower separated into florets (about 4 cups)

- 3/4 teaspoon kosher salt
- 1-quart low-sodium chicken broth
- 1/4 teaspoon freshly ground black pepper
- 1/4 teaspoon ground nutmeg
- 3/4 cup almond-cashew cream
- 1/4 cup chopped parsley
- 1/2 cup sliced almonds, toasted

Directions

- Heat the almond oil in a large soup pot over medium heat. Add the celery and cook until it begins to soften. Add the leek and continue to cook until both vegetables are soft.
- Steam a few cauliflower florets and set them aside for garnish. Add the remaining cauliflower, broth, salt, pepper, and nutmeg to the vegetable mixture and bring it to a boil. Simmer until the cauliflower is soft, about 10 minutes.
- Puree the soup in a blender or food processor. Stir in the almond-cashew cream. Serve each bowl of soup garnished with one tablespoon of the parsley, two tablespoons of the almonds, and a few reserved cauliflower florets.

Nutrition Facts

Carbohydrates: 14g| Protein: 7g| Fat: 14g| Saturated Fat: 1.5g| Sodium: 274mg| Fiber: 4.5g

115. SOUTHWEST WHITE BEAN STEW

Total Time: 20 minutes

Ingredients

- 3 cups white beans, cooked and drained
- One tablespoon canola oil
- 1/2 cup diced red onion
- 1 1/2 assorted bell peppers, diced
- Two jalapeños, seeded and diced
- Three garlic cloves, minced
- 1 cup low-salt chicken or vegetable broth
- Two tablespoons sherry or red wine vinegar
- One 14.5-ounce can of low-salt diced tomatoes
- One tablespoon kosher salt
- Two tablespoons chopped cilantro

Directions

- Puree 1 cup of the cooked beans and combine with the whole beans.
- Heat the oil in a soup pot over medium heat. Sauté the onions, bell peppers, jalapeños, and garlic in the oil until the onions are translucent, 4–5 minutes.
- Add the bean mixture and broth. Stir constantly until the beans are thoroughly heated, 3–4 minutes.
- Add the vinegar, tomatoes, and salt and remove from the heat when hot. Stir in the cilantro just before serving.

Nutrition Facts

Carbohydrates: 45g| Protein: 15g| Fat: 4g| Saturated Fat: 1/2g| Sodium: 321mg| Fiber: 11g

116. NEW ENGLAND CLAM CHOWDER

Total Time: 30 minutes

Ingredients

- One can (5 ounces) whole baby clams, undrained
- One baking potato, peeled and coarsely chopped
- 1/4 cup finely chopped onion
- 2/3 cup evaporated skimmed milk
- 1/4 teaspoon white pepper
- 1/4 teaspoon dried thyme
- One tablespoon reduced-fat margarine

Directions

- Drain clams, reserving juice. Add enough water to reserved liquid to measure 2/3 cup. Combine clam juice mixture, potato, and onion in a large saucepan. Bring to a boil over high heat; reduce heat and simmer for 8 minutes or until potato is tender.
- Add milk, pepper, and thyme to the saucepan. Increase heat to medium-high. Cook and stir for 2 minutes. Add margarine. Cook 5 minutes or until soup thickens, stirring occasionally.
- Add clams; cook and stir 5 minutes or until clams are firm.

Nutrition Facts

Carbohydrates: 30g| Protein: 14g| Fat: 4g| Saturated Fat: 1g| Cholesterol: 47mg| Sodium: 205mg| Fiber: 1g

117. ZESTY VEGETARIAN CHILI

Total Time: 50 Minutes

Ingredients

- One tablespoon canola or vegetable oil
- One large red bell pepper, coarsely chopped
- Two medium zucchini or yellow squash (or 1 of each), cut into 1/2-inch chunks.
- Four cloves garlic, minced
- One can (about 14 ounces) of fire-roasted diced tomatoes
- 3/4 cup chunky salsa
- Two teaspoons chili powder
- One teaspoon dried oregano
- One can (about 15 ounces) of no-salt-added red kidney beans, rinsed and drained
- 10 ounces extra-firm tofu, well-drained and cut into 1/2-inch cubes
- Chopped cilantro (optional)

Directions

- Heat oil in a large saucepan over medium heat. Add bell pepper; cook and stir for 4 minutes. Add zucchini and garlic; cook and stir for 3 minutes.
- Stir in tomatoes, salsa, chili powder, and oregano; bring to a boil over high heat. Reduce heat to low; simmer 15 minutes or until vegetables are tender.
- Stir in beans; simmer 2 minutes or until heated through. Stir in tofu; remove from heat. Ladle into bowls; garnish with chopped cilantro.

Nutrition Facts

Carbohydrates: 28g| Protein: 15g| Fat: 8g| Saturated Fat: 1g| Sodium: 432mg| Fiber: 8 g

118. BUTTERNUT SQUASH AND MILLET SOUP

Total Time: 1 Hour

Ingredients

- One red bell pepper
- One teaspoon canola oil
- 2 1/4 cups diced butternut squash or 1 (10-ounce) package frozen diced butternut squash
- One medium red onion, chopped
- One teaspoon curry powder
- 1/2 teaspoon smoked paprika
- 1/2 teaspoon salt
- 1/8 teaspoon black pepper
- 2 cups low-sodium chicken broth
- Two boneless skinless chicken breasts (about 4 ounces each), cooked and chopped
- 1 cup cooked millet

Directions

- Place bell pepper on rack in broiler pan 3 to 5 inches from heat source or hold over an open gas flame on a long-handled metal fork.
- Turn bell pepper often until blistered and charred on all sides.
- Transfer to food storage bag; seal bag and let stand 15 to 20 minutes to loosen skin.
- Remove loosened skin with a paring knife. Cut off the top and scrape out seeds; discard.
- Heat oil in a large saucepan over high heat. Add butternut squash, bell pepper, and onion; cook and stir 5 minutes.
- Add curry powder, paprika, salt, and black pepper. Pour in broth; bring to a boil. Cover and cook 7 to 10 minutes or until vegetables are tender.
- Purée soup in a saucepan with a hand-held immersion blender or batches in a food processor or blender. Return soup to saucepan. Stir in chicken and millet; cook until heated through.

Nutrition Facts

Carbohydrates: 19g| Protein: 16g| Fat: 3g| Saturated Fat: 1g| Cholesterol: 37mg| Sodium: 199mg| Fiber: 2g

119. CREAMY YELLOW SQUASH SOUP

Total Time: 40 minutes

Ingredients

- Nonstick cooking spray
- 1 pound yellow squash, cut into 1/4-inch slices
- One medium green bell pepper, chopped
- One medium onion, chopped
- 1/4 teaspoon dried thyme
- One teaspoon ground cumin, divided
- 1 3/4 cups reduced-sodium, 99% fat-free chicken broth
- 1 cup fat-free buttermilk
- One tablespoon diet margarine
- 1/4 teaspoon black pepper
- 2 ounces reduced-fat sharp Cheddar cheese, shredded

Directions

- 1 cup soup plus two tablespoons cheese
- Heat a Dutch oven over medium heat until hot. Lightly coat with cooking spray. Add squash, bell pepper, and onion. Spray vegetables with cooking spray. Cook and stir for 6 minutes or until the onion begin to brown.
- Add thyme, 1/2 teaspoon cumin, and broth. Bring to a boil over high heat. Reduce heat to a simmer. Cover. Cook 20 minutes.
- I am working in 1-cup batches, place mixture in blender or food processor. Cover. Purée. Repeat with remaining ingredients. Return soup to Dutch oven over medium heat. Add buttermilk, margarine, remaining 1/2 teaspoon cumin and pepper. Cook until heated through. Serve topped with cheese.

Nutrition Facts

Carbohydrates: 12g| Protein: 8g| Fat: 5g| Saturated Fat: 2g| Cholesterol: 11mg| Sodium: 401mg| Fiber: 2g

120. SWEET POTATO MINESTRONE

Total Time: 50 minutes

Ingredients

- One tablespoon extra virgin olive oil
- 3/4 cup diced onion
- 1/2 cup diced celery
- 2 cups diced peeled sweet potatoes
- One can (about 15 ounces) Great Northern beans, rinsed and drained
- One can (about 14 ounces) of no-salt-added diced tomatoes
- 3 cups water
- 3/4 teaspoon dried rosemary
- 1/2 teaspoon salt (optional)
- 1/8 teaspoon black pepper
- 2 cups coarsely chopped kale leaves (lightly packed)
- Four tablespoons grated Parmesan cheese

Directions

- Heat oil in a large saucepan or Dutch oven over medium-high heat. Add onion and celery; cook and stir 4 minutes or until the onion is softened.
- Stir water, sweet potatoes, beans, tomatoes, rosemary, salt, if desired, and pepper into a saucepan. Cover and bring to a simmer; reduce heat and simmer 30 minutes.
- Add kale; cover and cook 10 minutes or until tender.
- Ladle soup into bowls; sprinkle with cheese.

Nutrition Facts

Carbohydrates: 48g| Protein: 13g| Fat: 6g| Saturated Fat: 2g| Cholesterol: 4mg, Sodium: 189mg, Fiber: 11g

121. ITALIAN PASTA SOUP WITH FENNEL

Total Time: 20 minutes

Ingredients

- One tablespoon olive oil

- One small fennel bulb, trimmed and chopped into 1/4-inch pieces (1 1/2 cups)
- Four cloves garlic, minced
- 3 cups vegetable broth
- 1 cup uncooked small shell pasta
- One medium zucchini or yellow summer squash, cut into 1/2-inch chunks
- One can (about 14 ounces) of Italian-seasoned diced tomatoes
- 1/4 cup grated Romano or Parmesan cheese
- 1/4 cup chopped fresh basil
- Dash black pepper (optional)

Directions
- Heat oil in a large saucepan over medium heat. Add fennel; cook and stir for 5 minutes. Add garlic; cook and stir for 30 seconds. Add broth and pasta; bring to a boil over high heat. Reduce heat; simmer for 5 minutes. Stir in zucchini; simmer 5 to 7 minutes or until pasta and vegetables are tender.
- Stir in tomatoes; heat through. Ladle into shallow bowls; top with cheese, basil, and black pepper, if desired.

Nutrition Facts
Carbohydrates: 17g| Protein: 5g| Fat: 4g| Saturated Fat: 1g| Cholesterol: 3mg| Sodium: 430mg| Fiber: 2g

122. MOROCCAN LENTIL & VEGETABLE SOUP FOR DIABETICS
Total Time: 50-60 minutes

Ingredients
- One tablespoon olive oil
- 1 cup chopped onion
- Four cloves garlic, minced
- 1/2 cup dried lentils, rinsed and sorted
- 1 1/2 teaspoons ground coriander
- 1 1/2 teaspoons ground cumin
- 1/2 teaspoon ground cinnamon
- 1/2 teaspoon black pepper
- One container (32 ounces) low-sodium vegetable broth
- 1/2 cup chopped celery
- 1/2 cup chopped sun-dried tomatoes (not packed in oil)
- One yellow squash, chopped
- 1/2 cup chopped green bell pepper
- 1 cup chopped plum tomatoes
- 1/2 cup chopped fresh Italian parsley
- 1/4 cup chopped fresh cilantro or basil

Directions
- Heat oil in a medium saucepan over medium-high heat. Add onion and garlic; cook and stir 4 minutes or until the onion is tender. Stir in lentils, coriander, cumin, cinnamon, and black pepper; cook for 2 minutes. Add broth, celery, and sun-dried tomatoes; bring to a boil. Reduce heat to medium-low; cover and simmer for 25 minutes.
- Stir in squash and bell pepper; cover and cook 10 minutes or until lentils are tender.
- Top with plum tomatoes, parsley, and cilantro just before serving.

Nutrition Facts
Carbohydrates: 20g| Protein: 8g| Fat: 3g| Saturated Fat: 1g| Sodium: 264mg| Fiber: 2g

123. EASY-AS-PIE HOLIDAY SOUP
Total Time: 25-30 minutes

Ingredients
- One teaspoon canola oil
- 1/2 cup diced onion (1/2 medium onion)
- 1 cup peeled, diced apple (1 medium apple)
- 3/4 to 1 teaspoon pumpkin pie spice
- 1/4 teaspoon salt
- 1/4 teaspoon black pepper
- 1/2 cup fat-free, reduced-sodium chicken broth
- One box (12 ounces) frozen, cooked winter squash, thawed (see Tips)
- 1 cup fat-free evaporated milk
- Four tablespoons fat-free sour cream (optional)
- Pumpkin pie spice (optional)

Directions
- Heat oil in a large saucepan over medium-low heat. Add onion. Cook and stir for 3 minutes or until the onion are translucent. Do not brown. Add apple, spice, salt, and pepper. Cook and stir for 1 minute to coat apples. Add broth. Simmer, uncovered, 8 to 10 minutes or until apples are tender and the most stock has evaporated.
- Add thawed squash and milk to the apple mixture. Simmer, uncovered, 6 to 8 minutes or until flavors are blended and soup is hot. Ladle into bowls. Garnish with sour cream and pumpkin pie spice, if desired.

Nutrition Facts
Carbohydrates: 15g| Protein: 5g| Fat: 2g| Saturated Fat: 1g| Cholesterol: 2mg| Sodium: 160mg| Fiber: 1g

124. BROCCOLI & POTATO CHOWDER
Total Time: 25 minutes

Ingredients
- One can (about 14 ounces) fat-free reduced-sodium chicken broth
- 1 cup sliced leeks
- 1/2 cup cubed peeled potato
- 1/3 cup fresh or frozen corn
- One can (about 4 ounces) diced mild green chiles
- 3/4 teaspoon paprika
- 1 1/2 cups broccoli florets
- 3/4 cup evaporated skimmed milk
- Two tablespoons all-purpose flour
- Jalapeño pepper sauce (optional)

Directions
- In a medium saucepan, combine broth, leeks, potato, corn, chiles, and paprika. Bring to a boil. Reduce heat and simmer, covered, 10 to 15 minutes or until vegetables are tender. Add broccoli; simmer for 3 minutes.
- Whisk milk into flour. Stir into vegetable mixture. Cook, constantly stirring until soup comes to a boil and thickens slightly. Season to taste with pepper sauce, if desired.

Nutrition Facts

Carbohydrates: 51g| Protein: 19g| Fat: 1g| Saturated Fat: 1g| Cholesterol: 3mg| Sodium: 311mg| Fiber: 5g

125. VEGETARIAN CHILI WITH BROWN RICE

Total Time: 40 minutes

Ingredients

- One teaspoon canola oil
- One onion, chopped
- One green bell pepper, diced
- One red bell pepper, diced
- One stalk celery, diced
- One jalapeño pepper, minced
- One clove garlic, minced
- 2 cups fat-free vegetable broth
- One can (about 14 ounces) of no-salt-added diced tomatoes
- 1 cup cooked brown rice
- 1 cup no-salt-added canned pinto beans, rinsed and drained
- 1/2 teaspoon dried oregano
- 1/2 teaspoon chipotle chili powder
- 1/2 teaspoon salt
- 1/4 teaspoon black pepper
- 1/4 teaspoon ground cumin
- Six tablespoons shredded reduced-fat Cheddar cheese

Directions

- Heat oil in a large saucepan over medium-high heat. Add onion, bell peppers, celery, jalapeño, and garlic; cook and stir for 7 minutes.
- Add broth, tomatoes, rice, beans, oregano, chili powder, salt, black pepper, and cumin. Bring to a boil over high heat. Reduce heat to medium; cover and cook 15 minutes or until vegetables are tender. Uncover; cook 10 minutes or until thickened.
- Ladle Chili into bowls; top each serving with one tablespoon cheese.
- Jalapeño peppers can sting and irritate the skin, so wear rubber gloves when handling peppers and do not touch your eyes.

Nutrition Facts

Carbohydrates: 23g| Protein: 6g| Fat: 3g| Saturated Fat: 1g| Cholesterol: 5mg| Sodium: 378mg| Fiber: 5g

126. BUTTERNUT BISQUE

Total Time: 30 minutes

Ingredients

- One teaspoon margarine or butter
- One large onion, coarsely chopped
- One medium butternut squash (about 1 1/2 pounds), cut into 1/2-inch pieces
- Two cans (about 14 ounces each) reduced-sodium chicken broth, divided
- 1/2 teaspoon ground nutmeg
- 1/8 teaspoon white pepper
- Plain nonfat yogurt and chopped chives (optional)

Directions

- Melt margarine in a large saucepan over medium heat. Add onion; cook and stir for 3 minutes. Add squash, and one can make broth; bring to a boil over high heat. Reduce heat to low; cover and simmer 20 minutes or until squash is very tender.
- Purée soup in batches in the blender, returning the blended soup to saucepan after each set. (Or use a hand-held immersion blender.) Add remaining can of broth, nutmeg, and pepper. Simmer, uncovered, 5 minutes, stirring occasionally.
- Ladle soup into six serving bowls; serve with yogurt and chives, if desired.

Nutrition Facts

Carbohydrates: 14g| Protein: 5g| Fat: 1g| Saturated Fat: 1g| Sodium: 107mg| Fiber: 4g

127. MUSHROOM & CHICKEN SKILLET

Total Time: 15-20 minutes

Ingredients

- 1 pound boneless skinless chicken breasts, cut into bite-size pieces
- One can (about 14 ounces) fat-free chicken broth
- 1/4 cup hot water
- 1/2 teaspoon dried thyme
- 2 cups uncooked instant rice
- 8 ounces mushrooms, thinly sliced
- One can (10 3/4 ounces) 98% fat-free cream of celery soup, undiluted
- Chopped fresh parsley

Directions

- Cook chicken in broth and water in a 12-inch nonstick skillet until mixture comes to a full boil. Stir in thyme and rice. Place mushrooms on top. (Do not stir mushrooms into the rice.) Cover skillet; turn off the heat and let stand 5 minutes.
- Stir in soup; cook over low heat 5 minutes or until heated through. Sprinkle with parsley.

Nutrition Facts

Carbohydrates: 28g| Protein: 32g| Fat: 4g| Saturated Fat: 1g| Cholesterol: 67mg| Sodium: 774mg| Fiber: 2g

128. QUICK BROCCOLI SOUP

Total Time: 30 minutes

Ingredients

- 4 cups fat-free reduced-sodium chicken or vegetable broth
- 2 1/2 pounds broccoli florets
- One onion, quartered
- 1 cup low-fat (1%) milk
- 1/4 teaspoon salt (optional)
- 1/4 cup crumbled blue cheese

Directions

- Place broth, broccoli, and onion in a large saucepan; bring to a boil over high heat. Reduce heat to low; cover and simmer about 20 minutes or until vegetables are tender.
- Purée soup in blender and return to saucepan. Add milk and salt, if desired. Add water or additional broth, if needed.
- Ladle soup into serving bowls; sprinkle with cheese.

Nutrition Facts

Carbohydrates: 12g| Protein: 7g| Fat: 2g| Saturated Fat: 1g| Cholesterol: 6mg| Sodium: 175mg| Fiber: 3g

SALAD RECIPES

129. TOMATO CAPRESE SALAD

Preparation 10 Minutes
Serves 8 Persons

Ingredients

- 1 package prewashed baby arugula or mixed spring greens
- 25 fresh basil leaves
- 1 (8-ounce) package low-fat mozzarella
- 2 tomatoes cut into wedges
- ¼ cup extra-virgin olive oil juice of 1 lemon
- Fine-grained kosher salt and freshlyground pepper, to taste

Directions

- Place the arugula or greens in a large salad bowl.
- Tear up the basil leaves and add to the salad.
- Chop the mozzarella into bite-size pieces, and add them to the salad, along with the tomatoes.
- Drizzle the salad with the olive oil and lemon juice, and season with salt and pepper.
- Toss well to combine, and add more olive oil, lemon juice, or salt and pepper if needed.
- Nutrition Facts
- Calories per Serving: 157 cal Fat: 13g Protein: 7g Carbohydrates: 3g

130. EGG SALAD

Preparation 25 Minutes
Serves 6 Persons

Ingredients

- Black pepper – ¼ teaspoon
- Dijon mustard – 1 teaspoon
- Light mayonnaise – ¼ cup
- Hard-boiled eggs – 6 larges
- Celery (diced) – 1 stalk

Directions

- Start by cutting the hard-boiled eggs and putting the yolks in a glass bowl.
- Cut the egg whites into cubes.
- Add freshly ground black pepper, Dijon mustard, celery, and light mayonnaise to the yolks.
- Use the back of a fork to mash the yolk and combine it with the spices and seasonings.
- Add chopped egg whites to the yolk mixture.
- Serve right away with toast or salad leaves.

Nutrition Facts

Calories per Serving: 70 cal Fat: 4g Protein: 5g Carbohydrates: 2g

131. LETTUCE SALAD WITH HOT BACON DRESSING

Preparation 20 Minutes
Serves 6 Persons

Ingredients

- 5 pieces bacon
- ¼ cup sugar
- 1 Tbsp. cornstarch
- ½ tsp. salt 1 egg, beaten
- 1 cup fat-free milk
- ¼ cup vinegar
- 36 oz. ready-to-serve mixed lettuces, or 2 medium heads iceberg lettuce

Directions

- Sautée bacon in skillet until crisp.
- Remove bacon from heat and drain. Chop.
- Discard drippings.
- Add sugar, cornstarch, and salt to skillet.
- Blend together well.
- Add egg, milk, and vinegar, stirring until smooth.
- Cook over low heat, stirring continually, until thickened and smooth.
- When dressing is no longer hot, but still warm, toss with torn lettuce leaves and chopped bacon.
- Serve immediately.

Nutrition Facts

Calories per Serving: 60 cal Fat: 2g Protein: 3g Carbohydrates: 1g

132. ASPARAGUS-BERRY SALAD

Preparation 30 Minutes
Serves 4 Persons

Ingredients

- 1 lb fresh asparagus spears
- Cooking spray
- 2 tablespoons chopped pecans
- 1 cup sliced fresh strawberries
- 4 cups mixed salad greens
- ¼ cup fat- free balsamic vinaigrette dressing Cracked pepper, if desired

Directions

- Heat oven to 400°F.
- Line 15x10x1-inch pan with foil; spray with cooking spray.
- Break off tough ends of asparagus as far down as stalks snap
- easily.
- Cut into 1- inch pieces.
- Place asparagus in single layer in pan; spray with cooking spray. Place pecans in another shallow pan.
- Bake pecans 5 to 6 minutes or until golden brown, stirring occasionally.
- Bake as- paragus 10 to 12 minutes or until crisp-tender.
- Cool pecans and asparagus 8 to 10 minutes or until room temperature.
- In medium bowl, mix asparagus, pecans, strawberries, greens and dressing.
- Sprinkle with pepper.

Nutrition Facts

Calories per Serving: 90 cal Fat: 3g Protein: 4g Carbohydrates: 11g

133. POTATO SALAD

Preparation Time: 5 Minutes
Cooking Time: 15–20 Minutes.
Yield: 4 serving

Ingredients:

- 2 pounds small red potatoes

- Three tablespoons imitation bacon bits
- 2/3 cup fat-free Italian salad dressing
- Two packets of Splenda (or another artificial sweetener)
- One tablespoon cider vinegar
- 1/2 cup chopped parsley

Directions

- Leave skins on potatoes.
- Place potatoes in a medium saucepan and add enough cool water to cover them by at least an inch of water.
- Bring to a boil and cook until potatoes can be pierced with a fork, about 15 minutes.
- Drain and cool. Quarter the potatoes when cool enough to touch.
- Combine bacon bits, salad dressing, Splenda, vinegar, and parsley in a medium-sized bowl.
- Toss potato pieces in the bowl with dressing to coat.
- Serve warm or chilled.

Nutrition Facts: Information
Carbohydrates: 27g| Protein: 4g| Fat: 1g| Saturated Fat: <1g| Sodium: 344mg| Fiber: 3g

134. GRILLED ROMAINE AND ASPARAGUS SALAD

Preparation Time: 7 Minutes
Cooking Time: 6 Minutes
Yield: 4 serving
Ingredients

- One six-ounce head of romaine lettuce
- Nonstick cooking spray
- Aluminum foil
- Four medium spears or eight thin spears of fresh asparagus
- 1/4 cup thinly sliced red onion
- 12 grape tomatoes
- One tablespoon shredded Parmesan cheese
- 1/4 cup fat-free Italian salad dressing

Directions

- Heat grill. Cut lettuce head lengthwise in half, but do not trim off the base holding the leaves together; wash lettuce and pat dry.
- Spray a 12-inch piece of foil (or a larger piece, if needed) with nonstick cooking spray.
- Place lettuce halves on foil and place on the hot grill.
- Grill each side of halves for 2 minutes until slightly browned.
- Remove from grill and cool.
- Cut off base, then slice lettuce horizontally into ribbons, about 1 inch wide.
- While the grill is still hot, grill asparagus on the same foil, constantly turning until slightly browned. Slice asparagus diagonally into 1-inch pieces.
- Place lettuce and asparagus in a medium salad bowl and sliced onion, tomatoes, and Parmesan cheese.
- Toss, add dressing, then toss again.

Nutrition Information
Carbohydrates: 16g| Protein: 4 g| Fat: 2g| Sodium: 184mg| Fiber: 6g

135. PARSLEY, PEAR, AND WALNUT SALAD

Preparation Time: 5 Minutes
Chilling Time: 2 Hours
Yield: 2 serving
Ingredients

- 2 cups fresh curly parsley (about 1/3 pound)
- One medium Bosc pear (about 5 ounces)
- 1/2 cup chopped walnuts
- 1/4 cup Parmesan cheese, finely shredded
- 1/2 cup dried cranberries
- Ten red seedless grapes
- 1/4 cup fat-free raspberry vinaigrette salad dressing

Directions

- Wash and dry parsley, then remove stems and any discolored leaves.
- Chop parsley to make about 2 cups, and set aside. Cut the pear in half and remove the core with a melon baller.
- Leaving the skin on, cut pear into half-inch dice. Combine parsley, pear, walnuts, cheese, cranberries, and grapes in a medium salad bowl.
- Add dressing, and toss.
- Chill for 2 hours before serving for the best flavor.

Nutrition Facts: Information
Carbohydrates: 9g| Protein: 5g| Fat: 11g| Saturated Fat: 2g| Cholesterol: 4mg| Sodium: 164mg| Fiber: 2g

136. FALL HARVEST COLESLAW

Preparation Time: 10 Minutes
Chilling Time: 1 Hour
Yield: 1 serving
Ingredients:

- One head (one pound) green cabbage
- Two large carrots, peeled
- 1/2 cup chopped red onion
- 1/2 cup diced apple (any variety)
- 1/2 cup dried cranberries
- 1/4 cup poppy seed salad dressing
- 1/4 cup light mayonnaise

Directions

- Core cabbage and shred in a food processor; it will yield about 4 cups.
- Place cabbage in a large mixing bowl.
- Shred carrots in processor and combine with cabbage.
- Add remaining ingredients and stir well.
- Cover and chill in refrigerator at least 1 hour before serving.

Nutrition Information
Carbohydrates: 11g| Fat: 4g| Cholesterol: 1mg Sodium: 48mg| Fiber: 2g

137. CRUNCHY VEGETABLE SALAD

Preparation Time: 10 minutes
Yield: 2 serving
Ingredients:

- 4 ounces Romaine'sRomaine's hearts lettuce
- 1/2 cup sliced cucumber
- 1/4 cup chopped green pepper
- Four red radishes, thinly sliced
- Two green onions, chopped
- 12 cherry tomatoes
- Two tablespoons low-fat, shredded Cheddar cheese
- 1/4 cup light ranch-style salad dressing

- One tablespoon chopped chipotle peppers in adobo sauce
- One tablespoon fresh lime juice

Directions

- Tear or chop lettuce (should yield approximately 4 cups) and place in a large salad bowl.
- Add cucumber, green pepper, radishes, green onions, tomatoes, and cheese.
- Toss well. In a small bowl, mix salad dressing, chipotle peppers, and lime juice. Pour dressing over salad and toss again to combine.

Nutrition Facts: Information

Carbohydrates: 7g| Protein: 4g| Fat: 3g| Saturated Fat: 1g| Cholesterol: 2mg| Sodium: 255mg| Fiber: 2g

138. CREAMY CHOPPED CAULIFLOWER SALAD

Total: 15 mins
Servings: 6

Ingredients

- 5 tablespoons reduced-fat mayonnaise
- 2 tablespoons cider vinegar
- 1 small shallot, finely chopped
- 1/2 teaspoon caraway seeds, (optional)
- ¼ teaspoon freshly ground pepper
- 3 cups chopped cauliflower florets, (about 1/2 large head)
- 2 cups chopped heart of romaine
- 1 tart-sweet red apple, chopped

Directions:

- Whisk mayonnaise, vinegar, shallot, caraway seeds (if using), and pepper in a large bowl until smooth.
- Add cauliflower, romaine, and apple; toss to coat.

Nutrition Facts:

Calories: 68; Protein 1.5g; Carbohydrates 10.9g; Dietary Fiber 2.2g; Sugars 5.1g; Fat 2.6g; Saturated Fat 0.4g; Cholesterol 3.1mg

139. SPINACH & WARM MUSHROOM SALAD

Total: 30 mins
Servings: 4

Ingredients:

- 8 cups spinach, tough stems removed
- 2 cups coarsely chopped radicchio
- 2 tablespoons extra-virgin olive oil, divided
- 2 slices bacon, chopped
- 1 large shallot, halved and sliced (1/2 cup)
- 3 cups sliced mixed mushrooms, such as shiitake, oyster, and cremini
- ¼ teaspoon salt
- ¼ teaspoon ground pepper
- 2 tablespoons white balsamic vinegar
- ½ teaspoon honey

Directions:

- Combine spinach and radicchio in a large bowl.
- Heat 1 tablespoon oil in a large skillet over medium heat.
- Add bacon and shallot and cook, stirring, until the bacon is crisp, 4 to 5 minutes.
- Add mushrooms, salt, and pepper and cook, stirring, until the mushrooms are tender, 5 to 7 minutes.
- Remove from heat and stir in the remaining 1 tablespoon oil, vinegar, and honey, scraping up any browned bits.
- Immediately pour the warm vinaigrette over the spinach mixture and toss to coat.

Nutrition Facts:

Calories; Protein 4.7g; Carbohydrates 11.5g; Dietary Fiber 2.7g; Sugars 3.9g; Fat 8.8g; Saturated Fat 1.5g; Cholesterol 3.5mg;

140. MIXED GREEN SALAD WITH GRAPEFRUIT & CRANBERRIES

Total: 25 mins
Servings: 12

Ingredients:

- 2 red grapefruit
- ¼ cup extra-virgin olive oil
- 2 tablespoons minced scallions
- 1 tablespoon white-wine vinegar
- ¼ teaspoon salt
- ¼ teaspoon freshly ground pepper
- 8 cups torn butter lettuce
- 6 cups baby spinach
- 1 14-ounce can hearts of palm (see Shopping Tip), drained and cut into bite-size pieces
- ⅓ cup dried cranberries
- 1/3 cup toasted pine nuts

Directions:

- Remove the skin and white pith from grapefruit with a sharp knife. Working over a bowl, cut the segments from their surrounding membranes. Cut the segments in half on a cutting board and transfer to a large salad bowl. Squeeze the grapefruit peel and membranes over the original bowl to extract 1/4 cup grapefruit juice.
- Whisk oil, scallions, vinegar, salt, and pepper into the bowl with the grapefruit juice.
- Add lettuce, spinach, and hearts of palm to the salad bowl with the grapefruit segments. Just before serving, toss the salad with the dressing until well coated. Sprinkle cranberries and pine nuts on top.

Nutrition Facts:

Calories: 162; Protein 3.3g; Carbohydrates 14.9g; Dietary Fiber 3.2g; Sugars 8.4g; Fat 11.3g; Saturated Fat 1.3g;

141. MELON, TOMATO & ONION SALAD WITH GOAT CHEESE

Total: 30 mins
Servings: 8

Ingredient

- 1 cup very thinly sliced sweet white onion, separated into rings
- 1 small firm-ripe melon
- 2 large tomatoes, very thinly sliced
- 1 small cucumber, very thinly sliced
- ½ teaspoon kosher salt
- ¼ teaspoon freshly ground pepper
- 1 cup crumbled goat cheese
- ¼ cup extra-virgin olive oil
- 4 teaspoons balsamic vinegar
- ⅓ cup very thinly sliced fresh basil

Directions:

- Place onion rings in a medium bowl, add cold water to cover and a handful of ice cubes.
- Set aside for about 20 minutes. Drain and pat dry.

- Meanwhile, cut melon in half lengthwise and scoop out the seeds.
- Remove the rind with a sharp knife.
- Place each melon half cut-side down and slice crosswise into 1/8-inch-thick slices.
- Make the salad on a large platter or 8 individual salad plates. Begin by arranging a ring of melon slices around the edge.
- Top with a layer of overlapping tomato slices. Arrange a second ring of melon slices toward the center.
- Top with the remaining tomato slices.
- Tuck cucumber slices between the layers of tomato and melon. Sprinkle with salt and pepper.
- Top with goat cheese and the onion rings.
- Drizzle with oil and vinegar. Sprinkle with basil.

Nutrition Facts:

Calories: 194; Protein 4.7g; Carbohydrates 19.4g; Dietary Fiber 2.3g; Sugars 16g; Fat 11.6g; Saturated Fat 4g; Cholesterol 11.2mg;

142. THE ULTIMATE WEDGE SALAD RECIPE

Prep Time: 15 Minutes
Cook Time: 5 Minutes
Servings: 4 Servings

Ingredients:

For The Blue Cheese Dressing:
- ½ cup sour cream
- ½ cup mayonnaise
- 1/3 cup buttermilk
- 1 tablespoon apple cider vinegar
- ½ teaspoon salt
- ¼ teaspoon cracked black pepper
- ¼ teaspoon garlic powder
- ½ cup crumbled blue cheese

For The Wedge Salad:
- 8 slices bacon chopped
- 1 head iceberg lettuce
- 1 cup cherry or grape tomatoes halved
- 1 cup blue cheese dressing
- ½ cup chopped scallions
- ½ cup crumbled blue cheese

Directions:

- **Make The Dressing:** Set out a medium mixing bowl. Add the sour cream, mayonnaise, buttermilk, apple cider vinegar, salt, pepper, and garlic powder.
- Stir well. Then mix in the crumbled blue cheese.
- Cover and chill until ready to use. (If possible, make a day ahead, or early in the day, so the blue cheese has time to permeate the dressing.)
- **Cook The Bacon:** Set a skillet over medium heat. Place the chopped bacon in the skillet.
- Brown the bacon for 4-6 minutes until crispy, stirring regularly. Then scoop the bacon out of the skillet onto a paper towel-lined plate to drain off the grease.
- **Prep The Veggies:** Slice the tomatoes in half and chop the scallions.
- Then set the head of lettuce on the cutting board. Trim the root/core end a little.
- Cut the head in half, through the core. (This helps hold the wedges together.) Then cut each half in two, through the core.
- **Stack The Wedges:** Set each lettuce wedge on a plate.
- Drizzle with a generous amount of blue cheese dressing. (At least ¼ cup per salad.)
- Then sprinkle the tops with halved tomatoes, scallions, bacon, and more blue cheese crumbles. Finish each salad plate off with a bit of fresh cracked pepper. Serve cold.

Nutrition Facts:

Calories: 653kcal, Carbohydrates: 12g, Protein: 19g, Fat: 59g, Saturatedfat: 21g, Cholesterol: 84mg,

143. CRISPY BRUSSEL SPROUTS QUINOA SALAD RECIPE

Prep Time: 15 Minutes
Cook Time: 30 Minutes
Servings: 8

Ingredients:
- 1 1/4 cup dried lentils, choose a more firm lentil type
- 2/3 cup dried quinoa
- 3 cups water
- 3/4 teaspoon curry powder
- 8 ounces Brussels sprouts
- 1 cup thinly sliced shallots, about 3-4
- 2 tablespoons olive oil
- 1/2 cup DeLallo Sun-Dried Peppers, chopped
- 1/2 cup scallions, chopped
- 1/2 lemon, juiced
- Salt and pepper

Directions:

- Preheat the oven to 400 degrees F.
- Place the quinoa and lentils in a medium stockpot with 3 cups of water, 1 teaspoon salt, and 3/4 teaspoon curry powder.
- Bring to a boil, then cover and reduce the heat to medium-low. Cook for 25-30 minutes until the quinoa is fluffy and the lentils are cooked, but firm.
- Remove from heat, but keep covered until ready to use.
- Meanwhile, cut the Brussels sprouts in half and slice thin. Place them on a rimmed baking sheet with the sliced shallots and drizzle with olive oil.
- Toss to coat then spread them out thin and salt and pepper. Bake for 20-25 minutes, until crispy.
- Fluff the quinoa and lentils and move to a large bowl.
- Add the crispy Brussels sprouts and shallots, chopped sweet peppers, chopped scallions, and the juice of half a lemon.
- Toss and salt and pepper to taste. Serve immediately.

Nutrition Facts:

Calories: 214kcal, Carbohydrates: 33g, Protein: 11g, Fat: 5g, Saturatedfat: 1g,

144. HARVEST SALAD

Prep Time: 20 Minutes
Cook Time: 2 Minutes
Total Time: 22 Minutes
Servings: 4

Ingredients:

For The Cobb Salad:
- 2 romaine hearts roughly chopped
- 2 cups cooked chicken cut into cubes

- 2 cups roasted butternut squash cubes
- 6 slices thick-cut bacon cooked and crumbled
- 3 large hard-boiled eggs peeled and chopped
- 2 ripe avocadoes sliced
- 1 cup shelled pecans
- 1 tablespoon butter
- 1/4 teaspoon ground mustard
- 1/4 teaspoon garlic powder
- 1/4 teaspoon hot paprika
- 1/4 teaspoon salt

For The Creamy Corn And Poblano Dressing:
- 1 poblano pepper
- 1 clove garlic
- 2 ears corn on the cob cooked
- 2 limes juiced
- 1 teaspoon ground cumin
- 1 teaspoon salt
- 2/3 cup olive oil

Directions:
- Heat a skillet to medium-low heat. Melt the butter in the skillet, then add the pecans.
- Sprinkle the pecans with the ground mustard, garlic powder, paprika, and salt and toss to coat. Sauté for 3-5 minutes, stirring regularly to toast. Be careful not to burn the pecans.
- Pile the chopped romaine on a large platter. Arrange the chopped chicken, roasted butternut squash, bacon, pecans, eggs, and avocados in rows on top of the romaine.
- Preheat the oven to broil. Place the poblano pepper on a small baking sheet and set it on the top rack in the oven.
- Check the pepper every 1-2 minutes, turning when the skin is black and blistered. Remove the poblano from the oven when it's black on all sides. Place the pepper in a zip bag and allow it to steam for 10 minutes.
- Cut the corn off the cobs and place them in the blender. Add the garlic clove, lime juice, salt, and cumin. Once the pepper has steamed, removed the papery skin, stem, and seeds. Place the poblano flesh in the blender.
- Puree until smooth, then remove the ingredient cup from the lid and slowly pour in the olive oil to emulsify. Once the dressing is smooth and creamy, turn off the blender and pour the dressing into a serving bowl.

Nutrition Facts:
Calories: 860kcal, Carbohydrates: 20g, Protein: 16g, Fat: 83g, Saturatedfat: 17g, Cholesterol: 64mg, Sodium: 1139mg, Potassium: 741mg, Fiber: 6g, Sugar: 5g, Vitamin C: 52mg, Calcium: 94mg, Iron: 3mg

145. GREEK ORZO PASTA SALAD WITH LEMON VINAIGRETTE

Prep Time: 15 Minutes
Cook Time: 10 Minutes
Servings: 8 Servings
Ingredients:
- 1 pound dried orzo pasta
- 1 large red bell pepper seeded and diced
- 1 cup pitted olives (I used half kalamata and half green)
- 3 ounces sun-dried tomatoes chopped
- 1/3 cup diced red onion
- 1/3 cup chopped fresh basil
- 1/3 cup chopped fresh dill
- 1/3 cup chopped parsley
- For the Lemon Vinaigrette
- ½ cup fresh lemon juice
- ½ cup extra-virgin olive oil
- 1-2 teaspoons granulated sugar
- 1 clove garlic
- Salt and pepper

Directions:
- Set a large pot of salted water over high heat. Bring to a boil. Then cook the orzo as directed on the package. Drain.
- Meanwhile, set out a large salad bowl. Chop the bell pepper, onions, sun-dried tomatoes, and fresh herbs.
- In a small bowl (or measuring pitcher) whisk the lemon juice, olive oil, sugar, and garlic together. Set aside.
- Once the orzo is cooked and drained, place it in the salad bowl. Add in the bell peppers, olives, sun-dried tomatoes, onion, and all chopped herbs.
- Pour the lemon dressing over the salad and toss well. Cover and refrigerate until ready to serve.

Nutrition Facts:
Calories: 397kcal, Carbohydrates: 52g, Protein: 10g, Fat: 17g

146. CHUNKY STRAWBERRY SALAD WITH POPPYSEED DRESSING

Prep Time: 15 Minutes
Servings: 8 Servings
Ingredients:
- 2 cups fresh strawberries hulled and sliced
- 6 ounces fresh baby spinach
- 1 cup sliced radishes
- ¾ cup chopped roasted macadamia nuts
- 1/3 cup crumbled chevre goat cheese
- ¼ sliced red onion
- ¼ cup store-bought poppyseed dressing (or homemade)

Directions:
- Slice the strawberries, radishes, and onion. Chop the macadamia nuts.
- Set out a large salad bowl. Add the spinach leaves, sliced strawberries, radishes, chopped nuts, and onions. Pour the dressing over the top and toss to coat.
- Then sprinkle the top with crumbled goat cheese, and gently toss again.

Nutrition Facts:
Calories: 166kcal, carbohydrates: 8g, protein: 4g, fat: 14g

147. WILD RICE SALAD WITH BLUEBERRIES AND HERBS

Prep Time: 20 Minutes
Cook Time: 45 Minutes
Servings: 12 Servings
Ingredients
- 2 cups dry wild rice
- 2 cups fresh blueberries
- 1 cup chopped scallions
- ½ cup shelled pistachios chopped
- ½ cup roughly chopped mint leaves
- ½ cup fresh chopped dill
- 1 large juicy orange zested and juiced
- 1 juicy lime zested and juiced

- ¼ cup olive oil
- 1 tablespoon honey or agave
- Salt and pepper

Directions:
- Cook the rice according to the package instructions. (For wild rice, usually, 2 cups of rice requires 6 cups of water and approximately 45-50 minutes of covered cook time.) Allow the rice to cool.
- Meanwhile, chop the herbs and pistachios. Then zest and juice the citrus.
- Move the cooled wild rice to a large salad bowl. Add the blueberries, scallions, chopped pistachios, mint, dill, orange zest, and lime zest.
- In a measuring pitcher, combine the orange juice, lime juice, olive oil, honey, 1 ¼ teaspoon salt, and ½ teaspoon ground black pepper. Whisk well then pour over the rice mixture. Toss to coat.
- Taste, then add additional salt and pepper if needed.
- Cover and refrigerate until ready to serve.

Nutrition Facts:
Calories: 126kcal, Carbohydrates: 15g, Protein: 3g, Fat: 7g, Saturated Fat: 1g, Sodium: 4mg

Ginger Salad Dressing
Prep Time: 10 Minutes
Servings: 8 Servings
Ingredients
- 1 cup carrots roughly chopped
- ½ cup onion peeled and roughly chopped
- ¼ cup celery roughly chopped
- ½ cup rice vinegar
- 1/3 cup canola oil
- 3 tablespoons fresh grated ginger
- 2 tablespoons granulated sugar or honey
- 1-2 tablespoons soy sauce (I always buy GF and low sodium.)
- 1 small garlic clove

Directions:
- Roughly chop all the produce. Place in the blender.
- Add all other ingredients to the blender. If you are sensitive to sodium, start with 1 tablespoon of soy sauce. You can always add more if needed.
- Cover the blender and turn on high. Puree until smooth.
- Taste, then add more soy sauce if desired.
- Refrigerate until ready to serve.

Nutrition Facts:
Calories: 111kcal, Carbohydrates: 6g, Protein: 1g, Fat: 9g, Saturated Fat: 1g,

148. BUBBLY TACO SALAD BOWLS RECIPE

Prep Time: 5 Minutes
Cook Time: 13 Minutes
Servings: 4
Ingredients:
- 4 10-12 inch flour tortillas (XL burrito size)
- 4 tablespoons vegetable oil (or any flavorless oil)

Directions:
- Preheat the oven to 350 degrees F. Set 4 oven-safe cereal bowls on a large rimmed baking sheet. Then set a large 12-14 inch skillet on the stovetop over medium heat.
- Pour 1 tablespoon oil into the skillet. Once hot, place the tortilla in the skillet. Use tongs to swirl the tortilla to coat it in oil, flip it over, and swirl it again. It needs to be coated in oil, on both sides, right away.
- Pan-fry the tortilla for 30-45 seconds per side, allowing it to puff up with large bubbles. (The bigger the bubbles the better!) Flip and repeat. Make sure the tortilla isn't turning dark. It should be golden-brown.
- Use tongs to move the tortilla to one of the cereal bowls. Tuck it down into the bottom of the bowl, to create a bowl shape with the tortilla. Take care not to deflate the bubbles.
- Repeat with the remaining three tortillas. Once all the tortillas are flash-fried and shaped into bowls, bake for 9-10 minutes until very crispy. Cool and fill.

Nutrition Facts:
Calories: 124kcal, Carbohydrates: 1g, Protein: 1g, Fat: 14g, Saturated Fat: 11g, Sodium: 7mg, Sugar: 1g

Macaroni Salad With Potatoes
Prep Time: 15 Minutes
Cook Time: 14 Minutes
Servings: 16
Ingredients
- 3 pounds Russet potatoes, peeled and chopped into 1-inch cubes
- 12 ounces dried macaroni noodles
- 1/2 cup shredded onion
- 1 large carrot, shredded
- 10 ounces frozen peas
- 1/2 cup chopped scallions
- 2 1/2 cups low fat mayonnaise
- 1 cup sweet pickle relish
- 1 tablespoon apple cider vinegar
- 1 teaspoon yellow mustard
- 1 teaspoon ground allspice
- Salt and pepper

Directions:
- Cut the potatoes into 1-inch cubes and place them in a large stockpot.
- Fill the pot with cold water until it is one inch over the top of the potatoes. Set the pot over high heat and bring to a boil. Once boiling, add 1 tablespoon salt.
- Then set the timer and cook the potatoes for 5 minutes.
- After 5 minutes, stir in the macaroni noodles and continue boiling for 6-8 minutes, until the pasta is al dente.
- Meanwhile, in a medium bowl mix the mayonnaise, sweet pickle relish including juices, apple cider vinegar, mustard, allspice, 1/2 teaspoon salt, and pepper to taste. Stir until smooth.
- Then use a grater to shred the onions and carrot.
- Drain the potatoes and macaroni in a colander and place in a large salad bowl.
- Add in the onion, carrots, peas, and scallions. Pour the dressing over the top and mix until well combined.
- Cover the potato macaroni salad and refrigerate for at least 4 hours. If you have time to make it ahead, it tastes even better on day two!
- Keep refrigerated in an airtight container for up to one week.

Nutrition Facts:
Calories: 268kcal, Carbohydrates: 43g, Protein: 5g, Fat: 8g, Saturatedfat: 1g, Cholesterol: 5mg

149. CHICKEN SALAD

Prep Time: 20 Minutes
Cook Time: 3 Minutes
Servings: 12 Servings
Ingredients

- 1 whole rotisserie chicken, about 5 cups chopped chicken
- 1 ¼ – 1 ½ cups mayonnaise
- 1 cup chopped celery
- 1 cup diced apple, a firm variety
- ½ cup sweet pickle relish
- ½ cup toasted almonds
- ½ cup chopped scallions
- 2 tablespoons dijon mustard
- 1 tablespoon fresh chopped dill
- Salt and pepper

Directions:

- Place the almonds in a small dry skillet. Set over medium heat. Toss and brown for 3-5 minutes, until golden. Turn off the heat. Meanwhile, chop all the produce.
- Remove the skin from the chicken and pull the cooked meat off the bones. Place all the chicken meat on a cutting board and roughly chop. Discard the skin and bones.
- Set out a large mixing bowl. Place the chicken in the bowl. Then add the mayonnaise, celery, diced apple, sweet pickle relish, toasted almonds, scallions, Dijon mustard, and dill.
- Stir well to evenly mix all the ingredients. Taste, then salt and pepper as needed.
- Cover and chill until ready to serve. (Chicken salad always tastes better after it has time to rest and chill. If possible, make a day ahead.)

Nutrition Facts:
Calories: 268kcal, Carbohydrates: 4g, Protein: 18g, Fat: 20g

150. AMBROSIA SALAD RECIPE

Prep Time: 15 Minutes
Servings: 12

Ingredients

- 15 ounce can mandarin oranges
- 15 ounce can peach slices, drained
- 8 ounce can pineapple tidbits
- 5-ounce jar maraschino cherries stems removed
- ¾ cup fresh green grapes halved lengthwise
- ¾ cup sweetened coconut flakes
- ¾ cup mini marshmallows
- ½ cup chopped pecans, optional
- ¼ cup diced crystallized ginger, candied ginger
- 4 ounces sour cream
- 4 ounces cool whip
- Pinch of salt

Directions:

- Set a large colander in the sink. Pour the mandarin oranges, peaches, pineapple tidbits, and cherries into the colander.
- Once they are well-drained, chop each peach slice into 3-4 pieces. Remove all cherry stems, then cut the cherries in half.
- Cut the green grapes in half. Chop the pecans (if using) and dice the crystallized ginger pieces.
- Set out a large salad bowl. Pour the drained fruit into the bowl. Add the grapes, coconut, marshmallows, pecans, crystallized ginger, sour cream, and cool whip. Add a good pinch of salt and gently mix the salad until everything is well incorporated.
- Cover and refrigerate until ready to serve. Can be made up to 7 days in advance.

Nutrition Facts:
Calories: 172kcal, Carbohydrates: 27g, Protein: 2g, Fat: 7g, Saturated Fat: 3g, Cholesterol: 6mg

151. THE BEST MACARONI SALAD RECIPE

Prep Time: 15 Minutes
Cook Time: 10 Minutes
Servings: 12 Servings
Ingredients:

- 1 pound macaroni pasta
- 12 ounces roasted red pepper, (1 jar) drained and chopped
- 3/4 cup kale, finely chopped
- 1/2 cup cooked bacon, chopped
- 1/2 cup sweet pickle relish
- 1/2 cup scallions, chopped
- 1 1/2 cups mayonnaise, could be low fat
- 3 tablespoons apple cider vinegar
- 1 tablespoon granulated sugar
- 1 tablespoon hot sauce, i used frank's redhot
- 1 clove garlic, minced
- Salt and pepper

Directions:

- Bring a large pot of salted water to a boil. Cook the macaroni according to the package instructions, usually 7-10 minutes. Then drain and rinse with cold water.
- In a medium bowl mix the mayonnaise, apple cider vinegar, sugar, hot sauce, garlic, 1 teaspoon salt, and 1/2 teaspoon ground pepper.
- Pour the macaroni into a large bowl. Pour the dressing over the top. Then add the chopped roasted red peppers, kale, bacon, pickle relish, and scallions.
- Toss well to coat. Then refrigerate until ready to serve.

Nutrition Facts:
Calories: 362kcal, Carbohydrates: 34g, Protein: 5g, Fat: 22g, Saturated Fat: 3g, Cholesterol: 12mg

152. FRESH PEACH SALAD RECIPE WITH BASIL

Prep Time: 10 Minutes
Servings: 6
Ingredients

- 4-6 ripe peaches pitted and cut into bite-size pieces
- 1 tablespoon honey
- 6 basil leaves thinly sliced
- 1/2 cup lemon chevre or plain chevre with a little lemon zest
- Pinch of salt

Directions:

- Place the peaches in a bowl. Drizzle with honey and sprinkle with salt. Toss to coat.
- Gently fold in basil and chevre. Serve immediately.

Nutrition Facts:
Calories: 99kcal, Carbohydrates: 12g, Protein: 4g, Fat: 4g, Saturatedfat: 2g, Cholesterol: 8mg

153. SPICY SALAD RECIPE

Prep Time: 30 Minutes
Servings: 4
Ingredients
For The Dressing:
- 1/4 cup mayonnaise
- 2 tablespoon rice vinegar
- 1/2 teaspoon sugar
- 1 teaspoon sriracha sauce (chile sauce)
- 1/2 teaspoon paprika
- 1/2 teaspoon freshly grated ginger
- Pinch salt

For The Salad:
- 4 Kani sticks (1/2 pound imitation crab)
- 1 mango peeled and shredded
- 1 large cucumber (or three baby cucumbers) peeled and shredded
- 3/4 cup panko bread crumbs

Directions:
- Whisk the first seven ingredients together for the dressing. Taste for seasoning and salt and pepper as needed. Set aside.
- Shred the crab sticks by hand and place them in a large bowl. Shred the cucumber and mango in a food processor (or julienne by hand) and place in the bowl.
- Toss with the dressing and top with panko immediately before serving.

Nutrition Facts:
Calories: 178kcal, Carbohydrates: 16g, Protein: 2g, Fat: 11g, Saturated Fat: 1g, Cholesterol: 6mg

154. CUCUMBER SALAD

Prep Time: 15 Minutes
Servings: 6
Ingredients:
- 3 English cucumbers
- 1 tablespoon fresh chopped dill
- 1 clove garlic, minced
- 1 lemon, zested and juiced
- 1/2 cup plain greek yogurt
- 2 teaspoons granulated sugar
- Salt and pepper

Directions:
- Peel the cucumbers. Cut in half lengthwise. Then slice into thin pieces. Place the sliced cucumbers into a large bowl.
- Add the chopped dill, minced garlic, the zest of one lemon, 1 tablespoon of lemon juice, 1/2 cup plain greek yogurt, sugar, 1/2 teaspoon salt, and 1/4 teaspoon ground black pepper.
- Toss until the yogurt blends into a thin dressing. Taste, then salt and pepper as needed. Serve cold.

Nutrition Facts:
Calories: 38kcal, Carbohydrates: 7g, Protein: 2g, Fat: 0g, Saturatedfat: 0g, Cholesterol: 0mg, Sodium: 9mg, Potassium: 244mg, Fiber: 0g, Sugar: 4g, Vitamin A: 155iu, Vitamin C: 5.6mg, Calcium: 42mg, Iron: 0.4mg

155. MESSICAN SALAD

Preparation 30 Minutes
Serves 10 Persons
Ingredients
- 1 head lettuce
- ¾ lb. 93%-lean ground beef
- 2 tomatoes, chopped
- 16-oz. can kidney beans, drained
- ¾ cup freshly grated cheddar cheese
- ¼ cup diced onion
- ¼ cup sliced black olives, sliced
- 1 avocado, diced
- 2 oz. tortilla chips, crushed
- Sauce:
- 8 oz. fat-free Thousand Island dressing
- 1 Tbsp. dry low-sodium taco seasoning
- 1 Tbsp. hot sauce
- 1 Tbsp. sugar

Directions
- Wash lettuce and tear into bite-size pieces.
- Brown, drain, and cool ground meat.
- Combine all salad **Ingredients:** except tortilla chips.
- Set aside.
- Combine all sauce **Ingredients:**.
- Pour sauce over salad and toss thoroughly.
- Immediately before serving, add tortilla chips.

Nutrition Facts
Calories per Serving: 215 cal Fat: 8g Protein: 13g Carbohydrates: 23g

156. COBB SALAD

Preparation 20 Minutes
Serves 8 Persons
Ingredients
- 2 avocados, peeled, pitted, and chopped into bite-size pieces
- 2 tablespoons fresh lemon juice, plus more for seasoning
- 6 slices of turkey bacon, crumbled
- 1 tablespoon Dijon mustard
- 1 teaspoon granulated sucralose
- ½ cup extra-virgin olive oil
- Fine-grained kosher salt and freshly ground
- pepper, to taste
- 1 head romaine lettuce
- ½ cup reduced-fat blue cheese crumbles
- 2 hard-boiled eggs, sliced
- 1 cooked chicken breast (skin removed), chopped

Directions
- Toss the chopped avocado in lemon juice so it will not brown. Set aside.
- Cook the bacon on both sides over medium heat in a sauté pan or skillet, for about 5 minutes on each side, or until crisp.
- Line a plate with paper towels, remove each strip of bacon with a fork or tongs, and lay on the plate. Cover with a layer of paper towels to remove extra grease.
- In a small bowl, whisk together the 2 tablespoons lemon juice, mustard, and su- cralose, if using.

- Gradually add the oil in a steady and slow drizzle while whisking. Keep whisking until the dressing appears creamy, and the oil and lemon juice seem combined.
- Season with salt and pepper.
- Coarsely chop the romaine lettuce. Combine the romaine lettuce and the dress- ing in a large bowl, and toss well to combine.
- When ready to serve, place the salad in individual salad bowls or a large serving platter.
- Top the salad with the crumbled blue cheese, bacon, hard-boiled egg slices, chicken, and avocado.

Nutrition Facts

Calories per Serving: 379 cal Fat: 35g Protein: 11g Carbohydrates: 9g

157. MORROCCAN CARROT SALAD

Preparation 140 Minutes

Serves 5 Persons

Ingredients

Dressing

- ¼ cup orange juice
- 2 tablespoons olive oil
- 1 teaspoon orange peel
- 1 teaspoon ground cumin
- 1 teaspoon paprika
- ¼ teaspoon salt
- ⅛ to ¼ teaspoon ground red pepper
- ⅛ teaspoon ground cinnamon

Salad

- 1 bag (10 oz) julienne carrots
- 1 can (15 oz) chickpeas drained, rinsed
- ¼ cup golden raisins
- 3 tbs salted roasted almonds, chopped
- ¼ cup coarsely chopped fresh cilantro

Directions

- In small bowl, combine all dressing ingredients with whisk until ble nded; set aside.
- In large bowl, combine carrots, chickpeas and raisins; toss to combine.
- Add dressing; mix thoroughly.
- Cover and refrigerate at least 2 hours or overnight, stirring occasionally.
- Just before serving, sprinkle with almonds and cilantro.

Nutrition Facts

Calories per Serving: 310 cal Fat: 11g Protein: 10g Carbohydrates: 44g

158. 5 LAYER SALAD

Preparation 25 Minutes

Serves 6 Persons

Ingredients

- 1 cup frozen sweet peas
- 1 tablespoon water
- ⅓ cup plain fat-free yogurt
- ¼ cup reduced-fat mayonnaise
- 1 tablespoon cider vinegar
- 2 teaspoons sugar
- ½ teaspoon salt
- 3 cups coleslaw mix (shredded cabbage and carrots; from 16-oz bag)
- 1 cup shredded carrots (2 medium)
- 1 cup halved cherry tomatoes

Directions

- In small microwavable bowl, place peas and water.
- Cover with microwavable plastic wrap, folding back one edge ¼ inch to vent steam.
- Microwave on High 4 to 6 minutes, stirring after 2 minutes, until tender; drain.
- Let stand until cool.
- Meanwhile, in small bowl, mix yogurt, mayonnaise, vinegar, sugar and salt.
- In 1½- or 2-quart glass bowl, layer coleslaw mix, carrots, tomatoes and peas.
- Spread mayonnaise mixture over top.
- Refrigerate 15 minutes. Toss gently before serving.

Nutrition Facts

Calories per Serving: 100 cal Fat: 4g Protein: 3g Carbohydrates: 13g

159. CUCUMBER MANGO SALAD

Preparation 20 Minutes

Serves 4 Persons

Ingredients

- 1 small cucumber
- 1 medium mango
- ¼ teaspoon grated lime peel
- 1 tablespoon lime juice
- 1 teaspoon honey
- ¼ teaspoon ground cumin
- Pinch salt
- 4 leaves Bibb lettuce

Directions

- Cut cucumber lengthwise in half; scoop out seeds.
- Chop cucumber (about 1 cup).
- Score skin of mango lengthwise into fourths with knife; peel skin. Cut peeled mango lengthwise close to both sides of pit.
- Chop mango into ½-inch cubes.
- In small bowl, mix lime peel, lime juice, honey, cumin and salt. Stir in cucumber and mango.
- Place lettuce leaves on serving plates.
- Spoon mango mixture onto lettuce leaves.

Nutrition Facts

Calories per Serving: 50 cal Fat: 0g Protein: 0g Carbohydrates: 12g

160. TUNA MACARONI SALAD

Preparation 35 Minutes

Serves 10 Persons

Ingredients

- 1 cup elbow macaroni
- 1 cup whole-wheat elbow macaroni
- ½ cup nonfat mayonnaise
- ¾ teaspoon Dijon mustard
- 1½ teaspoons sucralose
- 1½ tablespoons white vinegar
- ¼ cup nonfat Greek yogurt Fine-grained kosher salt and freshly ground
- black pepper, to taste 2 (8-ounce) cans tuna in water 2 stalks celery, finely chopped
- 1 red onion, finely chopped
- 2 tablespoons finely chopped parsley
- ½ teaspoon paprika

Directions

- Cook the macaroni according to the package directions
- When done, rinse with cool water and drain completely.
- In a small bowl, whisk together the mayonnaise, mustard, sucralose, vinegar, yogurt or sour cream, and

season with salt and pepper to make the dressing.
- Combine the tuna, celery, red onion, parsley, and paprika in a large bowl.
- Stir the macaroni into the vegetables; then add the dressing, and stir well. Season with more salt and pepper, if needed.
- The pasta salad will taste best if you let it stand for a few hours in the refrigerator, and it can be stored for up to 3 days.

Nutrition Facts

Calories per Serving: 227 cal Fat: 10g Protein: 15g Carbohydrates: 18g

161. LAYERED MEXICAN SALAD

Total Time: 30-60 Minutes

Ingredients

- One package (10 ounces) shredded lettuce
- 1/2 cup chopped green onions (green and white parts)
- 1/2 cup fat-free sour cream
- 1/3 cup medium Picante sauce
- One medium lime halved
- One teaspoon sugar
- 1/2 teaspoon ground cumin
- One medium avocado, peeled, seeded, and chopped
- 3/4 cup (3 ounces) shredded reduced-fat sharp Cheddar cheese
- 2 ounces baked tortilla chips, coarsely crumbled

Directions

- Place lettuce evenly in a 13×9-inch baking pan. Sprinkle with green onions.
- Stir together sour cream, Picante sauce, juice from half of lime, sugar, and cumin in a small bowl. Spoon evenly over lettuce and green onions. Place avocado evenly over sour cream layer. Squeeze the remaining lime half evenly over the avocado layer. Sprinkle evenly with cheese.
- Cover with plastic wrap. Refrigerate until serving. Sprinkle with crumbled tortilla chips before serving.

Nutrition Facts

Carbohydrates: 13g| Protein: 5g| Fat: 5g| Saturated Fat: 2g| Cholesterol: 10mg| Sodium: 208mg| Fiber: 3g

162. ARUGULA SALAD WITH SUN-DRIED TOMATO VINAIGRETTE

Total Time: 30 minutes

Ingredients

- 1/4 cup sundried tomatoes (not packed in oil)
- Two tablespoons olive oil
- One tablespoon balsamic vinegar
- 1/4 teaspoon salt
- 1/4 teaspoon black pepper
- One package (5 ounces) baby arugula
- 1 cup halved grape tomatoes
- 1/4 cup shaved Parmesan cheese
- 1/4 cup pine nuts, toasted (optional)

Directions

- Combine sun-dried tomatoes, oil, vinegar, salt, and pepper in blender or food processor; blend until smooth.
- Combine arugula and grape tomatoes in a large bowl. Add dressing; toss to coat. Top with cheese and pine nuts, if desired.

Nutrition Facts

Carbohydrates: 6g| Protein: 4g| Fat: 9g| Saturated Fat: 2g| Cholesterol: 6mg| Sodium: 274g| Fiber: 1g

163. QUICK' ' N HEALTHY TACO SALAD

Total Time: 20-30 minutes

Ingredients

- Dressing
- 1/3 cup light sour cream
- 1/3 cup low-fat plain yogurt
- 1/2 cup chopped cilantro, loosely packed
- Two tablespoons lime juice (about one lime)
- 1/8 teaspoon garlic salt
- Salad
- Cooking spray
- One medium red bell pepper, diced
- 3/4 pound lean ground beef
- 1/2 teaspoon chili powder
- 3/4 cup salsa
- 6 cups chopped romaine lettuce
- Two green onions, sliced
- 3/4 cup reduced-fat Mexican blend cheese
- Two medium tomatoes, cut into wedges
- Reduced-fat tortilla strips, optional

Directions

- Combine all ingredients for dressing in a blender and blend until smooth.
- Spray a large nonstick skillet with cooking spray and place over medium heat. Add diced pepper and sauté for 3 to 4 minutes, or until slightly softened. Add the beef and chili powder to the pan and sauté for 5 to 6 minutes, or until the meat is well-browned. Stir in the salsa and cook for one minute to combine.
- Place 1 1/2 cups chopped lettuce onto each of the four plates. Top each salad with 3/4 cup of the meat mixture. Sprinkle on 1/4 of the green onions, three tablespoons cheese, and three tablespoons of dressing. Garnish with tomato wedges and optional tortilla strips, if desired.

Nutrition Facts

Carbohydrates: 11g| Sugars: 6g| Protein: 27g| Fat: 14g| Saturated Fat: 7g| Cholesterol: 45mg| Sodium: 460mg| Fiber: 3g

164. SANTA FE GRILLED VEGETABLE SALAD

Total Time: 40 minutes

Ingredients

- Two baby eggplants (about 6 ounces each), cut in half lengthwise
- One medium yellow summer squash, cut in half lengthwise
- One medium zucchini, sliced in half lengthwise
- One medium green bell pepper, quartered
- One medium red bell pepper, quartered
- One small onion, peeled and cut in half
- 1/2 cup orange juice
- Two tablespoons lime juice
- One tablespoon olive oil

- Two medium cloves garlic, minced
- One teaspoon dried oregano
- 1/4 teaspoon salt
- 1/4 teaspoon ground red pepper
- 1/4 teaspoon black pepper
- Nonstick cooking spray
- Two tablespoons chopped fresh cilantro

Directions

- Combine all ingredients except nonstick cooking spray and cilantro in a large bowl; toss to coat.
- Spray cold grid of grill with nonstick cooking spray. Prepare coals for direct grilling. Place vegetables on the grill, 2 to 3 inches from hot coals; reserve marinade. Grill 3 to 4 minutes per side, or until tender and lightly charred; cool 10 minutes. (Or, place vegetables on the rack of a broiler pan coated with nonstick cooking spray; reserve marinade. Broil 2 to 3 inches from heat 3 to 4 minutes per side, or until tender; cool 10 minutes.)
- Remove peel from eggplant, if desired. Slice vegetables into bite-size pieces; return to marinade. Stir in cilantro; toss to coat. Garnish as desired.

Nutrition Facts

Carbohydrates: 11g| Protein: 2g| Fat: 2g| Saturated Fat: 1g| Cholesterol: 1mg| Sodium: 70mg| Fiber: 1g

165. AVOCADO AND BLUEBERRY FRUIT SALAD

Total Time: 20 minutes

Ingredients

- Two tablespoons honey
- 1/4 cup plain nonfat yogurt
- 1/2 teaspoon ground cinnamon
- 1/4 cup fresh orange juice
- 1/8 teaspoon each salt and pepper
- One large, ripe avocado, cut into slices
- 2 cups fresh blueberries, rinsed and drained
- 2 cups peeled, diced apple
- 2 cups diced fresh mango
- 1 (5-ounce) package (8 cups) salad greens
- Two tablespoons chopped chives or green onion
- Two tablespoons toasted, coarsely chopped walnuts

Directions

- Whisk together dressing ingredients and set aside.
- Place avocado, blueberries, apple, and mango in a medium bowl and toss with four tablespoons salad dressing. Toss salad greens in a large bowl with the remainder of salad dressing, and distribute evenly between 6 salad plates. Place equal portions of the avocado mixture on each serving of greens. Sprinkle with chopped chives and toasted walnuts before serving.

Nutrition Facts

Carbohydrates: 33g| Protein: 3g| Fat: 6g| Saturated Fat: 1g| Sodium: 65mg| Fiber: 6g

166. CAPRESE SALAD

Total Time: 15 minutes

Ingredients

- Three medium tomatoes (3/4 pound total), cut into eight slices
- 2 (1-ounce) slices of part-skim mozzarella cheese, each cut into strips (24 strips total)
- 1/8 teaspoon salt
- Pinch black pepper
- Two teaspoons extra-virgin olive oil
- 1/4 cup thinly sliced fresh basil leaves

Directions

- Arrange tomatoes and cheese alternately on the plate, overlapping slightly. Sprinkle with salt and pepper and drizzle with oil. Scatter basil on top.

Nutrition Facts

Carbohydrates: 9g| Protein: 4g| Fat: 5g| Saturated Fat: 2g| Cholesterol: 9mg| Sodium: 165mg| Fiber: 1g

167. GINGER, ORANGE, AND SESAME DRESSING

Total Time: 40-50 minutes

Ingredients

- One tablespoon pure sesame oil
- Two tablespoons minced shallots
- One garlic clove, minced
- One tablespoon minced ginger
- Two teaspoons orange zest
- 3/4 teaspoon arrowroot
- 3/4 cup low-sodium chicken broth
- 1/4 cup fresh orange juice
- 1/4 cup rice wine vinegar
- One tablespoon reduced-sodium soy sauce
- 1/2 teaspoon kosher salt
- 1/2 teaspoon freshly ground black pepper

Directions

- Heat the sesame oil in a sauté pan over medium heat. Add the shallot, garlic, and ginger and sauté until soft. Add the orange zest and set it aside.
- Stir the arrowroot with one teaspoon of the chicken broth to form a paste. Bring the remaining broth, orange juice, and vinegar to a boil.
- Add the soy sauce to the arrowroot paste. Allow boiling until thickened and reduced slightly, stirring constantly. Remove from the heat and whisk in the salt, pepper, and reserved ginger mixture. Use warm as a sauce for the Spinach and White Bean main course or cool and use as a dressing.

Nutrition Facts

Carbohydrates: 2g| Fat: 1g| Sodium: 110mg| Fiber: 0g

168. GREENS AND BROCCOLI SALAD WITH POPPY VINAIGRETTE

Total Time: 10 minutes

Ingredients

- Four sun-dried tomato halves (not packed in oil)
- 3 cups torn leaf lettuce
- 1 1/2 cups broccoli florets

- 1 cup sliced mushrooms
- 1/3 cup sliced radishes
- Two tablespoons water
- One tablespoon balsamic vinegar
- One teaspoon vegetable oil
- 1/4 teaspoon chicken bouillon granules
- 1/4 teaspoon dried chervil or dried parsley
- 1/4 teaspoon dry mustard
- 1/8 teaspoon ground red pepper

Directions

- Pour boiling water over tomatoes in a small bowl to cover. Let stand 5 minutes; drain.
- Chop tomatoes. Combine tomatoes, lettuce, broccoli, mushrooms, and radishes in a large salad bowl.
- Combine two tablespoons of water, vinegar, oil, bouillon granules, chervil, mustard, and red pepper in a jar with a tight-fitting lid; shake well. Add to salad; toss gently.

Nutrition Facts

Carbohydrates: 9g| Protein: 3g| Fat: 2g| Saturated Fat: 1g| Sodium: 79mg| Fiber: 2g

169. BOUNTIFUL HARVEST VEGETABLE SALAD

Total Time: 20-25 minutes

Ingredients

- One tablespoon hazelnut or olive oil
- One small onion, finely chopped
- One clove garlic, finely chopped
- 3/4 cup malt vinegar
- One tablespoon brown sugar
- 1 cup chopped parsnips
- 1 cup chopped turnips
- 1/2 cup parsley and cilantro leaves
- 3 cups baby salad greens
- 1/2 cup toasted walnut pieces
- 1 cup chopped radish
- Salt and pepper to taste

Directions

- Heat oil in a large skillet over medium heat. Add onions and cook until golden brown, 5–7 minutes. Add garlic and cook for 30 seconds more. Stir in vinegar and sugar and bring just to a simmer. Remove from heat and keep dressing warm.
- Bring a large pot of salted water to a boil. Add parsnips and turnips and simmer until vegetables are just tender, 8–10 minutes. Drain well.
- Arrange parsley, cilantro, and salad greens on a platter and top with hot vegetables. Garnish with walnuts and radish. Drizzle with warm dressing, and serve immediately.

Nutrition Facts

- Protein: 3g| Fat: 9g| Saturated Fat: 8g| Sodium: 45mg| Fiber: 4g

170. ZUCCHINI RIBBON SALAD

Total Time: 10-15 minutes

Ingredients

- Two medium zucchini
- Two tablespoons chopped sun-dried tomatoes (not packed in oil)
- Two teaspoons olive oil
- One teaspoon fresh lemon juice
- One teaspoon white vinegar
- 1/8 teaspoon salt
- Two tablespoons shredded Parmesan cheese
- One tablespoon pine nuts, toasted

Directions

- Peel zucchini lengthwise into ribbons using a vegetable peeler until seeds are visible. Combine zucchini ribbons and sun-dried tomatoes in a medium bowl.
- Whisk oil, lemon juice, vinegar, and salt in a small bowl until well blended. Drizzle over zucchini and tomatoes; gently toss to coat.
- Divide salad evenly between 2 serving bowls. Top with cheese and pine nuts. Serve immediately.

Nutrition Facts

Carbohydrates: 9g| Protein: 5g| Fat: 10g| Saturated Fat: 2g| Cholesterol: 4mg| Sodium: 254mg| Fiber: 3g

171. GRAPE TOMATO SALAD WITH WHITE BEANS AND CUCUMBER

Total Time: 15 minutes

Ingredients

- 1 cup canned Great Northern beans, rinsed and drained
- 1 cup grape tomato halves
- 1 cup 1/2-inch diced cucumber
- Two tablespoons finely diced red onion
- One tablespoon finely chopped fresh cilantro
- One tablespoon extra-virgin olive oil
- One tablespoon lime juice
- 1/4 teaspoon salt
- 1/8 teaspoon black pepper

Directions

- Combine beans, tomatoes, cucumber, onion, and cilantro in a large bowl.
- Whisk oil, lime juice, salt, and pepper in a small bowl. Pour over salad and mix gently.

Nutrition Facts

Carbohydrates: 17g| Protein: 5g| Fat: 4g| Saturated Fat: 1g| Sodium: 291mg| Fiber: 4g

172. SPRINGTIME PANZANELLA

Total Time: 30 minutes

Ingredients

- Three tablespoons olive oil, divided
- Two cloves garlic, minced and divided
- Three slices of whole-wheat bread, cut into 1-inch cubes
- One teaspoon salt, divided
- 1 pound asparagus, cut into 1-inch pieces
- 1/4 cup chopped carrot
- 1/2 cup finely chopped red onion
- Two tablespoons white wine vinegar
- One tablespoon lemon juice
- 1/2 teaspoon deli-style mustard

- Two tablespoons shredded Parmesan cheese

Directions

- Preheat oven to 425°F. Spray baking sheets with nonstick cooking spray.
- Combine one tablespoon oil and one clove of garlic in a large bowl; mix well. Add bread cubes; toss to coat evenly. Spread in a single layer on a baking sheet.
- Combine one tablespoon oil, remaining one clove garlic, and 1/2 teaspoon salt in the same bowl. Add asparagus and carrot; toss to coat evenly. Spread on a separate baking sheet.
- Bake bread cubes and vegetables for 15 minutes, stirring once. Let stand 5 to 10 minutes to cool slightly.
- Meanwhile, combine onion, vinegar, remaining one tablespoon oil, lemon juice, mustard, and remaining 1/2 teaspoon salt in a small bowl; mix well. Add bread cubes and vegetables; gently toss to coat evenly. Top with cheese just before serving.

Nutrition Facts

Carbohydrates: 13g| Protein: 5g| Fat: 12g| Saturated Fat: 2g| Cholesterol: 2mg| Sodium: 722mg| Fiber: 3g

173. SIRLOIN STEAK ANTIPASTO SALAD

Total Time: 15 minutes

Ingredients

- Three cloves garlic, minced
- 1/2 teaspoon black pepper
- One beef top sirloin steak (about 1 pound and 3/4 inch thick), trimmed of fat
- 8 cups torn romaine lettuce
- 16 cherry tomatoes, halved
- 16 pitted kalamata olives, halved lengthwise
- One can (14 ounces) quartered artichoke hearts in water, rinsed, and drained
- 1/3 cup fat-free Italian or Caesar salad dressing
- 1/4 cup fresh basil, cut into thin strips

Directions

- Prepare grill for direct cooking or preheat broiler. Sprinkle garlic and pepper over steak.
- Grill steak over medium-hot coals or broil 4 inches from heat 4 minutes per side for medium-rare or until desired doneness. Transfer steak to cutting board; tent with foil. Let stand for at least 5 minutes.
- Meanwhile, combine lettuce, tomatoes, olives, and artichoke hearts in a large bowl. Add dressing; toss well. Transfer to four plates.
- Cut steak crosswise into thin slices; arrange over salads. Drizzle juices from the cutting board over steak. Sprinkle with basil.

Nutrition Facts

Carbohydrates: 21g| Protein: 30g| Fat: 7g| Saturated Fat: 2g| Cholesterol: 53mg| Sodium: 776mg| Fiber: 9g

174. PEAR AND CRANBERRY SALAD

Total Time: 10 minutes

Ingredients

- 1/2 cup canned whole berry cranberry sauce
- Two tablespoons balsamic vinegar
- One tablespoon olive or canola oil
- 12 cups (9 ounces) packed assorted bitter or gourmet salad greens
- Six small or four large ripe pears (about 1 3/4 pounds), cored and cut into 1/2-inch-thick slices
- 2 ounces blue or Gorgonzola cheese, crumbled

Directions

- Combine cranberry sauce, vinegar, and oil in a small bowl; mix well. Arrange greens on six serving plates. Arrange pears over greens; drizzle with dressing. Sprinkle with cheese. Serve immediately.

Nutrition Facts

Carbohydrates: 26g| Protein: 4g| Fat: 6g| Saturated Fat: 2g| Cholesterol: 7mg| Sodium: 165mg| Fiber: 2g

175. GREENS AND PEAR WITH MAPLE-MUSTARD DRESSING

Total Time: 15 minutes

Ingredients

- 1/4 cup maple syrup
- One tablespoon Dijon mustard
- One tablespoon olive oil
- One tablespoon balsamic or cider vinegar
- 1/8 teaspoon black pepper
- 4 cups torn mixed salad greens
- One medium red pear, cored and thinly sliced
- 1/4 cup sliced green onions
- Three tablespoons dried cherries
- Two tablespoons plus two teaspoons chopped walnuts, toasted

Directions

- Whisk maple syrup, mustard, oil, vinegar, and pepper in a small bowl until well blended.
- Combine greens, pear, green onions, cherries, and walnuts in a large serving bowl. Drizzle with dressing; gently toss to coat.

Nutrition Facts

Carbohydrates: 29g| Protein: 2g| Fat: 7g| Saturated Fat: 1g| Sodium: 112mg| Fiber: 3g

176. CHICKEN AND SPINACH SALAD

Total Time: 15 minutes

Ingredients

- 3/4 pound chicken tenders
- Nonstick cooking spray
- 4 cups shredded stemmed spinach
- 2 cups washed and torn romaine lettuce
- One large grapefruit, peeled and sectioned
- Eight thin slices of red onion, separated into rings
- Two tablespoons (1/2 ounce) crumbled blue cheese
- 1/4 cup prepared fat-free Italian salad dressing

- Assorted fresh greens (optional)

Directions

- Cut chicken into 2×1/2-inch strips. Spray a large nonstick skillet with cooking spray; heat over medium heat. Add chicken; cook and stir 5 minutes or until no longer pink in center. Remove from skillet.
- Divide spinach, lettuce, grapefruit, onion, cheese, and chicken among four salad plates. Combine citrus blend concentrate and Italian dressing in a small bowl; drizzle over salads.

Nutrition Facts

Carbohydrates: 4g| Protein: 23g| Fat: 4g| Saturated Fat: 1g| Cholesterol: 55mg| Sodium: 361mg| Fiber: 3g

177. CHICKEN AND CANTALOUPE SALAD WITH TOASTED PECANS

Total Time: 30-60 minutes

Ingredients

- 1/2 cup fat-free mayonnaise
- One tablespoon cider vinegar
- One tablespoon honey
- 1/2 teaspoon curry powder
- 1/4 teaspoon ground ginger
- 4 cups shredded cooked chicken
- 1 cup thinly sliced celery
- 1/4 cup thinly sliced red onion
- One small cantaloupe
- 1/2 cup toasted pecan halves, divided
- 6 cups Romaine or Boston lettuce leaves

Directions

- For the dressing, whisk together mayonnaise, vinegar, honey, curry powder, and ginger in a small bowl. Refrigerate until needed.
- For salad, place chicken in a medium bowl. Add celery and onion. Toss with dressing to mix.
- Peel and seed cantaloupe; cut half into small cubes and a half into eight wedges for garnish. Add cantaloupe cubes and 1/4 cup pecans to salad; toss lightly to mix.
- Line plates with lettuce leaves. Mound chicken mixture in the center. Garnish with cantaloupe wedges and sprinkle with remaining pecans.

Nutrition Facts

Carbohydrates: 27g| Protein: 44g| Fat: 14g| Saturated Fat: 2g| Cholesterol: 108mg| Sodium: 382mg| Fiber: 5g

178. FRUIT SALAD WITH CREAMY BANANA DRESSING

Total Time: 1 hour

Ingredients

- 2 cups fresh pineapple chunks
- 1 cup cantaloupe cubes
- 1 cup honeydew melon cubes
- 1 cup blackberries
- 1 cup sliced strawberries
- 1 cup seedless red grapes
- One medium apple, diced
- Two medium ripe bananas, sliced
- 1/2 cup vanilla nonfat Greek yogurt
- Two tablespoons honey
- One tablespoon lemon juice
- 1/4 teaspoon ground nutmeg

Directions

- Combine pineapple, cantaloupe, honeydew, blackberries, strawberries, grapes, and apple in a large bowl; gently mix.
- Combine bananas, yogurt, honey, lemon juice, and nutmeg in a blender or food processor; blend until smooth.
- Pour dressing over fruit mixture; gently toss to coat evenly. Serve immediately.

Nutrition Facts

Carbohydrates: 31g| Protein: 3g| Sodium: 15mg| Fiber: 4g

179. MAIN-DISH MEDITERRANEAN SALAD

Total Time: 1 hour 30 minutes

Ingredients

- One package (10 ounces) ready-to-use chopped romaine lettuce
- 1/2 pound fresh green beans, cooked and drained or one can (about 14 ounces) whole green beans, drained
- One package (5 1/2 ounces) solid white tuna, flaked
- 8 ounces cherry tomatoes, halved
- Two tablespoons olive oil
- Two tablespoons cider vinegar or white vinegar
- 1 1/2 teaspoons Dijon mustard
- 1/2 teaspoon black pepper

Directions

- Place lettuce, green beans, tuna, and tomatoes in a large bowl.

To Make The Dressing:

- Whisk oil, vinegar, mustard, and pepper in a small bowl until blended.
- Pour dressing over salad; toss well.
- Serve immediately.

Nutrition Facts

Carbohydrates: 9g| Protein: 13g| Fat: 8g| Saturated Fat: 1g| Cholesterol: 18mg| Sodium: 218mg, Fiber: 4g

180. FENNEL WHEAT BERRY SALAD

Total Time: 2 hours 30 minutes

Ingredients

- 3 cups water
- 1/2 cup wheat berries
- 1/4 teaspoon salt
- 3 cups coleslaw mix
- Two tablespoons balsamic vinegar
- One tablespoon olive oil
- One tablespoon honey
- 1 1/4 teaspoons whole fennel seeds, toasted

Directions

- Combine water and wheat berries in a medium saucepan.
- Bring to a boil. Reduce heat and simmer, covered, about 1 hour or until wheat berries are tender.
- Drain off any water.
- Place wheat berries in a large bowl; cover and refrigerate for at least 1 hour.

To Prepare Salad Dressing:

- Whisk together vinegar, olive oil, honey, and fennel seeds, if desired, in a small bowl.
- Add coleslaw mix to wheat berries.
- Drizzle with dressing; toss until coated.
- Serve immediately.

Nutrition Facts

Carbohydrates: 13g| Protein: 2g| Fat: 3g| Saturated Fat: 1g| Sodium: 102mg| Fiber: 2g

181. APPLE-WALNUT SALAD WITH BLUE CHEESE-HONEY VINAIGRETTE

Total Time: 30-60 minutes

Ingredients

- 1/4 cup chopped walnuts
- One tablespoon white wine vinegar
- Two teaspoons olive oil
- Two teaspoons honey
- 1/4 teaspoon salt
- 1/8 teaspoon black pepper
- Two tablespoons crumbled blue cheese
- One large head of Bibb lettuce, separated into leaves
- One small Red Delicious or other red apples, thinly sliced
- One small Granny Smith apple, thinly sliced

Directions

- Place walnuts in a small skillet over medium heat.
- Cook and stir 5 minutes or until fragrant and lightly toasted. Transfer to plate to cool.
- Whisk vinegar, oil, honey, salt, and pepper in a small bowl until well blended.
- Stir in cheese.
- Divide lettuce and apples evenly among four plates.
- Drizzle dressing evenly over each salad; top with walnuts.

Nutrition Facts

Carbohydrates: 18g| Protein: 3g| Fat: 8g| Saturated Fat: 2g| Cholesterol: 3mg| Sodium: 207mg| Fiber: 3g

182. SPINACH SALAD WITH POMEGRANATE VINAIGRETTE

Total Time: 30-50 minutes

Ingredients

- One package (5 ounces) baby spinach
- 1/2 cup pomegranate seeds (arils)
- 1/4 cup crumbled goat cheese
- Two tablespoons chopped walnuts, toasted
- 1/4 cup pomegranate juice
- Two tablespoons olive oil
- One tablespoon red wine vinegar
- One tablespoon honey
- 1/4 teaspoon salt
- 1/4 teaspoon black pepper

Directions

- Combine spinach, pomegranate seeds, goat cheese, and walnuts in a large bowl. Whisk pomegranate juice, oil, vinegar, honey, salt, and pepper in a small bowl until well blended. Pour over salad; gently toss to coat. Serve immediately.

Nutrition Facts

- Carbohydrates: 12g| Protein: 4g| Fat: 11g| Saturated Fat: 3g| Cholesterol: 4mg| Sodium: 210mg| Fiber: 1g

183. GARDEN PASTA SALAD

Total Time: 1 hour

Ingredients

- 6 cups (about 12 ounces) cooked penne pasta
- 2 cups shredded cooked boneless skinless chicken breasts
- 3/4 cup chopped red onion
- 3/4 cup chopped red or green bell pepper
- 3/4 cup sliced zucchini
- One can (4 ounces) sliced black olives, drained
- One teaspoon red pepper flakes
- One teaspoon salt (optional)
- One can (10 3/4 ounces) condensed reduced-fat reduced-sodium cream of chicken soup, undiluted
- 1/2 cup lemon juice
- 1/2 cup grated Parmesan cheese
- 1/2 cup chopped fresh basil (optional)
- 1/4 cup chopped fresh parsley (optional)

Directions

- Combine pasta, chicken, onion, bell pepper, zucchini, olives, red pepper flakes, and salt in a large bowl; toss lightly.
- Combine soup and lemon juice in a small bowl; mix well. Pour soup mixture over pasta salad; mix well.
- Sprinkle with Parmesan cheese, basil, and parsley.

Nutrition Facts

Carbohydrates: 33g| Protein: 18g| Fat: 10g| Saturated Fat: 2g| Cholesterol: 36mg| Sodium: 886mg| Fiber: 3g

184. BROWN RICE, ASPARAGUS, AND TOMATO SALAD

Total Time: 1 hour 30 minutes

Ingredients

- 1 cup instant brown rice
- 12 medium spears asparagus, cooked and cut into 1-inch pieces
- Two medium tomatoes
- 2 1/2 teaspoons lemon juice
- Two teaspoons olive oil
- 1/8 teaspoon salt
- 1/8 teaspoon black pepper
- 1/4 cup minced fresh chives or green onions
- Two teaspoons minced fresh dill

Directions

- Bring 1 cup water to a boil in a medium saucepan.
- Stir in rice. Bring water to a boil again. Reduce heat to low; cover and simmer for 5 minutes.
- Remove from heat. Stir rice; cover again.

- Let stand 5 minutes or until water is absorbed and rice is tender. Fluff with fork; set aside.
- Meanwhile, place asparagus in a large bowl.
- Core tomatoes over a separate bowl to catch the juice. Dice tomatoes, reserving liquid. Add tomatoes to asparagus.
- Whisk 1 1/2 tablespoons reserved tomato juice, lemon juice, oil, salt, and pepper in a small bowl until well blended. Stir in chives and dill.
- Add rice to the salad bowl. Pour in dressing; toss lightly to coat.

Nutrition Facts

Carbohydrates: 22g| Protein: 4g| Fat: 3g| Saturated Fat: 1g| Sodium: 97mg| Fiber: 3g

185. SPINACH SALAD WITH BEETS

Total Time: 30-60 minutes

Ingredients

- 6 cups (6 ounces) packed baby spinach or torn spinach leaves
- 1 cup canned pickled julienned beets, drained
- 1/4 cup thinly sliced red onion, separated into rings
- 1/4 cup fat-free croutons
- 1/3 cup low-fat raspberry vinaigrette salad dressing
- 1/4 cup real bacon bits
- Black pepper (optional)

Directions

- Combine spinach, beets, onion, and croutons in a large bowl. Add dressing; toss to coat.
- Divide evenly among four serving plates. Sprinkle with bacon bits and pepper, if desired

Nutrition Facts

Carbohydrates: 9g| Protein: 5g| Fat: 3g| Saturated Fat: 1g| Cholesterol: 5mg| Sodium: 740mg| Fiber: 2g

186. GREEN BEAN, WALNUT, AND BLUE CHEESE PASTA SALAD

Total Time: 30 minutes

Ingredients

- 2 cups uncooked Gemelli pasta
- 2 cups trimmed halved green beans
- Three tablespoons olive oil
- Two tablespoons white wine vinegar
- One tablespoon chopped fresh thyme
- One tablespoon Dijon mustard
- One tablespoon fresh lemon juice
- One teaspoon honey
- 1/4 teaspoon salt
- 1/4 teaspoon black pepper
- 1/2 cup chopped walnuts, toasted
- 1/2 cup reduced-fat crumbled blue cheese

Directions

- Cook pasta according to package directions, omitting salt. Add green beans during the last 4 minutes of cooking. Drain. Transfer to a large bowl.
- Meanwhile, whisk oil, vinegar, thyme, mustard, lemon juice, honey, salt, and pepper in a medium bowl until smooth and well blended.
- Pour dressing over pasta and green beans; toss to coat evenly. Stir in walnuts and cheese. Serve warm or cover and refrigerate until ready to serve.

Nutrition Facts

Carbohydrates: 25g| Protein: 7g| Fat: 12g| Saturated Fat: 2g| Cholesterol: 4mg| Sodium: 119mg| Fiber: 2g

187. HAM AND PINEAPPLE SALAD FOR ONE

Preparation time: 5 minutes

Ingredients

- 1/3 of 5-ounce package prewashed, mixed baby salad greens (about 2 cups)
- 2 ounces extra-lean, prepackaged, lower-sodium, deli-sliced ham, chopped
- Ten fresh snow peas, sliced in half
- 1/4 of a medium red or yellow bell pepper, cut into strips
- 1/2 cup unsweetened pineapple tidbits or chunks
- Two tablespoons fat-free ranch dressing

Directions

- Combine salad greens, ham, snow peas, pepper strips, and pineapple. Top with ranch dressing.

Nutrition Facts

- Carbohydrates: 30g| Protein: 13g| Fat: 2g| Cholesterol: 27mg| Sodium: 625mg, Fiber: 3g

188. WINTER FRUIT AND SPINACH SALAD

Preparation time: 5 minutes

Ingredients

- 2 cups baby spinach leaves, washed and drained
- One medium (about 3 inches in diameter) apple
- One medium pear (about 3 ounces)
- 1/4 cup chopped walnuts
- Two dried dates, chopped

Directions

- Place spinach leaves in a salad bowl. Core and dice apple and pear, leaving the skin on.
- Add to spinach leaves. Top with chopped walnuts and dates. Toss gently with salad tongs and serve.
- This salad does not need a dressing, but if desired, use a nonfat sauce or a drizzle of apple cider vinegar.

Nutrition Facts

- Carbohydrates: 27g| Protein: 2g| Fat: 1g| Sodium: 139mg| Fiber: 4g

189. COOL WHEAT BERRY SALAD

Preparation Time: 20 Minutes
Cooking Time: 35 Minutes.

Ingredients

- 1 cup soft wheat berries
- 4 cups water
- Pinch of salt, plus more to taste

- One large Gala or Fuji apple, chopped
- Two tablespoons lemon juice
- Four large stalks of celery, chopped
- 1/2–1 cup chopped jicama, optional
- 1/4 cup chopped parsley
- 1/2 cup sliced scallions, green and white portions
- 1/2–1 teaspoon curry powder, to taste
- 1/2 cup nonfat plain yogurt
- 8 ounces sliced, cooked chicken
- Seven walnut halves, toasted and chopped
- Head of lettuce

Directions

- Place wheat berries, water, and a pinch of salt in a pressure cooker and secure the lid.
- Bring to high pressure, lower heat, and cook for 35 minutes. Remove from heat and release stress quickly by running cold water over the cooker.
- Drain wheat berries and set them aside to cool.
- Toss chopped apple with lemon juice and cooled wheat berries and celery, jicama, parsley, and scallions.
- Mix curry powder and yogurt together for dressing.
- Add salt to taste. Mix dressing with wheat berries.
- Arrange a bed of lettuce on each plate, top with a cup wheat berry mixture, add chicken slices, and sprinkle with toasted nuts.

Nutrition Facts

Carbohydrates: 39g| Protein: 11g| Fat: 9g| Saturated Fat: 2g| Cholesterol: 17mg| Sodium: 244mg| Fiber: 8g

190. CUCUMBER YOGURT DRESSING

Total Time: 40 minutes

Ingredients

- One small cucumber, seeded and finely chopped
- 1/8 teaspoon salt
- 8 ounces nonfat yogurt
- Two tablespoons chopped celery
- Two tablespoons chopped onion
- One clove garlic, minced
- Dash white pepper

Directions

- Toss cucumber in a bowl with salt.
- Cover and chill for approximately 30 minutes.
- Drain moisture from cucumber.
- Combine cucumber with remaining ingredients; mix well.
- Store covered in refrigerator.

Nutrition Facts

- Carbohydrates: 2g| Protein: 1g| Sodium: 38mg

191. ASIAN VEGETABLE AND SOBA NOODLE SALAD

Preparation Time: 25 Minutes
Chilling Time: 1 Hour

Ingredients

- 5 ounces soba
- 3/4 cup coarsely sliced fresh red bell pepper
- 3/4 cup coarsely sliced fresh green bell pepper
- 1 cup sliced fresh red cabbage
- 1 cup peeled, matchstick-sliced fresh jicama
- 3/4 cup coarsely sliced green onions
- 3/4 cup matchstick-sliced unpeeled cucumber
- 1/4 cup chopped, unsalted peanuts
- One tablespoon sesame oil
- Two tablespoons rice vinegar
- Two cloves fresh garlic, minced
- One tablespoon low-sodium soy sauce
- 1/2 teaspoon black pepper

Directions

- Bring a medium pot of water to a boil.
- Add soba noodles, cover, and cook for about 5 minutes until noodles are tender yet firm.
- Place noodles in a strainer and rinse with cool water. In a large salad bowl, place sliced red pepper, green pepper, red cabbage, jicama, green onions, cucumber, and peanuts.
- Add cooled, drained noodles. In a small mixing bowl, whisk sesame oil, vinegar, minced garlic, soy sauce, and black pepper.
- Pour dressing over salad and toss ingredients until they are well distributed.
- Chill for approximately 1 hour before serving.

Nutrition Facts

Carbohydrates: 19g| Protein: 4g| Fat: 4g| Saturated Fat: 1g| Sodium: 222mg| Fiber: 3g

192. QUICK RAINBOW TORTELLINI VEGETABLE SALAD

Preparation Time: 6 Minutes
Cooking Time: 8 Minutes.

Ingredients

- 2 cups frozen Italian-blend mixed vegetables
- One package (9 ounces or about 2 1/2 cups) refrigerated cheese rainbow tortellini
- 1 cup chopped green pepper
- 1/4 cup reduced-fat Italian salad dressing

Directions

- Bring a large pot of water to a boil.
- Add frozen vegetables and cover, cooking for about 5 minutes.
- Add the tortellini and cook for an additional 3 minutes, until tortellini and vegetables are tender.
- Meanwhile, place chopped green pepper in a salad bowl.
- Drain tortellini and vegetables and add to the salad bowl.
- Cover with Italian salad dressing, toss thoroughly, and serve warm or chill until cool.

Nutrition Facts

Carbohydrates: 20g| Protein: 6g| Fat: 2g| Saturated Fat: 1g| Sodium: 308mg| Fiber: 2g

193. LUSCIOUS LOBSTER SALAD

Preparation Time: 15 Minutes
Chilling Time: At Least 30 Minutes

Ingredients

- 1 pound cooked lobster meat, cut into bite-size pieces
- One stalk of celery, finely chopped
- Two tablespoons fat-free tub margarine, melted
- 1/8 teaspoon black pepper
- Juice of 1/4–1/2 a lemon (to taste)
- 1/4 cup light mayonnaise (not salad dressing)

Directions

- Place lobster and celery in a medium bowl and drizzle with melted margarine.
- Toss to coat.
- Sprinkle evenly with pepper and lemon juice. Add mayonnaise and toss gently to coat.
- Cover and chill for at least 30 minutes to allow flavors to blend.

Nutrition Facts

Carbohydrates: 2g| Protein: 12g| Fat: 3g| Saturated Fat: <1g| Cholesterol: 41mg| Sodium: 298mg| Fiber: <1g

194. HOLD-THE-MAYO COLESLAW

Preparation Time: 4 1/2 hours

Ingredients

- 3/4 cup cold water
- Six tablespoons white vinegar
- 1/4 cup sugar
- 1/2 teaspoon salt
- 1 pound green cabbage, shredded
- 1/2 cup chopped green pepper
- 1/4 cup finely chopped celery
- 1/4 cup finely chopped radishes
- 1/2 cup grated carrots

Directions

- Combine water, vinegar, sugar, and salt in a deep bowl and stir until sugar and salt dissolve.
- Add the vegetables and toss thoroughly.
- Cover with plastic wrap.
- Marinate for at least 4 hours in the refrigerator.

Nutrition Facts

Carbohydrates: 21g| Sodium: 229mg| Fiber: 3g

195. GERMAN-STYLE POTATO SALAD

Preparation Time: 5 Minutes Once Potatoes Are Cool To Touch
Cooking Time: 15–20 Minutes.

Ingredients

- 2 pounds small red potatoes
- Three tablespoons imitation bacon bits
- 2/3 cup fat-free Italian salad dressing
- Two packets of Splenda (or another artificial sweetener)
- One tablespoon cider vinegar
- 1/2 cup chopped parsley

Directions

- Leave skins on potatoes. Place potatoes in a medium saucepan and add enough cool water to cover them by at least an inch of water. Bring to a boil and cook until potatoes can be pierced with a fork, about 15 minutes.
- Drain and cool.
- Quarter the potatoes when cool enough to touch. Combine bacon bits, salad dressing, Splenda, vinegar, and parsley in a medium-sized bowl. Toss potato pieces in the bowl with dressing to coat.
- Serve warm or chilled.

Nutrition Facts

Carbohydrates: 27g| Protein: 4g| Fat: 1g| Saturated Fat: <1g| Sodium: 344mg| Fiber: 3g

196. GRILLED ROMAINE AND ASPARAGUS SALAD

Preparation Time: 7 Minutes
Cooking Time: 6 Minutes

Ingredients

- One six-ounce head of romaine lettuce
- Nonstick cooking spray
- Aluminum foil
- Four medium spears or eight thin spears of fresh asparagus
- 1/4 cup thinly sliced red onion
- 12 grape tomatoes
- One tablespoon shredded Parmesan cheese
- 1/4 cup fat-free Italian salad dressing

Directions

- Heat grill. Cut lettuce head lengthwise in half, but do not trim off the base holding the leaves together; wash lettuce and pat dry.
- Spray a 12-inch piece of foil (or a larger piece, if needed) with nonstick cooking spray.
- Place lettuce halves on foil and place on the hot grill. Grill each side of halves for 2 minutes until slightly browned.
- Remove from grill and cool. Cut off base, then slice lettuce horizontally into ribbons, about 1 inch wide. While the grill is still hot, grill asparagus on the same foil, constantly turning until slightly browned.
- Slice asparagus diagonally into 1-inch pieces.
- Place lettuce and asparagus in a medium salad bowl and sliced onion, tomatoes, and Parmesan cheese. Toss, add dressing, then toss again.

Nutrition Facts

Carbohydrates: 16g| Protein: 4 g| Fat: 2g| Sodium: 184mg| Fiber: 6g

197. PARSLEY, PEAR, AND WALNUT SALAD

Preparation Time: 5 Minutes
Chilling Time: 2 Hours

Ingredients

- 2 cups fresh curly parsley (about 1/3 pound)
- One medium Bosc pear (about 5 ounces)
- 1/2 cup chopped walnuts
- 1/4 cup Parmesan cheese, finely shredded
- 1/2 cup dried cranberries

- Ten red seedless grapes
- 1/4 cup fat-free raspberry vinaigrette salad dressing

Directions

- Wash and dry parsley, then remove stems and any discolored leaves. Chop parsley to make about 2 cups, and set aside.
- Cut the pear in half and remove the core with a melon baller. Leaving the skin on, cut pear into half-inch dice.
- Combine parsley, pear, walnuts, cheese, cranberries, and grapes in a medium salad bowl.
- Add dressing, and toss. Chill for 2 hours before serving for the best flavor.

Nutrition Facts

Carbohydrates: 9g| Protein: 5g| Fat: 11g| Saturated Fat: 2g| Cholesterol: 4mg| Sodium: 164mg| Fiber: 2g

198. FALL HARVEST COLESLAW

Preparation Time: 10 Minutes
Chilling Time: 1 Hour

Ingredients

- One head (one pound) green cabbage
- Two large carrots, peeled
- 1/2 cup chopped red onion
- 1/2 cup diced apple (any variety)
- 1/2 cup dried cranberries
- 1/4 cup poppy seed salad dressing
- 1/4 cup light mayonnaise

Directions

- Core cabbage and shred in a food processor; it will yield about 4 cups. Place cabbage in a large mixing bowl.
- Shred carrots in processor and combine with cabbage.
- Add remaining ingredients and stir well.
- Cover and chill in refrigerator at least 1 hour before serving.

Nutrition Facts

Carbohydrates: 11g| Fat: 4g| Cholesterol: 1mg Sodium: 48mg| Fiber: 2g

199. CRUNCHY VEGETABLE SALAD WITH CHIPOTLE-RANCH DRESSING

Preparation Time: 10 minutes

Ingredients

- 4 ounces Romaine'sRomaine's hearts lettuce
- 1/2 cup sliced cucumber
- 1/4 cup chopped green pepper
- Four red radishes, thinly sliced
- Two green onions, chopped
- 12 cherry tomatoes
- Two tablespoons low-fat, shredded Cheddar cheese
- 1/4 cup light ranch-style salad dressing
- One tablespoon chopped chipotle peppers in adobo sauce
- One tablespoon fresh lime juice

Directions

- Tear or chop lettuce (should yield approximately 4 cups) and place in a large salad bowl.
- Add cucumber, green pepper, radishes, green onions, tomatoes, and cheese.
- Toss well. In a small bowl, mix salad dressing, chipotle peppers, and lime juice.
- Pour dressing over salad and toss again to combine.

Nutrition Facts

Carbohydrates: 7g| Protein: 4g| Fat: 3g| Saturated Fat: 1g| Cholesterol: 2mg| Sodium: 255mg| Fiber: 2g

DESSERT RECIPES

200. LEMON CHIFFON TOPPED WITH BERRIES

Preparation 90 Minutes
Serves 6 Persons

Ingredients

- Lemon (juiced) – 2 large (1/3 cup) S
- plenda (granulated) – ½ cup
- Eggs – 4 (large)
- Fresh berries – 3 cups

Directions

- Place a nonstick saucepan over a high flame. Add in the Splenda and lemon juice and let it heat through. Keep stirring until the sugar dissolves completely; once done, take off the flame. Let it cool down a bit.
- Take a small glass bowl and crack eggs into the same. Whisk well until nice and airy. Add in the lemon sugar. Mix gradually and continue whisking.
- Once the eggs and lemon mixture have fully incorporated, transfer into a pan placed on a medium-low flame.
- Continue whisking for about 2-3 minutes. Make sure the egg mixture is light and airy.
- Remove the pan from the heat and transfer the mixture into a bowl. Place it in the refrigerator for about an hour. The mixture will become thicker as it cools.
- Scoop the lemon chiffon into a dessert bowl using a spoon. Top with berries of your choice.

Nutrition Facts

Calories per Serving: 90 cal Fat: 4g Protein: 5g Carbohydrates: 11g

201. COCONUT PIE

Preparation 45 Minutes
Serves 8 Persons

Ingredients

- 4 large eggs, at room temperature
- 2 cups nonfat milk Sugar-free sweetener equivalent to 1 cup granulated sugar
- 4 teaspoons cornstarch
- ½ teaspoon salt
- ¾ cup flaked unsweetened coconut, toasted
- 1 single-crust 9-inch pie shell, premade

Directions

- Preheat the oven to 375 degrees F.
- In a large bowl, beat the eggs with a hand beater for about 5 minutes, or until very thick and pale-lemon colored.

- Whisk in the milk, sweetener, cornstarch, salt, and coconut until well combined.
- Pour the coconut mixture into the pie shell.
- Bake the pie for 30 minutes, or until a sharp knife inserted in the center comes out clean.
- Cool the pie on a wire rack.
- Serve at room temperature or chilled.

Nutrition Facts

Calories per Serving: 169 cal Fat: 10g Protein: 6g Carbohydrates: 13g

202. TANGERINE PANNA COTTA

Preparation 30 Minutes
Serves 4 Persons
Ingredients

- Gelatin (unflavored) – 2 sachets (7 Gr.)
- Cold water – 1 cup
- Evaporated milk (low-fat) – 1
- Granulated sweetener – 1 tbsp. And 2 tsp. Vanilla extract – 1 teaspoon Orange zest – 1 orange
- Orange juice – 1 cup

Directions

- Begin by preparing the vanilla cream layer
- Take a small nonstick saucepan and add ½ cup of water and 1 sachet of unflavored gelatin. Let it sit for 1 minute.
- Add the evaporated milk, vanilla, and 1 tablespoon of sugar substitute. Place it over a low flame and let the gelatin dissolve completely. This takes around 5 minutes.
- Once done, remove from the flame and pour it into 4 glasses. Place these glasses into the refrigerator for about 2 hours. The mixture should be set but not very firm. Now prepare the orange layer
- Take a small nonstick saucepan and add ½ cup water and 1 sachet of unflavored gelatin. Let it sit for 1 minute.

- Add the orange juice, orange zest, and around 2 teaspoons of the sugar substitute. Place the pan over a low flame and wait until the gelatin is dissolved completely. This will take around 5 minutes.
- Remove the mixture from the flame and let it reach room temperature. Pour all 4 glasses equally over the vanilla cream.
- Transfer the glasses into the refrigerator for at least 4 hours.
- The panna cotta is ready to be served.

Nutrition Facts

Calories per Serving: 130 cal Fat: 2g Protein: 10g Carbohydrates: 17g

203. CINNEMON APPLE SAUTE'

Preparation 22 Minutes
Serves 4 Persons
Ingredients

- Margarine (no trans-fat) – 1 tablespoon
- Apples (peeled and sliced) – 2 large
- Cinnamon (ground) – ½ teaspoon
- Vanilla extract – 1 teaspoon
- Water – 3 tablespoon
- Honey – 1 tablespoon

Directions

- Begin by peeling and slicing the apples.
- Now place a saucepan on a medium-high flame. Add the margarine and let it heat through.
- Toss in the sliced apples and cook for about 3 minutes. Keep stirring.
- Also, add the ground cinnamon, vanilla extract, water, and honey. Give it a nice stir.
- Reduce the flame to low and let it cook for about 12 minutes. Keep stirring to prevent it from sticking to the bottom.
- Serve

Nutrition Facts

Calories per Serving: 80 cal Fat: 2g Protein: 0g Carbohydrates: 14g

204. MIXED BERRY SNACK CAKE

Preparation 60 Minutes
Serves 8 Persons
Ingredients

- ¼ cup low-fat granola
- ½ cup buttermilk
- ⅓ cup packed brown sugar 2 tablespoons canola oil 1 teaspoon vanilla
- 1 egg
- 1 cup whole wheat flour
- ½ teaspoon baking soda
- ½ teaspoon ground cinnamon
- ⅛ teaspoon salt
- 1 cup mixed fresh berries

Directions

- Seat oven to 350°F. Spray 8- or 9-inch round pan with cooking spray.
- Place granola in resealable food-storage plastic bag; seal bag and slightly crush with rolling pin or meat mallet.
- Set aside.
- In large bowl, stir buttermilk, brown sugar, oil, vanilla and egg until smooth.
- Stir in flour, baking soda, cinnamon and salt just until moistened.
- Gently fold in half of the berries.
- Spoon into pan. Sprinkle with remaining berries and the granola.
- Bake 28 to 33 minutes or until golden brown and top springs back when touched in center.
- Cool in pan on cooling rack 10 minutes. Serve warm.

Nutrition Facts

Calories per Serving: 160 cal Fat: 5g Protein: 3g Carbohydrates: 26g

205. FUDGY BROWNIES

Preparation 33 Minutes
Serves 12 Persons
Ingredients

- Cocoa powder - 1/2 cup
- Stevia erythritol blend - ½ cup
- Baking soda - ¼ teaspoon
- Xanthan gum - 1/4 teaspoon
- Sea salt - 1/8 teaspoon

- Eggs - 2 large
- Avocado oil - ¼ cup
- Vanilla extract - 1 teaspoon
- Walnuts - 1/2 cup

Directions

- Start by preheating the oven by setting the temperature to 350 degrees Fahrenheit.
- Take a square baking dish and line it with a parchment paper sheet.
- In a medium-sized mixing bowl, add in the cocoa powder, baking
- soda, sweetener, sea salt and xanthan gum. Whisk until well combined.
- Take another mixing bowl and add in the eggs, vanilla extract and avocado oil. Whisk well.
- Pour the egg mixture over the cocoa powder mixture and mix until well blended.
- Now add in the walnuts and gently fold with the help of a spatula.
- Transfer the batter into the lined baking dish and place it in the preheated oven. Bake for around 25 minutes.
- .Once done, place it on a rack and let it stand until it reaches room temperature.
- Once the brownie is cool enough, lift the parchment paper from the sides and place it on flat surface.
- Cut the brownie into 12 equal-sized squares. Serve!

Nutrition Facts

Calories per Serving: 87 cal Fat: 8g Protein: 3g Carbohydrates: 3g

206. MAPLE AND CINNAMON PEACHES

Preparation 15 Minutes
Serves 4 Persons
Ingredients

- Maple syrup 1 tablespoon
- Nutmeg 0.125 teaspoons
- Cinnamon 0.5 teaspoons
- Lemon juice 1 medium
- Ripe peaches 4

Directions

- Preheat the grill until it gets to medium-high heat.
- Mix the nutmeg, maple syrup, lemon juice and cinnamon.
- Roll the peaches until they are fully and evenly coated.
- Grill the peaches for approximately 4 minutes until golden brown.
- Turn them once.

Nutrition Facts

Calories per Serving: 50 cal Fat: 0g Protein: 1g Carbohydrates: 12g

207. GINGERBREAD BISCUITS

Preparation 65 Minutes
Serves 4 Persons
Ingredients

- 1 cup white sugar
- 1/3 cup avocado oil
- 1/4 cup molasses
- 3 eggs
- 1 cup whole wheat flour
- 2 1/4 cups all-purpose flour
- 1 1/2 tbsps ground ginger
- 1 tbsp baking powder
- 1/2 tbsp ground cloves
- 3/4 tbsp ground cinnamon
- 1/4 tsp ground nutmeg

Directions

- Heat up oven to 375ºF.
- Prepare a greased cookie sheet.
- Add molasses, eggs, sugar and avocado oil into a big bowl and stir to combine.
- Add nutmeg, cinnamon, cloves, ginger, baking powder and flours into a separate bowl and mix well.
- Add flour mixture into the molasses mixture and mix until a stiff dough is formed.
- Split dough into two, and roll each half into the length of a cookie.
- Transfer dough rolls onto the prepared cookie sheet and pat down dough until flattened to 1/2" thickness.
- Transfer cookie sheet into the preheated oven, bake for 25 minutes and let sit until cooled.

- Slice cooled cookie rolls into 1/2" thick crosswise slices.
- Return sliced biscuits onto the cookie sheet and bake until crispy and toasted, for 5-7 minutes per side.

Nutrition Facts

Calories per Serving: 70 cal Fat: 2g Protein: 1g Carbohydrates: 12g

208. SESAME DATE AND ALMOND BALLS

Preparation 15 Minutes
Serves 4 Persons
Ingredients

- Pitted dates – 1 pound Butter – ¼ cup Water – ¼ cup
- Almonds (blanched) – ½ pound
- Vanilla extract – 1 teaspoon
- Cardamom (ground) – 1 teaspoon
- Cinnamon (ground) – ½ teaspoon
- Toasted sesame seeds – 1 cup
- Flax seed (ground) – 2 tablespoon

Directions

- Take a food processor and add in the dates, water, butter, vanilla, cinnamon, cardamom, and almonds.
- Process the **Ingredients:** into a smooth dough.
- Empty the prepared dough into a glass bowl.
- Use a spoon to scoop out the dough and form it into a ball. Repeat the process with the remaining dough.
- Spread both flaxseeds and sesame seeds onto the baking sheet.
- Dredge each ball into the seed mixture.
- Place them on a platter.

Nutrition Facts

Calories per Serving: 110 cal Fat: 7g Protein: 3g Carbohydrates: 12g

209. FRUITY OAT BARS

Preparation 40 Minutes
Serves 6 Persons
Ingredients

- 1/2 cup white sugar
- 1 1/3 cups quick cooking oats
- 1 tsp ground cinnamon

- 2 tsps baking powder
- 1/2 cup raisins
- 1/2 tsp baking soda
- 1/4 cup skim milk
- 1 cup bananas, mashed 1 tsp vanilla extract
- 2 egg whites

Directions

- Heat up oven to 350ºF.
- Add the dry **Ingredients:** into a bowl and mix well to combine.
- Add vanilla, milk, egg whites and bananas into another bowl and stir to combine.
- Add dry **Ingredients:** into the banana mixture and beat until well combined.
- Pour into a lightly sprayed 9-by-13" baking pan and transfer into the pre-heated oven.
- Bake mixture for about 35 minutes and let sit until cooled.
- Slice into bars and sprinkle with sugar and cinnamon, if desired.

Nutrition Facts

Calories per Serving: 72 cal Fat: 1g Protein: 2g Carbohydrates: 16g

210. BANANA SPLIT ICE CREAM PIE

Preparation Time: 25 Minutes
Freezing Time: 2 Hours
Standing Time: 10–15 Minutes

Ingredients

- One six-ounce commercial graham cracker crumb piecrust
- One banana (about 6 inches), sliced
- 2 cups reduced-fat, no-sugar-added vanilla ice cream, softened
- 2 cups reduced-fat, no-sugar-added chocolate ice cream
- 1/4 cup strawberry 100% fruit spread
- 1/2 cup fat-free whipped topping
- Eight maraschino cherries with stems, well-drained
- Three tablespoons lite chocolate syrup (such as Hershey's)

Directions

- Cover the bottom of the pie crust with banana slices. Spread softened vanilla ice cream over the banana slices, pressing it into spaces between bananas, making a smooth layer. Cover and freeze, about 1 hour or until ice cream is firm.
- Soften chocolate ice cream 20–30 seconds in the microwave or by allowing it to sit at room temperature for 10–15 minutes.
- Remove pie from the freezer and cover vanilla ice cream entirely with a layer of chocolate ice cream, smoothing it with a dull knife.
- Cover and return to the freezer until the ice cream is again hardened for about 1 hour.
- Before serving, allow the pie to soften slightly at room temperature for 10–15 minutes and warm the fruit spread.
- To help, cut the pastry into eight slices and put it on serving plates. Drizzle each piece with warm strawberry fruit spread.
- Top each with a dollop of whipped topping and a maraschino cherry, then drizzle with chocolate syrup. Serve immediately.

Nutrition Facts:

- Carbohydrates: 41g| Protein: 4g| Fat: 9g| Saturated Fat: 3g| Sodium: 190mg| Fiber: 1g

211. FRUIT & NUT QUINOA

Preparation Time: 25 Minutes
Standing Time: 10–15 Minutes

Ingredients

- 1 cup uncooked quinoa
- 2 cups water
- Two tablespoons finely grated orange peel, plus additional for garnish
- 1/4 cup fresh orange juice
- Two teaspoons olive oil
- 1/2 teaspoon salt
- 1/4 teaspoon ground cinnamon
- 1/3 cup dried cranberries
- 1/3 cup toasted pistachio nuts

Directions

- Place quinoa in fine-mesh strainer; rinse well under cold running water.
- Bring 2 cups water to a boil in a small saucepan; stir in quinoa.
- Reduce heat to low; cover and simmer 10 to 15 minutes, or until quinoa is tender and water is absorbed. Stir in 2 tablespoons orange peel.
- Whisk orange juice, oil, salt, and cinnamon in a small bowl.
- Pour over quinoa; gently toss to coat.
- Fold in cranberries and pistachios. Serve warm or at room temperature.
- Garnish with additional orange peel.

Nutrition Facts

Carbohydrates: 27g| Protein: 5g| Fat: 6g| Saturated Fat: 1g| Sodium: 198mg| Fiber: 3g

212. BEETS WITH HORSERADISH CREAM

Ingredients

- Four medium beets (about 2 inches in diameter)
- 1/3 cup low-fat sour cream
- 1 1/4 teaspoons prepared horseradish
- 1/4 teaspoon salt
- Pinch black pepper
- Cilantro (optional)

Directions

- Trim beets, leaving the root and 1 inch of stem. Scrub beets; place in large saucepan; cover with water. Cover; bring to a boil, reduce heat and boil 45 minutes, or until tender.
- Combine sour cream, horseradish, salt, and pepper in a small bowl.
- Remove beets from heat; drain. When cool, peel and cut into wedges. Transfer to plates and top with Horseradish Cream. Garnish with cilantro, if desired.

Nutrition Facts

Carbohydrates: 10g| Protein: 2g| Fat: 1g| Saturated Fat: 1g| Cholesterol: 7mg| Sodium: 231mg| Fiber: 2g

213. BLUEBERRY CUPCAKES WITH CREAM CHEESE FROSTING

Ingredients

- 1 1/2 cups all-purpose flour

- Two teaspoons baking powder
- 1/2 teaspoon baking soda
- 1/4 teaspoon salt
- 1/2 cup sugar substitute
- Two tablespoons unsalted butter softened
- Two tablespoons canola oil
- One large egg
- Two teaspoons grated lemon peel
- One teaspoon vanilla extract
- 1 1/4 cups plain low-fat yogurt
- 1 cup fresh blueberries
- 4 ounces reduced-fat cream cheese, cut into cubes
- One teaspoon vanilla extract
- 1/2 cup powdered sugar
- 1/4 cup sugar substitute

Directions

- Preheat oven to 350°F. Line 12 muffin standard (2 1/2-inch) muffin pan cups with paper baking cups; spray baking cups with nonstick cooking spray.
- Whisk flour, baking powder, baking soda, and salt in a medium bowl.
- Beat sugar substitute, butter, and oil in a large bowl with an electric mixer at medium speed until the mixture resembles coarse crumbs. Beat in egg, lemon peel, and vanilla. Alternately add flour mixture and yogurt, beginning and ending with flour mixture, beating well after each addition. Stir in blueberries.
- Spoon batter evenly into prepared muffin cups. Bake 20 to 30 minutes or until a toothpick inserted into the centers comes out clean. Cool in pan on wire rack 5 minutes. Remove from pan and cool completely.
- For frosting, beat cream cheese in a medium bowl with an electric mixer at medium speed until smooth. Beat in vanilla, powdered sugar, and sugar substitute at a low rate until blended; increase to high speed and beat until smooth (do not overbeat or frosting will be too thin). Refrigerate 15 to 30 minutes; spread evenly on cupcakes.

Nutrition Facts
Carbohydrates: 7g| Protein: 4g| Fat: 7g| Saturated Fat: 3g| Cholesterol: 29mg| Sodium: 251mg| Fiber: 1g

214. CHOCOLATE MINT SANDWICH COOKIES

Ingredients
Cookie Base:
- 1 1/2 cup almond flour
- 1/2 cup dutch processed cocoa powder
- 1/2 cup granulated Swerve, or sweetener of choice
- 1 tsp baking powder
- 1 tsp xanthan gum
- 6 tbsp unsalted butter, softened
- 1-2 tbsp cold water, if needed

Cream Filling:
- 6 tbsp unsalted butter, melted and cooled
- 1 cup powdered erythritol
- 2 tsp heavy cream
- 1/4 tsp non-alcohol mint extract
- Chocolate Coating:
- 5 oz Lily's Milk or Dark Chocolate
- 1/2 tsp coconut oil
- 1/4 tsp non-alcohol mint extract

Directions
Make The Cookies:
- Heat oven to 350°F and line a large cookie sheet with parchment.
- Whisk together the almond flour, cocoa powder, baking powder, sweetener, and xanthan gum.
- Cut in the soft butter and 1 tbsp cold water until a stiff dough forms. Use your hands to work the dough, and if it's too stiff, add another tbsp of water.
- Place the dough on a large piece of parchment and cover with plastic cling wrap. Roll into a thin round, about 1/4 inch thick, and use a round 2-inch cookie cutter (or small glass!) to cut the dough and place cookies on the prepared baking sheet.
- Re-roll the scraps and repeat until you are out of dough. Bake the cookies for 8–12 minutes; let cool before filling.

Make The Filling:
- Combine butter, powdered sweetener, and mint extract in a medium mixing bowl. Beat together until smooth, add the heavy cream, and continue to beat until light and fluffy. Taste and adjust the mint flavor to your preference.
- Spread or pipe filling onto half of the cooled cookies and top with another to make a sandwich.
- Melt the chocolate and coconut oil, stir in mint extract.
- Dip or drizzle in minty chocolate and arrange on a piece of wax paper or parchment. Let cool and serve!

215. PUMPKIN SPICE MINI DONUTS

Ingredients
- Nonstick cooking spray
- One tablespoon granulated sugar
- Two teaspoons ground cinnamon, divided
- 2 cups white whole-wheat flour
- 1/2 cup packed brown sugar
- 1 1/2 teaspoons baking powder
- 1/2 teaspoon salt
- 1/2 teaspoon ground ginger
- 1/2 teaspoon ground nutmeg
- 1/4 teaspoon baking soda
- 1/2 cup canned solid-pack pumpkin
- Two eggs
- 1/4 cup (1/2 stick) butter, softened
- 1/4 cup fat-free (skim) milk
- One teaspoon vanilla

Directions
- Preheat oven to 350°F. Spray 36 mini (1 3/4-inch) muffin cups with nonstick cooking spray. Combine granulated sugar and one teaspoon cinnamon in a small bowl; set aside.
- Combine flour, brown sugar, baking powder, remaining one teaspoon cinnamon, salt, ginger, nutmeg, and

baking soda in a medium bowl; mix well. Beat pumpkin, eggs, butter, milk, and vanilla in a large bowl with an electric mixer at medium speed until combined. Gradually add flour mixture, beating well after each addition. Spoon scant tablespoonful batter into each prepared muffin cup.

- Bake 12 minutes, or until a toothpick inserted into the centers comes out clean. Cool in pans on wire racks for 2 minutes.
- Working one at a time, dip doughnuts into cinnamon-sugar mixture, turning to coat evenly. Return to wire racks; let stand until set. Serve warm or cool ultimately.

Nutrition Facts

Carbohydrates: 19g| Protein: 3g| Fat: 3g| Saturated Fat: 2g| Cholesterol: 28mg| Sodium: 157mg| Fiber: 2g

216. MOCHA CRINKLE COOKIES

Ingredients

- 1 1/3 cups packed light brown sugar
- 1/2 cup vegetable oil
- 1/4 cup soft sour cream
- One egg
- One teaspoon vanilla
- 1 3/4 cups all-purpose flour
- 3/4 cup unsweetened cocoa powder
- Two teaspoons instant coffee granules
- One teaspoon baking soda
- 1/4 teaspoon salt
- 1/8 teaspoon black pepper
- 1/2 cup powdered sugar

Directions

- Beat brown sugar and oil in a large bowl with an electric mixer at medium speed until well blended. Add sour cream, egg, and vanilla; beat until well blended. Combine flour, cocoa, coffee granules, baking soda, salt, and pepper in a medium bowl; mix well. Beat into brown sugar mixture until well blended. Cover and refrigerate for 3 to 4 hours.
- Preheat oven to 350°F. Place powdered sugar in a shallow bowl. Shape dough into 1-inch balls; roll in powdered sugar. Place 2 inches apart on ungreased cookie sheets.
- Bake 10 to 12 minutes or until the tops of cookies are firm. Do not overbake. Remove to wire racks; cool completely.

Nutrition Facts

Carbohydrates: 7g| Fat: 1g| Saturated Fat: 1g| Cholesterol: 3mg| Sodium: 28mg

217. CHOCOLATE CINNAMON CAKE

Ingredients

- Nonstick cooking spray
- One package (about 15 ounces) devil's food cake mix
- 1 1/4 cups water
- 3/4 cup egg substitute or three eggs
- 1/3 cup canola oil
- One tablespoon instant coffee granules
- 1 1/2 to 2 teaspoons ground cinnamon
- 1/4 cup powdered sugar

Directions

- Preheat oven to 350°F. Coat 13×9-inch baking pan with nonstick cooking spray.
- Combine cake mix, water, egg substitute, oil, coffee granules, and cinnamon in a large bowl. Mix according to package directions. Spread batter in prepared pan.
- Bake 25 to 27 minutes or until a toothpick inserted into the center comes out clean. Cool completely in pan on wire rack. Just before serving, sift powdered sugar over the cake. (Use stencils to create designs, if desired.)

Nutrition Facts

Carbohydrates: 22g| Protein: 2g| Fat: 9g| Saturated Fat: 1 g| Sodium: 256mg, Fiber: 1g

218. EGGNOG SANDWICH COOKIES

Ingredients

- 1 cup (2 sticks) unsalted butter, softened
- 1 1/4 cups plus one tablespoon granulated sugar, divided
- One egg yolk
- 1/2 cup sour cream
- 2 1/2 cups all-purpose flour
- 1/4 teaspoon salt
- 1/2 teaspoon grated nutmeg
- 1/4 teaspoon ground ginger
- 1/2 cup (1 stick) butter, softened
- 1/4 cup shortening
- 2 1/2 cups powdered sugar
- Two tablespoons brandy or milk

Directions

- Preheat oven to 350°F. Lightly grease cookie sheets.
- Beat 1 cup butter and 1 1/4 cups granulated sugar in a large bowl with an electric mixer at medium speed until light and fluffy. Add egg yolk; beat until blended. Add sour cream; beat until well blended. Combine flour and salt in a small bowl; gradually add flour mixture to butter mixture, beating until well blended.
- Shape teaspoonfuls of dough into balls. Place on prepared cookie sheets; flatten slightly. Combine the remaining one tablespoon granulated sugar, nutmeg, and ginger in a small bowl; sprinkle over cookies.
- Bake 12 minutes or until edges are golden. Cool on cookie sheets for 5 minutes. Remove to wire racks; cool completely.
- Beat 1/2 cup butter and shortening in medium bowl until well blended. Add powdered sugar and brandy; beat until well blended. Spread or pipe filling on the flat side of half of the cookies. Top with remaining cookies, flat side down.

Nutrition Facts

Carbohydrates: 11g| Protein: 1g| Fat: 5g| Saturated Fat: 3g| Cholesterol: 14mg| Sodium: 10mg

219. CHOCOLATE-BAKED GRAPEFRUIT

Preparation Time: 5 Minutes
Baking Time: 5–7 Minutes

Ingredients

- One grapefruit (at room temperature)
- One tablespoon mini semisweet chocolate chips
- Two small strawberries

Directions

- Preheat oven to 350°F.
- Cut a thin slice off each end of the grapefruit (so that the grapefruit halves won't roll around) and slice grapefruit in half crosswise.
- Using a knife, gently cut around grapefruit sections to loosen them inside the skin; remove seeds.
- Sprinkle each grapefruit half evenly with 1/2 tablespoon chocolate chips.
- Place grapefruit halves in a pan and bake uncovered for 5 to 7 minutes, or until chocolate chips soften.
- Top each grapefruit half with a strawberry and serve immediately.

Nutrition Facts

Carbohydrates: 25g| Protein: 2g| Fat: 4g| Saturated Fat: 2g| Fiber: 2g

220. BLUEBERRY BLISS

Preparation Time: 10 Minutes

Ingredients

- 2 cups chilled, fresh blueberries (do not substitute unsweetened, frozen blueberries)
- 1/4 cup sugar-free, maple-flavored syrup
- Two teaspoons freshly grated orange or grapefruit zest
- 1/2 cup nonfat, no-sugar-added vanilla yogurt

Directions

- Place blueberries in a serving bowl. Add syrup and orange or grapefruit zest. Gently toss to coat blueberries. Fold in yogurt and serve right away.

Nutrition Facts

Carbohydrates: 12g| Protein: 1g| Fat: <1 g| Sodium: 43mg| Fiber: 2g

221. PUMPKIN CUSTARD

Ingredients

- Nonstick cooking spray
- One can (15 ounces) solid-pack pumpkin
- One teaspoon pumpkin pie spice
- 1/8 teaspoon salt
- 3/4 cup fat-free evaporated milk
- Three eggs or 3/4 cup egg substitute
- 1/4 cup packed dark brown sugar
- Two tablespoons chopped dried cherries
- Two tablespoons low-fat granola
- 4 cups boiling water

Directions

- Preheat oven to 350°F. Lightly spray 6 (6-ounce) custard cups with nonstick cooking spray. Place cups in a 13×9-inch baking pan. Stir pumpkin, pumpkin pie spice, and salt in a small bowl until blended.
- Heat milk in a small saucepan until steaming but not boiling. Meanwhile, whisk eggs and sugar in a medium bowl until smooth. Gradually whisk hot milk into the egg mixture. Whisk in pumpkin mixture. Spoon mixture evenly into prepared cups; sprinkle with cherries and granola.
- Place baking pan in oven; pour boiling water into the pan until water reaches halfway up sides of custard cups.
- Bake 25 to 30 minutes or until the knife inserted into the centers comes out clean. Remove cups to the wire rack. Serve custards warm or chilled.

Nutrition Facts

Carbohydrates: 24g| Protein: 7g| Fat: 3g| Saturated Fat: 1g| Cholesterol: 107mg| Sodium: 134mg| Fiber: 2g

222. CHOCOLATE CLUSTERS

Preparation Time: 15 Minutes

Ingredients

- 1 1/2 cups finely crushed vanilla wafers (about 45 wafers), graham cracker crumbs, or cornflake crumbs
- 2/3 cup unsweetened shredded coconut
- 2/3 cup powdered sugar plus additional powdered sugar for garnish
- 1/2 cup canned chocolate syrup
- One teaspoon vanilla

Directions

- Stir together the crushed vanilla wafers, coconut, and 2/3 cup powdered sugar in a bowl. Stir in the syrup and vanilla until well blended. Shape the dough into 1-inch balls and roll them in additional powdered sugar. Store tightly covered in a cool, dry place.

Nutrition Facts

- Carbohydrates: 13g| Protein: <1g| Fat: 2g| Saturated Fat: 1g| Sodium: 27mg| Fiber: <1g

223. SPLENDA FOUR INGREDIENT PEANUT BUTTER COOKIES

Ingredients

- 1 cup unsweetened peanut butter
- 1 cup Splenda Granulated Sweetener
- One large egg, beaten
- One teaspoon vanilla extract

Directions

- Preheat oven to 350°F. In a large bowl, add peanut butter, Splenda sweetener, egg, and vanilla extract. Stir until combined.
- Chill mixture for at least 10 minutes.
- Portion mixture into one tablespoon balls and place on an ungreased sheet pan. Press lightly with the tines of a fork to create a crosshatch pattern and flatten each cookie slightly.
- Bake for 8 minutes. Let cool on a sheet pan for at least 5 minutes before transferring to a wire rack to finish cooling.

- Enjoy while learning how Splenda Brand Sweeteners can help manage diabetes and reduce added sugars

Nutrition Facts

Carbohydrates: 4g| Protein: 3g| Fat: 7g| Saturated Fat: 1g| Cholesterol: 10mg| Sodium: 45mg| Fiber: 1g

224. SUMMER STRAWBERRY ORANGE CUPS

Ingredients

- 2 cups fresh strawberries, stems removed, divided
- One packet (1/4 ounce) unflavored gelatin
- Two tablespoons cold water
- Two tablespoons boiling water
- 1 1/2 cups reduced-fat (2%) milk
- 1/2 cup frozen orange juice concentrate
- One teaspoon vanilla

Directions

- Cut 1 cup strawberries into thin slices; place in the bottom of 6 (8-ounce) dessert bowls or custard cups.
- Combine gelatin and cold water in a small bowl; let stand 5 minutes. Add boiling water to softened gelatin; stir until completely dissolved.
- Combine milk, orange juice concentrate, and vanilla in a medium bowl; mix well. Let stand at room temperature for 20 minutes. Stir in gelatin mixture until well blended. Pour evenly over sliced strawberries in bowls. Refrigerate for 2 hours, or until completely set.
- Slice the remaining 1 cup strawberries; arrange on top of each dessert.

Nutrition Facts

Carbohydrates: 16g| Protein: 4g| Fat: 1g| Saturated Fat: 1g| Cholesterol: 5mg| Sodium: 29mg| Fiber: 1g

225. CAULIFLOWER PILAF

Preparation Time: 10 Minutes
Cooking Time: 10 Minutes.

Ingredients

- One large head cauliflower, cut into florets
- Two tablespoons extra-virgin olive oil
- Pinch asafetida
- 1/2 cup vegetable stock
- Sea salt
- 1/2 cup golden raisins
- 1/2 cup slivered almonds
- 1/4 cup chopped fresh flat-leaf Italian parsley

Directions

- In a food processor fitted with the metal blade, process the cauliflower florets until they resemble the texture of rice (you can also grate them on the large holes of a box grater). Set aside.
- In a medium skillet over medium-high heat, heat the olive oil. Add the asafetida and cook for about 45 seconds, constantly stirring until fragrant.
- Add the cauliflower and cook for 2 to 3 minutes, constantly stirring until it softens slightly.
- Stir in the vegetable stock and season to taste. Reduce the heat to low, cover, and cook for 5 minutes more until the cauliflower is tender.
- Remove from the heat and gently fold in the raisins, almonds, and parsley. Taste and adjust the seasonings. Serve.

Nutrition Facts

Carbohydrates: 21g| Protein: 5g| Fat: 13g| Saturated Fat: 2g| Sodium: 237mg| Fiber: 4g

226. ANGELIC MACAROONS

Ingredients

- One package (about 16 ounces) angel food cake mix
- 1/2 cup cold water
- One teaspoon almond extract
- One package (14 ounces) sweetened flaked coconut, divided
- 1/2 cup slivered almonds, coarsely chopped

Directions

- Preheat oven to 325°F. Line cookie sheets with parchment paper.
- Beat cake mix, water, and almond extract in a large bowl with an electric mixer at medium speed until well blended.
- Add half of the coconut; beat until blended.
- Add remaining coconut and almonds; beat until well blended. Drop dough by tablespoonfuls 2 inches apart onto prepared cookie sheets.
- Bake 22 to 25 minutes or until golden brown. Cool on cookie sheets for 3 minutes. Remove to wire racks; cool completely.

Nutrition Facts

Carbohydrates: 14g| Protein: 2g| Saturated Fat: 4g| Sodium: 86mg| Fiber: 1g

227. APPLE CINNAMON GRILL

Ingredients

- Four teaspoons vegetable-oil-and-yogurt spread
- 8 slices whole-grain cinnamon raisin bread
- 1/4 cup reduced-fat cream cheese
- One medium Granny Smith apple (about 5 ounces), thinly sliced
- 1/4 cup low-sugar red raspberry preserves
- 1/8 teaspoon ground cinnamon

Directions

- Spread 1/2 teaspoon spread onto one side of bread slices. Spread one tablespoon cream cheese on the opposite side of four bread slices. Arrange apple slices over cream cheese. Spread one tablespoon of preserves on the opposite side of the remaining four bread slices; sprinkle with cinnamon. Place on top of apples to create the sandwich.
- Spray a large nonstick skillet with nonstick cooking spray; heat over

medium heat. Grill sandwiches for 2 to 3 minutes on each side or until golden brown.

Nutrition Facts

Carbohydrates: 36g| Protein: 8g| Saturated Fat: 8g| Cholesterol: 10mg| Sodium: 300mg, Fiber: 3g

228. ANGELIC CUPCAKES

Preparation Time: Approximately 30 Minutes (Plus About 15 Minutes Preheating Time)

Ingredients

- One package (about 16 ounces) angel food cake mix
- 1 1/4 cups cold water
- 1/4 teaspoon peppermint extract (optional)
- Red food coloring
- 4 1/2 cups light whipped topping

Directions

- Preheat oven to 375°F. Line 36 standard (2 1/2-inch) muffin cups with paper baking cups.
- Beat cake mix, water, and peppermint extract, if desired, in a large bowl with an electric mixer at low speed for 2 minutes. Pour half of the batter into a medium bowl; fold in 9 drops of red food coloring. Alternate spoonfuls of white and pink batter in each prepared muffin cup, filling three-fourths full.
- Bake 11 minutes or until cupcakes are golden brown with deep cracks on top. Cool in pans for 10 minutes. Remove to wire racks; cool completely.
- Divide whipped topping between two small bowls. Add two drops of red food coloring to one bowl; stir gently until whipped topping is evenly colored. Frost cupcakes with pink and white whipped topping as desired.

Nutrition Facts

Carbohydrates: 13g| Protein: 1g| Fat: 1g| Saturated Fat: 1g| Sodium: 113mg|

229. CHOCOLATE CHIP FROZEN YOGURT

Ingredients

- 1 cup plain nonfat yogurt
- 1/2 cup fat-free half-and-half
- Two tablespoons sugar
- 1/4 teaspoon vanilla
- 1/4 cup mini semisweet chocolate chips

Directions

- Stir yogurt, half-and-half, sugar, and vanilla in a medium bowl until well blended.
- Freeze yogurt mixture in ice cream maker according to manufacturer's directions until soft. Add chocolate chips; freeze until firm.

Nutrition Facts

Carbohydrates: 14g| Protein: 3g| Fat: 2g| Saturated Fat: 1g| Cholesterol: 4mg| Sodium: 52mg| Fiber: 1g

230. ICE CREAM CAKE

Ingredients

- Five crushed sugar cones
- Three tablespoons unsalted butter, melted
- 2 pints (4 cups) no-sugar-added light ice cream, softened at room temperature, divided
- One container (8 ounces) reduced-fat whipped topping, thawed

Directions

- Spray 10-inch springform pan or deep-dish pie pan with nonstick cooking spray.
- Place sugar cone crumbs in a small bowl. Stir in butter until crumbs are evenly moistened. Press crumbs onto the bottom and partially up the side of the prepared pan. Refrigerate for 20 minutes.
- Spread one pint of ice cream into the crust with a rubber spatula. Freeze for 30 minutes or until firm. Spread the remaining pint of ice cream over the first layer. Freeze for 30 minutes or until firm. Spread whipped topping over ice cream; freeze for 2 hours or until firm. If desired, drizzle with fudge sauce after 30 minutes.
- Let soften in refrigerator 15 to 30 minutes; slice into wedges to serve.

Nutrition Information

Carbohydrates: 15g| Protein: 2g| Fat: 5g| Saturated Fat: 4g| Cholesterol: 11mg| Sodium: 35mg| Fiber: 1g

231. FROZEN BERRY ICE CREAM

Ingredients

- 8 ounces frozen unsweetened strawberries, partially thawed
- 8 ounces frozen unsweetened peaches, partially thawed
- 4 ounces frozen unsweetened blueberries, partially thawed
- Six packets sugar substitute
- Two teaspoons vanilla
- 2 cups sugar-free, low-fat vanilla ice cream
- 16 blueberries (optional)
- Four small strawberries halved (optional)
- Eight peach slices (optional)

Directions

- Combine partially thawed strawberries, peaches, blueberries, sugar substitute, and vanilla in a food processor. Process until coarsely chopped.
- Add ice cream; process until well blended.
- Serve immediately for semi-soft texture or freeze until ready to serve. (If frozen, let stand 10 minutes to soften slightly.) Garnish each serving with two blueberries for "eyes," 1 strawberry half for "nose," and one peach slice for "smile."

Nutrition Facts

Carbohydrates: 15g| Protein: 3g| Fat: 1g| Saturated Fat: 1g| Sodium: 23mg| Fiber: 1g

232. APPLE BUTTER ROLLS

Ingredients

- One package (11 ounces) refrigerated breadstick dough
- Two tablespoons apple butter
- 1 to 1 1/2 teaspoons orange juice
- 1/4 cup sifted powdered sugar

- 1/4 teaspoon grated orange peel (optional)

Directions

- Preheat oven to 350°F. Spray baking sheet with nonstick cooking spray; set aside.
- Unroll breadstick dough. Divide along perforations into 12 pieces. Gently stretch each piece to 9 inches in length. Twist ends of each element in opposite directions 3 to 4 times. Coil each twisted strip into a snail shape on the prepared baking sheet. Tuck ends underneath.
- Use thumb to make a slight indentation in the center of each breadstick coil. Spoon about 1/2 teaspoon apple butter into each indentation. Bake 11 to 13 minutes or until golden brown. Remove from baking sheet. Cool on a wire rack for 10 minutes.
- Meanwhile, stir enough orange juice into powdered sugar in a small bowl to make a pourable glaze. Stir in orange peel, if desired. Drizzle over rolls. Serve warm.

Nutrition Facts

Carbohydrates: 21g| Protein: 2g| Fat: 1g| Saturated Fat: 1g|Sodium: 186mg| Fiber: 1g

233. APPLE PECAN SPICE SQUARES

Ingredients

- One package (about 15 ounces) spice or carrot cake mix
- 1 1/4 cups water, divided
- Three eggs
- 1/2 cup plain fat-free yogurt
- 1/2 cup pecan pieces
- One unpeeled tart apple (such as Granny Smith), sliced
- One unpeeled baking apple (such as Red Delicious), sliced
- One tablespoon lemon juice (optional)
- One unpeeled ripe pear, sliced
- One teaspoon ground cinnamon
- 1/4 teaspoon ground nutmeg
- One tablespoon sucralose-based sugar substitute
- One tablespoon margarine or butter
- 1/2 teaspoon vanilla or vanilla, butter, and nut flavoring

Directions

- Preheat oven to 350°F. Spray jelly-roll pan with nonstick cooking spray.
- Beat cake mix, 1 cup water, eggs, and yogurt in a medium bowl according to package directions. Pour batter into prepared pan; smooth top.
- Bake 20 minutes or until a toothpick inserted into the center comes out clean. Cool completely in pan on wire rack.
- Cook and stir pecans in a large nonstick skillet over medium-high heat for about 2 minutes or until lightly browned. Remove to plate; set aside.
- Add remaining 1/4 cup water, apples, pear, lemon juice, cinnamon, and nutmeg to the same skillet; bring to a boil. Reduce heat to medium; cook 3 minutes or until fruit is crisp-tender. Remove from heat; gently stir in sugar substitute, margarine, vanilla, and pecans. Spoon evenly over cooled cake. Cut into 24 squares.

Nutrition Facts

Carbohydrates: 21g| Protein: 2g| Fat: 5g| Saturated Fat: 1g| Cholesterol: 27mg| Sodium: 158mg| Fiber: 1g

234. APPLE-CHEDDAR SCONES

Ingredients

- 1 cup all-purpose flour
- 1 cup white whole wheat flour
- Three tablespoons sugar
- 1 1/2 teaspoons baking powder
- 1/2 teaspoon salt
- 1/2 teaspoon ground cinnamon
- 1/4 teaspoon baking soda
- 1 Granny Smith apple, diced
- 1/2 cup (2 ounces) shredded reduced-fat sharp Cheddar cheese
- 1/3 cup natural or unsweetened applesauce
- 1/4 cup fat-free (skim) milk
- Three tablespoons melted butter
- One egg
- Nonstick cooking spray

Directions

- Preheat oven to 425°F. Line baking sheet with parchment paper.
- Combine all-purpose flour, white whole wheat flour, sugar, baking powder, salt, cinnamon, and baking soda in a large bowl; mix well. Stir in apple and cheese until well blended.
- Whisk applesauce, egg, milk, and butter in a small bowl until smooth and well blended. (Dough will be sticky.) stir into flour mixture until moistened.
- Knead dough on floured surface five times. Pat and stretch into an 8-inch circle. Slice diagonally into ten pieces. Place on prepared baking sheet. Spray tops with cooking spray.
- Bake 15 minutes or until lightly golden. Remove to wire rack; serve warm or cool completely.

Nutrition Facts

Carbohydrates: 26g| Protein: 5g| Fat: 6g| Saturated Fat: 3g| Cholesterol: 32mg| Sodium: 261mg| Fiber: 2g

235. APPLE AND OATMEAL COOKIE CRUMBLE

Ingredients

- 6 cups diced unpeeled apples
- 1/4 cup water
- 1/3 cup raisins
- 1/2 teaspoon ground cinnamon
- One teaspoon vanilla, butter, and nut flavoring or 1 1/2 teaspoons vanilla
- 3/4 cup oatmeal cookie mix
- One tablespoon canola oil

Directions

- Preheat oven to 400°F. Coat 11×7-inch baking pan with nonstick cooking spray. Stir together apples, water, raisins, cinnamon, and flavoring in a large bowl. Transfer to pan. Set aside.
- Stir cookie mix and oil with a fork in a medium bowl until well mixed. Sprinkle

evenly over the apple mixture. Bake for 17 minutes or until apples is tender. Let stand 30 minutes before serving.

Nutrition Facts

Carbohydrates: 32g| Protein: 4g| Fat: 5g| Saturated Fat: 1g| Sodium: 69mg| Fiber: 3g

236. GLAZED PLUM PASTRY

Ingredients

- Three tablespoons sucralose-sugar blend, divided
- Two tablespoons all-purpose flour
- One package (about 17 ounces) frozen puff pastry sheets, thawed
- Eight plums (about 2 pounds)
- 1/4 teaspoon ground cinnamon
- 1/3 cup sugar-free apricot preserves

Directions

- Preheat oven to 400°F. Combine two tablespoons of sucralose-sugar blend and flour in a small bowl. Line 18×12-inch baking sheet with parchment paper.
- Unfold pastry sheets on prepared baking sheets. Place pastry sheets side by side so fold lines are parallel to the length of the baking sheet. Arrange sheets, so they overlap 1/2 inch in the center. Press center seam firmly to seal. Trim ends so pastry fits on baking sheet. Prick the entire surface of the pie with a fork.
- Sprinkle flour mixture evenly over pastry to within 1/2 inch of edges. Bake 12 to 15 minutes or until pastry is slightly puffed and golden.
- Cut plums in half lengthwise; remove pits. Cut crosswise into 1/8-inch-thick slices. Arrange slices slightly overlapping in 5 rows down the length of pastry. Combine the remaining one tablespoon sucralose-sugar blend and cinnamon in a small bowl; sprinkle evenly over plums.
- Bake 15 minutes or until plums are tender and pastry is browned. Remove to wire rack.
- Microwave preserves in small microwavable bowl on HIGH 30 to 40 seconds or until melted. Brush preserves over plums. Cool 10 to 15 minutes before serving.

Nutrition Facts

Carbohydrates: 18g| Protein: 2g| Fat: 8g| Saturated Fat: 2g| Sodium: 53mg| Fiber: 1g

237. CHOCOLATE MOCHA PUDDING

Preparation Time: 20 Minutes
Chilling Time: 1 Hour

Ingredients

- 1 1/2 ounces unsweetened chocolate
- 2 1/2 cups skim milk
- 1/2 cup double-strength coffee (coffee made with twice as much instant granules or ground beans as usual)
- 1/4 cup cornstarch
- 3/4 cup sugar
- 1/8 teaspoon salt
- Fresh raspberries or strawberries for garnish (optional)

Directions

- Place the chocolate in a 2-quart, microwave-safe glass bowl and microwave at medium (50% power) for 2 to 3 minutes.
- Whisk the milk and coffee into the chocolate. In a separate bowl, combine the cornstarch, sugar, and salt; whisk this mixture into the milk mixture.
- Microwave the entire batter at High for 4 minutes.
- Whisk the mixture and continue cooking at High for 4 to 6 more minutes, whisking each minute until the pudding thickens.
- Pour the pudding into eight dessert cups and refrigerate for at least one hour before serving.
- Top with a few raspberries or strawberries for garnish.

Nutrition Facts

- Carbohydrates: 28g| Protein: 3g| Fat: 3g| Saturated Fat: 2g| Sodium: 77mg| Fiber: <1g

238. RAISIN-APRICOT LOAF CAKE MIX

Ingredients

- 2 cups all-purpose flour
- 1/2 teaspoon baking powder
- 1/4 teaspoon baking soda
- 1/4 teaspoon salt
- 1/2 cup sucralose-sugar blend
- 1/2 cup firmly packed light brown sugar
- 1/3 cup raisins
- 1/3 cup finely chopped dried apricots

Directions

- Level top of medicine in a pot. Sift together flour, baking powder, and baking soda in a mixing bowl. Add salt and toss to blend. I used a spoon and a funnel made of waxed paper, spoon flour mixture into a 1-quart wide-mouth jar, or another 1-quart decorative glass container.
- Place sugar blend and brown sugar into separate small, resealable plastic food storage bags. Seal bags. Mix raisins and apricots and place them into a small, resealable plastic food storage bag. Seal bag. Layer bags in a jar. Seal jar with its lid.
- Decorate jar lid with fabric tied with raffia, twine or ribbon, or other decorations. Attach a homemade recipe card to the jar describing how to use the mix.

Nutrition Facts

Fat: 16g| Saturated Fat: 5.1g| Polyunsaturated Fat: 7.4g| Monounsaturated Fat: 2.9g| Carbohydrates: 2.7g| Fiber: 0.3g| Sugar: 1.5g| Protein: 1.1gCalcium: 5.9mg| Iron: 2.5mg

239. ORANGE AND APRICOT CHIFFON CAKE

Ingredients

- Two medium-sized oranges
- 1/2 cup water
- 1/2 cup canola oil
- 1/2 teaspoon vanilla
- 1/2 teaspoon orange extract
- 2 1/4 cups cake flour

- One tablespoon baking powder
- 1/4 teaspoon salt
- 2/3 cup firmly packed light brown sugar
- 1/3 cup sucralose-sugar blend
- 1 cup finely chopped dried apricots
- Four extra-large egg yolks, at room temperature
- Eight extra-large egg whites, at room temperature
- 1/2 teaspoon cream of tartar
- 1/4 cup firmly packed light brown sugar

Directions

- Position rack in center of the oven and preheat to 325°F. Cut a round of parchment paper to fit the bottom of the pan and cut out a hole in the middle to fit the center tube of the pan.
- Finely grate the zest from oranges over a piece of waxed or parchment paper or a small bowl. Squeeze juice from oranges and place in a small saucepan. Simmer juice until it reduces to 2 tablespoons, taking care not to scorch or evaporate it.
- In a 2-cup liquid measure, combine water, canola oil, vanilla, orange extract, orange zest, and reduced orange juice.
- Sift together cake flour and baking powder in a large mixing bowl. Add salt, brown sugar, and sugar blend, and stir together. Make a well in the center of the mixture by pushing dry ingredients toward the sides of the bowl. Add the mixture of water, oil, and extracts, and egg yolks. I am using a rubber spatula or a whisk stir together until thoroughly combined.
- Place egg whites in a grease-free bowl of an electric stand mixer or sizeable grease-free mixing bowl. Using wire whip attachment or a hand-held mixer, whip egg whites on medium speed until they are foamy. Add cream of tartar and continue to beat. Slowly sprinkle in brown sugar and continue whipping until egg whites hold glossy and firm, but not stiff, peaks, about 5 minutes.

Fold egg whites into cake batter in 3 to 4 stages, blending thoroughly after each addition.

- Transfer mixture to tube pan. Use a rubber spatula to smooth and even the top. Bake for 1 hour until a cake tester inserted in the center of the cake comes out clean. Remove pan from oven and invert it over a cooling rack onto its feet or over a funnel or a thin necked bottle. Let cake hang to cool completely. Don't set the pan on a cooling rack on its base. This will cause the cake to collapse onto itself.
- Don't shake the cake out of the pan before it is fantastic. Once it is cool, use a thin-bladed knife or flexible blade spatula to run around the outer edge and inside the tube to help release cake from the pan. Invert cake onto a rack, then re-invert onto a serving plate. The cake will keep up to 4 days tightly wrapped in plastic wrap at room temperature.

Nutrition Facts

Carbohydrates: 41g| Protein: 5g| Fat: 9g| Saturated Fat: 1g| Cholesterol: 59mg| Sodium: 187mg| Fiber: 1g

240. ORANGE CUPCAKES WITH ORANGE-GINGER FROSTING

Ingredients

- 1 1/2 cups all-purpose flour
- 1/3 cup tapioca or potato starch
- 1/3 cup nonfat instant dry milk powder
- 1 1/2 teaspoons baking powder
- 1/4 teaspoon baking soda
- One teaspoon salt
- 1 cup sugar
- 3/4 cup sugar substitute
- Ten tablespoons unsalted butter
- Three large eggs
- 3/4 cup nonfat milk
- 1/4 cup nonfat half-and-half
- Two tablespoons fresh orange juice
- One teaspoon orange extract
- One teaspoon grated orange peel

- Orange-Ginger Frosting

Directions

- Preheat oven to 350°F. Place paper liners in 2 (12-cup) muffin tins.
- In a medium bowl, whisk together flour, tapioca, milk powder, baking powder, baking soda, and salt.
- Combine sugar, sugar substitute, and butter in a mixing bowl; beat on medium speed until creamy, about 1 to 2 minutes. Add eggs, one at a time, with motor running, scraping sides of the bowl to incorporate each egg.
- In a small bowl, blend milk and half-and-half; reserve. Alternatively, spoon flour mixture and milk mixture into sugar-butter-egg mixture; end with flour mixture; mix with a spatula just until smooth.
- In a small bowl, combine the last three ingredients; add to flour mixture; mix with a spatula until blended. Carefully spoon batter into paper liners, about 1/4 to 1/2 full. Bake 15 to 20 minutes, or until lightly browned, and centers spring back to the touch. Cool 5 minutes; remove cupcakes to wire racks to finish cooling before frosting.

Nutritional Value

Fat: 5.2g| Saturated fat: 1.4g| Carbohydrates: 18.6g| Sugar: 12.4g| Sodium: 221mg| Fiber: 2.6g| Protein: 12.8g| Cholesterol: 10mg

241. YOGURT LIME TARTLETS

Ingredients

- One refrigerated pie crust (half of the 15-ounce package)
- 1 cup plain nonfat Greek yogurt
- Two tablespoons honey
- One egg, lightly beaten
- Grated peel and juice of 1 lime
- Additional grated lime peel (optional)

Directions

- Preheat oven to 350°F. Unroll the pie dough onto a cutting board. Unroll pie crust on work surface. Cut out circles with a 3-inch round cookie cutter. Re-roll scraps of dough to cut out a total of

14 processes. Press dough into bottoms and up sides of prepared muffin cups.

- Stir yogurt, honey, egg, lime peel, and lime juice in a medium bowl until well blended. Spoon one tablespoon mixture into each muffin cup.

- Bake for 18 minutes or until set and crust is golden brown. Cool in pan on wire rack 5 minutes. Remove to wire rack; cool completely. Refrigerate at least 2 hours before serving. Garnish with additional lime peel.

Nutrition Facts

Carbohydrates: 12g| Protein: 2g| Fat: 5g| Saturated Fat: 2g| Cholesterol: 13mg| Sodium: 78mg| Fiber: 1g

242. BROWNED BUTTER SPRITZ COOKIES

Ingredients

- 1 1/2 cups (3 sticks) butter
- 1/2 cup granulated sugar
- 1/4 cup powdered sugar
- One egg yolk
- One teaspoon vanilla
- 1/8 teaspoon almond extract
- 2 1/2 cups all-purpose flour
- 1/4 cup cake flour
- 1/4 teaspoon salt
- Assorted decorating gels, decorating sugars, sprinkles, and decors.

Directions

- Melt butter in a medium heavy saucepan over medium heat until light amber, stirring frequently. Transfer butter to a large bowl. Cover and refrigerate for 2 hours or until solid.

- Preheat oven to 350°F. Let browned butter stand at room temperature for 15 minutes.

- Beat browned butter, granulated sugar, and powdered sugar in a large bowl with an electric mixer at medium speed until light and fluffy. Add egg yolk, vanilla, and almond extract; beat until well blended. Combine all-purpose flour, cake flour, and salt in a small bowl. Add flour mixture to butter mixture; beat until well blended.

- Fit cookie press with desired plate (or change plates for different shapes after the first batch). Fill the press with dough; press dough 1 inch apart on ungreased cookie sheets.

- Bake 10 minutes or until lightly browned. Cool on cookie sheets for 5 minutes. Remove to wire racks; cool completely. Decorate as desired.

Nutrition Facts

Carbohydrates: 4g| Protein: 1g| Fat: 3g| Saturated Fat: 2g| Cholesterol: 10mg| Sodium: 7mg| Fiber: 1g

243. DIABETIC SPICED BAKED APPLES RECIPE

Preparation Time: 15 Minutes
Baking Time: 45 Minutes

Ingredients

- Four large baking apples (approximately 9 ounces each)
- Two tablespoons sweetened dried cranberries
- Two tablespoons raisins
- 3/4 cup unsweetened apple juice
- 1/2 teaspoon allspice

Directions

- Preheat oven to 375°F.
- Remove the core of each apple, leaving 1/2 inch flesh at the bottom.
- Place cored apples in an 8" x 8" baking dish. Fill each apple with 1/2 tablespoon cranberries and 1/2 tablespoon raisins.
- Fill apple half full of apple juice and pour the remaining juice around them in the pan. Sprinkle apples evenly with allspice.
- Cover and bake for 45 minutes, or until tender when pierced with a fork.
- Spoon remaining baking juices over the apples and serve hot or chilled.

Nutrition Facts

Carbohydrates: 24g| Fiber: 4g

244. DIABETIC MACAROON

Ingredients

- 3/4 cup powdered erythritol, or the equivalent of stevia
- 2 1/2 cups unsweetened shredded coconut
- 1/2 cup unsweetened chocolate chips,
- Pinch of salt
- 1 1/2 teaspoons pure vanilla extract
- Two large egg whites

Directions

- Preheat oven to 350°F. Line a baking sheet with parchment paper. In a large bowl, combine all ingredients well by mixing with your hands.

- Wet your hands and then place 1 1/2 tablespoons of macaroon mixture on the baking sheet. Repeat this step with the remaining mixture, spacing macaroons about an inch apart.

- Bake macaroons until golden brown, 18 to 20 minutes. Allow cooling.

Nutrition Facts

Carbohydrates: 21g| Fat: 13g| Sodium: 33mg

245. AVOCADO ICE CREAM

Ingredients

- Three ripe avocados
- Three medium bananas, peeled, chopped, and frozen
- One teaspoon vanilla extract
- 1/4 cup favorite unsweetened milk (e.g., cow's, almond, cashew, etc.); can add one tablespoon at a time in addition as needed

Directions

- Cut avocados in half, remove pits, and scrape out the edible flesh into a food processor.

- Add frozen banana pieces and vanilla extract to a food processor.

- Process ingredients together until the mixture is smooth. Splash with milk as needed to soften the mix. You may need to stop processing and scrape the edges a time or two.

- Once smooth, lightly mix optional add-ins. (Read on for tasty flavor combinations!)
- Serve and enjoy, or freeze until use. Once frozen, the ice cream may need to be thawed before serving.

Nutrition Facts

Carbohydrates: 10g| Protein: 2g| Fat: 9g

246. FLOURLESS CHOCOLATE CAKE

Ingredients

- Three squares (1 ounce each) semisweet chocolate, chopped
- Three tablespoons margarine
- One tablespoon espresso powder or instant coffee granules
- Two tablespoons hot water
- Four eggs, separated
- Two egg whites
- 2/3 cup sugar, divided
- Three tablespoons unsweetened cocoa powder, sifted
- One teaspoon vanilla
- 1/2 teaspoon salt
- Thawed fat-free whipped topping (optional)
- Fresh raspberries (optional)
- Fresh mint leaves (optional)

Directions

- Preheat oven to 300°F. Grease 9-inch springform pan; line bottom of the pan with parchment paper.
- Melt chocolate and margarine in a small heavy saucepan over low heat, stirring frequently; cool. Dissolve espresso powder in hot water in a small bowl.
- Place six egg whites in a large bowl; set aside. Beat egg yolks in medium bowl with electric mixer at high speed for about 5 minutes, or until pale yellow. Add 1/3 cup sugar; beat about 4 minutes, or until mixture falls in ribbons from beaters. Slowly beat in melted chocolate mixture and espresso mixture at low speed just until blended. Beat in cocoa and vanilla just until blended.
- Add salt to egg whites; beat at high speed for 2 minutes or until soft peaks form. Beat in remaining 1/3 cup sugar until stiff peaks form. Stir a large spoonful of egg whites into the chocolate mixture. Fold chocolate mixture into egg whites until almost blended. Spoon batter into prepared pan.
- Bake for 1 hour or until the cake begins to pull away from the side of the pan. Cool on a wire rack for 10 minutes; run a thin spatula around the edge of the cake. Carefully remove the side of the pan. Cool completely. Invert cake; remove the bottom of pen and paper from the cake. Cover and refrigerate for at least 4 hours. Serve chilled with whipped topping, raspberries, and mint, if desired.

Nutrition Facts

Carbohydrates: 26g| Protein: 4g| Fat: 8g| Saturated Fat: 3g| Cholesterol: 85mg| Sodium: 240mg| Fiber: 1g

247. KETO CHERRY CHOCOLATE BROWNIES

Ingredients

- 6 tbsp butter
- 4 oz Lily's Dark Chocolate Baking Chips
- 1/2 cup almond flour
- 1/4 cup + 1 tbsp Dutch-process cocoa powder
- 1 cup allulose, or 3/4 cup erythritol
- 2 tbsp ground flaxseed meal
- 1/4 tsp xanthan gum
- Pinch salt
- Two large eggs, room temp
- 1 tsp vanilla extract
- 1 cup frozen dark sweet cherries - thawed, drained, and halved
- 2 oz Lily's Milk Chocolate Style Baking Chips, optional plus more on top

Directions

- Heat oven to 350°F and line an 8 x 8 baking pan with parchment. Crack the two eggs in a bowl to let them get closer to room temp and set your cherries out to thaw.
- Melt the butter in the microwave for 25 seconds in a glass bowl. Add the chocolate chips to the hot butter and stir until all of the chips are melted. Set aside.
- Whisk together the almond flour, cocoa powder, sweetener, ground flax, xanthan gum, and salt.
- Beat the eggs with a fork or a hand mixer until combined. Pour in the warm chocolate-butter mixture and stir. The batter will become very thick.
- Make sure your cherries are mostly drained of any excess liquid and slice each in half. Fold in the cherries and additional chocolate chips (if using) and spread into the prepared pan.
- Bake for 17–20 minutes and check for browning at the edges. The brownies are done when the center is still soft but doesn't jiggle.
- Remove from the oven and, if you are fancy, sprinkle a handful more of the chocolate chips on top and let them melt. Slice and enjoy!

Nutrition Facts

Carbohydrates: 5g| Protein: 1g| Fat: 1g| Saturated Fat: 1g| Sodium: 2mg| Fiber: 1g

AIR FRYER RECIPES

248. AIR-FRYER ROASTED VEGGIES

Prep Time: 20 mins
Cook Time: 10 mins
Total Time: 30 mins
Servings: 4

Ingredient

- ½ cup diced zucchini
- ½ cup diced summer squash
- ½ cup diced mushrooms
- ½ cup diced cauliflower
- ½ cup diced asparagus
- ½ cup diced sweet red pepper

- 2 teaspoons vegetable oil
- ¼ teaspoon salt
- ¼ teaspoon ground black pepper
- 1/4 teaspoon seasoning, or more to taste

Directions

- Preheat the air fryer to 360 degrees F (180 degrees C).
- Add vegetables, oil, salt, pepper, and desired seasoning to a bowl. Toss to coat; arrange in the fryer basket.
- Cook vegetables for ten minutes, stirring after five minutes.

Nutrition Facts

Protein: 1.4g| Carbohydrates: 3.4g| Fat: 2.4g| Sodium: 152.2mg.

249. MARINATED AIR FRYER VEGETABLES

Prep Time: 10 minutes
Cook Time: 15 minutes
Marinading time: 20 minutes
Total Time: 25 minutes
Servings: 4 servings

Ingredients

- Vegetables
- 2 green zucchini cut into ½ inch pieces
- 1 yellow squash cut into ½ inch pieces
- 4 oz button mushrooms cut in half
- 1 red onion cut into ½ inch pieces
- 1 red bell pepper cut into ½ inch pieces
- Marinade
- 4 Tbsp Olive Oil
- 2 Tbsp Balsamic Vinegar
- 1 Tbsp Honey
- 1 ½ tsp salt
- ½ tsp dried thyme
- ½ tsp dried oregano
- ¼ tsp garlic powder
- A few drops of liquid smoke optional
- Salt to taste

Directions

- Place marinade ingredients in a large bowl and whisk until combined. Place chopped vegetables in a bowl and stir until all vegetables are fully covered.
- Allow vegetables to marinate for 20-30 minutes.
- Place marinated vegetables in an air fryer basket and cook at 400 degrees Fahrenheit for 15-18 minutes, stirring every 5 minutes, until tender. Salt to taste.

Nutrition Facts

Calories: 200kcal | Carbohydrates: 16g | Protein: 3g | Fat: 15g | Saturated Fat: 2g | Sodium: 890mg | Potassium: 586mg | Fiber: 3g | Sugar: 12g | Vitamin A: 1225IU | Vitamin C: 67mg | Calcium: 34mg | Iron: 1mg

250. AIR FRYER VEGETABLES

Prep Time: 3 mins
Cook Time: 7 mins
Total Time: 10 mins

Ingredients

- 1/2 lb broccoli fresh
- 1/2 lb cauliflower fresh
- 1 TBSP olive oil
- 1/4 tsp seasoning can use pepper, salt, garlic salt - I prefer Flavor God Garlic Everything
- 1/3 c water

Directions

- In a medium bowl, mix vegetables, olive oil, and seasonings.
- Pour 1/3 c. water in the Air Fryer base to prevent smoking.
- Place vegetables in the air fryer basket.
- Cook at 400 degrees for 7-10 minutes.
- Shake vegetables to make sure they get evenly cooked about halfway through the 7-10 minutes.

Nutrition Facts

Calories: 65kcal | Carbohydrates: 7g | Protein: 3g | Fat: 4g | Saturated Fat: 1g | Sodium: 37mg | Potassium: 349mg | Fiber: 3g | Sugar: 2g | Vitamin A: 355IU | Vitamin C: 77.9mg | Calcium: 44mg | Iron: 0.8mg

251. AIRFRIED VEGETABLES

Prep time: 10 min
Cook time: 20 min
Total time: 30 min
Serves: 4

Ingredients

- 1 lb / 0.5kg of vegetables (broccoli, brussels sprouts, carrots, cauliflower, parsnips, potatoes, sweet potatoes, zucchini will all work), chopped evenly
- 1 Tbsp / 30 mL of cooking oil
- Some salt and pepper

Directions

Prep

- Preheat air fryer for about 5 minutes at 360F / 182C degrees.
- Evenly chop veggies and toss with oil and some salt and pepper. If making potato or sweet potato fries, soak them in water for ~30 minutes to draw out excess starch for crispier results, and then pat dry thoroughly with paper towels before tossing with oil.

Make

- Transfer veggies into frying compartment and fry for 15 to 20 minutes, stirring veggies every 5 to 8 minutes or so. Some veggies might need longer and some will need less – just use your judgment when you open the compartment to stir the veggies. You want the outside to be golden and crispy and the inside to be tender.
- Enjoy or toss with your favorite dipping sauce when done! If you need sauce ideas, check out 5 of our favorites.

Nutrition Facts

Calories: 172| Total Fat: 11g| Saturated Fat: 2g| Unsaturated Fat: 9g| Sodium: 577mg| Carbohydrates: 16g| Fiber: 6g| Sugar: 4g| Protein: 6g

252. AIR FRYER VEGETABLES

Prep Time: 10 minutes
Cook Time: 15 minutes
Total Time: 25 minutes
Servings: 4

Ingredients

- 380 g Broccoli
- 250 g Carrots
- 1 Large Bell pepper
- 1 Large Onion
- 1/2 teaspoon Black pepper
- 1 tablespoon Olive oil
- 1 teaspoon Seasoning vegetable, chicken, turkey seasoning, or any of choice.
- Salt to taste

Directions

- Wash and cut the vegetables into bite-size.
- Cut veggies on a white flat plate.
- Add them to a bowl and season with salt, black pepper, or any seasoning of choice, and olive oil. Mix so that the veggies are covered in the seasoning.
- Seasoning and olive oil added to the veggies.
- Add the seasoned veggies into the air fryer basket and air fry at a temperature of 175c for 15 minutes.
- Air fryer roasted vegetables in the air fryer basket.
- Toss the veggies in the basket halfway through cooking so that all sides are crisp.
- When done, take out the basket and serve.
- The finished dish displayed.

Nutrition Facts

Calories: 120kcal | Carbohydrates: 19g | Protein: 4g | Fat: 4g | Saturated Fat: 1g | Sodium: 78mg | Potassium: 657mg | Fiber: 6g | Sugar: 8g | Vitamin A: 12338IU | Vitamin C: 144mg | Calcium: 96mg | Iron: 2mg

253. ROASTED AIR FRYER VEGETABLES

Prep Time: 5 minutes
Cook Time: 12 minutes
Total Time: 17 minutes
Servings: 4

Ingredients

- 1 red bell pepper
- 1-2 yellow squash
- 1 zucchini
- 1/4 medium red onion
- 1 cup broccoli
- 1 tbsp olive oil
- 1/2 teaspoon salt
- 1/2 teaspoon garlic powder
- 1/8 teaspoon black pepper

Directions

- Cut up one red bell pepper, two small yellow zucchini squash, one zucchini, 1/2 a medium onion, and one cup of broccoli into similar sized chunks.
- Add the sliced vegetables into a large bowl and toss them with 1 tablespoon of olive oil, 1/2 teaspoon salt, 1/2 teaspoon garlic powder, and 1/8 teaspoon black pepper.
- Once the veggies a coated in the oil and seasoning, place them onto the bottom of your air fryer basket and roast for 10-12 minutes at 400 degrees Fahrenheit.

Nutrition Facts

Calories: 65kcal | Carbohydrates: 7g | Protein: 2g | Fat: 4g | Saturated Fat: 1g | Sodium: 305mg | Potassium: 391mg | Fiber: 2g | Sugar: 4g | Vitamin A: 1269IU | Vitamin C: 75mg | Calcium: 26mg | Iron: 1mg

254. AIR FRYER ROAST VEGETABLES

Prep Time: 5 Minutes
Cook Time: 10 Minutes
Total Time: 15 Minutes

Ingredients

- One large sweet potato
- One large potato
- One large carrot
- ¼ small pumpkin
- ½ tsp spice or herb mix, optional

Directions

- Wash the vegetables or peel if preferred, and cut into chunks no thicker than 1 inch (they can be as long as you like). Pat vegetables dry.
- Place vegetable pieces in an air fryer basket and spray with olive oil. Add spice if desired. Shake and spray with oil again.
- Cook in the air fryer at 360°F (180°C) for 5 minutes. Remove the basket and shake.
- Return to the air fryer and cook for a further 5-10 minutes until golden brown.

Nutrition Facts

Calories: 156| Unsaturated Fat: 0g| Sodium: 69mg| Carbohydrates: 35g| Fiber: 5g| Sugar: 6g| Protein: 4g

255. AIR FRYER VEGGIES

Prep Time: 5 mins
Cook Time: 20 mins
Total Time: 25 mins

Ingredients

- 3 cups mixed vegetables, cut into 1-inch pieces (cauliflower, broccoli, squash, carrots, beets, etc)
- 1 tablespoon olive oil
- 1/2 teaspoon kosher salt

Preparation

- Place the vegetables in a bowl and toss to coat with the oil and salt.
- Place the vegetables in the air fryer basket and cook at 375F degrees for 15-20 minutes or until golden and fork-tender.

Nutrition Facts

Total Fat: 11g| Sodium: 234mg| Carbohydrates: 16g| Fiber: 6g| Sugar: 4g| Protein: 6g

256. AIR FRYER "ROASTED" ASPARAGUS

Prep Time: 3 mins
Cook Time: 7 mins
Total Time: 10 mins
Servings: 4 servings

Ingredients

- 1 pound fresh asparagus, ends trimmed
- Oil spray or olive oil
- Salt, to taste
- Black pepper, to taste

Directions

- Coat the asparagus with oil spray or olive oil and season with salt and pepper. Lay the asparagus evenly in the air fryer basket.
- Make sure to coat the asparagus tips so they don't burn or dry out too fast. It is best to season before you put it in the air fryer basket.
- Too much excess salt in the air fryer baskets will often start to break down with coating.
- Air Fry at 380°F for 7-10 minutes, depending on thickness, shake, and turn asparagus halfway through cooking.
- Taste for seasoning & tenderness, then serve.

Nutrition Facts

Calories: 572kcal | Carbohydrates: 1g | Protein: 46g | Fat: 43g | Saturated Fat: 22g | Cholesterol: 168mg | Sodium: 219mg | Potassium: 606mg | Sugar: 1g | Calcium: 16mg | Iron: 4mg

257. AIR FRYER VEGETABLES

Prep Time: 10 minutes
Cook Time: 10 minutes
Servings: 6

Ingredients

- 2 zucchini cut into dials
- 2 yellow squash cut into dials
- 1 container mushrooms cut in half
- 1/2 c olive oil
- 1/2 onion sliced
- 3/4 tsp Italian seasoning
- 1/2 tsp garlic salt
- 1/4 tsp Lawry's seasoned salt

Directions

- Slice zucchini and yellow squash into dials. The thinner they are the softer they will get. I would recommend 3/4" thick so they all are the same consistency when done.
- Slice mushrooms in half. Put all vegetables in a bowl and toss together gently. (if you want to add 1/2-1 full precooked sausage link diced into bite-size pcs., add that now too)
- Pour olive oil on top and toss gently, then sprinkle in all seasonings in a bowl and gently toss one more time.
- Add half of your vegetables into your air fryer, close, and set to 400 degrees for 10 minutes. I did not bother shaking or tossing halfway through and they came out amazing.
- Remove, enjoy, and add another half at 400 degrees for 10 minutes to finish the cooking batch.

Nutrition Facts

Fat: 18g| Saturated Fat: 3g| Sodium: 201mg| Potassium: 355mg| Carbohydrates: 5g| Fiber: 2g| Sugar: 3g| Protein: 2g| Vitamin: A 261IU| Vitamin C: 23mg| Calcium: 26mg| Iron: 1mg

258. AIR FRYER CHIMICHANGAS

Prep Time: 15 mins
Cook Time: 20 mins
Total Time: 35 mins
Servings: 6

Ingredient

- 1 tablespoon vegetable oil
- ½ cup diced onion
- 2 cups shredded cooked chicken
- ½ (8 ounces) package Neufchatel cheese, softened
- 1 (4 ounces) can hot fire-roasted diced green chiles (such as Ortega)
- ¼ cup chicken broth
- 1 ½ tablespoons chicken taco seasoning mix (such as McCormick)
- ½ teaspoon salt
- ¼ teaspoon ground black pepper
- 6 (10 inches) flour tortillas
- 1 cup shredded Mexican cheese blend, or to taste
- Avocado oil cooking spray

Directions

- Heat oil in a medium skillet. Add onion and cook until soft and translucent, 4 to 6 minutes. Add chicken, Neufchatel cheese, diced chiles, chicken broth, taco seasoning, salt, and pepper. Cook and stir until mixture is well combined and Neufchatel has softened been incorporated.
- Heat tortillas in a large skillet or directly on the grates of a gas stove until soft and pliable. Place 1/3 cup chicken mixture down the center of each tortilla and top with a heaping tablespoon of Mexican cheese. Fold top and bottom of tortillas over the filling, then roll each into a burrito shape. Mist with cooking spray and place in the basket of an air fryer.
- Air fry at 400 degrees F (200 degrees C) for 4 to 6 minutes. Flip each chimichanga over, mist with cooking spray, and air fry until lightly browned, 2 to 4 minutes more.

Nutrition Facts

Calories: 455| Protein: 24.8g| Carbohydrates: 41g| Fat: 20.6g| Cholesterol: 69.8mg| Sodium: 1291.5mg.

259. AIR-FRIED SHRIMP

Prep Time: 5 mins
Cook Time: 10 mins
Total Time: 15 mins
Servings: 4

Ingredient

- 1 tablespoon butter, melted
- 1 teaspoon lemon juice
- ½ teaspoon garlic granules
- ⅛ teaspoon salt
- 1 pound large shrimp - peeled, deveined, and tails removed
- Perforated parchment paper
- ⅛ cup freshly grated parmesan cheese

Directions

- Place melted butter in a medium bowl. Mix in lemon juice, garlic granules, and salt. Add shrimp and toss to coat.

- Line air fryer basket with perforated parchment paper. Place shrimp in the air fryer basket and sprinkle with Parmesan cheese.
- Cook shrimp in the air fryer at 400 degrees F (200 degrees C) until shrimp are bright pink on the outside and the meat is opaque for about 8 minutes.

Nutrition Facts

Calories: 125| Protein: 19.6g| Carbohydrates: 0.5g| Fat: 4.6g Cholesterol: 182.4mg| Sodium: 329.7mg.

260. AIR FRYER POTSTICKERS

Prep Time: 10 mins
Cook Time: 25 mins
Total Time: 35 mins
Servings: 24

Ingredient

- ½ pound ground pork
- 1 (4 ounces) can water chestnuts, drained and chopped
- 1 (4 ounces) can shiitake mushrooms, drained and chopped
- 2 tablespoons soy sauce
- 2 tablespoons sesame oil
- 1 tablespoon Sriracha sauce
- 1 (12 ounces) package round dumpling wrappers

Directions

- Preheat an air fryer to 400 degrees F (200 degrees C).
- Combine ground pork, water chestnuts, shiitake mushrooms, sesame oil, soy sauce, and Sriracha in a large skillet over medium-high heat.
- Cook until pork is no longer pink, about 6 minutes.
- Remove from heat and let sit until cool enough to handle.
- Layout 8 dumpling wrappers on a clean work surface.
- Place a heaping teaspoonful of pork mixture in the middle of each wrapper.
- Pull both sides up like a taco and pinch the tops until sealed.
- Cook in batches in the preheated air fryer for 3 minutes. Use tongs to flip the potstickers and cook 3 minutes more. Transfer to a paper-towel-lined plate.
- Repeat with remaining dumpling wrappers and filling.

Nutrition Facts

Calories: 70| Protein: 2.7g| Carbohydrates: 8.7g| Fat: 2.6g| Cholesterol: 4.7mg| Sodium: 273.1mg.

261. LUMPIA IN THE AIR FRYER

Prep Time: 15 mins
Cook Time: 20 mins
Total: 35 mins
Servings: 16

Ingredient

- 1 pound Italian hot sausage links
- ½ cup finely sliced green onions
- ¼ cup diced onions
- ½ cup finely chopped carrots
- ½ cup finely chopped water chestnuts
- 2 cloves garlic, minced
- 2 tablespoons soy sauce
- ½ teaspoon salt
- ¼ teaspoon ground ginger
- 16 spring roll wrappers
- Avocado oil cooking spray

Directions

- Remove casing from sausage and cook in a skillet over medium heat until slightly browned 4 to 5 minutes. Add green onions, onions, carrots, and water chestnuts.
- Cook and stir until onions are soft and translucent, 5 to 7 minutes.
- Add garlic and cook for 1 to 2 minutes.
- Season with soy sauce, salt, and ginger.
- Stir until filling is well combined and remove from heat.
- Lay a spring roll wrapper at an angle. Place a scant 1/4 cup filling in the center of the wrapper. Fold bottom corner over filling and tuck in the sides to form a roll.
- Use your finger to lightly moisten edges with water. Repeat with remaining wrappers and filling. Mist each roll with avocado oil spray.
- Preheat an air fryer to 390 degrees F (198 degrees C).
- Place lumpia rolls in the basket, making sure they are not touching; cook in batches if necessary. Fry for 4 minutes; flip and cook until skins are crispy, about 4 minutes more.

Nutrition Facts

Calories: 98| Protein: 4.8g| Carbohydrates: 7.2g| Fat: 5.5g| Cholesterol: 11.9mg| Sodium: 471.1mg.

262. CAJUN AIR FRYER SALMON

Prep Time: 10 mins
Cook Time: 10 mins
Total Time: 20 mins
Servings: 2

Ingredient

- 2 (6 ounces) skin-on salmon fillets
- Cooking spray
- 1 tablespoon cajun seasoning
- 1 teaspoon brown sugar

Directions

- Preheat the air fryer to 390 degrees F (200 degrees C).
- Rinse and dry salmon fillets with a paper towel. Mist fillets with cooking spray. Combine Cajun seasoning and brown sugar in a small bowl. Sprinkle onto a plate. Press the flesh sides of fillets into the seasoning mixture.
- Spray the basket of the air fryer with cooking spray and place salmon fillets skin-side down. Mist salmon again lightly with cooking spray.
- Cook for 8 minutes. Remove from air fryer and let rest for 2 minutes before serving.

Nutrition Facts

Calories: 327| Protein: 33.7g| Carbohydrates: 4g| Fat: 18.5g|

Cholesterol: 99.1mg| Sodium: 810.8mg.

263. AIR FRYER LEMON PEPPER SHRIMP

Prep Time: 5 mins
Cook Time: 10 mins
Total Time: 15 mins
Servings: 2

Ingredient

- 1 tablespoon olive oil
- 1 lemon, juiced
- 1 teaspoon lemon pepper
- ¼ teaspoon paprika
- ¼ teaspoon garlic powder
- 12 ounces uncooked medium shrimp, peeled and deveined
- 1 lemon, sliced

Directions

- Preheat an air fryer to 400 degrees F (200 degrees C).
- Combine olive oil, lemon juice, lemon pepper, paprika, and garlic powder in a bowl. Add shrimp and toss until coated.
- Place shrimp in the air fryer and cook until pink and firm, 6 to 8 minutes. Serve with lemon slices.

Nutrition Facts

Calories: 215| Protein: 28.9g| Carbohydrates: 12.6g| Fat: 8.6g| Cholesterol: 255.4mg| Sodium: 528mg.

264. AIR FRYER MEATLOAF

Prep Time: 10 mins
Cook Time: 25 mins
Additional Time: 10 mins
Total: 45 mins
Servings: 4

Ingredient

- 1 pound lean ground beef
- 1 egg, lightly beaten
- 3 tablespoons dry bread crumbs
- 1 small onion, finely chopped
- 1 tablespoon chopped fresh thyme
- 1 teaspoon salt
- Ground black pepper to taste
- 2 mushrooms, thickly sliced
- 1 tablespoon olive oil, or as needed

Directions

- Preheat an air fryer to 392 degrees F (200 degrees C).
- Combine ground beef, egg, bread crumbs, onion, thyme, salt, and pepper in a bowl. Knead and mix thoroughly.
- Transfer beef mixture to a baking pan and smooth the top. Press mushrooms into the top and coat with olive oil. Place the pan into the air fryer basket and slide it into the air fryer.
- Set air fryer timer for 25 minutes and roast meatloaf until nicely browned.
- Let meatloaf rest at least 10 minutes before slicing into wedges and serving.

Nutrition Facts

Protein: 24.8g| Carbohydrates: 5.9g| Fat: 18.8g| Cholesterol: 125.5mg| Sodium: 706.5mg.

265. AIR FRYER BAKED POTATOES

Prep Time: 5 mins
Cook Time: 1 hr
Total Time: 1 hr 5 mins
Servings: 2

Ingredient

- 2 large russet potatoes, scrubbed
- 1 tablespoon peanut oil
- ½ teaspoon coarse sea salt

Directions

- Preheat air fryer to 400 degrees F (200 degrees C).
- Brush potatoes with peanut oil and sprinkle with salt. Place them in the air fryer basket and place the basket in the air fryer.
- Cook potatoes until done, about 1 hour. Test for doneness by piercing them with a fork.

Nutrition Facts

Protein: 7.5g| Carbohydrates: 64.5g| Fat: 7.1g| Sodium: 462.1mg.

266. AIR FRYER RIB-EYE STEAK

Prep Time: 5 mins
Cook Time: 15 mins
Additional Time: 2 hrs 5 mins
Total Time: 2 hrs 25 mins

Ingredient

- 2 rib-eye steaks, cut 1 1/2- inch thick
- 4 teaspoons grill seasoning
- ¼ cup olive oil
- ½ cup reduced-sodium soy sauce

Directions

- Combine steaks, soy sauce, olive oil, and seasoning in a large resealable bag. Marinate meat for at least 2 hours.
- Remove steaks from bag and discard the marinade. Pat excess oil off the steaks.
- Add about 1 tablespoon water to the bottom of the air fryer pan to prevent it from smoking during the cooking process.
- Preheat the air fryer to 400 degrees F (200 degrees C).
- Add steaks to air fryer and cook for 7 minutes. Turn steaks and cook for another 7 minutes until steak is medium-rare. For a medium steak, increase the total cook time to 16 minutes, flipping steak after 8 minutes.
- Remove steaks, keep warm, and let sit for about 4 minutes before serving.

Nutrition Facts

Protein: 44g| Carbohydrates: 7.5g| Fat: 49.1g| Cholesterol: 164.8mg| Sodium: 4043.7mg.

267. AIR FRYER COCONUT SHRIMP

Prep Time: 30 mins
Cook Time: 15 mins
Total Time: 45 mins

Ingredient

- ½ cup all-purpose flour
- 1 ½ teaspoon ground black pepper
- 2 large eggs
- ⅔ cup unsweetened flaked coconut
- ⅓ cup panko bread crumbs
- 12 ounces uncooked medium shrimp, peeled and deveined
- cooking spray
- ½ teaspoon kosher salt, divided
- ¼ cup honey
- ¼ cup lime juice
- 1 serrano chile, thinly sliced
- 2 teaspoons chopped fresh cilantro

Directions

- Stir together flour and pepper in a shallow dish. Lightly beat eggs in a second shallow dish.
- Stir together coconut and panko in a third shallow dish. Hold each shrimp by the tail, dredge in flour mixture, and shake off excess.
- Then dip floured shrimp in egg, and allow any excess to drip off.
- Finally, dredge in coconut mixture, pressing to adhere. Place on a plate.
- Coat shrimp well with cooking spray.
- Preheat air fryer to 400 degrees F (200 degrees C). Place 1/2 the shrimp in the air fryer and cook for about 3 minutes.
- Turn shrimp over and continue cooking until golden, about 3 minutes more.
- Season with 1/4 teaspoon salt. Repeat with remaining shrimp.
- Meanwhile, whisk together honey, lime juice, and serrano chile in a small bowl for the dip.
- Sprinkle fried shrimp with cilantro and serve with dip.

Nutrition Facts

Protein: 13.8g| Carbohydrates: 27.6g| Fat: 9.1g| Cholesterol: 147.1mg| Sodium: 316.4mg.

SIDE DISH RECIPES

268. BAKED PLANTAIN FOR DIABETICS

Preparation Time: 5 Minutes
Baking Time: 45 Minutes

Ingredients

- Two large, ripe plantains (skin blackened)

Directions

- Preheat oven to 350°F. Wash and dry plantains. Trim off both ends of each plantain.
- Make a slit in the peel of the plantain lengthwise. Place on a baking sheet and bake for approximately 45 minutes (turning over halfway through the baking) until plantain flesh is tender.
- Slice each plantain into three equal-sized pieces and serve in the skin.

Nutrition Facts

- Carbohydrates: 19g, Protein: 1g, Sodium: 2mg, Fiber: 1g

269. MICROWAVE LIMA BEAN CASSEROLE

Preparation Time: 45 Minutes (Includes Cooking Time)

Ingredients

- 2 cups fresh or frozen lima beans
- Four slices of uncooked turkey bacon (optional)
- Vegetable cooking spray
- 1/2 cup dry bread crumbs
- Two tablespoons margarine, melted
- 2 cups chopped fresh tomatoes
- 1/4 teaspoon ground black pepper
- 1/4 teaspoon celery salt
- 1/4 cup chopped onion

Directions

- Place lima beans in a microwave-safe dish with a small amount of water; microwave on high for 6 to 9 minutes, then let stand, covered, for 2 minutes.
- Drain. Spread 3 or 4 paper towels on a plate, arrange bacon on the towels, and microwave on High for 3 minutes.
- Test for crispness, and continue microwaving, if necessary, checking for doneness every 30 seconds. Spray a 6-cup casserole with cooking spray. Mix bread crumbs with margarine in a large bowl.
- Add lima beans, tomatoes, pepper, salt, and onions. Pour mixture into casserole.
- Microwave on High for 10 to 12 minutes, until the dish is bubbly. Crumble bacon on top.

Nutrition Facts

Carbohydrates: 21g, Protein: 7g, Fat: 6g, Saturated Fat: 1g, Sodium: 360mg, Fiber: 5g

270. POLISH CHILLED FISH IN HORSERADISH SAUCE

Preparation Time: 50 Minutes

Ingredients

- Two carrots
- Two stalks celery
- One sprig parsley
- One onion, quartered
- Five peppercorns
- One bay leaf
- 6 cups water
- Eight four-ounce fish fillets (carp, sole, pike, or similar fish)
- Two tablespoons margarine
- Three tablespoons flour
- Two tablespoons prepared horseradish sauce
- One teaspoon sugar
- Dash salt
- 1/2 cup light sour cream
- Two eggs, hard-boiled, peeled and diced
- 1 cup shredded lettuce

Directions

- Place carrots, celery, parsley, onion, peppercorns, bay leaf, and water in a large pot.
- Bring to a boil and simmer for 20 minutes. Strain broth and add fish fillets to hot vegetable broth, cooking for 6–10 minutes until the fish flakes easily.
- Remove fish from broth and arrange fillets on a serving platter: cover and chill.
- Strain and chill 3/4 cup of the remaining fish broth, reserving it for the sauce. In a saucepan, melt the margarine. Blend in flour until it forms a smooth paste.
- Add the cooled fish broth gradually, stirring constantly.
- Cook and stir until the sauce boils.
- Remove from heat and stir in horseradish sauce, sugar, a dash of salt, sour cream, and chopped hard-boiled eggs. Cool for 15 minutes.
- Pour the horseradish sauce over the chilled fish, garnish with shredded lettuce, and serve immediately.

Nutrition Facts

Carbohydrates: 5g, Protein: 24g, Fat: 6g, Saturated Fat: 2g, Sodium: 135mg,

271. COLORFUL VEGETABLE CASSEROLE

Preparation Time: 15 Minutes
Baking Time: 1 Hour

Ingredients

- Vegetable cooking spray

- One package (16 ounces) of frozen Italian-mix vegetables
- One large green pepper, cut into strips
- 1 pound baby carrots, halved
- One medium zucchini, unpeeled, cut into 1/2-inch slices
- Four medium tomatoes, quartered
- 1 cup celery, sliced
- Two tablespoons butter or margarine
- 1 1/2 cups chopped onion
- Two large cloves of garlic, minced
- Two teaspoons instant reduced-sodium chicken broth granules
- Two tablespoons cooking wine
- 1/2 teaspoon salt
- 1/2 teaspoon pepper

Directions

- Preheat oven to 325°F. Spray a 3-quart casserole or Dutch oven with cooking spray.
- Spread frozen vegetables in an even layer in the soup. Follow with layers of green pepper strips, baby carrots, zucchini slices, tomato pieces, and celery.
- Melt margarine in skillet. Add onion and garlic, sautéing until tender. Stir in broth granules, wine, salt, and pepper.
- Pour skillet mixture over vegetables. Cover casserole and bake for approximately 1 hour until vegetables are crisp-tender.

Nutrition Facts

Carbohydrates: 15g, Protein: 3g, Fat: 3g, Saturated Fat: <1g, Sodium: 227mg, Fiber: 4g

272. SPINACH ALMOND CASSEROLE

Preparation Time: 30 Minutes
Cooking Time: 30–35 Minutes.

Ingredients

- Two tablespoons sesame seeds
- 1/4 cup slivered almonds
- Two packages (10 ounces each) frozen chopped spinach
- 1/8 teaspoon black pepper
- One can (10 3/4 ounces) reduced-fat, low-sodium cream of mushroom soup concentrate
- 1/2 cup low-fat sour cream
- One can (8 ounces) sliced water chestnuts, drained
- Vegetable cooking spray

Directions

- Toast sesame seeds and almonds in a skillet just until slightly browned. Set aside.
- Cook spinach on the stove or in the microwave according to package directions, omitting salt.
- Drain spinach thoroughly by placing it in a colander and pressing it with a large spoon.
- In a large bowl, toss spinach with sesame seeds, almonds, pepper, soup, sour cream, and water chestnuts.
- Spray one 1/2-quart casserole with cooking spray and spoon in spinach mixture.
- Bake in a preheated 350°F oven for 30 to 35 minutes.

Nutrition Facts

- Carbohydrates: 11g, Protein: 4g, Fat: 5g, Saturated Fat: 1g, Sodium: 207mg, Fiber: 3g

273. GREEK CHRISTMAS BREAD

Preparation Time: 45 Minutes
Rising Time: 1 1/2 Hours Total
Baking Time: 35–40 Minutes

Ingredients

- 1 1/2 tablespoons yeast
- 1/2 teaspoon sugar plus 1/3 cup sugar
- One tablespoon flour plus 3 1/2 cups flour (may require up to 1/2 cup additional flour to make a stiff dough)
- Dash salt
- 1/4 cup warm water
- Three eggs
- 3/4 cup nonfat milk, scalded and cooled
- 1/2 teaspoon vanilla flavoring
- 1/3 cup margarine, melted and cooled
- 1/2 cup slivered almonds
- 1/4 cup yellow raisins
- 1/2 teaspoon grated lemon peel

Directions

- Combine yeast, 1/2 teaspoon sugar, one tablespoon flour, dash salt, and warm water in a bowl. Let stand in a warm place for 10 minutes until the mixture is bubbly and foamy. Add two eggs, 1/3 cup sugar, cooled milk, and vanilla, and stir well. Add melted margarine, almonds, raisins, and lemon peel.
- Add 3 1/2 cups flour a little bit at a time, stirring until a stiff, elastic dough forms. (Add up to 1/2 cup more flour as needed.)
- Turn dough out onto the floured surface and knead for five minutes.
- Place in an oiled bowl and cover with plastic wrap, then a damp towel. Let dough rise in a warm place for about 30 minutes, then punch down and turn over.
- Let rise again for 30 minutes until it is almost doubled in size.
- Shape into a round or oblong shape, place on a lightly oiled baking sheet, and let rise again for 30 minutes.
- Beat the remaining egg and brush about half of the egg mixture on the top of the entire surface of the dough.
- Discard leftover beaten egg and bake the bread at 350°F for approximately 35–40 minutes, until golden brown and done.

Nutrition Facts

Carbohydrates: 22g, Protein: 4g, Fat: 4g, Saturated Fat: 1g, Sodium: 53mg, Fiber: 1g

274. FRIED BROWN RICE FOR DIABETICS

Preparation Time: 5 Minutes
Cooking Time: Approximately 10 Minutes.
Standing Time: 7 Minutes

Ingredients

- Cooking spray
- Two teaspoons reduced-calorie margarine
- 1/4 cup liquid egg substitute
- One chopped green onion
- 1 1/2 cups instant brown rice
- 1 1/2 cups 50% less sodium, fat-free chicken broth
- 1/2 cup frozen peas and carrots, unthawed (alternatively, who can use unthawed frozen mixed vegetables)

Directions

- Coat a large, nonstick skillet with cooking spray; add margarine, and melt over medium heat.
- Add egg substitute and stir-fry until egg is set (like scrambled egg). Stir in onion, rice, broth, and peas, and carrots; stir to mix.
- Bring mixture to a boil over high heat, cover, reduce heat to medium-low, and simmer for 5 minutes.
- Remove from the heat, stir, and body.
- Let stand 7 minutes, fluff with a fork, and serve.

Nutrition Facts

- Carbohydrates: 16g, Protein: 4g, Fat: 2g, Saturated Fat: <1g, Sodium: 163mg, Fiber: 1g

275. RICH-TASTING RED CLAM SAUCE

Preparation Time: 10 Minutes
Cooking Time: 1 Hour And 5 Minutes.

Ingredients

- Two tablespoons olive oil
- 1/2 cup finely chopped onion
- Two large celery stalks, finely chopped
- Four cloves garlic, minced
- Two cans (14 1/2 ounces each) no-salt-added diced tomatoes
- One can (6 ounces) no-salt-added tomato paste
- Two cans (10 ounces each) whole clams, drained, with liquid reserved
- 1/8–1/4 teaspoon red pepper flakes
- Two teaspoons crushed dried oregano
- 1/4 teaspoon dried basil

Directions

- Heat olive oil in a large saucepan over medium-high heat.
- Add onion, celery, and garlic and cook, constantly stirring, until tender.
- Stir in tomatoes, tomato paste, liquid from clams, red pepper flakes to taste, oregano, and basil.
- Cover and simmer over low-medium heat for 50 minutes, or until tomatoes turn a deeper red and the sauce thickens; stir periodically to prevent sticking.
- Stir in clams and simmer 10 minutes more.
- Serve over rice or pasta. The sauce reheats well.

Nutrition Facts

Carbohydrates: 15g, Protein: 13g, Fat: 6g, Saturated Fat: 1g, Cholesterol: 440mg, Sodium: 3g, Fiber: 3g

276. BASMATI RICE PILAF

Preparation Time: About 1 Hour

Ingredients

- Two teaspoons olive oil
- Two cloves garlic, peeled and minced
- One large onion, peeled and finely chopped (1 cup)
- One teaspoon curry powder
- 4 cups water
- 2 cups basmati brown rice
- 1 cup frozen green peas, thawed
- 1 cup diced red pepper

Directions

- Heat oil in a large saucepan or Dutch oven. Add the garlic and onion, sautéing until tender.
- Stir in the curry powder, stirring to combine with the vegetables. Add water and bring ingredients to a boil.
- Stir in the rice, reduce heat to low, cover the pan, and simmer rice for 40 to 45 minutes until the water is almost completely absorbed.
- Add the peas and red pepper, and continue cooking the rice 5 minutes longer.

Nutrition Facts

Carbohydrates: 45g, Protein: 5g, Fat: 2g, Saturated Fat: <1g, Sodium: 17g, Fiber: 2g

277. MAKE-AHEAD MASHED POTATOES

Preparation Time: 30 Minutes
Baking Time: 45 Minutes

Ingredients

- 3 pounds potatoes, peeled and quartered
- 1/2 cup fat-free sour cream
- 4 ounces fat-free cream cheese
- One tablespoon butter-flavor spray
- 1/2 teaspoon salt (optional)
- 1/8 teaspoon pepper
- Skim milk

Directions

- Boil potatoes in water for about 20 minutes or until done.
- Drain water off and whip with a mixer until smooth. Add sour cream, cream cheese, butter-flavor spray, salt, and pepper, mixing well after each addition. If the potatoes are too thick, add 1/4 to 1/2 cup skim milk for desired consistency.
- Spray a 2-quart casserole pan with butter-flavor cooking spray and spread potatoes evenly in the pan. Cover and refrigerate. Who can make this recipe two to three days in advance? When ready to use, bake at 350°F for 45 minutes or until hot.

Nutrition Facts

- Carbohydrates: 24g, Protein: 5g, Sodium: 85mg

278. SAVORY BREAD DRESSING

Preparation Time: 20 Minutes
Baking Time: 30 Minutes

Ingredients

- Two tablespoons margarine
- 1/4 cup chopped onions
- 1/2 cup finely diced celery
- 8 cups herb-seasoned croutons for stuffing
- 1/4 teaspoon salt (optional)
- 1/4 teaspoon ground pepper
- 2 cups turkey or chicken broth
- One egg
- Cooking spray

Directions

- Melt margarine in a large skillet.
- Add onion and celery; cook until tender. Add croutons, salt, and pepper.
- Moisten with broth. Beat egg with a fork and stir into dressing mixture.
- Spray a 2-quart casserole with cooking spray and put the dressing in it.
- Bake, covered, at 350°F for 30 minutes.

Nutrition Facts

- Carbohydrates: 14g, Protein: 3g, Fat: 2g, Saturated Fat: 1g, Sodium: 276mg, Fiber: <1g

279. TURKEY GRAVY FOR DIABETICS

Preparation Time: 20 Minutes

Ingredients

- Five tablespoons cornstarch
- Five tablespoons water
- 3 cups turkey or chicken broth, defatted
- Salt and pepper as desired

Directions

- Mix cornstarch and water in a bowl until blended.
- Place turkey broth in a 1-quart saucepan and bring to a boil over medium heat.
- Slowly add the cornstarch mixture to the turkey broth, stirring until the gravy is thickened.
- Season to taste with salt and pepper.

Nutrition Facts

- Carbohydrates: 2g, Sodium: 223mg

280. DIABETIC STUFFED PEPPERS RECIPE

Preparation Time: 25 Minutes

Baking Time: 20 Minutes

Ingredients

- Four medium-size green peppers
- 1/2 pound extra-lean ground beef
- 1/2 cup chopped onion
- 1 cup drained, canned whole tomatoes
- 1 cup cooked wild rice
- One tablespoon Worcestershire sauce
- 1/2 teaspoon Italian seasoning
- 1/2 cup soft bread crumbs
- Vegetable cooking spray
- 1 cup canned tomato sauce

Directions

- Slice off the stem end of peppers and remove and discard seeds and membranes.
- Submerge the peppers in a pan of boiling water and cook for 5 to 10 minutes; drain. Brown ground beef and onion in a nonstick skillet over medium heat.
- Drain and pat dry with paper towels. Return meat mixture to skillet.
- Add tomatoes, breaking them into pieces with a cooking spoon, and cook until liquid evaporates.
- Remove meat mixture from heat; stir in wild rice, Worcestershire sauce, and Italian seasoning.
- Spoon 1/2-cup portions of rice mixture into peppers; sprinkle evenly with bread crumbs. Place peppers in a baking dish coated with cooking spray.
- Bake at 350°F for 20 minutes or until lightly browned. Spoon tomato sauce over peppers and return to oven until heated.

Nutrition Facts

- Carbohydrates: 34g, Protein: 19g, Fat: 4g, Saturated Fat: <1g, Sodium: 653mg, Fiber: 5g

281. ORZO STUFFED PEPPERS

Preparation Time: 25 Minutes

Baking Time: 45 Minutes

Ingredients

- 8 ounces orzo or another small pasta shape
- Two teaspoons oil
- Two cloves garlic, minced
- One medium onion, chopped
- 1/2 teaspoon thyme
- One tablespoon chopped fresh parsley
- 1/2 cup grated Parmesan cheese
- 1 1/2 plus 1/2 cups low-sodium chicken broth
- 3 ounces reduced-fat provolone cheese, grated and divided into halves
- Six red bell peppers
- Three teaspoons dry bread crumbs

Directions

- Preheat oven to 350°F. Prepare pasta according to package directions; drain and set aside. Heat oil in a medium saucepan; add garlic, onion, and celery.
- Cover and cook until vegetables are soft.
- Remove from heat. Stir in pasta, thyme, parsley, Parmesan cheese, 1/2 cup of the chicken broth, and half of the provolone cheese.
- Cut tops off the peppers and remove seeds.
- Cut a small piece off the bottoms so peppers will stand upright. Spoon the pasta mixture into each pepper and set it in a baking dish.
- Sprinkle each pepper with 1/2 teaspoon bread crumbs. Sprinkle the remaining half of the provolone on top of the peppers.
- Pour the remaining 1 1/2 cups of broth around peppers. Bake 45 minutes until lightly browned on top and tender.
- Serve immediately.

Nutrition Facts

- Carbohydrates: 38g, Protein: 14g, Fat: 7g, Saturated Fat: 3g, Sodium: 383mg, Fiber: 3g

282. LEMON-PEPPER-GLAZED VEGGIE TOSS

Preparation Time: 20 Minutes

Cooking Time: Approximately 10 Minutes.

Ingredients

- 1/2 packet saccharin sweetener
- Two teaspoons cornstarch
- 1/4 teaspoon lemon pepper seasoning
- Two tablespoons fresh-squeezed lemon juice
- One tablespoon water
- Cooking spray
- One teaspoon corn oil
- 1 cup julienned carrots
- 3 cups cauliflower florets
- 1/4 cup water
- 1 cup asparagus sliced into 2-inch pieces

Directions

- In a small bowl, whisk together sweetener, cornstarch, lemon pepper seasoning, lemon juice, and water. Set aside.
- Coat an excellent, nonstick wok with cooking spray. Preheat wok, then add oil. When the oil is hot, add carrots and cook for 2 minutes, stirring constantly. Add cauliflower and water and continue cooking 2 minutes more, stirring constantly. Add asparagus and cook for an additional 2 minutes, stirring constantly. Stir in lemon mixture and

cook 20–30 seconds, or until the glaze thickens. Serve immediately.

Nutrition Facts

Carbohydrates: 4g, Protein: 2g, Fat: 1g, Saturated Fat: <1g, Sodium: 56mg, Fiber: 2g

283. BLACK BEAN AND VEGETABLE ENCHILADAS

Preparation Time: 15 Minutes
Baking Time: 20 Minutes

Ingredients

- Vegetable cooking spray
- One can plus one can (16 ounces each) black beans, rinsed and drained
- 1 cup chopped onion
- One green pepper, chopped
- Two tablespoons vegetable broth
- 1 cup plus 1 cup Picante sauce
- 12 medium corn tortillas
- 1 cup chopped tomatoes
- 1/2 cup reduced-fat shredded Cheddar cheese
- 1/2 cup reduced-fat shredded mozzarella cheese
- 3 cups shredded lettuce
- Light sour cream for garnish (optional)

Directions

- Preheat oven to 350°F and coat a 9"x13" baking pan with vegetable cooking spray.
- Mash one can of the beans with a spoon or in a blender or food processor; set aside. Sauté the onion and green pepper in the vegetable broth until tender, about 2 to 3 minutes.
- Add 1 cup Picante sauce, the mashed beans, and the can of whole beans. Stir the mixture and heat thoroughly.
- Spoon about 1/3 cup of the bean mixture down the center of each tortilla and roll it up.
- Place the tortillas seam-side down in the baking pan. Combine the remaining cup of Picante sauce and the tomatoes; spoon over enchiladas.
- Cover with foil and bake for 15 minutes.
- Uncover, sprinkle with cheeses, and bake, uncovered, for five more minutes.

- To serve, place 1/2 cup lettuce on each plate and top with two enchiladas. Garnish with sour cream, if desired.

Nutrition Facts

- Carbohydrates: 59g, Protein: 15g, Fat: 5g, Saturated Fat: 2g, Sodium: 807mg, Fiber: 12g

284. ZESTY BROCCOLI SALAD

Preparation Time: 15 Minutes
Chilling Time: 1–2 Hours

Ingredients

- 4 cups fresh small broccoli florets
- 1 cup thinly sliced purple onion rings
- 1/2 cup sweetened, dried cranberries
- 1/2 cup reduced-fat Italian dressing
- Two tablespoons dry-roasted sunflower seeds

Directions

- Combine all ingredients in a serving dish and toss to coat well.
- Refrigerate for 1–2 hours to allow flavors to blend.
- Toss again before serving.

Nutrition Facts

- Carbohydrates: 10g, Protein: 2g, Fat: 3g, Saturated Fat: <1g, Sodium: 110mg, Fiber:2g

285. EXOTIC AMARETTO MAROON CARROTS

Preparation Time: 10 Minutes
Cooking Time: 8–9 Minutes.

Ingredients

- 1 pound maroon carrots (who can substitute plain carrots)
- Two tablespoons water
- 1 1/2 tablespoons reduced-calorie stick margarine, melted
- One tablespoon Amaretto

Directions

- Peel carrots and slice them into 1-inch pieces. Place in a microwave-safe dish, add two tablespoons of water and cover with a lid or microwave-safe plastic wrap.
- Microwave on 100% for 8–9 minutes, or until tender when pierced with a fork.
- Drain water.

- In a small bowl, stir together melted margarine and Amaretto.
- Drizzle evenly over carrots and toss to coat.

Nutrition Facts

Carbohydrates: 12g, Protein: 1g, Fat: 3g, Saturated Fat: 1g, Sodium: 50mg, Fiber: 4g

286. COUNTRY-STYLE COLLARD GREENS

Preparation Time: 15 Minutes
Cooking Time: 50–55 Minutes.

Ingredients

- One tablespoon corn oil
- 1/2 cup chopped onion (about one small onion)
- One teaspoon (or one clove) minced garlic
- 1 pound collard greens, trimmed and chopped (about two large bunches)
- Two cans (14.5 ounces each) fat-free, reduced-sodium chicken broth
- One teaspoon packed brown sugar
- 1 1/2 teaspoons liquid smoke flavoring
- 1/4 teaspoon red pepper flakes

Directions

- Heat oil in a large pot. Add onion and garlic and cook, frequently stirring, until onion is tender, taking care not to burn the garlic.
- Add greens, chicken broth, brown sugar, liquid smoke flavoring, and red pepper flakes.
- Cover, bring to a boil, reduce heat to medium and simmer 30 minutes, or until greens are tender; stir periodically.
- Remove the lid from the pan and continue cooking until most of the liquid evaporates (about 15–20 minutes more).

Nutrition Facts

Carbohydrates: 10g, Protein: 3g, Fat: 4g, Saturated Fat: 1g, Sodium: 550mg, Fiber: 3g

287. LUSCIOUS LENTILS

Preparation Time: 15 Minutes
Soaking Time: 1 Hour

Cooking Time: Approximately 1 3/4 Hours

Ingredients

- 2 cups dried lentils, rinsed and picked over for small stones or debris
- 3 quarts cold water
- 6 cups low-sodium chicken broth
- 2 1/2 cups water
- One can (14 1/2 ounces) no-salt-added diced tomatoes, undrained
- Two teaspoons olive oil
- One large onion, finely chopped
- 1/2 teaspoon dried thyme
- One teaspoon minced garlic
- 1/4 teaspoon coarse ground black pepper
- One tablespoon dried parsley
- 1/2 cup plus one tablespoon chopped green onions (approximately five green onions)
- Six tablespoons reduced-fat sour cream

Directions

- Soak lentils in the 3 quarts of cold water for 1 hour.
- Drain. In a large pan, combine soaked lentils, broth, 2 1/2 cups water, tomatoes, olive oil, onion, thyme, and garlic; stir to mix.
- Cover and bring to a boil over high heat.
- Reduce heat to medium and simmer for about 1 1/2 hours, or until lentils are tender.
- Stir periodically, add more water if a thinner broth is desired, or cook on medium-low for thicker consistency (some broth should remain).
- Stir in pepper and parsley, and simmer 5 minutes longer.
- Serve alone or over-cooked brown rice.
- Top each serving with one tablespoon green onions and two teaspoons sour cream.

Nutrition Facts

- Carbohydrates: 35g, Protein: 17g, Fat: 3g, Saturated Fat: 1g, Sodium: 72mg, Fiber: 7g

288. DILL GREEN BEANS

Preparation Time: 5 Minutes
Cooking Time: Approximately 10 Minutes.

Ingredients

- 6 cups water
- One package (14 ounces) frozen whole green beans, thawed
- Two tablespoons extra virgin olive oil
- Two tablespoons cider vinegar
- 1/4 cup finely chopped green onion
- Two tablespoons chopped fresh dill
- 1/4 teaspoon salt
- 1/4 teaspoon black pepper

Directions

- Bring water to boil in a large saucepan; add green beans and cook about 10 minutes or until tender when pierced with a fork (beans should retain their bright green color).
- Meanwhile, in a small bowl, whisk together olive oil, vinegar, green onion, dill, salt, and pepper. Drain cooked beans well.
- Drizzle dill sauce over the beans and toss gently to coat well.

Nutrition Facts

Carbohydrates: 3g, Protein: 1g, Fat: 3g, Saturated Fat: <1g, Sodium: 60mg, Fiber: 1g

289. WHERE'S-THE-BEEF BEAN BURGERS

Preparation Time: 15 Minutes
Cooking Time: 4–6 Minutes.
Standing Time: 15 Minutes

Ingredients

- One can (15 ounces) pinto beans, rinsed and drained
- 1/2 15-ounce can black beans, rinsed and drained
- 1/2 cup uncooked quick-cooking oats
- 1/4 cup liquid egg substitute
- 1/4 cup no-salt-added ketchup
- 1/8 teaspoon garlic powder
- 1/4 teaspoon liquid smoke
- Two dashes of cayenne pepper
- Two green onions, finely chopped
- Cooking spray
- Two tablespoons corn oil

Directions

- Combine rinsed and drained pinto and black beans in a large bowl; mash well using a potato masher.
- Stir in oats, egg substitute, ketchup, garlic powder, liquid smoke, cayenne pepper, and green onions; mix well.
- Allow mixture to stand 15 minutes to thicken, then shape into 5 (4-inch) patties approximately 1/2-inch in thickness.
- Coat a large, nonstick skillet with cooking spray, add oil, and warm over medium to medium-high heat.
- Add burgers and cook 2–3 minutes on each side, or until lightly browned; turn using a large spatula to prevent burgers from breaking apart.
- Serve on whole-wheat buns topped with favorite burger toppings.

Nutrition Facts

Carbohydrates: 29g, Protein: 9g, Fat: 7g, Saturated Fat: 1g, Sodium: 305mg, Fiber: 8g

290. INSTANT REFRIED BEANS RECIPE FOR DIABETICS

Preparation Time: 20 minutes

Ingredients

- 1 pound dried pinto beans
- 1/2 tablespoon chili powder
- One tablespoon ground cumin
- 1/8 teaspoon garlic powder
- Two dashes of cayenne pepper
- Two teaspoons salt
- One tablespoon dried minced onion
- 2 1/2 cups water

Directions

- Preheat oven to 350°F. Look beans over and discard any foreign material.
- Quickly rinse beans and drain well to prevent them from absorbing water.
- Turn beans out on a dry towel and pat dry.
- Place beans in a single layer in a 9" x 13" baking pan and bake 4–5 minutes, frequently stirring, to dry beans.
- Pour beans out onto a dry towel to cool to room temperature.
- Using a blender, coffee grinder (make sure it's free of coffee bean powder), or food mill, process cooled beans in small

batches until they're the consistency of flour (larger lumps will add crunch to your beans).
- Pour processed beans into a bowl and add remaining dry ingredients. Stir until well mixed.
- Store in an airtight container until ready to prepare. You will have about 3 cups of bean mix.

To Prepare:
- Place 2 1/2 cups water in a medium-size saucepan and bring to a boil over high heat.
- Add 3/4 cup bean mix to boiling water and mix with a wire whisk until combined. There may be a few lumps that add texture.
- Return to a boil over medium-high heat, cover, reduce heat to low-medium and simmer for 11–12 minutes, or until thickened; periodically remove the lid and stir beans.
- Beans will continue to thicken as they cool. Thin, as needed, with hot water.

Nutrition Facts

Carbohydrates: 15g, Protein: 5g, Fat: <1g, Sodium: 245mg, Fiber: 9g

291. SPICY BLACK BEAN BURRITOS

Preparation Time: 25 Minutes

Ingredients
- Two cans (15 ounces each) black beans, rinsed and drained
- 1 cup frozen corn, thawed
- 1 cup cooked rice
- 16 ounces mild Picante sauce
- 1/4 teaspoon lime juice
- 1/4 teaspoon ground cumin
- 10 (8-inch) flour tortillas
- Fat-free sour cream (optional)

Directions
- Place beans in a nonstick skillet over medium heat. Mash about half of the beans with a fork or the back of a spoon.
- Add corn, rice, Picante sauce, lime juice, and cumin. Stir to combine. Cook over medium heat, frequently stirring, until hot and bubbly.
- Warm tortillas, if desired. Spoon 1/2 cup bean mixture down the center of each flour tortilla. Fold tortilla around filling. Top with a dollop of fat-free sour cream if desired.
- Bean filling can be made ahead and frozen or refrigerated until serving time. Warm over low-medium heat on the stove or in the microwave.

Nutrition Facts

Carbohydrates: 66g, Protein: 10g, Fat: 4g, Saturated Fat: <1g, Sodium: 995mg, Fiber: 5g

292. DIABETIC SUMMER SQUASH SIDE DISH RECIPE

Preparation Time: 10 Minutes
Cooking Time: Approximately 7 Minutes.

Ingredients
- Cooking spray
- One teaspoon olive oil
- Four small yellow squash (approximately 5 inches long), quartered and sliced 1/4-inch thick (about 2 cups total)
- Two medium zucchini (around 6-7 inches long), quartered and sliced 1/4-inch wide (about 2 cups total)
- 1 cup thinly sliced onion, separated into rings
- 3/4 teaspoon parslied garlic salt

Directions
- Coat an excellent, nonstick wok with cooking spray.
- Preheat wok, then add oil.
- When the oil is hot, add yellow squash, zucchini, and onion.
- Cook, constantly stirring, for 4-5 minutes, or until the squash is crisp-tender.
- Sprinkle with parslied garlic salt and toss to coat. Serve immediately.

Nutrition Facts

Carbohydrates: 5g, Protein: 1g, Fat: 1g, Saturated Fat: <1g, Sodium: 222 mg, Fiber: 1g

293. ASPARAGUS WITH MUSTARD VINAIGRETTE

Preparation Time: 20 Minutes

Ingredients
- 1 pound fresh asparagus, preferably thin spears
- Two teaspoons Dijon-style mustard
- Three tablespoons red wine vinegar
- One teaspoon granulated sugar
- 1/4 teaspoon salt
- 1/4 teaspoon black pepper
- One tablespoon minced fresh parsley
- Two tablespoons olive oil

Directions
- Wash asparagus and trim the ends. If stems are tough, remove the outer layer with a vegetable peeler.
- Drop asparagus into boiling water and cook approximately 8 minutes or until desired texture is reached; drain.
- Measure mustard into a bowl. Whisk in vinegar, sugar, salt, pepper, and parsley.
- Whisk in olive oil until the mixture is blended.
- Pour over cooked asparagus.
- Serve warm.

Nutrition Facts

Carbohydrates: 3g, Protein: 1g, Fat: 5g, Saturated Fat: <1g, Sodium: 121mg, Fiber: 1g

294. BLACK BEANS AND RICE

Preparation Time: 20 Minutes

Ingredients
- One can (15 ounces) black beans, undrained
- 1/4 teaspoon garlic salt
- Two dashes of cayenne pepper
- 1/4 teaspoon lime juice
- One can (14.5 ounces) diced tomatoes seasoned with basil, garlic, and oregano
- 3 cups cooked brown rice
- 1/2 ripe avocado (about 5 ounces), chopped into bite-size pieces
- 1/4 cup crumbled garlic-herb or plain Feta cheese

Directions
- Place beans with their liquid in a small saucepan and stir in garlic salt, cayenne pepper, and lime juice.
- Simmer over medium heat until heated through. In another small saucepan, warm tomatoes over medium heat until heated through. Put 3/4 cup hot rice on each plate and top

with one-fourth of the beans and one-fourth of the tomatoes.
- Sprinkle each serving with one-fourth of the chopped avocado and one-fourth of the cheese.

Nutrition Facts
- Carbohydrates: 60g, Protein: 12g, Fat: 9g, Saturated Fat: 3g, Sodium: 1,190mg, Fiber: 10g

295. GINGER-CARAWAY CARROTS

Preparation Time: 15–20 Minutes

Ingredients
- Two tablespoons butter or margarine, melted
- Two tablespoons brown sugar
- 1/2 teaspoon ground ginger
- 1/2 teaspoon caraway seeds
- 1 pound peeled baby carrots

Directions
- Mix butter or margarine, brown sugar, ginger, and caraway seeds.
- Set aside.
- Place carrots in a microwave-safe dish.
- Add about 2 to 3 tablespoons of water to cover the bottom of the word.
- Cover the dish with a lid or plastic wrap.
- Microwave on High until tender, approximately 8 to 10 minutes, stirring halfway through cooking time.
- Remove the container from the microwave and drain any water that remains.
- Add sauce, toss to cover carrots, and return to microwave; cook on High for 1 minute.
- Remove from microwave, stir, and place carrots in a serving dish.

Nutrition Facts
- Carbohydrates: 13g, Protein: <1g, Fat: 4g, Saturated Fat: <1g, Sodium: 74mg, Fiber: 2g

296. STIR-FRIED SNOW PEAS

Preparation Time: 15 Minutes
Cooking Time: Approximately 7 Minutes.

Ingredients
- Cooking spray
- One teaspoon sesame oil (who may substitute corn oil or canola oil)
- 3/4 pound snow peas, strings removed
- 1/4 teaspoon salt

Directions
- Coat an excellent, nonstick wok with cooking spray. Preheat wok, then add oil. When the oil is hot, add snow peas.
- Cook, constantly stirring, for 4–5 minutes, or until pods are crisp-tender.
- Sprinkle with salt and toss to coat. Serve immediately.

Nutrition Facts
- Carbohydrates: 4g, Protein: 1g, Fat: 1g, Saturated Fat: <1g, Sodium: 97mg, Fiber: 1g

297. CORNY ZUCCHINI MEDLEY

Preparation Time: 10 Minutes
Cooking Time: Approximately 15 Minutes.
Standing Time: 4–5 Minutes

Ingredients
- Cooking spray
- 1 1/2 teaspoons olive oil
- One clove garlic, minced
- One small onion, finely chopped
- Two dashes of hot pepper sauce (such as Tabasco)
- 2 cups frozen corn, thawed
- 2 cups chopped zucchini (approximately 9 ounces)
- 1/3 cup finely shredded, reduced-fat Monterey Jack cheese
- Four slices of turkey bacon, cooked, drained, and crumbled
- 1/4 cup finely diced tomato

Directions
- Coat a nonstick skillet with cooking spray, add olive oil, and warm over medium heat.
- Add garlic and onion; cook, frequently stirring, for 2–3 minutes, or until onion is translucent.
- Stir in hot pepper sauce. Add corn and zucchini and cook until crisp-tender, about 10 minutes; stir frequently.
- Spoon vegetables into a serving dish and sprinkle evenly with cheese, bacon, and tomato.
- Allow standing 4–5 minutes for the cheese to melt.

Nutrition Facts
- Carbohydrates: 13g, Protein: 5g, Fat: 4g, Saturated Fat: 1g, Sodium: 147mg, Fiber: 2g

298. ARTICHOKE SANDWICH SPREAD

Preparation Time: 5 Minutes
Chilling Time: 1 Hour

Ingredients
- 8 ounces fat-free cream cheese
- Two tablespoons light mayonnaise (not salad dressing–style mayonnaise)
- 1 cup drained marinated artichoke hearts, finely chopped
- Two tablespoons marinade from artichokes

Directions
- Place cream cheese in a mixing bowl and whip with an electric mixer until fluffy.
- Whip in mayonnaise.
- Stir in chopped artichoke hearts and marinade.
- Store in an airtight container in the refrigerator and chill for at least 1 hour to allow flavors to blend.
- Spread on thinly sliced whole wheat bread.

Nutrition Facts
- Carbohydrates: 2g, Protein: 3g, Fat: 2g, Saturated Fat: <1g, Sodium: 117mg

299. SEASONED BRUSSELS SPROUTS

Preparation Time: 25 Minutes

Ingredients
- 6 cups water
- 1 pound tiny Brussels sprouts
- Three tablespoons reduced-calorie margarine
- One green onion, finely chopped
- One teaspoon (or one clove) minced garlic
- One teaspoon salt
- 1/8 teaspoon ground ginger
- One tablespoon slivered almonds, toasted and chopped

Directions

- Bring the 6 cups of water to a boil in a large pan.
- Add the Brussels sprouts to the boiling water.
- Cook 6–7 minutes (or until tender when pierced with a fork; do not overcook), then drain well.
- Meanwhile, cut an "x" in the stem end of the sprouts for more even cooking. Set aside.
- Melt margarine in a large, nonstick skillet over medium heat.
- Add green onion, garlic, salt, and ginger.
- Cook, frequently stirring until onion softens.
- Add sprouts and gently toss to coat.
- Heat 1–2 minutes, then sprinkle with toasted almonds.

Nutrition Facts

Carbohydrates: 8g, Protein: 3g, Fat: 4g, Saturated Fat: 1g, Sodium: 460mg, Fiber: 3g

300. GREEN BEAN AND RED PEPPER SAUTÉ

Preparation Time: 30 Minutes

Ingredients

- 1 pound fresh green beans, ends trimmed
- Two tablespoons olive oil
- One large red bell pepper, cut into strips
- One teaspoon lemon juice
- 1/4 cup chopped salted cashews
- Dash of black pepper

Directions

- In a large kettle, bring 3 quarts of water to a boil.
- Add green beans and return water to a spot.
- Cook, uncovered, for 8 to 10 minutes until crisp-tender.
- Plunge beans into cold water to stop cooking. Beans may be covered and refrigerated overnight at this point.
- Heat oil in a large saucepan or wok until hot. Sauté red pepper over medium heat for 2 to 3 minutes. Stir in beans, lemon juice, cashews, and pepper.
- Cook and stir gently until thoroughly heated, about 6 to 8 minutes. Transfer to a serving platter and serve immediately.

Nutrition Facts

Carbohydrates: 7g, Protein: 2g, Fat: 7g, Saturated Fat: 1g, Sodium: 40mg, Fiber: 2g

301. BALSAMIC-BASIL SLICED TOMATOES

Preparation Time: 10 Minutes

Ingredients

- Two medium ripe tomatoes (about 4 ounces each) or one large tomato (about 8 ounces)
- One teaspoon olive oil
- One tablespoon balsamic vinegar
- 1/8 teaspoon coarse ground black pepper
- 1/4 cup snipped fresh basil
- Two tablespoons finely crumbled garlic-herb Feta cheese (who can substitute plain Feta)

Directions

- Slice tomatoes and lay them on a serving platter.
- Drizzle evenly with olive oil and balsamic vinegar.
- Sprinkle evenly with cracked pepper, snipped basil, and cheese.
- Divide into four equal portions and serve right away.

Nutrition Facts

Carbohydrates: 4g, Protein: 1g, Fat: 2g, Saturated Fat: 1g, Sodium: 60mg, Fiber: 1g

302. TANGY STEAMED GREEN BEAN SALAD

Preparation Time: 10 Minutes
Cooking Time: 7 Minutes

Ingredients

- 1 pound fresh whole green beans, washed, ends trimmed off
- Two tablespoons extra-virgin olive oil
- Two tablespoons red wine vinegar
- One tablespoon Dijon-style mustard
- One tablespoon water
- 1/4 teaspoon garlic powder
- 1/4 teaspoon black pepper
- Four green onions, finely chopped
- Ten cherry tomatoes, cut in half

Directions

- Steam green beans in a steamer (or use a steaming basket in a saucepan) for about 5 minutes until bright green and still slightly crisp.
- Immediately rinse under cold running water until cool to the touch. Drain.
- Place in a serving dish. In a small bowl, combine olive oil, red wine vinegar, mustard, water, and garlic powder with a small whisk or spoon.
- Pour over green beans.
- Add green onions and tomatoes, toss well, and serve.

Nutrition Facts

Carbohydrates: 12g, Protein: 3g, Fat: 7g, Sodium: 62mg, Fiber: 5g

303. SQUASH AND CORN

Preparation Time: 10 Minutes
Cooking Time: 20–25 Minutes.

Ingredients

- 1 pound zucchini, sliced lengthwise
- Three roasted green chilies, peeled and seeded (who used banana peppers in testing; alternatively, half a four 1/2-ounce can of roasted, diced chilies can be used)
- Cooking spray
- One teaspoon corn oil
- One small onion, finely chopped
- One teaspoon of real bacon bits
- 2 cups frozen corn, thawed (who can also use fresh corn cut from the cob)
- 1/4 cup water
- 1/4 teaspoon salt

Directions

- Dice zucchini into 1/2-inch pieces.
- Thinly slice chilies. Coat a large nonstick skillet with cooking spray, add oil, and warm over medium-high heat.
- Add onion and cook, frequently stirring, until translucent, about 3–4 minutes.
- Add bacon bits and corn and cook 2–3 minutes more, stirring frequently.
- Add water, squash, chilies, and salt; stir to mix.

- Cover pan, reduce heat to medium, and simmer 10–15 minutes, or until corn and zucchini are tender; stir occasionally.

Nutrition Facts

Carbohydrates: 11g, Protein: 3g, Fat: 1g, Saturated Fat: <1g, Cholesterol: <1mg, Sodium: 91mg, Fiber: 2g

304. BLACK BEAN AND RICE RECIPE FOR DIABETICS

Preparation Time: 20 Minutes

Ingredients

- 1 (15-ounce) can black beans, rinsed and drained
- 1 (12-ounce) jar thick and chunky mild salsa
- 1 (8 3/4-ounce) can no-salt-added corn, drained
- 4 cups cooked brown rice
- 1 cup (4 ounces) shredded Monterey Jack cheese

Directions

- Combine black beans, salsa, and corn in a saucepan and warm over medium heat until bubbly (approximately 10 minutes). Spoon 1/2 cup bean mixture over 1/2 cup hot, cooked rice. Sprinkle with two tablespoons of cheese and serve.

Nutrition Facts

Carbohydrates: 59g, Protein: 11g, Fat: 6g, Saturated Fat: 2g, Sodium: 444mg, Fiber: 4g

305. GINGERED SNOW PEAS

Preparation Time: 2 Minutes

Ingredients

- 6 ounces fresh snow peas
- Two medium carrots (6–8 inches in length)
- One teaspoon peanut oil
- One tablespoon minced shallots
- One teaspoon minced ginger
- One teaspoon lite (low-sodium) soy sauce

Directions

- Wash and drain snow peas. Remove pod string with a sharp knife if necessary.
- Using a vegetable peeler, shave the carrots into thin strips until you reach the inner core layer of the carrot; discard the core.
- You should get about 1/2 cup or more of shavings from the two carrots. Heat peanut oil in a medium skillet or wok over medium-high heat.
- Add shallots and ginger and stir, then add snow peas and stir-fry for approximately 2 minutes until peas are bright green and still crisp.
- Next, add soy sauce and carrot shavings and stir-fry for only 30–60 seconds more. (Overcooking the carrots will cause them to shrink considerably.)

Nutrition Facts

Carbohydrates: 7g, Protein: 2g, Fat: 1g, Sodium: 69 mg, Fiber: 2g

306. ROASTED WINTER VEGETABLE BLEND

Preparation Time: 15 Minutes

Ingredients

- Two medium carrots, peeled
- One medium sweet potato, peeled
- One large russet potato
- One medium turnip, peeled
- One medium parsnip, peeled
- One large onion, peeled
- Two tablespoons tomato paste
- One tablespoon olive oil
- Two teaspoons Italian herb blend
- Black pepper to taste

Directions

- Preheat oven to 400°F. Cut carrots, sweet potato, potato, turnip, parsnip, and onion into chunks. Place in a large bowl.
- Mix tomato paste and olive oil into vegetables, stirring well to coat all surfaces. Sprinkle with an herb blend and black pepper.
- Spread on the shallow baking sheet or pan so that vegetables are in a single layer.
- Bake 40–45 minutes, turning vegetables once with a spatula during cooking, until vegetables are fork-tender.

Nutrition Facts

Carbohydrates: 26g, Protein: 2g, Fat: 2g, Sodium: 45mg, Fiber: 4g

BEEF PORK AND LAMB

307. ITALIAN STYLE PORK CHOPS

Preparation 540 Minutes

Serves 6 Persons

Ingredients

- 1 large onion, coarsely chopped
- 6 pork chops (bone in), trimmed
- 1 teaspoon dried basil
- 1 teaspoon dried oregano
- 4 teaspoons minced garlic
- ½ teaspoon fine-grained kosher salt
- ½ teaspoon freshly ground black pepper
- 6 large tomatoes, chopped, with accumulated juices
- 4 teaspoons balsamic vinegar
- 2 medium zucchini, diced
- 4 teaspoons cornstarch
- 4 teaspoons cold water

Directions

- Place half the onion in a slow cooker. Place three of the pork chops over the onion.
- Sprinkle them with half the basil, oregano, garlic, salt, and pepper. Repeat these layers with the remaining onion, pork chops, herbs, garlic, salt, and pepper.
- Top the layers with the tomatoes, balsamic vinegar, and zucchini.
- Cover and cook on low heat for 8 to 9 hours or on high heat for 4 to 5 hours.
- Use a slotted spoon to transfer the pork chops and vegetables to a serving plate and cover to keep warm.
- Pour the cooking juices from the slow cooker into a medium saucepan, and place it over medium-high heat.
- Whisk together the cornstarch and water in a small bowl, and add it to the cook- ing juices. Cook until the sauce is thick and bubbling.
- Serve the sauce over the pork chops and vegetables.

Nutrition Facts

Calories per Serving: 333 cal Fat: 20g Protein: 21g Carbohydrates: 17g

308. PORK LOIN CHOPSTOPPED WITH PEACH SALSA

Preparation 28 Minutes

Serves 4 Persons

Ingredients

- Pork loin chops (no bones) – 1 pound
- Black pepper – ¼ teaspoon
- Garlic powder – ½ teaspoon
- Peaches (peeled and diced) – 2
- Dried oregano – 1 teaspoon
- Green pepper (diced finely) – ½
- Red onion (diced finely) – 1/3 cup
- Olive oil – 1 teaspoon
- Rice wine vinegar – 1 tablespoon
- Cilantro leaves (chopped) – 1 teaspoon
- Stevia – 1 packet

Directions

- Start by preparing the grill by placing coal inside the same and lighting it.
- While the grill is heating up, season the pork loin chops with garlic powder, oregano, and pepper.
- Place the pork chops on the grill and cook them for about 4 minutes on a medium flame. Flip over and cook for another 4 minutes.
- Take a small glass bowl and add the peaches, red onion, green pepper, olive oil, rice wine vinegar, sugar substitute, and freshly chopped cilantro. Give it a nice toss.
- For plating – place 1 pork chop on a platter and top it with ¼ of the peach salsa mixture.
- Serve right away!

Nutrition Facts

Calories per Serving: 205 cal Fat: 9g Protein: 22g Carbohydrates: 10g

309. MARVELOUS MEATBALLS

Makes about 26 meatballs

Ingredients:

- 1 pound Sharron's Pork Sausage
- 1 1/2 pounds ground beef
- 3/4 cup pork rinds, ground
- 1/4 cup onion, minced
- 2 tablespoons parsley flakes
- 1/4 teaspoon dry mustard powder
- 1 teaspoon seasoning salt
- 3 cloves garlic, minced
- 1/4 teaspoon lemon pepper
- 2 eggs
- 1/3 cup Almond Milk unsweetened, or cream

Directions:

- Combine all of the ingredients in a large mixing bowl. Mix well and allow the meat mixture to rest at least 5 minutes.
- Form the meat into 2" balls.
- Bake them in a 9" x 13" x 2" baking pan about 20 minutes at 375 F, or barbecue over medium coals the same amount of time.
- They are done when they feel firm to the touch, no longer mushy.
- This easy meal can be served with your choice of dipping sauces.
- Freeze leftover meatballs for a quick meal!
- Reheat at 375 F for about 25 minutes or until hot.

Per Meatball.

Carbohydrates: 1 g Fiber: 1 g Protein: 11 g Fat: 17 g Calories: 205

310. MEATBALL SOUP

Makes about 10 servings

Ingredients:

- 1/2 medium onion, chopped
- 4 cloves garlic, minced
- 1 to 2 tablespoons lard
- Seasoning salt, to taste
- 6 cups beef Rich Stock (page 254)
- 1 carrot, chopped (optional)
- 3 stalks celery, chopped
- 3 cups cabbage, chopped into 1" cubes
- 1 1/2 cups broccoli (or cauliflower) stems, peeled and chopped or chopped zucchini
- 1 bay leaf
- 1/2 teaspoon marjoram, dried
- 1/8 teaspoon fennel/anise seed
- 1/2 tablespoon parsley
- Salt and lemon pepper to taste

Directions:

- In a 5-quart pot with a lid, cook the onion and the garlic in the lard with seasoning salt until they are beginning to become slightly golden, about 10 minutes.
- Add all of the remaining ingredients, except the meatballs, cover the pot, and simmer while preparing the meatballs, about 30 minutes.
- Meanwhile, prepare the meatballs.
- Bake them on a baking sheet for about 15 minutes.
- Add the cooked meatballs to the soup and simmer covered for another 20 minutes.

Nutrition Facts:

Carbohydrates: 5 g Fiber: 2 g Protein: 30 g Fat: 46 g Calories: 588

311. TACO MEAT

Makes about 6 servings

Ingredients:

- 1 1/2 pounds ground beef
- 1/2 medium onion, chopped (about 1/2 cup)
- 2 cloves garlic, minced or 1 tsp garlic powder
- 2 tablespoons butter
- 1/4 cup water (didn't add this)
- 2 teaspoons hot chili oil (added only half)
- 1 teaspoon lemon pepper (1 1/2 tsp Penzey's Singapore Seasoning as substitute for the lemon pepper and cumin)
- 1/2 teaspoon oregano
- 1 teaspoon sea salt
- 1/2 teaspoon cumin, ground
- 1/2 teaspoon Sweet & Slender (or the same of SteviaPlus) 1/4 tsp powdered stevia

Directions:

- In a large skillet, brown the ground beef and drain it in a large colander.
- While the beef is draining, cook the onion and garlic in the butter until golden, about 5 minutes.
- Add the beef and remaining ingredients.
- Simmer until most of the moisture has evaporated, about 5 minutes.

Nutrition Facts:

Carbohydrates: 2 g Fiber: 1g Protein: 19 g Fat: 36 g Calories: 409

312. ORANGE CINNAMON BEEF STEW

Serving Size: 4 servings
Overall Time: 2½ hours and 20 mins
Ingredients:

- Beef stew (2 lbs., grass fed. Cut in 1" pcs and pat dry)
- Salt (1 tsp.) + pepper (1 tsp.)
- Coconut oil (2-3 tbsp)
- Medium onion (1 medium, diced)
- Carrot (1, diced)
- Celery (1 stalk, diced)
- Garlic (2 cloves, minced)
- Orange (½ cup plus zest)
- Balsamic vinegar (¼ cup)
- Water (4 cups)
- Ground cinnamon (2 tsp.)
- Bay leaves (3)
- Rosemary (1 tbsp., finely chopped)
- Fresh thyme (1 tbsp., finely chopped)
- Fresh sage (1 tbsp., finely chopped)
- Small rutabagas (4 small, spiralized)

Directions:

1. Heat oven to 350 degrees Fahrenheit.
2. In a Dutch oven, heat coconut oil over the medium high flame. Add a layer of meat pieces ensuring that enough space is in between each piece. Dribble with pepper and salt and fry until all sides are golden brown. Transfer to a plate and set aside. Continue in batches until all pieces are done, adding more oil if necessary, so that pot bottom does not burn or stick.
3. After pieces of meat have been browned and removed from Dutch oven; place onions, celery, carrot, and garlic in a pot and sauté until fragrant, roughly 1. min.
4. Add orange juice and mix well. Now, add browned meat, zest, water, balsamic vinegar, salt, cinnamon, bay leaves and pepper.
5. Bake in the oven until meat is extremely tender, almost falling apart, roughly 2 - 2 ½ hours.
6. Mix in thyme, rosemary, and sage and cook for a further 10-15 minutes.
7. In the meantime, place rutabaga into a steaming basket; add a pinch of salt and steam over a pot of boiling water for about 5 minutes, until firm.
8. Serve immediately (for a tasty boost of healthy fat, add a dribble of extra-virgin olive.)

Nutritional Info:
Calories: 447   Carbs: 21g

313. BEEF & PUMPKIN STEW

Serving Size: 4 servings
Overall Time: 6 hours and 5 mins
Ingredients:

- Steak (¾ lb., stewing)
- Pumpkin (½ lb.)
- Coconut oil (6 tbsp.)
- Sage (1 tsp.)
- Mixed herbs (1 tsp.)
- Rosemary (2 tsp.)
- Thyme (2 tbsp.)
- Salt & pepper

Directions:

1. Set slow cooker on high. Remove excess fat from your stewing steak and place steak in the slow cooker. Add 3 tbsp. of coconut oil; rub in a dash of pepper and salt. Put to cook for 60 mins on high temperature.
2. Transfer steak from slow cooker to a bowl. Add the seasoning and remaining portion of coconut oil and combine thoroughly. Return to slow cooker along with pumpkin and cook for another 3 hours on low.
3. Garnish with fresh herbs and serve.

Nutritional Info:
Calories: 263   Carbs: 12g

314. PIE WITH MUSHROOMS, SMOKED CHEDDAR, BACON, AND SOUR CREAM

Makes 9 servings
Ingredients:

- 3 lb (1.3 kg) lean ground beef
- 1 cup (240 ml) finely diced onion
- 1 cup (240 ml) finely diced celery
- 1/4 tsp (1.2 ml) dried thyme or 1 tsp. (2.5 ml) fresh thyme leaves
- 1 Tbsp (15 ml) tomato paste
- Sea salt and freshly ground black pepper
- 2 Tbsp (30 ml) unsalted butter
- 1/2 lb (227 g) mushrooms, coarsely chopped
- 2 lb (908 g) cauliflower, trimmed
- 2 cups (480 ml) shredded smoked cheddar cheese
- 1/4 cup (60 ml) sour cream
- 2 Tbsp (30 ml) unsalted butter
- 1 large egg
- 8 bacon slices, cooked until crisp and crumbled
- Paprika

Directions:

- To make the beef: Place the beef in a large pot and cook over high heat, crumbling the meat with a spoon until it loses its raw, red color. Stir in the onion, celery, thyme, and tomato paste. Season lightly with saltand pepper.
- Cover tightly, turn the heat to low, and cook for 20 minutes, stirring occasionally. Add a touch of water if the mixture looks too dry; it should look juicy but not wet.
- Heat the butter in a large frying pan over high heat until the foam subsides. Add mushrooms and cook briskly until the water has evaporated and the mushrooms are soft. Add the mushrooms to the beef mixture and cook for 10 minutes longer.
- To make the cauliflower puree: Chop the cauliflower, including the core, into chunks.
- Place in a large potand add enough water to cover the pieces by 1 inch (2.5 em). Bring to a boil over high heat and cook until extremely tender, about 20 minutes.
- Drain well. Transfer to a food processor and blend until smooth. Remove 1 cup of the puree and stir into the pot with the beef.
- To the remaining cauliflower in the food processor, add the cheese, sour cream, and butter; blend well.
- Add the egg and blend until smooth. Add the bacon and pulse once or twice to combine.
- Preheat the oven to 350 F (175 C). Spread the beef mixture in a 9 X 9-inch

(22.5 X 22.5-cm) deep baking dish. Cover with the cauliflower mixture and smooth the top. Sprinkle with the paprika or make crisscross lines, dots, or whatever strikes your fancy.
- Place the baking dish on a large rimmed baking sheet to catch any drips. Bake for 45 minutes, or until bubbly and browned. Let sit for 10 minutes before serving.

Nutrition Facts:

Carbohydrates: 9.1 g Fiber: 3.3 g Protein: 42.9 g Fat: 29.5 g Calories: 475

315. SLIGHTLY ITALIANO MEAT LOAF

Makes 12 servings

Ingredients:
- 1/4 lb. (112 g) pancetta, diced
- 3 large eggs
- 3 lb. (1.3 kg) lean ground beef
- 1/2 cup (120 ml) freshly grated Parmesan cheese
- 2 Tbsp. (30 ml) finely chopped fresh parsley
- 1/2 cup (120 ml) finely chopped onion
- 2 garlic cloves, minced
- 1 tsp. (5 ml) sea salt
- 1/2 tsp. (2.5 ml) freshly ground black pepper
- 2 Tbsp. (30 ml) finely diced sun-dried tomatoes

Directions:
- Preheat the oven to 350 F (175 C).
- Place the pancetta in a food processor and process until finely ground. Add the eggs and pulse to combine.
- Place in a large bowl and add the beef, cheese, parsley, onion, garlic, salt, pepper, and tomatoes.
- Mix well with your hands and pack into a 12 x 4 1/2-inch (30 x 11.5 cm) loaf pan.
- Bake for 1 1/4 hours. Let cool for 15 minutes before slicing.

Nutrition Facts:

Carbohydrates: 1.2 g Fiber: 0.2 g Protein: 27.6 g Fat: 12.7 g Calories: 236

316. STUFFED CABBAGE ROLLS

Makes 4 servings

Ingredients:
- 1 pound lean ground beef
- 1 egg
- 1/4 cup cream or Almond Milk (page 240
- 2 tablespoons minced onion, dried, or 1/4 cup fresh
- 1/2 teaspoon seasoning salt
- 1/4 teaspoon lemon pepper
- 1/2 teaspoon Italian seasonings
- 4 large cabbage leaves

Directions:
- Combine the beef, egg, cream, and seasonings well in a mixing bowl.
- Divide the meat into 4 equal parts and form each into a small loaf shape. Set them aside.
- Bring a medium-sized pot of water to a boil.
- Turn it off and place the cabbage leaves into the pot for 5 minutes, until they are soft and pliable.
- Place the leaves on a large plate or cutting board.
- Put a piece of meat on a cabbage leaf and wrap it end over end, tucking the ends, as if it were a small burrito.
- Place the rolls into an 8" square baking dish, and pour the stewed tomatoes or tomato sauce over the top.
- Bake at 350 F for about 45 minutes to 1 hour, or until they test at 170 F with a meat thermometer.

Nutrition Facts:

Carbohydrates: 3 g Fiber: 1 g Protein: 22 g Fat: 28 g Calories: 363

317. CHEESESTEAK LETTUCE CUPS

Ingredients:
- 3 ounces lean beef steak
- 1/3 cup sliced mushrooms
- 1/4 cup tinly sliced onions
- 1 slice fat-free American cheese
- 2 leaves romaine, butter or green leaf lettuce

Directions
- Slice meat into thin strips. Coat medium pan with non-stick cooking spray.
- Add mushrooms and onions; cook over medium heat for 5 minutes, stirring occasionally, until onions are slightly browned. Set aside.
- Remove pan from heat and re-coat with non-stick cooking spray.
- Cook steak strips over medium heat for 1-2 minutes, flipping halfway through.
- Break cheese slice into small strips.
- Place cheese on top of meat--still in the pan-- and continue to cook until cheese melts.
- Remove from heat; mix beef strips with veggies and serve on lettuce leaves.

Nutritional Facts

Calories 197 Protein 13.5 g Fat 7.5 g (3 g saturated) Cholesterol 55 mg Carbohydrates 7 g

318. SLOW COOKER CORNED BEEF AND CABBAGE

Servings: 4

Ingredients:
- 4 cups Hot Water
- 2 tbsp Cider Vinegar
- 2 tbsp Splenda
- 1/2 tsp Pepper -- Freshly Ground
- 1 Large Onion -- Cut Into Wedges
- 3 lb Corned Beef -- 1.5kg With Spices
- 1 Cabbage
- Cored And Cut into 10 Wedges

Directions
- In a 6 quart - 6litre crock pot, combine the water, vinegar, splenda, pepper, and onions, mixing well.
- Place the corned beef into the mixture.
- Cover and cook on high heat for 4 hours.
- Remove the lid and scatter the cabbage wedges over the top.
- Cover and continue cooking on high 3 to 4 hours longer, or until the beef is tender.
- To serve, carve the beef into slices and serve with the cabbage, with some of the cooking liquid spooned over the beef to keep it moist.

Nutritional Facts

248 Calories 20g Fat (70.5% calories from fat) 9g Protein 10g Carbohydrate 2g Dietary Fiber 35mg Cholesterol

319. SIRLOIN STEAK STRIPS

Servings: 8

Ingredients:
- 2 lb Beef, top sirloin steak, lean, raw
- 1 pinch salt and pepper (to taste)
- 1 tsp minced garlic
- 1/2 cup red wine (dry)
- 1/2 cup fat free unsalted beef broth
- 2 tbsp dijon mustard
- 3 tbsp chopped parsley

Directions
- Cut the steak into strips about 3/4 inch thick, and heat a large skillet coated with non-stick cooking spray over medium high heat.
- Sauté the steak on both sides until it is done, about 5 to 7 minutes, and season with the salt and pepper.
- Remove the meat, and add the garlic and wine to the pan, and boil until reduced by half, stirring well, and add the beef broth and mustard, stirring until blended.
- Boil until slightly thickened, and add the parsley, and return the meat to the pan, heat with the sauce, and serve.

Nutritional Facts

Calories 239.1 Total Carbs 1.8g Dietary Fiber 0.1g Sugars 0.1g

320. SPICY BEEF ROAST

Servings: 10

Ingredients:
- 1 3-1/2 to 4 pound boneless beef chuck roast
- Salt and black pepper
- 2 Tbsp cooking oil (optional) (Although there is
- a healthier oil out there called smart beat)
- 1/2 cup water
- 1 Tbsp Worcestershire Sauce
- 1 Tbsp tomato paste
- 2 cloves garlic, minced
- Several dashes bottled hot pepper sauce
- 1 Tbsp cornstarch
- 1 Tbsp cold water
- 1 Tbsp prepared horseradish
- 1/2 tsp salt

Directions
- Trim fat from meat. If necessary, cut meat to fit into a 3/1/2 to 4-1/2 quart slow cooker.
- Sprinkle meat with salt and pepper.
- If desired, in a large skillet cook meat in hot oil over medium heat until brown on all sides.
- Drain off fat. Place meat in cooker, In a small bowl combine the 1/2 cup water, the Worcestershire sauce, tomato paste, garlic, and hot pepper sauce.
- Pour over meat in slow cooker.
- Cover and cook on low-heat for 10-12 hours or on high=heat setting for 5 to 6 hours.
- Transfer meat to a serving platter, reserving cooking liquid, Cover meat with foil to keep warm.
- For gravy, strain cooking liquid and skim fat.
- Transfer liquid to a medium saucepan,
- In a small bowl combine corn starch and the Tblsp water; stir into liquid in saucepan.
- Cook and stir over medium heat until thickened and bubblu. Cook and stir for 2 minutes more.
- Stir in the horseradish an 1/2 tspn salt. Serve gravy with meat.

Nutritional Facts

Calories 203 Fat 6 g Cholesterol 94mg Sodium 227 mg Carbohydrates 2 g Protein 34 g

321. CHIPOTLE CHEESEBURGERS

Servings : 6

Ingredients:
- 2 pounds (910 g) ground beef
- 6 chipotle chiles canned in adobo
- sauce, minced
- ½ cup (32 g) chopped cilantro
- 2 cloves garlic, crushed
- ¼ cup (40 g) minced onion
- ½ teaspoon salt
- 6 ounces (170 g) Monterey Jack
- cheese, sliced

Directions:
- Plunk everything but the cheese into a big bowl and use clean hands to mush everything together until very well blended.
- Form into 6 burgers about 1 inch (2.5 cm) thick. Put your burgers on a plate and stick them in the fridge to chill for a good hour—it makes them easier to handle on the grill.
- Get your fire going—you'll want your gas grill on medium or a little lower or well-ashed charcoal.
- Grill the burgers for a good 7 to 10 minutes per side or until juices run clear, keeping down flare-ups with a water bottle.
- When the burgers are almost done, top with the cheese and let it melt. Serve with Chipotle Sauce Exclusive of Chipotle Sauce.

Nutritional Info:

Carbohydrate 1 g fibre 1g , protein. 33 grams

322. SIMPLE GRILLED LAMB CHOPS

Prep Time: 10 mins

Cook Time: 6 mins

Additional Time: 2 hrs

Total Time: 2 hrs 16 mins

Servings: 6

Ingredient
- ¼ cup distilled white vinegar
- 2 teaspoons salt
- ½ teaspoon black pepper
- 1 tablespoon minced garlic
- 1 onion, thinly sliced
- 2 tablespoons olive oil
- 2 pounds lamb chops

Instructions
- Mix together the vinegar, salt, pepper, garlic, onion, and olive oil in a large resealable bag until the salt has dissolved. Add lamb, toss until coated, and marinate in the refrigerator for 2 hours.
- Preheat an outdoor grill for medium-high heat.
- Remove lamb from the marinade and leave any onions on that stick to the meat. Discard any remaining marinade. Wrap the exposed ends of the bones with aluminum foil to keep them from burning. Grill to desired doneness, about 3 minutes per side for medium.

The chops may also be broiled in the oven for about 5 minutes per side for medium.

Nutrition Facts

Calories: 519; Protein 25g; Carbohydrates 2.3g; Fat 44.8g; Cholesterol 112mg; Sodium 861mg.

323. ROAST LEG OF LAMB

Prep Time: 15 mins
Cook Time: 1 hr 45 mins
Additional Time: 10 mins
Total Time: 2 hrs 10 mins
Servings: 12
Ingredient

- 4 cloves garlic, sliced
- 2 tablespoons fresh rosemary
- Salt to taste
- Ground black pepper to taste
- 5 pounds leg of lamb

Instructions

- Preheat oven to 350 degrees F (175 degrees C).
- Cut slits in the top of the leg of lamb every 3 to 4 inches, deep enough to push slices of garlic down into the meat. Salt and pepper generously all over the top of the lamb, place several sprigs of fresh rosemary under and on top of the lamb. Place lamb on roasting pan.
- Roast in the preheated oven until the lamb is cooked to your desired doneness, about 1 3/4 to 2 hours. Do not overcook the lamb, the flavor is best if the meat is still slightly pink. Let rest at least 10 minutes before carving.

Nutrition Facts

Calories: 382; Protein 35.8g; Carbohydrates 0.4g; Fat 25.3g; Cholesterol 136.1mg; Sodium 136.3mg.

324. ROASTED LAMB BREAST

Prep Time: 30 mins
Cook Time: 2 hrs 25 mins
Total Time: 2 hrs 55 mins
Servings: 4
Ingredient

- 2 tablespoons olive oil
- 2 teaspoons salt
- 2 teaspoons ground cumin
- 1 teaspoon freshly ground black pepper
- 1 teaspoon dried Italian herb seasoning
- 1 teaspoon ground cinnamon
- 1 teaspoon ground coriander
- 1 teaspoon paprika
- 4 pounds lamb breast, separated into two pieces
- ½ cup chopped Italian flat-leaf parsley
- ⅓ cup white wine vinegar, more as needed
- 1 lemon, juiced
- 2 cloves garlic, crushed
- 1 teaspoon honey
- ½ teaspoon red pepper flakes
- 1 pinch salt

Instructions

- Preheat oven to 300 degrees F (150 degrees C).
- Combine chopped parsley, vinegar, fresh lemon juice, garlic, honey, red pepper flakes, and salt in a large bowl. Mix well and set aside.
- Whisk olive oil, salt, cumin, black pepper, dried Italian herbs, cinnamon, coriander, and paprika in a large bowl until combined.
- Coat each lamb breast in the olive oil and spice mixture and transfer to a roasting pan, fat side up.
- Tightly cover the roasting pan with aluminum foil and bake in the preheated oven until the meat is tender when pierced with a fork, about 2 hours.
- Remove lamb from the oven and cut into four pieces.
- Increase oven temperature to 450 degrees F (230 degrees C).
- Line a baking sheet with aluminum foil and place lamb pieces on it. Brush the tops of each piece with fat drippings from the roasting pan.
- Bake lamb until meat is browned and edges are crispy about 20 minutes.
- Increase the oven's broiler to high and brown lamb for 4 minutes. Remove from oven.
- Serve lamb topped with parsley and vinegar sauce.

Nutrition Facts

Calories: 622; Protein 46.2g; Carbohydrates 7.7g; Fat 45.3g; Cholesterol 180.4mg; Sodium 1301.6mg.

325. MOROCCAN LAMB STEW WITH APRICOTS

Prep Time: 30 mins
Cook Time: 1 hr 55 mins
Total Time: 2 hrs 25 mins
Servings: 4
Ingredient

- 2 pounds boneless leg of lamb, cut into 1-inch cubes
- 2 teaspoons ground coriander
- 1 teaspoon ground cumin
- 1 teaspoon sweet paprika
- ½ teaspoon cayenne pepper
- ½ teaspoon ground cardamom
- ½ teaspoon ground turmeric
- 2 teaspoons kosher salt
- 2 tablespoons olive oil
- 2 cups finely chopped onion
- 4 cloves garlic, minced
- 1 tablespoon minced fresh ginger root
- 2 (3 inches) cinnamon sticks
- 2 cups low-sodium chicken stock
- 1 cup dried apricots, halved
- 2 (3 inches) orange peel strips
- 1 tablespoon honey
- ¼ cup chopped fresh cilantro
- ¼ cup toasted pine nuts

Instructions

- Combine lamb, coriander, cumin, paprika, cayenne, cardamom, turmeric, and salt in a large bowl; toss together until lamb is evenly coated.
- Heat oil in a large Dutch oven or tagine over medium heat. Add onions; cook, stirring occasionally until soft and translucent, about 5 minutes. Stir in garlic, ginger, and cinnamon; cook, stirring frequently, until fragrant, about 1 minute. Add seasoned lamb; cook, stirring frequently until light brown, being careful not to caramelize, about 2 minutes. Add chicken stock and bring to a gentle boil over medium heat. Reduce heat to low and simmer, covered, until the lamb is just tender, about 1 hour and 15 minutes.

- Stir in apricots, orange peels, and honey; continue to simmer over low heat, uncovered, until the liquid has thickened slightly and lamb is fork-tender, about 30 minutes. Remove from the heat, discard cinnamon sticks and orange peels.
- Divide evenly among 4 bowls. Garnish each bowl with a tablespoon each of cilantro and pine nuts.

Nutrition Facts

Calories: 553; Protein 44.5g; Carbohydrates 40.9g; Fat 24.8g; Cholesterol 125.5mg; Sodium 1129.7mg.

326. SLOW COOKER LAMB CHOPS

Prep Time: 15 mins
Cook Time: 4 hrs 30 mins
Additional Time: 5 mins
Total Time: 4 hrs 50 mins
Servings: 6
Ingredient

- ½ cup red wine
- ½ sweet onion, roughly chopped
- 3 tablespoons honey
- 2 tablespoons Dijon mustard
- 2 tablespoons lemon juice
- 4 garlic cloves, minced
- 1 tablespoon ground thyme
- 1 tablespoon dried rosemary
- 2 teaspoons ground basil
- 1 teaspoon salt
- 1 teaspoon coarse ground black pepper
- ¼ cup tapioca starch
- 1 ½ pound sirloin lamb chops, room temperature

Instructions

- Combine red wine and onion in a slow cooker.
- Whisk honey, mustard, lemon juice, garlic, thyme, rosemary, basil, salt, and pepper together in a small bowl until well blended. Add tapioca starch and whisk until well combined. Let sit until the mixture is thickened, at least 5 minutes.
- Dip lamb chops in the mustard mixture and massage until fully coated.
- Place chops in a single layer over the red wine and onion mixture in the slow cooker. Pour the remaining mustard mixture on top.
- Cover slow cooker and cook on Low until an instant-read thermometer inserted into the center of a chop reads at least 130 degrees F (54 degrees C), about 4 1/2 hours.

Nutrition Facts

Calories: 209; Protein 13g; Carbohydrates 18.5g; Fat 7.7g; Cholesterol 43.6mg; Sodium 550.5mg.

327. GRILLED LEG OF LAMB STEAKS

Prep Time: 10 mins
Cook Time: 10 mins
Additional Time: 30 mins
Total: 50 mins
Servings: 4
Ingredient

- 4 bone-in lamb steaks
- ¼ cup olive oil
- 4 large cloves garlic, minced
- 1 tablespoon chopped fresh rosemary
- Salt and ground black pepper to taste

Directions:

- Place lamb steaks in a single layer in a shallow dish. Cover with olive oil, garlic, rosemary, salt, and pepper. Flip steaks to coat both sides. Let sit until steaks absorb flavors, about 30 minutes.
- Preheat an outdoor grill for high heat and lightly oil the grate. Cook steaks until browned on the outside and slightly pink in the center, about 5 minutes per side for medium. An instant-read thermometer inserted into the center should read at least 140 degrees F (60 degrees C).

Nutrition Facts

Calories: 327; Protein 29.6g; Carbohydrates 1.7g; Fat 21.9g; Cholesterol 92.9mg; Sodium 112.1mg.

328. EASY MEATLOAF

Prep Time: 10 mins
Cook Time: 1 hr
Total Time: 1 hr 10 mins
Servings: 8
Ingredient

- 1 ½ pounds ground beef
- 1 egg
- 1 onion, chopped
- 1 cup milk
- 1 cup dried bread crumbs
- Salt and pepper to taste
- 2 tablespoons brown sugar
- 2 tablespoons prepared mustard
- ⅓ cup ketchup

Directions:

- Preheat oven to 350 degrees F (175 degrees C).
- In a large bowl, combine the beef, egg, onion, milk, and bread OR cracker crumbs. Season with salt and pepper to taste and place in a lightly greased 9x5-inch loaf pan, or form into a loaf and place in a lightly greased 9x13-inch baking dish.
- In a separate small bowl, combine the brown sugar, mustard, and ketchup. Mix well and pour over the meatloaf.
- Bake at 350 degrees F (175 degrees C) for 1 hour.

Nutrition Facts

Calories: 372; Protein 18.2g; Carbohydrates 18.5g; Fat 24.7g; Cholesterol 98mg; Sodium 334.6mg.

329. CLASSIC MEATLOAF

Prep: 30 mins
Cook: 45 mins
Total: 1 hr 15 mins
Servings: 10
Meatloaf Ingredients:

- 1 carrot, coarsely chopped
- 1 rib celery, coarsely chopped
- ½ onion, coarsely chopped
- ½ red bell pepper, coarsely chopped
- 4 white mushrooms, coarsely chopped
- 3 cloves garlic, coarsely chopped
- 2 ½ pounds ground chuck
- 1 tablespoon Worcestershire sauce
- 1 egg, beaten
- 1 teaspoon dried Italian herbs
- 2 teaspoons salt
- 1 teaspoon ground black pepper
- ½ teaspoon cayenne pepper
- 1 cup plain bread crumbs
- 1 teaspoon olive oil

Glaze Ingredients:

- 2 tablespoons brown sugar

- 2 tablespoons ketchup
- 2 tablespoons dijon mustard
- Hot pepper sauce to taste

Instructions

- Preheat the oven to 325 degrees F.
- Place the carrot, celery, onion, red bell pepper, mushrooms, and garlic in a food processor, and pulse until very finely chopped, almost to a puree. Place the minced vegetables into a large mixing bowl, and mix in ground chuck, Worcestershire sauce, and egg. Add Italian herbs, salt, black pepper, and cayenne pepper. Mix gently with a wooden spoon to incorporate vegetables and egg into the meat. Pour in bread crumbs. With your hand, gently mix in the crumbs with your fingertips just until combined, about 1 minute.
- Form the meatloaf into a ball. Pour olive oil into a baking dish and place the ball of meat into the dish. Shape the ball into a loaf, about 4 inches high by 6 inches across.
- Bake in the preheated oven just until the meatloaf is hot, about 15 minutes.
- Meanwhile, in a small bowl, mix together brown sugar, ketchup, Dijon mustard, and hot sauce. Stir until the brown sugar has dissolved.
- Remove the meatloaf from the oven. With the back of a spoon, smooth the glaze onto the top of the meatloaf, then pull a little bit of glaze down the sides of the meatloaf with the back of the spoon.
- Return meatloaf to the oven, and bake until the loaf is no longer pink inside and the glaze has baked onto the loaf, 30 to 40 more minutes. An instant-read thermometer inserted into the thickest part of the loaf should read at least 160 degrees F (70 degrees C). Cooking time will depend on the shape and thickness of the meatloaf.

Nutrition Facts

Calories: 284; Protein 21.6g; Carbohydrates 14.8g; Fat 14.9g; Cholesterol 85.3mg; Sodium 755.4mg.

330. SALISBURY STEAK

Prep Time: 20 mins
Cook Time: 20 mins
Total Time: 40 mins
Servings: 6

Ingredient

- 1 (10.5 ounces) can condense French onion soup
- 1 ½ pounds ground beef
- ½ cup dry bread crumbs
- 1 egg
- ¼ teaspoon salt
- ⅛ teaspoon ground black pepper
- 1 tablespoon all-purpose flour
- ¼ cup ketchup
- ¼ cup water
- 1 tablespoon Worcestershire sauce
- ½ teaspoon mustard powder

Instructions

- In a large bowl, mix together 1/3 cup condensed French onion soup with ground beef, bread crumbs, egg, salt, and black pepper. Shape into 6 oval patties.
- In a large skillet over medium-high heat, brown both sides of patties. Pour off excess fat.
- In a small bowl, blend flour and remaining soup until smooth. Mix in ketchup, water, Worcestershire sauce, and mustard powder. Pour over meat in skillet. Cover, and cook for 20 minutes, stirring occasionally.

Nutrition Facts

Calories: 440; Protein 23g; Carbohydrates 14.1g; Fat 32.3g; Cholesterol 127.5mg; Sodium 818.3mg.

331. LEEK AND PORK STIR FRY

Total Time: 40 mins

Ingredients

- 1 pound pork shoulder thinly sliced (about 500g)
- 2 Tablespoon oyster sauce
- 2 Tablespoon soy sauce
- 1 Tablespoon sesame oil
- 1 teaspoon garlic powder
- 1 teaspoon onion powder
- 1 teaspoon corn starch
- 1/2 teaspoon black pepper
- 1 cup of leek cleaned and sliced diagonally about 1/2 inch wide

Instructions

- In a large bowl, mix the pork slices with all the seasoning ingredients. Marinate for at least 30 minutes.
- Lightly grease the inside of the cake barrel.
- Put the marinated pork sliced inside the cake barrel. Air fry at 380F (190C) for about 8 minutes, stirring once in the middle
- Add the leek to the pork and mix. Air fry again at 380F (190C) for another 4-5 minutes until the pork is cooked through.

Nutrition

Calories: 186kcal | Carbohydrates: 11g | Protein: 16g | Fat: 9g | Saturated Fat: 2g | Cholesterol: 46mg

332. HEARTY MEATBALL SOUP

Prep Time: 10 mins
Cook Time: 45 mins

Ingredients

Meatball Ingredients:

- 1 pound ground meat I used ground turkey, about 500g
- 1/4 cup yellow onion finely chopped
- 1/2 cup Panko breadcrumb
- 1/2 tablespoon Italian seasoning
- 2 tablespoon grated Parmesan cheese
- 1 tablespoon soy sauce
- 2 teaspoon corn starch
- 1 teaspoon garlic powder
- 1 teaspoon onion powder
- 1/4 teaspoon black pepper or to taste

Soup Ingredients:

- 2 tablespoon olive oil
- 1 stalk celery diced
- 2 tablespoon garlic chopped
- 1/4 cup yellow onion diced
- 1/4 cup tomato ketchup
- 1/2 cup carrot diced
- 1 large zucchini diced
- 1/4 cup wine I used rice wine
- 1 can crushed tomatoes
- 1/2 can corn kernels
- 2 cup broth I used chicken
- 1 tablespoon Italian seasoning
- 2 teaspoon garlic powder

- Salt and pepper to taste

Directions:

- Line the fryer basket with a grill mat or a sheet of lightly greased aluminum foil.
- In a large bowl, combine all the meatball ingredients. Take about 1 tablespoonful of the mixture and roll it into a ball. Place the meatballs into the fryer basket. Spritz the meatballs with oil and air fry at 380F (190C) for about 8 minutes, shake the basket once in the middle.
- In the meantime, pour olive oil into a pot and saute garlic, celery, and onion until fragrant. Add in the rest of the soup ingredient and bring it to boil.
- When the meatballs are done, transfer them to the pot. Fill the pot with water just enough to cover all the ingredients. Let it simmer for about 30 minutes.
- Serve on its own or with pasta or bread.

Nutrition

Calories: 476kcal | Carbohydrates: 22g | Protein: 24g | Fat: 31g | Saturated Fat: 10g | Cholesterol: 83mg

333. ITALIAN PORK CHOPS

Preparation 30 Minutes

Serves 4 Persons

Ingredients

- 4 cloves garlic, sliced
- 4 thick pork chops, fat trimmed
- 1 small yellow onion, cut into rings
- ½ cup low-fat mozzarella cheese
- 1 (28-ounce) can diced tomatoes
- 1 teaspoon paprika
- 1 teaspoon dried oregano
- 1 chicken bouillon cube
- Salt and pepper to taste

Directions

- Preheat the oven to 400°F (200°C).
- Grease a baking pan with some cooking spray.
- Season the pork chops with pepper.
- Grease a medium saucepan or skillet with cooking spray and heat it over medium heat.

- Add the pork chops and stir-cook for 2 minutes per side until evenly brown.
- Add the garlic and onion rings and stir-cook for 1–2 minutes until softened.
- Add the spices, tomato and bouillon cube; simmer for 2–3 minutes.
- Pour in the tomato sauce.
- Add the mixture to the baking pan, top with the cheese, and bake for about 20 minutes until the top is golden brown.
- Let cool slightly and serve warm.

Nutrition Facts

Calories per Serving: 405 cal Fat: 17g Protein: 43g Carbohydrates: 16g

334. PORK CHOPS WITH ONION GRAVY

Preparation 20 Minutes

Serves 4 Persons

Ingredients

- Pork chops (boneless) - 4
- Sea salt - 1 teaspoon
- Black pepper - 1/4
- teaspoon Olive oil - 2 tablespoons
- Onion (sliced) - 1 large
- Garlic (minced) - 2 cloves
- Fresh thyme - 1 tablespoon
- Chicken broth - 1 cup
- Cream cheese - 1.5 ounce

Directions

- Begin by adding garlic powder, onion powder, black pepper and sea salt in a glass bowl. Mix well to combine. Place the pork chops into a shallow dish and generously season both sides of the meat with the prepared spice mix.
- Place a Dutch oven on medium-high flame and pour in the olive oil. Once the oil heats through, place the seasoned pork chops into the Dutch oven and cook for around 3 minutes; flip over and cook for another 3 minutes. Make sure that the pork chops are nicely browned.
- Once the pork chops are done, transfer onto a plate and keep aside.
- Reduce the flame under the Dutch oven to medium and toss in the onions into the same.
- Cook the onions in the pork fat for around 20 minutes.

- The onions should be nicely caramelized.
- While the onions caramelize, let us heat the oven by setting the temperature to 375 degrees Fahrenheit.
- Once the onions are cooked, add in the thyme leaves and minced garlic and stir for about a minute. Now pour the chicken stock into the Dutch oven and use a wooden spoon to scrape out the browned bits.
- Bring the gravy to a boil and cook for another 3 minutes or until the
- sauce becomes thicker. Put off the flame. 10.Toss in the cream cheese and mix until the cheese is well incorporated with other **Ingredients:** of the gravy.
- Return the seared pork chops to the sauce and top them with some onion gravy. Cover the Dutch oven with a lid. Place the Dutch oven into the oven and bake for around 25 minutes. Serve

Nutrition Facts

Calories per Serving: 541 cal Fat: 35g Protein: 48g Carbohydrates: 5g

335. BLACKBERRY PULLED PORK SHOULDER

Preparation 600 Minutes

Serves 10 Persons

Ingredients

- 2–3-lb. pork shoulder
- 1 large onion, chopped
- 2 pints fresh blackberries
- ¼ cup brown sugar
- 1 tsp. salt
- 2 tsp. garlic powder
- ½ tsp. red pepper
- 1 tsp. apple cider vinegar

Directions

- Place the pork shoulder in the crock and place the onion on top.
- Puree the blackberries and pass them through a sieve or strainer t o separate the puree from the seeds.
- Mix the remaining **Ingredients:** with the blackberry puree.
- Pour the blackberry puree over the contents of the crock.

- Cover and cook on Low for 8–10 hours.
- Remove the roast and pull between two forks to shred.
- Stir back through the liquid in the crock.

Nutrition Facts

Calories per Serving: 215 cal Fat: 12g Protein: 26g Carbohydrates: 8g

336. SLOW COOKER PORK TENDERLOIN

Preparation 250 Minutes
Serves 6 Persons

Ingredients

- 2-lb. pork tenderloin, cut in half lengthwise, visible fat removed
- 1 cup water
- ¾ cup red wine
- 3 Tbsp. light soy sauce
- 1 envelope salt-free onion soup mix
- 6 cloves garlic, peeled and chopped
- freshly ground pepper

Directions

- Place pork tenderloin pieces in slow cooker.
- Pour water, wine, and soy sauce over pork.
- Turn pork over in liquid several times to completely moisten.
- Sprinkle with dry onion soup mix.
- Top with chopped garlic and pepper.
- Cover. Cook on Low 4 hours.

Nutrition Facts

Calories per Serving: 220 cal Fat: 4g Protein: 37g Carbohydrates: 6g

337. SMOPKY PORK CHOPS AND TOMATOES

Preparation 35 Minutes
Serves 4 Persons

Ingredients

- Diced Roma tomatoes 2 medium
- Canola oil 2 tablespoons
- 5-ounce b1-in pork chops 4
- Black pepper 0.5 teaspoon
- Salt 0.375 teaspoons divided
- Garlic powder 0.25 teaspoons
- Dried thyme leaves 0.5 teaspoons
- Smoked paprika 1 teaspoon
- All-purpose flour 0.25 cups

Directions

- Mix the paprika, garlic powder, flour, thyme, pepper and 0.25 teaspoons of salt in a shallow bowl.
- Evenly coat all pork chops.
- In a large nonstick pan, pour in the oil and heat it using medium- high heat.
- Place the pork into the pan and on each side, cook 4 minutes.
- Repeat until the pork chops are thoroughly cooked.
- Add in the remaining 0.125 teaspoons of salt and the diced tomatoes.
- Cook until tomatoes are heated.

Nutrition Facts

- Calories per Serving: 205 cal Fat: 9g Protein: 22g Carbohydrates: 10g

338. PORK CHOPS WITH APPLE STUFFING

Preparation 60 Minutes
Serves 4 Persons

Ingredients

- 6 bone-in pork chops, at least 1-inch
- thick, about 2 lbs. total
- 1 Tbsp. canola oil
- ¼ cup chopped celery
- ¼ cup chopped onion 3 apples, peeled, cored, and diced
- ¼ cup sugar
- ½ cup bread crumbs, or cracker crumbs
- ¼ tsp. salt
- ¼ tsp. pepper
- 2 tsp. chopped parsley

Directions

- Cut a pocket about 1½-inch deep into the side of each chop for stuffing. Heat oil in skillet. Stir celery and onion into oil in skillet.
- Cook over medium until tender, stirring frequently. Stir in diced apples. Sprinkle with sugar.
- Cover skillet. Cook apples over low heat until tender and glazed.
- Stir in bread crumbs.
- Stir in salt, pepper, and parsley.
- Spreading open the pocket in each chop with your fingers, stuff with mixture.
- Place half of stuffed chops in skillet. Brown on both sides over me dium to high heat. Remove browned chops to platter. Cover to k eep warm.
- Repeat Step 9 with remaining chops. Return other chops to skillet Reduce heat.
- Add a few tablespoons of water. Cover. Cook slowly over low he at until done, about 20–25 minutes.

Nutrition Facts

Calories per Serving: 205 cal Fat: 9g Protein: 22g Carbohydrates: 10g

339. INDONESIAN PORK TENDERLOIN

Preparation 30 Minutes
Serves 4 Persons

Ingredients

- ¼ cup fresh lime juice
- 1 teaspoon lime zest
- 1 tablespoon low-sodium soy sauce
- 5 teaspoons grated fresh gingerroot
- 1 teaspoon crushed red pepper flakes
- 4 teaspoons minced garlic
- 1½ pounds pork tenderloin, trimmed of fat

Directions

- In a medium bowl, whisk together everything except the pork tenderloin, and pour half the marinade into a large, resealable plastic bag. (Reserve the other half of the marinade in a bowl in the refrigerator.)
- Add the pork to the bag and seal it, turning a few times to coat the meat.
- Store the bag in the refrigerator at least 3 hours or overnight

- Preheat the barbecue grill to medium-high heat, and take the pork out of the re- frigerator.
- Drain the pork and grill for about 15 minutes, turning and basting with the re- served marinade until the internal temperature reads 160 degrees F.
- Serve warm

Nutrition Facts

Calories per Serving: 263 cal Fat: 6g Protein: 45g Carbohydrates: 5g

340. ROASTED LEG LAMB

Preparation 165 Minutes
Serves 12 Persons
Ingredients

- 6 pound bone-in lamb leg, trimmed
- 1 cup of chicken broth
- Marinade:
- 1/3 cup fresh minced rosemary
- 2 tablespoons of Dijon mustard 2 tablespoons of olive oil
- 8 minced garlic cloves
- 1 teaspoon soy sauce reduced-sodium
- 1/2 teaspoon salt
- 1/2 teaspoon pepper

Directions

- Preheat your oven to 325degrees F.
- Combine marinade ingredients and coat the lamb. Refrigerate with cover overnight.
- Place the lamb on a rack using a shallow roasting pan with the fat side up.
- Bake without cover for 1 ½ hours.
- Pour the broth then cover loosely using foil.
- Bake for another 1 ½ hours or until meat turns to your desired doneness
- Cool lamb for 10 to 15 minutes before slicing.

Nutrition Facts

Calories per Serving: 246 cal Fat: 11g Protein: 32g Carbohydrates: 6g

341. LAMB CHOPS CURRY

Preparation 40 Minutes
Serves 2 Persons
Ingredients

- 8 ounces bone-in loin chops of lamb
- 1 tablespoon of canola oil
- 3/4 cup of orange juice
- 2 tablespoons teriyaki sauce
- 2 teaspoons of grated orange zest
- 1 teaspoon of curry powder
- 1 garlic clove, minced
- 1 teaspoon cornstarch
- 2 tablespoons of cold water

Directions

- Brown lamb chops on both sides over canola oil.
- Combine the next five ingredients and pour over the skillet.
- Cover and let it simmer for 15 to 20 minutes or until lamb turns tender.
- Remove from heat and keep warm.
- Combine the last two ingredients until smooth.
- Stir into the pan drippings and bring to boil for 2 minutes or until it thickens.
- Serve with steamed rice if desired

Nutrition Facts

Calories per Serving: 337 cal Fat: 17g Protein: 30g Carbohydrates: 15g

342. GRILLED LAMB CHOPS

Preparation 15 Minutes
Serves 4 Persons
Ingredients

- 8 ounces lamb loin chops

Marinade:

- 1 small sliced onion
- 2 tablespoons of red wine vinegar
- 1 tablespoon of lemon juice
- 1 tablespoon of olive oil
- 2 teaspoons fresh minced rosemary
- 2 teaspoons of Dijon mustard
- 1 minced garlic clove
- 1/2 teaspoon pepper
- 1/4 teaspoon salt
- 1/4 teaspoon of ground ginger

Directions

- Coat the lamb chops with the combined marinade mixture. Cover and refrigerate for 4 hours or overnight.
- Drain and discard marinade.
- Lightly oil your grill rack.
- Grill lamb chops 4 to 7 minutes on each side over medium heat.
- Grill until it reaches your desired doneness

Nutrition Facts

Calories per Serving: 164 cal Fat: 8g Protein: 21g Carbohydrates: 1g

343. PORK AND CABBAGE

Preparation 25 Minutes
Serves 8 Persons
Ingredients

- 2 lbs. pork steaks, or chops, or shoulder, bone-in, trimmed of fat
- ¾ cup chopped onions
- ¼ cup chopped fresh parsley, or 2 Tbsp. dried parsley
- 4 cups shredded cabbage
- 1 tsp. salt
- ⅛ tsp. pepper
- ½ tsp. caraway seeds
- ⅛ tsp. allspice
- ½ cup beef broth 2 medium cooking apples, cored and sliced
- ¼-inch thick

Directions

- Place pork in slow cooker.
- Layer onions, parsley, and cabbage over pork.
- Combine salt, pepper, caraway seeds, and allspice.
- Sprinkle over cabbage.
- Pour broth over cabbage.
- Cover. Cook on Low 5–6 hours.
- Add apple slices 30 minutes before serving.

Nutrition Facts

Calories per Serving: 149 cal Fat: 5g Protein: 18g Carbohydrates: 9g

344. GLAZED HAM BALLS

Preparation 70 Minutes
Serves 20 Persons

Ingredients

- 1 cup crushed pineapple, undrained
- 2⅔ Tbsp. Splenda Brown Sugar Blend
- 1 Tbsp. vinegar
- 2–3 Tbsp. prepared mustard
- 1 lb. 50%-reduced-fat bulk sausage
- ½ cup cooked ground ham
- ¾ cup bread crumbs, crackers
- ½ cup egg substitute
- ½ cup ketchup, or milk
- ⅛ cup chopped onion
- ¼ tsp. pepper, optional

Directions

- In a mixing bowl, mix together pineapple, Splenda, vinegar, and mustard. Set aside.
- In a large mixing bowl, thoroughly combine sausage, ham, bread crumbs, egg substitute, ketchup, and onion.
- Shape into 20 1½-inch balls. Place in well-greased shallow baking dish.
- Spoon pineapple mixture over ham balls.
- Cover. Bake at 350°F for 25 minutes.
- Uncover. Continue baking for 25 more minutes.

Nutrition Facts

Calories per Serving: 100 cal Fat: 4g Protein: 7g Carbohydrates: 8g

345. CORNED BEEF BRISKET

Preparation 360 Minutes
Serves 6 Persons

Ingredients

- Corned beef brisket (flat-cut) – 1 (5 pounds)
- Browning sauce – 1 tablespoon
- Vegetable oil – 1 tablespoon
- Onion (sliced) – 1
- Garlic (sliced) – 6 cloves Water – 2 tablespoons

Directions

- Start by preheating the oven by setting the temperature to 275 degrees Fahrenheit.
- Place the brisket in a shallow dish and brush both sides gently with the browning sauce.
- Take a large nonstick skillet and add the vegetable oil. Place it over a medium-high flame and let it completely heat through.
- Place the brisket into the skillet and cook for about 8 minutes on both sides.
- Make sure the brisket forms a dark brown crust.
- Take a roasting pan and place the brisket on the rack set inside the same.
- Scatter chopped garlic and onion on top of the brisket. Add some water to the roasting pan. Use aluminum foil to cover the pan.
- Place the pan in the preheated oven and roast until the meat becomes tender to the touch. This would take about 6 hours.
- Once done, remove the foil and transfer onto a serving platter.

Nutrition Facts

Calories per Serving: 455 cal Fat: 33g Protein: 30g Carbohydrates: 5g

346. STIR-FRYED BEEF & ZUCCHINI WITH PESTO

Preparation 20 Minutes
Serves 6 Persons

Ingredients

- Beef (ground) - 1 pound
- Sea salt - 1 teaspoon
- Black pepper - ½ teaspoon
- Zucchini - 2 medium
- Garlic (minced) - 2 cloves
- Basil pesto - ¾ cup
- Goat cheese (crumbled) - ½ cup
- Fresh parsley (chopped) - 2 tablespoons

Directions

- Wash zucchini under running tap water and wipe it dry using a kitchen towel. Cut it lengthwise and then further cut them into semi-circles about ½ inch thick. Keep aside.
- Take a large nonstick skillet and place it on medium flame. Lightly grease the pan with cooking spray.
- Once the pan is hot enough, toss in the garlic and sauté until it becomes fragrant, stirring continuously. This will take about a minute.
- Add in the ground beef and give it a nice stir. Generously season the meat with black pepper and salt. Stir well and cook for another 8-10 minutes.
- 5.Once the meat is browned, add in the zucchini. Keep stirring and cook for about 6 minutes. The zucchini should be tender yet crunchy.
- 6.Put off the flame and add in the basil pesto. Also add in the fresh parsley and goat cheese. Give it a nice mix.

Nutrition Facts

Calories per Serving: 468 cal Fat: 37g Protein: 30g Carbohydrates: 4,5g

347. HEARTY POT ROAST

Preparation 180 Minutes
Serves 12 Persons

Ingredients

- 4-lb. beef roast, ideally rump roast
- 4 medium red potatoes, cut in thirds
- 3 medium carrots, quartered
- 2 ribs celery, chopped 2 medium onions, sliced
- ½ cup flour 6-oz. can tomato paste
- ¼ cup water
- 1 tsp. instant beef bouillon, or 1 beef bouillon cube
- ¼ tsp. pepper

Directions

- Place roast in 9×13-inch baking pan or roasting pan.
- Arrange vegetables around roast.
- Combine flour, tomato paste, water, bouillon, and pepper in small bowl.
- Pour over meat and vegetables.
- Cover. Roast at 325°F for 2–2½ hours, or until meat thermometer registers 170°F.
- Allow meat to stand for 10 minutes.
- Slice and place on platter surrounded by vegetables.

Nutrition Facts

Calories per Serving: 305 cal Fat: 8g Protein: 36g Carbohydrates: 22g

348. MUSHROOM AND WALNUT MEAT LOAF

Preparation 45 Minutes

Serves 4 Persons

Ingredients

- Finely chopped walnuts 0.5 cups
- Fat-free milk 0.5 cups
- Panko breadcrumbs 1 cup
- Beaten egg 1
- Freshly ground black pepper 0.25 tsp
- Sea salt 0.5 teaspoons
- Italian seasoning 1 teaspoon
- Rehydrated tomatoes 0.33 cups
- Diced red bell pepper 0.33 cups
- Finely chopped mushrooms 1 pound
- Chopped onion 1 large
- Olive oil 1 tablespoon
- Cooking spray

Directions

- Preheat the oven to 350 degrees Fahrenheit. Take 4 ramekins that hold 8 ounces and coat them with a nonstick spray.
- In a pan, add the oil and then put it on medium heat.
- Add the onions and mushrooms, and cook them for 10 minutes until they are browned. Stir in the sundried tomatoes and red pepper, saute for about 8 minutes.
- Add the salt and pepper and Italian seasoning. Saute for 1 more minute.
- Take the mushroom mixture and put it into a large bowl. Let it sit for about 2 minutes so that it is able to cool.
- Add the breadcrumbs, walnuts, milk, and egg. Gently mix all of these together and then evenly divide it into the individual ramekins. Press down so that the mixture is even with the top of the ramekin.
- Grab a baking sheet and place the ramekins on top. Let it cook for 30 to 35 minutes after putting it into the oven.

Nutrition Facts

Calories per Serving: 250 cal Fat: 15g Protein: 13g Carbohydrates: 45g

349. GREEK STEAK WRAPS

Preparation 25 Minutes

Serves 6 Persons

Ingredients

- ¼ cup balsamic vinegar
- 2 tablespoons olive oil
- 1 tablespoon minced garlic
- 1 tablespoon dried oregano
- 1 tablespoon dried basil Lemon zest and juice from
- 1 lemon
- Freshly ground black pepper, to taste
- 1 (18-ounce) flank steak, trimmed completely of fat
- 6 whole-wheat tortillas
- 2 cups shredded lettuce
- 1 medium red onion, sliced thinly 2 cups halved cherry tomatoes

Directions

- Combine the balsamic vinegar, olive oil, garlic, oregano, basil, and lemon zest and juice, and season with pepper.
- Pour the mixture into a large, resealable plastic bag.
- Add the steak to the marinade in the bag, turning the bag to coat. Place the sealed bag in the refrigerator on a plate for at least 4 hours or overnight.
- Turn the bag over several times so that the steak marinates
- evenly.
- Preheat a barbecue grill to medium-high heat.
- Take the steak out of the bag and discard the marinade. Grill the steak 5 minutes per side, or until it is the desired doneness. Remove the steak from the heat and let it rest for at least 10 minutes.
- Slice the steak diagonally into thin strips.
- Fill the 6 tortillas with sliced steak, lettuce, onion, and cherry tomatoes, and serve.

Nutrition Facts

Calories per Serving: 347 cal Fat: 13g Protein: 28g Carbohydrates: 28g

350. BEEF STROGANOFF

Preparation 15 Minutes

Serves 5 Persons

Ingredients

- Egg noodles (whole-grain) – 5 ounces
- Olive oil – 2 teaspoons
- Beef tenderloin (boneless) tips 450 g
- Button mushrooms (white) – 1 ½ cups
- Onion (minced) – ½ cup
- All-purpose flour – 1 tablespoon
- Dry white wine – ½ cup
- Dijon mustard – 1 teaspoon
- Beef broth – 1 can
- Sour cream – ½ cup Salt – ¼ teaspoon
- Black pepper – ¼ teaspoon

Directions

- Begin by slicing the tenderloins into strips measuring ½ inch. Also, slice the button mushrooms and set aside.
- Place a stockpot over a high flame and fill it with water.
- Once it comes to a boil, add the noodles and cook them as per the package instructions. Once done, drain the excess water and set aside.
- While the noodles are cooking, place a saucepan on a high flame. Pour in the oil and let it heat through. Add the meat and cook for 3 minutes.
- Remove the meat from the pan and set aside.
- Toss in the minced onion and sliced mushrooms. Cook for around 5 minutes.
- Add the flour and let it cook for 1 minute. Pour in the wine and give it a nice stir (this will help deglaze the pan).
- Let it simmer for a couple of minutes. Now add the Dijon mustard and stir in the beef broth. Lower the flame and cook for around 5 minutes.
- Add the sliced beef to the pan and cook for around 3 minutes.
- Also add the sour cream, pepper, and salt, then cook for another 30 seconds.
- Transfer onto a platter and serve with prepared egg noodles.

Nutrition Facts

Calories per Serving: 275 cal Fat: 7g Protein: 23g Carbohydrates: 29g

351. GARLIC ROASTED RIB

Preparation 140 Minutes
Serves 1 Persons

Ingredients

- Rib roast (4-bone standing) - 1
- Sea salt - 1 ½ tablespoon
- Black pepper - 1 teaspoon
- Butter (melted) - 6 tablespoons
- Italian seasoning - 2 tablespoons
- Garlic (minced) - 10 cloves
- Parsley (finely chopped) – for garnish

Directions

- Start by placing a roasting rack into a roasting pan. Now place the rib onto the rack with the fatty side facing up.
- Generously season the meat with black pepper and salt and let it sit at room temperature for at least an hour.
- When the meat is almost done resting, let the oven preheat at 450 degrees Fahrenheit.
- Take a small glass mixing bowl and add in the melted butter, minced garlic and Italian seasoning. Mix well.
- Use a brush to evenly apply the seasoned butter over the ribs. Make sure the meat is evenly coated.
- Place the rib into the oven and roast uncovered for at least 25 minutes. The top of the meat should be dark golden.
- Once done, take the roasted rib out and cover it with a foil. Return to the oven and reduce the temperature of the oven to 350 degrees Fahrenheit. Cook for about 65 to 85 minutes depending upon the doneness desired. (refer to the note)
- Once done, remove the rib and let it rest for about 20 minutes before you carve and serve. Garnish with freshly chopped parsley.

Nutrition Facts

Calories per Serving: 575 cal Fat: 51g Protein: 24g Carbohydrates: 0g

352. BEEF STEW

Preparation 120 Minutes
Serves 6 Persons

Ingredients

- Freshly ground black pepper 1/2 tsp
- Vinegar (red wine) 1 tablespoon
- Minced thyme 1 tablespoon fresh
- Frozen peas 1 cup
- Peeled carrots 3 medium
- Russet potatoes 2 large
- Minced garlic cloves 3
- Coarsely chopped onion 1 large
- Low-fat, chicken broth 4 cups
- divided Cleaned, quartered and steamed cremini mushrooms 1.5 pounds
- Cubed top round 2 pounds
- Olive oil 3 tablespoons
- Seasoning (Italian) 1 tablespoon
- Whole-wheat pastry flour 2 tablespoons

Directions

- Combine the Italian season and flour in a container.
- In a Dutch oven, use medium heat for the olive oil.
- Coat the beef cubes in the flour and Italian seasoning and then brown in the Dutch oven.
- Deglaze the pan after removing the browned beef cubes. Pour in
- 0.25 cups of chicken broth and the mushrooms. Sauté these until they are browned.
- Deglaze the pan after removing the mushrooms. Pour in 0.25 cups of broth. Toss in the garlic and onions. Allow these to sauté for about 4 minutes.
- Place the beef back into the pot and pour in the rest of the broth. Allow this to come to a boil. Once boiling, cover it and allow it to simmer for 45 minutes on low heat. Stir occasionally.
- Toss in the potatoes and carrots. Let all of this cook for about 45 additional minutes.
- Toss in the peas, red wine vinegar, mushrooms, thyme and black pepper. Mix all **Ingredients:** thoroughly.

Nutrition Facts

Calories per Serving: 450 cal Fat: 7g Protein: 25g Carbohydrates: 8g

353. MERLOT MARINATED BEEF KEBEB

Preparation 60 Minutes
Serves 4 Persons

Ingredients:

- ½ cup Merlot or other dry red wine
- 1 tablespoon brown sugar
- 2½ tsp extra virgin olive oil, divided
- 1 teaspoon Dijon mustard 2 garlic cloves, minced
- 1-pound top sirloin or flank steak, trimmed of all visible fat and cut into 1-inch pieces 8 small cremini mushrooms
- 8 cherry tomatoes
- 1 yellow bell pepper, cut into 1-inch pieces
- 1 red onion, cut into 8 wedges
- ½ teaspoon kosher salt
- ¼ teaspoon freshly ground pepper

Directions

- Combine the wine, sugar, 2 teaspoons of the oil, the mustard, and garlic in a shallow dish and stir until the sugar dissolves.
- Add the steak, turn to coat, cover, and refrigerate at least 6 hours or up to 12 hours.
- Preheat the broiler. Brush the rack of a broiler pan with the remaining ½ teaspoon oil.
- Remove the beef from the marinade and discard the marinade.
- Thread the beef, mushrooms, tomatoes, bell pepper, and onion onto eight 8- to 10-inch metal skewers.
- Sprinkle with the salt and ground pepper.
- Place the kebabs on the broiler rack and broil, turning occasionally 6 to 8 minutes for medium-rare, or to the desired degree of doneness.
- Divide the kebabs among 4 plates and serve at once.

Nutrition Facts

Calories per Serving: 208 cal Fat: 7g Protein: 26g Carbohydrates: 8g

354. BEEF AND BROCCOLI STIR-FRY

Preparation 45 Minutes

Serves 4 Persons

Ingredients

- 1/3 cup Chicken Stock or low-sodium chicken broth
- 2 tablespoons reduced-sodium soy sauce
- 1 tablespoon cornstarch 1 teaspoon Asian sesame oil
- 1/4 teaspoon chili-garlic paste
- 6 teaspoons canola oil, divided
- 1 pound top sirloin, trimmed of all visible fat and cut into
- 1/4-inch-thick slices
- 2 Tbs. minced fresh ginger
- 2 garlic cloves, minced
- 4 cups broccoli florets
- 1 small red bell pepper, thinly sliced
- 4 scallions, cut into
- 2-inch pieces
- 1/4 cup chopped fresh cilantro

Directions

- Combine the stock, soy sauce, cornstarch, sesame oil, and chili-garlic paste in a small bowl and stir until the cornstarch dissolves and set aside.
- Heat a large wok or nonstick skillet over medium-
- high heat. Add 2 teaspoons of the canola oil and tilt the pan to coat the bottom evenly. Add half of the beef and cook, stirring constantly, until lightly browned, 2 to 3 minutes. Transfer the beef to a plate. Repeat with 2 teaspoons of the remaining canola oil and the remaining beef.
- Wipe out the wok with paper towels. Add the remaining 2 teaspoons canola oil to the wok over medium-high heat.
- Add the ginger and garlic and cook, stirring constantly, until fragrant, 30 seconds. Add the broccoli, bell pepper, and scallions and cook, stirring constantly, until crisp-tender, 5 minutes.
- Stir in the beef and the stock mixture and cook, stirring constantly, until the sauce is thickened, 30 seconds. Remove from the heat and stir in the cilantro. Divide evenly among 4 plates and serve at once.

Nutrition Facts

Calories per Serving: 269 cal Fat: 13g Protein: 29g Carbohydrates: 10g

355. GRILLED STEAK WITH SWEET PEPPER SALSA

Preparation 45 Minutes

Serves 8 Persons

Ingredients

- 4 beef steaks, trimmed and chopped
- 1 tablespoon and 2 teaspoons olive oil, divided
- 1 tablespoon garlic powder
- 1 teaspoon ground paprika
- 2 teaspoons dried oregano
- 1 teaspoon dried thyme
- 1 teaspoon freshly ground black pepper
- 1/2 teaspoon cayenne pepper
- 2 red bell peppers, cored, seeded, and cut
- 1 yellow bell pepper, cored, seeded, and cut
- 1 orange bell pepper, cored, seeded, and cut
- 2 tablespoons balsamic vinegar
- 2 teaspoons chopped fresh basil

Directions

- Brush the steaks with 2 teaspoons of the olive oil, and set aside.
- In a small bowl stir together the garlic powder, paprika, oregano, thyme, pepper, and cayenne.
- Rub the spice and herb mixture all over the meat. Cover the steaks, and chill them for at least 1 hour.
- Preheat grill to medium-high heat.
- Toss the peppers in a small bowl with the rest of the olive oil and the balsamic vinegar to coat. Grill the peppers until softened and lightly charred, turning.
- Remove them from the grill and chop them coarsely. Transfer them to a bowl and add the basil; stir to combine, then set aside.
- Place the steaks on the barbecue, and grill until desired doneness, turning once, about 12 to 15 minutes total for medium rare.
- Cut the steaks in half, and serve with the grilled peppers

Nutrition Facts

Calories per Serving: 355 cal Fat: 24g Protein: 28g Carbohydrates: 6g

356. SHREDDED BEEF FOR TACOS

Preparation 380 Minutes

Serves 8 Persons

Ingredients

- 2-lb. round roast, cut into large chunks, trimmed of fat
- 1 large onion, chopped
- 2 Tbsp. canola oil
- 2 serrano chilies, chopped
- 3 cloves garlic, minced
- 1 tsp. salt
- 1 cup water

Directions

- Brown meat and onion in oil. Transfer to slow cooker.
- Add chilies, garlic, salt, and water.
- Cover.
- Cook on High 6–8 hours.
- Pull meat apart with two forks until shredded.

Nutrition Facts

Calories per Serving: 184 cal Fat: 9g Protein: 22g Carbohydrates: 4g

357. SLOW COOKER CHIPOTLE BEEF STEW

Preparation 540 Minutes

Serves 6 Persons

Ingredients

- 12 oz frozen whole kernel corn
- 1 lb boneless beef top sirloin, trimmed of fat, cut into 1-inch cubes
- 1 chipotle chile in adobo sauce, finely chopped
- 2 large onions, chopped (2 cups)
- 2 poblano chiles, seeded, diced
- 3 cloves garlic, chopped
- 2 cans diced tomatoes, undrained
- 1 1/2 teaspoons ground cumin
- 1/2 teaspoon salt
- 1/4 teaspoon cracked black pepper

Directions

- Spray 4- to 5-quart slow cooker with cooking spray.
- In small microwavable bowl, microwave corn uncovered on High 2 minutes or until thawed.
- In slow cooker, place corn and all remaining stew **Ingredients:**; mix well.
- Cover and cook on Low heat setting 8 to 10 hours (or High heat setting 4 to 5 hours).
- Divide stew evenly among 6 bowls.
- To serve, top with avocado, tortilla chips, cilantro and sour cream.

Nutrition Facts

Calories per Serving: 310 cal Fat: 10g Protein: 25g Carbohydrates: 30g

358. BLACK PEPPER AND COFFEE STEAK

Preparation 15 Minutes
Serves 4 Persons

Ingredients

- ½ cup ground coffee
- ¼ cup brown sugar
- 4 teaspoons ground ginger
- 2 teaspoons garlic powder 2 teaspoons dried rosemary
- 2 teaspoons cumin
- 1 teaspoon paprika
- 1 teaspoon cayenne
- 6-ounce sirloin steaks
- Salt and pepper

Directions

- In a small bowl, stir together the coffee, brown sugar, ginger, garlic powder, rose- mary, cumin, paprika, and cayenne.
- Season the steaks with salt and pepper and then rub all over with the coffee-spice mixture.
- Cover with plastic wrap and let it marinate in the refrigerator for 1 hour.
- Preheat the oven to 425°F.
- Heat a cast iron skillet over high heat until almost smoking; add the steaks and sear, about 3 minutes per side.
- Transfer the pan to the oven and roast for about 5 minutes (or longer if you prefer a more thoroughly cooked piece of meat).

- Remove from the heat and let sit for about 5 minutes before serving.

Nutrition Facts

Calories per Serving: 400 cal Fat: 22g Protein: 35g Carbohydrates: 16g

359. GARLIC AND LIME BEEF ROAST WITH CILANTRO PESTO

Preparation 35 Minutes
Serves 8 Persons

Ingredients

- 4 garlic cloves, minced
- 1 tablespoon grated lime zest
- 2 teaspoons ground cumin
- ¼ teaspoon ground cayenne
- ¼ teaspoon freshly ground pepper
- 1 (2-pound) eye of round roast, trimmed of all visible fat
- 1 teaspoon kosher salt
- 2 teaspoons extra virgin olive oil Cilantro Pesto (to serve)

Directions

- To make the roast, combine the garlic, lime zest, cumin, cayenne, and pe pper in a small bowl and stir to mix well.
- Cut about 16 deep slits into the roast.
- Insert a pinch of the garlic mixture into each slit.
- Place the roast in a shallow dish, cover, and refrigerate overnight or up to 24 hours.
- Preheat the oven to 325°F.
- Sprinkle the roast with the salt.
- Heat a large heavy-bottomed ovenproof skillet over medium-high heat.
- Add the oil and tilt the pan to coat the bottom evenly.
- Cook the roast, turning occasionally, until well browned on all sides, about 6 minutes.
- Transfer to the oven and bake, turning once, until thermometer inserted into the center of the roast reads 145°F, 40 to 45 minutes.
- 1Cover the roast loosely with foil and let stand about 10 minutes. Cut into thin slices and divide evenly among 8 plates. Serve with the pesto.

Nutrition Facts

Calories per Serving: 246 cal Fat: 14g Protein: 26g Carbohydrates: 2g

360. SESAME BEEF STIR-FRY

Preparation 45 Minutes
Serves 4 Persons

Ingredients

- ½ cup fresh orange juice
- 3 teaspoons soy sauce
- 1 tablespoon grated fresh gingerroot
- 2 teaspoons toasted sesame oil
- 1 teaspoon cornstarch
- Zest from ½ orange
- 1 teaspoon olive oil
- 8 ounces boneless beef sirloin, thinly sliced on a bias
- 2 garlic cloves, minced
- ½ cup bias-sliced green onions
- 1 cup snow peas, cut in half
- 1 cup bean sprouts
- 2 oranges, peeled and sectioned

Directions

- In a small bowl whisk together the orange juice, tamari, gingerroot, sesame oil, cornstarch, and orange zest; set aside.
- Place a large skillet over medium-high heat and add the olive oil. Stir-fry the beef for 4 minutes until desired doneness.
- Add the garlic, green onions, snow peas, and bean sprouts, and stir-fry for about 4 minutes.
- Move the meat and vegetables to the side of the pan and add the sauce.
- Stir until the sauce has thickened and is bubbly. Stir the meat and vegetables into the sauce to coat.
- Add the orange segments and toasted sesame seeds.
- Serve over hot, cooked brown rice (½ cup per serving).

Nutrition Facts

Calories per Serving: 410 cal Fat: 11g Protein: 34g Carbohydrates: 44g

361. BROILED DIJON BURGERS

Preparation 25 Minutes
Serves 6 Persons

Ingredients
- ¼ cup fat-free egg product or 2 egg whites
- 2 tablespoons fat-free (skim) milk
- 2 teaspoons Dijon mustard sauce
- ¼ teaspoon salt
- ⅛ teaspoon pepper
- 1 cup soft bread crumbs
- 1 small onion, finely chopped (⅓ cup)
- 1 lb extra-lean ground beef
- 6 whole-grain burger buns, split, toasted

Directions
- Set oven control to broil.
- Spray broiler pan rack with cooking spray.
- In medium bowl, mix egg product, milk, mustard, salt and pepper.
- Stir in bread crumbs and onion.
- Stir in beef.
- Shape mixture into 6 patties, each about ½ inch thick.
- Place patties on rack in broiler pan.
- Broil with tops of patties about 5 inches from heat 6 minutes.
- Turn; broil until meat thermometer inserted in center of patties reads 160°F, 4 to 6 minutes longer.
- Serve patties in buns.

Nutrition Facts
Calories per Serving: 250 cal Fat: 8g Protein: 22g Carbohydrates: 23g

362. BEEF GRAVY SUPREME
Makes 8 servings

Ingredients:
- 1/2 cup sour cream right before serving.
- **Ingredients:**
- 1/2 large sweet onion, chopped
- 1 tablespoon lard
- 2 pounds ground beef
- 2 stalks celery, chopped
- 4 cloves garlic, minced
- 2 tablespoons fresh parsley, chopped
- 1 mint leaf (1/2 teaspoon, approximately), chopped
- 1/2 teaspoon fresh lemon thyme, chopped
- 1/2 teaspoon lemon pepper
- 1/8 teaspoon dry mustard powder
- 1 teaspoon seasoning salt
- 1/8 teaspoon Stevia Plus or 1/2 packet sucralose
- 1/8 teaspoon hot chili oil or a few grains of cayenne
- 1 1/2 cups water or beef or pork Rich Stock (page 254)
- 1 tablespoon arrowroot mixed into 1/2 cup water

Directions:
- In a small skillet, cook the onion in the lard until translucent and it begins to brown around the edges.
- Meanwhile, in a large skillet with a lid, brown the ground beef. Drain it.
- Add the cooked onion with its juices. Stir in the celery, garlic, parsley, mint, lemon thyme, lemon pepper, mustard powder, seasoning salt,
- Stevia Plus, chili oil, and water or stock. Cover and simmer 45 minutes to 1 hour.
- Just before serving, add the arrowroot/water mixture to the boiling gravy and stir.

Nutrition Facts:
Effective carbohydrates: 2 g Carbohydrates: 3 g Fiber: 1 g Protein: 19 g Fat: 32 g Calories: 382

363. SMOTHERED BURGERS
Servings: 4

Ingredients:
- 4 -pound (150 g) hamburger patties
- 2 tablespoons (28 g or 30 ml)
- butter or olive oil
- ½ cup (80 g) sliced onion
- ½ cup (35 g) sliced mushrooms

Directions:
- Dash of Worcestershire sauce
- Cook the burgers by your preferred method.
- While the burgers are cooking, melt the butter or heat the oil in a small, heavy skillet over medium-high heat.
- Add the onion and mushrooms and sauté until the onions are translucent.
- Add a dash of Worcestershire sauce, stir, and spoon over the burgers.

Nutritional Info:
Carbohydrates 2g, protein. 27 g

364. LOW CARB CABBAGE ROLLS
Serving Size: 12 cabbage rolls
Overall Time: 5 hours and 10

Ingredients:
- Cabbage leaves (12, Napa)
- Beef (1 lb., ground)
- Parmesan (1 cup)
- Garlic (2 cloves, minced)
- Onion powder (1 tsp.)
- Parsley (1 handful)
- Pepper (1/2 tsp.)
- Marinara sauce (1 cup, no sugar added)

Directions:
- Set a saucepan over high heat with about a cup of water and allow to come to a boil. Once boiling, add in your cabbage and cook until slightly tender (about 3 minutes) then quickly cool.
- Pour half of your marinara into your slow cooker.
- Now let's make some cabbage rolls! Begin by combining all your **Ingredients:** except cabbage and marinara sauce in a medium bowl and stir to combine.
- Lay your cabbage leaves on a flat surface and spoon your filling evenly into the leaves. Roll your cabbage leaves to create a roll then place them seam side down in your slow cooker.
- Top with remaining marinara sauce and set to cook on medium heat for 5 hours. Enjoy!

Nutritional Info:
Calories: 242 Carb: 14.2g

365. BEEF & BROCCOLI
Serving Size: 4 servings
Overall Time: 6 hours and 15 minutes

Ingredients:
- Flank steak (2 lbs., sliced in 2" chunks)
- Coconut aminos (2/3 cup)
- Beef broth (1 cup)
- Stevia (3 tbsp.)
- Ginger (1 tsp., grated)
- Garlic (3 cloves, minced)
- Red Pepper Flakes (1/2 tsp.)
- Salt (1/2 tsp.)
- Broccoli (1 head, chopped in florets)

- Bell pepper (1, red, cut into 1" pieces)
- Sesame seeds (1 tsp., garnish)

Directions:

- Set your slow cooker to pre-heat on low.
- Add all your **Ingredients:**, except vegetables, and sesame seeds and leave to cook for about 5 hours.
- Add your vegetables, stir and resume cooking for another hour on low.
- Top with sesame seeds, serve, and serve!

Nutritional Info:
Calories: 430 Carbs: 11g

366. BEEF PECAN

Makes 10 servings

Ingredients:

Sauce:
- 1/2 small onion, chopped
- 4 tablespoons butter
- 3 stalks celery, chopped
- 3/4 teaspoon sea salt
- 1/4 teaspoon marjoram
- 1 teaspoon parsley flakes
- 1/2 teaspoon seasoning salt
- Pinch pepper
- 1/2 cup beef Rich Stock
- 1 3/4 cups half-and-half, cream
- Casserole base:
- 1 1/3 pounds ground beef
- 1/2 teaspoon seasoning salt
- 1 6" head cauliflower, including
- Cooking oil spray
- Topping:
- 3/4 cup almonds, ground
- 1/3 cup soy protein powder
- 1/2 teaspoon sea salt
- 1/4 teaspoon Sweet & Slender
- 1/4 teaspoon SteviaPlus
- 4 tablespoons butter, chilled
- 3/4 cup pecan pieces, broken

Directions:

- In a 4-quart saucepan with a lid, cook the onion in the butter over medium heat until golden, about 10 minutes.
- Add the celery, sea salt, marjoram, parsley, seasoning salt, pepper, and stock to the pan, cover it, and bring it to a boil over medium heat. Reduce the heat to low and simmer it for 10 minutes, until the celery becomes soft.
- Remove the lid, pour in the 1 3/4 cups half-and-half, and heat it over medium-low heat until it is steaming. It is very important that you not boil your half-and-half. Add the half-and-half/arrowroot mixture and set the sauce aside.
- While the onions and celery are cooking, brown the ground beef in a medium-sized frying pan over medium heat with the seasoning salt. When the beef is thoroughly browned, drain it, and set it aside.
- Using a food processor with a chopping blade, finely chop the cauliflower into small pieces that resemble rice.
- A pulsing action works best for this task. Put the chopped cauliflower into a large bowl and set it aside.
- To make the topping, add all of the topping **Ingredients:** EXCEPT the pecans to the food processor bowl,
- and pulse until well combined. Pour the topping into a small mixing bowl and add the broken pecan pieces.
- Set it aside.
- When the sauce is done, add the ground beef and mix it well. Spray a 9" x 13" baking dish with cooking oil spray, and spread the cauliflower evenly over the bottom of the dish.
- Pour the beef and cream mixture over the cauliflower, making sure that all of the cauliflower is covered with the sauce.
- 1Sprinkle the topping evenly over the beef mixture. Bake at 350 F for 35 to 40 minutes, or until the sauce is bubbling and topping is golden brown.
- 1Remove the casserole from the oven and allow it to rest 5 to 10 minutes before serving.

Nutrition Facts:
Effective Carbohydrates: 6 g Carbohydrates: 8 g Fiber: 2 g Protein: 16 g Fat: 42 g Calories: 466

367. BEEF STEW WITH PUMPKIN

Makes 8 Servings

Ingredients:

- 2 pounds beef stew meat
- 2 tablespoons lard
- 1/2 teaspoon seasoning salt
- 1 medium sweet onion, chopped
- 1 clove elephant garlic or 2 cloves garlic, minced
- 2 bay leaves
- 4" tops from 1 bunch celery or 2 large stalks celery, chopped
- 2 small turnips, cut into 3/4" cubes
- 2 carrots, cut into 1/2" chunks (optional)
- 1/2 head cabbage, cut into 1 1/2" cubes
- 1/2 teaspoon seasoning salt
- 1/4 teaspoon basil
- 1/4 lemon pepper
- 1 cup pumpkin puree

Directions:

- Place the stew meat and lard into a 5-quart stockpot. Season it with 1/2 teaspoon seasoning salt.
- Cook over medium heat until the meat loses most of its redness, about 5 minutes.
- Add the onion and garlic, and continue to cook until the onion is translucent, about 3 to 4 minutes.
- Add the bay leaves, celery, turnips, carrots, cabbage, 1/2 teaspoon seasoning salt, basil, and lemon pepper.
- Cover tightly and allow to simmer on low 4 to 6 hours.
- After that time, remove the bay leaves and add the pumpkin to the pot. Simmer uncovered 5 minutes.

Nutrition Facts:
Carbohydrates: 7 g Fiber: 2 g Protein: 33 g Fat: 27 g Calories: 406

368. CHEESEBURGER CASSEROLE

Makes 8 servings

Ingredients:

- 1 pound ground beef
- medium-sized onion or 1 tablespoon dried minced onion
- 4 cloves garlic or 1 teaspoon garlic granules
- 2 slices low-carb bread, cut into 1/2" to 1" cubes
- 1/2 tablespoon olive oil
- 1/2 teaspoon ground sage

- 1/2 tablespoon dried parsley flakes
- 1/2 teaspoon dried rosemary
- 1/4 teaspoon dried marjoram
- 8 drops hot chili oil (about 1/8 teaspoon) or a few grains of cayenne
- 1/2 teaspoon lemon pepper
- 1 tablespoon coconut oil or olive oil
- 1/2 tablespoon butter
- 1/2 teaspoon sea salt
- 1 teaspoon seasoning salt, divided
- 4 eggs
- 2/3 cup yogurt or kejir (sour cream could be used as well)
- 3/4 cup shredded cheese (Cheddar, Colby, or a blend)
- 2 tablespoons grated Parmesan cheese
- Basil, for garnish
- Garlic granules, for garnish

Directions:

- Brown the beef, onions, and garlic in a frying pan over medium heat, about 6 to 8 minutes. Drain it.
- Toss the bread cubes with the olive oil in a 9" x 13" baking pan. Bake in a 350 F oven for about 5 to 8 minutes, until they are nearly dry. Add the beef and seasonings (including 1/2 teaspoon of seasoning salt) to the baking dish and stir it well.
- Combine the eggs, remaining 1/2 teaspoon of seasoning salt, and yogurt in a small dish, mixing well. Pour it over the bread and sausage mixture. Do not stir.
- Sprinkle the cheeses over the top of the casserole. Garnish it with a very small amount of basil and garlic granules.
- Bake the casserole for about 25 minutes at 350 F.
- Refrigerate any leftovers and reheat in the microwave on medium power until they are warm.

Nutrition Facts:

Carbohydrates: 3 g Fiber: 0 g Protein: 18 g Fat: 22 g Calories: 286

369. CHEESE CASSEROLE

Makes 6 Servings

Ingredients:

- 1 1/2 cups sour cream
- 2 eggs
- 1 1/4 cups cheese, shredded (Colby, Monterey jack, Cheddar, mozzarella, etc.)
- 1/4 teaspoon paprika
- 1 1/2 tablespoons minced onion, dried
- 1 teaspoon seasoning salt
- 1/4 teaspoon lemon pepper
- 1 pound cauliflower, chopped into 1/2" pieces (approximately 5 cups, either fresh or frozen)
- 1 pound beef franks, cut into bite-sized pieces
- 1 tablespoon parsley flakes
- Cooking oil spray

Directions:

- In a large mixing bowl, stir together the sour cream, eggs, cheese, and spices (except the parsley).
- Mix thoroughly with a wire whisk, if available. Stir the cauliflower and franks into the cheese mixture.
- Spray a 9" x 13" x 2" pan with cooking oil spray and pour the cauliflower-and-cheese mixture into the pan.
- Spread the mixture evenly and sprinkle it with the parsley flakes.
- Bake it at 350 F for about 25 to 35 minutes, or until it is bubbly and golden.

Nutrition Facts:

Carbohydrates: 8 g Fiber: 2 g Protein: 18 g Fat: 38 g
Calories: 440

370. CHILI BEEF

Preparation Time: 15 minutes
Cooking Time: 25 minutes
Servings: 4

Ingredients:

- 8 ounces lean ground beef
- 4 minced garlic cloves
- 3/4 teaspoon of salt, divided
- 1/4 teaspoon pepper
- 3 teaspoons of olive oil, divided
- 1 medium sliced red onion
- 2 medium zucchinis, sliced
- 1 medium-size green pepper
- 1-28 ounces can dice tomatoes, undrained
- 1 teaspoon of red wine vinegar
- 1 teaspoon of dried basil
- 1 teaspoon of dried thyme

Directions:

- Sauté beef in ¼-teaspoon salt, garlic, pepper, and a teaspoon of oil over medium heat until the beef turns brown. Drain and remove. Keep warm.
- Using the same skillet, pour the remaining oil and sauté onion. Add zucchini and green pepper and stir-cook for 4 to 6 minutes until crisp-tender.
- Stir in the remaining **Ingredients:**. Add beef and cook until heated through—suggested serving over pasta or brown rice.

371. FILLET STEAK WITH DEEP-FRIED ONIONS

Preparation: 30 minutes
Marinade: 24 hours
Cooking Time: 15 minutes
Serves 6

Ingredients:

- 2 lb (900 g) fillet steak
- 3½ oz (100 g) ginger
- 3 tbsp vegetable oil generous
- ¾ cup (200 ml) sweet soy sauce - scant
- 1 tsp sweet paprika
- 1 bunch small onions or scallions
- 1 quart (1 liter) oil for frying
- 5 oz (150 g) mesclun salad
- 1 bunch chives, cut into short lengths
- 1 bunch chervil
- 2 tbsp sherry vinegar
- 3 tbsp olive oil
- salt, freshly ground pepper

Directions:

- The day before, peel and chop the ginger.
- Cut the beef fillet into two lengthways and heat the vegetable oil in a skillet.
- Cook the beef over high heat for 3–4 minutes to seal all over.
- Transfer to a plate. Skim the fat from the skillet then deglaze with generous ¾ cup (200 ml) sweet soy sauce. Add the chopped ginger and the sweet paprika.
- Season generously with pepper and add salt. Reduce until syrupy.

- Put the beef pieces back into the skillet and coat with sauce. Cook for 3–4 minutes over high heat so the surface of the beef becomes "lacquered" in appearance (it should remain rare inside). Place on a rack and cool.
- Wrap tightly in plastic wrap. Chill for 24 hours in the refrigerator.
- The next day, peel the onions, leaving a bit of green stalk attached to their bulbs. Heat the oil for deep-frying to about 355 °F (180 °C) and fry the onions for 5–6 minutes. Drain on absorbent paper towels and season with salt.
- Wash the mesclun and the herbs. Mix the sherry vinegar and the olive oil in a salad bowl and season with salt and pepper. Add the mesclun, chives, and chervil.
- Take the beef out of the refrigerator, discard the plastic wrap, and cut it into slices ¼–½ in (8–10 mm) thick. Arrange on plates with the onions andpour over a little soy sauce. Serve with the salad.

372. RIB OF BEEF

Preparation: 50 minutes
Cooking time: 1½ hours
Standing time: 10 minutes
Serves 6

Ingredients:

- 2 rib steaks weighing about 1½ lb (700 g) each
- 6 large floury potatoes
- 6 small sprigs thyme
- 4 shallots, peeled and chopped
- 2½ cups (600 ml) Burgundy
- 1 tbsp superfine sugar
- generous 1 cup (250 ml) veal broth
- 7 oz (200 g) black grapes, washed
- 7 oz (200 g) Époisses cheese (unpasteurized cow's milk cheese)
- generous 1 tbsp thick sour cream
- 3 tbsp grapeseed oil
- salt, freshly ground pepper

Directions:

- Pre-heat the oven to 355 °F (180 °C).
- Wash the potatoes but leave them unpeeled. Cut 6 pieces of aluminum foil and place 1 sprig of thyme and 1 potato in each. Season with salt and pepper.
- Wrap the potatoes in the foil and place in an ovenproof dish. Bake in the oven for 45 minutes.
- Meanwhile, put the shallots in a large saucepan with the wine and sugar.
- Season with salt and pepper. Reduce the mixture by two-thirds over medium heat. Pour in the veal broth and reduce again, to obtain a smooth sauce. At the end of the cooking time, add the washed grapes.
- Keep this sauce hot in a double boiler.
- Take the potatoes out of the oven, and leave them to cool a little. Discard the aluminum foil, cut a lid in the potatoes, and carefully scoop out the filling.
- Reserve the potato skins. Put the potato filling in a bowl with half the Époisses cheese, cut into small pieces, and the sour cream.
- Season with salt and pepper. Spoon this mixture into the potato skins and place them in an ovenproof dish.
- Slice the remaining Époisses cheese and use to cover the tops of the potatoes.
- 1Heat the grapeseed oil in a skillet and brown the ribs of beef for 2 minutes on each side before placing on a baking tray.
- 1Cook in the oven for 10–15 minutes, depending on whether you like your meat rare, medium, or well done. Take the beef out of the oven and rest it for 10 minutes wrapped in aluminum foil.
- 1Meanwhile, place the potatoes under the broiler to reheat and brown.
- 1Thinly slice the meat and serve with the stuffed potatoes and the Burgundy sauce.

373. STEAK WITH MUSTARD SAUCE

Preparation: 30 minutes
Chilling time: overnight
Cooking time: 3 hours
Serves 6

Ingredients:

- 2 lb (900 g) chuck under blade steak in one piece
- 1 carrot
- 1 leek, white part only
- 1 bunch celery
- 1 onion
- 2 cloves
- 1 bouquet garni
- 1 head frisée salad
- 1 bunch red spring onions
- generous 2 tbsp strong mustard
- 1 anchovy fillet, preserved in oil
- 3 tbsp aged wine vinegar
- ½ cup (100 ml) olive oil - salt, freshly ground pepper

Directions:

- The day before, peel and trim the carrot, leek, celery, and onion, studding the onion with the cloves.
- Truss up the piece of beef with twineas you would a roast and place it in a large saucepan.
- Cover with cold water and bring to a boil. Discard the water, drain the rolled meat, and put it back into the cleaned-out saucepan.
- Add the carrot, onion, celery, leek, and the bouquet garni. Season with salt and pepper.
- Pour in enough cold water to cover, bring to a boil, and cook, covered, for 3 hours over low heat, skimming the surface regularly.
- Take off the heat and cool the chuck steak in the saucepan.
- Drain the meat and reserve ½ cup (100 ml) of the cooking liquid. Wrap it tightly in several layers of plastic wrap. Put the meat and reserved cooking broth in the refrigerator to chill overnight.
- The next day, wash the salad. Peel and thinly slice the red onions. Take the meat out of the refrigerator, discard the plastic wrap, and thinly slice the rolled steak.
- Discard the twine. Strain the reserved broth.
- Put the mustard in a high-sided container and add the anchovy fillet, vinegar, olive oil, and strained broth. Season with salt and pepper.
- 1Blend with a hand blender until you have a smooth salad dressing.
- 1Divide the salad, red onions, and the chuck steak slices among 6 plates or

bowls then add a generous amount of salad dressing to each. (Sprinkle with a few golden croutons fried in oil if desired.)

374. BEEF FILLET WITH PORT

Preparation: 35 minutes
Cooking time: 45 minutes
Standing time: 15 minutes
Serves 6

Ingredients:

- 3 lb 11 oz (1.2 kg) beef fillet in one piece
- 3¼ lb (1.5 kg) floury potatoes
- 3½ oz (100 g) capers in vinegar
- 3 tbsp grapeseed oil
- 1¼ cups (300 ml) milk
- generous 4 tbsp thick sour cream
- 13 tbsp (180 g) butter
- 14 oz (400 g) button mushrooms
- 1¼ cups (300 ml) port
- generous 1 cup (250 ml) veal broth
- salt, freshly ground pepper

Directions:

- Pre-heat the oven to 400 °F (200 ° C).
- Peel the potatoes and cut them into large pieces. Cook for 20 minutes in a saucepan filled with salted water.
- Drain the capers and chop. Heat the milk in a saucepan.
- Drain the potatoes and mash through a ricer, add the hot milk, 3 tablespoons sour cream, 9 tablespoons of butter (130 g), cut into pieces, and the capers.
- Season with salt and pepper. Keep the mashed potatoes warm in a bain-marie.
- Place the meat in an ovenproof dish. Pour over grapeseed oil and dot with 1½ tablespoons (20 g)of diced butter; season with salt and pepper.
- Cook in the oven for 10 minutes then lower the temperature to 355 °F (180 °C) and cook for a further 10–15 minutes.
- Meanwhile, wash and thinly slice the mushrooms. Heat the remaining butter in a skillet and cook the mushrooms for 5–7 minutes.
- Season with salt and pepper then transfer to a plate. Deglaze the skillet with the port and reduce by two-thirds. Pour in the veal broth, season with salt and pepper, and reduce by half. Add the remaining sour cream, bring to a boil, and cook for 3 minutes over high heat, whisking constantly.
- Add the mushrooms to the sauce and keep warm.
- 1Take the meat out of the oven, wrap in aluminium foil, and rest for 15 minutes. Thinly slice the meat and serve immediately with the preflavored mashed potatoes and the mushroom sauce.

375. GRILLED FLANK STEAK WITH CUMIN AIOLI

Makes 6 servings

Ingredients:

- 1 Tbsp (15 ml) cumin seeds
- 1 large egg
- 1 tsp (5 ml) Dijon mustard
- 1/2 tsp (2.5 ml) sea salt
- 1 garlic dove, minced
- 1/2 cup (120 ml) vegetable oil
- 4 tsp (20 ml) freshly squeezed lemon juice
- 1/2 cup (120 ml) extra-virgin olive oil
- 3 Tbsp (45 ml) extra-virgin olive oil
- 1/2 tsp (2.5 ml) sea salt
- 2 garlic doves, minced
- 1/2 tsp (2.5 ml) freshly ground black pepper
- 1-21/2 lb (1.1 kg) flank steak

Directions:

- To make the cumin aioli: Place the cumin seeds in a small frying pan and stir over medium heat for 2minutes, or until they darken a shade.
- Remove from the heat.
- Finely grind half of the cumin seeds in a coffee grinder or with a mortar and pestle.
- In a blender or food processor, combine the egg, mustard, salt, garlic, and the ground cumin seeds.
- Process briefly to blend. With the motor running, add the vegetable oil in a slow, steady stream.
- Pour in the lemon juice and then slowly add the olive oil until the aioli is emulsified.
- If the mixture seems too thick, add a spoonful or two of water. Scrape the aioli into a bowl and stir in the whole cumin seeds.
- Cover and refrigerate.
- To make the steak: In a small bowl, mix the oil, salt, garlic, and pepper. Spread on both sides of the steak.
- Cover and refrigerate up to overnight.
- 1Preheat the grill or broiler. Grill or broil the steak for 3 to 4 minutes on each side for medium-rare.
- 1Remove the steak from the heat and let it sit for a few minutes.
- 1Slice very thinly across the grain and serve with the aioli on the side.

Nutrition Facts:

Carbohydrates: 1.5 g Fiber: 0.3g
Protein: 42.7 g Fat: 58 g
Calories: 701

376. ROAST BEEF MELT

Ingredients:

- 2 slices leftover roast beef
- 2 green pepper slices -- cut
- in 2 inch pieces
- 3 mushrooms -- sliced
- 2 onion slice -- cut in 2 inch
- pieces1 tablespoon butter
- 2 tablespoons LC Ranch
- Dressing
- Mozzarella cheese to cover

Directions:

- The quantities are approximate - add to your liking. Place roast beef on a heat proof plate or pan.
- Saute vegetables in butter until tender-crisp and place on top of beef.
- Spread dressing over the vegetables and top with mozzarella cheese.
- Broil until cheese is hot and bubbly.
- This is a quick and easy way to use up leftover roast.

Nutrition Facts:

Effective carbohydrates: 6.6 g
Carbohydrates: 8.1 g Fiber: 1.5 g
Protein: 43.7 g Fat: 48.3 g Calories: 648

377. RED HOT SIRLOIN

Ingredients:

- 1 pound Beef top sirloin
- 1/2 cup FRANK"S Red Hot
- 3 tablespoons butter
- Salt a Fresh cracked pepper

Directions:

- Season the sirloin with salt and pepper and grill till desired doneness.
- In a saucepan over low heat melt butter and hot sauce together until mixture is hot and blended.
- Pour directly over hot sirloin and serve.

Nutrition Facts:

Carbohydrates: 1.1 g Fiber: 6.5 g Protein: 53.7 g Fat: 28.3 g Calories: 348

378. HAMBURGERS

Makes 4 servings

Ingredients:

- 1 lb ground beef
- Salt and black pepper to taste
- 1 clove garlic, minced (optional)
- 1 Tbsp chopped parsley (optional)
- 1 Tbsp chopped chives or scallions (optional)
- 1 Tbsp olive oil or butter (if ground beef is very lean)

Directions:

- If you just want a simple burger, season beef with salt and pepper and form into 4 patties.
- Add the garlic and/or parsley and chives to the beef mixture if you like an added flavor. Slowly preheat a skillet.
- Add oil or butter if beef is lean. Saute patties about 3 minutes per side.
- Pour pan drippings over burgers.

Nutrition Facts:

Carbohydrates: .4 g Protein: 4 oz

379. KEEMA

Makes 4 servings

Ingredients:

- 1/4 cup (60 ml) vegetable oil
- 2 bay leaves
- 1 3-inch (7.5-cm) cinnamon stick
- 1 1/2 cups (36000) finely chopped onion
- 1 Tbsp. (15 00) grated fresh ginger
- 5 garlic cloves, minced
- 1 Tbsp. (15 ml) ground coriander
- 1 Tbsp. (15 00) ground cumin
- 1 tsp. (500) turmeric
- 1 Tbsp. (15 ml) tomato past
- e2 lb. (908 g) lean ground beef
- 1/2 cup (120 ml) water
- 1/4 tsp. (1.2 00) freshly grated nutmeg
- 1/4 tsp. (1.2 00) ground mace
- 1 tsp. (5 00) sea salt
- 1/4 to 1/2 tsp. (1.2 to 2.5 ml) cayenne pepper

Directions:

- Heat the oil in a large pot over high heat. Add the bay leaves and cinnamon.
- Cook for a few moments until the bay leaves darken. Add the onion, ginger, and garlic.
- Cook, stirring occasionally, over medium heat until the onion turns dark brown.
- Add the coriander, cumin, and turmeric.
- Cook for 2 minutes. Stir in the tomato paste.
- Add the beef and cook, breaking up the pieces, until browned. Add the water, nutmeg, mace, salt, and cayenne to taste. Turn the heat to low.
- Cover and simmer for 1 hour, stirring frequently and adding more water as needed to prevent the mixture from sticking. Remove the bay leaves.
- After adding the water and spices, cover the pot and bake at 300 F (150 C) for 1 hour, checking occasionally to make sure that the water has not evaporated.
- This is great with a spinach salad, zucchini, or green beans.

Nutrition Facts:

Carbohydrates: 8.1 g Fiber: 1.5 g Protein: 43.7 g Fat: 48.3 g Calories: 648

380. LOW-CARB STROGANOFF STEW

Makes 8 servings

Ingredients:

- 1 medium onion, chopped
- 3 cloves garlic, minced
- 3 stalks celery, chopped
- 2 turnips, cut up
- 2 pounds beef stew meat, cubed
- 1 1/2 cups cabbage, chopped
- 1 teaspoon seasoning salt
- 1/2 teaspoon lemon pepper
- 1/4 teaspoon paprika
- 1/2 teaspoon dill weed, dried
- 1 1/2 teaspoons lime juice (fresh is always best!)
- 1/2 cup water
- 1 1/2 cups sour cream

Directions:

- Combine all of the **Ingredients:**, except the sour cream, in a large pot with a lid.
- Cover the pot and bring the stew to a simmer.
- Simmer over medium-low heat for about 20 to 30 minutes, or until the vegetables are becoming tender.
- In the last 5 minutes of cooking, add the sour cream.

Nutrition Facts:

Carbohydrates: 7 g Fiber: 1 g Protein: 34 g Fat: 33 g
Calories: 461

381. MANDARIN BEEF SAUTE

Makes 4 servings

Ingredients:

- 1 Tbsp roasted sesame oil (see Note 1)
- 1/2 tsp minced fresh ginger
- 1/3 tsp crushed red pepper flakes (optional)
- 1/3 cup sliced button mushrooms
- 1 lb thinly sliced lean beef (see Note 2)
- 1 Tbsp soy sauce
- 2 Tbsp cider vinegar

Directions:

- In a large heavy skillet, heat oil on a low temperature.

- Add ginger, red pepper flakes, and mushrooms, then saute for 2-3 minutes.
- Add sliced beef to the skillet and increase temperature to a medium-high setting.
- Stir continuously for 3-4 minutes. Stir in soy sauce and vinegar.
- Immediately remove skillet from burner and serve warm.
- This recipe will keep in the refrigerator for 3-4 days.
- It will store in the freezer for 2-3 months.

Nutrition Facts:
Carbohydrates: 1.2 g Protein: 4.1 oz

382. MARVELOUS MEATBALLS

Makes about 26 meatballs

Ingredients:
- 1 pound Sharron's Pork Sausage
- 1 1/2 pounds ground beef
- 3/4 cup pork rinds, ground
- 1/4 cup onion, minced
- 2 tablespoons parsley flakes
- 1/4 teaspoon dry mustard powder
- 1 teaspoon seasoning salt
- 3 cloves garlic, minced
- 1/4 teaspoon lemon pepper
- 2 eggs
- 1/3 cup Almond Milk unsweetened, or cream

Directions:
- Combine all of the **Ingredients:** in a large mixing bowl. Mix well and allow the meat mixture to rest at least 5 minutes.
- Form the meat into 2" balls.
- Bake them in a 9" x 13" x 2" baking pan about 20 minutes at 375 F, or barbecue over medium coals the same amount of time.
- They are done when they feel firm to the touch, no longer mushy.
- This easy meal can be served with your choice of dipping sauces.
- Freeze leftover meatballs for a quick meal!
- Reheat at 375 F for about 25 minutes or until hot.

Nutrition Facts:
Per Meatball.
Carbohydrates: 1 g Fiber: 1 g Protein: 11 g Fat: 17 g
Calories: 205

383. MEATBALL SOUP

Makes about 10 servings

Ingredients:
- 1/2 medium onion, chopped
- 4 cloves garlic, minced
- 1 to 2 tablespoons lard
- Seasoning salt, to taste
- 6 cups beef Rich Stock (page 254)
- 1 carrot, chopped (optional)
- 3 stalks celery, chopped
- 3 cups cabbage, chopped into 1" cubes
- 1 1/2 cups broccoli (or cauliflower) stems, peeled and chopped or chopped zucchini
- 1 bay leaf
- 1/2 teaspoon marjoram, dried
- 1/8 teaspoon fennel/anise seed
- 1/2 tablespoon parsley
- Salt and lemon pepper to taste

Directions:
- In a 5-quart pot with a lid, cook the onion and the garlic in the lard with seasoning salt until they are beginning to become slightly golden, about 10 minutes.
- Add all of the remaining **Ingredients:**, except the meatballs, cover the pot, and simmer while preparing the meatballs, about 30 minutes.
- Meanwhile, prepare the meatballs.
- Bake them on a baking sheet for about 15 minutes.
- Add the cooked meatballs to the soup and simmer covered for another 20 minutes.

Nutrition Facts:
Carbohydrates: 5 g Fiber: 2 g Protein: 30 g Fat: 46 g Calories: 588

384. NIGHTSHADE-FREE TACO MEAT

Makes about 6 servings

Ingredients:
- 1 1/2 pounds ground beef
- 1/2 medium onion, chopped (about 1/2 cup)
- 2 cloves garlic, minced or 1 tsp garlic powder
- 2 tablespoons butter
- 1/4 cup water (didn't add this)
- 2 teaspoons hot chili oil (added only half)
- 1 teaspoon lemon pepper (1 1/2 tsp Penzey's Singapore Seasoning as substitute for the lemon pepper and cumin)
- 1/2 teaspoon oregano
- 1 teaspoon sea salt
- 1/2 teaspoon cumin, ground
- 1/2 teaspoon Sweet & Slender (or the same of SteviaPlus) 1/4 tsp powdered stevia

Directions:
- In a large skillet, brown the ground beef and drain it in a large colander.
- While the beef is draining, cook the onion and garlic in the butter until golden, about 5 minutes.
- Add the beef and remaining ingredients
- Simmer until most of the moisture has evaporated, about 5 minutes.

Nutrition Facts:
Carbohydrates: 2 g Fiber: 1g Protein: 19 g Fat: 36 g Calories: 409

385. BREAKFAST CASSEROLE

Serving Size: 6 servings
Overall Time: 6 hours and 10 minutes

Ingredients:
- Coconut oil (2 tbsp.)
- Leek (1 ⅓ cups, sliced)
- Garlic (2 tsp., mince)
- Kale (1 cup, chopped)
- Egg (8 large)
- Butternut squash (⅔ cups, peeled, cored, grated)
- Beef sausage (1 ½ cups)

Directions:

- Set a skillet with coconut oil over medium heat and allow to melt.
- Once melted, add in your garlic, kale, and leeks then sauté until fork tender.
- Combine all your **Ingredients:**, including your cooked veggies, to your slow cooker basket and all eggs, butternut squash, beef sausage and sautéed vegetables.
- Allow to cook for 6 hours on low. Serve, and enjoy.

Nutritional Info:

Calories: 280   Carbs: 7.2g

386. BEEF TIPS IN CROCKPOT

Serving Size: 8 servings

Prepl Time: 8 hours and 10 minutes

Ingredients:

- Stew meat (2 lbs. Lean)
- Lipton onion soup mix (2 envelopes)
- Mushroom soup (2 cans, 10.5 oz., 98% fat free)
- Red wine (1 cup; beef broth can be used as substitute)
- Sliced mushrooms (2 cans; 8 oz., drained)

Directions:

- In a crock pot, combine all **Ingredients:**.

Cook on low for 6-8 hours.

Nutritional Info:

Calories: 302   Carbs: 1.2g

387. ORANGE CINNAMON BEEF STEW

Serving Size: 4 servings

Overall Time: 2½ hours and 20 mins

Ingredients:

- Beef stew (2 lbs., grass fed. Cut in 1" pcs and pat dry)
- Salt (1 tsp.) + pepper (1 tsp.)
- Coconut oil (2-3 tbsp)
- Medium onion (1 medium, diced)
- Carrot (1, diced)
- Celery (1 stalk, diced)
- Garlic (2 cloves, minced)
- Orange (½ cup plus zest)
- Balsamic vinegar (¼ cup)
- Water (4 cups)
- Ground cinnamon (2 tsp.)
- Bay leaves (3)
- Rosemary (1 tbsp., finely chopped)
- Fresh thyme (1 tbsp., finely chopped)
- Fresh sage (1 tbsp., finely chopped)
- Small rutabagas (4 small, spiralized)

Directions:

- Heat oven to 350 degrees Fahrenheit.
- In a Dutch oven, heat coconut oil over the medium high flame. Add a layer of meat pieces ensuring that enough space is in between each piece. Dribble with pepper and salt and fry until all sides are golden brown. Transfer to a plate and set aside. Continue in batches until all pieces are done, adding more oil if necessary, so that pot bottom does not burn or stick.
- After pieces of meat have been browned and removed from Dutch oven; place onions, celery, carrot, and garlic in a pot and sauté until fragrant, roughly min.
- Add orange juice and mix well. Now, add browned meat, zest, water, balsamic vinegar, salt, cinnamon, bay leaves and pepper.
- Bake in the oven until meat is extremely tender, almost falling apart, roughly 2 - 2 ½ hours.
- Mix in thyme, rosemary, and sage and cook for a further 10-15 minutes.
- In the meantime, place rutabaga into a steaming basket; add a pinch of salt and steam over a pot of boiling water for about 5 minutes, until firm.
- Serve immediately (for a tasty boost of healthy fat, add a dribble of extra-virgin olive.)

Nutritional Info:

Calories: 447   Carbs: 21g

388. BEEF & PUMPKIN STEW

Serving Size: 4 servings

Overall Time: 6 hours and 5 mins

Ingredients:

- Steak (¾ lb., stewing)
- Pumpkin (½ lb.)
- Coconut oil (6 tbsp.)
- Sage (1 tsp.)
- Mixed herbs (1 tsp.)
- Rosemary (2 tsp.)
- Thyme (2 tbsp.)
- Salt & pepper

Directions:

- Set slow cooker on high.
- Remove excess fat from your stewing steak and place steak in the slow cooker.
- Add 3 tbsp. of coconut oil; rub in a dash of pepper and salt.
- Put to cook for 60 mins on high temperature.
- Transfer steak from slow cooker to a bowl. Add the seasoning and remaining portion of coconut oil and combine thoroughly. Return to slow cooker along with pumpkin and cook for another 3 hours on low.
- Garnish with fresh herbs and serve.

Nutritional Info:

Calories: 263   Carbs: 12g

389. PIE WITH MUSHROOMS, SMOKED CHEDDAR, BACON, AND SOUR CREAM

Makes 9 servings

Ingredients:

- 3 lb (1.3 kg) lean ground beef
- 1 cup (240 ml) finely diced onion
- 1 cup (240 ml) finely diced celery
- 1/4 tsp (1.2 ml) dried thyme or 1 tsp. (2.5 ml) fresh thyme leaves
- 1 Tbsp (15 ml) tomato paste
- Sea salt and freshly ground black pepper
- 2 Tbsp (30 ml) unsalted butter
- 1/2 lb (227 g) mushrooms, coarsely chopped
- 2 lb (908 g) cauliflower, trimmed
- 2 cups (480 ml) shredded smoked cheddar cheese
- 1/4 cup (60 ml) sour cream
- 2 Tbsp (30 ml) unsalted butter
- 1 large egg
- 8 bacon slices, cooked until crisp and crumbled
- Paprika

Directions:

- To make the beef: Place the beef in a large pot and cook over high heat, crumbling the meat with a spoon until it loses its raw, red color. Stir in the onion, celery, thyme, and tomato paste. Season lightly with salt and pepper.

- Cover tightly, turn the heat to low, and cook for 20 minutes, stirring occasionally. Add a touch of water if the mixture looks too dry; it should look juicy but not wet.
- Heat the butter in a large frying pan over high heat until the foam subsides. Add mushrooms and cook briskly until the water has evaporated and the mushrooms are soft. Add the mushrooms to the beef mixture and cook for 10 minutes longer.
- To make the cauliflower puree: Chop the cauliflower, including the core, into chunks.
- Place in a large potand add enough water to cover the pieces by 1 inch (2.5 em). Bring to a boil over high heat and cook until extremely tender, about 20 minutes.
- Drain well. Transfer to a food processor and blend until smooth. Remove 1 cup of the puree and stir into the pot with the beef.
- To the remaining cauliflower in the food processor, add the cheese, sour cream, and butter; blend well.
- Add the egg and blend until smooth. Add the bacon and pulse once or twice to combine.
- Preheat the oven to 350 F (175 C). Spread the beef mixture in a 9 X 9-inch (22.5 X 22.5-cm) deep baking dish. Cover with the cauliflower mixture and smooth the top. Sprinkle with the paprika or make crisscross lines, dots, or whatever strikes your
- fancy.
- 1Place the baking dish on a large rimmed baking sheet to catch any drips. Bake for 45 minutes, or until bubbly and browned. Let sit for 10 minutes before serving.

Nutrition Facts:

Carbohydrates: 9.1 g Fiber: 3.3 g Protein: 42.9 g Fat: 29.5 g Calories: 475

390. SLIGHTLY ITALIANO MEAT LOAF

Makes 12 servings

Ingredients:

- 1/4 lb. (112 g) pancetta, diced
- 3 large eggs
- 3 lb. (1.3 kg) lean ground beef
- 1/2 cup (120 ml) freshly grated Parmesan cheese
- 2 Tbsp. (30 ml) finely chopped fresh parsley
- 1/2 cup (120 ml) finely chopped onion
- 2 garlic cloves, minced
- 1 tsp. (5 ml) sea salt
- 1/2 tsp. (2.5 ml) freshly ground black pepper
- 2 Tbsp. (30 ml) finely diced sun-dried tomatoes

Directions:

- Preheat the oven to 350 F (175 C).
- Place the pancetta in a food processor and process until finely ground. Add the eggs and pulse to combine.
- Place in a large bowl and add the beef, cheese, parsley, onion, garlic, salt, pepper, and tomatoes.
- Mix well with your hands and pack into a 12 x 4 1/2-inch (30 x 11.5 cm) loaf pan.
- Bake for 1 1/4 hours. Let cool for 15 minutes before slicing.

Nutrition Facts:

Carbohydrates: 1.2 g Fiber: 0.2 g Protein: 27.6 g Fat: 12.7 g Calories: 236

391. STUFFED CABBAGE ROLLS

Makes 4 servings

Ingredients:

- 1 pound lean ground beef
- 1 egg
- 1/4 cup cream or Almond Milk (page 240
- 2 tablespoons minced onion, dried, or 1/4 cup fresh
- 1/2 teaspoon seasoning salt
- 1/4 teaspoon lemon pepper
- 1/2 teaspoon Italian seasonings
- 4 large cabbage leaves

Directions:

- Combine the beef, egg, cream, and seasonings well in a mixing bowl.
- Divide the meat into 4 equal parts and form each into a small loaf shape. Set them aside.
- Bring a medium-sized pot of water to a boil.
- Turn it off and place the cabbage leaves into the pot for 5 minutes, until they are soft and pliable.
- Place the leaves on a large plate or cutting board.
- Put a piece of meat on a cabbage leaf and wrap it end over end, tucking the ends, as if it were a small burrito.
- Place the rolls into an 8" square baking dish, and pour the stewed tomatoes or tomato sauce over the top.
- Bake at 350 F for about 45 minutes to 1 hour, or until they test at 170 F with a meat thermometer.

Nutrition Facts:

Carbohydrates: 3 g Fiber: 1 g Protein: 22 g Fat: 28 g Calories: 363

392. TANGERINE-BEEF STIR-FRY

Eating Light Participants 4

Ingredients:

- 2 tangerines 8 tangerines
- 1/4 cup sherry,
- 1 tbsp. ginger, fresh,
- 1 tsp. sesame oil
- 1 tsp. cornstarch
- 1 tbsp. cornstarch 4 tbsp.
- 2 tbsp. soy sauce, low sodium 8 tbsp.
- 1 lb. flank steak, cut into 1/8 in. slices
- 4 tsp. oil,
- 1 large pepper, red, thinly sliced
- 6 oz. snow peas, strings removed
- 3 onions, green cut into 1 in pieces

Directions:

- To prepare for group:
- With veggie peeler, remove peel in strips from tangerines. Bag peel. Remove remaining pith.
- Hold tangerine over 2 cup measuring cup and cut on either side of membranes to remove each segment, allowing fruit and juice to drop into cup.
- Squeeze juice from remaining membranes until mixture equals 1/2 cup. Discard seeds, if any.
- Stir in sherry, ginger,sesame oil, and 1 tsp. of cornstarch. Bag.
- Mix soy sauce and 1 tbsp. of cornstarch. Bag with beef.
- Bag pepper, peas, and green onion together.
- Cooking Day:

- Thaw.
- In a non-stick, 12 inch skillet on med-high heat, heat 2 tsps oil until hot.
- Add strips of peel and cook until lightly browned. Transfer to a bowl.
- To same skillet, add veggies and toss to coat with oil, cook 1 minute. Add 1/2 cup water and cook 2 minutes or until veggies are tender-crisp. Transfer to bowl with peel.
- To same skillet, add 1 tsp. oil and heat until very hot. Add half of beef mixture and cook until beef is lightly browned, stirring frequently. Transfer to bowl. Repeat with remaing 1 tsp. oil and beef.
- Add juice mixture to skillet and heat to boiling. Boil 1 minute. Return beef mixture to skillet and heat through.

Nutrition Facts
Calories 330 fiber 4g Protein 25g cholest 59 mg Carbs 17g sodium 385 mg Total Fat 18g Sat Fat 6g

393. PHILLY CHEESESTEAK LETTUCE CUPS

Ingredients:
- 3 ounces lean beef steak
- 1/3 cup sliced mushrooms
- 1/4 cup tinly sliced onions
- 1 slice fat-free American cheese
- 2 leaves romaine, butter or green leaf lettuce

Directions
- Slice meat into thin strips. Coat medium pan with non-stick cooking spray.
- Add mushrooms and onions; cook over medium heat for 5 minutes, stirring occasionally, until onions are slightly browned. Set aside.
- Remove pan from heat and re-coat with non-stick cooking spray.
- Cook steak strips over medium heat for 1-2 minutes, flipping halfway through.
- Break cheese slice into small strips.
- Place cheese on top of meat--still in the pan-- and continue to cook until cheese melts.
- Remove from heat; mix beef strips with veggies and serve on lettuce leaves.

Nutritional Facts
Calories 197 Protein 13.5 g Fat 7.5 g (3 g saturated) Cholesterol 55 mg Carbohydrates 7 g

394. LOW-CARB BEEF STROGANOFF

Ingredients:
- 1 1/2 lb beef tenderloin -- thin strips
- 2 tbsp all-purpose flour
- 2 tbsp butter
- 2 tbsp olive oil
- 1 1/2 cups beef bouillon
- 1/4 cup sour cream
- 2 tbsp tomato paste
- 1/2 tsp paprika
- salt to taste

Directions
- Dredge beef in flour. In a heavy skillet, melt butter with oil. Brown the beef (about 5 minutes).
- Slowly add bouillon to beef, stirring well.
- Bring to a boil. Combine sour cream, tomato paste, paprika, and salt.
- Slowly stir sour cream mixture into beef mixture.
- Turn heat to low and bring to a bare simmer.
- Cook 15-20 minutes, stirring frequently and never allowing mixture to boil.

Nutritional Facts:
652 Calories 55g Fat (76.5% calories from fat) 32g Protein 6g Carbohydrate

395. INDIAN RED CURRY

Ingredients:
- 1 lb beef stew
- 1 tbsp butter
- 1/2 tsp curry paste -- or powder
- 1 dash cinnamon, cardamom, and pepper
- 1 cup canned coconut milk
- 1/2 cup red pepper
- 1 tsp paprika
- 1 garlic clove

Directions
- Brown meat and garlic in butter, then add spices and stir fry few minutes.
- Add red pepper and coconut milk.
- Reduce heat and simmer til done (2-3 hours, add water if necessary.)

Nutritional Facts
248 Calories 20g Fat (70.5% calories from fat) 9g Protein
10g Carbohydrate

396. SLOW COOKER CORNED BEEF AND CABBAGE

Ingredients:
- 4 cups Hot Water
- 2 tbsp Cider Vinegar
- 2 tbsp Splenda
- 1/2 tsp Pepper -- Freshly Ground
- 1 Large Onion -- Cut Into Wedges
- 3 lb Corned Beef -- 1.5kg With Spices
- 1 Cabbage cored And Cut into 10 Wedges

Directions
- In a 6 quart - 6litre crock pot, combine the water, vinegar, splenda, pepper, and onions, mixing well.
- Place the corned beef into the mixture.
- Cover and cook on high heat for 4 hours.
- Remove the lid and scatter the cabbage wedges over the top.
- Cover and continue cooking on high 3 to 4 hours longer, or until the beef is tender.
- To serve, carve the beef into slices and serve with the cabbage, with some of the cooking liquid spooned over the beef to keep it moist.

Nutritional Facts
248 Calories 20g Fat (70.5% calories from fat) 9g Protein
10g Carbohydrate 2g Dietary Fiber 35mg Cholesterol

397. SIRLOIN STEAK STRIPS

Ingredients:
- 2 lb Beef, top sirloin steak, lean, raw
- 1 pinch salt and pepper (to taste)
- 1 tsp minced garlic
- 1/2 cup red wine (dry)
- 1/2 cup fat free unsalted beef broth
- 2 tbsp dijon mustard
- 3 tbsp chopped parsley

Directions

- Cut the steak into strips about 3/4 inch thick, and heat a large skillet coated with non-stick cooking spray over medium high heat.
- Sauté the steak on both sides until it is done, about 5 to 7 minutes, and season with the salt and pepper.
- Remove the meat, and add the garlic and wine to the pan, and boil until reduced by half, stirring well, and add the beef broth and mustard, stirring until blended.
- Boil until slightly thickened, and add the parsley, and return the meat to the pan, heat with the sauce, and serve.

Nutritional Facts

Calories 239.1 Total Carbs 1.8g Dietary Fiber 0.1g Sugars 0.1g

398. SPICY BEEF ROAST

Servings: 10

Ingredients:

- 1 3-1/2 to 4 pound boneless beef chuck roast
- Salt and black pepper
- 2 Tbsp cooking oil (optional) (Although there is
- a healthier oil out there called smart beat)
- 1/2 cup water
- 1 Tbsp Worcestershire Sauce
- 1 Tbsp tomato paste
- 2 cloves garlic, minced
- Several dashes bottled hot pepper sauce
- 1 Tbsp cornstarch
- 1 Tbsp cold water
- 1 Tbsp prepared horseradish
- 1/2 tsp salt

Directions

- Trim fat from meat. If necessary, cut meat to fit into a 3/1/2 to 4-1/2 quart slow cooker.
- Sprinkle meat with salt and pepper.
- If desired, in a large skillet cook meat in hot oil over medium heat until brown on all sides.
- Drain off fat. Place meat in cooker, In a small bowl combine the 1/2 cup water, the Worcestershire sauce, tomato paste, garlic, and hot pepper sauce.
- Pour over meat in slow cooker.
- Cover and cook on low-heat for 10-12 hours or on high=heat setting for 5 to 6 hours.
- Transfer meat to a serving platter, reserving cooking liquid, Cover meat with foil to keep warm.
- For gravy, strain cooking liquid and skim fat.
- Transfer liquid to a medium saucepan,
- In a small bowl combine corn starch and the Tblsp water; stir into liquid in saucepan.
- 1Cook and stir over medium heat until thickened and bubblu. Cook and stir for 2 minutes more.
- 1Stir in the horseradish an 1/2 tspn salt. Serve gravy with meat.

Nutritional Facts

Calories 203 Fat 6 g Cholesterol 94mg Sodium 227 mg

Carbohydrates 2 g Protein 34 g

399. TERIYAKI KABOBS

Servings: 1

Ingredients:

- 1/3 C. soy sauce
- 2 T. vegetable oil
- 1 T. brown sugar
- 1 garlic clove, minced
- 1 tsp. ground ginger
- 1 tsp. seasoned salt
- 1 1/2 lb. boneless sirloin steak, cut into 1 1/4–inch cubes
- 12 whole mushrooms
- 1 large green pepper, cut into 1 1/2–inch pieces
- 1 large onion, cut into wedges
- 12 cherry tomatoes

Directions

- In a bowl, combine soy sauce, oil, brown sugar, garlic, ginger and salt; mix well.
- Pour half of the marinade into a large resealable plastic bag or shallow glass container; add beef and turn to coat.
- Seal or cover; refrigerate for 4 to 8 hours, turning occasionally.
- Cover and refrigerate remaining marinade.
- Drain meat; discard marinade.
- On metal or soaked bamboo skewers, alternate meat, mushrooms, green pepper, onion and cherry tomatoes; leaving 1/4 inch between each.
- Grill, uncovered, over medium heat for 3 minutes on each side.
- Baste with reserved marinade.
- Continue turning and basting for 8 to 10 minutes or until meat is cooked thoroughly.

Nutritional Facts

264 calories 590 mg sodium 79 mg cholesterol 5 gm carbohydrate 39 gm protein 10 gm fat

400. MEATLOAF

Servings: 1

Ingredients:

- 1 pound ground skinless turkey breast
- 1 pound lean ground beef
- 1/2 medium onion, minced
- 1 clove garlic, minced
- 3 tablespoon minced fresh parsley
- 1 egg
- 1/4 cup low-fat (1%) milk
- 1 teaspoon dry mustard
- 1/4 teaspoon salt
- 1/4 teaspoon ground white pepper
- 1/8 teaspoon nutmeg
- 2 slices white bread, lightly toasted
- and made into coarse crumbs
- 2 tablespoons ketchup
- 2 tablespoons water

Directions

- Preheat the oven to 350 degrees F.
- In a large bowl, combine the meats with your hands or a large fork.
- Blend in the onion, garlic, and parsley; set aside.
- In a medium bowl, whisk the egg until frothy, about 1 minute.
- Add the milk, mustard, salt, pepper, and nutmeg and whisk to blend.
- Add the bread crumbs and let stand for 5 minutes.
- Add the egg mixture to the meat mixture and blend well, about 1 minute.

- Spread evenly into a 9x5-inch loaf pan. In a small bowl, combine the ketchup and water until blended.
- Spread on top of the meat. Bake until the meat is no longer pink, about 90 minutes.

Nutritional Facts

244 calories 690 mg sodium 77 mg cholesterol 10 gm carbohydrate 29 gm protein 10 gm fat

401. BLEU BURGER

Serving : 1

Ingredients:

- ½ pound (150 g) hamburger patty
- 1 tablespoon (8 g) crumbled blue
- cheese
- 1 teaspoon finely minced sweet
- red onion

Directions:

- Cook the burger by your preferred method.
- When it's almost done to your liking, top with the bleu cheese and let it melt.
- Remove from the heat, put it on plate, and top with onion.

Nutritional Info

Carbohydrates 0.9g, 27 g of protein.

402. CHIPOTLE CHEESEBURGERS

Servings : 6

Ingredients:

- 2 pounds (910 g) ground beef
- 6 chipotle chiles canned in adobo
- sauce, minced
- ½ cup (32 g) chopped cilantro
- 2 cloves garlic, crushed
- ¼ cup (40 g) minced onion
- ½ teaspoon salt
- 6 ounces (170 g) Monterey Jack
- cheese, sliced

Directions:

- Plunk everything but the cheese into a big bowl and use clean hands to mush everything together until very well blended.
- Form into 6 burgers about 1 inch (2.5 cm) thick. Put your burgers on a plate and stick them in the fridge to chill for a good hour—it makes them easier to handle on the grill.
- Get your fire going—you'll want your gas grill on medium or a little lower or well-ashed charcoal.
- Grill the burgers for a good 7 to 10 minutes per side or until juices run clear, keeping down flare-ups with a water bottle.
- When the burgers are almost done, top with the cheese and let it melt. Serve with Chipotle Sauce Exclusive of Chipotle Sauce.

Nutritional Info:

Carbohydrate 1 g fibre 1g , protein. 33 grams

403. GRILLED LAMB CHOPS WITH GARLIC AND HERBS

Prep Time: 15 mins
Cook Time: 20 mins
Total Time: 35 mins

Ingredients

- Eight lamb chops, loin, or rib 1-1 1/2 inches thick
- 2 -3 cloves garlic, peeled
- 2 tablespoons olive oil
- 1 1/2 teaspoons fresh rosemary, finely chopped or 1/2 teaspoon dried
- 1 1/2 teaspoons fresh thyme, or 1/2 teaspoon dried
- 1/4 teaspoon salt
- Freshly ground black pepper

Directions

- Smash garlic cloves, drizzle with a bit of olive oil and salt and chop/grind it until it forms a paste.
- Scrape into a bowl, add the herbs and pepper and combine thoroughly. Rub the paste over the chops. If possible, cover and refrigerate for at least 30 minutes for the flavors to meld and the chops to marinate.
- Preheat a grill pan or cast-iron skillet over medium-high heat. Cook the chops for 2 minutes on each side.
- Reduce the heat to medium-low and cook until desired degree of doneness.
- Cook about 3 minutes more for medium-rare. The exact cooking time depends on the size of the chops.
- Set aside on a cutting board to rest for 5 minutes before serving.

Nutrition FactsValue

Carbohydrates: 1g| Protein: 84g| Fat: 31g| Saturated Fat: 11g| Cholesterol: 257mg| Sodium: 347mg| Potassium: 1083mg| Fiber: 1g| Vitamin A: 90IU| Vitamin C: 3mg| Calcium: 47mg| Iron: 8mg

404. GRILLED LAMB LOIN CHOPS WITH CORN ON THE COB AND GRILLED ROMAINE

Prep Time: 30 minutes
Cook Time: 10 minutes
Total Time: 44 minutes

Ingredients

For The Marinade/Sauce:

- 3 cloves garlic minced
- Zest from 1 lemon
- ¼ cup dijon mustard
- ½ tsp salt
- ½ tsp black pepper
- ¼ cup avocado oil
- ¼ cup water

Lamb Loin Chops:

- 1 lb (5-6) lamb loin chops

Veggies:

- 4 ears of corn husks removed
- 2 heads of romaine
- 1 Tbsp softened butter

Directions

For The Marinade:

- Pre-heat your grill. Ideally, we want to get the grill temperature above 400 degrees before putting the lamb loin chops on so it doesn't hurt to give it a nice long time to warm up!
- While your grill is heating, remove the lamb loin chops from the refrigerator, and combine the garlic, lemon zest, Dijon mustard, salt and pepper, oil, and water in a bowl. Whisk to combine.
- Place the lamb loin chops on a plate or in a glass dish. Use 2/3 of the lemon garlic mixture as your lamb marinade, reserving the final 1/3 for the romaine.
- Rub both sides of all of your lamb loin chops with 2/3 of the marinade, and let them sit for 30 minutes to an hour on

the counter to marinate. Remember, to keep the other 1/3 of the marinade for the romaine lettuce.

For The Veggies:

- Cut your heads of romaine lettuce in half length-wise and brush each half (on the cut side) with the remaining 1/3 of your marinade.
- Next, rub 1 Tbsp of softened butter on the ears of corn.
- Let's grill!
- Once your grill is heated, add all of your food to the grill and close the lid. (Make sure to place the cut heads of romaine cut side down on the grill grates.) Let the food cook for 5-6 minutes.
- After 5-6 minutes, carefully open the grill, and flip your lamb loin chops, flip your ears of corn, and remove the heads of romaine from the grill. You can place the romaine heads on a platter next to the grill while you wait for the corn and lamb loin chops to finish cooking.
- Return the lid to the grill, and let the lamb loin chops and corn cook for an additional 5 minutes.
- Using your meat thermometer, check your lamb loin chops to ensure they have reached 135 degrees F. Once they have, remove them along with your corn from the grill.
- Serve everything together and enjoy!

Nutrition FactsValue

Carbohydrates: 26g | Protein: 25g | Fat: 48g | Saturated Fat: 17g | Sodium: 742mg | Fiber: 9g | Sugar: 6g

405. MOUSSAKA

Prep Time: 30 minutes
Cook Time: 1 hour 30 minutes
Total Time: 2 hours

Ingredients

For The Vegetable Layers

- 1 medium onion sliced
- 2 large potatoes peeled & sliced into 0.5 cm thick slices (maris pipers work well)
- 2 whole aubergines sliced into 0.5 cm thick slices
- 2 medium courgettes sliced into 0.5 cm thick slices
- 3 tsp fresh thyme (or dried)
- Plenty olive oil
- Plenty salt and ground black pepper for seasoning

For The Meat Layer

- 1 tbsp olive oil
- 1 medium onion diced
- 500 grams minced lamb, beef, quorn or meat-free alternative
- 1 whole clove of garlic minced
- 200 grams chopped tin of tomatoes
- 1 tbsp tomato purée
- ½ tsp ground cinnamon
- 1 pinch ground cloves
- Salt & ground black pepper for seasoning

For The GD Friendly White Sauce

- 500 grams Greek yogurt full fat
- 3 large egg yolks
- 100 grams Parmesan cheese grated
- 50 grams feta cheese crumbled or cheddar grated
- 1 good pinch freshly ground black pepper
- 1 good pinch ground nutmeg

Directions

For The Vegetable Layers

- Pre-heat the oven to 200c and brush a roasting pan with olive oil
- Add 1 sliced onion and potatoes to a bowl. Add a glug of olive oil and season with salt & black pepper and a good pinch of thyme. Turn the ingredients in the bowl to coat them
- Place the onion and potatoes into the oiled roasting pan and bake for 20 minutes until softened and slightly golden
- Add the aubergine to the bowl, add a glug of olive oil, seasoning, and thyme and turn to coat all piece well
- Remove the potatoes from the oven and cover with the aubergine slices so that it forms a layer. Bake in the oven for another 20 minutes
- Add the courgette slices to the bowl, repeating the oil, seasoning, and thyme process, and add to the cooked layer of aubergine
- Place the tray back in the oven to bake for another 20 minutes then remove and set it aside

For The Meat Layer

- Add a tbsp of olive oil to a pan and heat on high. Add the onion and caramelized to high heat, then add the garlic
- Add the cinnamon and a pinch of ground cloves and cook for 1 minute
- Add a tbsp of tomato puree to the pan and mix. Then add the mince and season with salt & ground black pepper. Cook through until the mince has browned
- Add the tinned tomatoes and cook until most of the liquid evaporates, leaving the mince quite dry (You do not want the meat to be too wet or this will cause the moussaka to turn into slop!)
- Spread the mince over the cooked vegetables and flatten with a spoon

For The GD Friendly White Sauce

- Add the yogurt, egg yolks, cheese, and spices to a bowl and whisk
- Add the yogurt mixture on top of the meat layer and sprinkle with more parmesan, feta, or cheddar if you wish
- Place the tray back into the oven to bake for 20-25 minutes, or until the top is golden and bubbling
- You can serve this hot, but it is better after it has been left to sit for a little while. Serve with a Greek side salad

Nutrition FactsValue

Calories: 550kcal | Carbohydrates: 33g | Protein: 35g | Fat: 31g | of which saturates: 14g | Fibre: 5g | sugars: 9g

406. LOW CARB HAMBURGER HELPER

Total Time: 25 Minutes

Ingredients

- 1 lb ground lamb (can sub ground beef)
- 1/2 tsp cumin
- 1/2 tsp dried oregano
- 1/2 tsp salt
- 1/4 tsp pepper
- 1 tbsp butter
- 1 tsp minced garlic

- 1 medium zucchini, spiralized or julienned
- 1/2 cup crumbled feta
- Additional salt and pepper to taste

Directions

- Add ground lamb to a large skillet over medium heat, breaking up any clumps with the back of a wooden spoon.
- Sprinkle with cumin, oregano, salt, and pepper, and sauté until cooked for about 10 minutes. Use a slotted spoon to remove the lamb from a plate or bowl, leaving drippings in the pan.
- Add butter to the pan. When melted, add garlic and sauté until fragrant, about 1 minute.
- Add zucchini noodles to pan and sauté until just softened, about 2 minutes.
- Add lamb back into pan and toss with noodles. Sprinkle with feta and any additional salt and pepper.

Nutrition Facts

Cholesterol: 106mg| Energy: 436 kcal| Total Fat: 31.49g| Carbohydrate: 8.68g| Protein: 24.41g| Dietary Fiber: 2.48g

407. SLOW-COOKED ROAST LEG OF LAMB

Preparation Time: 15 mins
Cooking Time: 1 h 40 mins

Ingredients

- 460g lamb's leg
- 1 clove garlic
- 1 tbsp olive oil 15ml
- 1 pinch salt [optional] 0.2g
- Ground pepper to taste [optional]
- 1/2 onions, coarsely chopped 100g
- 1 sprig rosemary, fresh 5g
- 1/4 cup red wine 65mL

Before You Start

- You should estimate 3 ½ h per kilo of meat.
- A baking dish or casserole with a tight-fitting lid is necessary for this recipe.

Directions

- Preheat the oven to 140°C/275°F.
- Peel the garlic cloves and slice them in half lengthwise. Cut small slits in one surface of the lamb with a sharp knife and put a piece of garlic into each slit.
- Heat the oil in a casserole or roasting pan over medium heat. Brown the lamb thoroughly on each side until golden, about 7-8 min. Add salt and pepper, then remove the lamb from the pan and set aside.
- Coarsely chop the onion and sauté in the same pan, 4-5 min until translucent and soft. Put the lamb back into the pan, add the rosemary sprigs and wine. Cover and cook in the middle of the oven. Calculate 3 ½ h per kilo of meat. When ready, the meat will fall apart when inserting a fork.
- Serve.

Nutrition Facts

Fat: 13g| Saturated: 3.5g| Cholesterol: 90mg| Sodium: 70mg| Carbohydrate: 5g| Fiber: 1g| Sugars: 2g| Net Carbs: 4g| Protein: 30g

408. LAMB SHANKS WITH BARLEY, GARDEN PEAS, AND MINT

Prep Time: 15 Minutes
Cook Time: 2 Hours

Ingredients

- 1 tbsp Olive oil
- 4 Large lamb shanks
- 1 Brown onion, chopped
- 4 cups Chicken stock
- 1 1/2 cups Pearl barley
- 1 1/2 cups Garden peas
- 1 Handful mint leaves
- 1 Large orange grated zest and juice

Directions

- Preheat the oven to 180°C/350°F (fan 160°C/315°F).
- Place a large casserole dish on the stovetop over medium-high heat. Pour in the oil and, when hot, add the shanks and brown all over, turning occasionally, for about 8 minutes. Push the shanks to the side of the dish slightly and reduce the heat.
- Add the onion and cook for about 8 minutes, or until golden. Pour in the stock, bring to a lively simmer, cover, and place in the oven for about 1½ hours, or until the shanks are tender.
- Rinse the barley, drain, and add it to the casserole dish, making sure it is covered in liquid. If not, add a little more stock. Cover and cook for about 25–30 minutes, or until the barley is al dente, adding the peas in the last 5 minutes of cooking.
- Roughly chop half of the mint and stir it in with the orange zest and juice, and salt and pepper to taste. Using forks, pull the meat from the bone and serve with the barley and pea mixture, garnished with the remaining mint leaves.

Nutrition Facts:

Calories: 235kcal | Carbohydrates: 20g | Protein: 6g | Fat: 13.5g | Saturated Fat: 2g | Sodium: 685mg | Potassium: 395mg | Fiber: 6g | Sugar: 2g

409. LIGHTER LAMB HOTPOT

Preparation Time: Less Than 30 Mins
Cooking Time: 1 To 2 Hours

Ingredients

- 3 tsp olive oil
- 600g/1lb 5oz lamb leg steaks, all visible fat removed (500g/1lb 2oz after the fat is cut off), cut into bite-size pieces
- 2 onions, roughly chopped
- 2 garlic cloves, thickly sliced
- 250g/9oz celery (about 4 stalks), thickly sliced
- 400g/14oz carrots (about 4 medium carrots), peeled and thickly sliced
- Small handful fresh rosemary, finely chopped
- Few sprigs of fresh thyme
- 1 tbsp plain flour
- 1 beef stock pot diluted to make 500ml/18fl oz stock
- 2 tbsp worcestershire sauce
- 2 tbsp tomato purée
- 650g/1lb 7oz floury potatoes, ideally maris piper, cut into thick slices
- Salt and freshly ground black pepper

Directions

- Preheat the oven to 160C/140C Fan/Gas
- Heat 1 teaspoon of the oil in a large heavy-bottomed casserole over medium to high heat. Brown the lamb on all sides in two batches for 3-4

minutes per batch. Transfer to a plate using a slotted spoon.
- Add another teaspoon of oil to the pan and add the onions, garlic, celery, and carrots and fry, stirring, for 3-4 minutes. Add the rosemary and thyme and fry for another minute. Sprinkle over the flour and cook for 2 minutes, stirring all the time to cook the flour.
- Return the lamb to the pan, pour in the stock, and stir in the Worcestershire sauce and tomato purée, then bring to a boil.
- Layer the potatoes on top in two overlapping layers, seasoning between the layers. Cover with the lid and bake in the oven for 1½ hours, or until the lamb and the potatoes are tender.
- Remove the lid and increase the oven temperature to 200C/180C Fan/Gas Brush the potatoes with the final teaspoon of oil and bake for a further 15 minutes, or until the top is nicely browned.

Nutrition Facts

Calories: 299kcal | Carbohydrates: 29g | Protein: 9g | Fat: 15g | Saturated Fat: 8g | Cholesterol: 112mg | Sodium: 436mg | Potassium: 180mg | Fiber: 2g | Sugar: 5g | Vitamin A: 535IU | Calcium: 134mg | Iron: 2.4mg

410. LAMB GYROS

Total Time: 50 Minutes

Ingredients

- 1 lb lamb ground, or ground chicken for a lower fat option
- 3 cloves garlic minced
- 1/2 onion finely diced
- 2 tsp oregano dried
- 1 tsp basil dried
- 1 tsp mint leaves dried
- 1/2 tsp salt
- 6 pita bread whole wheat, pocketless
- 1-1/2 cup tomato cherry, halved
- 1-1/2 cup cucumber diced
- 3/4 cup olives Kalamata, halved
- 3 cups arugula
- 6 Tbsp dressing Greek vinaigrette or a creamy dairy-free ranch, like Tessemae

Directions

- Combine lamb, garlic, onion, oregano, basil, mint, and salt. Mix with hands until just incorporated. Cover and refrigerate for 1 hour.
- Preheat oven to 350º F. Takes the lamb out of the fridge and form into a rectangular loaf. Place on a baking sheet lined with foil. Bake for about 20 minutes, until lamb reaches an internal temperature of 130º F.
- Remove from oven and let cool. Slice lamb thinly and lay pieces in a single layer back onto the baking sheet. Broil for about 10 minutes, until hot and browned.
- Divide lamb among the 6 pitas and top with tomato, cucumber, olives, arugula, and a drizzle of desired dressing.

Nutrition FactsValue

Carbohydrates: 35g | Protein: 19g | Fat: 30g | Sodium: 755mg | Potassium: 369mg | Fiber: 5g | Iron: -25mg

411. TURMERIC LAMB CHOPS WITH CRISPY POTATOES AND BROCCOLI

Active Time: 20 Mins
Total Time: 20 Mins

Ingredients

- 1 tablespoon water
- 12 ounces baby Yukon Gold potatoes, quartered (about 2 1/2 cups)
- 3 tablespoons olive oil, divided
- 2 teaspoons ground cumin
- 1 teaspoon ground turmeric
- 1 1/4 teaspoons kosher salt, divided
- 1/2 teaspoon black pepper, divided
- 8 (3-oz.) lamb loin chops
- 1 (12-oz.) pkg. fresh steam-in-bag broccoli florets
- 1 tablespoon unsalted butter, softened
- 1 lemon, cut into wedges

How To Make It

- Place 1 tablespoon water and potatoes in a medium microwave-safe bowl; cover with plastic wrap. Microwave at high 4 minutes or until tender. Spread potatoes in a single layer on a paper towel-lined baking sheet; let dry 3 for minutes.
- Combine 1 tablespoon oil, cumin, turmeric, 1/2 teaspoon salt, and 1/4 teaspoon pepper in a small bowl. Rub spice mixture evenly over lamb chops.
- Heat 1 tablespoon oil in a large cast-iron skillet over medium-high. Add lamb chops to pan; cook 3 minutes on each side for medium-rare or until desired degree of doneness. Remove chops from pan; let stand 5 minutes.
- Return pan to medium-high. Add remaining 1 tablespoon oil. Add potatoes, 1/2 teaspoon salt, and remaining 1/4 teaspoon pepper; cook 3 to 4 minutes or until crisp.
- Cook broccoli according to package directions. Place broccoli, remaining 1/4 teaspoon salt, and butter in a bowl; toss to coat. Serve with lamb, potato mixture, and lemon wedges.

Nutrition Facts

Fat: 24g| Satfat: 7g| Unsatfat: 15g| Protein: 40g| Carbohydrate: 22g| Fiber: 5g| Sodium: 766mg| Sugars: 2g

412. ROASTED EGGPLANT WITH SPICED LAMB

Prep Time: 5 mins
Cook Time: 40 minutes

Ingredients

- Roasted eggplant with spiced lamb
- 1 large eggplant (500g), halved lengthways
- 2 teaspoon olive oil
- 350-gram cauliflower, chopped coarsely
- 150 gram lean minced (ground) lamb
- 1 teaspoon each ground cumin and coriander
- 2 tablespoon water
- 2 teaspoon pomegranate molasses
- 1/2 cup (140g) fat-free natural yogurt
- 2 teaspoon lemon juice
- 1 clove garlic, crushed
- 2 tablespoon currants
- 1/2 cup fresh coriander leaves (cilantro)
- 1/2 teaspoon sumac

Directions

- Roasted eggplant with spiced lamb
- Preheat oven to 200°C. Line a large oven tray with baking paper.

- Using a sharp knife, score the eggplant flesh diagonally. Drizzle with half the oil. Place flesh-side down on the tray. Roast for 10 minutes. Add cauliflower to tray; drizzle with remaining oil. Roast a further 30 minutes or until tender.
- Meanwhile, heat a medium oiled non-stick frying pan over high heat; cook lamb, spices, and the water, stirring, until browned. Add pomegranate molasses. Remove from heat.
- Combine yogurt, juice, and garlic in a small bowl.
- Serve eggplant topped with cauliflower, lamb, currants, and coriander. Spoon over the yogurt mixture and sprinkle with sumac.

Nutrition Facts
Total Fat: 15.8g | Saturated Fat: 3.4g | Carbohydrates: 7.4g | Fibre: 0.2g | Protein: 8.5g

413. HONEY SPICED LAMB CASSEROLE

Prep Time: 10 Minutes
Cook Time: 10 Minutes

Ingredients
- 2 tsp smoked paprika
- 2 tsp ground cumin
- 1 tsp ground ginger
- 1 tsp ground turmeric
- Pinch ground nutmeg
- 2 tsp extra virgin olive oil
- 500g lamb leg steaks, trimmed of fat, cut into 2.5cm pieces
- 4 cloves garlic, peeled
- 1 brown onion, cut into wedges
- 3 carrots, cut into chunks
- 500g piece pumpkin, peeled, deseeded, and chopped
- 60ml (¼ cup) honey
- 1 massel ultracube salt reduced vegetable stock cube
- 375ml (1½ cups) boiling water
- 3 zucchini, cut into chunks
- Chopped flat-leaf parsley, to serve
- Lemon zest, to serve
- 4 x 30g slices wholemeal sourdough or gluten-free bread, toasted or chargrilled, to serve

Directions
- Preheat oven to 150°C (fan-forced). Put paprika, cumin, ginger, turmeric, nutmeg, and 1 tbsp of the oil in a medium bowl and stir to combine. Add lamb and toss to coat. Heat remaining oil in a large ovenproof and ovenproof casserole dish with a lid over medium-high heat. Add lamb and cook, tossing, for 2 minutes or until the meat changes color.
- Add garlic, onion, carrot, and pumpkin to the pan and stir to combine. Put honey, stock cube, and boiling water in a heatproof jug and stir to combine. Add to pan and bring to a simmer. Cover. Transfer to oven and bake for 1½ hours, stirring once. Add zucchini and stir. Return to oven and cook for a further 30 minutes or until zucchini is tender and lamb is soft.
- Divide casserole (including juices) between shallow serving bowls. Sprinkle over parsley and lemon zest. Serve with toast.

Nutrition FactsInfo
Protein: 36g, Total Fat: 11g, Sat. Fat: 2.7g, Carbs: 47g, Fiber: 1g, Sodium: 456mg.

414. JUICY LAMB BURGERS

Prep Time: 8 Min
Cook Time: 8 Min

Ingredients
- 454g lean ground lamb (ask the butcher to bone lamb, trim off visible fat, and grind)
- 1/2 cup dry whole-wheat breadcrumbs
- 1/4 cup rehydrated sundried tomatoes (diced)
- 1/4 cup fresh parsley (minced)
- Shallots
- 1/4 cup (finely minced)
- 2 tsp grated pecorino romano cheese
- 1/4 tsp kosher salt
- 1/4 tsp freshly ground black pepper
- 4 slice tomatoes
- 4 lettuce leaves

Directions
- Combine all the ingredients for the burger, handling the meat as little as possible. Form into four patties.
- Heat a cast-iron skillet over medium-high heat. Add the patties and cook for 3-4 minutes per side. Serve with tomato and lettuce on a whole-grain bun or serve bunless.

Nutrition Facts
Fat: 5g| Saturated Fat: 2g| Cholesterol: 60mg| Sodium: 240mg| Carbohydrate: 15g| Dietary Fiber: 3g| Total Sugars: 3g| Protein: 22g| Potassium: 620mg| Phosphorus: 240mg

415. SHEPHERD'S PIE – DIABETIC FRIENDLY

Prep Time: 20 Minutes
Cook Time: 60 Minutes

Ingredients
- 175g lean minced lamb
- 1 onion, chopped
- 2 carrots, peeled and grated
- Pinch cinnamon
- Pinch mixed herbs
- 2 tsp plain flour
- 1 tsp worcestershire sauce
- 1 tbsp brown sauce
- 200ml beef stock
- 1 tsp oil
- 1 leek, finely sliced
- 450g floury potatoes, peeled and chopped
- 2 tbsp milk
- 2 tbsp light creme fraiche
- 2 tbsp parmesan, grated

Directions
- Place the lamb, onion, and carrot into a non-stick pan, and cook for 5-6 minutes until the lamb is browned. Drain off any excess fat. Stir in the cinnamon, herbs, flour, Worcestershire sauce, brown sauce, and stock, bring to boil, and simmer gently for 10 minutes.
- Heat the oil in a small pan, add the leeks and fry for 3-4 minutes until tender. Preheat the oven to 200°C/400°F/gas mark
- Place the potatoes into a pan of boiling water and simmer for 12-15 minutes until cooked. Drain then mash together with the milk and crème Fraiche until smooth. Stir through the leeks and season with black pepper.

- Spoon the mince into a medium oven-proof dish and smooth over the potato and leek mixture then sprinkle over the Parmesan.
- Cook for 20-30 minutes, until golden and bubbling.

Nutrition FactsInfo

Protein: 26g| Carbohydrates: 58g| Fat: 12g

416. LAMB, SWEET POTATO, AND ALMOND SLOW-COOKED CURRY

Prep Time: 6 Minutes
Cook Time: 8 Hour

Ingredients

- 1kg lamb leg steak, trimmed
- 1kg orange sweet potato
- 1 large brown onion
- 3 cloves garlic
- 1 red chili
- 2 tsp ground cumin
- 2 tsp garam masala
- 400g canned chopped tomatoes
- 375mL coconut flavored evaporated milk
- 250g spinach leaves
- ½ cup (60g) ground almonds
- 1/3 cup (45g) slivered almonds
- 1/3 cup fresh coriander

Directions

- Cut lamb and sweet potato into 5cm pieces. Combine with sliced onion and place in the slow cooker with crushed garlic, chopped chili, spices, tomatoes and evaporated milk. Cook in slow cooker on low for about 8 hours.
- Add spinach and ground almonds. Cook on high for 5 minutes or until the spinach wilts.
- Serve sprinkled with slivered almonds and chopped coriander.

Nutrition FactsValue

Carbohydrate: 36g| Total fat: 24g| Saturated fat: 6g| Dietary fiber: 11g| Sodium: 261mg

417. MOROCCAN LAMB STEW

Total Time: 1 Hour 30 Minutes

Ingredients

To Make Moroccan Lamb Stew, You'll Need:

- 3 tbsp. olive oil
- 500g lean lamb steaks, diced
- 1 medium onion, finely sliced
- 2 garlic cloves, finely chopped
- 1 medium potato
- 400g tinned plum tomatoes
- 1 medium red bell pepper, sliced
- 220g tinned chickpeas
- 1 small aubergine
- 250ml boiling water
- 2 tbsp. red wine vinegar
- 1 tbsp. fresh coriander, finely chopped
- Salt and freshly ground pepper to taste

Directions

- Preheat the oven to Gas Mark 4 or 180°C.
- Heat half the oil in a large saucepan on high heat, and brown the pieces of lamb for 5 minutes.
- Lower the heat and add the rest of the oil. Fry the onions and garlic for 4 minutes.
- Pop the lamb, onions, and garlic into a large ovenproof dish.
- Throw in the potato, tomatoes, red bell pepper, chickpeas, aubergine, boiling water, and red wine vinegar.
- Season to taste with salt and freshly ground pepper. Mix thoroughly, and cook for 1 hour and 15 minutes until the lamb is cooked.

Nutrition Facts

Total Fat: 17g | Saturated Fat: 4g | Carbohydrates: 30g | Fibre: 6g | Protein: 40g

418. HERB-CRUSTED RACK OF LAMB

Total Time: 50-60 Minutes

Ingredients

- 4 cloves garlic, minced
- 1/2 cup chopped fresh rosemary leaves
- 1/4 cup chopped fresh mint leaves
- Salt to taste
- Freshly ground black pepper
- 1 rack of new zealand lamb, fully french trimmed
- 1/2 cup chopped fresh parsley leaves
- 1 cup plain bread crumbs
- 1 tablespoon Dijon mustard

Directions

- In a small bowl, mix the garlic, salt, pepper, rosemary, and mint. Rub the mixture over the lamb and refrigerate for an hour or overnight.
- Meanwhile, combine the bread crumbs and parsley in a small bowl. Season with salt and pepper and set aside.
- Spray a roasting pan with nonstick spray and place it in the oven. Preheat the oven to 500F.
- Place the lamb, meat-side down in the hot roasting pan and cook for 10 minutes. Remove the lamb from the oven and reduce the heat to 400F.
- Turn the lamb meat-side up and brush the meat with the mustard. Spread the crumb mixture over the mustard and press it onto the meat. Return to the oven and cook for 10 minutes more to brown the bread crumbs.
- Let the meat rest for 5 minutes. Carve the racks into chops and serve.

Nutrition Facts

Fat: 12g| Saturated Fat: 1g| Fiber: 0.5g| Sodium: 302mg| Cholesterol: 189mg| Protein: 35g| Carbohydrates: 23g

419. DIABETIC BRAISED LAMB WITH CARROTS

Prep Time: 25 Min
Cook Time: 2 Hr 10 Min

Ingredients

- 1 Tbsp coconut oil
- 2 lb lamb shoulder chops
- 1 large onion (sliced)
- 1/2 c mushrooms (quartered)
- 3 clove garlic (sliced)
- 1/4 tsp allspice
- 1 tsp smoked paprika
- 3-5 sprig(s) of fresh thyme (or 3/4 teaspoon dried)
- 2-3 branches of fresh rosemary (or 1 teaspoon dried)
- 1/2 tsp salt
- 2 bay leaves
- 1/2 tsp freshly ground black pepper
- 1c white wine
- 2c chicken broth (no salt added)
- 1-2c beef broth

- 8 medium carrots (sliced about 2" on diagonal) or mixed root vegetables
- 1 Tbsp dijon mustard

How To Make Diabetic Braised Lamb With Carrots

- Preheat oven to 325 degrees F. Lightly seasons your lamb with salt and pepper. In a large oven-proof dutch oven, heat the coconut oil over medium-high heat Brown the lamb on each side for approx 1-2 minutes. Remove from the pot and set aside.
- Add the onions, mushrooms, and garlic to the pot and cook for about 3 minutes until the onions begin to soften.
- Stir in allspice, paprika, salt & pepper, bay leaves, and add the wine. Then add the carrots and chicken broth. Bring to a boil and allow to cook for about 3 minutes.
- Return meat to the pot and lay on top of veggies and sauce. Divide mustard and spread on top of each shoulder chop. Top with thyme sprigs and rosemary. Add enough beef broth to bring the liquid to cover the sides of the lamb. Cover and place in the oven for 2 hours.
- Do NOT check the meat while it's cooking. Just let it cook undisturbed for 2 hours. Remove meat and serve with veggies and broth. Use the leftovers (if there are any) for a great veggie and barley soup the next day or freeze it for another day.

Nutritional Value

Carbohydrates: 9g | Protein: 12g | Fat: 22g | Saturated Fat: 8g | Polyunsaturated Fat: 1g | Monounsaturated Fat: 4g | Cholesterol: 104mg | Sodium: 366mg | Potassium: 331mg | Fiber: 1g | Vitamin A: 400IU | Vitamin C: 21.5mg | Calcium: 90mg | Iron: 1.3mg

420. LAMB KEBABS WITH VERDANT SALSA

Total Time: 1 Hour 30 Minutes

Ingredients

To Make Lamb Kebabs With Verdant Salsa, You'll Need:

Kebab Mix

- 400g minced lamb
- 2 tsp. garlic, peeled and finely chopped
- 2 tsp. ginger, peeled and finely chopped
- 1 large onion, peeled and finely chopped
- 2 tsp. ground coriander
- 2 tsp. ground cumin
- ¼ tsp. ground black pepper
- 1 tbsp. fresh coriander, finely chopped
- 4 metal skewers

Verdant Salsa Mix

- 3 spring onions, chopped
- 1 tbsp. olive oil
- 4 tomatoes, chopped roughly
- 1 tbsp. pitted olives of your choice
- 1 bunch of coriander, chopped
- 1 bunch of parsley, chopped
- Juice and grated rind of a lemon

Directions

- Mix the mince, onion, ginger, garlic, coriander, cumin, pepper, and salt in a mixing bowl.
- Form 16 balls out of the mince mixture.
- Put each ball around the tip of a metal skewer and flatten slightly.
- Place the meatballs on a baking sheet and cover, then refrigerate them for an hour.
- Pop all the salsa ingredients in a bowl and mix them.
- Cook the skewered lamb kebabs under a preheated grill, turning now and again until the lamb is cooked through.
- This will take 15 minutes.
- Serve hot with the salsa.
- Mmm, delicious!

Nutrition Facts

Total Fat: 21g | Saturated Fat: 9g | Carbohydrates: 9g | Fibre: 2.2g | Protein: 18g

421. GARLICKY MUSTARD LAMB CHOPS

Total Time: 30 Minutes

Ingredients:

- 4 cloves, garlic, minced
- 1 teaspoon Dijon mustard
- 1/2 teaspoon pepper
- 1/4 teaspoon dried thyme
- 1/8 teaspoon salt
- 1 teaspoon chopped fresh parsley
- 2 teaspoons lemon juice
- 1 tablespoon olive oil
- 4 (5-ounce) lean lamb loin chops

Directions:

- Preheat the broiler. In a small bowl, combine all ingredients except lamb chops; mix well.
- Trim fat from lamb chops. Spread garlic mixture over both sides of chops. Place chops on a lightly greased rack in a broiler pan. Broil 6 to 7 minutes on each side or the desired degree of doneness.

Nutrition Facts

Total Fat: 23g | Saturated Fat: 9.6g | Protein: 37g | Cholesterol: 120mg | Sodium: 192mg | Total Carbohydrates 1.4g | Dietary Fiber: 0.2g | Sugars: 0.1g

422. LAMB AND VEGETABLE STEW

Total Time: 6-7 Hour 30 Minutes

Ingredients

- 2 cups sliced mushrooms
- 1 large red bell pepper, diced
- 1 large carrot, cut into 1/2-inch-thick slices
- 1 small unpeeled new potato, diced
- 1 small parsnip, cut into 1/2-inch-thick slices
- 1 large leek, white part only, chopped
- 1 clove garlic, minced
- 1/2 cup reduced-sodium chicken broth
- 1/2 teaspoon dried thyme
- 1/4 teaspoon dried rosemary
- 1/8 teaspoon black pepper
- 12 ounces lamb shoulder meat, cut into 1-inch pieces
- 2 tablespoons all-purpose flour

Directions

- Place mushrooms, bell pepper, carrot, potato, parsnip, leek, and garlic in the slow cooker. Add chicken broth, thyme, rosemary, and black pepper; stir. Add

lamb. Cover; cook on LOW for 6 to 7 hours.
- Combine flour and 2 tablespoons of liquid from the slow cooker in a small bowl. Stir flour mixture into slow cooker. Cover; cook 10 minutes. Stir in salt, if desired.

Nutrition Facts
Carbohydrates: 55g, Protein: 21g, Fat: 4g, Saturated Fat: 1g, Cholesterol: 82mg, Sodium: 82mg, Fiber: 3g

423. MAPLE AND SAGE PORK CHOPS

Total Time: 20 Minutes

Ingredients
- 2 tablespoons finely chopped fresh sage, plus additional for garnish
- 2 teaspoons olive oil
- 1/2 teaspoon salt
- 4 boneless pork chops (about 4 ounces each)
- 2 teaspoons maple syrup

Directions
- Combine 2 tablespoons of sage, oil, and salt in a small bowl. Rub mixture evenly over pork chops. Place on rimmed baking sheet.
- Broil pork chops for 4 minutes. Turn over; brush evenly with syrup. Broil for 4 minutes or until pork chops are browned and barely pink in the center. Garnish with additional sage.

Nutrition Facts
Carbohydrates: 2g, Protein: 25g, Fat: 10g, Saturated Fat: 3g, Cholesterol: 62mg, Sodium: 342mg

424. STUFFED PORK TENDERLOIN

Preparation Time: 10 minutes
Cooking Time: 40 minutes.

Ingredients
- 1 pound pork tenderloin
- 1/2 cup cooked wild rice
- 5 baby carrots, finely chopped
- 1/2 cup chopped mushrooms
- 1/2 teaspoon oregano
- 1/4 teaspoon garlic powder
- Nonstick cooking spray

Directions
- Preheat oven to 375°F. Cut tenderloin down the long side approximately 2/3 way through and spread open (butterfly style).
- Combine wild rice, carrots, mushrooms, oregano, and garlic powder in a small bowl. Spoon mixture into the cut seam, then fold over to close.
- Seal with small skewers or tie with string (about 5 ties should do). Spray the baking pan with nonstick cooking spray and add meat.
- Cook 30–40 minutes until meat reaches 160°F when tested with a meat thermometer.
- Let rest 10 minutes before slicing.

Nutrition Facts
Carbohydrates: 5g, Protein: 3g, Fat: 4g, Saturated Fat: 1g, Cholesterol: 83mg, Sodium: 76mg, Fiber: 1g

425. MAPLE AND APPLE PORK CHOPS

Preparation Time: 3 Minutes
Cooking Time: 15 Minutes

Ingredients
- Nonstick cooking spray
- 4 boneless pork chops (about 1 pound)
- 2 small apples (2–2 1/2 inches in diameter)
- 1/8 cup lite, maple-flavored syrup
- 1/8 cup water

Directions
- Spray large skillet with nonstick cooking spray.
- Heat over medium heat, then add pork chops to the pan so that they are not touching each other.
- Brown pork chops on both sides, approximately 2 minutes on each side. Core apples (leaving the skin on), then dice to yield approximately 1 1/2 cups.
- Sprinkle apples into a hot skillet. In a small bowl, combine maple-flavored syrup and water and stir until well combined.
- Pour liquid into skillet, and cover.
- Cook approximately 5–7 minutes on medium heat until pork chops are cooked through and internal temperature is 160°F.

Nutrition Facts
Carbohydrates: 14g, Protein: 29g, Fat: 10g, Saturated Fat: 4g, Cholesterol: 80mg, Sodium: 88mg, Fiber: 1g

426. GRILLED PORK CHOPS WITH CHERRY SAUCE

Preparation Time: 4 Minutes
Cooking Time: 30 Minutes

Ingredients
- 12 cherries, stemmed and pitted
- 4 ounces unsweetened apple juice
- 1–1 1/4 pounds boneless lean pork chops
- 1/4 teaspoon thyme
- 1 tablespoon honey
- 1 teaspoon balsamic vinegar
- 1 tablespoon cornstarch

Directions
- Combine cherries and apple juice in a small saucepan over low heat for 15 minutes.
- While cooking sauce, heat grill.
- Grill pork chops for approximately 3–4 minutes on each side until cooked through (internal temperature should be 160°F).
- Pour hot apple juice and cherries into a small food processor and add thyme, honey, balsamic vinegar, and cornstarch.
- Pulse a few times.
- Add the sauce back to saucepan over low heat and stir until thickened, about 3 minutes.
- Pour sauce (approximately 1/2 cup) evenly over cooked pork chops and serve.

Nutrition Facts
Carbohydrates: 11g, Protein: 29g, Fat: 3g, Saturated Fat: 1g, Cholesterol: 78mg, Sodium: 263mg

427. STUFFED PORK TENDERLOIN WITH COLLARD GREENS

Preparation Time: 15 Minutes
Cooking Time: 50 Minutes

Ingredients
- 1 pound lean pork tenderloin

- 12 dried apricot halves (about 1/2 cup)
- 1 teaspoon black pepper
- 1 teaspoon onion powder
- 1 teaspoon oregano
- 1 pound collard greens, stemmed, washed, and drained, but not dry
- 1 tablespoon extra-virgin olive oil
- 3/4 cup diced onion
- 1 clove garlic, minced
- 2 dashes salt

Directions

- Heat oven to 400°F. Line a baking pan with nonstick aluminum foil (or use regular aluminum foil sprayed with nonfat cooking spray).
- Place tenderloin on a cutting board, and use a slightly oiled (olive oil) sharpening steel or boning knife to make a hole in the center of the tenderloin all the way through. Stuff dried apricots into the cavity, working from one end at a time and making sure to stuff them into the middle. Place tenderloin in the pan and sprinkle with black pepper, onion powder, and oregano.
- Cook for 45 minutes, or until a meat thermometer reads at least 160°F. If you prefer your pork well done, cook until the thermometer reads 170°F.
- Remove and let rest 5 minutes before slicing.
- While meat is resting, roll a collard leaf into a tight roll.
- Using a sharp slicing knife, slice into thin strips.
- Repeat until all of the greens resemble green ribbons. Heat oil in a large skillet over medium-high heat and add onion and garlic.
- Cook until onions are almost transparent. Add greens (which should still be damp) and sauté, moving rapidly until greens have relaxed and deepened in color, 2–3 minutes. If the mixture starts to stick to the pan, add 1 tablespoon water. Remove greens from heat.
- To serve, place approximately 1 cup of greens on a dinner plate. Cut tenderloin into 1 1/2-inch slice. Place meat slices on top of greens.

Nutrition Facts

Carbohydrates: 19g, Protein: 35g, Fat: 9g, Saturated Fat: 2g, Cholesterol: 90mg, Sodium: 89mg, Fiber: 6g

428. GRILLADES OF PORK

Preparation Time: 15 Minutes

Cooking Time: Approximately 45–50 Minutes.

Ingredients

- 1/4 cup all-purpose flour
- 1/2 teaspoon creole seasoning blend (available in the spice aisle)
- 1 pound pork cutlets, trimmed of fat
- Cooking spray
- 1 tablespoon plus 1 teaspoon canola oil
- 1 large green bell pepper, sliced into thin strips
- 2 teaspoons (or 2 cloves) minced garlic
- 1 small onion, thinly sliced into rings
- 3/4 cup finely chopped celery
- 3/4 cup water
- 3 1/3 cups hot cooked brown rice

Directions

- In a large zip-top bag, combine flour and Creole seasoning blend. Shake to mix well. Add pork cutlets one at a time to the bag and shake to coat well.
- Coat a large, nonstick skillet with cooking spray.
- Add 1 tablespoon oil and heat over medium-high heat.
- Add pork cutlets and brown for 2–3 minutes on each side (may need to do in batches depending on the size of the skillet).
- Remove cutlets to a plate. Add remaining 1 teaspoon oil to the skillet and heat.
- Decrease the heat to medium and add pepper, garlic, onion, and celery; cook until onions are translucent, about 5 minutes.
- Stir in water and return cutlets to the skillet. Bring to a boil; reduce heat to medium-low, and cover.
- Simmer for about 25–30 minutes, or until cutlets are tender. Stir occasionally. Serve each cutlet with 2/3 cup hot brown rice.

Nutrition Facts

Carbohydrates: 39g, Protein: 24g, Fat: 8g, Saturated Fat: 2g, Cholesterol: 59mg, Sodium: 128mg, Fiber: 4g

429. CROCK-POT VEGETABLE SOUP

Preparation Time: 15 Minutes

Cooking Time: 4 Hours

Ingredients

- 2 bags (16 ounces each) frozen mixed vegetables
- 1 can (28 ounces) Italian-style crushed tomatoes
- 1 pound lean stew beef, cut into bite-size pieces
- 1 envelope (1 ounce) dry onion soup mix
- 2 cubes reduced-sodium beef bouillon
- 1 1/2 cups water

Directions

- Place all ingredients in a Crock-Pot and stir to combine.
- Cover and cook on high for 4 hours.
- Stir once halfway through, being careful to stir and replace the lid quickly to prevent heat loss.

Nutrition Facts

Carbohydrates: 15g, Protein: 20g, Fat: 3g, Saturated Fat: 1g, Sodium: 328mg, Fiber: 2g

430. JUMBLETTI

Preparation Time: 5 Minutes

Cooking Time: Approximately 35 Minutes.

Ingredients

- 1 pound ground round
- 1 tablespoon sodium-free beef bouillon granules
- 2 cups warm water
- 1 bag (16 ounces) frozen vegetable soup blend mixed vegetables, thawed
- 2 cans (8 ounces each) no-salt-added tomato sauce
- 1 can (14 1/2 ounces) no-salt-added diced tomatoes
- 1 1/2 teaspoons Italian seasoning blend

- 1/8 teaspoon black pepper
- 1/8 teaspoon garlic powder
- Juice of 1 fresh lemon
- 2 cups cooked (about 4 ounces dry) elbow macaroni

Directions

- In a large pan, brown ground round and drain well.
- Meanwhile, dissolve bouillon granules in warm water. Add bouillon, vegetables, tomato sauce, diced tomatoes, Italian seasoning, black pepper, garlic powder, and lemon juice to meat; stir well to combine. Cover, bring to a simmer over medium heat, and cook 15 minutes, or until vegetables are tender; stir frequently.
- Stir in cooked macaroni and cook an additional 5 minutes, or until heated through.

Nutrition Facts

- Carbohydrates: 22g, Protein: 13g, Fat: 2g, Saturated Fat: 1g, Sodium: 94mg, Fiber: 2 g

431. BALSAMIC BEEF, MUSHROOMS, AND ONIONS

Total Time: 30 Minutes

Ingredients

- 2 large sweet onions, sliced
- 3 teaspoons olive oil, divided
- 1/2 teaspoon salt, divided
- 4 to 5 teaspoons balsamic vinegar, divided
- 3 ounces (about 1 cup) mushrooms, sliced
- 1 boneless beef top sirloin (about 1 pound), cut into 1/2-inch-thick slices
- 1/4 teaspoon dried thyme
- 1/4 to 1/2 teaspoon black pepper

Directions

- Heat large nonstick skillet over medium heat. Add onions; cook and stir for 15 minutes.
- Stir in 2 teaspoons oil and 1/4 teaspoon salt. Add 3 teaspoons balsamic vinegar, 1 teaspoon at a time, stirring to scrape up browned bits.
- Reduce heat to medium-low. Add mushrooms; cook and stir 4 to 5 minutes or until mushrooms are tender. Transfer to a medium bowl. Cover and set aside.
- Increase heat to medium-high. Add remaining 1 teaspoon oil. Add beef; sprinkle with remaining 1/4 teaspoon salt, thyme, and pepper. Cook 4 to 6 minutes or until browned.
- Turn off heat. Drizzle the remaining 2 teaspoons of balsamic vinegar over beef. Stir in vegetables. Serve immediately.

Nutrition Facts

Carbohydrates: 7g, Protein: 26g, Fat: 9g, Saturated Fat: 2g, Cholesterol: 53mg, Sodium: 360mg, Fiber: 1g

432. KOREAN-STYLE BEEF AND PASTA

Total Time: 8 Hours 30 Minutes

Ingredients

- 1 beef top round steak (about 3/4 pound)
- 2 tablespoons reduced-sodium soy sauce
- 1 tablespoon rice wine
- 2 teaspoons sugar
- 1 package (about 6 ounces) medium rice noodles
- Korean-Style Dressing
- 2 cups thinly sliced napa cabbage
- 1 3/4 cups thinly sliced red and/or yellow bell peppers
- 1 medium carrot, shredded
- 2 green onions, thinly sliced

Directions

- Freeze beef until partially firm; cut into very thin slices.
- Whisk soy sauce, rice wine, and sugar in a large bowl until smooth and well blended. Add beef slices; toss to coat evenly. Cover and refrigerate for 8 hours or overnight.
- Drain beef; discard marinade. Prepare grill for direct cooking over medium-high heat. Grill beef for 2 to 3 minutes or until desired doneness.
- Place rice noodles in a medium bowl. Cover with hot water; let stand 15 minutes or until tender. Drain; cut noodles into 3-inch lengths.
- Meanwhile, prepare Korean-Style Dressing; set aside.
- Combine cabbage, bell peppers, carrot, green onions, and beef in a medium bowl. Add Korean-Style Dressing; toss to coat evenly. Serve over noodles.

Nutrition Facts

Carbohydrates: 24g, Protein: 13g, Fat: 4g, Saturated Fat: 1g, Cholesterol: 29mg, Sodium: 668mg, Fiber: 1g

433. STUFFED EGGPLANT

Total Time: 1 Hour 30 Minutes

Ingredients

- Nonstick cooking spray
- 2 eggplants (about 8 to 12 ounces each), halved lengthwise
- 1 teaspoon salt
- 1 1/2 teaspoons chopped garlic
- 1 teaspoon black pepper
- 1 pound boneless beef sirloin steak, trimmed of visible fat and cut into 1/4-inch strips
- 2 cups sliced red and green bell peppers
- 2 cups sliced mushrooms
- 1/4 cup water
- Pinch paprika
- Chopped fresh parsley

Directions

- Preheat oven to 450°F. Spray baking dish with cooking spray.
- Place eggplant halves face-up in a large baking dish. Pierce cut sides with a fork in approximately 8 places. Sprinkle each eggplant half with 1/4 teaspoon salt. Cover with foil; bake for 45 minutes.
- Meanwhile, spray a large nonstick skillet with cooking spray. Add garlic and black pepper; cook over medium heat for 2 minutes, stirring lightly. Add beef; cook and stir for 5 minutes.
- Add bell peppers; cook 5 minutes. Add mushrooms; cook 5 minutes. Add water; stir and cover. Remove skillet from heat.
- Remove eggplant from oven, let cool 5 minutes. Mash cooked eggplant centers with a fork, but do not break shells.
- Top each half with one-fourth beef mixture; blend with mashed eggplant.

Cover with foil; bake 15 minutes. Remove from oven. Garnish with paprika and parsley.

Nutrition Facts

Carbohydrates: 12g, Protein: 25g, Fat: 5g, Saturated Fat: 2g, Cholesterol: 42mg, Sodium: 348mg, Fiber: 4g

434. CHEDDAR STUFFED BEEF BURGER

Total Time: 50-60 Minutes

Ingredients

- Nonstick cooking spray
- 2 large baking potatoes, washed and dried
- 12 ounces extra-lean ground sirloin
- 1/2 teaspoon dried thyme
- 4 slices fat-free sharp Cheddar cheese
- 1/8 cup water
- 4 slices beefsteak tomato
- 4 romaine lettuce leaves

Directions

- Preheat oven to 450°F. Lightly coat a baking sheet with cooking spray. Cut each potato crosswise into 8 round slices. Place slices on a baking sheet. Bake for 25 to 30 minutes or until lightly browned.
- Mix the ground sirloin and thyme in a mixing bowl. Form into 8 balls.
- Fold each slice of cheese in half 4 times, forming a cube.
- Press cheese cube in between 2 ground sirloin balls, sealing cheese inside. Form into a patty by flattening to approximately 1 1/2-inch thick. Repeat for 3 more patties.
- Lightly coat a deep skillet with cooking spray. Heat skillet over medium-high heat. Add stuffed patties and cook for 3 minutes on each side. Add water; cover and cook for 6 minutes.
- Place each burger on a slice of potato. Top with a tomato slice, lettuce leaf, and another slice of potato.

Nutrition Facts

Carbohydrates: 26g, Protein: 26g, Fat: 3g, Saturated Fat: 1g, Cholesterol: 40mg, Sodium: 369mg, Fiber: 3g

435. GRILLED STEAK AND BLACK BEAN TACOS

Total Time: 20-30 Minutes

Ingredients

- 1 teaspoon ground cumin
- 1 teaspoon chili powder
- 1 teaspoon garlic salt
- 12 ounces skirt steak, trimmed of fat
- 4 slices red onion (1/4 inch thick)
- Nonstick cooking spray
- 2 cloves garlic, minced
- 1/2 cup salsa
- 1 cup canned no-salt-added black beans, rinsed and drained
- 1/2 cup chopped fresh tomato
- 8 corn tortillas, warmed
- 1/2 cup chopped fresh cilantro
- Lime wedges and lime juice (optional)

Directions

- Prepare grill for direct cooking. Combine cumin, chili powder, and garlic salt in a small bowl; sprinkle evenly over both sides of the steak. Coat steak and onion slices lightly with nonstick cooking spray.
- Grill steak and onions, covered, over medium-high heat 4 to 5 minutes per side or until steak is barely pink in center and onion is tender.
- Spray large skillet with cooking spray; heat over medium heat. Add garlic; cook and stir for 30 seconds. Add beans, salsa, and tomato; cook and stir 5 minutes or until heated through.
- Slice steak crosswise into thin strips; separate onion slices into rings. Serve in warm tortillas with salsa mixture and cilantro. Garnish with lime wedges and lime juice, if desired.

Nutrition Facts

Carbohydrates: 26g, Protein: 23g, Fat: 9g, Saturated Fat: 3g, Cholesterol: 65mg, Sodium: 400mg, Fiber: 3g

436. BEEF WITH CABBAGE AND CARROTS

Total Time: 30 Minutes

Ingredients

- 3/4 pound 90% lean ground beef
- 4 cups shredded cabbage
- 1 1/2 cups shredded carrot (1 large carrot)
- 1/2 teaspoon caraway seeds
- 2 tablespoons seasoned rice vinegar
- Salt and black pepper

Directions

- Brown ground beef in a large skillet. Drain. Reduce heat to low. Stir in cabbage, carrot, and caraway seeds; cover. Cook 10 minutes or until vegetables are tender, stirring occasionally. Stir in vinegar. (Add 1 tablespoon water for extra moistness, if desired.) Season with salt and pepper to taste.

Nutrition Facts

Carbohydrates: 7g, Protein: 18g, Fat: 3.5g, Saturated Fat: 1g, Cholesterol: 45mg, Sodium: 220mg, Fiber: 2g

437. DIABETIC BEEF AND ARTICHOKE CASSEROLE RECIPE

Total Time: 45 Minutes

Ingredients

- 3/4 pound 95% lean ground beef
- 1/2 cup sliced mushrooms
- 1/4 cup chopped onion
- 1 clove garlic, minced
- 1 can (14 ounces) artichoke hearts, drained and chopped
- 1/2 cup dry bread crumbs
- 1/4 cup (1 ounce) grated parmesan cheese
- 1 tablespoon chopped fresh rosemary leaves or 1 teaspoon dried rosemary
- 1 1/2 teaspoons chopped fresh marjoram or 1/2 teaspoon dried marjoram
- Salt and black pepper
- 3 egg whites

Directions

- Preheat oven to 400°F. Spray 1-quart casserole with nonstick cooking spray.
- Brown beef 6 to 8 minutes in a medium skillet over medium-high heat, stirring to break up meat. Drain fat. Add mushrooms, onion, and garlic; cook and stir 5 minutes or until tender.

- Combine ground beef mixture, artichokes, bread crumbs, cheese, rosemary, and marjoram; gently mix. Season with salt and pepper
- Beat egg whites in medium bowl with electric mixer at high speed until stiff peaks form; fold into ground beef mixture. Spoon into prepared casserole.
- Bake 20 minutes or until edges are lightly browned.

Nutrition Facts
Carbohydrates: 24g, Protein: 28g, Fat: 7g, Saturated Fat: 3g, Cholesterol: 55mg, Sodium: 330mg, Fiber: 9g

438. HOLIDAY STUFFED BEEF TENDERLOIN

Total Time: 1 Hour 20 Minutes

Ingredients
- 4 teaspoons olive oil, divided
- 2 shallots, minced
- 1 package (8 ounces) sliced cremini mushrooms
- 3 cloves garlic, minced and divided
- 1 tablespoon chopped fresh thyme, plus additional for garnish
- 1 1/2 teaspoons chopped fresh parsley, plus additional for garnish
- 1/4 cup dry sherry or red wine vinegar
- 2 to 3 pounds beef tenderloin
- 1/2 cup fresh whole wheat bread crumbs
- 1 teaspoon salt
- 1/2 teaspoon black pepper

Directions
- Preheat oven to 425°F.
- Heat 2 teaspoons oil in a large skillet over medium heat. Add shallots; cook and stir 5 minutes or until tender. Add mushrooms, cook and stir 8 minutes or until softened. Stir in 1 clove garlic, 1 tablespoon thyme, and 1 1/2 teaspoon parsley; cook and stir 1 minute.
- Pour dry sherry into skillet. Bring to a boil over medium heat; boil 2 minutes or until sherry is reduced by about half. Cool slightly.
- Cut beef tenderloin lengthwise. (Do not cut all the way through). Open up beef; cover with plastic or waxed paper. Pound using a meat mallet to 1/2-inch thickness.
- Stir bread crumbs into mushroom mixture; spread evenly onto center of beef, leaving a 1-inch border around edges. Roll up beef jelly-roll style. Secure with kitchen string at 1-inch intervals. Place beef on rack in shallow roasting pan.
- Combine the remaining 2 teaspoons oil, 2 cloves garlic, salt, and pepper in a small bowl. Rub mixture evenly over beef.
- Roast 35 to 40 minutes for medium-rare (135°F) or until the desired doneness is reached. Remove roast to carving board; tent loosely with foil. Let stand 15 to 20 minutes before carving and serving. Sprinkle with additional thyme and parsley, if desired.

Nutrition Facts
Carbohydrates: 5g, Protein: 21g, Fat: 9g, Saturated Fat: 3g, Cholesterol: 59mg, Sodium: 381mg, Fiber: 1g

439. CALDO DE RES

Total Time: 2 Hour 40 Minutes

Ingredients
- 12 cups of water
- 2 pounds beef shank, crosscut
- 2 cloves of peeled garlic
- 1 stalk of celery, cut into 1/2-inch pieces
- 4 ounces of onion, peeled and diced
- 12 ounces of russet potatoes, peeled and cut into 1-inch pieces
- 12 ounces of chayote, cut into 8 wedges
- 1 ear of corn, husked, cut into 1-inch pieces
- 1 pound of cabbage, cut into 6 wedges
- 8 ounces of carrots, peeled and cut into 1-inch pieces
- 12 ounces of zucchini, cut into 1-inch pieces
- 1/4 bunch of cilantro, roughly chopped
- Salt to taste

Directions
- Chop beef shank into large chunks, keeping some attached to the bone (the bone marrow is an important element of the recipe).
- In a large stock pot, add meat, water, garlic, celery, and onions.
- Bring to a boil and then reduce heat to medium.
- Cover and simmer for 2 hours, skimming off any foam and fat.
- Add potatoes, chayote, and corn, and then simmer for 15–20 minutes.
- Add cabbage, carrots, zucchini, and cilantro.
- Cover, cook for 15 minutes, and taste for seasoning. Adjust the salt if needed.
- Serve in a large bowl and garnish with lemon wedges.

Nutrition Facts
Carbohydrates: 20g, Protein: 20g, Fat: 7g, Saturated Fat: 2g, Cholesterol: 33mg, Sodium: 1091mg, Fiber: 3g

440. CHEF LALA'S GOODNESS PLATTER

Total Time:

Ingredients
Steak:
- 1 pound skirt steak, fat trimmed, butterflied
- 1 cup water
- 1 teaspoon soy sauce, low sodium
- 1/2 medium brown onion, peeled, sliced
- 1/4 cup cilantro, rough chop
- 1 garlic cloves, peeled, sliced
- 1 teaspoon extra-virgin olive oil
- 1/2 orange, juiced
- to taste salt and pepper

Hummus:
- 1 1/2 cups freshly cooked chickpeas (or 15 ounces can drain)
- 1/4 cup fresh lemon juice (1 large lemon)
- 1/4 cup well-stirred tahini
- 1 small garlic clove, minced

- 2 tablespoons extra-virgin olive oil, and more for serving
- to taste salt
- 2–3 tablespoons water
- Dash ground paprika for garnish

Roasted Veggies:
- 1 cup sweet potato, sliced into half-moons
- 1 package mushrooms
- 8 ounces asparagus, sliced
- 1–2 tablespoons olive oil
- to taste salt and pepper
- More goodness:
- 1 avocado ripe, sliced
- 8 ounces baby tomatoes
- 16 ounce mixed green
- 1 red baby bell pepper sliced

Directions

Steak Directions:
- In a large bowl, combine water, soy sauce, brown onion, cilantro, garlic, olive oil, orange, and salt & pepper.
- Add meat to marinate, making sure it is completely covered.
- Cover and refrigerate for at least two hours.
- Heat grill to medium (you should be able to hold your hand about 4 inches above the grate for six to eight seconds). If using charcoal, it should be glowing orange with a light layer of ash.
- Place meat on the grill.
- Turn steak once during cooking.

Hummus Directions:
- In the bowl of a food processor, combine the tahini and lemon juice and process for 1 minute, scrape the sides and bottom of the bowl then process for 30 seconds more. This extra time helps whip the tahini, for a smooth and creamy hummus.
- Add the olive oil, minced garlic, and a 1/2 teaspoon of salt to the whipped tahini and lemon juice. Process for 30 seconds, scrape the sides and bottom of the bowl then process another 30 seconds or until well blended. Add half of the chickpeas to the food processor and process for 1 minute. Scrape sides and bottom of the bowl, then add remaining chickpeas and process until thick and quite smooth; 1 to 2 minutes.
- Most likely the hummus will be too thick or still have tiny bits of chickpea. To fix this, with the food processor turned on, slowly add 2 to 3 tablespoons of water until you reach the perfect consistency.
- Taste for salt and adjust as needed. Serve hummus with a drizzle of olive oil and a dash of paprika.
- Cook to desired doneness (5 minutes on each side for medium-rare).

Roasted Veggies Directions:
- Preheat oven to 350 F. Place sweet potato, mushrooms, and asparagus on a baking pan. Drizzle with oil and lightly sprinkle with salt and pepper. Bake for 15 minutes or until tender.

Final Assembly Directions:
- There is no right or wrong way to assemble this dish. Some people prefer to toss it like a salad, I prefer to keep each item separated layered over the mixed greens so I can see the colors and textures which compliment the beauty of the clean delicious ingredients. Enjoy!

Nutrition Facts

Carbohydrates: 34g, Protein: 26g, Fat: 26g, Saturated Fat: 8g, Cholesterol: 44mg, Sodium: 510mg, Fiber: 11g

441. CRANBERRY-GLAZED PORK CHOPS

Preparation Time: 35 Minutes

Ingredients
- 4 half-inch-thick lean, bone-in pork chops (about 6 ounces each)
- 1/4 teaspoon garlic powder
- 1/4 teaspoon black pepper
- 1/4 teaspoon salt
- Cooking spray
- 1 teaspoon corn oil
- 1 medium onion (about 6 ounces), sliced and separated into rings
- 1/3 cup plus 1 tablespoon cold water
- 1 tablespoon packed brown sugar
- 1 teaspoon cornstarch
- 3 tablespoons balsamic vinegar
- 1/4 cup sweetened, dried, orange-flavored cranberries (plain sweetened, dried cranberries can be substituted)

Directions
- Trim fat from pork chops. Sprinkle chops evenly with garlic powder, pepper, and salt. Coat a large nonstick skillet with cooking spray, add 1 teaspoon corn oil, and heat over medium-high heat. Add chops and cook 10–12 minutes, or until nicely browned and no longer pink in the center; turn once during cooking. Remove chops from the skillet and cover to keep them warm. Decrease the heat to medium-low. Add onion and 1 tablespoon water to the skillet. Cook covered for 8–10 minutes, or until the onions are tender and begin to turn golden; remove the lid and stir periodically. Stir in brown sugar and cook uncovered until sugar dissolves, about 1 minute. Meanwhile, whisk together cornstarch, remaining 1/3 cup cold water, and vinegar. Stir into the onions. Stir in cranberries. Cook until sauce is bubbly and slightly thickened; stirring frequently. Add chops and heat through, about 4–5 minutes.

Nutrition Facts

Carbohydrates: 16g, Protein: 20g, Fat: 8g, Saturated Fat: 3g, Sodium: 200mg, Fiber: 1g

442. SMOKED SAUSAGE PITA POCKETS

Preparation Time: 30 Minutes
Baking Time: 7–10 Minutes

Ingredients
- Cooking spray
- 1/2 cup fat-free beef broth
- 1 medium onion (about 6 ounces), thinly sliced and separated into strips
- Pepper, sliced into thin strips
- 4 ounces fresh mushrooms, sliced
- 7 ounces low-fat smoked sausage (such as Healthy Choice), sliced into bite-size pieces
- 5 whole-wheat pita pocket halves (6 1/2–inch diameter)
- 1/4 cup plus 1 tablespoon finely shredded, reduced-fat mild Cheddar cheese

- 1/4 cup fat-free salad dressing-style mayonnaise (such as fat-free Miracle Whip)
- 1 teaspoon prepared yellow mustard

Directions

- Preheat oven to 350°F.
- Coat a large nonstick skillet with cooking spray. Add beef broth and bring to a boil over medium-high heat. Add onion, pepper, and mushrooms, cover, and continue cooking over medium-high heat until tender; stir periodically. If all the liquid evaporates, add 2–3 tablespoons of water to the vegetables. Reduce heat to medium, add sliced smoked sausage, and cook uncovered, stirring periodically, until sausage is heated through and liquid evaporates.
- Spoon about 1/2 cup meat filling into each pita pocket. Stand up-filled pita pockets in a small baking dish. Press 1 tablespoon cheese over the filling in each pita pocket. Bake uncovered until cheese is melted, about 7–10 minutes.
- Meanwhile, stir together salad dressing and mustard in a small bowl. Place a dollop on top of the cheese in each pita pocket and serve.

Nutrition Facts

Carbohydrates: 29g, Protein: 12g, Fat: 4g, Saturated Fat: 2g, Sodium: 640mg, Fiber: 4g

443. FETTUCCINE AND VEGETABLE SALAD

Preparation Time: 25 Minutes

Ingredients

- 6 ounces fettuccine, uncooked, broken in half
- 2 cups broccoli flowerets
- 1 cup sliced carrots
- 1 cup sliced celery
- 1/2 cup commercial fat-free creamy italian salad dressing
- 1/2 teaspoon pepper
- 12 cherry tomatoes, halved
- 3/4 pound cooked chicken, turkey, beef, or pork

Directions

- Cook fettuccine according to package directions, omitting salt and oil. Drain and rinse under cold water; drain again and set aside. Meanwhile, cook broccoli, carrots, and celery in a small amount of boiling water or steam until crisp-tender, about 5–6 minutes. Drain and plunge vegetables into cold water for 1 minute; drain again. Combine cooked fettuccine and vegetables in a large bowl. Add dressing and pepper and stir well. Gently fold in tomatoes. Cut meat into bite-size pieces or strips and arrange over salad. Serve immediately, or chill until serving time.

Nutrition Facts

Carbohydrates: 20g, Protein: 17g, Fat: 3g, Saturated Fat: <1g, Sodium: 196mg, Fiber: 2g

444. STIR-FRY BEEF AND SPAGHETTI

Preparation Time: 20 Minutes

Marinating Time: 30 Minutes

Cooking Time: 10 Minutes.

Ingredients

- 3 plus 1 tablespoon cornstarch
- 1/3 cup low-sodium soy sauce, divided
- 1 clove garlic, minced
- 1/2 teaspoon ground ginger
- 1/4 teaspoon pepper
- 12 ounces boneless beef round steak, trimmed of fat and cut into thin strips
- 2 cups cold water
- 8 ounces spaghetti, fusilli, or linguine, uncooked
- 2 plus 1 teaspoon oil
- 2 medium carrots, thinly sliced
- 1 large onion, cut into bite-size chunks
- 1 package (10 ounces) frozen cut green beans, thawed and drained
- Toasted sesame seeds (optional)

Directions

- In a small bowl, blend 1 tablespoon of the cornstarch and 1 tablespoon of the soy sauce with garlic, ginger, and pepper. Add beef; marinate for 30 minutes in the refrigerator. In another small bowl, blend the remaining 3 tablespoons of cornstarch into the water; stir in the remaining soy sauce; set aside. Prepare pasta according to package directions; drain. Add 1 teaspoon of the oil to pasta and toss to coat. In a nonstick skillet, heat the remaining 2 teaspoons of oil. Add meat mixture and stir-fry for 1 minute. Remove meat from the pan. Add carrots and onion and stir-fry until tender-crisp. Stir in meat, green beans, and the water and cornstarch mixture. Cook, stirring constantly until the mixture is translucent and thick. Arrange hot pasta on a serving platter and top with meat mixture. Garnish with sesame seeds, if desired.

Nutrition Facts

Carbohydrates: 44g, Protein: 18g, Fat: 5g, Saturated Fat: 1g, Sodium: 713mg, Fiber: 4g

445. BEEF AND BROCCOLI STROGANOFF

Preparation Time: 20 Minutes

Cooking Time: 30 Minutes.

Ingredients

- 1 pound frozen round steak, partially thawed
- 6 tablespoons all-purpose flour, divided
- Cooking spray
- 1 tablespoon canola oil
- 1 clove garlic, minced
- 4 ounces fresh mushrooms, sliced
- 1 small onion, finely diced
- 2 tablespoons reduced-calorie margarine
- 1 tablespoon Worcestershire sauce
- 1/4 teaspoon black pepper
- 1/2 teaspoon dry dill weed
- 1 cube reduced-sodium beef bouillon dissolved in 1 1/2 cups warm water
- 1 cup fat-free sour cream
- 2 cups lightly steamed small broccoli florets
- 4 cups cooked cholesterol-free egg noodles (about 12 ounces dry)

Directions

- Remove fat from steak and slice meat across the grain into bite-size pieces.
- Place 3 tablespoons of flour in a large, zip-top plastic bag. Add meat and shake to coat.
- Spray a large nonstick skillet with cooking spray. Add oil and warm over medium heat. Add meat and brown on

both sides. Stir in garlic, mushrooms, and onion; cook for 5 minutes.
- Add margarine and cook until melted.
- Stir in 2 tablespoons of flour until liquid forms a paste. Stir in Worcestershire sauce, pepper, dill weed, and bouillon dissolved in water.
- Continue cooking uncovered for 10 minutes, stirring frequently.
- Mix remaining 1 tablespoon of flour into the sour cream, then add to meat mixture. Cook for 5 minutes, stirring frequently, but do not boil. Toss in steamed broccoli.
- Place cooked noodles on a serving dish and top with meat mixture.

Nutrition Facts

Carbohydrates: 32g, Protein: 19g, Fat: 7g, Saturated Fat: 2g, Sodium: 190mg, Fiber: 2g

446. CLASSIC BEEF STEW

Preparation Time: 20 Minutes
Cooking Time: 20–25 Minutes

Ingredients

- 1 tablespoon canola oil
- 1 pound stew beef or buffalo
- 1 large onion, chopped into 1-inch chunks
- 1/2 cup red wine
- 3 large cloves garlic, cut in half
- 1 cup low-sodium broth (beef, chicken, or vegetable)
- 3 medium (3–4 ounces each) red-skinned potatoes, scrubbed and quartered
- 2 large carrots, peeled
- 1/2 teaspoon dried thyme
- 1/2 teaspoon dried oregano
- 2 bay leaves
- Salt and pepper to taste
- 1–2 tablespoons chopped fresh parsley

Directions

- Heat canola oil in a pressure cooker until hot, add meat, and brown. Add onion and cook about 5 minutes more.
- Add wine, garlic, and broth and bring to a boil. Scrape browned bits of cooked meat from the bottom of a pressure cooker. Place lid on cooker and cook at high pressure 15 minutes.
- Quick-release pressure. Open the cooker and add potatoes, carrots, thyme, oregano, and bay leaves. Replace lid and cook at high temperature for 5 minutes.
- Quick-release pressure and remove the lid. Cut cooked carrots into large chunks.
- Add salt and pepper to taste and chopped parsley before serving.
- Simmer stew uncovered if you desire a thicker consistency.

Nutrition Facts

Carbohydrates: 20g, Protein: 27g, Fat: 6g, Saturated Fat: 1g, Cholesterol: 80mg, Sodium: 233mg, Fiber: 3g

447. JALAPEÑO CHEESEBURGERS

Preparation time: 5 minutes
Cooking time: 10 minutes

Ingredients

- 2 ounces (4 slices) Sargento Deli-Style Reduced Fat Pepper Jack Cheese
- 1 pound 85% lean ground beef
- 4 drops liquid hot pepper sauce
- 4 whole-grain, light hamburger buns
- 4 slices tomato
- 1/4 cup lightly chopped cilantro

Directions

- Preheat grill. Cut cheese slices into half-inch pieces. In a medium-size bowl, combine cheese, ground beef, and hot pepper sauce, and mix well.
- Shape meat into four equal patties. Slightly depress the center of each patty.
- Grill burgers for approximately 5 minutes on each side until meat is cooked through.
- Place burger on bottom of a hamburger bun, top with 1 slice tomato and a quarter of the chopped cilantro.
- Add top bun and serve.

Nutrition Facts

Carbohydrates: 16g, Protein: 28g, Fat: 21g, Saturated Fat: 7g, Cholesterol: 77mg, Sodium: 301mg, Fiber: 2g

448. MINI MARINATED BEEF SKEWERS

Total Time: 3 Hour

Ingredients

- 1 beef top round steak (about 1 pound)
- 2 tablespoons reduced-sodium soy sauce
- 1 tablespoon dry sherry
- 1 teaspoon dark sesame oil
- 2 cloves garlic, minced
- 18 cherry tomatoes (optional)

Directions

- Cut beef crosswise into 18 (1/8-inch-thick) slices. Place in a large resealable food storage bag. Combine soy sauce, sherry, oil, and garlic in a small cup; pour over beef. Seal bag; turn to coat. Marinate in 2the refrigerator for at least 30 minutes or up to 2 hours.
- Meanwhile, soak 18 (6-inch) wooden skewers in water for 20 minutes.
- Preheat broiler. Drain beef; discard marinade. Weave beef accordion-style onto skewers. Place on rack of broiler pan.
- Broil 4 to 5 inches from heat for 2 minutes. Turn skewers over; broil 2 minutes more or until beef is barely pink.
- Garnish each skewer with 1 cherry tomato. Serve warm.

Nutrition Facts

Carbohydrates: 2g, Protein: 20g, Fat: 4g, Saturated Fat: 1g, Cholesterol: 60mg, Sodium: 99mg, Fiber: 1g

449. APRICOT BRISKET

Total Time: 3 Hour

Ingredients

- 1 cup chopped dried apricots, divided
- 1 cup canned diced tomatoes, divided
- 2 teaspoons ground cumin
- 1 teaspoon salt, divided
- 1 clove garlic
- 1/4 teaspoon ground cinnamon
- 1 medium onion, thinly sliced
- 2 large carrots, cut into 1-inch pieces
- 1 small beef brisket (about 2 to 3 pounds), trimmed of fat
- 1/2 teaspoon black pepper
- 1 1/2 cups low-sodium beef broth
- 2 tablespoons cornstarch
- 2 tablespoons cold water
- Chopped parsley (optional)

Directions

- Preheat oven to 325°F.
- Combine 1/2 cup chopped apricots, 1/2 cup tomatoes, cumin, 1/2 teaspoon salt, garlic, and cinnamon in the food processor. Process using on/off pulses until coarsely combined.
- Place onion and carrots on the bottom of the roasting pan. Place brisket on top. Cut several small slits across the top of brisket; gently spoon apricot mixture into slits. Sprinkle brisket with remaining 1/2 teaspoon salt and pepper. Spread remaining 1/2 cup diced tomatoes over brisket; top with remaining 1/2 cup apricots. Drizzle broth over brisket. Cover with foil.
- Roast 2 to 2 1/2 hours. Transfer brisket to carving board; tent with foil and let stand 15 minutes.
- Pour pan juices and vegetables into a medium saucepan. Stir cornstarch into the water in a small bowl until smooth and well blended. Stir into pan juices; simmer until thickened, about 5 minutes.
- Carve brisket crosswise into thin slices; serve with onion, carrots, tomatoes, apricots, and pan juices. Sprinkle with parsley, if desired.

Nutrition Facts

Carbohydrates: 17g, Protein: 20g, Fat: 4g, Saturated Fat: 1g, Cholesterol: 53mg, Sodium: 380mg, Fiber: 2g

450. PORK STIR-FRY

Preparation Time: 20 Minutes
Cooking Time: 15 Minutes

Ingredients

- 3 tablespoons reduced-sodium soy sauce
- 1/4 cup cold water
- 1 tablespoon cornstarch
- 1/8 to 1/4 teaspoon red pepper flakes (not ground red pepper)
- 1/4 teaspoon garlic powder
- Cooking spray
- 1 teaspoon corn oil
- 1/2 pound lean, boneless pork loin chops with fat trimmed, cut into bite-size pieces
- 1/4 cup hot water
- 1 red pepper, cut into bite-size pieces
- 1 cup coarsely chopped onion
- 2 cups fresh broccoli florets
- 8 ounces fresh mushrooms, thickly sliced
- 1 can (8 ounces) pineapple chunks canned in juice, drained
- 1 can (11 ounces) mandarin oranges canned in light syrup, rinsed, and drained
- Hot rice (optional)

Directions

- In a small bowl, whisk together soy sauce, cold water, cornstarch, red pepper flakes, and garlic powder. Set aside.
- Coat a cool, nonstick wok with cooking spray. Preheat wok, then add oil. When the oil is hot, add pork cubes and cook for 3-4 minutes, stirring constantly. Remove pork from wok and set aside. Add hot water, pepper, onion, and broccoli, and cook 2-3 minutes, stirring constantly. Add mushrooms and cook an additional 2-3 minutes, stirring constantly. Add cooked pork back to the wok. Stir the soy sauce mixture well and pour it over the ingredients in the wok. While stirring constantly, heat for 1 minute or until the sauce thickens and bubbles. Add pineapple and mandarin oranges and toss gently to coat. Serve immediately (over hot rice if desired).

Nutrition Facts

Carbohydrates: 30g, Protein: 27g, Fat: 8g, Saturated Fat: 2g, Sodium: 518mg, Fiber: 4g

451. DIRTY RICE

Preparation Time: 15 Minutes
Cooking Time: 45–50 Minutes

Ingredients

- 1 pound ground round (ground beef)
- 1 medium onion, finely chopped
- 1 green bell pepper, finely chopped
- 1/2 cup finely chopped celery
- 2 teaspoons (or 2 cloves) minced garlic
- 1/2 teaspoon salt
- 1/8–1/4 teaspoon cayenne pepper (more or less to taste)
- 1/4 teaspoon ground black pepper
- 1/8 teaspoon paprika
- 1/4 teaspoon dried oregano
- 1 teaspoon dried parsley
- 1 tablespoon low-sodium Worcestershire sauce
- 1 cup uncooked brown rice
- 1 can (14 ounces) 50%reduced-sodium fat-free beef broth
- I cup water

Directions

- Brown ground round in a large, nonstick skillet. Drain off any fat. Stir in the remaining ingredients. Cover and bring to a boil over high heat, reduce heat to medium and simmer 30–35 minutes, or until rice is tender; stir periodically.

Nutrition Facts

- Carbohydrates: 29g, Protein: 20g, Fat: 5g, Saturated Fat: 2g, Cholesterol: 47mg, Sodium: 367mg, Fiber: 2g

452. BEEFY BARLEY MUSHROOM SOUP

Preparation Time: 25 Minutes
Cooking Time: 50 Minutes

Ingredients

- Cooking spray
- 1 pound lean stew beef or trimmed, diced sirloin steak, cut into bite-size pieces
- 2 cups water plus 4 cups water
- 1/2 cup red wine (optional)
- 2 tablespoons reduced-calorie margarine
- 2 large carrots, diced
- 1 medium onion, finely diced
- 2 medium celery stalks, finely diced
- 8 ounces fresh mushrooms, sliced (porcini, shiitake, or gourmet blend are suggested)
- 3 cloves garlic, minced
- 4 cups 50% less sodium, fat-free beef broth
- 1 cup quick barley
- 1/8 teaspoon black pepper
- 1/2 teaspoon dried thyme
- 1/3 cup reduced-fat sour cream
- 1/4 cup chopped fresh parsley
- Salt to taste (optional)

Directions

- Coat a large, nonstick skillet with cooking spray, add meat, and brown over medium-high heat for about 5–7 minutes. Add 2 cups water and the wine; simmer uncovered over medium heat while sautéing vegetables.
- In a large stockpot, melt margarine over medium heat. Add carrots, onion, celery, mushrooms, and garlic; sauté for 7–8 minutes or until onions are translucent. Add meat and cooking liquid to the stockpot. Stir in broth, remaining 4 cups water, barley, black pepper, and thyme. Cover and simmer 30 minutes over medium heat, or until barley is soft; stir occasionally. Remove from heat and stir in sour cream, parsley, and salt (if desired). Serve. Reheats well.

Nutrition Facts

Carbohydrates: 19g, Protein: 12g, Fat: 6g, Saturated Fat: 2g, Sodium: 209mg, Fiber: 4g

453. CHEESEBURGERS

Preparation Time: 8 Minutes
Cooking Time: 14 Minutes.

Ingredients

- Nonstick cooking spray
- 1 teaspoon salt-free, herb-and-spice steak seasoning such as Mrs. Dash
- 6 slices reduced-fat sharp Cheddar cheese
- 2 tomatoes, sliced
- 1 onion, sliced
- 6 lettuce leaves
- 2 tablespoons mustard
- 3 tablespoons ketchup
- 6 100% whole wheat buns

Directions

- Heat grill to medium. Shape ground beef into 6 equal patties.
- Spray both sides of burgers with nonstick cooking spray, then sprinkle with herb-and-spice seasoning. Place burgers on the grill and cook on one side for about 5 minutes. Flip the burgers and cook for 2–5 minutes on the other side.
- Place the cheese slices on top of the burgers and cook for another 2–4 minutes, or until the meat juices are no longer pink. For the last 2–4 minutes of cooking, place the buns on the grill to warm.
- Place the burgers on the buns and top with tomato, onion, lettuce, mustard, and ketchup.

Nutrition Facts

Carbohydrates: 28g, Protein: 36g, Fat: 14g, Saturated Fat: 7g, Cholesterol: 90mg, Sodium: 670mg, Fiber: 4g

454. GARLIC GRILLED BEEF BROCHETTES

Total Time: 30 Minutes

Ingredients

- 1/3 cup light Caesar salad dressing
- 3 cloves garlic, minced
- 1 pound beef tenderloin tips or steaks, cut into 1 1/2-inch chunk
- 1 small red onion (or 1/2 medium), cut into 1/2-inch-thick wedges
- 1 large red or yellow bell pepper (or 1/2 of each), cut into 1-inch chunks
- 2 tablespoons chopped fresh thyme or rosemary

Directions

- Heat grill to medium-high heat. Combine dressing and garlic in a shallow dish. Add tenderloin, onion, and bell pepper; toss to coat well and let stand 20 minutes.
- Alternately thread meat and vegetables onto 4 long metal skewers. Brush any remaining marinade from the dish the shover meat and vegetables.
- Grill skewers on covered grill 5 minutes on each side. (Tenderloin will be pink in center and vegetables will be crisp-tender.) Top with thyme.

Nutrition Facts

Carbohydrates: 8g, Protein: 27g, Fat: 12g, Saturated Fat: 3g, Cholesterol: 85mg, Sodium: 313mg, Fiber: 1g

455. SPICY PORK CHOP SUPPER

Preparation Time: 25 Minutes
Baking Time: 35–40 Minutes

Ingredients

- 2 tablespoons + 1 tablespoon chili seasoning mix
- 2 tablespoons all-purpose flour
- 4 boneless, 1/2 inch–thick pork loin chops (about 4 ounces each)
- Cooking spray
- 1 1/2 teaspoons corn oil
- 1 cup uncooked instant white rice
- 1 cup water
- 1 can (8 ounces) tomato sauce
- 1/2 cup coarsely chopped onion
- 1/2 cup coarsely chopped yellow pepper

Directions

- Preheat oven to 350°F. Combine 2 tablespoons chili seasoning mix and flour in a large zip-top bag. Add pork chops, seal bag, and shake to coat well.
- Coat a large, nonstick skillet with cooking spray, add oil, and heat until oil is hot. Add chops and sprinkle with the remaining coating.
- Brown pork chops quickly over medium-high heat (about 3–4 minutes on each side). Remove from heat and set aside.
- Coat a 2-quart casserole dish with cooking spray; set aside. In a large bowl, stir together the remaining 1 tablespoon chili seasoning mix, rice, water, and tomato sauce.
- Pour into casserole dish.
- Arrange pork chops over rice and sprinkle with onion, yellow pepper, and green pepper.
- Bake, covered, for 35–40 minutes, or until rice is bubbly and pork chops are no longer pink in the center.

Nutrition Facts

Carbohydrates: 34g, Protein: 39g, Fat: 9g, Saturated Fat: 4g, Sodium: 965mg, Fiber: 2g

456. HASH BROWN BREAKFAST CASSEROLE FOR DIABETICS

Total Time: 4 Hours 30 Minutes

Ingredients

- 3 cups refrigerated or frozen hash brown potatoes, thawed
- 1 1/2 cups (6 ounces) finely chopped extra-lean ham
- 3/4 cup (3 ounces) shredded reduced-fat Cheddar cheese
- 1/4 cup sliced green onions

- 1 can (12 ounces) evaporated fat-free (skim) milk
- 1 tablespoon all-purpose flour
- 1 cup cholesterol-free egg substitute
- 1/2 teaspoon black pepper

Directions

- Lightly spray an 8-inch square baking dish with nonstick cooking spray. Layer potatoes, ham, cheese, and green onions in the prepared dish.
- Gradually whisk evaporated milk into flour in a medium bowl. Stir in egg substitute and pepper; pour over potato mixture. Cover; refrigerate for 4 hours or overnight.
- Preheat oven to 350°F. Bake, uncovered, 55 to 60 minutes or until knife inserted into the center comes out clean. Let stand 10 minutes before serving.

Nutrition Facts

Carbohydrates: 24g, Protein: 21g, Fat: 9g, Saturated Fat: 3g, Cholesterol: 19mg, Sodium: 748mg, Fiber: 1g

457. BEEF MEATBALLS ON BOK CHOY NESTS

Preparation Time: 10 Minutes
Cooking Time: 15–17 Minutes

Ingredients

- 1 pound lean ground beef (8% fat or less)
- 1/4 cup chopped green onions
- 1 beaten egg white
- 1/4 cup chopped water chestnuts
- 1 slice whole-wheat bread
- 3/4 teaspoon Chinese five-spice powder
- 1/2 teaspoon ground red pepper
- 1 teaspoon lite (low-sodium) soy sauce
- 1 teaspoon minced garlic plus 1 teaspoon minced garlic
- Nonstick cooking spray
- 1 pound bok choy, washed and patted dry
- 1/2 cup low-sodium, fat-free chicken broth
- 1 teaspoon sesame oil (or canola oil)

Directions

- Meatballs
- Preheat oven to 350°F. Combine beef, green onions, egg white, and water chestnuts in a medium-size mixing bowl. Tear the slice of bread into fingernail-sized pieces into the bowl.
- Add five-spice powder, red pepper, soy sauce, and 1 teaspoon garlic, and mix well. Mold into 24 one-inch meatballs.
- Heat a nonstick skillet over medium heat. Spray with nonstick cooking spray and cook the meatballs in the skillet in small batches so they brown evenly. Quickly brown on all sides, turning frequently, but do not cook through. Place meatballs on a baking sheet or dish sprayed with nonstick cooking spray in a single layer. Place in oven and bake an additional 10 minutes until cooked through.
- Bok choy nests
- While meatballs are cooking in the oven, cut 2 inches off bottom(s) of bok choy and discard. Cut remaining stalks and leaves into bite-size pieces, slicing horizontally across the leaves. Heat chicken broth in a wok or large skillet over medium-high heat. When liquid begins to boil, add the second teaspoon of garlic, sesame oil, and bok choy pieces. Stir-fry over medium-high heat for about 3–4 minutes; bok choy should retain its crispness.
- To serve, remove hot bok choy with large tongs or a slotted spoon and make a small nest on each of the four plates. Center six meatballs within the bok choy nest.

Nutrition Facts

Carbohydrates: 7g, Protein: 28g, Fat: 7g, Saturated Fat: 3g, Cholesterol: 70mg, Sodium: 427mg, Fiber: 2g

458. ESTOFADO DE BISTEC CON PAPAS

Total Time: 45 Minutes

Ingredients

- 1 1/2 pounds beef shoulder roast, sliced into 2-inch pieces
- 1 tablespoon grapeseed oil
- 1 teaspoon granulated garlic
- 1 teaspoon black pepper
- 1 teaspoon salt
- 1 cup water
- 1 packet bouillon with chicken flavor
- 2 medium russet potatoes, peeled, sliced into rounds
- 1/2 medium white onion, thinly sliced
- 2 medium tomatoes, sliced in rounds
- 1 can of tomato sauce (8 oz)
- 2 tablespoons canned pickled jalapeno or
- Serrano peppers with juice

Directions

- Heat the oil in a large sauté pan and add beef.
- Add granulated garlic, pepper, and salt and stir to combine.
- Brown meat over medium-high heat for 15 minutes and stir in water and bouillon.
- Lower heat, cover, and simmer for 10 minutes.
- Uncover pan and layer in potatoes, then onion, and then tomatoes.
- Pour tomato sauce and serrano and pickled juice over the casserole.
- Cover and cook for 10–15 minutes, until the potatoes are tender.

Nutrition Facts

Carbohydrates: 16.5g, Protein: 22g, Fat: 9g, Sodium: 605mg

SMOOTHIES RECIPES

459. KIWI VANILLA YOGURT SMOOTHIE

Prep Time: 5 mins
Total Time: 5 mins

Ingredients

- 8 fl. oz. (237 ml) Glucerna Shake, Homemade Vanilla flavor
- 6 oz. low-fat Greek yogurt
- 1 medium kiwi fruit, sliced
- 4 ice cubes

Directions

- Combine the Glucerna Shake (Homemade Vanilla), Greek yogurt, kiwi fruit, and ice cubes in a high-speed blender.
- Process for 20 seconds or until smooth.
- Pour in serving glasses.

- Serve and enjoy.

Nutrition Facts

Fat: 5.2g| Saturated fat: 1.4g| Carbohydrates: 18.6g| Sugar: 12.4g| Sodium: 221mg| Fiber: 2.6g| Protein: 12.8g| Cholesterol: 10mg

460. DRAGON FRUIT SMOOTHIE BOWL

Prep Time: 3 Mins
Cook Time: 2 Mins
Total Time: 5 Minutes

Ingredients

- 3/4 cup frozen fruit (we used dragon fruit, mangoes, strawberries, and peaches)
- 1 cup spinach
- 1/2 cup Greek yogurt
- 1/2 Avocado

Directions

- Add ingredients to blender or food processor.
- Blend on high until smooth. As needed, pause and scrape the edges with a spoon or spatula to incorporate all ingredients.
- Enjoy!

Nutrition Facts

Carbs: 295g| Fiber: 8g| Net Carbs: 21g| Protein: 15g

461. THE ULTIMATE GREEN SMOOTHIE RECIPE

Prep Time: 5 minutes

Ingredients

- 35g (1 cup, firmly packed) baby spinach leaves
- 1 Lebanese cucumber, chopped
- 1 green apple, unpeeled, cored, chopped
- 250ml (1 cup) coconut water
- ½ cup ice cubes

Directions

- Put all ingredients in a blender. Cover and blend until smooth.
- Pour smoothie between 2 glasses and serve immediately.

Nutrition Facts

Protein: 2g| Total Fat: 0.3g| Satfat: 0.1g| Carbs: 16g| Fiber: 3g| Sodium: 38mg.

462. PEACH SMOOTHIE (DIABETIC)

Prep Time: 10m
Ready In: 10 minutes

Ingredients

- 2 cups fat-free soy beverage (no-fat 500ml)
- 2 medium bananas (400g, chopped coarsely)
- 4 medium peaches (600g, chopped coarsely)
- 1/2 teaspoon ground cinnamon

Directions:

- Blend or process ingredients, in batches, until smooth.

Nutrition Facts

Total Fat: 0.6g| Saturated Fat: 0.1g| Sodium: 2.9mg| Total Carbohydrate: 34.7g| Dietary Fiber: 4g| Sugars: 19.9g| Protein: 5.2 g| Calcium: 34.8mg| Iron: 2mg| Vitamin C: 15mg|

463. DIABETES-FRIENDLY CHOCOLATE CHIA SMOOTHIE RECIPE

Total Time: 10 min
Prep Time: 5 min
Cook Time: 5 min

Ingredients

- ½ cup unsweetened almond milk
- 2 tablespoons chia seeds
- ½ teaspoon cinnamon
- 1 ½ medium frozen bananas, cut into chunks
- 1 ½ cups unsweetened almond milk
- 2 tablespoons cocoa powder
- 2 tablespoons peanut butter powder

Preparation

- In a medium bowl, whisk together almond milk, chia seeds, and cinnamon. Let sit for at least 10 minutes for the chia seeds to swell and absorb the liquid.
- Combine the banana, almond milk, cocoa powder, and peanut butter powder in a blender. Puree until well combined.
- Divide the chia pudding between two glasses. Top with the smoothie and serve immediately.

Nutrition FactsValue

Fat: 8g| Carbs: 31g| Protein: 6g

464. LOWER CARB STRAWBERRY SMOOTHIE

Cook Time: 5 minutes
Total Time: 5 minutes

Ingredients

- 5 medium strawberry
- 1 cup unsweetened soy milk (or unsweetened almond milk)
- 1/2 cup low-fat Greek-style yogurt
- 6 ice cubes

Directions

- Place all ingredients in a blender and blend until smooth.
- Pour into a glass and garnish with a strawberry.

Nutrition Facts

Fat: 6g| Saturated Fat: 1g| Polyunsaturated Fat: 0.1g| Monounsaturated Fat: 0.03g| Cholesterol: 8mg| Sodium: 161mg| Potassium: 520mg| Carbohydrates: 11g| Fiber: 2g| Sugar: 6g| Protein: 16g

465. BALANCED BLOOD SUGAR SMOOTHIE

Total Time: 10 minutes

Ingredients

- 1/2 cup Greenspring Mix
- 1/2Banana
- 1/2Pear, cored
- 1 1/2 cup almond milk, unsweetened
- 1 tsp rolled, gluten-free
- 1/2 tsp Cinnamon, ground

Directions

- Add ingredients in the order listed and blend until smooth.
- Enjoy!

Nutrition Facts

Total Fat: 3.9g| Saturated Fat: 0.4g| Sodium: 273.3mg|Carbs: 34.6g| Dietary Fiber: 6.2g| Sugar: 18.9g| Protein: 3g

466. SPINACH SMOOTHIE (LOW-CARB & GLUTEN-FREE)

Prep Time: 5 minutes
Total Time: 5 minutes

Ingredients

- 2 tablespoons nut butter of choice
- ½ cup plain Greek yogurt
- ½ avocado (pitted)
- ¼ cup milk (or almond milk)
- 1 teaspoon vanilla extract
- 2 cups fresh spinach
- A few drops of sweetener (to taste)
- 1 cup ice

Directions

- Add all of the ingredients except the ice to a blender.
- Blend until smooth.
- Add the ice and pulse until the ice is mostly crushed.
- Blend until the mixture is smooth and creamy.

Nutrition Facts

Fat: 16.1g| Saturated Fat: 2.7g| Polyunsaturated Fat: 0.7g| Monounsaturated Fat: 3.5g| Cholesterol: 8.1mg| Sodium: 66.9mg| Potassium: 473.8mg| Carbohydrates: 11g| Fiber: 4.4g| Sugar: 4.8g| Protein: 11.1g| Net carbs: 6.6g

467. PINEAPPLE KALE SMOOTHIE

Prep Time: 5 minutes
Total Time: 5 minutes

Ingredients

- 1 cup 0% fat Greek yogurt
- 1½ cups cubed pineapple
- 3 cups baby kale
- 1 cucumber
- 2 tbsp, hemp seeds

Directions

- Put all the ingredients in a blender (I use a Nutribullet) and blend until the smoothie has an even and silky consistency.
- Find yourself a spot in the sun and enjoy!

Nutrition Facts

Fat: 5.7g| Saturated Fat: 0.3g| Polyunsaturated Fat: 2.7g| Monounsaturated Fat: 0.5g| Cholesterol: 5mg| Sodium: 80mg| Potassium: 743mg| Carbohydrates: 31.6g| Fiber: 6.4g| Sugar: 19.1g| Protein: 13.8g

468. BERRY DELICIOUS SMOOTHIE PACK

Total Time: 4 hours

Ingredients

- ¾ cup nonfat vanilla Greek yogurt
- 1 cup frozen strawberries
- ½ cup frozen blackberries
- ¼ cup frozen raspberries
- ¼ cup frozen blueberries
- 2 cups coconut water

How To Make It

- Spoon yogurt into an ice cube tray; freeze for 3 to 4 hours.
- Pop frozen yogurt cubes out of the ice cube tray and place them into a quart-size plastic freezer bag along with berries. (Or, to make individual portions, divide the fruit and yogurt cubes evenly between five freezer bags.) Label the bag and store it in the freezer.
- When ready to serve, pour the contents of the bag into a blender, add coconut water, and blend until smooth. (If using individual-portion bags, add only enough coconut water to reach desired thickness

Nutrition Facts

Fiber: 1g| Total Fat: 0g| Protein: 3g| Total Carbohydrate: 13g

469. TROPICAL PARADISE GREEN SMOOTHIE PACK

Total Time: 10 Minutes

Ingredients

- 2 cups spinach
- 1 avocado, diced
- 1 cup frozen pineapple chunks
- 1 cup frozen mango chunks
- ½ cup ice cubes
- 1 cup water
- 1 cup apple juice

How To Make It

- Place the first five ingredients in a plastic freezer bag. (Or, to make individual portions, divide these ingredients evenly between four freezer bags.) Label the bag and store it in the freezer.
- When ready to serve, pour the contents of the bag into a blender. Add water and apple juice. Blend until smooth. (If using individual-portion bags, add only ¼ cup apple juice and ¼ cup water.)

Nutrition Facts

Fiber: 5g| Total Fat: 7g| Protein: 1g| Total Carbohydrate: 27g

470. CHOCOLATE PEANUT BUTTER & BANANA SMOOTHIE PACK

Total Time: 4 Hours

Ingredients

- 1 large banana, diced
- ½ cup peanut butter
- ½ cup plain Greek yogurt
- 1 cup chocolate almond milk

How To Make It

- Spoon yogurt and peanut butter into separate sections of an ice cube tray; freeze for 3 to 4 hours.
- Pop frozen yogurt and peanut butter cubes out of the ice cube tray and place them into a quart-size plastic freezer bag along with a banana. (Or, to make individual portions, divide ingredients evenly between two freezer bags.) Label the bag and store it in the freezer.
- When ready to serve, pour the contents of the bag into a blender, add chocolate almond milk, and blend until smooth. (If using an individual-portion bag, add only ½ cup chocolate almond milk.)

Nutrition Facts

Fiber: 5g| Total Fat: 18g| Protein: 14g| Total Carbohydrate: 39g

471. LOW CARB DIABETIC BREAKFAST SMOOTHIE

Prep Time: 3 minutes

Ingredients

- 3/4 cup frozen mixed berries
- 2 scoops of protein powder
- 1/2 cup desiccated coconut
- 1 cup almond milk - or use coconut milk

- 1 Tablespoon flaxseed oil - or olive oil
- 1/4 teaspoon vanilla extract
- 1/4 teaspoon ground cinnamon
- 5-10 drops liquid stevia - optional for extra sweetness
- 1/4 cup water - if it's too thick for your liking

Directions

- Place everything into a blender and blend until smooth.
- Pour into a glass and you're good to go.

Nutrition Facts

Total Carbs:27g| Net Carbs:15g| Fiber:12g

472. GREEN SMOOTHIE

Prep Time: 5 minutes
Total Time: 5 minutes

Ingredients

- 100 grams baby spinach fresh or frozen partially defrosted
- 1 whole kiwi peeled and chopped
- ½ whole ripe avocado pitted and diced
- 200 ml tinned coconut milk (or almond, soy, or lalacto free milk)
- ½ whole lime the juice of
- 1 tbsp flaxseed milled or ground
- Ice cubes to the consistency liked
- Sugar-free syrup optional to taste

Directions

- Combine spinach, kiwi, avocado, coconut milk, and some cream from the top of the tin, lime, and milled flaxseed in a blender
- Add the desired amount of ice cubes and blitz to create a texture and consistency you like
- Add sugar-free syrup or sweetener to sweeten to your taste

Nutrition FactsValue

Carbohydrates: 12g | Protein: 9g | Fat: 47g | of which saturates: 38g | Fibre: 5g | of which sugars: 1g

473. AYURVEDIC DIGESTIVE TEA

Total Time: 10 Minutes

Ingredients

- 1/2 teaspoon whole cumin seed
- 1/2 teaspoon whole coriander seed
- 1/2 teaspoon fennel seed
- 1/2 teaspoon dried rose petals

Directions

- Place all the ingredients in an 8- to 10-ounce cup.
- Heat water on the stovetop and pour over the spices.
- Steep spices and rose petals for about 5 minutes.
- Sip while it is warm. You may strain out the spices if you prefer but this is not required.

Nutrition Facts

Carbohydrates: 11g| Protein: 1g| Fat: 1g| Saturated Fat: 1g| Sodium: 14mg| Fiber: 1g

474. SPICED CITRUS TEA

Total Time: 10 Minutes

Ingredients

- 1 Spiced Citrus Teabag
- Boiling water
- 1 to 2 teaspoons orange juice
- Honey (optional)
- Orange slices (optional)

Directions

- Place tea bag in cup or mug. Pour boiling water over tea bag; steep 3 to 5 minutes. Remove tea bag, pressing out liquid.
- Discard tea bag. Serve with orange juice and honey, if desired. Garnish with orange slices.

Nutrition Facts

Sodium: 2.5 mg

475. TROPICAL GREEN SHAKE

Total Time: 10 Minutes

Ingredients

- 1 cup ice cubes
- 1 cup packed stemmed kale
- 1 cup frozen tropical fruit mix
- 1/2 cup reduced-sugar orange juice beverage
- 2 tablespoons honey or agave nectar

Directions

- Combine ice, kale, tropical fruit mix, orange juice, and honey in a blender; blend until smooth.
- Pour into two glasses.

Nutrition Facts

Carbohydrates: 32g| Protein: 2g| Sodium: 20mg| Fiber: 1g

476. HONEYDEW AGUA FRESCA

Total Time: 10-20 Minutes

Ingredients

- 1/4 large honeydew melon, rind removed and cubed
- 1/4 cup fresh mint leaves
- 1/4 cup fresh lime juice (juice of 2 limes)
- 2 tablespoons sugar
- 1 1/2 cups club soda, chilled
- 4 lime wedges
- 4 mint sprigs

Directions

- Combine melon, mint leaves, lime juice, and sugar in blender; blend until smooth. (Mixture may be blended in advance and chilled for several hours.)
- Pour into a 4-cup measuring cup and stir in enough club soda to measure 4 cups.
- Pour into four glasses. Garnish with lime wedges and mint sprigs. Serve immediately.

Nutrition Facts

Carbohydrates: 24g| Protein: 1g| Sodium: 51mg| Fiber: 2g

477. MINT-GREEN TEA COOLERS

Total Time: 10 Minutes

Ingredients

- 2 bags of green tea
- 4 thin slices of fresh ginger (about 1 inch)
- 7 or 8 large fresh mint leaves, roughly torn
- 2 cups boiling water
- 2 cups crushed ice

Directions

- Place tea bags, ginger, and mint leave in a teapot or 2-cup heatproof measuring cup. Add boiling water; steep for 4 minutes. Remove tea bags, ginger, and mint leaves; discard. Cool tea to room temperature.

- Pour 1 cup crushed ice into each of the two tall glasses. Divide tea between glasses.

Nutrition Facts

Carbohydrates: 1g| Protein: 1g| Fat: 1g| Saturated Fat: 1g| Sodium: 1mg| Fiber: 1g

478. BANANA-BERRY SMOOTHIE RECIPE FOR DIABETICS

Total Time: 10 minutes

Ingredients

- 1 cup ice cubes
- 1 medium banana (approximately 6 inches long), sliced and frozen
- 1/2 cup frozen blueberries (not thawed)
- 1 container (8 ounces) nonfat, artificially sweetened vanilla yogurt
- 1/4 cup skim milk

Directions

- Place ice cubes at the bottom of the blender and add banana slices, blueberries, yogurt, and milk. Cover and blend in pulses until smooth, stopping frequently to stir down the ice. Serve right away. Freeze leftovers in an airtight, microwave-safe container and thaw in the microwave until slushy.

Nutrition Facts

Carbohydrates: 28g| Protein: 6g| Fat: <1g| Sodium: 80mg| Fiber: 3g

479. SIMPLE SPICED TEA MIX FOR DIABETICS

Preparation Time: 5 minutes

Ingredients

- 2 cups artificially sweetened instant iced tea mix with lemon
- 2 tubs (0.5 ounces each) powdered sugar-free orange breakfast drink mix (such as Tang)
- 1 tub (0.5 ounces) powdered sugar-free lemon-lime drink mix (such as Crystal Light)
- 1 tablespoon cinnamon
- 1 1/2 teaspoons ground cloves

Directions

- Combine all ingredients in a bowl and mix well. Store in an airtight container. To serve, put 1 1/2 teaspoons tea mix into a mug and add 8 ounces hot water. Stir well.

Nutrition Facts

- Carbohydrates: 1g| Protein: <1g| Sodium: 11mg

480. BLACKBERRY LEMONADE

Preparation Time: 10 Minutes

Ingredients

- 3 cups fresh blackberries (or thawed unsweetened frozen blackberries)
- 3 cups plus 4 cups cold water
- 6 packets NutraSweet (may add more or useless depending on sweetness of blackberries)
- 1 tub (approximately 1/2 ounce) sugar-free pink lemonade mix
- 9 sprigs of fresh mint

Directions

- Place blackberries, 3 cups of water, NutraSweet, and drink mix in a blender, cover, and process until smooth. Pour half of the fruit mixture through a fine wire-mesh strainer into a 2-quart pitcher. Use a large spoon to help force juice through the strainer. Discard solids in the strainer and rinse out. Strain remaining fruit mixture. Add 4 cups of water to blackberry lemonade in a pitcher. Stir well. Serve over ice and garnish each glass with a fresh mint sprig.

Nutrition Facts

Carbohydrates: 4g| Protein: 1g| Fat: 1g

481. BANANA RASPBERRY REFRESHER

Preparation Time: 2 Minutes

Ingredients

- 4 ounces nonfat, artificially sweetened raspberry cultured yogurt
- 1/2 ripe banana, cut into chunks
- 1/4 cup skim milk
- 1/2 cup ice cubes (approximately 5 cubes)

Directions

- Place all ingredients in a blender. Cover, and process until smooth and frothy. Serve immediately.

Nutrition Facts

Carbohydrates: 34g| Protein: 7g| Fat: 1g| Saturated Fat: 1g| Sodium: 85mg| Fiber: 3g

482. CHOCOLATE HAZELNUT COFFEE

Preparation Time: 10 Minutes (To Brew Coffee)

Ingredients

- 6 ounces hot coffee
- 1 tablespoon chocolate hazelnut spread, such as Nutella
- 1 packet artificial sweetener
- 1 tablespoon skim milk

Directions

- Stir all ingredients together in a mug and serve.

Nutrition Facts

Carbohydrates: 10g| Protein: 1g| Fat: 5g| Saturated Fat: 1g| Sodium: 13mg| Fiber: 1g

483. CANTALOUPE COOLER

Preparation time: 5 minutes

Ingredients

- 1 cup cubed cantaloupe
- 1/2 cup nonfat, no-sugar-added vanilla yogurt
- 1/4 teaspoon lemon juice
- 1 packet NutraSweet
- Dash cinnamon

Directions

- Combine all ingredients in a blender and blend until smooth.

Nutrition Facts

Carbohydrates: 20g| Protein: 6g| Fat: <1g|Sodium: 128mg| Fiber: 2g

484. TOFU BERRY SMOOTHIE

Preparation Time: 10 Minutes

Ingredients

- 1 cup frozen raspberries
- 1 cup fresh strawberries, cut into bite-size pieces
- 1/2 cup soy milk, unsweetened (shake before pouring)
- 1/3 pound (5 1/2 ounces) soft tofu, cut into bite-size pieces
- 1 cup ice
- 1/2 cup light whipped topping

- 4 tablespoons Splenda or other artificial sweeteners
- 1 teaspoon vanilla extract
- 1 teaspoon lemon juice

Directions

- Place all ingredients in a blender. Puree until smooth. Serve immediately.

Nutrition Facts

Carbohydrates: 10g| Protein: 6g| Fat: 3g| Saturated Fat: 1g| Sodium: 10mg| Fiber: 4g| Soy Protein: 5g

485. ORANGE SPICE COFFEE MIX

Preparation Time: 5 Minutes
Brewing Time: 5 Minutes.

Ingredients

- 1/2 pound freshly ground coffee
- 1/2 cup dried orange peel (can be found in the spice section of the grocery store)
- 4 teaspoons ground cloves
- 4 teaspoons ground cinnamon

Directions

- Place all ingredients in a large zip-top bag and shake to combine. Use 5 level tablespoons with 12 cups water (use more or less to suit taste). Brew coffee according to automatic-drip coffeemaker directions.

Nutrition Facts

Carbohydrates: 1g| Protein: <1g| Sodium: 5mg

486. CHOCOLATE AVOCADO SMOOTHIE

Prep Time: 5 minutes
Cook Time: 0 minutes
Total Time: 5 minutes

Ingredients

- 1/2 ripe avocado
- 3 tbsp. cocoa powder
- 1 cup full-fat coconut milk
- 1/2 cup water
- 1 tsp. lime juice
- Pinch mineral salt
- 6-7 drops liquid Stevia
- Fresh mint (for decoration)

Directions

- Add all of the ingredients to a blender.
- Blend on high speed until smooth and creamy. If desired, add more liquid Stevia to taste.
- Garnish with fresh mint if desired and serve.

Nutrition FactsValue

Sat Fat: 23.4g| Poly unsat Fat: 0.7g| Mono unsat Fat: 4g| Sodium: 180.2mg| Potassium: 307.7mg| Carbohydrates: 12.1g| Fiber: 5.5g| Sugar: 2.4g| Protein: 2.3g

DIABETIC SAUCES, DIPS, AND DRESSING

487. KETO RANCH DRESSING

Prep Time:5 minutes
Cook Time:0 minutes
Resting time:1 hour
Total Time:1 hour 5 minutes

Ingredients

- 3/4 cup mayonnaise
- 3/4 cup sour cream
- 2 tbsp. fresh parsley
- 1 tbsp. fresh dill
- 1 tbsp. fresh chives
- 2 garlic cloves
- 1/2 tsp. onion powder
- 1/2 tsp. salt
- 1/2 tsp black pepper
- 1/4 cup milk of choice
- Lemon juice (optional)

Directions

- Wash the fresh herbs and dry them completely so the excess water won't dilute the dressing. Chop them finely.
- Mince the garlic, then use a garlic press or a fork to press it into a paste.
- Add all of the ingredients to a small mixing bowl.
- Whisk together until the ranch is smooth, creamy, and there are no lumps. Adjust to taste with salt, pepper, and lemon juice, keeping in mind that the flavors will develop in the refrigerator.
- Cover and refrigerate for at least 3 – 4 hours or overnight.

Nutrition Facts

Fat: 16g| Saturated Fat: 5.1g| Polyunsaturated Fat: 7.4g| Monounsaturated Fat: 2.9g| Cholesterol: 6.9mg| Sodium: 242.9mg| Potassium: 87.6mg| Carbohydrates: 2.7g| Fiber: 0.3g| Sugar: 1.5g| Protein: 1.1g| Vitamin A: 12.4IU| Vitamin C: 10.4mg| Calcium: 5.9mg| Iron: 2.5mg| Net carbs: 2.4g

488. CHEESY ARTICHOKE DIP

Cook Time: 15 Min

Ingredients

- 2 (13.75-ounce) cans artichoke hearts in water, drained and chopped
- 1 (4-ounce) can mild diced green chilies, drained
- 6 tablespoons reduced-fat mayonnaise
- 1 1/2 cup reduced-fat finely shredded Cheddar cheese, divided

Directions:

- Preheat oven to 350 degrees F. Coat a 2-cup baking dish with cooking spray.
- In a bowl, combine all the ingredients, except 1/2-cup of cheddar cheese. Spoon into baking dish. Sprinkle with remaining cheese.
- Bake 15 minutes, or until mixture bubbles and is heated through.

Nutrition Facts

Fat: 4.2g| Saturated Fat: 1.6g|Protein: 4.4g|Sodium: 284mg|Total Carbohydrates: 4.8g| Dietary Fiber: 0.7g| Sugars: 0.9g

489. LOW CARB BBQ SAUCE

Prep Time: 5 mins
Cook Time: 35 mins
Total Time: 40 mins

Ingredients

- 8 ounces canned tomato sauce
- 1 Tablespoon onion powder
- ¼ teaspoon garlic powder
- 1 Tablespoon chili powder
- 2 Tablespoons Worcestershire sauce with no added sugar
- 2 Tablespoons mustard dijon or regular

- ⅛ teaspoon stevia concentrated powder or ¼ teaspoon liquid
- ¼ teaspoon monk fruit concentrated powder or ½ teaspoon liquid
- 2 teaspoons liquid smoke optional for a smokey flavor
- 1 teaspoon sea salt
- 2 Tablespoons apple cider vinegar

Directions
- Mix all ingredients in a small saucepan.
- Bring to a boil, reduce to low, and simmer uncovered for about 30 minutes, stirring occasionally. If desired, cook boneless skinless meat in the sauce and shred for BBQ pulled pork or chicken.

Nutrition Facts
Carbohydrates: 2g | Protein: 0g | Fat: 0g | Saturated Fat: 0g | Cholesterol: 0mg | Sodium: 362mg | Potassium: 107mg | Fiber: 0g | Sugar: 1g | Vitamin A: 280IU | Vitamin C: 1.8mg | Calcium: 11mg | Iron: 0.5mg

490. FAT-FREE HONEY MUSTARD SAUCE

Prep Time: 5 minutes
Total Time: 5 minutes

Ingredients
- 1/4 cup honey
- 1/2 cup plain nonfat greek yogurt
- 1/4 cup dijon mustard
- 1 tablespoon yellow mustard
- 1/2 teaspoon salt
- Pepper to taste
- Juice of 1 lemon

Directions
- Simply whisk all ingredients together and chill in the fridge for 30 minutes to an hour.
- Keep refrigerated for up to a week.

Nutrition Facts
Sodium: 110mg | Carbohydrates: 9g | Sugar: 9g | Protein: 2g

491. CHICKEN MARINADE FOR GRILLING

Prep Time: 2 mins
Total Time: 2 mins

Ingredients
- ½ cup olive oil
- ¼ cup liquid aminios or soy sauce
- ¼ teaspoon stevia concentrated powder see note
- ¼ teaspoon monk fruit liquid extract see note
- 2 teaspoons Worcestershire sauce
- 2 tablespoons apple cider vinegar
- 2 teaspoons garlic powder
- 1 teaspoon ginger
- 1 teaspoon black pepper
- ¼ teaspoon chili powder

Directions
- Whisk all ingredients together in a small bowl.
- Pour marinade over chicken in large plastic zipper bags.
- Allow chicken to marinate for at least an hour.
- Brush leftover marinade on chicken during grilling.

Nutrition Facts
Calories: 99 | Carbohydrates: 0.8g | Protein: 0.9g | Fat: 10.8g | Sodium: 384mg | Fiber: 0.1g

492. HOMEMADE PESTO SAUCE: NUT FREE

Prep time: 5 mins
Total time: 5 mins

Ingredients
- 1-1/3 cup loosely packed basil leaves
- 4 teaspoons minced garlic
- 1/4 teaspoon salt
- 1/4 teaspoon pepper
- 2/3 cup extra virgin olive oil
- 2/3 cup grated Parmesan cheese
- Optional for those without nut allergies: 4 tablespoons pine nuts

Directions
- In a food processor, pulse basil, garlic, salt, pepper (add pine nuts if using) until chopped.
- Add in half the olive oil and cheese and pulse to blend, add in the rest and continue to pulse until combined.
- Makes 1 cup.
- Keep refrigerated.

Nutrition Facts
Fat: 10g | Sodium: 63mg | Protein: 2g | Cholesterol: 4mg

493. SPICY GUACAMOLE

Prep Time: 10 minutes
Total Time: 10 minutes

Ingredients
- 2 Haas avocados, ripe
- 1/4 red onion
- 1 jalapeno
- 1tblsp fresh lime juice
- Sea salt

Directions
- Cut open the avocados, remove the pits and spoon the flesh into a bowl.
- Dice the red onion and jalapeno; roll the lime to make it easier to squeeze.
- Begin breaking down avocado pieces and smash them into desired consistency.
- Add chopped vegetables and lime juice; continue mixing and smashing.
- Finish with an extra squeeze of lime juice and sprinkle sea salt over top.

Nutrition Facts
8g Total Carbs | 3g Net Carbs | 12g Fat | 1g Protein

494. CHOPPED CHICKEN SALAD

Prep Time: 5 minutes
Cook Time: 30 minutes
Total Time: 35 minutes

Ingredients
- Baked chicken
- 2 lbs. boneless skinless chicken thighs
- Olive oil spray
- ½ tsp. pepper
- ½ tsp. garlic powder
- ½ tsp. onion powder
- ½ tsp. salt
- Salad
- 3 cups kale, chopped into bite-sized pieces
- 1 cup Brussel sprouts, chopped into bite-sized slices
- 1 cup purple cabbage, sliced
- 1 carrot, cut in ribbons with a mandolin (or sliced thinly)
- 1 red onion, sliced thinly
- 1 small stalk of fennel, sliced thinly (divided)

- ¼ cup pomegranate seeds
- 1 cucumber, chopped into bite-sized pieces
- 1 tomato, diced
- ¼ cup crumbled feta (optional)
- Garlic Citrus Vinaigrette
- ¼ cup extra virgin olive oil
- 1 ½ lemon, juiced (approximately 4 tbsp. juice)
- ½ tsp. salt
- ½ tsp. pepper
- 1 garlic cloves, minced
- 1 tsp. minced fennel

Directions

- Preheat oven to 375ºF (190ºC). Spray a small pan with olive oil spray and spread seasonings on both sides of chicken thighs.
- Place in pan and bake for 30 minutes or until the thickest part of the thigh reads 165 degrees. Set aside and allow to cool.
- While the chicken is baking, prepare the salad ingredients. Chop the kale, Brussels sprouts, and cucumber. Thinly slice the purple cabbage, carrot, red onion, and fennel. Dice the tomato. Toss the ingredients into a large bowl, then place them in the refrigerator until needed.
- Combine all vinaigrette ingredients in a mason jar and shake vigorously. Place in the refrigerator until needed.
- Once the chicken has cooled, chop it into bite-sized pieces and place it over the salad. Drizzle on vinaigrette and toss.

Nutrition Facts

Fat: 16.6g| Saturated Fat: 3.7g| Polyunsaturated Fat: 1.5g| Monounsaturated Fat: 6.7g| Cholesterol 105mg| Sodium 415.3mg| Potassium: 675.8mg| Carbohydrates 14.7g| Fiber 3.8g| Sugar 5.2g| Protein 30.6g

495. MEDITERRANEAN ROASTED PEPPER DIP

Prep Time: 5 Min

Ingredients:

- 1 (7-ounce) jar roasted red peppers, drained and patted dry
- 1 (15-ounce) can chickpeas, rinsed and drained
- 1 (16-ounce) non-fat Greek yogurt
- 2 tablespoons chopped fresh basil
- 1 garlic clove
- 1/8 teaspoon black pepper

Directions:

- Place all the ingredients in a blender jar and process until thoroughly blended. Serve immediately, or store in the refrigerator in an airtight container until ready to use.

Nutrition Facts

- Fat: 0.5g| Saturated Fat: 0.1g| Protein: 4.3g| Sodium: 111mg| Total Carbohydrates: 5.7g| Dietary Fiber: 1.2g| Sugars: 1.2g

496. TANGY SPINACH DIP

Chill Time: 2 Hr

Ingredients:

- 1 (10-ounce) package frozen chopped spinach, thawed and drained
- 1/3 cup finely chopped green onions
- 1 tablespoon lemon juice
- 1 (8-ounce) container reduced-fat sour cream
- cayenne pepper
- 1/2 teaspoon garlic powder

Directions:

- Squeeze spinach between paper towels to completely remove excess moisture.
- Place all ingredients in a food processor or blender and process until smooth.
- Cover and refrigerate at least 2 hours before serving.

Nutrition Facts

Fat: 2.8g| Saturated Fat: 1.7g| Protein: 2.3g| Cholesterol: 6.6mg| Sodium: 31mg| Total Carbohydrates2.7g| Dietary Fiber: 0.8g| Sugars: 0.3g

497. SOUTH-OF-THE-BORDER BEAN DIP

Cook Time: 10 Min

Ingredients:

- 2 (15-1/2-ounce) cans pinto beans, rinsed and drained, divided
- 1 cup salsa, divided
- 1 teaspoon canola oil
- 1 onion, finely chopped
- 1 green bell pepper, finely chopped
- 3 cloves garlic, minced
- 1 tablespoon dried cilantro
- 2 teaspoons ground cumin
- 3/4 teaspoon salt
- 1/2 cup (2 ounces) shredded Cheddar cheese
- 1 tomato, chopped

Directions:

- In a blender or food processor, combine 1 can of beans and 1/4 cup salsa; blend or process until smooth.
- In a large nonstick skillet, heat the oil over medium heat and sauté the onion, bell pepper, and garlic for 5 to 7 minutes, or until tender. Add the bean mixture, cilantro, cumin, salt, and the remaining can of beans and 3/4 cup salsa; mix well. Bring to a boil, reduce the heat to low, and simmer for 5 minutes, stirring frequently.
- Pour the mixture into a shallow serving dish, top with Cheddar cheese and tomato, and serve warm.

Nutrition Facts

Fat: 1.8g| Saturated Fat: 0.9g| Protein: 4.6g| Cholesterol: 4.2mg| Sodium: 393mg| Total Carbohydrates: 11g| Dietary Fiber: 3.1g| Sugars: 1.6g

498. PARMESAN SPINACH DIP

Cook Time: 30 Min

Ingredients:

- 2 (10-ounce) packages frozen chopped spinach, thawed and squeezed dry
- 1 (8-ounce) package reduced-fat cream cheese, softened
- 1/2 cup freshly grated Parmesan cheese (1 tablespoon reserved for topping)
- 1/3 cup fat-free mayonnaise
- 2 tablespoons fresh lemon juice
- 1 teaspoon garlic powder
- 1 (8-ounce) can sliced water chestnuts, drained and chopped

Directions:

- Preheat oven to 350 degrees F. Coat a 2-quart casserole dish or 9-inch pie plate with cooking spray.
- In a medium bowl, beat spinach, cream cheese, all but the reserved 1 tablespoon Parmesan cheese, mayonnaise, lemon juice, and garlic powder until well blended. Stir in water chestnuts then spoon mixture into prepared pie plate. Sprinkle with reserved 1 tablespoon Parmesan cheese then cover with aluminum foil.
- Bake 15 minutes; remove foil and cook an additional 15 to 20 minutes, or until heated through. Serve immediately.

Nutritional

Total Fat: 3.9g| Saturated Fat: 2.1g| Protein: 4.3g| Cholesterol: 12mg| Sodium: 207mg| Total Carbohydrates: 6.2g| Dietary Fiber: 1.7g| Sugars: 2.1g

499. ITALIAN-STYLE CAPONATA

Cook Time: 30 Min

Ingredients:

- 2 tablespoons vegetable oil
- 1 large unpeeled eggplant (about 1-1/2 pounds), coarsely chopped
- 1 medium onion, chopped
- 2 tablespoons garlic powder
- 1/2 cup chopped pimiento-stuffed green olives
- 3 ribs celery, chopped
- 1 (8-ounce) can tomato sauce
- 1/4 cup white vinegar
- 1/3 cup packed light brown sugar
- 2 dashes of hot pepper sauce (optional)

Directions:

- In a large saucepan, heat the oil over medium-high heat. Add the eggplant, onion, and garlic powder and sauté for about 5 minutes, or until the eggplant begins to soften, stirring occasionally.
- Stir in the remaining ingredients and cook over medium-low heat for 25 minutes to allow the flavors to marry.
- Serve immediately or allow to cool, then cover and chill until ready to serve.

Nutrition Facts

Fat: 2.2g| Saturated Fat: 0.3g| Protein: 0.8g| Sodium: 116mg| Total Carbohydrates: 8.7g| Dietary Fiber: 1.7g| Sugars: 6.2g

500. SPRINGTIME DIP

PREP Time: 5 Min

Ingredients:

- 1 cup fat-free Greek yogurt
- 1/2 cup low-fat buttermilk
- 1 teaspoon fresh lemon juice
- 1 tablespoon chopped fresh dill
- 1/2 teaspoon garlic powder
- 1/4 teaspoon black pepper
- 1/2 teaspoon grated lemon peel

Directions:

- In a small bowl, whisk together all the ingredients until well combined. Serve, or cover, and chill until ready to serve.

Nutritional

Total Fat: 0.2g| Saturated Fat: 0.1g| Protein: 5.0g| Cholesterol: 0.8mg| Sodium: 37mg| Total Carbohydrates: 3.0g| Dietary Fiber: 0.1g| Sugars: 2.7g

501. CHEESY PARTY BAKE

Cook Time: 20 Min

Ingredients:

- 1/2 cup reduced-fat mayonnaise
- 2 cups shredded reduced-fat Swiss cheese
- 1 teaspoon garlic powder
- 1 scallion, sliced thin
- Paprika for sprinkling

Directions:

- Preheat oven to 350 degrees F.
- In a bowl, combine all ingredients except paprika.
- Spoon into a 1-quart baking dish, sprinkle with paprika and bake 20 to 25 minutes or until golden and cheese is melted.

Nutrition Facts

Fat: 3.2g| Saturated Fat: 0.8g| Protein: 4.0g| Cholesterol: 7.4mg| Sodium: 86mg| Total Carbohydrates: 1.3g| Sugars: 0.5g

502. CRANBERRY-NUT SPREAD

Chill Time: 30 Min

Ingredients:

- 1 (8-ounce) package reduced-fat cream cheese, softened
- 1/2 cup sweetened dried cranberries
- 2 teaspoons finely grated orange peel
- 1/4 cup chopped toasted walnuts

Directions:

- In a medium bowl, combine all ingredients and mix well. Refrigerate 30 minutes, or until ready to serve. Serve with celery or thin wholegrain crackers.

Nutrition Facts

Fat: 3.4g| Saturated Fat: 1.4g| Protein: 1.4g| Cholesterol: 7.7mg| Sodium: 67mg|Total Carbohydrates: 4.6g| Dietary Fiber: 0.4g| Sugars: 3.3g

503. IN-A-WINK GUACAMOLE DIP

Prep: 10 Min

Ingredients:

- 2 ripe avocados, halved, with seeds removed
- 1 teaspoon grated onion
- 2 teaspoons lime juice
- 1/4 teaspoon garlic powder

Directions:

- Cut avocados into quarters and peel. In a medium bowl, mash avocado with a fork.
- Add remaining ingredients and mix well.
- Serve, or cover tightly, and refrigerate for 1 hour. This is best served the same day.

Nutritional

Total Fat: 15g| Saturated Fat: 2.1g| Protein: 2.1g| Sodium: 7.2mg|Total Carbohydrates: 9.0g| Dietary Fiber: 6.8g| Sugars: 0.8g

504. BOO-TIFUL BEAN DIP

Ingredients:

- 2 (15-ounce) no salt added pinto beans, rinsed and drained, divided
- 1 cup salsa, divided (see tip)
- 2 tablespoons chopped fresh cilantro, plus extra for garnish
- 2 teaspoons ground cumin
- 1/4 cup finely shredded reduced-fat Cheddar cheese

Directions:

- In a blender or food processor, combine 1 can of beans and 1/4 cup salsa; blend or process until smooth.
- In a medium bowl, combine bean mixture, cilantro, cumin, salt, and the remaining can of beans and 3/4 cup salsa; mix well.
- Spoon the mixture into a serving dish; sprinkle with Cheddar cheese and extra cilantro. Cover and refrigerate until ready to serve.

Nutrition Facts

Fat: 0.6g| Saturated Fat: 0.3g| Protein: 2.9g| Cholesterol: 1.1mg| Sodium: 169mg| Total Carbohydrates: 8.4g| Dietary Fiber: 2.5g| Sugars: 0.9g

505. SUN-DRIED TOMATO PESTO DIP

Cook Time: 25 Min

Ingredients:

- 2 (8-ounce) packages of reduced-fat cream cheese, softened
- 1/2 cup grated Parmesan cheese
- 1/3 cup light mayonnaise
- 2 tablespoons fresh lemon juice
- 1 teaspoon garlic powder
- 1/2 teaspoon onion powder
- 1/2 cup (approximately 10) sun-dried tomatoes, reconstituted and chopped (see note)
- 1/2 cup walnuts, toasted
- 1/3 cup packed fresh basil leaves
- 1 tablespoon grated Parmesan cheese

Directions:

- Preheat the oven to 350°F. Coat a 9-inch pie plate with cooking spray.
- In a medium bowl, beat the cream cheese, 1/2 cup Parmesan cheese, the mayonnaise, lemon juice, garlic powder, and onion powder until well blended.
- In a blender or food processor, combine the sun-dried tomatoes, walnuts, and basil; process until finely chopped.
- Add the tomato mixture to the cream cheese mixture; mix well then spoon into the pie plate. Sprinkle the remaining 1 tablespoon Parmesan cheese over the top.
- Bake for 25 to 30 minutes, or until heated through. Serve immediately.

Nutrition Facts

Fat: 9.1g| Saturated Fat: 3.6g| Protein: 4.4g|Cholesterol: 20mg| Sodium: 224mg| Total Carbohydrates: 4.6g| Dietary Fiber: 0.5g| Sugars: 2.7g

506. TANGY ONION DIP

Chill Time: 1 Hr

Ingredients:

- 1 package (8-ounce) reduced-fat cream cheese, softened
- 1 carton (8-ounce) fat-free sour cream
- 1/2 cup reduced-sugar ketchup or chili sauce
- 1 packet (1-ounce) dry onion soup mix
- 1 tablespoon fresh lemon juice

Directions:

- Beat cream cheese in a bowl until smooth. Stir in the remaining ingredients and mix well.
- Cover and refrigerate for at least 1 hour.

Nutrition Facts

Fat: 1.7g| Saturated Fat: 1.0g| Protein: 1.4g| Cholesterol: 7.1mg| Sodium: 239mg| Total Carbohydrates: 4.5g| Dietary Fiber: 0.2g| Sugars: 1.3g

DIABETIC FISH AND SEAFOOD RECIPES

507. CRUSTED SALMON

Preparation 22 Minutes

Serves 4 Persons

Ingredients

- ¼ cup olive oil
- 1 tablespoon honey
- ¼ cup bread crumbs
- ½ cup finely chopped almonds, lightly toasted
- ½ teaspoon dried thyme Fine-grained kosher salt and freshly ground black pepper, to taste
- 4 (4-ounce) salmon steaks

Directions

- Preheat the oven to 350 degrees F.
- Combine the olive oil with the honey. (Soften the honey in the microwave for 15 seconds, if necessary, for easier blending.)
- In a shallow dish, combine the bread crumbs, almonds, and thyme, and season with salt and pepper.
- Coat the salmon with the olive oil mixture and then the almond mixture.
- Place the salmon on a baking sheet brushed with olive oil and bake 8 to 12 minutes, or until the almonds are lightly browned and the salmon is firm.

Nutrition Facts

Calories per Serving: 565 cal Fat: 27g Protein: 24g Carbohydrates: 14g

508. CLAM SPAGHETTI

Preparation 30 Minutes

Serves 4 Persons

Ingredients

- ¼ cup olive oil 1 medium onion, diced
- 1 medium green bell pepper, cored, seeded, and diced
- 4 garlic cloves, minced
- ½ cup chopped fresh flat-leaf parsley, chopped
- ⅓ teaspoon cayenne pepper Fine-grained kosher salt and freshly ground black pepper,
- 3 dozen or so clams, depending on their size
- ½ cup white wine
- 1 pound whole-wheat spaghetti
- 1 lemon, cut into wedges for garnish
- ½ cup freshly grated, low-fat Parmesan cheese for garnish

Directions

- Heat the olive oil in a large skillet over medium heat.
- Add the onion, pepper, and garlic, and cook until the onion is translucent.
- Add the parsley and cayenne pepper, season with salt and pepper, and set aside.
- Bring a pot of water to a boil. Add the clams and boil for 10 minutes, or until they open (discard any unopened clams). Remove the clams from the pot,

reserv- ing the liquid, and shell half of them.
- Return the skillet to medium-high heat. Add the shelled clams to the skillet, along with the remaining clams, white wine, and 2 cups of the liquid used to boil the clams.
- Cook the pasta according to the package **Directions** for al dente, drain, and place in a large serving dish.
- Ladle the clam mixture over the pasta, and toss to serve. Garnish with lemon wedges and Parmesan cheese.

Nutrition Facts

Calories per Serving: 647 cal Fat: 21g Protein: 32g Carbohydrates: 92g

509. COD GRATIN

Preparation 30 Minutes

Serves 4 Persons

Ingredients

- ½ cup olive oil, divided
- 1-pound fresh cod
- 1 cup black kalamata olives, pitted and chopped
- 4 leeks, trimmed and sliced
- 1 cup whole-wheat bread crumbs
- ¾ cup low-sodium chicken stock
- Fine-grained kosher salt and freshly ground black pepper, to taste

Directions

- Preheat the oven to 350 degrees F. Brush 4 gratin dishes and a large baking dish with the olive oil.
- Place the cod in the large baking dish, and bake for 5 to 7 minutes. Cool and cut into 1-inch pieces.
- Heat the remaining olive oil in a large skillet.
- Add the olives and leeks, and cook over medium-low heat until the leeks are tender.
- Add the bread crumbs and chick- en stock, stirring to mix.
- Gently fold in the pieces of cod.
- Divide the mixture between the 4 gratin dishes, and drizzle with olive oil. Season
- with salt and pepper.
- Bake for 15 minutes or until warmed through.

Nutrition Facts

Calories per Serving: 578 cal Fat: 36g Protein: 25g Carbohydrates: 32g

510. FISH FILLET CRUSTED WITH CUMIN

Preparation 10 Minutes

Serves 4 Persons

Ingredients

- Cumin (ground) – 1 tablespoon
- Thyme – ¼ teaspoon
- Paprika – 1 teaspoon
- Lemon pepper – ½ teaspoon
- Halibut fish fillets – 1 pound
- Canola oil – ½ tablespoon
- Parsley (chopped) – 2 tablespoons
- Lime wedges – 4

Directions

- Take a shallow dish and add the cumin, paprika, lemon pepper, and thyme.
- Mix well to combine.
- Rub both sides of the fillets generously with the prepared spice mix.
- Take a large cast-iron pan and place it over a medium flame. Pour in the canola oil and let it heat through.
- Place the fish fillets into the pan and cook for 4 minutes on each side or until the fish turns opaque.
- Transfer onto a platter and sprinkle with parsley. Serve with lemon wedges

Nutrition Facts

Calories per Serving: 130 cal Fat: 4g Protein: 22g Carbohydrates: 1g

511. HERB AND PARMESAN CRUSTED FISH

Preparation 15 Minutes

Serves 4 Persons

Ingredients

- Almonds (chopped) – 1/3 cup
- Dry bread crumbs (plain) – ¼ cup
- Parmesan cheese (grated) – 3 Tbs.
- Garlic powder – ½ teaspoon Paprika – ½ teaspoon
- Parsley flakes – ½ teaspoon
- Black pepper (freshly ground) – ¼ tbs.
- Tilapia fillets – 1 pound
- Olive oil

Directions

- Begin by preheating the oven by setting the temperature to 450 degrees Fahrenheit.
- Take a baking pan and line it with an aluminum foil sheet.
- Take a shallow dish and add the chopped almonds, parmesan cheese, bread crumbs, garlic powder, paprika, black pepper, and parsley flakes. Mix well to combine.
- Place the fish on a plate and use a brush to gently grease the fish on both sides with olive oil.
- Dredge the fish with the almond and seasoning mixture. Make sure both sides of the fish are evenly coated.
- Place the coated fish onto the baking pan and bake for about 12 minutes.
- You should be able to flake the fish using a fork

Nutrition Facts

Calories per Serving: 225 cal Fat: 9g Protein: 29g Carbohydrates: 7g

512. HALIBUT WITH VEGETABLES

Preparation 25 Minutes

Serves 4 Persons

Ingredients

- 1 pound green beans, trimmed
- 2 red bell peppers, seeded and cut into strips
- 1 onion, sliced
- Zest and juice of 2 lemons
- 3 garlic cloves, minced
- 2 tablespoons extra-virgin olive oil
- 1 teaspoon dried dill 1 teaspoon dried oregano
- 4 halibut fillets
- ½ teaspoon salt
- ¼ teaspoon freshly ground black pepper

Directions

- Preheat the oven to 400ºF (205ºC). Line a baking sheet with parchment paper.
- In a large bowl, toss the green beans, bell peppers, onion, lemon zest and juice, garlic, olive oil, dill, and oregano.
- Use a slotted spoon to transfer the vegetables to the prepared baking sheet in a single layer, leaving the juice behind in the bowl.

- Gently place the halibut fillets in the bowl, and coat in the juice. Transfer the fillets to the baking sheet, nestled
- between the vegetables, and drizzle them with any juice left in
- the bowl.
- Sprinkle the vegetables and halibut with the salt and pepper.
- Bake for 15 to 20 minutes until the vegetables are just tender and the fish flakes apart easily.

Nutrition Facts

Calories per Serving: 235 cal Fat: 9g Protein: 23g Carbohydrates: 16g

513. CHIPOTLE SPICY FISH TACOS

Preparation 20 Minutes
Serves 4 Persons
Ingredients

- Olive oil - 2 tablespoons
- Yellow onion (diced) – 1/2 small
- Jalapeño (chopped) – 1
- Garlic (pressed) - 2 cloves
- Chipotle peppers soaked in adobo sauce - 4 ounces
- Butter - 2 tablespoons
- Mayonnaise - 2 tablespoons
- Haddock fillets - 1 pound
- Tortillas (low carb) - 4

Directions

- Take a large nonstick pan and place it on medium-high flame. Pour in the olive oil and let it shimmer.
- Toss in the diced onion and sauté them for around 5 minutes. Keep stirring to prevent the onions from browning.
- Reduce the flame and add in the chopped garlic and jalapeno. Stir and cook for around 2 minutes.
- Take the chipotle peppers out of the adobo sauce and chop them finely. Transfer the chopped chipotle and adobo sauce to the hot pan. Add in the mayonnaise, butter and fish fillets to the pepper sauce and stir well.
- Cook the fish for around 8 minutes or until the fish is completely cooked. Divide into four equal portions
- To prepare the taco shells, take a tortilla and fry them for around 2 minutes on both sides on high flame.
- Place the taco onto a plate and let each taco cool in the desired shape. Fill each taco shell with ¼ of the fish mixture.
- Top with freshly chopped chives and serve hot!

Nutrition Facts

Calories per Serving: 300 cal Fat: 20g Protein: 24g Carbohydrates: 7g

514. ASPARAGUS WITH SCALLOPS

Preparation 25 Minutes
Serves 4 Persons
Ingredients

- 3 tsp. extra-virgin olive oil, divided
- 1 pound asparagus, trimmed and cut into 2-inch segments
- 1 tablespoon butter
- 1 pound sea scallops
- ¼ cup dry white wine Juice of
- 1 lemon
- 2 garlic cloves, minced
- ¼ teaspoon freshly ground black pepper

Directions

- In a large skillet, heat 1½ teaspoons of oil over me- dium heat.
- Add the asparagus and sauté for 5 to 6 minutes until
- just tender, stirring regularly. Remove from the skillet and cover with aluminum foil to keep warm.
- Add the remaining 1½ teaspoons of oil and the butter to the skillet. When the butter is melted and sizzling, place the scallops in a single layer in the skillet.
- Cook for about 3 minutes on one side until nicely browned. Use tongs to gently loosen and flip the scallops, and cook on the other side for another 3 minutes until browned and cooked through.
- Remove and cover with foil to keep warm.
- In the same skillet, combine the wine, lemon juice, garlic,
- and pepper. Bring to a simmer for 1 to 2 minutes, stirring to mix in any browned pieces left in the pan.
- Return the asparagus and the cooked scallops to the skillet to coat with the sauce. Serve warm.

Nutrition Facts

Calories per Serving: 253 cal Fat: 7g Protein: 26g Carbohydrates: 14g

515. SESAME TUNA STEAK

Preparation 21 Minutes
Serves 2 Persons
Ingredients

- Tuna steaks - 2 (6-ounce)
- Soy sauce – 2 tablespoons
- Sesame oil - 1 tablespoon
- Sesame seeds - 1 teaspoon
- Salt - as per taste

Pepper - as per taste

Directions

- Begin by placing the ahi tuna steak into a shallow dish and generously season with pepper and salt.
- Take a small bowl and add in the sesame oil and soy sauce. Whisk well and pour over the ahi tuna steak.
- Flip over and place the dish aside for around 15 minutes at room temperature.
- Take a nonstick pan and place it over medium flame.
- Once the pan is hot, place the marinated ahi tuna steaks and cook for about 3 minutes.
- Flip over and cook for another 3 minutes.
- Once done, transfer onto a wooden block and slice into slices measuring about ½ inch in thickness.
- Transfer onto a serving platter and garnish with a sprinkle of black and white sesame seeds.
- Serve hot!

Nutrition Facts

Calories per Serving: 255 cal Fat: 9g Protein: 40g Carbohydrates: 1g

516. SHRIMP CREOLE

Preparation 110 Minutes
Serves 8 Persons
Ingredients

- 1¾ lbs. raw shrimp, peeled
- pepper, to taste
- 2 Tbsp. canola oil
- 1 cup chopped onion
- 1 cup chopped celery

- ½ cup chopped bell pepper
- 8-oz. can no-salt-added tomato paste
- 8-oz. can no-salt-added tomato sauce
- 1 Tbsp. Louisiana hot sauce
- 2½ cups water
- 3 cloves garlic, minced
- 1 cup chopped green onions
- parsley
- rice

Directions

- Peel shrimp.
- Pepper to taste and set aside.
- In a heavy saucepan, heat oil. Sauté onion, celery, and pepper until wilted.
- Add tomato paste and cook 5 minutes over low heat, stirring constantly.
- Add tomato sauce, hot sauce, and water. Cook for 1 hour, stirring occasionally.
- Stir in shrimp and garlic. Cook another 15 minutes.
- Sprinkle with green onions and parsley. Cook 2–3 more minutes.
- Serve with rice.

Nutrition Facts

Calories per Serving: 150 cal Fat: 4g Protein: 15g Carbohydrates: 13g

517. TUNA BAKE WITH CHEESE SWIRLS

Preparation 55 Minutes
Serves 8 Persons

Ingredients

- ½ cup diced green bell pepper
- ½ cup chopped onion
- 2 Tbsp. canola oil
- 6 Tbsp. flour
- 2 cups fat-free milk
- 6½- or 7-oz. can or pouch tuna
- Cheese Swirls:
- 1½ cups reduced-fat buttermilk biscuit
- mix
- ¾ cup grated 50%-less fat cheddar cheese
- ½ cup fat-free milk 2 chopped pimentos (from jar)

Directions

- In saucepan, sauté green pepper and onion in oil until soft but not brown.
- Blend in flour and cook over low heat a few minutes to get rid of raw flour taste.
- Gradually stir in milk. Cook over low heat, stirring continually until smooth.
- Add tuna. Spoon into greased 9×13-inch baking pan. Set aside.
- To make cheese swirls, prepare biscuits with milk according to package **Directions**.
- On lightly floured board, roll out to 8×13-inch rectangle.
- Sprinkle with cheese and chopped pimento. Press into dough to help adhere.
- Roll up jelly-roll fashion. Cut roll into 8 slices.
- Flatten slightly and place on top of tuna mixture.
- Bake at 450°F for 25 minutes, or until tuna mix is bubbly and biscuits are browned.

Nutrition Facts

Calories per Serving: 215 cal Fat: 7g Protein: 13g Carbohydrates: 25g

518. TILAPIA FILLET WITH FRUITY SALSA

Preparation 30 Minutes
Serves 4 Persons

Ingredients

- 1/2 lb. (quartered) raspberries
- 1/2 (peeled, cored and chopped) fresh pineapple
- 1 (peeled, seeded and diced) large mango
- 3 (peeled and diced) kiwifruit
- 2 tbsps fresh parsley, finely chopped
- 1/2 cup grape tomatoes 1 1/2 lbs. tilapia fillets 1 tbsp balsamic vinegar
- 1/2 tsp seasoned pepper blend

Directions

- Add balsamic vinegar, parsley, tomatoes, mango, kiwifruit, raspberries and pineapple into a bowl and toss until combined.
- Add avocado oil into a skillet over med-high heat.
- Season tilapia fillets with the pepper blend.
- Add the seasoned fish into the hot pan and saute for 2-3 minutes on each side, until fish is opaque and white.
- Serve salsa with cooked tilapia.

Nutrition Facts

Calories per Serving: 305 cal Fat: 3g Protein: 36g Carbohydrates: 35g

519. MEDITERRANEAN TUNA CUPS

Preparation 15 Minutes
Serves 5 Persons

Ingredients

- White albacore tuna in water, flaked and drained 10 ounces
- Garlic salt 0.25 teaspoons
- Lemon juice 2 tablespoons fresh
- Red onion 0.33 cups chopped
- Pitted and chopped Kalamata olives 0.33 cups
- Non-fat, plain Greek yogurt 0.66 cups
- Cucumbers 3 medium

Directions

- Slice each cucumber into 10 pieces, discarding the ends. Keep the cucumber shell and use a 0.5 teaspoon to scoop out the insides.
- Make sure that there is a thin layer on the bottom of each slice so that it can accommodate the tuna mixture.
- Stir together the olives, garlic, yogurt, onion and lemon juice.
- Blend until the mixture is smooth.
- Add in the tuna and stir again until it is all blended.
- Take approximately 1 tablespoon of the tuna mix and put it into the cucumber cup.
- Repeat this until all 10 of the cucumber cups are filled with tuna.
- Keep this refrigerated until eating

Nutrition Facts

Calories per Serving: 150 cal Fat: 1g Protein: 6g Carbohydrates: 2g

520. ROASTED SEA BASS

Preparation 20 Minutes
Serves 6 Persons

Ingredients

¼ cup olive oil

6 sea bass filets

Fine-grained kosher salt and freshly ground black pepper, to taste

¼ cup dry white wine

3 teaspoons fresh dill

2 teaspoons fresh thyme

1 garlic clove, minced

Directions

Preheat the oven to 425 degrees F.

Brush the bottom of a roasting pan with olive oil.

Place the fish in the pan and brush the fish with oil.

Season the fish with salt and pepper.

Combine the remaining Ingredients: and pour them over the fish.

Bake for 10 to 15 minutes, depending on the size of the fish.

Sea bass is done when the flesh is firm and opaque.

Nutrition Facts

Calories per Serving: 213 cal Fat: 12g Protein: 24g Carbohydrates: 0g

521. SHRIMP STEWED IN CURRY BUTTER

Yield: 2 servings

Ingredients:

6 tablespoons (85 g) butter

2 teaspoons curry powder

1 teaspoon minced garlic or 2 cloves garlic, crushed

24 large, raw, "easy peel" shrimp

Directions:

Melt the butter in a large, heavy skillet over lowest heat. Stir in the curry powder and garlic and then add the shrimp in a single layer.

Cook for 3 to 5 minutes per side or until the shrimp are pink right through.

Transfer to serving plates and scrape the extra curry butter over them.

Nutrition Facts:

2 grams of carbohydrates, 1 gram of fiber 15 grams of protein.

522. SAIGON SHRIMP

Yield: 3 servings

Ingredients:

- Scant 1/2 teaspoon salt
- Scant 1/2 teaspoon pepper
- 1 1/2 teaspoons Splenda
- 3 scallions
- 4 tablespoons (60 ml) peanut or canola oil
- 1 pound (455 g) large shrimp, shelled and deveined
- 1 1/2 teaspoons chili garlic paste
- 2 teaspoons minced garlic

Directions:

- Mix together the salt, pepper, and Splenda in a small dish or cup. Slice the scallions thinly and set them aside.
- Gather all the ingredients except the scallions together—the actual cooking of this dish is lightning fast! In a wok or heavy skillet over highest heat, heat the oil.
- Add the shrimp and stir-fry for 2 to 3 minutes or until they're about two-thirds pink.
- Add the chili garlic paste and garlic and keep stir-frying.
- When the shrimp are pink all over and all the way through, sprinkle the salt, pepper, and Splenda mixture over them and stir for just another 10 seconds or so.
- Turn off the heat and divide the shrimp between 3 serving plates.
- Top each serving with a scattering of sliced scallion and serve.

Nutrition Facts:

2 grams of carbohydrates 1 gram of fiber, 25 grams of protein.

288 calories

523. BASIL-LIME SHRIMP

Yield: 4 servings

Ingredients:

- 1/2 cup (120 ml) lime juice
- 1/2 cup (120 ml) olive oil
- 1/4 cup (10 g) fresh basil—Just compact sprigs into your measuring cup.
- 4 teaspoons (16 g) brown mustard
- 1/4 teaspoon Splenda
- 4 scallions—thinly sliced, including the crisp part of the green
- 1/2 pound (225 g) shrimp

Directions:

- Put everything from the lime juice through the Splenda in your blender and run it just for a second or two.
- Pour the mixture into a big nonreactive pan and place over medium heat.
- Bring to a simmer, turn the heat down to keep it just simmering, and let it cook until it's reduced by about half.
- While that's happening, slice your scallions.
- When the lime juice mixture is reduced, lay the shrimp in it, in one layer if possible. (
- Let them poach for about two minutes and then flip and give them another couple of minutes, just until they're firm and pink.
- Serve drizzled with the sauce, with the slicedscallion sprinkled over the top.

Nutrition Facts:

438 calories, 30 grams fat, 35 grams protein, 6 grams carbohydrate, 1 gram dietary fiber, and 5 grams usable carb.

524. SHRIMP IN BRANDY CREAM

Yield: 3 or 4 servings

Ingredients:

- 1 pound (455 g) shrimp, shelled and deveined
- 4 tablespoons (55 g) butter
- 1/3 cup (80 ml) brandy
- 3/4 cup (175 ml) heavy cream

Directions:

- Sauté the shrimp in the butter over medium-high heat until cooked throug 4 to 5 minutes.
- Add the brandy, turn up the heat, and let it boil hard for a minute or so to reduce.
- Stir in the cream and heat through.
- Thicken the sauce a bit with guar or xanthan if you like and then serve.

Nutrition Facts:

2 grams of carbohydrates and 26 grams of protein.

525. SHRIMP IN CURRIED COCONUT MILK

Ingredients:

- 1/2 onion
- 1/2 green pepper
- 2 tablespoons (28 ml) coconut oil
- 2 teaspoons cumin
- 2 teaspoons curry powder
- 1 1/2 teaspoons ground coriander
- 1 1/2 teaspoons chopped garlic
- 1 cup (235 ml) unsweetened coconut milk
- 1/2 teaspoon salt or Vege-Sal
- 1/4 teaspoon chili garlic paste
- 3 cups (384) frozen cooked salad shrimp, thawed

Directions:

- Throw your onion and green pepper in the food processor and pulse until they're chopped fine. In a heavy-bottomed skillet, start them sautéing in the coconut oil over medium heat.
- When the onion and pepper are starting to soften, throw in the spices.
- Sauté another few minutes, add the garlic, and give it just another minute.
- Add the coconut milk and stir the whole thing up. Stir in the salt and chili garlic paste, too.
- Now add the thawed, drained shrimp, stir it in, and turn the burner up a little.
- Simmer for a minute or two, thickening with a little guar, xanthan, or glucomannan if you think it needs it.
- Then serve—with spoons, to get all of the sauce!

Nutrition Facts:

Each with 235 calories, 11 grams fat, 28 grams protein, 6 grams carbohydrate, 1 gram dietary fiber, and 5 grams usable carb.

526. SALMON IN GINGER CREAM

Yield: 3 servings.

Ingredients:

- 2 tablespoons (28 g) butter
- 2 pieces salmon fillet, 6 ounces (170 g) each, skin still attached
- 1 teaspoon minced garlic or 2 cloves garlic, crushed
- 2 scallions, finely minced
- 2 tablespoons (2 g) chopped cilantro
- 4 tablespoons (60 ml) dry white wine
- 2 tablespoons (16 g) grated gingerroot
- 4 tablespoons (60 g) sour cream
- Salt and pepper

Directions:

- Melt the butter in a heavy skillet over medium-low heat and start sautéing the salmon in it—you want to sauté it for about 4 minutes per side.
- While the fish is sautéing, crush the garlic, mince the scallions, and chop the cilantro.
- When both sides of the salmon have sautéed for 4 minutes, add the wine to the skillet, cover, and let the fish cook an additional 2 minutes or so until done through.
- Remove the fish to serving plates.
- Add the garlic, scallions, cilantro, and ginger to the wine and butter in the skillet, turn the burner up to medium-high, and let them cook for a minute or two.
- Add the sour cream, stir to blend, and salt and pepper to taste.
- Spoon thesauce over the fish and serve.

Nutrition Facts:

5 grams of carbohydrates and 1 gram of fiber, and 36 grams of protein

527. BUTTERED SALMON WITH CREOLE SEASONINGS

Yield: 2 or 3 servings.

Ingredients:

- 12 ounces (340 g) salmon fillet, in two or three pieces
- 1 teaspoon purchased Creole seasoning
- 1/4 teaspoon dried thyme
- 4 tablespoons (55 g) butter
- 1 teaspoon minced garlic or 2 cloves garlic, minced

Directions:

Sprinkle the skinless side of the salmon evenly with the Creole seasoning and thyme.

Melt the butter in a heavy skillet over medium-low heat and add the salmon, skin side down.

Cook 4 to 5 minutes per side, turning carefully.

Remove to serving plates, skin side down, and stir the garlic into the butter remaining in the pan.

Cook for just a minute, then scrape all the garlic butter over the salmon, and serve.

Nutrition Facts

2 grams of carbohydrates, 35 grams of protein.

528. GLAZED, GRILLED SALMON

Yield: 2 servings

Ingredients:

- 2 tablespoons (3 g) Splenda
- 1 1/2 teaspoons dry mustard
- 1 tablespoon (15 ml) soy sauce
- 1 1/2 teaspoons rice vinegar
- 1/4 teaspoon blackstrap molasses
- 12 ounces (340 g) salmon fillet, cut into 2 or 3 serving-size pieces

Directions:

- Mix together the Splenda, mustard, soy sauce, vinegar, and molasses in a small dish.
- Spoon out 1 tablespoon (15 g) of this mixture and set it aside in a separate dish.
- Place the salmon fillets on a plate and pour the larger quantity of the soy sauce mixture over it, turning each fillet so that both sides come in contact with the seasonings. Let the fish sit for a few minutes—just 2 or 3—with the skinless side down in the seasonings.
- Now, you get to choose how you want to cook the salmon. I do mine on a stove top grill, but you can broil it, do it in a heavy skillet sprayed with nonstick cooking spray, cook it on your electric tabletop grill, or even do it on your outdoor grill. However you cook it, it will need about 5 minutes per side.
- When the salmon is cooked through, remove it to serving plates and drizzle the reserved seasoning mixture over each piece before serving.

Nutrition Facts:

3 grams of carbohydrates, and 35 grams of protein.

529. SALMON IN CITRUS VINAIGRETTE

Yield: 4 servings

Ingredients:

- 1 tablespoon (15 ml) coconut oil
- 24 ounces (680 g) salmon fillet in 4 servings
- 1/2 cup (120 ml) vinaigrette (I used Paul Newman's light red wine vinegar
- and olive oil.) 1/2 cup (120 ml) lemon juice
- 2 1/2 tablespoons (4 g) Splenda, or the equivalent in liquid Splenda
- 1/4 teaspoon orange extract
- 1 teaspoon brown mustard
- 1 teaspoon chili powder
- 2 tablespoons (28 ml) lime juice

Directions:

- Spray a big skillet with nonstick cooking spray and put it over medium heat.
- Throw in the coconut oil and when it's melted, slosh it around and then add the salmon.
- While the salmon is getting a little touch of gold, throw everything else in the blender and run the thing.
- Okay, go back and flip your salmon. Let it get a little gold on the other side, too.
- Now add the vinaigrette mixture and turn the burner up to medium-high. Let the whole thing cook another five minutes or until the salmon is done through.
- Plate the salmon and turn up the burner. Boil the vinaigrette hard until it's reduced and starting to get a little syrupy. Pour over the salmon and serve.

Nutrition Facts:

384 calories, 25 grams fat, 34 grams protein, 5 grams carbohydrate

530. MAKES 8 CAKES

Ingredients:

- 1 1/2 lb (680 g) boneless, skinless salmon filet
- 2 Tbsp (30 ml) mayonnaise
- 1 Tbsp (15 ml) finely chopped green onion tops
- 1 Tbsp (15 ml) finely chopped fresh dill
- 1 Tbsp (15 ml) freshly squeezed lemon juice
- 3/4 (3.7 ml) Sea salt
- Freshly ground black pepper
- 2 Tbsp (30 ml) vegetable oil

Directions:

- With a knife, chop the fillet into 1/4 inch (0.6-cm) pieces and place in a bowl.
- Add the mayonnaise, green onion, dill, lemon juice, salt, and pepper to taste.
- Stir rapidly in the same direction for 1 minute. This helps the cakes stick together.
- Form into 8 patties. You can refrigerate them, uncovered, for up to 6 hours or until ready to cook.
- Heat the oil in a large heavy or nonstick frying pan over medium-high heat.
- Add the cakes and cook until lightly browned, 2 to 3 minutes.
- Turn over and cook for an additional 2 to 3 minutes, or until browned.

Nutrition Facts:

Carbohydrates: 0.3 g Fiber: 0.1 g Protein: 17.1 g Fat: 15 g Calories: 209

531. EXTRA-CRISPY FISH WITH LEMON-DILL DIP

Servings: 4

Ingredients:

- 2 (1-ounce) bags low-carb soy chips. finely ground
- 4 (8-ounce) fish fillets, about 1/4 inch thick
- 2 tablespoons canola oil, divided
- 1/2 cup mayonnaise
- 3 tablespoons chopped fresh dill
- 2 teaspoons grated lemon zest
- 1/4 teaspoon pepper

Directions

- Spread ground chips on a piece of waxed paper or paper plate.
- Dredge fillets in chips to coat on both sides Heat 1 tablespoon of the oil in a large non-stick skillet over med heat.
- Add half the fish and cook until just opaque inside and golden brown outside. 3 to 4 minutes per side.
- Carefully transfer to plates and tent with foil to keep warm. Repeat with remaining tablespoon oil and fish.
- Combine mayonnaise, dill, and zest in a small bowl.
- Season with pepper and serve alongside fish.

Nutritional Facts

carbs 3 g fiber 2g protein 51 g fat 32.5 calories 520 prep time 5 minutes cook time 14 minutes

532. SALMON TERIYAKI

Makes 6 servings

Ingredients:

- 1 cup Kikkoman soy sauce
- 3 Tbsp Da Vinci sugar-free hazelnut syrup
- 1/2 tsp dry mustard
- 2 cloves garlic, minced
- 1/4 cup chopped parsley
- 1/4 cup dry red wine
- 6 salmon fillets, 4 oz each
- 4 Tbsp butter (1/2 stick)
- 1 Tbsp lemon zest

Directions:

- Combine soy sauce, syrup, mustard, garlic, parsley, and wine.
- Mix well.
- Place salmon in a ceramic or glass dish and pour marinade over it.
- Cover with plastic wrap, refrigerate, and marinate 4 hours.
- Remove salmon from refrigerator about 30 minutes before ready to grill.
- Melt butter in small saucepan.
- Add lemon zest.
- Remove salmon from marinade and grill 6-8 minutes, basting with butter sauce.

Nutritional Facts:

Carbohydrates: 0.73 g Protein: 4.9 OZ

533. TUNA CASSEROLE

Makes 4 Servings

Ingredients:

Sauce ingredients:

- 1 cup sour cream

- 2 eggs
- 1/2 tablespoon minced onion, dried
- 1 teaspoon dill weed
- 1/2 teaspoon orange zest
- 1/2 teaspoon seasoning salt

Other ingredients:

- 1 pound cauliflower, cut into bite-sized pieces (may be fresh or frozen)
- 1 6-ounce can of tuna, drained
- Cooking oil spray
- 1 1/2 cups cheese, shredded (Monterey jack, Co-Jack, Cheddar, or a blend)

Directions:

- Combine the sauce ingredients in a mixing bowl with a wire whisk.
- Mix the cauliflower into the sauce, then the tuna.
- Spray a 9" x 13" baking dish with cooking oil spray and pour the cauliflower mixture into the baking dish.
- Top it with the cheese. Bake it at 350F for about 25 minutes or until the cheese is thoroughly melted and starting to become golden brown.

Nutrition Facts:

Carbohydrates: 10 g Fiber: 3 g Protein: 27 g Fat: 28 g Calories: 390

534. DILLY TUNA SALAD

Prep Time: 15 Minutes

Yield: 2 servings

Ingredients:

- 1 cup (284 g) light tuna, in water, drained
- 1/4 cup (25 g) celery, chopped
- 2 tablespoons (28 g) low-fat mayonnaise
- 3 tablespoons (12 g) fresh dill, chopped
- 2 tablespoons (20 g) white onions, ciced
- Pepper to taste

Directions:

1. Mix all ingredients well.

Nutritional Info:

26 g water; 66 calories (66% from fat, 7% from protein, 27% from carb); 1 g Protein; 5 g total fat; 1 g saturated fat; 0 g monounsaturated fat; 0 g polyunsaturated fat; 5 g carb; 1 g fiber; 1 g sugar; 39 mg

535. GRILLED HADDOCK WITH PEACH-MANGO SALSA

Prep Time: 15 Minutes

Servings: 4; Serving Size: 1/2 recipe

Ingredients:

- 2 tablespoons olive oil
- 2 tablespoons lime juice
- 1/2 teaspoon salt
- 1/2 teaspoon ground pepper
- 1 pound haddock, cut into 4 fillets
- Nonstick cooking spray
- 2 cups Fresh Peach-Mango Salsa

Directions:

1. Mix olive oil, lime juice, salt, and pepper in a shallow dish; add haddock. Turn and coat fish with marinade.
2. Heat gas grill or broiler. Spray large piece of aluminum foil with nonstick cooking spray. Place fillets on foil; cook 7–8 minutes on each side or until fish is tender when pierced with a fork.
3. Top each piece of fish with 1/2 cup Fresh Peach-Mango Salsa.

Nutritional Analysis:

Calories: 204 Protein: 22g arbohydrates: 11g Fat: 8g Saturated Fat: 1g Cholesterol: 65mg Sodium: 467mg Fiber: 2g

536. SESAME SHRIMP AND ASPARAGUS

Prep Time: 15 Minutes

Servings: 4; Serving Size: 1/2 recipe

Ingredients:

- 2 teaspoons canola oil
- 2 cloves garlic, chopped
- 1 tablespoon grated fresh gingerroot
- 1 pound medium shrimp
- 2 tablespoons dry white wine
- 1/2 pound asparagus, cut diagonally into 1" pieces
- 2 cups cooked whole-grain pasta
- 1/2 teaspoon sesame seeds
- 1/2 cup thinly sliced scallions
- 1 teaspoon sesame oil

Directions:

1. Heat oil in wok or large nonstick skillet. Stir-fry garlic, gingerroot, and shrimp over high heat until shrimp begins to turn pink, about 2 minutes.
2. Add white wine and asparagus; stir-fry an additional 3–5 minutes.
3. Add pasta, sesame seeds, scallions, and sesame oil; toss lightly and serve.

Nutritional Analysis (per serving):

Calories: 257 Protein: 28g Carbohydrates: 23g Fat: 6g Saturated Fat: 1g Cholesterol: 172mg Sodium: 173mg Fiber: 3g

537. PARMESAN CRUSTED CATFISH

Prep Time: 25 Minutes

Yield: 8 servings

Ingredients:

- 8 catfish fillets
- 1 cup (115 g) bread crumbs
- 3/4 cup (75 g) parmesan cheese, grated
- 1/4 cup (15 g) fresh parsley, chopped
- 1 teaspoon paprika
- 1/2 teaspoon oregano
- 1/4 teaspoon basil
- 1/2 teaspoon pepper
- 1/2 cup (112 g) melted butter

Directions:

- Pat fish dry.
- Combine bread crumbs, cheese, and seasonings; stir well.
- Dip catfish in butter and roll each in crumb mixture.
- Arrange fish in well-greased 13 x 9 x 2-inch (33 x 23 x 5 cm) baking dish.
- Bake at 375°F (190°C, or gas mark 4) about 25 minutes or until fish flakes easily when tested with a fork.

Nutritional Info:

127 g water; 412 calories (60% from fat, 30% from protein, 10% from carb); 30 g Protein; 27 g total fat; 12 g saturated fat; 10 g monounsaturated fat; 3 g polyunsaturated fat; 10 g carb; 1 g fiber; 1 g sugar; 418 mg phosphorous; 151 mg calcium; 2 mg iron; 311 mg sodium;

538. SPICY "FRIED" FISH FILLET

Prep Time: 35 Minutes

Servings: 4; Serving Size: 1/2 recipe

Ingredients:

- 1/2 cup cornmeal

- 1/2 teaspoon salt
- 1 teaspoon chipotle seasoning
- 1 egg
- 2 tablespoons 1% milk
- 16 ounces flounder, cut into 4 pieces
- 2 tablespoons olive oil

Directions:

1. Combine cornmeal, salt, and chipotle seasoning in shallow dish.
2. Beat egg and milk together in shallow dish.
3. Dip fish in egg mixture; coat each fillet with cornmeal mixture.
4. Heat olive oil in nonstick skillet; brown fillets until golden and crispy, about 6–7 minutes each side.

Nutritional Analysis (per serving):

Calories: 230 Protein: 24g Carbohydrates: 9g Fat: 10g Saturated Fat: 2g Cholesterol: 116mg Sodium: 412mg Fiber: 1g

539. FRESH TOMATO AND CLAM SAUCE WITH WHOLE-GRAIN LINGUINE

Prep Time: 35 Minutes

Servings: 4; Serving Size: 1/2 recipe

Ingredients:

- 3 dozen (36) littleneck clams
- 2 tablespoons olive oil
- 5 cloves garlic, chopped
- 1/2 cup chopped red bell pepper
- 4 cups peeled and chopped fresh tomatoes
- 3 tablespoons chopped fresh parsley
- 1 tablespoon chopped fresh basil
- 1/2 teaspoon salt
- 1/2 teaspoon red pepper flakes
- 1/2 teaspoon dried oregano
- 1/2 cup dry white wine
- 8 ounces whole-grain linguine

Directions:

- Before preparing this dish (preferably several hours or more), place clams in bowl of cold water with handful of cornmeal added; keep refrigerated.
- When ready to cook, rinse and scrub clams.
- Heat olive oil, garlic, and chopped red pepper in a deep skillet.
- Add tomatoes, parsley, basil, salt, red pepper flakes, and oregano; bring to quick boil, then reduce heat and simmer 15–20 minutes.
- Stir in white wine; add clams on top of tomato sauce. Cover and steam until clams open.
- Meanwhile, boil water and cook pasta to al dente.
- Serve tomato sauce and clams over pasta.

Nutritional Analysis (per serving):

Calories: 361 Protein: 13g Carbo: 60g Fat: 8g Saturated Fat: 1g Cholesterol: 7mg Sodium: 356 mg Fiber: 8g

540. HONEY-SOY BROILED SALMON

Prep Time: 35 Minutes

Servings: 4

Ingredients:

- 1 scallion, minced
- 2 tablespoons reduced-sodium soy sauce
- 1 tablespoon rice vinegar
- 1 tablespoon honey
- 1 teaspoon minced fresh ginger
- 1 pound center-cut salmon fillet,
- skinned (see Tip) and cut into 4 portions
- 1 teaspoon toasted sesame seeds

Directions:

- Whisk scallion, soy sauce, vinegar, honey and ginger in a medium bowl until the honey is dissolved.
- Place salmon in a sealable plastic bag, add 3 tablespoons of the sauce and refrigerate; let marinate for 15 minutes.
- Reserve the remaining sauce.
- Preheat broiler. Line a small baking pan with foil and coat with cooking spray.
- Transfer the salmon to the pan, skinned-side down. (Discard the marinade.)
- Broil the salmon 4 to 6 inches from the heat source until cooked through, 6 to 10 minutes.

Nutritional Analysis (per serving):

Calories: 257 Protein: 28g Carbohydrates: 23g

541. FETA-SPINACH SALMON ROAST

Prep Time: 15 Minutes

Servings: 4

Ingredients:

- 3 ounces cream cheese, softened
- 3/4 cup crumbled feta
- 2 scallions, thinly sliced, including the crisp part of the green
- 1/2 cup fresh spinach, chopped
- 2 skinless salmon fillets of roughly equal size and shape, totaling 3/4 pound
- Olive oil

Directions:

1. Preheat the oven to 350°F.
2. Combine the cream cheese and feta, mashing and stirring with a fork until well blended.
3. Add the scallions and spinach, and combine well.
4. Spread the mixture evenly over one salmon fillet. (The filling will be about 3/4 inch thick.) Top with the second salmon fillet. Brush both sides with olive oil, turning the whole thing over carefully with a spatula.
5. Place the loaf on a shallow baking pan, and bake for 20 minutes. Slice carefully with a sharp, serrated knife.

542. BARBECUED SEA-BASS

Prep Time: 35 Minutes

Servings: 4

Ingredients:

- 1 pound (455 g) sea bass fillets
- Barbecue Rub (sugar free)
- 4 slices bacon
- 2 tablespoons (30 ml) lemon juice

Directions:

- Cut your sea bass fillets into serving portions.
- Sprinkle both sides liberally with the barbecue rub.
- Spray your big, heavy skillet with nonstick cooking spray, and place over medium-low heat.
- Using a sharp kitchen shears, snip your bacon into small pieces, straight into the skillet.
- Stir it about for a moment.
- As soon as a little grease starts to cook out of the bacon, clear a couple of spaces for the fish, and put the fish in the pan.

- Cover and set your oven timer for 4 minutes.
- When time is up, flip the fish, and stir the bacon around a bit, so it will cook evenly.
- Re-cover the pan, and set the timer for another 3 to 4 minutes.
- Peek at your fish at least once; you don't want to overcook it!
- When the fish is flaky, remove to serving plates, and top with the browned bacon bits.
- Pour the lemon juice in the skillet, stir it around, and pour over the fish.

Nutritional Analysis (per serving):
Calories: 357 Protein: 58g Carbohydrates: 13g

543. EASY TUNA CASSEROLE

Prep Time: 35 Minutes
Servings: 4
Ingredients:

- 2 6-ounce (170 g) cans chunk-style tuna
- 1/2 cup (60 g) chopped celery
- 1/3 cup (35 g) sliced scallions, including the crisp part of the green shoot
- 1 large head cauliflower
- 1/2 -2/3 cup (115-160 g) sour cream
- 1/2 cup (120 g) mayonnaise
- 2 teaspoons yellow mustard
- 1/2 teaspoon Dried thyme
- Salt and pepper to taste
- 1-2 small zucchini, scrubbed, sliced
- 1-2 cups (180 g) shredded Monterey Jack or cheddar cheese
- 1 small tomato, chopped (optional)

Directions:

- Preheat oven to 350°F (180 °C).
- Drain and flake the tuna.
- In a large bowl, combine tuna, celery, and green onion.
- Using only the white tops of the cauliflower, slice the cauliflower completely from stems and stalks.
- Steam until fork tender (don't allow to get too soft) and add to tuna.
- In a small bowl, combine sour cream, mayonnaise, mustard, thyme, and salt and pepper.
- Blend into the tuna mixture.
- Spoon half the mixture into a buttered 2-quart (1.9 L) casserole.
- Top with half the zucchini.
- Repeat layers. Top with cheese.
- Bake for 30 to 40 minutes or until hot and bubbly.
- Sprinkle with the chopped tomato, and serve.

544. DEVILED CRAB

Prep Time: 25 Minutes
Servings: 2
Ingredients:

- 1/2 pound (225 g) claw or back fin crab meat
- 4 tablespoons (60 g) mayonnaise
- 1/2 teaspoon paprika
- 1 hard-boiled egg, diced
- 2 tablespoons (30 g) butter, melted
- 2 tablespoons (30 g) Worcestershire sauce
- 2 tablespoons (30 ml) very dry sherry
- 1/4 teaspoon Tabasco
- 1/4 teaspoon salt
- 1 tablespoon (15 g) Dijon mustard
- 3 tablespoons (45 g) grated Parmesan cheese
- 1/4 teaspoon nutmeg, fresh grated if possible

Directions:

- Preheat oven to 350°F (180 °C).
- Clean crab meat and ensure there aren't any shell fragments in it.
- Reserve 1 tablespoon of mayonnaise and the paprika.
- Combine all other ingredients, mixing well, and placing in a small casserole or 4 seafood baking dishes or 4 clean crab shells.
- Frost the top of the crab mixture with mayo and then sprinkle with paprika.
- Bake 20 minutes.
- Place dish(es) under the broiler for 1 minute or until the mayo topping puffs up and browns slightly.

545. FISH CAKES

Prep Time: 55 Minutes
Servings: 8; **Serving Size:** 2 patties
Ingredients:

- 1-pound catfish fillet
- 2 green onions, minced
- 1 banana pepper, cored, seeded, and chopped
- 2 cloves garlic, minced
- 1 tablespoon grated or minced fresh ginger
- 1 tablespoon Bragg Liquid Aminos
- 1 tablespoon lemon juice
- 1 teaspoon grated lemon zest
- Nonstick cooking spray

Directions:

- Preheat oven to 375°F.
- Combine fish with green onions, banana pepper, garlic, ginger, Bragg Liquid Aminos, lemon juice, and lemon zest in food processor; process until chopped and mixed.
- Add Old Bay Seasoning if using; stir to mix.
- Form fish mixture into patties of about 2 tablespoons each; you should have sixteen patties total.
- Place patties on baking sheet treated with nonstick cooking spray; bake 12–15 minutes or until crisp.

Nutritional Analysis (per serving):
Calories: 66 Protein: 11g Carbohydrates: 1g Fat: 2g
Saturated Fat: 1g Cholesterol: 41mg Sodium: 112mg

546. SLOW-ROASTED SALMON

Prep Time: 25 Minutes
Servings: 4; **Serving Size:** 1 fillet
Ingredients:

- 2 teaspoons extra-virgin olive oil
- 4 (5-ounce) salmon fillets with skin, at room temperature
- 1 cup finely minced fresh chives
- Sea or kosher salt and freshly ground white pepper to taste (optional)
- Nonstick cooking spray
- Sage sprigs for garnish

Directions:

1. Preheat oven to 250°F. Rub 1/2 teaspoon of olive oil into flesh side of each salmon fillet. Completely cover fillets with chives; gently press into flesh. Season with salt and pepper if desired.

2. Place fillets skin-side down on nonstick oven-safe skillet or foil-lined

cookie sheet treated with nonstick spray; roast 25 minutes. Garnish with sage sprigs.

Nutritional Analysis (per serving):

Calories: 257 Protein: 25g Carbohydrates: 1g Fat: 16g Saturated Fat: 3g Cholesterol: 710mg Sodium: 69mg Fiber: 1g

547. SALMON PATTIES

Prep Time: 45 Minutes

Servings: 5; Serving Size: 1 patty

Ingredients:

- 2 cups flaked cooked salmon (no salt added)
- 6 soda crackers, crushed
- 1 egg
- 1/2 cup skim milk
- 1 small onion, chopped
- 1 tablespoon chopped fresh parsley
- 1 tablespoon unbleached all-purpose flour
- 1 tablespoon olive oil
- Ener-G Pure Rice Flour (optional)

Directions:

1. Place flaked salmon in a bowl. Add crushed crackers, egg, milk, onion, parsley, and flour; mix well. Gently form five patties.

2. Heat oil in nonstick skillet over medium heat. (Optional: Lightly dust patties with some Ener-G Pure Rice Flour for crispier patties.) Fry on both sides until browned, about 5 minutes per side.

Nutritional Analysis (per serving):

Calories: 168 Protein: 17g Carbohydrates: 3g Fat: 9g Saturated Fat: 2g Cholesterol: 70mg Sodium: 92mg

548. TRADITIONAL STOVETOP TUNA-NOODLE CASSEROLE

Prep Time: 35 Minutes

Servings: 4; Serving Size: 1/2 recipe

Ingredients:

- 1 1/2 cups egg noodles (yields 2 cups when cooked)
- 1 recipe Condensed Cream of Mushroom Soup (see recipe in Chapter 4)
- 1 teaspoon steamed chopped onion
- 1 tablespoon steamed chopped celery
- 1/2 cup skim milk
- 1 ounce shredded (to yield 1/2 cup) American, Cheddar, or Colby cheese
- 1 cup frozen mixed peas and carrots
- 1 cup steamed sliced fresh mushrooms
- 1 can water-packed tuna, drained

Directions:

1. Cook egg noodles according to package directions. Drain and return to pan.

2. Add all remaining ingredients to pan; stir to blend. Cook over medium heat, stirring occasionally until cheese is melted.

Nutritional Analysis (per serving):

Calories: 245 Protein: 20g Carbohydrates: 33g Fat: 4g Saturated Fat: 2g Cholesterol: 46mg Sodium: 241mg

549. CRAB CAKES WITH SESAME CRUST

Servings: 5; Serving Size: 2 cakes

Ingredients:

- 1 pound (16 ounces) lump crabmeat
- 1 egg
- 1 tablespoon minced fresh ginger
- 1 small scallion, finely chopped
- 1 tablespoon dry sherry
- 1 tablespoon freshly squeezed lemon juice
- 6 tablespoons real mayonnaise
- 1/2 cup lightly toasted sesame seeds

Directions:

1. Preheat oven to 375°F. In large bowl, mix together crab, egg, ginger, scallion, sherry, lemon juice, mayonnaise, and seasonings if using.

2. Form the mixture into ten equal cakes. Spread sesame seeds over sheet pan; dip both sides of cakes to coat them. Arrange cakes on baking sheet treated with nonstick spray. Typical baking time is 8–10 minutes, depending on thickness of cakes.

Nutritional Analysis (per serving):

Calories: 108 Protein: 9g Carbohydrates: 3g Fat: 6g Saturated Fat: 1g Cholesterol: 45mg Sodium: 171mg

550. SMOKED SHRIMP AND CHEESE QUESADILLAS

Servings: 4; Serving Size: 1 quesadilla

Ingredients:

- 4 (8") flour tortillas
- 4 teaspoons olive oil
- 2 ounces part-skim mozzarella or other mild cheese (such as fontina or baby Swiss)
- 1 jalapeño or banana pepper, finely chopped
- 2 cloves garlic, crushed
- 4 ounces smoked shrimp
- 1 cup thinly sliced red onion
- 1/2 cup roughly chopped fresh cilantro

Directions:

- Preheat oven to 375°F.
- Lightly brush one side of each tortilla with some olive oil.
- Mix cheese, pepper, and garlic with remaining olive oil; spread 1/2 of cheese mixture in center of oiled half of each tortilla.
- Top with shrimp, red onion, and cilantro; fold tortilla in half to cover ingredients.
- Place tortillas in baking pan treated with nonstick spray.
- Bake 3–5 minutes or until nicely browned and cheese is melted. Serve with your choice of tomato salsa.

Nutritional Analysis (per serving):

Calories: 272 Protein: 11g Carbohydrates: 32g Fat: 11g Saturated Fat: 3g Cholesterol: 39mg Sodium: 428mg Fiber: 3g

551. CREAMY SHRIMP PIE WITH RICE CRUST

Servings: 4; Serving Size: 1/2 recipe

Ingredients:

- 1 1/2 cups cooked white rice
- 2 teaspoons dried parsley
- 2 tablespoons grated onion
- 1 teaspoon olive oil
- 1 tablespoon butter
- 1 clove garlic, crushed
- 1 pound shrimp, peeled and deveined

- 1 recipe Condensed Cream of Mushroom Soup (see recipe in Chapter 4)
- 1 teaspoon lemon juice
- 1 cup sliced steamed mushrooms

Directions:

1. Preheat oven to 350°F. Combine rice, parsley, and onion; mix well. Use olive oil to coat 10" pie plate; press rice mixture evenly around sides and bottom. This works best if the rice is moist; if necessary, add 1 teaspoon of water.

2. Melt butter in deep, nonstick skillet over medium heat; sauté garlic. Add shrimp; cook, stirring frequently, until pink, about 5 minutes.

3. Add soup and lemon juice to skillet; stir until smooth and thoroughly heated, about 5 minutes. (If the soup seems too thick, add some water 1 teaspoon at a time.) Stir mushrooms into soup mixture; pour over rice "crust." Bake 30 minutes or until lightly browned on top. Serve hot.

Nutritional Analysis (per serving):

Calories: 273   Protein: 26g
Carbohydrates: 27g Fat: 6g

552. BARLEY-SPINACH-FISH BAKE

Servings: 4; Serving Size: 1/2 recipe

Ingredients:
- 1/2 tablespoon olive oil
- 1/2 cup chopped scallions
- 1 clove garlic, minced
- 1/2 teaspoon dried rosemary
- 1/2 teaspoon ground marjoram
- 1/2 teaspoon salt
- 1 cup cooked pearl barley
- 5 ounces (1/2 box) frozen chopped spinach, thawed and drained
- 1/2 cup chopped sun-dried tomatoes
- 4 (12") squares of aluminum foil
- 4 (4-ounce) fish fillets
- 3 tablespoons white wine
- Salt and freshly ground pepper to taste

Directions:

1. Preheat oven to 400°F (or outdoor grill can be used).

2. Heat oil in medium nonstick skillet; add scallions and sauté 2 minutes. Add garlic, rosemary, marjoram, and salt; continue to cook another 3 minutes until scallions are tender. Add cooked barley, spinach, and sun-dried tomatoes; mix well.

3. Place aluminum foil squares on work surface; place a fish fillet in center of each square. Divide barley mixture equally; place on top of each fillet. Sprinkle with white wine, salt, and pepper.

4. Fold aluminum foil loosely to enclose filling. Place packets on baking sheet (or directly on grill if using outdoor grill); bake 15 minutes or until fish is tender and flakes easily.

Nutritional Analysis (per serving):

Calories: 239   Protein: 26g
Carbohydrates: 15g Fat: 8g Saturated Fat: 1g Cholesterol: 67mg Sodium: 418mg Fiber: 3g

553. GRILLED SALMON WITH ROASTED PEPPERS

Servings: 4; Serving Size: 1 steak

Ingredients:
- 4 (4-ounce) salmon steaks
- 1 tablespoon reduced-sodium soy sauce
- 1 tablespoon brown sugar
- 1 tablespoon olive oil
- 2 large roasted red bell peppers, cut into strips
- 1 tablespoon balsamic vinegar
- 1/2 teaspoon dried thyme
- 1/2 teaspoon freshly ground pepper

Directions:

1. Place salmon in shallow dish. Mix together soy sauce, brown sugar, and olive oil; pour over salmon and cover both sides with marinade. Set aside.

2. Sprinkle roasted pepper strips with balsamic vinegar, thyme, and pepper. Set aside.

3. Heat grill. Remove salmon from the marinade; grill over medium heat approximately 8 minutes on one side.

4. Turn and grill on other side until salmon is cooked and tender, about 4–5 minutes longer. Remove from heat.

5. Top each salmon steak with marinated roasted red peppers.

Nutritional Analysis (per serving):

Calories: 269   Protein: 24g
Carbohydrates: 8g Fat: 16g Saturated Fat: 3g Cholesterol: 67mg Sodium: 321mg Fiber: 1g

554. BAKED BREAD CRUMB–CRUSTED FISH WITH LEMON

Servings: 6; Serving Size: 1/2 recipe

Ingredients:
- 2 large lemons
- 1/2 cup bread crumbs
- Nonstick cooking spray
- 1 1/2 pounds (24 ounces) halibut fillets

Directions:

1. Preheat oven to 375°F. Wash 1 lemon; cut into thin slices. Grate 1 tablespoon of zest from the second lemon, then juice it. Combine grated zest and bread crumbs in small bowl; stir to mix. Set aside.

2. Put lemon juice in shallow dish; arrange lemon slices in bottom of baking dish treated with nonstick spray. Dip fish pieces in lemon juice; set on lemon slices in baking dish.

3. Sprinkle bread crumb mixture evenly over fish pieces along with salt and pepper if using; bake until crumbs are lightly browned and fish is just opaque, 10–15 minutes.

4. Serve immediately using lemon slices as garnish.

Nutritional Analysis (per serving, without salt):

Calories: 137   Protein: 24g
Carbohydrates: 5g Fat: 3g
Saturated Fat: 1g Cholesterol: 36mg Sodium: 73mg Fiber: 2g

555. BAKED RED SNAPPER ALMANDINE

Servings: 4; Serving Size: 1/2 recipe

Ingredients:
- 1 pound (16 ounces) red snapper fillets
- Sea or kosher salt and freshly ground white or black pepper to taste (optional)

- 4 teaspoons all-purpose flour
- 2 teaspoons olive oil
- 2 tablespoons ground raw almonds
- 2 teaspoons unsalted butter
- 1 tablespoon lemon juice

Directions:
1. Preheat oven to 375°F. Rinse red snapper fillets and dry between layers of paper towels. Season with salt and pepper if using; sprinkle with flour, front and back.
2. In an ovenproof nonstick skillet, sauté fillets in olive oil until nicely browned on both sides, about 5 minutes per side.
3. Combine ground almonds and butter in microwave-safe dish.
4. Microwave on high 30 seconds or until butter is melted; stir to combine.
5. Pour almond-butter mixture and lemon juice over fillets; bake 3–5 minutes or until almonds are nicely browned.

Nutritional Analysis (per serving, without salt):
Calories: 178 Protein: 24g Carbohydrates: 3g Fat: 7g Saturated Fat: 2g Cholesterol: 47mg Sodium: 73mg Fiber: 1g

556. A-TASTE-OF-ITALY BAKED FISH

Servings: 4; Serving Size: 1/2 recipe
Ingredients:
- 1 pound (16 ounces) cod fillets
- Nonstick cooking spray
- 1 (14-ounce) can stewed tomatoes
- 1/2 teaspoon dried minced onion
- 1/2 teaspoon dried minced garlic
- 1/2 teaspoon dried basil
- 1/2 teaspoon dried parsley
- 1/2 teaspoon dried oregano
- 1/2 teaspoon sugar
- 1 tablespoon grated Parmesan cheese

Directions:
1. Preheat oven to 375°F. Rinse cod with cold water and pat dry with paper towels.
2. In 2–3-quart baking pan or casserole treated with nonstick cooking spray, combine remaining ingredients; mix.
3. Arrange fillets over mixture, folding thin tail ends under; spoon mixture over fillets.
4. For fillets about 1" thick, bake uncovered 20–25 minutes or until fish is opaque and flaky.

Nutritional Analysis (per serving):
Calories: 128 Protein: 22g Carbohydrates: 7g Fat: 1g Saturated Fat: 0g Cholesterol: 50mg Sodium: 312mg

557. SALMON CASSEROLE

Yield: 6 servings
Ingredients:
- 1 pound (455 g) potatoes, peeled and sliced
- 1 1/2 pounds (680 g) salmon fillets
- 1 tablespoon (4 g) chopped fresh dill
- 1/4 cup (60 ml) oil, heated
- 1/2 cup (120 ml) white wine
- 1/4 cup (60 ml) sherry
- 1/2 cup (115 g) fat-free sour cream
- 2 tablespoons (30 g) grated horseradish

Directions:
- Boil potatoes until almost done, about 10 to 15 minutes.
- Layer in a large ovenproof casserole.
- Place the salmon on top. Sprinkle with the dill.
- Cover and cook at 350°F (180°C, gas mark 4) for 25 minutes.
- Remove from the oven and pour the heated oil, wine, and sherry over.
- Continue to cook uncovered until salmon is done.
- Stir together sour cream and horseradish and pour over top.

Nutritional Info:
162 g water; 346 calories (58% from fat, 23% from protein, 19% from carb); 19 g protein; 21 g total fat; 4 g

558. SALMON HASH

Yield: 4 servings
Ingredients:
- 1 tablespoon (15 ml) vegetable oil
- 1/2 cup (80 g) chopped onion
- 1/2 cup (75 g) green bell peppers, chopped
- 1/2 cup (75 g) red bell peppers, chopped
- 1/8 teaspoon pepper
- 1 clove garlic, crushed
- 2 medium potatoes, diced and cooked
- 1 6 ounces (455 g) salmon

Directions:
- Heat oil in 1 Q-inch (25 cm) nonstick skillet over medium-high heat.
- Saute onion, bell peppers, pepper, and garlic in oil.
- Stir in potatoes and salmon.
- Cook uncovered, stirring frequently, until hot.

Nutritional Info:
282 g water; 336 calories (27% from fat, 34% from protein, 39% from carb); 28 g Protein; 10 g total fat; 2 g

559. BAKED SNAPPER WITH ORANGE-RICE DRESSING

Servings: 4; Serving Size: 1/2 recipe
Ingredients:
- 1/2 cup chopped celery
- 1/2 cup chopped onion
- 1/2 cup orange juice
- 1 tablespoon lemon juice
- 1 teaspoon grated orange zest
- 1 1/2 cups cooked rice
- Water as needed to moisten rice
- 1 pound (16 ounces) red snapper fillets
- 2 teaspoons unsalted butter
- 2 tablespoons ground raw almonds

Directions:
1. Preheat oven to 350°F.
2. In a microwave-safe bowl, mix celery and onion with juices and orange zest;
3. Microwave on high 2 minutes or until mixture comes to a boil.
4. Add rice; stir to moisten, adding water 1 tablespoon at a time if necessary to thoroughly coat rice.
5. Cover and let stand 5 minutes.
6. Rinse fillets and pat dry between paper towels. Prepare baking dish with nonstick

spray. Spread rice mixture in dish; arrange fillets on top. Season fillets with salt and pepper if using.

7. Combine butter and almonds in a microwave-safe bowl; microwave on high 30 seconds or until butter is melted. Stir; spoon over top of fillets.

8. Cover and bake 10 minutes. Remove cover and bake another 5–10 minutes or until fish flakes easily when tested with a fork and almonds are lightly browned.

Nutritional Analysis (per serving, without salt):

Calories: 257 Protein: 26g Carbohydrates: 25g Fat: 5g Saturated Fat: 2g Cholesterol: 47mg Sodium: 83mg Fiber: 1g

560. SHRIMP MICROWAVE CASSEROLE

Servings: 4; Serving Size: 1/2 recipe
Ingredients:
- 1 1/2 cups uncooked egg noodles (to yield four 1/2 -cup servings)
- 1 cup chopped green onion
- 1 cup chopped green pepper
- 1 cup sliced mushrooms
- 1 recipe Condensed Cream of Celery Soup
- 1 teaspoon Homemade Worcestershire
- 4 drops Tabasco (optional)
- 1/2 cup diced canned pimientos
- 1/2 cup pitted chopped olives
- 1/2 cup skimmed milk
- 1/2 pound (8 ounces) cooked, deveined, shelled shrimp

Directions:

1. Cook egg noodles according to package directions; drain and keep warm.

2. Place green onion and green pepper in covered microwave-safe dish; microwave on high 1 minute. Add mushrooms; microwave another minute or until all vegetables are tender.

3. Add soup, Worcestershire sauce, Tabasco (if using), pimiento, olives, and milk; stir well. Microwave covered 1–2 minutes until mixture is hot and bubbly.

4. Add cooked shrimp and noodles; stir to mix. Microwave 30 seconds–1 minute or until mixture is hot.

Nutritional Analysis (per serving):
Calories: 196 Protein: 18g Carbohydrates: 27g Fat: 2g

561. CRUNCHY "FRIED" CATFISH FILLETS

Servings: 4; Serving Size: 1/2 recipe
Ingredients:
- 4 catfish fillets
- 1 egg white (from a large egg), room temperature
- 1/2 cup bread crumbs
- 1/2 cup enriched white cornmeal
- 1 teaspoon grated lemon zest
- 1/2 teaspoon crushed dried basil
- 1/2 cup all-purpose flour
- 1/2 teaspoon kosher or sea salt (optional)
- 1/2 teaspoon lemon pepper

Directions:

1. Preheat oven to 450°F; treat shallow baking pan with nonstick spray. Rinse catfish and dry between layers of paper towels.

2. In shallow dish, beat egg white until frothy. In another dish, combine bread crumbs, cornmeal, lemon zest, and basil. In third dish, combine flour, salt (if using), and lemon pepper.

3. Dip fish into flour mixture to coat one side of each fillet. Shake off any excess flour mixture, then dip flour-covered side of fillet into egg white. Next, coat covered side of fillet with bread crumb mixture.

4. Arrange prepared fillets side by side, coated-side up, on prepared baking pan.

5. Tuck in any thin edges.

6. Bake 6–12 minutes or until fish flakes easily with a fork.

Nutritional Analysis (per serving, without salt):
Calories: 244 Protein: 21g Carbohydrates: 18g Fat: 9g Saturated Fat: 2g Cholesterol: 53mg Sodium: 248mg Fiber: 1g

562. BAKED ORANGE ROUGHY WITH SPICY PLUM SAUCE

Servings: 4; Serving Size: 1/2 recipe
Ingredients:
- 1 pound (16 ounces) orange roughy fillets
- 1 teaspoon paprika
- 1 bay leaf
- 1 clove garlic, crushed
- 1 apple, peeled, cored, and cubed
- 1 teaspoon grated fresh ginger
- 1 small red or Spanish onion, chopped
- 1 teaspoon olive oil
- 1/2 cup Plum Sauce (see recipe in Chapter 6)
- 1/2 teaspoon Chinese five-spice powder
- 1 teaspoon frozen unsweetened apple juice concentrate
- 1/2 teaspoon Bragg Liquid Aminos
- 1/2 teaspoon blackstrap molasses
- 1 1/2 cups cooked brown rice

Directions:
- Preheat oven to 400°F.
- Treat baking dish with nonstick spray.
- Rinse orange roughly and pat dry between paper towels.
- Rub both sides of fish with paprika; set in prepared dish.
- In covered microwave-safe bowl, mix bay leaf, garlic, apple, ginger, onion, and oil;
- Microwave on high 3 minutes or until apple is tender and onion is transparent.
- Stir; discard bay leaf and top fillets with mixture. Bake uncovered 15–18 minutes or until fish is opaque.
- While fish bakes, add Plum Sauce to microwave-safe bowl.
- Add five-spice powder, apple juice concentrate, Liquid Aminos, and molasses.
- Microwave on high 30 seconds; stir, add a little water if needed to thin ixture, and microwave another 15 seconds.
- Cover until ready to serve.
- If necessary, bring back to temperature by microwaving mixture another 15 seconds just prior to serving.

Nutritional Analysis (per serving):
Calories: 221 Protein: 19g Carbohydrates: 31g Fat: 3g Saturated Fat: 1g Cholesterol: 23mg Sodium: 101mg

563. GRILLED TUNA WITH HONEY MUSTARD

Yield: 4 servings

Ingredients:
- 1/3 cup (80 ml) red wine vinegar
- 1 tablespoon (11 g) spicy brown mustard
- 1 tablespoon (20 g) honey
- 3 tablespoons (45 ml) extra virgin olive oil
- 1 pound (455 g) tuna steaks

Directions:
- Combine the first 4 ingredients in a jar or covered container; shake to mix well.
- Put tuna in a food storage bag; add the mustard mixture.
- Seal the bag and let marinate for about 20 minutes.
- Heat the grill.
- Remove the tuna from the marinade and pour the marinade in a small saucepan.
- Bring marinade to a boil; remove from heat and set aside.
- Grill the tuna over high heat for about 2 minutes on each side or until done as desired.
- Drizzle with the hot marinade.

Nutritional Info:
100 g water; 275 calories (53% from fat, 40% from protein, 7% from carb); 27 g protein; 16 g total fat; 3 g

564. SWEET ONION–BAKED YELLOWTAIL SNAPPER

Servings: 4; Serving Size: 1/2 recipe

Ingredients:
- 2 cups sliced Vidalia onions
- 1 tablespoon balsamic vinegar
- 2 teaspoons brown sugar
- 4 teaspoons olive oil
- 1 pound (16 ounces) skinless yellowtail snapper fillets
- 1 tablespoon Madeira Sauce (see recipe in Chapter 6)

Directions:
1. In covered microwave-safe dish, microwave onion on high 5 minutes or until transparent. Carefully remove cover; stir in vinegar and brown sugar. Cover; allow to sit several minutes so onion absorbs flavors.
2. Heat a nonstick pan on medium-high heat; add olive oil. Transfer steamed onion mixture to pan; sauté until browned but not crisp.
3. Cook until all liquid has evaporated from pan, stirring often.
4. Onions should have a shiny and dark caramelized color. (This can be prepared 2–3 days in advance; store tightly covered in refrigerator.)
5. Preheat oven to 375°F. Rinse snapper in cold water and dry between paper towels.
6. Arrange on baking sheet treated with nonstick spray.
7. Spoon caramelized onions over tops of fillets, pressing to form a light crust over top of fish.
8. Bake 12–15 minutes or until fish flakes easily with a fork.
9. Serve immediately with Madeira Sauce divided on four plates with fish placed on top.

Nutritional Analysis (per serving):
Calories: 189 Protein: 25g Carbohydrates: 13g Fat: 4g Saturated Fat: 1g Cholesterol: 42mg Sodium: 77mg

565. STIR-FRIED GINGER SCALLOPS WITH VEGETABLES

Servings: 4; Serving Size: 1/2 recipe

Ingredients:
- 1 pound (16 ounces) scallops
- 1 teaspoon peanut or sesame oil
- 1 tablespoon chopped fresh ginger
- 2 cloves garlic, minced
- 4 scallions, thinly sliced (optional)
- 1 teaspoon rice wine vinegar
- 2 teaspoons Bragg Liquid Aminos
- 1/2 cup low-fat, reduced-sodium chicken broth
- 2 cups broccoli florets
- 1 teaspoon cornstarch
- 1/2 teaspoon toasted sesame oil

Directions:
1. Rinse scallops and pat dry between layers of paper towels. If necessary, slice scallops so they're uniform size. Set aside.
2. Add peanut oil to heated nonstick deep skillet or wok; sauté ginger, garlic, and scallions if using 1–2 minutes, being careful ginger doesn't burn. Add vinegar, Liquid Aminos, and broth; bring to a boil. Remove from heat.
3. Place broccoli in large covered microwave-safe dish; pour chicken broth mixture over top. Microwave on high 3–5 minutes depending on preference. (Keep in mind that vegetables will continue to steam for a minute or so if cover remains on dish.)
4. Heat skillet or wok over medium-high temperature. Add scallops; sauté 1 minute on each side. (Do scallops in batches if necessary; be careful not to overcook.)
5. Remove scallops from pan when done; set aside. Drain (but do not discard) liquid from broccoli; return liquid to bowl and transfer broccoli to heated skillet or wok.
6. Stir-fry vegetables to bring up to serving temperature.
7. Meanwhile, in small cup or bowl, add enough water to cornstarch to make a slurry or roux. Whisk slurry into reserved broccoli liquid; microwave on high 1 minute.
8. Add toasted sesame oil; whisk again. Pour thickened broth mixture over broccoli; toss to mix.
9. Add scallops back to broccoli mixture; stir-fry over medium heat to return scallops to serving temperature. Serve over rice or pasta; adjust exchange approximations accordingly.

Nutritional Analysis (per serving):
Calories: 145 Protein: 22g Carbohydrates: 8g Fat: 3g Saturated Fat: 1g Cholesterol: 37mg Sodium: 373mg

566. SCALLOPS AND SHRIMP WITH WHITE BEAN SAUCE

Servings: 4; Serving Size: 1/2 recipe

Ingredients:
- 1/2 cup finely chopped onion, steamed
- 2 cloves garlic, minced
- 2 teaspoons olive oil, divided
- 1/2 cup dry white wine
- 1/2 cup tightly packed fresh parsley leaves
- 1/2 cup tightly packed fresh basil leaves
- 1 1/2 cups canned, drained, and rinsed cannellini (white) beans
- 1/2 cup low-fat reduced-sodium chicken broth
- 1/2 pound (8 ounces) shrimp, shelled and deveined
- 1/2 pound (8 ounces) scallops

Directions:

1. In nonstick saucepan, sauté onion and garlic in 1 teaspoon of oil over moderately low heat for about 5 minutes until onion is soft.
2. Add wine; simmer until wine is reduced by half. Add parsley, basil, 1/2 cup of beans, and chicken broth; simmer, stirring constantly for 1 minute.
3. Transfer bean mixture to blender or food processor; purée. Pour purée back into saucepan; add remaining beans and simmer 2 minutes.
4. In nonstick skillet, heat remaining 1 teaspoon of oil over moderately high heat until it is hot but not smoking. Sauté shrimp 2 minutes on each side or until cooked through.
5. Using slotted spoon, transfer shrimp to plate; cover to keep warm.
6. Add scallops to skillet; sauté 1 minute on each side or until cooked through.
7. To serve, divide bean sauce between four shallow bowls and arrange shellfish over top.

Nutritional Analysis (per serving):
Calories: 231 Protein: 27g Carbohydrates: 18g Fat: 4g Saturated Fat: 1g Cholesterol: 105mg

567. SMOKED MUSSELS AND PASTA

Servings: 4; Serving Size: 1/2 recipe

Ingredients:
- 1 1/2 cups uncooked pasta (to yield 2 cups cooked pasta)
- 1/2 cup chopped leek
- 4 ounces smoked mussels, drained of all excess oil
- 1/2 teaspoon ground cayenne pepper
- 1/2 teaspoon dried oregano
- 1/2 cup nonfat cottage cheese
- 1/2 cup nonfat plain yogurt
- 2 teaspoons grated Parmesan cheese
- 2 teaspoons extra-virgin olive oil
- Cracked black pepper to taste

Directions:

1. Cook pasta according to package directions; drain and set aside. In covered microwave-safe bowl, microwave leek on high 2–3 minutes or until limp and translucent.
2. Add mussels and cayenne pepper; stir. Cover and microwave on high 30 seconds to heat mussels.
3. In blender, combine oregano, cottage cheese, yogurt, and Parmesan cheese; process until smooth.
4. Combine cottage cheese and mussel mixtures; microwave on high until warm, about 30 seconds.
5. Toss pasta with olive oil; stir in mussel mixture.
6. Divide into four portions and serve immediately, topped with cracked pepper.

Nutritional Analysis (per serving):
Calories: 206 Protein: 10g Carbohydrates: 22g Fat: 8g Saturated Fat: 2g Cholesterol: 31mg Sodium: 371mg Fiber: 1g

568. TUNA STEAKS

Yield: 2 servings

Ingredients:
- 6 ounces (170 g) tuna steaks
- 2 tablespoons (30 ml) olive oil
- 2 tablespoons (30 ml) lemon juice
- 1/2 teaspoon black pepper, fresh ground

Directions:
- Combine the olive oil and lemon juice.
- Marinate the steaks in the mixture at least 30 minutes,
- turning occasionally.
- Heat a skillet over high heat. Add the steaks and cook 2 minutes.
- Sprinkle with pepper, turn over, and cook 2 minutes longer.

Nutritional Info: 72 g water; 247 calories (65% from fat, 33% from protein, 3% from carb); 20 g protein; 18 g total fat; 3 g

569. SALMON PINWHEELS

Total: 30 mins

Servings: 4

Ingredients
- 1/2 cup coarse dry breadcrumbs, preferably whole-wheat (see Tip)
- 1 tablespoon extra-virgin olive oil
- 1 tablespoon whole-grain mustard
- 1 tablespoon chopped shallot
- 1 tablespoon lemon juice
- 1 teaspoon chopped rinsed capers
- 1 teaspoon chopped fresh thyme, or 1/2 teaspoon dried
- 1 ¼ pounds center-cut salmon fillet, skinned and cut lengthwise into 4 strips
- 4 teaspoons low-fat mayonnaise

Directions:
- Preheat oven to 400 degrees F. Coat a 9-by-13-inch baking dish with cooking spray.
- Mix breadcrumbs, oil, mustard, shallot, lemon juice, capers, and thyme in a small bowl until combined.
- Working with one at a time, spread each salmon strip with 1 teaspoon mayonnaise.
- Spread about 3 tablespoons of the breadcrumb mixture over the mayonnaise.
- Starting at one end, roll the salmon up tightly, tucking in any loose filling as you go. Insert a toothpick through the end to keep the pinwheel from unrolling. Place in the prepared dish.
- Repeat with the remaining salmon strips.

- Bake the pinwheels until just cooked through, 15 to 20 minutes. Remove the toothpicks before serving.

Nutrition

Calories: 257; protein 29.9g; carbohydrates 8.9g; dietary fiber 1.1g; sugars 0.6g; fat 10.3g; saturated fat 1.9g; cholesterol

570. FISH AMANDINE

Active: 15 mins
Total: 20 mins
Servings: 4

Ingredients

- 4 (4 ounces) fresh or frozen skinless tilapia, trout, or halibut fillets, 1/2- to 1-inch thick
- ¼ cup buttermilk
- ½ cup panko bread crumbs or fine dry bread crumbs
- 2 tablespoons chopped fresh parsley or 2 teaspoons dried parsley flakes
- ½ teaspoon dry mustard
- ¼ teaspoon salt
- ¼ cup sliced almonds, coarsely chopped
- 2 tablespoons grated Parmesan cheese
- 1 tablespoon butter, melted
- ⅛ teaspoon crushed red pepper

Instructions

- Thaw fish, if frozen. Preheat oven to 450 degrees F. Grease a shallow baking pan; set aside. Rinse fish; pat dry with paper towels. Measure the thickness of fish.
- Pour buttermilk into a shallow dish. In another shallow dish, combine bread crumbs, parsley, dry mustard, and salt.
- Dip fish into buttermilk, then into crumb mixture, turning to coat. Place coated fish in the prepared baking pan.
- Sprinkle fish with almonds and Parmesan cheese; drizzle with melted butter.
- Sprinkle with crushed red pepper. Bake 4 to 6 minutes per 1/2-inch thickness of fish or until fish flakes easily when tested with a fork.

Nutrition

Calories: 209; protein 26.2g; carbohydrates 6.7g; dietary fiber 0.9g; sugars 1g; fat 8.7g; saturated fat 3.2g; cholesterol 66.9mg

571. SALMON & ASPARAGUS WITH LEMON-GARLIC BUTTER SAUCE

Active: 10 mins
Total: 25 mins
Servings: 4

Ingredients

- 1 pound center-cut salmon fillet, preferably wild, cut into 4 portions
- 1 pound fresh asparagus, trimmed
- ½ teaspoon salt
- ½ teaspoon ground pepper
- 3 tablespoons butter
- 1 tablespoon extra-virgin olive oil
- ½ tablespoon grated garlic
- 1 teaspoon grated lemon zest
- 1 tablespoon lemon juice

Directions:

- Preheat oven to 375 degrees F. Coat a large rimmed baking sheet with cooking spray.
- Place salmon on one side of the prepared baking sheet and asparagus on the other. Sprinkle the salmon and asparagus with salt and pepper.
- Heat butter, oil, garlic, lemon zest, and lemon juice in a small skillet over medium heat until the butter is melted.
- Drizzle the butter mixture over the salmon and asparagus. Bake until the salmon is cooked through and the asparagus is just tender, 12 to 15 minutes.

Nutrition

Serving Size: 1 Piece, Salmon & About 5 Spears Asparagus Per Serving: 270 calories; protein 25.4g; carbohydrates 5.6g

572. CHINESE STEAMED FISH

Yield: 2 servings

Ingredients:

- 12 ounces (340 g) fish fillets
- 2 tablespoons (28 ml) dry sherry
- 1 tablespoon (15 ml) soy sauce
- 2 teaspoons grated gingerroot
- 1/2 teaspoon minced garlic or 1 clove garlic, crushed
- 1 1/2 teaspoons toasted sesame oil
- 1 or 2 scallions, minced (optional)

Directions:

- Lay the fish fillets on a piece of heavy-duty aluminum foil and turn the edges up to form a lip.
- Mix together the sherry, soy sauce, gingerroot, garlic, and sesame oil.
- Fit a rack—a cake-cooling rack works nicely—into a large skillet.
- Pour about 1/4 inch (6 mm) of water in the bottom of the skillet and turn the heat to high. Place the foil with the fish on it on the rack.
- Carefully pour the sherry mixture over the fish.
- Cover the pan tightly.
- Cook for 5 to 7 minutes or until the fish flakes easily.
- Serve with minced scallions as a garnish, if desired.

Nutrition Info:

2 grams of carbohydrates, and 31 grams of protein.

573. SWORDFISH VERACRUZ

Yield: 4 servings, each

Ingredients:

- 24 ounces (680 g) swordfish steaks
- 1/2 cup (120 ml) ruby red grapefruit juice—I like to use fresh-squeezed.
- 1/2 teaspoon ground cumin
- 1 tablespoon oil
- 1/4 cup (65 g) salsa verde

Directions:

- Cut the swordfish into 4 servings and place on a plate with a rim.
- Mix together the grapefruit juice and the cumin and pour it over the steaks, turning them to coat both sides.
- Let the swordfish steaks sit in the grapefruit juice for 5 minutes or so.
- Spray a large, heavy skillet with nonstick cooking spray and place over medium heat.
- When the skillet is hot, add the oil and then the fish. Sauté for 4 minutes per side.
- Then pour in the grapefruit juice from the plate and let the fish cook in it for another minute or two, turning once.
- Place the fish on serving plates, top each serving with a tablespoon of salsa verde, and serve.

574. DIJON SALMON WITH GREEN BEAN PILAF

Total: 30 mins

Servings: 4

Ingredients:

- 1 ¼ pound wild salmon, skinned and cut into 4 portions
- 3 tablespoons extra-virgin olive oil, divided
- 1 tablespoon minced garlic
- ¾ teaspoon salt
- 2 tablespoons mayonnaise
- 2 teaspoons whole-grain mustard
- ½ teaspoon ground pepper, divided
- 12 ounces pretrimmed haricots verts or thin green beans, cut into thirds
- 1 small lemon, zested and cut into 4 wedges
- 2 tablespoons pine nuts
- 1 8-ounce package precooked brown rice
- 2 tablespoons water
- Chopped fresh parsley for garnish

Directions:

- Preheat oven to 425 degrees F. Line a rimmed baking sheet with foil or parchment paper.
- Brush salmon with 1 tablespoon oil and place on the prepared baking sheet. Mash garlic and salt into a paste with the side of a chef's knife or a fork. Combine a scant 1 teaspoon of the garlic paste in a small bowl with mayonnaise, mustard, and 1/4 teaspoon pepper. Spread the mixture on top of the fish.
- Roast the salmon until it flakes easily with a fork in the thickest part, 6 to 8 minutes per inch of thickness.
- Meanwhile, heat the remaining 2 tablespoons of oil in a large skillet over medium-high heat. Add green beans, lemon zest, pine nuts, the remaining garlic paste, and 1/4 teaspoon pepper; cook, stirring, until the beans are just tender, 2 to 4 minutes. Reduce heat to medium. Add rice and water and cook, stirring, until hot, 2 to 3 minutes more.
- Sprinkle the salmon with parsley, if desired, and serve with the green bean pilaf and lemon wedges.
- All wild salmon--and now some farmed--is considered a sustainable choice. For farmed, ask for fish that's raised in the land- or tank-based systems.

Nutrition Facts:

Serving Size: 4 Oz. Fish & 1 Cup Pilaf Per Serving: 442 calories; protein 32.2g; carbohydrates 21.6g; dietary fiber

575. FISH PIE

Preparation time: 10 minutes Cooking time: 1 hour and 10 minutes Servings:6

Ingredients:

- 1 red onion, chopped
- 2 salmon fillets, skinless and cut into medium pieces
- 2 mackerel fillets, skinless and cut into medium pieces
- 3 haddock fillets and cut into medium pieces
- 2 bay leaves
- ¼ cup ghee+ 2 tbsp. ghee
- 1 cauliflower head, florets separated
- 4 eggs
- 4 cloves
- 1 cup whipping cream
- ½ cup water
- A pinch of nutmeg, ground
- 1 tsp. Dijon mustard
- 1 cup cheddar cheese, shredded+ ½ cup cheddar cheese, shredded
- Some chopped parsley
- Salt and black pepper to the taste
- 4 tbsp. chives, chopped

Directions:

- Put some water in a pan, add some salt, bring to a boil over medium heat, add eggs, , cook them for 10 minutes, take off heat, drain, leave them to cool down, peel and cut them into quarters.
- Put water in another pot, bring to a boil, add cauliflower florets, cook for 10 minutes, drain them, transfer to your blender, add ¼ cup ghee, pulse well and transfer to a bowl.
- Put cream and ½ cup water in a pan, add fish, toss to coat and heat up over medium heat.
- Add onion, cloves and bay leaves, bring to a boil, reduce heat and simmer for 10 minutes.
- Take off heat, transfer fish to a baking dish and leave aside.
- return pan with fish sauce to heat, add nutmeg, stir and cook for 5 minutes.
- Take off heat, discard cloves and bay leaves, add 1 cup cheddar cheese and 2 tbsp. ghee and stir well.
- Place egg quarters on top of the fish in the baking dish.
- Add cream and cheese sauce over them, top with cauliflower mash, sprinkle the rest of the cheddar cheese, chives and parsley, introduce in the oven at 400 degrees F for 30 minutes.
- Leave the pie to cool down a bit before slicing and serving.

Nutrition Facts:

- cal.300, fat 45, fiber 3, carbs 5, protein 26
- Baked Fish
- Preparation time: 10 minutes Cooking time: 30 minutes Servings: 4

Ingredients:

- 1 pound haddock
- 3 tsp. water
- 2 tbsp. lemon juice
- Salt and black pepper to the taste
- 2 tbsp. mayonnaise
- 1 tsp. dill weed
- Cooking spray
- A pinch of old bay seasoning

Directions:

- Spray a baking dish with some cooking oil.
- Add lemon juice, water and fish and toss to coat a bit.
- Add salt, pepper, old bay seasoning and dill weed and toss again.
- Add mayo and spread well.
- Introduce in the oven at 350 degrees F and bake for 30 minutes.
- Divide between plates and serve.

Nutrition Facts:

cal.104, fat 12, fiber 1, carbs 0.5, protein 20

576. TILAPIA

Preparation time: 10 minutes Cooking time: 10 minutes Servings: 4

Ingredients:

- 4 tilapia fillets, boneless

- Salt and black pepper to the taste
- ½ cup parmesan, grated
- 4 tbsp. mayonnaise
- ¼ tsp. basil, dried
- ¼ tsp. garlic powder
- 2 tbsp. lemon juice
- ¼ cup ghee
- A pinch of onion powder

Instructions:

• Spray a baking sheet with cooking spray, place tilapia on it, season with salt and pepper, introduce in preheated broiler and cook for 3 minutes.
• Turn fish on the other side and broil for 3 minutes more.
• In a bowl, mix parmesan with mayo, basil, garlic, lemon juice, onion powder and ghee and stir well.
• Add fish to this mix, toss to coat well, place on baking sheet again and broil for 3 minutes more.

Nutrition Facts:

cal.175, fat 10, fiber 0, carbs 2, protein 17

577. TROUT AND SPECIAL SAUCE

Preparation time: 10 minutes Cooking time: 10 minutes Servings: 1

Ingredients:

- 1 big trout fillet
- Salt and black pepper to the taste
- 1 tbsp. olive oil
- 1 tbsp. ghee
- Zest and juice from 1 orange
- A handful parsley, chopped
- ½ cup pecans, chopped

Directions::

• Heat up a pan with the oil over medium high heat, add the fish fillet, season with salt and pepper, cook for 4 minutes on each side, transfer to a plate and keep warm for now.
• Heat up the same pan with the ghee over medium heat, add pecans, stir and toast for 1 minutes.
• Add orange juice and zest, some salt and pepper and chopped parsley, stir, cook for 1 minute and pour over fish fillet.
• Serve right away.

Nutrition Facts:

cal.200, fat 10, fiber 2, carbs 1, protein 14

578. PEACH SALMON

Yield: 4 servings

Ingredients:

• 24 ounces (680 g) salmon fillet in four servings
• 3 tablespoons (42 g) butter
• 2 fresh peaches
• 1/4 onion
• 1 teaspoon chopped garlic
• 1 1/2 teaspoons curry powder
• 2 tablespoons (28 ml) lemon juice
• 1/4 cup (6 g) Splenda or its equivalent in sweetness
• salt and pepper

Directions:

• Start the salmon sautéing in the butter over medium heat and cover it with a tilted lid.
• Peel your peaches, halve, and remove the pits. Throw the peaches, onion, garlic, and curry powder in your food processor and pulse until the peach is chopped medium-fine. Go flip your salmon.
• Mix together the lemon juice and Splenda. When your salmon is donethrough, plate it.
• Pour the lemon juice mixture in the skillet and stir it around, scraping up the yummy brown bits.
• Add the peach mixture and cook for just aminute or two, stirring.
• Salt and pepper to taste and then spoon over the salmon and serve.

Nutrition Facts:

309 calories, 15 grams fat, 35 grams protein, 9 grams carbohydrate, 1 gram dietary fiber

579. SKILLET BARBECUED SALMON

Yield: 4 servings

Ingredients:

• 1/4 cup (115 g) bacon grease
• 24 ounces (680 g) salmon fillets, 1-inch (2.5 cm) thick and cut into four servings
• 2 tablespoons (28 ml) pineapple juice, or sugar-free pineapple syrup

• 1/4 cup (60 ml) soy sauce
• 1 1/3 tablespoons (20 ml) rice vinegar
• 1 1/3 tablespoons (20 ml) lemon juice
• 2 teaspoons olive oil
• 1/2 cup (12 g) Splenda
• 1/8 cup erythritol
• 1/3 teaspoon molasses
• 1/2 teaspoon pepper
• 1/3 teaspoon cayenne
• 1/3 teaspoon paprika
• 1/8 teaspoon garlic

Directions:

• Put your big, heavy skillet over medium-high heat and throw in the bacon grease.
• When it's hot, add the fillets. Let them sizzle there while you mix together everything else.
• Flip your fillets after 4 to 5 minutes and let them get golden on the other side, too.
• Now pour in the sauce and flip the fillets again to coat.
• Let them simmer in the sauce until they're done through.
• Then plate the fillets and turn up the burner.
• Boil the sauce until it's syrupy, pour over the fillets, and serve.

Nutrition Facts:

366 calories, 21 grams fat, 35 grams protein, 7 grams carbohydrate

580. BACON AND SALMON BAKE

Makes 6 Servings

Ingredients:

• 1/2 cup sweet onion, chopped
• 1/2 teaspoon lemon thyme, fresh, or dried regular thyme
• 1 tablespoon butter
• 1 8-ounce package cream cheese, softened
• 2 eggs
• 1 tablespoon parsley flakes
• 1/4 teaspoon lemon pepper
• 1/2 cup bacon, cooked and chopped
• 2 cans salmon, drained, large bones and skin removed
• Topping:
• 2 tablespoons Romano cheese (or Parmesan)

- 1/2 cup Monterey jack cheese, shredded
- 1 teaspoon chives, snipped

Directions:

- In a small frying pan over medium heat, cook the onions and thyme in the butter until the onions are golden, about 5 minutes.
- Set them aside to cool.
- Combine the cream cheese, eggs, parsley, and lemon pepper in a mixing bowl and mix well.
- Stir in the bacon
- and salmon. Pour this mixture into a 9" x 13" baking dish.
- Sprinkle the topping over the salmon mixture.
- Bake at 350 F for about 25 minutes, or until the cheese is bubbling and golden.

Nutrition Facts:

Carbohydrates: 3 g Fiber: 1 g Protein: 15 g Fat: 23 g Calories: 278

581. CHEESY SALMON CASSEROLE

Makes 6 Servings

Ingredients:

- 6 eggs
- 6 cloves garlic, minced
- 3 tablespoons butter
- 1 1/2 cups half-and-half
- 3 tablespoons lemon juice, fresh
- 2-14 ounce cans salmon, skin and bones removed, juices reserved
- 1/4 teaspoon sea salt
- 1/8 teaspoon lemon pepper
- 1/4 teaspoon oregano
- 1/4 cup soy protein
- Cooking oil spray
- 1 cup mozzarella or Monterey jack cheese, shredded

Directions:

- Hard cook the eggs: Place the whole eggs into a medium-sized pan with a lid and cover them with water.
- Add a pinch of salt, cover the pan, and bring it to a boil over medium heat.
- Once it reaches a full, rolling boil, turn the heat off and allow the pan to rest on the burner for 10 minutes. Then place the eggs into a bowl filled with cold water to cool them, so that they are easy to handle.
- While the eggs are resting, cook the garlic in the butter in a 4- to 6-quart pot until it is becoming translucent, about 4 minutes.
- Stir in the half-and-half, lemon juice, juice reserved from the canned salmon, sea salt, lemon pepper, and oregano.
- Bring this mixture to a boil over medium heat; then stir in the soy protein.
- Blend it as thoroughly as possible and remove it from the heat. Stir in the canned salmon and set the cream mixture aside.
- Slice the eggs and place them evenly across the bottom of a 9" x 13" baking dish that has been sprayed with cooking oil spray.
- Carefully spread the salmon mixture atop the egg slices. Sprinkle it with the shredded cheese and bake it for about 25 minutes at 350 F, or until the cheese is bubbling and the top is golden brown.

Nutrition Facts:

Carbohydrates: 5 g Fiber: 1 g Protein: 21 g Fat: 23 g Calories: 313

582. TUNA AND SPINACH BAKE

Makes 4 servings

Ingredients:

- 2 Tbsp unsalted butter
- 1/2 cup finely chopped onion
- 2-10 oz bags ready-to-use spinach
- 2-6 oz cans chunk light tuna, drained and flaked
- 3 large eggs
- 3/4 cup whipping cream
- 1/2 tsp sea salt
- 4 oz aged cheddar cheese, shredded

Directions:

- Preheat the oven to 350 F (175 C). Melt the butter in a large frying pan over medium heat.
- Add the onion and stir for about 2 minutes, or until the onion is soft.
- Add the spinach and cook until wilted. Spread the spinach mixture in an 8 x 8-inch (20 x 20-cm) baking dish.
- Top with the tuna. In a small bowl, lightly beat the eggs with a fork.
- Beat in the cream and salt. Pour over the tuna. Sprinkle evenly with the cheese.
- Bake for 40 minutes, or until set and the top is lightly browned.

Nutrition Facts:

Carbohydrates: 8.7 g Fiber: 4.1 g Protein: 38.7 g Fat: 36.9 g Calories: 515

583. EASY SALMON OR TUNA PATTIES

Makes 4 Patties

Ingredients:

- 1-6 oz (170 g) can salmon or tuna
- 1 large ege, lightly beaten
- 2 Tbsp (30 ml) minced green onion
- Sea salt and freshly ground black pepper
- 1 Tbsp (15 ml) extra-virgin olive oil
- 1 Tbsp (15 ml) unsalted butter

Directions:

- Drain the fish well, place in a medium bowl, and mash it up with a fork.
- Stir in the egg and green onion.
- Season to taste with salt and pepper. Heat the oil and butter in a large frying pan over medium to medium-high heat until bubbly.
- Drop the fish mixture from a large spoon to make 4 equal mounds. Press them flat with the back of the spoon. Cook until golden brown underneath.
- Use a large pancake turner to gently turn the patties over; turn them only once or they'll break.
- Brown the other side.

Nutrition Facts:

Carbohydrates: 0.6 g Fiber: 0.1 g Protein: 10.4 g (salmon) 11.6 g (tuna) Fat: 10.8 g (salmon) 7.7 g (tuna) Calories: 142 (salmon) 120 (tuna)

584. SALMON CAKES

Makes 8 Cakes

Ingredients:

- 1 1/2 lb (680 g) boneless, skinless salmon filet
- 2 Tbsp (30 ml) mayonnaise
- 1 Tbsp (15 ml) finely chopped green onion tops
- 1 Tbsp (15 ml) finely chopped fresh dill

- 1 Tbsp (15 ml) freshly squeezed lemon juice
- 3/4 (3.7 ml) Sea salt
- Freshly ground black pepper
- 2 Tbsp (30 ml) vegetable oil

Directions:
- With a knife, chop the fillet into 1/4 inch (0.6-cm) pieces and place in a bowl.
- Add the mayonnaise, green onion, dill, lemon juice, salt, and pepper to taste.
- Stir rapidly in the same direction for 1 minute. This helps the cakes stick together.
- Form into 8 patties. You can refrigerate them, uncovered, for up to 6 hours or until ready to cook.
- Heat the oil in a large heavy or nonstick frying pan over medium-high heat.
- Add the cakes and cook until lightly browned, 2 to 3 minutes.
- Turn over and cook for an additional 2 to 3 minutes, or until browned.

Nutrition Facts:
Carbohydrates: 0.3 g Fiber: 0.1 g Protein: 17.1 g Fat: 15 g Calories: 209

585. SALMON WITH LEMON LIME BUTTER

Servings: 4

Ingredients:
- 1/2 tsp grated lemon zest
- 1/2 tsp grated lime zest
- 2 tbs room-temp butter
- 1 1/2 lbs salmon fillet
- 1/4 tsp salt
- 1/3 c water

Directions
- Stir lemon/lime zests into butter, put mixture onto a piece of plastic wrap and roll to form 1" cylinder.
- Either refrigerate, or if in a hurry put in freezer to firm while you cook the fish.
- Put fish in microwave baking dish. Pour in water and sprinkle fish with salt.
- Cover with plastic wrap and poke several holes in it.
- Microwave on MEDIUM for 6 min. then flip fish and cook 2 minutes.
- Top each portion with slices of lemon lime butter and serve.

Nutritional Facts
Cal. 290 Protein 33g Fat 16g Sodium 268mg Carb .06g

586. GRILLED GLAZED SALMON

Ingredients:
- 2 tablespoons olive oil
- 1 teaspoon water
- 1/2 cup red wine vinegar
- 2 cloves crushed garlic
- 1 teaspoon garlic salt
- 1/2 teaspoon freshly ground black pepper
- 2 teaspoons dried basil
- 1/2 cup No Calorie Sweetener
- Granulated
- 1 1/3 pounds salmon fillet

Directions
- In a shallow baking pan, combine the olive oil, water, red wine vinegar, garlic, garlic salt, black pepper and basil.
- Place salmon filet in the marinade meat side down, if skin is still on.
- Marinate for 30 minutes.
- Preheat an outdoor grill for medium heat and lightly oil grate. Coat the salmon filet lightly with No Calorie Sweetener.
- Place on grill and cook 12 minutes per side. Baste with marinade periodically while cooking. Salmon is done, when it flakes easily with a fork.

Nutritional Facts
Calories 360 Calories from Fat 210 Total Fat 23g Saturated Fat 4g Cholesterol 90mg Sodium 540mg Total Carbs 6g

587. GINGER MUSTARD FISH

Yield: 4 servings

Ingredients:
- 4 (6 ounce, or 175 g) fish fillets,
- such as tilapia, cod, or orange roughly
- 4 tablespoons (56 g) butter
- 2 teaspoons minced garlic or 4
- cloves garlic, crushed
- 2 teaspoons grated ginger
- 2 teaspoons spicy brown or Dijon
- mustard
- 1 tablespoon (15 ml) water

Directions
- In a large, heavy skillet, start sautéing the fish in the butter over medium-low heat; 4 to 5 minutes per side should be plenty.
- Remove the fish to a plate.
- Add the garlic, ginger, mustard, and water to the skillet and stir everything together well.
- Put the fish back in, turning it over once, carefully, to make sure both sides get acquainted with the sauce.
- Let it cook for another minute or so and then serve. Scrape the sauce out of the skillet over the fish.

Nutrition Facts:
1 gram of carbohydrates, and 31 grams of protein.

588. AIOLI FISH BAKE

Yield: 1 serving

Ingredients:
- 1 fillet (about 6 ounces, or 170 g)
- of mild, white fish
- 2 tablespoons (30 ml) Aioli Sauce
- 1 tablespoon (6.3 g) grated
- Parmesan cheese

Directions:

7. Preheat the oven to 350°F (180°C, or gas mark 4).

8. Spray a shallow baking pan (a jelly roll pan is ideal) with nonstick cooking spray.

9. Working right on the baking pan, spread a fillet thickly with Aioli

10. Sauce and sprinkle ½ tablespoon of Parmesan over that.

11. Turn the fillet over carefully and spread Aioli and sprinkle the remaining Parmesan on other side.

12. Bake for 20 minutes and serve.

Aioli Sauce

Ingredients
- 1 cup oil

- 1 egg
- 1 egg yolk
- 1 tablespoon Dijon mustard
- 2 teaspoons lemon juice
- 1/2 teaspoon coarse salt
- 1 garlic cloves (or 1 1/2 teaspoons minced garlic)

Directions:
- Place all ingredients in a large cup.
- Blend with an immersion blending, working from the bottom up, until ingredients are combined and thick

Nutritional Info

1 gram of carbohydrates, and 32 grams of protein.

589. FISH AND ASPARAGUS WITH TARRAGON MUSTARD SAUCE

Yield: 2 servings

Ingredients:
- 12 ounces (340 g) fish fillets whiting, tilapia, sole, flounder, or any other mild white fish
- 10 asparagus spears
- 2 tablespoons (30 g) sour cream
- 1 tablespoon (15 g) mayonnaise
- ¼ teaspoon dried tarragon
- ½ teaspoon Dijon or spicy brown mustard

Directions:
- Snap the bottoms off the asparagus spears where they break naturally.
- Place the asparagus in a large glass pie plate, add 1 tablespoon (15 ml) of water, and cover by placing a plate on top.
- Microwave on high for 3 minutes. While the asparagus is microwaving, stir together the sour cream, mayonnaise, tarragon, and mustard.
- Remove the asparagus from the microwave, take it out of the pie plate, and set it aside.
- Drain the water out of the pie plate.
- Place the fish fillets in the pie plate and spread 2 tablespoons (30 ml) of the sour cream mixture over them.
- Re-cover the pie plate and microwave the fish for 3 to 4 minutes on high.
- Open the microwave, remove the plate from the top of the pie plate, and arrange the asparagus on top of the fish.
- Re-cover the pie plate and cook for another 1 to 2 minutes on high.
- Remove the pie plate from the microwave and take the plate off.
- Place the fish and asparagus on serving plates.
- Scrape any sauce that's cooked into the pie plate over the fish and asparagus.
- Top each serving with the reserved sauce and serve.

Nutrition Facts:

4 grams of carbohydrates and 2 grams of fiber

590. TRUITE AU BLEU

Ingredients:
- Water
- Cider vinegar
- Bay leaves
- Peppercorns or coarse cracked pepper
- Salt or Vege-Sal
- Trout, cleaned and beheaded, but with the skin still on—about 10 ounces
- (280 g) per serving as a main course, or 5 or 6 ounces (140 to 170 g)
- per serving as a first course Butter

Directions:
- You'll need a pan big enough for the trout to lie flat stainless steel, enamelware, anodized aluminum, or stove-top glassware.
- Next, you make up a solution of water and vinegar, just enough to completely cover the trout.
- The proportions you want are roughly 3 or 4 parts water to 1 part vinegar.
- I find that 1 1/2 quarts (1.4 L) of water and 1 1/2 cups (355 ml) of vinegar are about right for my pan.
- Pour this solution in your pan and turn the burner to high.
- Stir in 1 or 2 bay leaves, 1/2 tablespoon of pepper per quart (950 ml), and 1 teaspoon of salt or Vege-Sal per quart (950 ml). Bring this mixture to a simmer. Simply lower the trout into the simmering solution, turn the burner to medium-low, and let the fish simmer for about 5 minutes. Lift the fish carefully out of the simmering solution and serve with a pitcher of melted butter to pour over the fish. Yield: Servings will depend on how many fish you cook, of course.

Nutrition Facts:

Carbohydrates 1g per serving, and 59 grams of protein

591. SEA BASS WITH TAPENADE CREAM SAUCE

Yield: 2 servings

Ingredients:
- 12 ounces (340 g) sea bass fillet
- 3 tablespoons (45 ml) olive oil
- 1/4 medium onion
- 1/2 teaspoon minced garlic or 1 clove garlic, crushed
- 2 tablespoons (16 g) tapenade
- 1 tablespoon (15 ml) balsamic vinegar
- 1 teaspoon lemon juice
- 3 tablespoons (45 ml) heavy cream
- Salt and pepper

Directions:
- If the bass is in one piece, cut it into two equal portions. Brush with 1 tablespoon (15 ml) of the olive oil and put it under a broiler set on High, 3 or 4 inches (7.5 to 10 cm) from the heat.
- The length of time the fish will need to broil will depend on its thickness. I use fillets about 1 1/2-inch (3.8 cm) thick, and they take about 5 to 6 minutes per side.
- While the fish is broiling, slice the quarter-onion in half lengthwise and then slice as thinly as possible.
- Put the rest of the olive oil in a medium-size skillet over medium heat and add the onion and garlic.
- Sauté together for 3 to 4 minutes.
- Add the tapenade, stir in, and sauté for a few more minutes.
- Now, stir the vinegar and lemon juice into the mixture in your skillet and let it cook down for 1 to 2 minutes.
- Stir in the cream and let the whole thing cook down for another minute.
- When the fish is done, place it on two serving plates.

- Salt and pepper the sauce to taste, spoon over the fish, and then serve.

Nutrition Facts:

4 grams of carbohydrates, and 32 grams of protein.

592. CHILI-BACON SCALLOPS

Yield: 3 to 4 servings

Ingredients:

- 8 slices bacon
- 1 pound (455 g) bay scallops
- 2 teaspoons chili powder

Directions:

- Put your big, heavy skillet over medium heat and snip the bacon into it in bits about 1/4 inch (6 mm) wide. Let that fry.
- Sprinkle the chili powder all over the scallops; I sprinkled both sides and then stirred them up to make sure they were evenly seasoned.
- When the bacon bits are about halfway to done, add the scallops to the skillet and spread them out in a single layer.
- Let them cook for about 5 minutes, turning them a few times, until they're done through and the bacon bits are crisp.
- Serve with the bacon bits and pour the grease over the top!

Nutrition Facts:

177 calories, 7 grams fat, 23 grams protein, 3 grams carbohydrate,

593. GREEK ROASTED FISH WITH VEGETABLES

Active: 35 mins

Total: 55 mins

Servings: 4

Ingredients

- 1 pound fingerling potatoes, halved lengthwise
- 2 tablespoons olive oil
- 5 garlic cloves, coarsely chopped
- ½ teaspoon sea salt
- ½ teaspoon freshly ground black pepper
- 4 5 to 6-ounce fresh or frozen skinless salmon fillets
- 2 medium red, yellow, and/or orange sweet peppers, cut into rings
- 2 cups cherry tomatoes
- 1 ½ cups chopped fresh parsley (1 bunch)
- ¼ cup pitted kalamata olives, halved
- ¼ cup finely snipped fresh oregano or 1 Tbsp. dried oregano, crushed
- 1 lemon

Directions:

- Preheat oven to 425 degrees F. Place potatoes in a large bowl.
- Drizzle with 1 Tbsp. of the oil and sprinkle with garlic and 1/8 tsp. of the salt and black pepper; toss to coat.
- Transfer to a 15x10-inch baking pan; cover with foil. Roast 30 minutes.
- Meanwhile, thaw salmon, if frozen. Combine, in the same bowl, sweet peppers, tomatoes, parsley, olives, oregano, and 1/8 tsp. of the salt and black pepper. Drizzle with remaining 1 Tbsp. oil; toss to coat.
- Rinse salmon; pat dry. Sprinkle with remaining 1/4 tsp. salt and black pepper.
- Spoon sweet pepper mixture over potatoes and top with salmon. Roast, uncovered, 10 minutes more or just until salmon flakes.
- Remove zest from the lemon. Squeeze juice from lemon over salmon and vegetables. Sprinkle with zest.

Nutrition

Serving Size: 4 Ounces Salmon And 1 1/2 Cups Vegetable Per Serving: 422 calories; protein 32.9g; carbohydrates 31.5g;

594. MOqUECA

Active: 30 mins

Servings: 8

Ingredient

- 1 pound fresh crabmeat (preferably claw meat), cleaned and picked over
- 1 pound raw shrimp (16-20 per pound), peeled and deveined if desired
- ¼ cup lemon juice
- 1 ½ tablespoons dendê (red palm oil; see Tip) or canola oil
- 3 cups sliced red bell peppers
- 2 ½ cups sliced green bell peppers
- 2 ½ cups sliced red onions
- ½ cup minced fresh cilantro, plus more for garnish
- 4 large cloves garlic, minced
- ¼ cup tomato paste
- ¾ teaspoon salt
- ¾ teaspoon ground pepper
- 2 14-ounce cans of coconut milk
- 2 cups clam juice or fish stock
- 4 cups cooked brown rice

Directions:

- Combine crab, shrimp, and lemon juice in a medium bowl.
- Heat oil in a large pot over medium-high heat. Add red peppers, green peppers, and onions; cook, stirring occasionally, until beginning to soften, about 4 minutes.
- Add cilantro, garlic, tomato paste, salt, and pepper; cook, stirring, for 1 minute.
- Add coconut milk and clam juice (or fish stock) and bring to a simmer.
- Reduce heat to maintain a simmer, cover, and cook until the peppers are softened, 8 to 10 minutes.
- Add the crab and shrimp and return to a simmer over medium heat.
- Cover and cook until the shrimp is cooked through, 3 to 4 minutes more. Serve the chowder over rice. Garnish with cilantro, if desired.

Nutrition Facts:

Serving Size: 1 ⅓ Cups Chowder & ½ Cup Rice Per Serving: 485 calories; fat 26g; cholesterol 112mg; sodium 686mg; carbohydrates 39g;

595. HERBY MEDITERRANEAN FISH WITH WILTED GREENS & MUSHROOMS

Active: 25 mins

Total: 25 mins

Servings: 4

Ingredients

- 3 tablespoons olive oil, divided
- ½ large sweet onion, sliced
- 3 cups sliced cremini mushrooms
- 2 cloves garlic, sliced
- 4 cups chopped kale
- 1 medium tomato, diced

- 2 teaspoons Mediterranean Herb Mix (see Associated Recipes), divided
- 1 tablespoon lemon juice
- ½ teaspoon salt, divided
- ½ teaspoon ground pepper, divided
- 4 (4 ounces) cod, sole, or tilapia fillets
- Chopped fresh parsley, for garnish

Instructions

- Heat 1 Tbsp. oil in a large saucepan over medium heat. Add onion; cook, stirring occasionally, until translucent, 3 to 4 minutes.
- Add mushrooms and garlic; cook, stirring occasionally until the mushrooms release their liquid and begin to brown, 4 to 6 minutes.
- Add kale, tomato, and 1 tsp. herb mix. Cook, stirring occasionally until the kale is wilted and the mushrooms are tender 5 to 7 minutes.
- Stir in lemon juice and 1/4 tsp. each salt and pepper. Remove from heat, cover, and keep warm.
- Sprinkle fish with the remaining 1 tsp. herb mix and 1/4 tsp. each salt and pepper.
- Heat the remaining 2 Tbsp. oil in a large nonstick skillet over medium-high heat.
- Add the fish and cook until the flesh is opaque, 2 to 4 minutes per side, depending on thickness.
- Transfer the fish to 4 plates or a serving platter.
- Top and surround the fish with the vegetables; sprinkle with parsley, if desired.

Nutrition

Serving Size: 1 Piece Fish + 1/2 Cup Vegetables Per Serving: 214 calories; protein 18g; carbohydrates 11g;

596. GARLICY PEPPERED CREOLE SALMON FILLETS

Preparation Time: 40 minutes
Servings 4
Ingredients:

- 1/3 cups fre lime juice
- 1/3 cups Worcestershire sauce
- 3 tsp.s avocado oil
- 1/4 cups chopped fresh chives
- 2 minced garlic cloves
- 1/4 tsp.s onion powder
- 1 tsp. lemon thyme
- 1/4 tsp.s ground black pepper
- 1/4 tsp.s white pepper
- 1 tsp. dried oregano
- 4 salmon fillets

Instructions:

- Thoroughly mix the lime juice, Worcestershire sauce, avocado oil, fresh chives, garlic, and onion powder together to make the marinade.
- Add the salmon fillets to the marinade, then refrigerate for 20 to 25 minutes reserve some marinade.
- Add lemon thyme, black pepper, white pepper and oregano to taste, to season the salmon fillets.
- Heat the seasoned salmon fillets on a preheated grill.
- Cook seasoned salmon for 10 to 12 minutes, but ensure you turn over the salmon once, and brush the seasoned salmon with the reserved marinade.

Nutrition Facts:

Calories: 266 Fat: 11.5g; Carbs: 5.6g; Protein:34.9g; Sugars: 4.2g

597. LOW-CARB PARSLEY MASHED CAULIFLOWER WITH FISH CUTLETS

Preparation Time: 35 minutes
Servings 4
Ingredients:

- 1 pound, 3/4-inch-thick swordfish cutlets
- 1/2 tsp. celery salt
- freshly ground mixed peppercorns
- 1/2 tsp. dried marjoram
- 1/2 tsp. dried basil
- 1/2 tsp. crushed dried sage
- 1 ½ tbsp.s butter at room temperature
- 1 tbsp. fresh lime juice
- 1/2 cup roughly chopped fresh chives
- 1-pound cauliflower broken into florets
- 1/4 cup heavy cream
- 2 tbsp.s butter
- 1/4 cup freshly grated Colby cheese
- Salt and pepper to taste
- 1 tbsp. finely chopped fresh parsley

Directions Facts:

- Set your grill to high heat and rub fish with salt, peppercorns, marjoram, basil, and sage. Thereafter, whisk butter with fresh lime juice and reserve mixture.
- Grill swordfish cutlets for 8 minutes, coat with whisked mixture, then turn the fish cutlet over and brush the other side with the whisked butter/lime mixture.
- After turning over, grill for another 8 minutes, then transfer to a serving platter and sprinkle fresh chives over grilled meal.
- Cook the cauliflower in a microwave-safe bowl rubbed with cream and butter. Set the microwave to high, and heat for 10 to 12 minutes.
- Add Colby cheese to the mixture before pulsing in your food processor until the mixture becomes creamy. Add parsley, salt and pepper to taste, then serve with grilled fish cutlets.

Nutrition: Calories: 404 Fat: 22.2g; Carbs: 5.7g; Protein:43.5g; Sugars: 2.9g

598. FISH PIE

Preparation time: 10 minutes
Cooking time: 1 hour and 10 minutes
Servings:6

Ingredients:

- 1 red onion, chopped
- 2 salmon fillets, skinless and cut into medium pieces
- 2 mackerel fillets, skinless and cut into medium pieces
- 3 haddock fillets and cut into medium pieces
- 2 bay leaves
- ¼ cup ghee+ 2 tbsp. ghee
- 1 cauliflower head, florets separated
- 4 eggs
- 4 cloves
- 1 cup whipping cream
- ½ cup water
- A pinch of nutmeg, ground
- 1 tsp. Dijon mustard
- 1 cup cheddar cheese, shredded+ ½ cup cheddar cheese, shredded
- Some chopped parsley
- Salt and black pepper to the taste
- 4 tbsp. chives, chopped

Directions:

- Put some water in a pan, add some salt, bring to a boil over medium heat, add eggs, , cook them for 10 minutes, take off heat, drain, leave them to cool down, peel and cut them into quarters.
- Put water in another pot, bring to a boil, add cauliflower florets, cook for 10 minutes, drain them, transfer to your blender, add ¼ cup ghee, pulse well and transfer to a bowl.
- Put cream and ½ cup water in a pan, add fish, toss to coat and heat up over medium heat.
- Add onion, cloves and bay leaves, bring to a boil, reduce heat and simmer for 10 minutes.
- Take off heat, transfer fish to a baking dish and leave aside return pan with fish sauce to heat, add nutmeg, stir and cook for 5 minutes.
- Take off heat, discard cloves and bay leaves, add 1 cup cheddar cheese and 2 tbsp. ghee and stir well.
- Place egg quarters on top of the fish in the baking dish.
- Add cream and cheese sauce over them, top with cauliflower mash, sprinkle the rest of the cheddar cheese, chives and parsley, introduce in the oven at 400 degrees F for 30 minutes.
- Leave the pie to cool down a bit before slicing and serving.

Nutrition: cal.300, fat 45, fiber 3, carbs 5, protein 26

599. BAKED FISH

Preparation time: 10 minutes **Cooking time:** 30 minutes **Servings:** 4

Ingredients:
- 1 pound haddock
- 3 tsp. water
- 2 tbsp. lemon juice
- Salt and black pepper to the taste
- 2 tbsp. mayonnaise
- 1 tsp. dill weed
- Cooking spray
- A pinch of old bay seasoning

Instructions:
- Spray a baking dish with some cooking oil.
- Add lemon juice, water and fish and toss to coat a bit.
- Add salt, pepper, old bay seasoning and dill weed and toss again.
- Add mayo and spread well.
- Introduce in the oven at 350 degrees F and bake for 30 minutes.
- Divide between plates and serve.

Nutrition: cal.104, fat 12, fiber 1, carbs 0.5, protein 20

600. TROUT AND GHEE SAUCE

Preparation time: 10 minutes
Cooking time: 10 minutes
Servings: 4

Ingredients:
- 4 trout fillets
- Salt and black pepper to the taste
- 3 tsp. lemon zest, grated
- 3 tbsp. chives, chopped
- 6 tbsp. ghee
- 2 tbsp. olive oil
- 2 tsp. lemon juice

Instructions:
- Season trout with salt and pepper, drizzle the olive oil and massage a bit.
- Heat up your kitchen grill over medium high heat, add fish fillets, cook for 4 minutes, flip and cook for 4 minutes more.
- Meanwhile, heat up a pan with the ghee over medium heat, add salt, pepper, chives, lemon juice and zest and stir well.
- Divide fish fillets on plates, drizzle the ghee sauce over them and serve.

Nutrition: cal.320, fat 12, fiber 1, carbs 2, protein 24

601. CHAR-GRILLED FISH KEBABS WITH PESTO POTATOES

Total Time: 50-60 mins

Ingredients
- Kebabs
- 200g Mackerel fillet
- 200g Kingfish fillet
- 200g Salmon fillet
- 200g Ling fillet
- 12 Shallots
- ¼ cup Olive oil
- 1.5 tbsp Red Wine Vinegar
- 1 clove Garlic, crushed
- Pinch Salt & Black Pepper
- Salad
- 750g baby Carisma Potatoes, quartered
- 6 cups baby spinach leaves
- 6 cups Broccolini
- 375g mini Roma Tomatoes or Cherry Tomatoes, halved
- 3 tbsp Basil Pesto

Sides
- 3 small Corn Cobs cut in half or 6 small frozen Corn Cobs

Directions
- Preheat the oven to 200o or 180oC fan-forced. Place potato quarters on the oven tray and toss in the olive oil. Season with salt, pepper, and roast in the oven for 40-45 minutes or until tender and golden. Please note- cooking times may vary slightly depending on your oven.
- Cut mackerel, kingfish, salmon, and ling each into 12 equal-sized cubes and place them in a large shallow bowl.
- Make garlic marinade: whisk olive oil, red wine vinegar, and garlic together. Pour over fish and toss well to combine. Cover with plastic wrap and set aside for 30 minutes.
- Meanwhile, bring a steamer saucepan of water to a boil. Add corn and broccolini to the steamer and cook until just soft.
- Transfer cooked potatoes to a bowl, add the baby spinach, broccoli, and halved tomatoes. Add the pesto and toss to coat well.
- Cut green onions into 4 cm lengths. On the bamboo skewer, place a piece of green onion, then thread on one piece of each fish, finishing with a piece of green onion. Repeat with remaining fish and green onion to make 12 skewers.
- Heat a barbecue or char-grill plate to cook kebabs for about a minute on each of 4 sides or until fish is opaque.
- Serve 2 fish kebabs with pesto potato salad and corncob.

Nutrition Facts

Carbohydrate: 28.5g| Total Fat: 25g| Saturated Fat: 4.11g| Dietary fibre: 16.3g| Sodium: 366mg

602. GRILLED SALMON

Prep Time: 1 hr
Cook Time: 12 mins

Ingredients
- 4 6 oz Salmon Fillets
- 1 garlic clove minced
- 1 teaspoon smoked paprika
- 1/4 teaspoon cayenne pepper
- 2 tablespoons parsley chopped fine
- 2 tablespoon thyme
- 1 tablespoon rosemary
- The juice of 1 lemon
- 1/2 cup extra virgin olive oil
- 2 tablespoons soy sauce

Directions
- Rinse salmon fillets and pat dry.
- Arrange the fillets' skin side down on a baking dish.
- Rub each fillet with herb and spice mixture, making sure to coat each fillet well.
- Combine olive oil, soy sauce, and the juice of one lemon in a bowl.
- Whisk together and pour over the fillets.
- Seal and chill. Marinate for 30-45 minutes.
- Heat grill pan or outdoor grill until piping hot.
- Brush grill grates with olive oil to prevent the fish from sticking.
- Remove fish from the marinade and place it on a very hot grill.
- When the salmon starts to lighten in color, about 6 minutes use a spatula to flip it over on the grill.
- Cook for another 6 minutes or until fish flakes easily with a fork.
- Remove with spatula, garnish with lemon.
- Enjoy.

Nutritional Value
Carbohydrates: 9g | Protein: 12g | Fat: 22g | Cholesterol: 104mg | Sodium: 366mg | Potassium: 331mg | Fiber: 1g | Calcium: 60mg

603. EASY LOW CARB BAKED FISH

Prep Time: 5 minutes
Cook Time: 25 minutes
Total Time: 30 minutes

Ingredients
- 3 oz Fish fillets- 1 per person
- ¼ tsp Seafood seasoning of choice I use Old Bay Low Sodium Seasoning
- Paprika
- Salt and pepper
- Lemon quarters

Directions
- Preheat oven to 375 degrees.
- Line a baking pan with parchment paper or foil.
- Place fillets on pan and season liberally with seafood seasoning, paprika, salt, and pepper.
- Bake for 25 minutes or until fish flakes easily.
- Serve with lemon quarters.

Nutrition Facts
Sodium: 44mg | Potassium: 256mg | Protein: 17g | Iron: 0.5mg

604. SALMON & SHRIMP PASTA

Prep Time: 5 minutes
Cook Time: 20 minutes
Total Time: 25 minutes

Ingredients
- 2½ oz. salmon
- 2½ oz. shrimp
- 1½ oz. whole wheat pasta
- 2 tbsp. light sour cream
- ¼ tsp. curry powder
- ¼ tsp. paprika
- ¼ tsp. black pepper
- Chives (optional)

Directions
- Cook the salmon in the oven at 400 F (200 C) for about 15 min. (depending on how large the piece is). Remove the skin and any brown fat after cooking.
- Cook the pasta according to the instructions on the package. You want the pasta to be done around the same time as the salmon, so based on how long the pasta needs to boil, wait until the salmon only has that long left to cook before placing the pasta in the boiling water.
- Cook the shrimp for 2-3 minutes in lightly salted water until they just start turning pink. You also want the shrimp to finish cooking around the same time as the salmon and pasta, so wait until those ingredients only have a few minutes left before cooking your shrimp. Alternatively, you could buy your shrimp pre-cooked, in which case you'll just skip this step.
- Flake the salmon into small pieces.
- Add the pasta, flaked salmon, and shrimp to a bowl and mix.
- In a small bowl, mix the sour cream and spices until combined. Drizzle over the pasta.
- Garnish with chives to taste.

Nutrition Facts
Fat: 10.1g | Saturated Fat: 2g | Polyunsaturated Fat: 0.1g | Monounsaturated Fat: 0.2g | Cholesterol: 154.7mg | Sodium: 330.9mg | Potassium: 44.3mg | Carbohydrates: 32.1g | Fiber: 5.2g | Sugar: 1.6g | Protein: 39g

605. SEAFOOD SAUSAGE GUMBO

Prep Time: 10 minutes
Cook Time: 55 minutes
Total Time: 1 hour 5 minutes

Ingredients
- 12 ounces spicy chicken or turkey sausage links (cut into 1-inch slices)
- 2 tablespoons olive oil (extra virgin)
- 1 cup onions (diced)
- ½ cup red bell pepper (chopped)
- ½ cup green bell pepper (chopped)
- 2 cloves garlic (finely minced)
- 2½ cups chicken broth or stock
- 1½ cups crushed tomatoes (no-salt-added)
- ½ teaspoon ground cumin
- ¼ teaspoon cayenne pepper
- ¼ teaspoon kosher salt
- ¼ teaspoon freshly ground black pepper
- 1 bay leaf
- ¾ pound shrimp (peeled and deveined)
- ½ pound scallops
- 6 ounces lump crabmeat
- 1 tablespoon fresh parsley (chopped)

Directions
- In a large stockpot or Dutch oven, sauté the sausage over medium heat

until it starts to brown. Precooked sausage will take about 5 minutes, the un-cooked sausage will take about 15 minutes.
- Transfer the browned sausage to a plate lined with paper towels.
- In the same pot, add the oil along with the onions, bell peppers, and garlic. Stir to combine, then cook for about 10 minutes or until the onions start to become translucent.
- Add the chicken broth, tomatoes, cumin, cayenne, salt, pepper, and bay leaf to the pot.
- Increase the heat to medium-high and bring to a boil, then reduce the heat and simmer, uncovered, for about 30 minutes.
- Add the shrimp and scallops to the pot and simmer for about 5 minutes.
- Add the crab and sausage, then simmer for another 5 minutes or until everything is heated through.
- Ladle into 6 bowls and garnish with fresh parsley.

Nutrition Facts

Fat: 12.6g| Saturated Fat: 2.2g| Polyunsaturated Fat: 2.4g| Monounsaturated Fat: 1.7g| Cholesterol: 94.6mg| Sodium: 672.5mg| Potassium: 560.6mg| Carbohydrates: 16.2g| Fiber: 2.6g| Sugar: 4.3g| Protein: 28.5g

606. CUMIN-CRUSTED FISH FILLETS

Total Time: 15 Minutes

Ingredients

- 1/2 to 1 Tbsp ground cumin
- 1/4 tsp thyme
- 1 tsp paprika
- 1/2 tsp lemon pepper
- 1 lb white fish fillets (like walleye, halibut, or cod)
- 1/2 Tbsp canola oil
- 2 Tbsp chopped parsley
- Lemon or lime wedges

Directions

- In a small bowl, mix cumin, thyme, paprika, and lemon pepper.
- Rub spice mixture on both sides of fillets.

- In a large skillet, set over medium heat, heat canola oil. Add fish fillets and cook until browned on both sides and fish is opaque in the center about 4 minutes per side.
- Sprinkle with parsley and serve immediately with lemon or lime wedges.

Nutrition Facts

Fat: 3.5g| Fiber: 1g| Sodium: 100mg| Cholesterol: 100mg| Protein: 22g| Carbohydrates: 1g

607. SALMON WITH CILANTRO-LIME SALSA

Preparation Time: 10 To 15 Minutes
Cooking Time: 10 To 15 Minute

Ingredients

- Salmon
- 6-8 ounces skin-on salmon (2 fillets)
- 1/4 teaspoon each kosher salt and pepper (mixed)
- 1/2 teaspoon each chili powder, garlic powder, and paprika (mixed)
- 1 tablespoon of olive oil
- Cilantro-Lime Salsa
- 1 tablespoon of chopped cilantro
- 1/2 teaspoon of lime juice
- 1/2 teaspoon garlic clove
- 1/4 cup of quartered cherry tomatoes
- 1 tablespoon of diced red onion
- 1/2 tablespoon of olive oil
- Salt and pepper to taste

Directions

- Combine the first six ingredients for Cilantro-Lime Salsa in a bowl. Add salt and pepper mixture to taste. Set aside or place in the refrigerator until ready to use.
- Pat the salmon skin dry with a paper towel. This step is necessary for nice, crispy skin. Season the skin with half of your salt and pepper mix.
- Season the flesh side of the salmon with the salt and pepper mix and the chili powder, garlic powder, and paprika mix.
- Heat 1 tablespoon of olive oil in a skillet over medium-high heat.
- Once the oil is shimmering, place the salmon skin-side down; hold down for 10 to 15 seconds until it relaxes and lies flat.
- Cook for about 5 minutes over medium-high heat before flipping over. If you feel resistance as you try to flip the salmon, let it cook a couple of minutes longer. Tip: You should be able to slide the spatula relatively easily under the fish when getting ready to flip it.
- Turn down the heat, flip to the flesh side and let it cook over medium heat for about 3 to 5 minutes, until golden brown. Depending on the thickness of the salmon, you may want to cook it a little longer or less.
- The fish should be opaque (pink) when done. Test for doneness by slightly cutting open the thickest part of the salmon. If it flakes, you're done!
- Serve the salmon topped with the Cilantro-Lime Salsa and your choice of side.

Nutrition Facts

Carbohydrates: 4g, Protein: 18g, Fat: 14g, Cholesterol: 634mg, Sodium: 289mg, Fiber: 1g

608. TARRAGON SEAFOOD PASTA SALAD

Preparation Time: 35 Minutes

Ingredients

- Water
- 2 tablespoons curry powder
- 8 ounces uncooked penne (tubular pasta)
- 3/4 pound medium shrimp, cooked and peeled (fully-cooked thawed frozen shrimp work well)
- 4 ounces smoked salmon, diced
- 1 1/2 cups lightly steamed, coarsely chopped asparagus
- 1 tablespoon chopped fresh tarragon (or 1 teaspoon dry)
- 1 teaspoon fresh-squeezed lemon juice
- 1/4 teaspoon coarse ground black pepper
- 3 tablespoons olive oil
- 1/4 teaspoon salt

Directions

- Fill a large saucepan 3/4 full of water and stir in curry powder until dispersed. Add pasta and cook according to package directions, omitting any salt. Drain well, cool with cold running water, and drain again; place in a large serving bowl. Add shrimp, salmon, and asparagus. In a small bowl, stir together the tarragon, lemon juice, salt, and pepper. Using a whisk, briskly whisk in the oil while pouring it in a steady stream. Pour dressing over pasta and toss gently to coat well. Serve right away. Slightly warm leftovers in the microwave before serving.

Nutrition Facts

Carbohydrates: 23g, Protein: 16g, Fat: 7g, Saturated Fat: 1g, Sodium: 450mg, Fiber: 2g

609. DILLED SALMON PASTA WITH ASPARAGUS

Preparation Time: 30 Minutes

Ingredients

- 2 tablespoons margarine
- 2 tablespoons olive oil
- 1/2 medium red onion, sliced
- 1 pound fresh asparagus, trimmed and cut diagonally into 1-inch lengths
- 4 ounces smoked salmon, sliced into thin strips
- 1/4 teaspoon ground black pepper
- 16 ounces tubular pasta (such as penne or ziti)
- 2 tablespoons chopped fresh dill

Directions

- Heat the margarine and oil in a large skillet. Add the onion and cook, stirring over low heat until tender, about 5 minutes. Add the asparagus and sauté until crisp-tender, about 5 minutes. Add the salmon to the skillet. Sprinkle with pepper, and stir the mixture to blend. Bring a large pot of water to boil and cook the pasta until al dente, about 8–10 minutes. Drain pasta and return it to the cooking pot. Add the asparagus mixture. Stir in the dill and toss to blend.

Nutrition Facts

Carbohydrates: 46g, Protein: 11g, Fat: 8g, Saturated Fat: 1g, Sodium: 148mg, Fiber: 3g

610. SUN-DRIED TOMATO SEASONED SALMON

Preparation Time: 5 Minutes

Marinating Time: 30 Minutes

Baking Time: 18–21 Minutes

Ingredients

- 2 eight-ounce salmon fillets (about 1 1/2 inches thick
- 1/4 cup purchased sun-dried tomato vinaigrette
- Cooking spray

Directions

- Place salmon fillets in a zip-top bag and pour vinaigrette over them. Seal bag and shake gently to coat. Marinate for 30 minutes in the refrigerator.
- Preheat oven to 450°F. Coat a baking dish with cooking spray. Place salmon in the baking dish with the skin side down. Pour marinade over salmon. Bake uncovered until fish flakes, about 18–21 minutes (6–7 minutes per 1/2-inch thickness of the fillet). Remove skin and cut each fillet in half.

Nutrition Facts

Carbohydrates: 1g, Protein: 23g, Fat: 6g, Saturated Fat: 1g, Sodium: 220mg

611. GIRL CHEF'S GRILLED LOBSTER

Total Time: 1 Hour 20 Minutes

Ingredients

- 1/2 pound 16–20 count shrimp
- 2 cloves garlic, smashed and finely chopped
- Extra virgin olive oil
- Kosher salt
- Two 1 1/4 to 1 1/2 pound lobsters
- 1 lemon, cut in half
- 4 ears of corn
- 1-pint cherry tomatoes, cut in half
- 1/2 small red onion, thinly sliced
- 6 tablespoons red wine vinegar
- 5 fresh basil leaves, cut into chiffonade

Directions

- In a large bowl, toss the shrimp with the garlic, 2 tablespoons olive oil, and a generous sprinkle of salt. Let the shrimp sit at room temperature for 30 minutes.
- Bring a large pot of well-salted water to a boil. Squeeze both halves of the lemon into the water and drop in the lemon halves.
- Plunge the lobsters into the water, cover, and cook for 4 minutes. Carefully remove the lobsters from the water and let them cool. The lobsters will NOT be cooked through at this point.
- Preheat a grill to medium.
- Cover half the grill with 2 layers of aluminum foil and place the shrimp in a single layer on the foil (this will prevent the shrimp from falling through the grates). Grill the shrimp on both sides, until pink and opaque, 2 to 3 minutes per side. Remove the shrimp and transfer it to a large bowl.
- While the shrimp are cooking, use the other half of the grill to cook the corn until charred on all sides, about 10 minutes. Remove the corn and let cool. Cut the corn off the cob and add it to the bowl with the shrimp. Holding the corn vertically on your cutting board, run your knife up the cobs to get the lovely little remnants of the corn kernels and add these to the bowl as well. Be sure to get these...they are sweet and delicious and not to be missed!
- Toss the cherry tomatoes and onions with the shrimp and corn. Add the vinegar and a few drops of olive oil. Stir to combine and season with salt. Taste and reseason if needed. Reserve.
- Twist the claws of the lobsters and set them aside. Using a large, very sharp knife, cut the lobsters in half lengthwise. Commit to this you can do it! Remove the contents of the cavity and discard. Save the tomalley (the green stuff) and the coral (the red stuff), for another purpose if desired.
- Place the lobster's cut side down on the grill along with the claws. Grill the lobster for 10 minutes and the claws for 15 minutes, being sure to turn the claws halfway through cooking.

- Transfer the lobsters to serving plates 2 halves, cut side up, and 2 claws per plate. To serve, add the basil to the shrimp corn mixture and spoon it into the cavity of each lobster.

Nutrition Facts

Carbohydrates: 25g, Protein: 25g, Fat: 10g, Saturated Fat: 1g, Cholesterol: 150mg, Sodium: 479mg, Fiber: 3g

612. GRILLED SEA SCALLOPS WITH A WATERMELON THREE-WAY & DANDELION GREENS

Total Time: 1 Hour

Ingredients

- 1-pound wedge watermelon
- 1 cup champagne or white wine vinegar
- 2 tablespoons sugar
- 2 tablespoons kosher salt, plus more for seasoning
- Pinch of crushed red pepper
- 8 large sea scallops
- 2 to 3 tablespoons extra virgin olive oil, plus more as needed
- 1 watermelon radish (about the size of a kiwi), peeled and julienned
- 1 cup dandelion greens, cut into 1/2 inch-wide ribbons
- 1/2 small red onion, thinly sliced

Directions

- Carefully cut the rind off the watermelon. Using a mandolin or a sharp vegetable peeler, shave the rind into wide ribbons about 1/8 inch thick. In a large bowl, combine the vinegar, sugar, salt, and red pepper. Add the watermelon rind ribbons and let stand at room temperature for at least an hour (BTW – this can be done yesterday).
- Meanwhile, dice the watermelon flesh into 1/2-inch pieces and reserve.
- When the watermelon pickles are done, heat the grill.
- Brush the scallops with olive oil and season with salt. Place on the grill and cook until grill marks appear, about 1 minute, then rotate the scallops 90 degrees and let the grill marks develop in the other direction (what you're going for here are those lovely crosshatch grill marks!). Turn the scallops over and repeat; the scallops are done when they're no longer translucent, about 2 minutes on each side.
- While the scallops cook, drain the rind pickles, reserving their liquid. Toss the reserved watermelon, the rind pickles, watermelon radish, dandelion greens, and red onion together in a large bowl. Dress the salad with 2 tablespoons of pickling liquid and some olive oil. TASTE! Adjust seasonings and dressing if needed.
- Arrange the deliciously dressed salad in a tall pile just off the center of the four salad plates. Cut the scallops equatorially (through the middle, like the equator) and lay the disks slightly overlapping, grill side up, on the salad. Drizzle with a little olive oil.

Nutrition Facts

Carbohydrates: 19g, Protein: 5g, Fat: 8g, Saturated Fat: 1g, Cholesterol: 7mg, Sodium: 296mg, Fiber: 3g

613. BLACKENED SHRIMP WITH TOMATOES AND RED ONION

Total Time: 30 Minutes

Ingredients

- 1 1/2 teaspoons paprika
- 1 teaspoon Italian seasoning
- 1/2 teaspoon garlic powder
- 1/4 teaspoon black pepper
- 1/2 pound (about 24) small raw shrimp, peeled (with tails on)
- 1 tablespoon canola oil
- 1/2 cup sliced red onion, separated into rings
- 1 1/2 cups halved grape tomatoes
- Lime wedges (optional)

Directions

- Combine paprika, Italian seasoning, garlic powder, and pepper in a small bowl; add to resealable food storage bag. Add shrimp, seal bag, and shake to coat.
- Coat large skillet with nonstick cooking spray; heat over medium-high heat. Heat oil then adds shrimp and cook, turning occasionally, 4 minutes or until shrimp are pink and opaque.
- Add onion and tomatoes; cook, mixing occasionally, 1 minute or until tomatoes are hot and onion is slightly wilted.
- Serve with lime wedges, if desired.

Nutrition Facts

Carbohydrates: 5g, Protein: 13g, Fat: 5g, Saturated Fat: 1g, Cholesterol: 86mg, Sodium: 88mg, Fiber: 1g

614. SPINACH, CRAB, AND ARTICHOKE DIP

Total Time: 50 min

Ingredients

- 1 can (6 1/2 ounces) crabmeat, drained and shredded
- 1 package (10 ounces) frozen chopped spinach, thawed and squeezed nearly dry
- 1 package (8 ounces) reduced-fat cream cheese
- 1 jar (about 6 ounces) marinated artichoke hearts, drained and finely chopped
- 1/4 teaspoon hot pepper sauce
- Melba toast or whole-grain crackers (optional)

Directions

- Pick out and discard any shell or cartilage from crabmeat. Combine crabmeat, spinach, cream cheese, artichokes, and hot pepper sauce in a 1 1/2-quart slow cooker. Cover; cook on high 1 1/2 to 2 hours or until heated through, stirring after 1 hour. Serve with melba toast, if desired.

Nutrition Facts

Carbohydrates: 3g, Protein: 6g, Fat: 7g, Saturated Fat: 3g, Cholesterol: 29mg, Sodium: 295mg, Fiber: 1g

615. SOUTHERN CRAB CAKES WITH RÉMOULADE DIPPING SAUCE

Total Time: 30 Minutes

Ingredients

- 10 ounces fresh lump crabmeat
- 1 1/2 cups fresh white or sourdough bread crumbs, divided
- 1/4 cup chopped green onions
- 1/2 cup fat-free or reduced-fat mayonnaise, divided

- 1 egg white, lightly beaten
- 2 tablespoons coarse-grained or spicy brown mustard, divided
- 3/4 teaspoon hot pepper sauce, divided
- 2 teaspoons olive oil, divided
- Lemon wedges (optional)

Directions

- Preheat oven to 200°F. Pick out and discard any shell or cartilage from crabmeat. Combine crabmeat, 3/4 cup bread crumbs, and green onions in a medium bowl.
- Add 1/4 cup mayonnaise, egg white, 1 tablespoon mustard, and 1/2 teaspoon hot pepper sauce; mix well.
- Using 1/4 cup mixture per cake, shape into 8 (1/2-inch-thick) cakes.
- Roll crab cakes lightly in the remaining 3/4 cup bread crumbs.
- Heat a large nonstick skillet over medium heat; add 1 teaspoon oil.
- Add 4 crab cakes; cook 4 to 5 minutes per side or until golden brown. Transfer to serving platter; keep warm in the oven.
- Repeat with the remaining 1 teaspoon oil and crab cakes.
- For the dipping sauce, combine the remaining 1/4 cup mayonnaise, 1 tablespoon mustard, and 1/4 teaspoon hot pepper sauce in a small bowl; mix well.
- Serve crab cakes warm with dipping sauce and lemon wedges, if desired.

Nutrition Facts

Carbohydrates: 8g, Protein: 7g, Fat: 2g, Saturated Fat: 1g, Cholesterol: 30mg, Sodium: 376mg, Fiber: 1g

616. SHRIMP CAPRESE PASTA

Total Time: 30 Minutes

Ingredients

- 1 cup uncooked whole wheat penne
- 2 teaspoons olive oil
- 2 cups coarsely chopped grape tomatoes
- 4 tablespoons chopped fresh basil, divided
- 1 tablespoon balsamic vinegar
- 2 cloves garlic, minced
- 1/4 teaspoon salt
- 1/8 teaspoon red pepper flakes
- 8 ounces medium raw shrimp (with tails on), peeled and deveined
- 1 cup grape tomatoes, halved
- 2 ounces fresh mozzarella pearls

Directions

- Cook pasta according to package directions, omitting salt. Drain, reserving 1/2 cup cooking water. Set aside.
- Heat oil in a large skillet over medium heat. Add 2 cups chopped tomatoes, reserving 1/2 cup pasta water, 2 tablespoons basil, vinegar, garlic, salt, and red pepper flakes. Cook and stir 10 minutes or until tomatoes begin to soften.
- Add shrimp and 1 cup halved tomatoes to skillet; cook and stir 5 minutes or until shrimp turn pink and opaque. Add pasta; cook until heated through.
- Divide mixture evenly among four bowls. Top evenly with cheese and the remaining 2 tablespoons of basil.

Nutrition Facts

Carbohydrates: 15g, Protein: 5g, Fat: 2g, Saturated Fat: 1g, Cholesterol: 2mg, Sodium: 160mg, Fiber: 1g

617. SCALLOP AND ARTICHOKE HEART CASSEROLE

Total Time: 50-60 Minutes

Ingredients

- 1 package (9 ounces) frozen artichoke hearts, cooked and drained
- 1 pound scallops
- 1 teaspoon canola or vegetable oil
- 1/4 cup chopped red bell pepper
- 1/4 cup sliced green onions
- 1/4 cup all-purpose flour
- 2 cups low-fat (1%) milk
- 1 teaspoon dried tarragon
- 1/4 teaspoon salt
- 1/4 teaspoon white pepper
- 1 tablespoon chopped fresh parsley
- Dash paprika

Directions

- Preheat oven to 350°F.
- Cut large artichoke hearts lengthwise into halves. Arrange artichoke hearts in an even layer in 8-inch square baking dish.
- Rinse scallops; pat dry with a paper towel. If scallops are large, cut them into halves. Arrange scallops evenly over artichokes.
- Heat oil in a medium saucepan over medium-low heat. Add bell pepper and green onions; cook and stir 5 minutes or until tender. Stir in flour. Gradually stir in milk until smooth. Add tarragon, salt, and white pepper; cook and stir over medium heat 10 minutes or until sauce boils and thickens. Pour sauce over scallops.
- Bake, uncovered, for 25 minutes or until bubbling and scallops are opaque. Sprinkle with parsley and paprika before serving.

Nutrition Facts

Carbohydrates: 23g, Protein: 26g, Fat: 4g, Saturated Fat: 1g, Cholesterol: 43mg, Sodium: 438mg, Fiber: 4g

618. BARBECUED SHRIMP OVER TROPICAL RICE

Total Time: 30 Minutes

Ingredients

- 20 frozen large raw shrimp, peeled and deveined (26 to 30 per pound)
- 1/2 cup uncooked brown rice
- 1/2 cup barbecue sauce
- 2 teaspoons fresh grated ginger
- 1 cup chopped fresh mango (about 1 medium mango)
- 2 tablespoons finely chopped red onion
- 1 tablespoon chopped fresh cilantro
- 1 tablespoon finely chopped and seeded jalapeño pepper
- 2 teaspoons lime juice

Directions

- Thaw shrimp according to package directions.
- Cook brown rice according to package directions, omitting salt; set aside.
- Meanwhile, thread shrimp onto 4 metal skewers, leaving 1/8-inch space between shrimp. In a small bowl stir together barbecue sauce and ginger. Grill shrimp on the greased rack of an uncovered grill directly over medium

heat for 6 to 7 minutes or until shrimp are opaque, turning once and brushing frequently with sauce mixture.

• Stir mango, onion, cilantro, jalapeño, and lime juice into hot rice. Spoon onto serving plates. Serve shrimp on top of the rice mixture.

Nutrition Facts

Carbohydrates: 37g, Protein: 9g, Fat: 2g, Saturated Fat: 1g, Cholesterol: 53mg, Sodium: 396mg, Fiber: 2g

619. SHRIMP & CAPER VERMICELLI

Total Time: 20-30 Minutes

Ingredients

• 1 medium tomato, seeded and chopped
• 1/4 cup chopped parsley
• 3 tablespoons capers, rinsed and drained
• 2 tablespoons dry white wine or low-sodium broth
• 1 1/2 tablespoons extra virgin olive oil
• 1 clove garlic, minced
• 1/2 teaspoon grated lemon peel
• 2 tablespoons lemon juice
• 1/4 teaspoon salt
• 1/8 to 1/4 teaspoon red pepper flakes
• 6 ounces uncooked dry vermicelli, broken in thirds
• 10 ounces peeled fresh or frozen and thawed raw medium shrimp
• 2 ounces reduced-fat feta, crumbled (plain or basil and sun-dried tomato variety)

Directions

• Combine tomato, parsley, capers, wine, lemon juice, oil, garlic, lemon peel, salt, and red pepper flakes in a large bowl; set aside.
• Cook pasta according to directions on the package, omitting any salt or fat. After 6 minutes of cooking, add shrimp to pasta. Return to a boil and cook 4 to 5 minutes or until shrimp is pink and opaque. Drain well. Add to tomato mixture, and toss well.
• Place shrimp mixture in a pasta bowl or place equal amounts on each of four dinner plates. Sprinkle evenly with cheese.

Nutrition Facts

Carbohydrates: 35g| Protein: 23g| Fat: 9g| Saturated Fat: 2g| Cholesterol: 113mg| Sodium: 646mg| Fiber: 2g

620. SHRIMP AND WATERMELON CEVICHE

Total Time: 1 Hour 45 Minutes

Ingredients

• 1 pound medium raw shrimp, peeled and deveined
• 1/2 cup plus 2 tablespoons lime juice, divided
• 1 cup finely chopped seedless watermelon
• 1/2 cup finely chopped jicama
• 1/2 cup finely chopped red onion
• 1/2 cup chopped fresh cilantro
• 1 jalapeño pepper, minced
• 56 water crackers

Directions

• Remove tails from shrimp; discard. Chop shrimp into small pieces.
• Combine shrimp and 1/2 cup lime juice in a medium bowl. Cover and refrigerate for 1 hour or until shrimp are pink and opaque. Drain; discard juice.
• Meanwhile, combine watermelon, jicama, onion, cilantro, jalapeño, and the remaining 2 tablespoons lime juice in a large bowl. Gently stir in shrimp. Cover and refrigerate for at least 30 minutes to allow flavors to develop.
• Serve on or with water crackers.

Nutrition Facts

Carbohydrates: 7g, Protein: 3g, Fat: 1g, Cholesterol: 20mg, Sodium: 132mg, Fiber: 1g

621. PESTO PASTA WITH SCALLOPS

Total Time: 30 Minutes

Ingredients

• 8 ounces whole-wheat rotini or other curly whole wheat pasta
• 5 1/2 teaspoons olive oil, divided
• 12 ounces asparagus (about 20 asparagus), cut into 2-inch-pieces
• 8 ounces cherry tomatoes, halved (about 2 cups)
• 1/2 teaspoon black pepper, divided
• 12 ounces large sea scallops
• 1 tablespoon lemon juice
• 1 clove garlic, crushed
• 1/4 teaspoon salt
• 6 tablespoons prepared pesto
• 3 tablespoons fat-free sour cream
• Pinch red pepper flakes (optional)
• Fresh basil for garnish

Directions

• Prepare pasta according to package directions, omitting any salt or fat. Set aside and keep warm.
• Meanwhile, heat 1 1/2 teaspoon's oil in a medium skillet over medium heat. Cook asparagus for 5 minutes, stirring occasionally. Toss in tomatoes and turn heat to low. Sprinkle with 1/4 teaspoon black pepper, cover, and continue cooking for about 5 additional minutes. (Stir occasionally to prevent sticking.) Add asparagus and tomatoes to pasta and keep warm.
• Toss scallops with 1 teaspoon oil, lemon juice, garlic, and 1/4 teaspoon black pepper in a large bowl. (Do not marinate.)
• In the same skillet, heat the remaining 1 tablespoon oil over medium-high heat. Add scallops and sprinkle with salt. Cook about 3 minutes per side until scallops are opaque.
• Combine pesto and sour cream in a small bowl; add to vegetable and pasta mixture, mix well. Add red pepper flakes, if desired. Arrange scallops on top and garnish with fresh basil.

Nutrition Facts

Carbohydrates: 37g, Protein: 17g, Fat: 11g, Saturated Fat: 1g, Cholesterol: 19mg, Sodium: 383mg, Fiber: 5g

622. HOT SHRIMP WITH COOL SALSA

Total Time: 20 Minutes

Ingredients

• 1/4 cup salsa
• 4 tablespoons fresh lime juice, divided
• 1 teaspoon honey
• 1 clove garlic, minced
• 2 to 4 drops hot pepper sauce
• 1 pound large shrimp, peeled and deveined, with tails intact
• 1 cup finely diced honeydew melon

- 1/2 cup finely diced unpeeled cucumber
- 2 tablespoons minced parsley
- 1 green onion, finely chopped
- 1 1/2 teaspoons sugar
- 1 teaspoon olive oil
- 1/4 teaspoon salt

Directions

- To make a marinade, combine salsa, 2 tablespoons lime juice, honey, garlic, and hot pepper sauce in a small bowl. Thread shrimp onto skewers. Brush shrimp with marinade; set aside.
- To make salsa, combine the remaining 2 tablespoons of lime juice, melon, cucumber, parsley, onion, sugar, oil, and salt in a medium bowl; mix well.
- Grill shrimp over medium coals for 4 to 5 minutes or until shrimp turn pink, turning once. Serve with salsa.

Nutrition Facts

Carbohydrates: 8g, Protein: 19g, Fat: 2g, Saturated Fat: 1g, Cholesterol: 175mg, Sodium: 398mg, Fiber: 1g

623. FRESH GARLIC SHRIMP LINGUINE

Total Time: 20 Minutes

Ingredients

- 6 ounces uncooked multigrain linguine or spaghetti, broken in half
- 1/2 pound raw shrimp, peeled and ceveined
- 1/4 cup grated Parmesan cheese
- 3 tablespoons diet margarine
- 1 clove garlic, minced
- 1/2 teaspoon seafood seasoning
- 1/4 cup finely chopped fresh parsley (optional)
- 1/8 teaspoon salt (optional)

Directions

- Cook linguine according to package directions, omitting salt and fat, about 7 minutes or until al dente.
- Add shrimp; cook 3 to 4 minutes or until shrimp are pink and opaque.
- Drain; transfer to a medium bowl. Add cheese, margarine, garlic, and seafood seasoning; toss gently to coat.
- Add parsley and salt, if desired; toss to combine.

Nutrition Facts

Carbohydrates: 30g, Protein: 21g, Fat: 7g, Saturated Fat: 2g, Cholesterol: 91mg, Sodium: 242mg, Fiber: 3g

624. WARM SHRIMP, ARTICHOKE, AND PARMESAN SALAD

Total Time: 20 Minutes

Ingredients

- 1 can (14 ounces) water-packed quartered artichoke hearts
- 20 frozen cooked tail-on premium shrimp (12 ounces)
- 1/2 cup fat-free Italian salad dressing
- 1 bag (12 ounces) salad blend
- 1/4 cup (1 ounce) shredded Parmesan cheese

Directions

- Drain and rinse artichoke hearts. Combine with shrimp and dressing in a large, deep skillet. Cover and cook over medium heat for 10 minutes, stirring occasionally.
- Divide salad blend among 4 dinner plates. Top salad with the shrimp-artichoke mixture. Sprinkle with cheese.

Nutrition Facts

Carbohydrates: 21g, Protein: 24g, Fat: 3g, Saturated Fat: 1g, Cholesterol: 133mg, Sodium: 757mg, Fiber: 7g

625. SPICY FISH TACOS

Cook Time: 10 Min

Ingredients:

- 1/2 cup reduced-fat mayonnaise
- 1/4 cup reduced-fat sour cream
- 1 teaspoon hot sauce
- 2 tablespoons lemon juice
- 2 (8-ounce) tilapia fillets or other firm-fleshed fish fillets
- 1/8 teaspoon cayenne pepper
- 1/4 teaspoon onion powder
- 4 (6-inch) flour tortillas
- 1 cup shredded red cabbage

Directions:

- Preheat oven to broil. Line a broiler pan with aluminum foil; coat with cooking spray.
- In a medium bowl, whisk together mayonnaise, sour cream, hot sauce, and lemon juice. Refrigerate sauce until ready to use.
- Sprinkle fish on both sides with cayenne pepper and onion powder.
- Broil fillets about 5 inches from heat for 3-5 minutes on each side or until fish flakes easily. Cut fillets in half lengthwise.
- On each tortilla, place half a fillet, 1/4 cup shredded cabbage, and 2 tablespoons sauce. Roll or fold the tortilla. Serve immediately.

Nutrition Facts

Total Fat: 16g| Saturated Fat: 3.9g| Protein: 27g| Cholesterol: 72mg| Sodium: 513mg| Total Carbohydrates: 21g| Dietary Fiber: 1.1g| Sugars: 3.6g

626. GREEK FESTIVAL FISH

Cook Time: 20 Min

Ingredients:

- 2 tablespoons olive oil
- 8 scallions, thinly sliced
- 2 cloves garlic, minced
- 4 tomatoes, chopped
- 1/2 cup dry white wine
- 2 tablespoons finely chopped parsley
- 1 teaspoon dried oregano
- 1 teaspoon black pepper
- 6 white-fleshed fish fillets (2 pounds total) such as tilapia, flounder, or sole
- 1 (4-ounce) package crumbled feta cheese

Directions:

- Preheat the oven to 400 degrees. Coat a 9-inch by a 13-inch baking dish with cooking spray.
- In a medium skillet, heat the oil over medium heat. Add the scallions and garlic and sauté until tender. Add the tomatoes, wine, parsley, oregano, and pepper. Simmer for 5 minutes, or until the sauce thickens. Remove from the heat.
- Place half of the sauce mixture in the baking dish. Arrange the fish fillets over the sauce and cover them with the remaining sauce. Sprinkle with the feta cheese.
- Bake for 15 to 18 minutes, or until the fish flakes easily with a fork. Serve immediately.

Nutrition Facts

Total Fat: 18g| Saturated Fat: 5.6g| Trans Fat: 0.1g| Protein: 28g| Cholesterol: 104mg| Sodium: 375mg| Total Carbohydrates: 5.9g| Dietary Fiber: 1.5g| Sugars: 3.1g

627. ALMOND CRUSTED FISH FILLETS

Cook Time: 30 Min

Ingredients:

- 1 tablespoon sugar
- 3/4 teaspoon ground cinnamon
- 1/4 teaspoon ground red pepper
- 1/2 teaspoon salt
- 1 1/2 pound white-fleshed fish fillets
- 1 egg white, beaten
- 2 cups sliced almonds
- 2 tablespoons butter, plus more as needed
- 1/4 cup olive oil, plus more as needed
- 1/2 cup Amaretto liqueur

Directions:

- In a small bowl, combine sugar, cinnamon, red pepper, and salt; mix well. Season fillets with 1 teaspoon of the mixture, reserving the remaining mixture.
- Place egg white in a shallow dish; place almonds in another shallow dish. Dip each fillet in egg white then in almonds, coating completely.
- In a large skillet, melt butter with oil over medium heat. Add half of the fillets and cook 5 minutes then turn fillets and cook 2 to 3 more minutes, or until fish flakes easily with a fork; transfer to a serving platter and cover to keep warm. Repeat with remaining fillets, adding additional butter and oil as needed.
- Add reserved sugar mixture and amaretto to skillet; reduce heat to low and cook 1 to 2 minutes, or until thickened, stirring constantly. Pour over fillets and serve immediately.

Nutrition Facts

- Total Fat: 43g| Saturated Fat: 7.6g| Trans Fat: 0.2g| Protein: 42g|Cholesterol: 139mg| Sodium: 506mg| Total Carbohydrates: 31g|Dietary Fiber: 5.9g| Sugars: 8.1g

628. FLORENTINE FISH ROLL-UPS

Prep Time: 10 Mins
Cook Time: 18 Mins

Ingredients:

- 1 (10-ounce) package frozen chopped spinach, thawed and well-drained
- 2 tablespoons grated Parmesan cheese
- 1/4 teaspoon garlic powder
- 1/4 teaspoon salt
- 1/4 teaspoon black pepper
- 4 (6-ounce) white-fleshed fish fillets, such as sole, flounder, or tilapia
- Cooking spray
- 1/2 teaspoon paprika

Directions:

- Preheat the oven to 350 degrees. Coat a rimmed baking sheet with cooking spray.
- In a medium bowl, combine the spinach, Parmesan cheese, garlic powder, salt, and pepper; mix well.
- Spread the spinach mixture evenly over the fish fillets. Roll up jellyroll style and place seam side down on the baking sheet.
- Lightly coat the fish with the cooking spray and sprinkle with the paprika. Bake for 18 to 22 minutes, or until the fish flakes easily with a fork.

Nutrition Facts

Total Fat: 11g| Saturated Fat: 2.7g| Trans Fat: 0.1g| Protein: 30g| Cholesterol: 96mg| Sodium: 403mg| Total Carbohydrates: 3.4g| Dietary Fiber: 2.2g| Sugars: 0.5g

629. FIESTA FISH TACOS

Total Time: 30 Minutes

Ingredients:

- Juice of 1/2 lime
- 2 cloves garlic, minced
- 1 tablespoon olive oil
- 1 pound tilapia fillets
- 1/2 cup chopped green bell pepper
- 1/2 cup chopped red bell pepper
- 1 tablespoon minced cilantro
- 1 cup cherry or grape tomatoes
- 4 (6-inch) whole-wheat tortillas
- 2 cups shredded lettuce
- 1 cup cubed mango

- Black pepper, to taste

Directions:

- Mix lime juice, garlic, and olive oil in a glass bowl.
- Add tilapia and marinate in the refrigerator for 1 hour.
- Place tilapia in a glass baking dish surrounded by green and red bell pepper, minced cilantro, and tomatoes.
- Bake at 350 degrees F for 10 minutes or until fish flakes easily.
- Divide fish and veggies into 4 servings and place on each of the warmed tortillas.
- Top with lettuce, cubed mango, and a sprinkling of black pepper.
- Before You Start Cooking!

Nutrition Facts

Total Fat: 8.7g| Saturated Fat: 2.2g| Protein: 28g| Cholesterol: 57mg| Sodium: 346mg| Total Carbohydrates: 33g| Dietary Fiber: 5.3g| Sugars: 11g

630. PEPPERED SHRIMP SKEWERS

Total Time: 45 Minutes

Ingredients

- 1/3 cup teriyaki sauce
- 1/3 cup ketchup
- 2 tablespoons dry sherry or water
- 2 tablespoons reduced-fat peanut butter
- 1 teaspoon hot pepper sauce
- 1/4 teaspoon ground ginger
- 32 large raw shrimp (about 1 1/2 pounds), peeled and deveined, with tails on
- 2 large yellow bell peppers
- 32 fresh sugar snap peas, trimmed

Directions

- Soak 16 (12-inch) wooden skewers in water for at least 20 minutes before assembling kabobs.
- Preheat broiler. Coat rack of broiler pan with nonstick cooking spray; set aside.
- Combine teriyaki sauce, ketchup, sherry, peanut butter, pepper sauce, and ginger in a small saucepan. Bring to a boil, stirring constantly. Reduce heat to low; simmer, uncovered, 1 minute. Remove from heat; set aside.

- Cut each bell pepper lengthwise into 4 quarters; remove stems and seeds. Cut each quarter crosswise into 4 equal pieces. Thread 2 shrimp, 2 bell pepper pieces, and 2 sugar snap peas onto each skewer; place on prepared pan. Brush with teriyaki sauce mixture.
- Broil skewers 4 inches from heat 3 minutes; turn. Brush with teriyaki sauce mixture; broil 2 minutes or until shrimp turn pink and opaque. Discard any remaining teriyaki sauce mixture.

Nutrition Facts
Carbohydrates: 7g, Protein: 10g, Fat: 2g, Saturated Fat: 1g, Cholesterol: 66mg, Sodium: 245mg, Fiber: 1g

631. SAUTÉED SHRIMP RECIPE FOR DIABETICS

Preparation Time: 10 Minutes
Cooking Time: 5 Minutes

Ingredients
- 4 sun-dried tomato halves
- 1/4 cup hot water
- 1 tablespoon olive oil
- 1/2 pound cooked and peeled shrimp (20–24 count size)
- 1 cup baby spinach leaves, rinsed and drained
- 1 teaspoon dried basil
- 1/4 teaspoon black pepper

Directions
- Place sun-dried tomato halves into a small bowl.
- Pour hot water over the tomatoes and set aside for 10 minutes, stirring occasionally. After 10 minutes, remove tomatoes from the water, reserving the water for later use.
- Chop tomatoes and set them aside. In a large sauté pan, heat olive oil.
- Add cooked shrimp and sauté.
- Add chopped tomato and spinach, then pour in the 1/4 cup reserved hot water and continue cooking.
- Add dried basil and black pepper, stir until combined, and serve immediately.

Nutrition Facts
Carbohydrates: 4g, Protein: 25g, Fat: 8g, Saturated Fat: 2g, Cholesterol: 221mg, Sodium: 346mg, Fiber: 1g

632. SPICY SHRIMP APPETIZERS

Preparation Time: 2 Minutes
Cooking Time: 10 Minutes

Ingredients
- 2 quarts water
- 1 pound shelled and cooked medium frozen shrimp (21–24 count)
- 1/4 cup no-added-salt tomato paste
- 1/2 teaspoon minced garlic
- 1/2 teaspoon crushed red pepper
- 1 teaspoon olive oil
- 1 teaspoon basil
- 1/4 teaspoon black pepper
- 2–3 drops hot pepper sauce
- 24 toothpicks
- 3 leaf lettuce leaves for presentation

Directions
- Bring 2 quarts of water to a boil in a large saucepan over medium heat.
- Add frozen shrimp and cook approximately 3 minutes until shrimp are heated through. Drain.
- In a small bowl, whisk together tomato paste, garlic, crushed red pepper, olive oil, basil, black pepper, and hot sauce.
- Pour mixture into a large skillet and heat at low heat, stirring constantly.
- Add hot, cooked shrimp and stir to coat with sauce. Place 1 toothpick in each shrimp.
- Serve immediately on a large plate covered with 3 lettuce leaves.

Nutrition Facts
Carbohydrates: 2g, Protein: 14g, Fat: 2g, Saturated Fat: 1g, Cholesterol: 112mg, Sodium: 65mg

633. TRIPLE-QUICK SHRIMP AND PASTA

Total Time: 10 min

Ingredients
- 4 ounces uncooked whole grain rotini pasta
- 8 ounces small shrimp (with tails), peeled
- 4 ounces asparagus spears, trimmed and broken into 2-inch pieces
- 1 cup grape tomatoes, quartered
- 1/2 cup light olive oil vinaigrette
- 2 cloves garlic, minced
- 2 teaspoons chopped fresh rosemary
- 1/4 cup chopped fresh basil
- 1/4 cup grated Parmesan cheese

Directions
- Cook pasta according to package directions, omitting salt and fat. Add shrimp during the last 4 minutes of cooking. Add asparagus during the last 3 minutes of cooking; cook until shrimp are pink and opaque. Drain and return to saucepan.
- Add tomatoes, vinaigrette, garlic, and rosemary. Toss until well blended. Stir in basil and Parmesan cheese.

Nutrition Facts
Carbohydrates: 27g, Protein: 16g, Fat: 7g, Saturated Fat: 1g, Cholesterol: 76mg, Sodium: 766mg, Fiber: 3g

634. CRAB SOUP

Preparation Time: 15 Minutes
Cooking Time: 25 Minutes

Ingredients
- 1 can (10 3/4 ounces) Campbell's Healthy Request Cream of Chicken soup
- 1 1/2 cups water
- 1/4 cup skim milk
- 1/2 pound Yukon Gold potatoes, washed and peeled
- 2 ounces whole white mushrooms (about 2 large)
- 1 can (6 ounces) lump crabmeat, drained
- 2 tablespoons chopped red bell pepper
- 1/4 teaspoon black pepper
- 1/4 teaspoon onion powder

Directions
- In a 2-quart saucepan, combine soup, water, and milk and stir well to combine into a smooth mixture.
- Place the saucepan on the stove over medium heat.
- Finely dice potatoes (should yield about 1 1/4 cups) and add to liquid.
- Remove stems from mushrooms and wipe away visible dirt with a small brush or paper towel.
- Chop mushrooms and add to saucepan, along with drained

crabmeat, bell pepper, black pepper, and onion powder.
- Bring to a gentle boil, then cover and simmer for approximately 15 minutes until potatoes are soft, then serve.

Nutrition Facts

Carbohydrates: 18g, Protein: 8g, Fat: 2g, Saturated Fat: 1g, Cholesterol: 3mg, Sodium: 485mg, Fiber: 2g

635. GREEK SHRIMP

Preparation Time: 40 Minutes

Ingredients

- 1 tablespoon olive oil
- 1 large onion, chopped
- 1/4 cup chopped fresh parsley
- 1 clove garlic, minced
- 1/2 teaspoon sugar
- 1 1/2 pounds roma tomatoes, peeled and chopped
- 1 cup dry white wine
- 1 pound cooked medium-size shrimp, peeled and deveined (frozen, fully cooked shrimp, thawed, may be used for convenience)
- 1/4 cup grated mizithra cheese

Directions

- Warm the oil in a large, nonstick skillet over medium heat. Add onion and sauté until tender, about 3–4 minutes. Stir in parsley, garlic, and sugar.
- Add tomatoes and cook uncovered until they soften and the liquid evaporates about 8–10 minutes; stir frequently.
- Add wine and cook until liquid evaporates about 10 minutes.
- Add shrimp and cook, stirring occasionally, for 2–3 minutes, or until shrimp are heated through.
- Transfer to a serving dish and top with cheese.
- Can be served over cooked brown rice.

Nutrition Facts

- Carbohydrates: 15g, Protein: 21g, Fat: 5g, Saturated Fat: 1g, Sodium: 528mg, Fiber: 2g

636. CLASSIC GUMBO

Preparation Time: 3 Hours

Ingredients

- 1 1/2 quarts water
- 8 ounces crabmeat
- 5 ounces shrimp
- 2 bay leaves
- 2 lemon wedges
- 2 slices onion
- 1 teaspoon plus 1/2 teaspoon cayenne pepper
- 1 teaspoon black pepper
- 1 tablespoon chopped parsley
- 1 pound okra, sliced
- 4 tablespoons vegetable oil
- 2 medium tomatoes, chopped
- 1 onion, diced
- 1 green pepper, diced
- 2 tablespoons flour
- 1 teaspoon thyme
- 3 1/2 cups prepared white rice

Directions

- In a large pot, bring 1 1/2 quarts water to a boil and add crabmeat, shrimp, bay leaves, lemon wedges, onion slices, 1 teaspoon cayenne pepper, and black pepper.
- Boil for 10 minutes. Remove shrimp and crabmeat and set in the refrigerator. Strain stock and set aside.
- Sauté sliced okra in 1 tablespoon of vegetable oil in a large skillet. When soft and lightly browned, place in a large pot.
- Add chopped tomatoes to okra and cook over low heat, stirring often. In a skillet with 1 tablespoon of the vegetable oil sauté green peppers and onion until tender.
- Add to okra and tomatoes and cook, stirring often. In the skillet, add 2 tablespoons of flour and stir until slightly browned (if it burns, discard flour and start over again).
- Add the remaining 2 tablespoons of vegetable oil to the flour and stir until the mixture is slightly bubbly. Stir in 1 cup of the reserved stock and cook until thickened.

- Add this liquid to the pot with vegetables. Stir thoroughly, keeping the heat on low.
- Add additional stock to create a thick, stewlike consistency. Stir in thyme and 1/2 teaspoon cayenne pepper. Cover and cook over low heat for an additional two hours.
- Add reserved crabmeat and shrimp to gumbo and blend, adding additional stock if needed.
- Cover and continue to heat for another 30 minutes. Prepare rice
- To serve, place 1/2 cup boiled white rice in a large soup bowl and top with 1 cup gumbo.
- Serve immediately.

Nutrition Facts

Carbohydrates: 29g, Protein: 15g, Fat: 9g, Saturated Fat: 1g, Sodium: 146mg, Fiber: 3g

637. SHRIMP AND BEET SMÖRGÅSOR

Preparation Time: 8 Minutes

Ingredients

- 1/4-inch-thick slice French or Italian Bread
- 1 teaspoon reduced-fat margarine spread
- 2 slices canned, chilled pickled beets, drained and blotted on paper towels
- 2 large shrimp, cooked, peeled, deveined, and chilled
- 1 teaspoon chopped green pepper

Directions

- Spread a thin layer of margarine on bread, and layer with pickled beets, shrimp, and green pepper. Serve immediately, as beets may bleed into sandwiches.

Nutrition Facts

Carbohydrates: 23g| Protein: 8g| Fat: 3g| Sodium: 390 mg| Fiber: 2g

638. SHRIMP PO'BOY

Preparation Time: 20 Minutes

Ingredients

- 1 loaf French bread, about 24 inches long and 2 1/2 inches wide
- 2 cups shredded iceberg lettuce
- 2 medium tomatoes, thinly sliced

- 8 ounces cooked shrimp, chilled

Cajun Remoulade:
- 4 tablespoons fat-free mayonnaise
- 1/2 tablespoon Creole or Dijon mustard
- 1/2 tablespoon sweet pickle relish
- 1 hard-boiled egg, diced
- 2 tablespoons minced onion
- 2 tablespoons chopped fresh parsley
- 1/2 teaspoon Worcestershire sauce
- 1/2 teaspoon salt-free Creole seasoning

Directions
- Cut French bread crosswise into four pieces, each about 6 inches long, and split open each section.
- Prepare Cajun remoulade by mixing mayonnaise, mustard, relish, egg, onion, parsley, Worcestershire sauce, and Creole seasoning in a small mixing bowl.
- Chill remoulade while assembling a sandwich. Place French bread sections on a baking sheet and toast in a 375°F oven for 5 minutes.
- Bread should be crispy, but not browned.
- Remove from oven and fill each sandwich with 1/2 cup shredded lettuce, 1/4 of the tomato slices, 2 ounces (approximately 1/3 cup) shrimp, and 3 tablespoons Cajun remoulade.
- Serve immediately.

Nutrition Facts
- Carbohydrates: 56g| Protein: 23g| Fat: 6g| Saturated Fat: 1g| Sodium: 899mg| Fiber: 4g

639. FISH CREOLE

Total Time: 20-30 Minutes

Ingredients
- 4 (3-ounce) fish fillets
- 2 tablespoons lemon juice
- 2 tablespoons finely chopped onion
- 4 tablespoons reduced-fat margarine, divided
- 1/2 cup chopped green peppers
- 1 cup chopped canned tomatoes, undrained
- Pepper to taste
- 2 teaspoons flour

Directions
- Preheat oven to 350 degrees F.
- Place fish fillets in a baking pan coated with nonstick cooking spray.
- Mix lemon juice, onion, and 2 tablespoons of melted margarine. Pour mixture over fish. Bake uncovered or until fish flakes easily with a fork, about 15 minutes.
- While fish is baking, prepare the creole sauce; saute green pepper in the remaining margarine. Add tomatoes and pepper. Stir in flour. Simmer until the mixture is heated.

Nutrition Facts
Fat: 9g| Fiber: 1g| Sodium: 338mg| Cholesterol: 37mg| Protein: 25g| Carbohydrates: 7g| Sugars: 4g

640. SEAFOOD KABOBS

Total Time: 30-60 Minutes

Ingredients
- 2 tablespoons lime juice
- 1 tablespoon olive oil
- 1 clove garlic, crushed
- 1/8 teaspoon salt
- 1/4 teaspoon freshly ground black pepper
- 2 teaspoons fresh snipped dill
- 12 large shelled deveined shrimp (6 ounces meat)
- 7 large sea scallops (6 ounces)
- 1 medium zucchini cut into 1-inch pieces (2 cups)
- 1 medium yellow squash cut into 1-inch pieces (2 cups)

Directions
- Preheat grill or broiler.
- Mix lime juice, olive oil, garlic, salt, pepper, and dill. Add shrimp, scallops, and vegetables and set aside to marinate for 15 minutes. Turn once during this time.
- Alternate vegetables, shrimp, and scallops on 4 skewers. Grill or broil 3-4 inches from the heat source for 2-1/2 minutes per side. Do not overcook the fish. Sprinkle with salt and pepper.
- Place skewers on 2 dinner plates or remove seafood and vegetables from skewers onto 2 plates and serve.

Nutrition Facts
Fat: 5g| Saturated Fat: 7g| Fiber: 4g| Sodium: 314mg| Cholesterol: 157mg| Protein: 34g| Carbohydrates: 12g

641. PRIMAVERA FISH FILLETS

Total Time: 60 Minutes

Ingredients
- 4 (4-ounce) fresh or frozen orange roughy fillets
- 2 tablespoons unsalted butter
- 1 tablespoon fresh lemon juice
- 1/4 teaspoon freshly ground black pepper
- 1 garlic clove, minced
- 1-1/2 cups fresh broccoli florets
- 1 cup fresh cauliflower florets
- 1 cup julienne-cut carrots
- 1 cup sliced fresh white mushrooms
- 1/2 cup diagonally sliced celery
- 1/8 teaspoon salt
- 1/4 teaspoon dried basil
- 2 tablespoons grated Parmesan cheese

Directions
- Heat the oven to 450 degrees. Thaw roughy if frozen. Place 1 tablespoon butter into a 13x9-inch glass or ceramic baking dish and melt in the oven. Place roughy fillets in melted butter and turn to coat, arranging fillets in a single layer. Sprinkle with lemon juice and pepper. Bake for 5 minutes. Remove from the oven.
- While fish is baking, melt the remaining 1 tablespoon butter in a large skillet over medium-high heat. Add garlic and cook until lightly browned. Add broccoli, cauliflower, carrots, mushrooms, celery, salt, and basil. Cook, stirring, for 5 to 6 minutes or until vegetables are crisp-tender.
- Spoon hot vegetables into the center of the baking dish, moving fish to the sides of the dish. Sprinkle vegetables and fish with Parmesan cheese.
- Return the dish to the oven and bake an additional 3 to 5 minutes or until fish flakes easily with a fork.

Nutritional
Fat: 11g| Sodium: 216mg| Cholesterol: 38mg| Protein: 28g| Carbohydrates: 7g

642. FISH WITH CHINESE GINGER SCALLION SAUCE

Total Time: 20-30 Minutes

Ingredients

- 2 Tbsp. canola oil
- 1-1/2 cups thinly sliced scallion, white and green parts
- 2 tsp. grated fresh ginger
- 1/2 tsp. sugar
- 1/4 tsp. salt
- 1 tsp. grated orange zest
- Freshly ground pepper, preferably white, to taste
- 4 (4-oz.) pieces tilapia or other mild, flaky white fish

Directions

- Preheat the broiler.
- Heat oil in a small skillet over medium heat. Mix in scallions to coat them with oil.
- Add ginger, sugar, and salt. Cook, stirring until sugar dissolves and scallions are tender but still bright green, 3-4 minutes.
- Off the heat, mix in the zest. Season sauce generously with pepper.
- Set skillet aside so it keeps warm while the fish cooks.
- Arrange fish on a baking sheet and coat with cooking spray.
- Season fish lightly with salt and ground pepper. Broil until fish is opaque in the center at the thickest point, about 6 minutes.
- Divide fish among four dinner plates. Top each piece with one-fourth of the sauce. Serve immediately.

Nutrition Facts

Fat: 9g| Sodium: 210mg| Protein: 23g| Carbohydrates: 3g

643. SEAFOOD KABOBS HAWAIIAN

Total Time: 50-60 Minutes

Ingredients

- 1/2 cup dry sherry
- 1 teaspoon sesame oil
- 2 tablespoons grated fresh ginger
- 2 tablespoons tamari soy sauce
- 2 tablespoons pineapple juice concentrate
- 1 pound fresh sea scallops or shrimp, peeled and deveined
- 1 large mango, peeled and cut into wedges
- 1/2 papaya, peeled and cut into wedges
- 1 large red pepper, seeded and cut into large squares

Directions

- In a medium bowl, combine the sherry, sesame oil, ginger, soy sauce, and pineapple juice concentrate. Add the shrimp or scallops. Let the shellfish marinate for 30 minutes in the refrigerator.
- Prepare an outside grill or oven broiler by placing the rack 6 inches from the heat source. Remove the shrimp or scallops from the marinade. Reserve the remaining marinade. Thread the shellfish onto wooden skewers and alternate them with the mango, papaya, and red pepper.
- Place the skewers on the grill and frill for about 5 minutes, turning and basting with the marinade.

Nutrition Facts

Fat: 2g| Sodium: 429mg| Cholesterol: 95g| Protein: 16g| Carbohydrates: 20g

644. SIZZLIN' CATFISH

Cook Time: 5 Min

Ingredients:

- 2 tablespoons vegetable oil
- 4 (4-ounce) catfish fillets
- 1/8 teaspoon salt
- 1/4 teaspoon black pepper
- 1 tablespoon lemon juice
- 1/4 pound fresh mushrooms, sliced
- 1 onion, chopped
- 1/4 cup chopped fresh parsley

Directions:

- In a large skillet, heat the oil over medium heat.
- Season the catfish fillets with salt and pepper. Add to the skillet and sprinkle with lemon juice. Add the remaining ingredients to the skillet. Cook for 3 to 4 minutes per side, or until the fish flakes easily with a fork.
- Serve the fish topped with vegetables.

Nutrition Facts

Total Fat: 14g| Saturated Fat: 2.4g| Trans Fat: 0.1g| Protein: 18g| Cholesterol: 62mg| Sodium: 188mg| Total Carbohydrates: 3.1g| Dietary Fiber: 0.7g| Sugars: 1.4g

645. FAST 'N' FIERY GRILLED CATFISH

Cook Time: 15 Min

Ingredients:

- 1 tablespoon chopped fresh basil
- 1 teaspoon crushed red pepper
- 1 teaspoon garlic powder
- 1/2 teaspoon salt
- 1/2 teaspoon black pepper
- 4 (6-ounce) farm-raised catfish fillets
- 2 tablespoons canola oil

Directions:

- Preheat the grill to medium-high heat. Coat a hinged grill basket with nonstick cooking spray.
- In a small bowl, combine the basil, crushed red pepper, garlic powder, salt, and black pepper; mix well.
- Rinse the fish with cold water and pat dry with a paper towel. Rub the oil over both sides of the fish, then rub both sides with the seasoning mixture, coating evenly.
- Place the fish in the grill basket and grill for 7 to 9 minutes, or until cooked through and firm to the touch, turning the basket over once during cooking.

Nutrition Facts

Total Fat: 17g| Saturated Fat: 2.8g|Trans Fat: 0.1g| Protein: 26g| Cholesterol: 94mg| Sodium: 458mg| Total Carbohydrates: 0.7g| Dietary Fiber: 0.2g

646. SESAME-CRUSTED SWORDFISH

Cook Time: 10 Min

Ingredients:

- 1/2 cup lemon juice
- 1/4 cup vegetable oil
- 2 cloves garlic, minced
- 1/2 teaspoon salt
- 1/2 teaspoon black pepper
- 4 (4-ounce) swordfish steaks (1/2-inch-thick)
- 2 teaspoons sesame seeds

Directions:

- In a shallow dish, combine all the ingredients except the swordfish and sesame seeds; mix well. Add the swordfish and coat completely. Cover and marinate in the refrigerator for 2 hours, turning occasionally.
- Coat a grill pan with cooking spray and heat over medium-high heat.
- Remove the swordfish from the marinade; discard the marinade. Grill the fish for 4 to 5 minutes; turn the fish, sprinkle with sesame seeds, and grill for 4 to 5 more minutes, or until it flakes easily with a fork. Serve immediately.

Nutrition Facts

Total Fat: 22g| Saturated Fat: 3.7g| Trans Fat: 0.1g| Protein: 23g| Cholesterol: 75mg| Sodium: 384mg| Total Carbohydrates: 2.9g| Dietary Fiber: 0.4g| Sugars: 0.8g

647. LOUISIANA BROILED CATFISH

Cook Time: 12 Min

Ingredients:

- 4 (4-ounce) catfish fillets, rinsed and patted dry
- Cooking spray
- 2 teaspoons Creole seasoning
- 1 lemon, cut into wedges

Directions:

- Preheat broiler. Coat a broiler pan with cooking spray.
- Coat both sides of fillets with cooking spray and sprinkle with seasoning.
- Place fillets on prepared pan about 5 inches from heat. Broil each side for about 6 minutes, or until fish is crispy and flakes easily with a fork. Serve with lemon wedges.

Nutrition Facts

Total Fat: 6.8g| Saturated Fat: 1.5g| Trans Fat: 0.1g| Protein: 18g| Cholesterol: 62mg| Sodium: 267mg| Total Carbohydrates: 2.5g| Dietary Fiber: 0.8g| Sugars: 0.7g

648. ASIAN FISH

Cook Time: 10 Min

Ingredients:

- 4 (4-ounce) halibut fillets
- 2 tablespoons light soy sauce
- 1/3 cup dry sherry
- 1 tablespoon brown sugar
- 3/4 teaspoon ground ginger
- 1 (6-ounce) package frozen snow peas, thawed
- 1 (15-ounce) can whole baby corn, drained

Directions:

- Coat a large skillet with cooking spray and heat over medium-high heat until hot.
- Add the fillets to the skillet and cook for 3 to 4 minutes per side, or until the fish flakes easily with a fork. Remove the fillets to a platter and cover to keep warm.
- In a small bowl, combine the soy sauce, sherry, sugar, and ginger; add to the hot skillet. Cook over high heat for 2 minutes, or until the mixture begins to thicken, stirring constantly to loosen the particles on the bottom of the skillet.
- Add the snow peas and corn, stirring until heated through. Return the fish to the skillet, turning to coat with the sauce.
- Serve the fish topped with vegetables and sauce.

Nutritional

Total Fat: 1.5g| Saturated Fat: 0.3g| Protein: 24g| Cholesterol: 56mg| Sodium: 663mg| Total Carbohydrates: 14g| Dietary Fiber: 2.3g| Sugars: 6.3g

649. ENSENADA SHRIMP TOSTADAS

Preparation Time: 25 Minutes

Ingredients

- 1 tablespoon vegetable oil
- 2 tablespoons lemon juice
- 1 teaspoon plus 1 teaspoon chili powder
- 1/2 teaspoon ground cumin
- 12 ounces medium-size cooked shrimp
- 1/3 cup fat-free sour cream
- 1/3 cup fat-free mayonnaise
- 1/4 cup fresh cilantro, chopped
- 1 can (4 ounces) diced green chilies
- 6 6-inch corn tortillas
- Nonstick cooking spray
- 3 cups shredded fresh cabbage
- 3 ripe medium tomatoes, chopped
- 3/4 cup chopped white onion

Directions

- Heat vegetable oil in skillet. In a medium bowl, pour lemon juice, 1 teaspoon chili powder, and cumin over shrimp and toss lightly. Pour into hot skillet and heat through, approximately 5 minutes.
- Prepare the dressing by mixing fat-free sour cream, fat-free mayonnaise, cilantro, chilies, and 1 teaspoon chili powder.
- Heat corn tortillas on both sides in a skillet sprayed with nonstick cooking spray.
- To prepare each tostada, place a hot corn tortilla on the serving dish. Place 1/3 cup hot shrimp mixture on tortilla. Top with 1/2 cup shredded cabbage, 1/2 chopped tomato, and 2 tablespoons chopped onion. Pour 1/4 cup dressing over and serve immediately. Garnish with additional cilantro if desired.

Nutrition Facts

Carbohydrates: 24g| Protein: 16g| Fat: 4g| Saturated Fat: 1g| Sodium: 354mg| Fiber: 4g

DIABETIC VEGETARIAN AND VEGAN RECIPES

650. STUFFED EGGPLANT

Preparation 75 Minutes

Serves 8 Persons

Ingredients

- 2 large eggplants
- 1 medium onion, chopped
- 4 tomatoes, chopped
- 3 medium green bell peppers, chopped
- 1 rib celery, chopped
- 2 Tbsp. olive oil
- ½ cup egg substitute
- 1 tsp. salt
- 1 tsp. pepper
- ½ cup freshly grated

- Parmesan cheese
- ¼ tsp. cayenne pepper, optional
- ½ tsp. grated garlic, optional

Directions

- Cut eggplants in half and scrape out seeds. Parboil 15 minutes
- After eggplant halves have drained, remove pulp within ½- inch of outer "shell." Chop pulp. Set aside.
- Place eggplant shells, cut-side up, in 12×24-inch baking dish.
- Empty stockpot of water. Place onion, tomatoes, peppers, and celery, and olive oil in stockpot. Cook until soft and almost a purée. Remove from heat.
- Stir in eggplant pulp, egg substitute, salt, and pepper.
- Fill eggplant halves with the mixture. Sprinkle with cheese.
- Distribute any leftover stuffing in baking dish around
- eggplant halves.
- Bake at 350°F for 30 minutes, or until eggplant is tender and cheese is brown

Nutrition Facts

Calories per Serving: 100 cal Fat: 4g Protein: 7g Carbohydrates: 8g

651. CREAMED SPINACH

Preparation 25 Minutes

Serves 6 Persons

Ingredients

- 2 tablespoons olive oil, divided
- 1 medium red onion or 2 shallots, finely chopped
- Fine-grained kosher salt, to taste
- 1 tablespoon all-purpose flour
- ½ cup 1 percent milk
- ⅛ teaspoon freshly grated nutmeg
- ½ teaspoon ground white pepper or pinch of cayenne pepper
- 2 (10-ounce) packages prewashed baby spinach
- 2 tablespoons freshly grated Parmesan cheese

Directions

- Heat 1 tablespoon of the olive oil in a sauté pan over medium heat, and add in the onion or shallots and season with salt.
- Cook for 5 minutes or until the onion is softened and translucent at the edges.
- Add the rest of the olive oil and the flour, and whisk constantly for 3 minutes until a golden, nutty-smelling paste is formed. (Just whisk the onion or shallots with the paste; there's no need to remove them from pan.)
- Slowly pour in the milk while whisking constantly.
- Add the nutmeg and the white or cayenne pepper, and continue to whisk until a thick sauce is formed.
- Add the baby spinach to the hot sauce, and stir until wilted.
- Serve hot, sprinkled with Parmesan cheese.

Nutrition Facts

Calories per Serving: 91cal Fat: 7g Protein: 2g Carbohydrates: 4g

652. SOUR CREAM MASHED POTATOES

Preparation 40 Minutes

Serves 8 Persons

Ingredients

- 3 pounds waxy potatoes such as Yukon Gold or round white, peeled and chopped into large pieces
- 2 teaspoons fine-grained kosher salt, divided, plus more to taste
- 2 tablespoons unsalted butter
- 1½ cups
- 1 percent milk or lowfat buttermilk
- 1 cup nonfat sour cream
- Freshly ground black pepper, to taste

Directions

- Add the potatoes to a pot and cover with cold water.
- Add 2 teaspoons of salt.
- Place the pot over high heat and bring to a boil.
- Cook the potatoes for 15 to 20 minutes, until tender (test by piercing with a fork or sharp knife), and drain them in a colander.
- To mash the potatoes, use a food mill, a potato ricer, a potato masher, or the paddle attachment on the stand mixer.
- While mashing, add the butter, milk or buttermilk, and the sour cream and combine, but don't overmix.
- Season with salt and pepper, and serve

Nutrition Facts

Calories per Serving: 180 cal Fat: 3g Protein: 5g Carbohydrates: 34g

653. ASPARAGUS BAKE

Preparation 45 Minutes

Serves 6 Persons

Ingredients

- 5 medium potatoes, sliced
- 2 medium onions, diced
- 2 cups fresh, chopped asparagus
- salt and pepper
- 2 Tbsp. trans-fat free tub margarine
- 3 oz. 75%-less-fat cheddar cheese slices

Directions

- Lay potatoes in greased 2-qt. casserole dish. Sprinkle with salt and pepper.
- Sprinkle diced onions over potatoes.
- Add asparagus.
- Add salt and pepper, to taste.
- Dot top with pieces of margarine.
- Cover tightly.
- Bake at 325°F for 45–60 minutes, or until potatoes are tender when poked with a fork.
- Remove from oven and lay sliced cheese over hot vegetables to melt.

Nutrition Facts

Calories per Serving: 195 cal Fat: 4g Protein: 8g Carbohydrates: 32g

654. GLAZED CARROTS

Preparation 240 Minutes

Serves 8 Persons

Ingredients

- 32-oz. (2 lbs.) pkg. baby carrots
- 3 Tbsp. brown sugar substitute to equal
- 2 Tbsp. sugar
- ½ cup orange juice
- 2 Tbsp. margarine
- ¾ tsp. cinnamon

- ¼ tsp. nutmeg
- 2 Tbsp. cornstarch
- ¼ cup water

Directions

- Combine all ingredients except cornstarch and water in slow cooker.
- Cover. Cook on Low 3–4 hours until carrots are tender crisp.
- Put carrots in serving dish and keep warm, reserving cooking juices.
- Put reserved juices in small saucepan.
- Bring to boil.
- Mix cornstarch and water in small bowl until blended.
- Add to juices. Boil one minute or until thickened, stirring constantly.
- Pour over carrots and serve

Nutrition Facts

Calories per Serving: 108 cal Fat: 0.5g Protein: 1g Carbohydrates: 0.5g

655. BROCCOLI AND SQUASH MEDLEY

Preparation 30 Minutes
Serves 7 Persons

Ingredients

- 2 bags (12 oz each) frozen broccoli cuts
- 2 cups cubed peeled butternut squash
- ½ cup orange juice 1 tablespoon butter or margarine, melted
- ½ cup sweetened dried cranberries
- ½ cup finely chopped pecans, toasted
- 1 tablespoon grated orange peel
- ½ teaspoon salt

Directions

- Cook broccoli as directed on bag; set aside.
- Meanwhile, in 12-inch skillet, cook squash in orange juice
- over medium-low heat 8 to 10 minutes, stirring frequently, until tender but firm.
- Stir in butter, broccoli, cranberries, pecans, orange peel and salt; toss to coat.
- Serve immediately.

Nutrition Facts

Calories per Serving: 80 cal Fat: 1g Protein: 1g Carbohydrates: 10g

656. CREAMED PEAS AND MUSHROOMS

Preparation 40 Minutes
Serves 8 Persons

Ingredients

- 20-oz. pkg. frozen peas
- ½ cup mushroom caps
- 1 Tbsp. onion, minced
- 2 Tbsp. trans-fat-free tub margarine
- 2 Tbsp. flour
- 1½ cups fat-free half-and-half
- 3 Tbsp. reduced-fat Velveeta cheese
- ¼ tsp. salt

Directions

- Cook peas in boiling salted water until tender.
- Sauté mushroom caps and onion in oil until lightly browned.
- Add to peas.
- Stir flour into remaining drippings.
- Add half-and-half gradually, cooking and stir- ring until slightly thickened.
- Turn heat to low and add cheese.
- Stir until dissolved.
- Combine with peas and mushrooms.

Nutrition Facts

Calories per Serving: 115 cal Fat: 4g Protein: 6g Carbohydrates: 8g

657. ASPARAGUS PEPPER STIR-FRY

Preparation 25 Minutes
Serves 4 Persons

Ingredients

- 1 lb fresh asparagus spears
- 1 teaspoon canola oil
- 1 medium red, yellow bell pepper, cut into ¾-inch pieces
- 2 cloves garlic, finely chopped
- 1 tablespoon orange juice
- 1 tablespoon reduced-sodium soy sauce
- ½ teaspoon ground ginger

Directions

- In a mixing bowl, mix together pineapple, Splenda, vinegar, and mustard.
- Set aside.
- In a large mixing bowl, thoroughly combine sausage, ham, bread crumbs, egg substitute, ketchup, and onion.
- Shape into 20 1½-inch balls.
- Place in well-greased shallow baking dish.
- Spoon pineapple mixture over ham balls.
- Cover. Bake at 350°F for 25 minutes.
- Uncover.
- Continue baking for 25 more minutes.

Nutrition Facts

Calories per Serving: 40 cal Fat: 1,5g Protein: 2g Carbohydrates: 6g

658. SWEET POTATO CASSEROLE

Preparation 80 Minutes
Serves 10 Persons

Ingredients

- 6 medium to large sweet potatoes
- 1 cup whole pecans
- 2 tablespoons brown sugar
- 2 teaspoons cinnamon
- Pinch of fine-grained kosher salt, plus more, to taste
- 1 tablespoon unsalted butter
- 1 tbs sugar-free imitation maple
- 1 teaspoon pure vanilla extract
- ½ teaspoon freshly grated nutmeg or ½ teaspoon ground nutmeg
- 1 egg Olive oil cooking spray

Directions

- Preheat the oven to 400 degrees F.
- Pierce each of the sweet potatoes several times with a fork, and bake for about 45 minutes or until tender.
- Alternately, cook the pierced yams on the high setting in the microwave for 10 minutes.
- Stop halfway through to check the yams and adjust time accordingly, if necessary.
- Rotate the yams if necessary. Set aside to cool for about 10 minutes.
- Grind the pecans in a food processor or blender. Add the sweetener, cinnamon, pinch of salt, and butter, and process until blended.

- Cut the sweet potatoes in half, and scoop out the flesh, discarding the skins.
- Purée the sweet potatoes in a blender or food processor.
- Add the maple syrup or honey, vanilla, and nutmeg.
- Add in the egg and purée. Season with salt.
- Spray a baking dish with olive oil cooking spray.
- Add the sweet potato purée, and sprinkle the pecan topping on. Bake for 10 to 15 minutes, or until the topping is crisp and has browned.

Nutrition Facts

Calories per Serving: 169 cal Fat: 9g Protein: 3g Carbohydrates: 21g

659. TOMATO AND VEGGIE GAZPACHO

Preparation 15 Minutes

Serves 6 Persons

Ingredients

- Tomatoes (ripe) – 2 pounds
- Zucchini (medium) – 2
- Cucumbers – 2 large
- Red onion – 1 small
- Garlic (peeled) – 4 cloves
- Red bell pepper – 1 large
- Balsamic vinegar – 1 tablespoon
- Vegetable juice – 1 cup
- Salt – as per taste
- Pepper – as per taste

Directions

- Start by taking a food processor and adding the ripe tomatoes, zucchini, cucumbers, red onion, garlic, and bell pepper.
- Pulse until the veggies are finely chopped.
- Transfer the veggie mix into a large glass mixing bowl.
- Now add the vegetable juice, pepper, salt, and balsamic vinegar.
- Mix until well combined.
- Place the bowl into the refrigerator and chill for about 1 hour.
- Once chilled, serve it by topping with fresh basil.

Nutrition Facts

Calories per Serving: 85 cal Fat: 0.5g Protein: 4g Carbohydrates: 19g

660. BULGUR, GRAPE, AND KALE SALAD

Total Time: 30 Minutes

Ingredients

- 2 cups water
- 1 cup bulgur
- Kosher salt
- 1 cup pecan halves, toasted and roughly chopped
- 2 cups seedless California grapes, halved
- 2 cups packed kale or Swiss chard leaves, finely slivered
- 1/2 cup Italian parsley, chopped
- 1/4 cup scallions, thinly sliced
- 1/4 cup lemon juice
- 2 tablespoons extra virgin olive oil
- 2 teaspoons lemon zest, finely grated
- Pinch cayenne
- Black pepper

Directions

- Bring 2 cups of water to a boil in a medium saucepan.
- Stir in bulgur and 1/2 teaspoon salt and remove from heat.
- Cover and let stand 20 minutes
- Drain well and press to extract any excess water.
- Let cool and stir in the remaining ingredients.
- Season well with salt and black pepper.
- Serve room temperature or chilled.

Nutrition Facts:

Calories: 289| Fat: 17g| Sodium: 181mg| Protein: 6g| Carbohydrates: 33g

661. ASPARAGUS AND EDAMAME SALAD

Total Time: 10 Minutes

Ingredients

- 1 bunch asparagus, cut into 2-inch pieces
- 8 cups green leaf lettuce leaves, torn
- 1 cup sliced radishes
- 1 fennel bulb, thinly sliced
- 1 cup frozen shelled edamame, thawed
- 1/4 cup fresh mint leaves, torn
- 1 hard-boiled egg, chopped
- 1/4 cup fresh lemon juice
- 1/2 cup extra-virgin olive oil
- 1/2 teaspoon kosher salt
- 1/2 teaspoon granulated sugar

Directions

- Bring a medium saucepan of salted water to a boil.
- Add asparagus and cook 1 minute or until crisp-tender.
- Immediately plunge in ice water; drain completely.
- In a large bowl, toss together lettuce leaves, asparagus, radishes, fennel, edamame, mint, and egg.
- In a small bowl, whisk together lemon juice, olive oil, salt, and sugar.
- Drizzle desired amount over salad and toss.

Nutrition Facts

Fat: 16g| Saturated Fat: 2.5g| Fiber: 2g| Sodium: 160 mg| Cholesterol: 20mg| Protein: 4g| Carbohydrates: 6g| Sugars: 1g

Roasted Asparagus With Bacon

Total Time: 30 Minutes

Ingredients

- 2 pounds fresh asparagus, trimmed
- 2 tablespoons olive oil
- 1 (12-ounce) package Jennie-O Turkey Bacon, chopped
- Directions
- Heat oven to 425F.
- Place asparagus on a large rimmed baking sheet.
- Toss asparagus with olive oil and turkey bacon.
- Spread in a single layer.
- Roast 15 to 20 minutes or until asparagus in the crisp-tender.

Nutrition Facts

Fat: 11g| Saturated Fat: 2g| Fiber: 2g| Sodium: 370 mg| Cholesterol: 30mg| Protein: 8g| Carbohydrates: 4g| Sugars: 2g

662. FRESH PEAS WITH MINT

Total Time: 10 Minutes

Ingredients

- 2 cups sugar snap peas, blanched
- 2 cups frozen peas, thawed
- 1/4 cup sliced green onion
- 2 tablespoons butter
- 1 tablespoon fresh mint, finely chopped
- Salt and pepper, to taste

Directions

- In a large skillet over medium-high heat, cook sugar snap peas, peas, and green onion in butter for 4 to 5 minutes or until heated.
- Stir in mint.
- Season with salt and pepper.

Nutrition Facts

Fat: 2g| Saturated Fat: 1g| Fiber: 2g| Sodium: 20mg| Cholesterol: 5mg| Protein: 2g| Carbohydrates: 7g| Sugars: 3g

663. VEGETABLE SOUP WITH SHIRATAKI AND EDAMAME

Total Time: 20 Minutes

Ingredients

- 1 (8 oz) package Skinny Noodles Spinach Fettuccine (shirataki noodles), drained, rinsed, cut to 4-inch pieces, and set aside
- 4 cup vegetable broth
- 1 clove garlic, crushed
- 1 cup chopped carrots
- 1 cup chopped celery
- 1/2 cup shelled edamame
- 1/2 cup chopped onion
- Salt and pepper to taste

Directions

- Pour broth in a pot and add all ingredients except Skinny Noodles Spinach Fettuccine.
- Bring to a boil; lower heat and cook for 5-10 minutes until vegetables are fork-tender.
- Add Skinny Noodles, and cook for another 5-7 minutes.
- Add salt and pepper to taste and serve hot.

Nutrition Facts

Fat: 1g| Fiber: 4g| Protein: 3g| Carbohydrates: 11g

664. PORTABELLO MUSHROOM STROGANOFF

Total Time: 20 Minutes

Ingredients

- 2 (8 oz) packages Skinny Noodles Spinach Fettuccine
- 2-3 Tbsp olive oil
- 1 large onion, diced
- 1 lb. portobello mushrooms, sliced
- 1-1/2 Cup vegetable broth
- 1 cup fat-free sour cream
- 2 Tbsp cornstarch
- Salt and pepper to taste

Directions

- Drain Skinny Noodles Spinach Fettuccine into a colander and rinse well with warm water. Drain and set aside.
- Add olive oil to a large skillet on medium heat. Stir in onion and cook until soft; turn heat up to medium-high, add mushrooms and cook until browned and limp. Remove to a bowl and set aside.
- Add broth to the same skillet, stirring and mixing any onion/mushroom bits from the skillet.
- Bring to a boil and cook to reduce mixture by 30 percent.
- Reduce heat and add back the mushroom/onion mixture.
- Remove pan from heat.
- Mix the sour cream and cornstarch, and pour into the skillet to blend with the mushroom/onion mixture.
- Return the skillet to the burner, add salt and pepper to taste, and stir until the sauce thickens.
- Meanwhile, microwave drained Skinny Noodles Spinach Fettuccine for 2 minutes. Drain again and top with thicken the sauce.

Nutrition Facts

Fat: 7g| Fiber: 5g| Cholesterol: 5mg| Protein: 5g| Carbohydrates: 26g

665. FRESH ASPARAGUS TOPPED WITH SUNNY-SIDE-UP EGGS

Total Time: 15 Minutes

Ingredients

- 1 bunch asparagus, woody ends trimmed
- Cooking spray
- 2 Eggland's Best large eggs
- 1 tablespoon olive oil (optional)
- 1 teaspoon Parmesan cheese (optional)
- 1 teaspoon breadcrumbs (optional)
- 1/4 cup chopped red peppers (optional)

Directions

- Fill a medium saucepan with water and bring to a boil. Submerge asparagus and cook for approximately 2 minutes, maintaining a bright green color and slight crunch. Immediately remove asparagus and shock it in a bowl of ice water. Reserve.
- Coat medium-size skillet with cooking spray. Crack two Eggland's Best eggs into the pan and cook over medium heat until the whites set and the edges of the eggs are cooked.
- Place asparagus on the plate, making an even layer. Remove eggs from the pan using a slotted spatula and place them on top of asparagus. Top with a drizzle of olive oil and garnish with Parmesan cheese, bread crumbs, or red peppers, if desired. Can also be served on two pieces of whole-wheat toast.

Nutrition Facts

Fat: 11g| Saturated Fat: 5g| Fiber: 1g| Sodium: 86 mg| Cholesterol: 176mg| Protein: 7g| Carbohydrates: 2g

Sweet Corn Soup With Crab And Asparagus

Total Time: 20 Minutes

Ingredients

- 1-1/2 pounds fresh asparagus
- 1/4 cup water
- 4 cups fat-free, low-sodium chicken broth
- 1 (15-ounce) can no-salt-added cream-style corn
- 2 teaspoons low-salt soy sauce
- 1/2 teaspoon salt

- 2 tablespoons cornstarch
- 2 tablespoons cold water
- Egg substitute equivalent to 3 eggs, or 3 large eggs
- 2 (6-ounce) cans crabmeat, rinsed and drained
- 1/2 teaspoon toasted sesame oil
- 6 medium green onions (green part only), finely chopped
- Chili garlic sauce to taste (optional)

Directions

- Trim the asparagus and cut it into 1-inch pieces. Put in a microwave-safe dish with 1/4 cup water. Microwave, covered, on 100 percent power (high) for 5 minutes, or until tender-crisp. Don't overcook. Drain well.
- In a large saucepan, bring the broth to a boil over high heat. Stir in corn, soy sauce, and salt. Return to a boil. Meanwhile, put the cornstarch in a cup. Add 2 tablespoons of water, stirring to dissolve. Pour into the broth mixture, stirring constantly.
- Pour the egg substitute into the boiling soup in a thin stream. Remove from the heat.
- To serve, spoon 1/2 cup asparagus into each bowl. Ladle the broth mixture over each serving. Top with crabmeat and sesame oil. Sprinkle the green onions over each serving.
- Serve the chili garlic sauce on the side.

Nutrition Facts

Fat: 1g| Sodium: 278mg| Cholesterol: 38mg| Protein: 15g| Carbohydrates: 17g

666. POTATO, BROCCOLI, AND FENNEL SALAD

Total Time: 15 Minutes

Ingredients

- 8 large Idaho potatoes (about 4 pounds), well-scrubbed, cut into 3/4-inch chunks
- 1/2 teaspoon salt
- 4 cups chopped broccoli (about 1 bunch)
- 2 cups (16 ounces) favorite ranch salad dressing
- 3 cups chopped fennel (about one large bulb), with core and tops, removed
- 1 large red onion, quartered and very thinly sliced (about 1 1/2 cups)
- 1/2 cup diced green olives with pimento (optional)
- Salt and pepper to taste
- Leaf lettuce, for garnish
- Cherry tomatoes or sliced tomatoes, for garnish

Directions

- Fill large stockpot half full of water, add salt, and bring to boiling over high heat. Add potatoes and bring them back to boiling over high heat; reduce heat to medium and boil for three minutes.
- Add broccoli to potatoes and bring back to boiling over high heat. Reduce heat to medium again, and cook until desired doneness (1-3 minutes). Potatoes and broccoli should both be firm. Drain well in a colander.
- Transfer potatoes and broccoli to a large mixing bowl, add ranch dressing and let cool. Stir in fennel, onions, and olives, if using. Taste and season with salt and pepper, if desired. Serve on a bed of leaf lettuce with ripe tomatoes as garnish.

Nutrition Facts

Fat: 18g| Sodium: 480mg| Cholesterol: 10mg| Protein: 4g| Carbohydrates: 28g

667. SPINACH WITH GARLIC, RAISINS, AND PEANUTS

Total Time: 10-15 Minutes

Ingredients

- 1 tablespoon peanut oil
- 2 garlic cloves, thinly sliced
- A pinch dried hot red pepper flakes
- 1 small red bell pepper, cored, seeded, and cut into thin strips
- 2 pounds fresh baby spinach*, rinsed and spun
- 1/4 cup golden raisins
- 1/4 cup unsalted dry-roasted peanuts, chopped
- Salt and freshly ground black pepper

Directions

- In a large non-stick skillet, heat oil over medium-high heat; add garlic and red pepper flakes and cook, shaking pan here and there, just until edges of garlic are brown.
- Add red bell pepper and cook, tossing or stirring, another minute. Add spinach, raisins, and peanuts; using tongs, flip spinach from underneath to over on top to distribute a mixture and evenly cook.
- Saute just until wilted and released water has mostly evaporated about 2 minutes. Season with salt and pepper.

Nutrition Facts

Fat: 9g| Protein: 9g| Carbohydrates: 12g

668. SESAME SUGAR SNAP PEAS

Total Time: 10-15 Minutes

Ingredients

- 2 tsp. extra virgin olive oil
- 2 cloves garlic, finely minced
- 1 lb. sugar snap peas, trimmed
- 1 Tbsp. reduced-sodium soy sauce
- 1/2 tsp. sesame seed oil (can use toasted sesame seed oil)
- Pinch of crushed red pepper flakes or to taste
- 1 tsp. honey
- 1 Tbsp. toasted sesame seeds

Directions

- Place oven rack in highest position and preheat broiler.
- In a mixing bowl, whisk together olive oil and garlic. Add snap peas and toss to coat well.
- On the baking dish, place snap peas in a single layer. Broil until tender, about 5-6 minutes.
- While peas are cooking, mix soy sauce, sesame oil, pepper flakes, and honey.
- After removing snap peas from the oven, gently toss with soy sauce mixture. Garnish with sesame seeds.
- Serve hot or chilled as a side dish. Hot is most common.

Nutrition Facts

Fat: 4g| Saturated Fat: 5g| Fiber: 3g| Sodium: 140mg| Protein: 3 g| Carbohydrates: 11g

669. BROCCOLI RABE SAUTE

Total Time: 10-20 Minutes

Ingredients

- 2 Tbsp canola oil (30 mL)
- 3 bunches rapini (broccoli rabe), about 3 1/4 lb (1.5 kg), rinsed, trimmed, and cut into 3-inch (7.6 cm) pieces
- 3 large garlic cloves, minced or crushed
- 1/2 tsp salt (2 mL)
- 1-1/2 (375 mL) cups diced roasted red bell pepper, from one 12-oz jar (341mL)
- 3 Tbsp slivered almonds, toasted (45 mL)

Directions

- Heat a very large Dutch oven over medium-high heat.
- Add canola oil to pan; add rapini, garlic, and salt.
- Toss well, reduce heat to medium-low, and cover.
- Cook for 10 minutes or until rapini are tender, turning a few times while cooking.
- Add roasted pepper and toasted almonds, toss and serve.

Nutrition Facts

Fat: 5g| Fiber: 1g| Sodium: 55mg| Protein: 7g| Carbohydrates: 11g

670. BALSAMIC BRUSSELS SPROUTS

Total Time: 20-30 Minutes

Ingredients

- 10 oz. fresh Brussels sprouts, the smallest available
- 2-3 Tbsp. extra-virgin olive oil
- 1-2 garlic clove (or to taste), finely minced
- 1-1/2 Tbsp. balsamic vinegar, or to taste
- 1/4 cup minced red bell pepper
- 1 Tbsp. finely chopped flat-leaf parsley
- Salt and freshly ground black pepper, to taste

Directions

- Steam the Brussels sprouts just until tender, either on top of the stove or in a microwave at medium power.
- While the sprouts are cooking, whisk together the olive oil with vinegar and garlic. Set the dressing aside.
- When the sprouts are done, drain them well and place them in a shallow serving bowl. Re-blend dressing and drizzle over sprouts. Sprinkle top of sprouts with red pepper and parsley. Season to taste with salt and pepper. Serve hot.

Nutrition Facts

Fat: 7g| Saturated Fat: 1g| Fiber: 2g| Sodium: 195mg| Protein: 2g| Carbohydrates: 8g

671. PARMESAN-CRUSTED HALIBUT WITH SPICY BRUSSELS SPROUTS

Total Time: 50-60 Minutes

Ingredients

Halibut:

- Canola oil cooking spray
- 1/4 cup all-purpose gluten-free flour
- 2 egg whites
- 1 Tbsp fat-free milk
- 1 1/2 cup corn flakes, lightly crushed
- 1/4 fresh parsley, rinsed and chopped
- 1/4 tsp salt
- 1/4 tsp black pepper
- 1/4 tsp garlic powder
- 4 Pacific/Alaskan halibut fillets (4 oz/125 g each), rinsed and pat dry
- 1/4 cup grated Parmesan cheese
- 1 lemon, cut into wedges

Brussels Sprouts:

- 2 packages (10 oz/300g) Brussels sprouts, rinsed and sliced in half
- 1 Tbsp canola oil
- 1/8 tsp red pepper flakes
- 1/4 tsp garlic powder
- 1/8 tsp salt
- 1 tsp Parmesan cheese

Directions

- Preheat oven to 425F (220C) and place oven rack in the upper third of the oven.
- Coat the baking sheet with canola oil cooking spray and set it aside.
- In a shallow bowl, place flour. In another shallow bowl, combine egg whites and milk. In the third shallow bowl, combine corn flakes and parsley.
- Sprinkle halibut with a pinch of salt, pepper, and garlic powder. Lightly dust each fish fillet with flour, dip in egg mixture, then coat with corn flake-parsley mixture. Place on baking sheet.
- Sprinkle each fillet with 1 Tbsp
- Parmesan cheese and bake for 15 to 17 minutes until fish is opaque and flakes when pulled apart with a fork. Set aside and keep warm.
- In a large bowl, toss Brussels sprouts with 1 Tbsp canola oil, red pepper flakes, garlic powder, salt, and Parmesan cheese.
- Transfer to a baking sheet that has been coated with canola oil cooking spray and roast for 10 minutes until tender, turning every 2-3 minutes.
- Serve alongside halibut with a fresh lemon wedge.

Nutrition Facts

Fat: 9g| Saturated Fat: 2g| Fiber: 4g| Sodium: 540mg| Cholesterol: 40mg| Protein: 33g| Carbohydrates: 25g

672. SPINACH SALAD WITH SEARED BOK CHOY, GINGER, AND CILANTRO

Total Time: 10-15 Minutes

Ingredients

- 1 Tbsp canola oil
- 1 bunch bok choy, rinsed well and chopped (4 cups)
- 1/3 cup chopped whole green onions
- 2 cloves garlic, minced
- 1 tsp minced fresh ginger
- 1 Tbsp reduced-sodium soy sauce
- 1/4 tsp freshly ground black pepper
- 2 Tbsp chopped fresh cilantro
- 4 cups fresh baby spinach leaves

Directions

- In a large skillet, heat canola oil over medium-high heat.
- Add bok choy, green onions, garlic, and ginger and cook 2-3 minutes or until bok choy is tender-crisp.
- Add soy sauce and pepper, stir to coat, and cook for 1 minute. Remove from heat and stir in cilantro.

- Arrange spinach leaves on a serving platter. Spoon bok choy mixture over spinach and serve.

Nutrition Facts

Fat: 3.5g| Fiber: 2g| Sodium: 140mg| Protein: 1g| Carbohydrates: 5g

673. ROASTED BEET AND CARROT SALAD

Total Time: 40 Minutes

Ingredients

Salad:

- 2 medium beets (about 8 oz/225 g total), peeled, cut into 8 wedges each 2
- 1 medium carrot (about 3 oz/85 g), peeled, cut in half lengthwise, and cut into 2-inch pieces 1
- 1 medium parsnip (about 3 oz/85 g), peeled, quartered lengthwise, and cut into 2-inch pieces 1
- 1 tsp canola oil 5 mL
- 4 cups (about 4 oz/ 115 g) packed spring greens 1 L
- 1/2 cup thinly sliced red onion 125 mL
- 1/4 cup golden raisins (optional) 60 mL
- 1/4 cup (1 oz/ 28 g) pecan pieces, toasted 60 mL

Vinaigrette:

- 3 Tbsp balsamic vinegar 45 mL
- 1 Tbsp plus 2 tsp (10 mL) canola oil 15 mL
- 1/8 tsp dried red pepper flakes .5 mL
- 1 medium clove garlic, minced 1
- 1/4 tsp salt 1 mL
- 1/4 tsp coarsely ground black pepper 1 mL

Directions

- Preheat oven to 425 F (220 C).
- Coat a foil-lined baking sheet with cooking spray. Place beets, carrots, and parsnips on a baking sheet. Drizzle evenly with 1 tsp (5 mL) canola oil and toss gently, yet thoroughly, to coat lightly. Arrange vegetables in a single layer and bake for 10 minutes; stir and bake an additional 7 minutes or until beets are just tender when pierced with a fork. Remove from heat and let stand to cool slightly about 10 minutes.
- Combine vinaigrette ingredients in a small jar, secure lid, and shake well to blend thoroughly.
- Arrange equal amounts of salad greens on four salad plates. In the following order, top with equal amounts of onion, roasted vegetables, raisins, and pecans. Spoon vinaigrette evenly overall. Serve immediately for peak flavors.

Nutrition Facts

Fat: 12g| Saturated Fat: 1g| Fiber: 3g| Sodium: 185 mg| Protein: 2g| Carbohydrates: 14g

674. SPINACH, FETA, AND GRAPE TOMATO OMELET

Total Time: 20 Minutes

Ingredients

- 2 cups egg substitute (500 mL)
- 3 Tbsp fat-free milk (45 mL)
- 2 cups (2oz/60 g) loosely packed baby spinach (500 mL)
- 2 Tbsp chopped fresh basil leaves (30 mL)
- 1 Tbsp canola oil (15 mL)
- 1 cup grape tomatoes, quartered (250 mL)
- 1/2 tsp chopped fresh rosemary leaves (2 mL)
- 1/2 cup (2 oz/60 g) reduced-fat feta cheese (125 mL)

Directions

- Combine egg substitute and milk in a medium bowl and whisk until well blended.
- Place spinach and basil in another medium bowl; set aside.
- Heat canola oil in a small nonstick skillet over medium-high heat. Add tomatoes and rosemary, and cook 2 minutes or until soft, stirring frequently.
- Add to bowl with spinach and basil, toss, and cover to allow spinach to wilt slightly and flavors to blend while preparing omelets.
- Reduce heat to medium. Wipe skillet clean with a damp paper towel. Coat skillet with canola oil cooking spray and place over medium heat until hot. Pour half of the egg mixture into the skillet.
- Cook 5 minutes; as eggs begin to set, gently lift the edge of the omelet with a spatula and tilt the skillet so the uncooked portion flows underneath.
- When the egg mixture is set, spoon half of the tomato mixture over half of the omelet.
- Top with half of the feta cheese.
- Loosen the omelet with a spatula and fold it in half. Slide the omelet onto a serving plate and cover with foil to keep warm.
- Repeat with remaining ingredients.

Nutrition Facts:

Fat: 6g| Saturated Fat: 1.5g| Fiber: 1g| Sodium: 445mg| Cholesterol: 5mg| Protein: 16g| Carbohydrates: 5g

675. VIETNAMESE PHO

Total Time: 1 Hour 30 Minutes

Ingredients

Soup Ingredients:

- 1/2 lb sirloin tip, sliced very thinly (250 g)
- 1-1/2 Tbsp canola oil, divided (20 mL)
- 1 small onion, sliced into thin rings
- 4 cups sodium-reduced beef stock (1 L)
- 2 cups water (500 mL)
- 1 Tbsp freshly grated ginger (15 mL)
- 1 stalk lemongrass chopped or 3 Tbsp (45 mL) dried lemongrass
- 1/2 tsp whole black peppercorns (2 mL)
- 1 cinnamon stick
- 4 oz ounces rice vermicelli noodles (125 g)
- 2 cups bean sprouts (500 mL)

Garnish Ingredients:

- 1 lime, quartered
- 1/2 cup each fresh basil, mint, and cilantro (125 mL) each
- 1 small jalapeno pepper, thinly sliced (optional)
- 1 tbsp fish sauce (15 mL)

Directions

- In a large saucepan, heat 1 Tbsp (15 mL) canola oil over medium heat. Add beef and cook for about 2-3 minutes. It wonÂt be cooked through. Set aside.

- Add 1/2 Tbsp (7.5 mL) canola oil to the saucepan.
- Add onions and cook for about 3 minutes.
- Add beef stock, water, ginger, lemongrass, peppercorns, and cinnamon stick, simmer for about 1 hour.
- Meanwhile, place rice vermicelli in a bowl and cover it with very hot water. Place lid on top and allow to sit for about 3 minutes.
- Prepare garnish plate: Arrange limes, basil, mint, cilantro, jalapeno, and a small bowl of fish sauce on a plate.
- Add beef to the stock mixture and cook to desired doneness.
- To serve: Divide rice vermicelli and sprouts evenly in 4 bowls. Pour hot broth-beef mixture over top. Garnish as desired from the garnish plate.

Nutrition Facts

Fat: 9g| Saturated Fat: 2g| Fiber: 3| Sodium: 115mg| Cholesterol: 35mg| Protein: 20g| Carbohydrates: 27g

676. CHICKEN SALAD STUFFED AVOCADO

Total Time: 10-20 Minutes

Ingredients

- 2 medium avocados
- Juice of 1 lime
- 2 cups chopped cooked chicken breast, about 1/2-inch pieces
- 2 Tbsp. chopped red cabbage
- 2 Tbsp. diced carrots
- 2 Tbsp. diced radish
- 4 tsp. spicy brown mustard
- 1/2 tsp. garlic powder
- 1 tsp. extra virgin olive oil
- Salt and freshly ground black pepper, to taste
- Lime wedges for garnish

Directions

- Carefully cut avocados in half lengthwise.
- Remove pits. Scoop out pulp into mixing bowl and set avocado shells aside.
- Add lime juice and mash avocado.
- Add chicken, cabbage, carrots, radish, mustard, garlic powder, olive oil, salt, and pepper to taste and mix gently to combine.
- Spoon mixture into avocado shells, mounding in the center, and serve immediately with lime wedges.
- Or serve immediately on whole-grain bread for sandwiches or whole-wheat tortilla for wraps.

Nutrition Facts

Fat: 16g| Saturated Fat: 2g| Fiber: 6g| Sodium: 146mg| Protein: 29g| Carbohydrates: 8g

677. GARLIC SNOW PEAS WITH CILANTRO

Total Time: 5 Minutes

Ingredients

- 3 teaspoons canola oil, divided
- 3 cups fresh (or frozen and thawed) snow peas, patted dry and trimmed
- 4 medium cloves garlic, minced
- 1/4 teaspoon salt
- 1/4 to 1/2 cup chopped fresh cilantro leaves

Directions

- Working in two batches, heat 1-1/2 teaspoons canola oil in a large nonstick skillet over medium-high heat.
- Add half of the snow peas; cook 3 minutes or until just beginning to brown on edges, using two utensils to toss easily.
- Add half of the garlic and cook 30 seconds, stirring constantly. Set aside on a separate plate.
- Repeat with remaining 1-1/2 teaspoons canola oil, snow peas, and garlic.
- When cooked, return the reserved snow peas to skillet; add salt and cilantro, and toss gently, yet thoroughly.
- Serve immediately for peak flavors.

Nutrition Facts

Fat: 2.5g| Sodium: 100mg| Protein: 2g| Carbohydrates: 4g

678. SPINACH VEGETABLE KUGEL

Total Time: 1 Hour 30 Minutes

Ingredients

- 10 oz. package (300g) fresh spinach
- 2 onions, chopped
- 1 stalk celery, chopped
- 1 red pepper, chopped
- 3 carrots, grated
- 1 cup mushrooms, chopped
- 1 tablespoon olive oil
- 2 eggs plus 2 whites (or 3 eggs)
- 3/4 teaspoon salt
- 1/4 teaspoon each pepper and garlic powder
- 1/2 teaspoon dried basil
- 1/4 cup matzo meal

Directions

- Preheat oven to 350 degrees F. Wash spinach thoroughly. Remove and discard tough stems. Cook spinach in a covered saucepan until wilted, about 3 minutes (or microwave on HIGH for 4 minutes). Don't add any water. The water clinging to the leaves will provide enough steam to cook it. Cool and squeeze dry.
- Heat oil in a non-stick skillet on medium heat. Saute onion, celery, red pepper, and carrots for 5 minutes, until golden.
- Add mushrooms and cook 5 minutes longer (or cook vegetables uncovered in the microwave for 6 to 8 minutes on HIGH).
- Chop spinach coarsely. Combine with remaining ingredients and mix well.
- Pour into a sprayed 7" x 11" Pyrex casserole. Bake uncovered at 350F for 45 to 50 minutes, until firm. Cut into squares to serve.

Nutrition Facts

Fat: 2.7g| Protein: 4g| Carbohydrates: 11g

679. SAUTEED SPINACH WITH GARLIC

Total Time: 15 Minutes

Ingredients

- 1 pound raw spinach
- 2 tablespoons olive oil
- 1 fresh tomato
- 2 cloves garlic

Directions

- Wash spinach thoroughly and drain.
- Saute tomato and garlic in olive oil in a large saute pan.

- Add spinach, cover, and cook over low heat for 5 minutes, stirring a few times.
- Add salt and pepper to taste.
- Cook, uncovered, 5 minutes longer, stirring occasionally.

Nutrition Facts

Fat: 7g| Sodium: 94mg| Protein: 3.9g| Carbohydrates: 4g

680. LEMON ASPARAGUS AND CARROTS

Total Time: 25 Minutes

Ingredients

- 1/2 pound carrots, small
- 1 dash lemon pepper
- 8 ounces asparagus spears, frozen or fresh
- 1/8 cup lemon juice

Directions

- Wash, trim and peel small carrots.
- Place carrots in a steamer basket above boiling water.
- Cover and steam for about 15 minutes or till crisp-tender.
- Rinse carrots in cold water; drain.
- In the meantime, cook frozen asparagus spears according to the package.
- Rinse asparagus in cold water, drain.
- Cover and chill drained carrots and asparagus.
- To serve, arrange carrots and asparagus on a platter.
- Sprinkle with a little lemon juice and lemon pepper.

Nutrition Facts:

Sodium: 19mg| Protein: 1g| Carbohydrates: 6g

681. GREEN BEANS WITH MUSHROOMS

Total Time: 15 Minutes

Ingredients

- 2 pound fresh green beans
- 4-5 teaspoons water
- 1 cup fresh mushrooms, quartered
- 1 teaspoon garlic
- 2 teaspoons olive oil

Directions

- In a frying pan or saute pan, add 4-5 teaspoon water. Bring to boil.
- Add Green Beans and lower heat to medium-high and cover.
- When Green Beans are fork-tender, take off the heat and drain water.
- In another frying pan or saute pan, on medium-high heat, saute olive oil, garlic, and mushrooms for about 5-7 minutes.
- Add Green Beans and toss.
- Serve Hot.

Nutrition Facts

Fat: 5g| Protein: 2g| Carbohydrates: 5g

682. BAKED STUFFED ONIONS WITH SPINACH FETA

Total Time: 60 Minutes

Ingredients

- 2 large sweet or Spanish onions (about 1-1/2 pounds total, peeled)
- 2 teaspoons olive oil
- 1 clove garlic
- One 10-ounce package of frozen chopped spinach, thawed and squeezed dry
- 1 teaspoon fresh lemon juice
- 1/4 teaspoon freshly ground pepper
- 1/4 cup bread crumbs
- 1/4 cup (1 ounce) crumbled feta cheese

Directions

- Place the onions in a large saucepan and cover with water.
- Bring to a boil and cook until the onions are partially tender about 10 to 15 minutes.
- Drain and cool; cut the onions in half crosswise. Scoop out the center of each onion half, leaving a 1/2-inch shell.
- Reserve the centers. If necessary, cut a small piece from the end of each onion shell so the shells will stand upright.
- Prepare a shallow baking dish large enough to hold the onion halves in one layer with non-stick pan spray. Place the onions in the prepared dish, hollowed sides up.
- Preheat the oven to 350 degrees F.
- Chop the reserved centers of the onions. Saute in oil with the garlic in a medium saucepan until tender, about 5 minutes.
- Stir in the spinach, lemon juice, and pepper; cook until the liquid evaporates.
- Remove from the heat; stir in the bread crumbs and cheese
- Fill the onion shells with the spinach mixture. Cover with foil and bake for about 25 minutes. Serve hot.

Nutrition Facts

Fat: 4g| Sodium: 187mg| Cholesterol: 6mg| Protein: 5g| Carbohydrates: 22g

683. SUGAR SNAP PEAS AND CARROTS

Total Time: 10 Minutes

Ingredients

- 1 tsp. canola oil
- 1 small garlic clove, minced
- 1 tsp. grated or minced ginger
- 8 oz. sugar snap peas
- 3 baby carrots, cut lengthwise in 8 strips
- 3 Tbsp. chicken or vegetable broth, or water
- Salt and freshly ground black pepper, to taste
- 2 large basil leaves, cut crosswise in thin strips

Directions

- Heat oil in a medium non-stick skillet over medium-high heat.
- Saute garlic and ginger until fragrant, about 30 seconds.
- Add peas and carrots to the pan, stirring to coat them with oil. Add broth or water.
- Cook, stirring occasionally, until peas are tender-crisp, about 4 minutes.
- Season to taste with salt and pepper. Mix in basil and serve.

Nutrition Facts

- Fat: 1g| Sodium: 109mg| Protein: 2g| Carbohydrates: 7g

684. SPINACH SAUTE WITH MUSHROOMS

Total Time: 10 Minutes

Ingredients

- 2 tablespoons olive oil
- 2 cloves garlic, minced
- 1 cup mushrooms, sliced

- 3 bunches spinach (about 2 pounds), stemmed and washed
- 1 tablespoon lemon juice
- Salt and pepper, to taste

Directions

- In a skillet over medium heat, heat the oil. Add the mushrooms and garlic and saute for 3 minutes.
- Add the spinach, cover, and steam for 2 minutes. Add the lemon juice, salt, and pepper. Serve immediately.

Nutrition Facts

Fat: 7g| Sodium: 132mg| Protein: 5g| Carbohydrates: 7g

685. MARINATED ASPARAGUS, TOMATO, AND HEARTS OF PALM

Total Time: 40 Minutes

Ingredients

- 8 ounces fresh asparagus, trimmed, cut into 2-inch pieces (about 2 cups)
- 1 pound Italian plum tomatoes, cut into 1/4-inch slices
- 14-ounce can heart of palm, rinsed and drained
- 1/4 cup thinly sliced yellow onion

Dressing Ingredients:

- 1/4 cup red wine vinegar
- 2 tablespoons dry red wine (regular or nonalcoholic)
- 2 teaspoons sugar or sugar substitute
- 1/4 teaspoon pepper

Directions

- Steam asparagus for 3 minutes, or until tender-crisp. Immediately put asparagus in a shallow glass baking dish.
- Add a layer of tomatoes, then one of the hearts of palm, and one of onion.
- In a small bowl, whisk together dressing ingredients until sugar has dissolved. Pour over vegetables.
- Cover dish and refrigerate for 30 minutes, stirring occasionally.

Nutrition Facts

Fat: 1g| Sodium: 181mg| Protein: 3g| Carbohydrates: 10g

686. ROASTED STUFFED PORTOBELLO MUSHROOMS WITH SPINACH-CILANTRO PESTO

Total Time: 40-45 Minutes

Ingredients

- 8 large portobello mushrooms (5-6 inches diameter)
- Vegetable cooking spray
- 1 cup finely chopped zucchini
- 1 cup shredded carrots
- 3 green onions and tops, thinly sliced
- 4 tablespoons dry unseasoned breadcrumbs
- Spinach-Cilantro pesto (recipe follows)
- Salt and pepper, to taste
- 1/2 cup (2 ounces) shredded reduced-fat mozzarella cheese

Directions

- Remove and chop mushroom stems.
- Spray large skillet with cooking spray; heat over medium heat until hot. Saute mushroom stems, zucchini, carrots, and green onions until crisp-tender, 8 to 10 minutes. Stir in breadcrumbs and pesto.
- Season to taste with salt and pepper.
- Spoon vegetable mixture onto mushrooms.
- Spray aluminum-foil-lined jelly roll pan with cooking spray; arrange mushrooms on a pan.
- Roast mushrooms at 425 degrees until mushrooms are tender, about 20 minutes, sprinkling with cheese the last 5 minutes of roasting time.

Nutritional Value

Carbohydrates: 19g, Protein: 1g, Sodium: 2mg, Fiber: 1g

687. GREEN BEANS AND RED ONION SALAD

Total Time: 20-30 Minutes

Ingredients

- 1 10-oz package French-cut green beans
- 1/2 red onion, thinly sliced
- 4 tablespoons non-fat Italian dressing

Directions

- Cook green beans according to package directions, drain and place in serving dish; toss gently with red onion slices and dressing and serve warm or at room temperature.

Nutrition Facts

Sodium: 150mg| Protein: 1g| Carbohydrates: 7g

688. ASPARAGUS WITH PINE NUTS AND PIMENTO

Total Time: 10 Minutes

Ingredients

- 1 pound to 1-1/4 pound fresh asparagus
- 1 cup water
- 2 tablespoons fresh lime juice
- 1/4 cup diced pimento
- 1 tablespoon toasted pine nuts

Directions

- Rinse asparagus and snap off tough ends.
- In a large skillet, bring water to a boil and add asparagus.
- Cover and steam asparagus until bright green, 2 to 3 minutes.
- Remove from heat, drain and arrange on a platter.
- Sprinkle with lime juice.
- Garnish with pimento and pine nuts. Serve warm or chilled.

Nutrition Facts

Fat: 2g| Sodium: 6mg| Carbohydrates: 7g

689. CORN AND TOMATO POLENTA

Total Time: 40 Minutes

Ingredients

- 1-quart water
- 1/4 teaspoon salt
- 1 cup yellow cornmeal
- 1/2 cup Tomato Sauce
- 1 teaspoon dried leaf oregano
- 1/2 cup whole-kernel corn and drained
- 1/2 teaspoon crushed red pepper flakes
- Pepper to taste

Directions

- In a heavy 3-quart saucepan, bring water and salt to a boil.
- Slowly pour cornmeal into the saucepan so that water does not stop boiling, stir to keep smooth.
- Reduce heat and simmer 20 to 25 minutes, stirring often until mixture is stiff.

- Meanwhile, in a small saucepan, heat tomato sauce, oregano, corn, hot pepper flakes, and pepper.
- When cornmeal is stiff, turn half into a serving dish and top with half the sauce.
- Layer remaining cornmeal and sauce and let rest to 5 to 10 minutes.
- Cut in squares and serve.

Nutrition Facts
Sodium: 208mg| Carbohydrates: 23g

690. ROASTED ASPARAGUS

Total Time: 15 Minutes

Ingredients
- 1 lb fresh asparagus
- 2 tbsp Parmesan cheese, shredded
- 2 tsp olive oil
- 1 lemon, cut into wedges

Directions
- Preheat oven to 500 degrees.
- Arrange in a single layer in a shallow baking pan. With a pastry brush, paint the oil on the asparagus spears.
- Roast until tender but still crisp, 8 to 10 minutes, depending on the thickness of stalks. Turn spears occasionally for even cooking and to avoid browning.
- Place asparagus spears on a serving platter. Sprinkle with cheese. Serve with lemon wedges.

Nutrition Facts
Fat: 7g| Sodium: 71mg| Cholesterol: 3mg| Protein: 4g| Carbohydrates: 6g

691. ASPARAGUS CHEF SALAD

Total Time: 5 Minutes

Ingredients
- 2-1/2 lb. asparagus, trimmed
- 8 oz. mushrooms, sliced
- 2 oz. part-skim julienne Swiss cheese
- 2 oz. lean julienne ham
- 1 Tbsp. finely chopped onion
- 1 orange, peeled and cubed

Dressing:
- 1 pkg. lemon and herb salad dressing mix
- 2 Tbsp. water
- 1/4 cup vinegar
- 1/4 cup vegetable oil

Directions
- Chop asparagus into bite-sized pieces and place in a microwave-proof casserole dish. Add 2 Tbsp. water, cover, and Microwave for 2 minutes. Drain. Measure remaining ingredients into a salad bowl. Add asparagus when completely cool.
- Prepare dressing in a shaker container and add approximately 1/3 of it to the salad. Save remaining dressing for greens and fresh vegetables.

Nutrition Facts:
Fat: 5g| Sodium: 347mg| Cholesterol: 25mg

692. COUSCOUS WITH VEGETABLES

Total Time: 10 Minutes

Ingredients
- 5 ounces frozen green peas, thawed and drained, OR any other quick-cooking vegetable (1 cup)
- 1/2 cup minced onion
- 1/2 cup thinly sliced fresh mushrooms (about 2 ounces)
- 2 tablespoons dry white wine (regular or nonalcoholic)
- 1/2 teaspoon crushed garlic or 1/4 teaspoon garlic powder
- 2 tablespoons finely snipped fresh parsley
- 1/2 teaspoon dried basil, crumbled
- 1/8 teaspoon pepper
- 1/2 cup uncooked couscous

Directions
- In a medium nonstick saucepan, saute peas, onion, mushrooms, wine, and garlic over medium-high heat for 3 to 5 minutes, stirring often.
- Stir in parsley, basil, and pepper. Remove from heat. Meanwhile, prepare couscous using package directions. Stir together all together in a large serving bowl.

Nutrition Facts
Sodium: 5mg| Protein: 4g| Carbohydrates: 16g

693. ROMAINE, RED ONION, AND FENNEL SALAD WITH TART LIME DRESSING

Total Time: 10 Minutes

Ingredients
- 1 cup Romaine lettuce
- 1-1/2 cups fennel bulb, shredded
- 1 cup cauliflowers
- 1/2 cup red onion, sliced thinly
- Tart Lime Dressing
- 1/2 cup lime juice, fresh
- 1 tbsp olive oil
- 1 cup garlic, minced
- 1/4 tsp salt
- 1/4 tsp ground pepper
- 1/4 tsp paprika

Directions
Salad:
- Wash, dry, and tear lettuce into bite-sized pieces.
- Arrange lettuce pieces in a salad bowl; toss with shredded fennel, cauliflowers, and red onion. Prepare Tart Lime
- Dressing. Sprinkle dressing over salad and toss just before serving.

Tart Lime Dressing:
- Combine all ingredients and mix well.

Nutrition Facts
Fat: 3g| Protein: 2g| Carbohydrates: 6g

694. SOOTHING CUCUMBER MINT SOUP

Total Time: 20 Minutes

Ingredients
- 1 medium onion, chopped
- 1 large garlic clove
- 3 tbsp low-fat margarine
- 3 medium cucumbers, peeled, thinly sliced
- 3 tbsp flour
- 2 cups chicken broth
- 2 tbsp fresh mint, chopped
- 1 cup plain, low-fat yogurt
- 1 cup half & half
- Salt & pepper to taste

Directions
- In a large skillet, over medium heat, sauté onion and garlic in margarine until soft. Add cucumbers and cook until soft; about 5 to 8 minutes.
- Stir in flour, cooking for 1 minute. Add broth and increase heat to medium-high; bring to a boil. Reduce heat and simmer for 5 minutes.

- Puree cucumber mixture in a blender in batches. Pour into a bowl with the chopped mint. Cover and chill.
- Before serving, blend in yogurt and a half and half. Season to taste with salt and white pepper. Garnish with mint sprigs or chopped mint leaves.

Nutrition Facts

Fat: 8g| Sodium: 375mg| Cholesterol: 15mg| Protein: 7g| Carbohydrates: 15g

695. SAUTEED SPINACH

Total Time: 20 Minutes

Ingredients

- 1 pound raw spinach
- 2 tablespoons olive oil
- 1 fresh tomato
- 2 cloves garlic

Directions

- Wash spinach thoroughly and drain.
- Saute tomato and garlic in olive oil in a large saute pan.
- Add spinach, cover, and cook over low heat for 5 minutes, stirring a few times.
- Add salt and pepper to taste.
- Cook, uncovered, 5 minutes longer, stirring occasionally.

Nutrition Facts

Fat: 7g| Sodium: 94mg| Protein: 3.9g| Carbohydrates: 4g

696. BROCCOLI WITH ASIAN TOFU

Total Time: 30 Minutes

Ingredients

- 1 pkg (16 oz) firm tofu, drained
- 2 Tbsp lite soy sauce
- 1 tsp sesame oil (optional)
- 1/2 Tbsp brown sugar
- 1 tbsp fresh ginger root, finely chopped or shredded (or 1 tsp ground ginger)
- 1 lb fresh broccoli, rinsed and cut into individual spears
- 1 Tbsp peanut oil or vegetable oil
- 1/4 tsp crushed red pepper
- 4 Tbsp garlic, peeled and thinly sliced (about 8 cloves)
- 1 tbsp sesame seeds (optional)
- Cooking spray

Directions

- Slice tofu into eight pieces. Place on a plate or flat surface covered with three paper towels.
- Top with four more paper towels. Top with another flat plate or cutting board.
- Press down evenly and gently to squeeze out moisture.
- Throw away paper towels.
- Replace with fresh paper towels and press again. (The more liquid you remove, the more sauce the tofu will absorb.)
- Place tofu in a bowl just big enough to hold all eight pieces lying on their widest side without overlapping.
- In a small bowl, stir to thoroughly combine soy sauce, sesame oil, brown sugar, and ginger into a marinade, and stir thoroughly. Pour over tofu.
- Carefully turn the tofu several times to coat well. Set aside.
- Meanwhile, heat a large nonstick saute pan coated with cooking spray.
- Add broccoli and saute for about 5 minutes, until it turns bright green and becomes tender and crispy. Remove broccoli from the pan and set aside.
- Heat a grill pan or flat saute pan over high heat.
- Drain tofu, reserving marinade. Place on grill pan to heat for about 3 minutes.
- Gently turn. Heat the second side for 3 minutes.
- At the same time, in the saute pan over medium-low heat, warm the peanut oil, crushed red pepper, and garlic until the garlic softens and begins to turn brown, about 30 seconds to 1 minute.
- Add broccoli and reserved marinade, and gently mix until well-coated.
- Place two slices of tofu on each plate with one-quarter of the broccoli and marinade mixture. Sprinkle with sesame seeds (optional).

Nutrition Facts

Fat: 11g| Saturated Fat: 2g| Fiber: 4g| Sodium: 341mg| Protein: 14g| Carbohydrates: 13g

DIABETIC POULTRY (CHICKEN) RECIPES

697. CHICKEN MARSALA

Preparation 45 Minutes

Serves 4 Persons

Ingredients

- ¼ cup olive oil
- 4 boneless, skinless chicken breasts,
- pounded thin Fine-grained kosher salt and freshly ground black pepper, to taste
- ¼ cup whole-wheat flour
- ½ pound mushrooms, sliced
- 1 cup marsala wine
- 1 cup chicken stock
- ¼ cup chopped fresh flat-leaf parsley

Directions

- Heat the olive oil in a large skillet on medium-high heat.
- Season the chicken breasts with salt and pepper; then dredge them in flour.
- Sauté them in the olive oil until golden brown.
- Transfer them to an oven-safe plate, and keep warm in the oven on low.
- Sauté the mushrooms in the same pan.
- Add the wine and chicken stock, and bring to a simmer.
- Simmer for 10 minutes, or until the sauce is reduced and thickened slightly.
- Return the chicken to the pan, and cook it in the sauce for 10 minutes.
- Transfer everything to a serving dish and sprinkle with the parsley

Nutrition Facts

Calories per Serving: 437 cal Fat: 11g Protein: 57g Carbohydrates: 12g

698. BRAISE CHICKEN WITH WILD MUSHROOM

Preparation 120 Minutes

Serves 4 Persons

Ingredients

- ¼ cup dried porcini mushrooms
- ¼ cup olive oil
- 3 slices low-salt turkey bacon, chopped
- 1 chicken, cut into pieces

- Fine-grained kosher salt and freshly ground
- black pepper, to taste
- 1 small celery stalk, diced
- 1 small dried red chile, chopped
- ¼ cup vermouth or white wine
- ¼ cup tomato purée
- ¼ cup low-salt chicken stock
- ½ teaspoon arrowroot powder
- ¼ cup chopped fresh flat-leaf parsley
- 4 teaspoons fresh thyme, chopped
- 1 tablespoon fresh tarragon

Directions

- Place the mushrooms in a small bowl, and pour boiling water over them. Allow them to stand for 20 minutes to soften. Strain and chop, reserving the liquid.
- Heat the olive oil in a heavy stew pot on medium heat. Add the bacon and cook until it is browned and slightly crisp. Drain the bacon on a paper towel.
- Season the chicken with salt and pepper, and add it to the oil and bacon drip-pings.
- Cook for 10 to 15 minutes, turning halfway through the cooking time so that both sides of the chicken are golden brown.
- Add the celery and chopped chile, and cook for 3 to 5 minutes or until soft.
- Deglaze the pan with the wine, using a wooden spoon to scrape up the brown bits stuck to the bottom.
- Add the tomato purée, chicken stock, arrowroot powder, and mushroom liquid.
- Cover and simmer on low for 45 minutes.
- Add the fresh chopped herbs and cook an additional 10 minutes, or until the sauce thickens. Season with salt and pepper.
- Serve with wilted greens or crunchy green beans.

Nutrition Facts

Calories per Serving: 306 cal Fat: 20g Protein: 22g Carbohydrates: 6g

699. CHICKEN STIR-FRY

Preparation 20 Minutes
Serves 4 Persons

Ingredients

- Garlic (minced) – 1 clove
- Olive oil – 1 tablespoon
- Black pepper – ½ teaspoon
- Cornstarch – 2 teaspoon
- Stir-fry vegetables – 1 bag (14-oz)
- Soy sauce – 2 tablespoons
- Shredded chicken (cooked) – 1 ½ cups
- Chicken broth (low-sodium) – 1 cup

Directions

- Se Begin by placing a non-stick pan on a high flame.
- Pour in the olive oil and add the frozen stir-fry vegetables.
- Cook for about 7 minutes. Keep stirring.
- While the veggies are cooking, add the soy sauce, broth, garlic, black pepper, and cornstarch to a glass mixing bowl.
- Whisk until well combined.
- Transfer the broth mixture and chicken to the veggies and cook for around 7 minutes or until the sauce thickens and the chicken is nicely heated.
- Keep stir-ring.
- Transfer onto a platter and serve with rice or noodles.

Nutrition Facts

Calories per Serving: 180 cal Fat: 8g Protein: 13g Carbohydrates: 9g

700. HERB ROASTED CHICKEN

Preparation 420 Minutes
Serves 4 Persons

Ingredients

- 3–4-lb. whole roasting chicken (or smaller depending on the size of your slow cooker), gizzards removed
- 2–3 Tbsp. olive oil
- 2 tsp. rosemary
- 1 tsp. thyme
- 1 tsp. sage 2–3 Tbsp. poultry seasoning

Directions

- Truss the legs/wings of your bird.
- Rub it all over with olive oil.
- Place balled-up foil in the bottom of your crock to keep the bird from floating in the juices.
- Place the chicken on top, breast-side down
- Mix together the rosemary, thyme, sage, and poultry seasoning.
- Pat this all over the bird
- Cover and cook on Low for 7 hours.

Nutrition Facts

Calories per Serving: 361 cal Fat: 13g Protein: 56g Carbohydrates: 2g

701. MANDARIN CHICKEN SALAD

Preparation 160 Minutes
Serves 6 Persons

Ingredients

- 3 cups cut-up cooked chicken
- ¾ cup sliced green grapes
- 2 medium stalks celery, thinly sliced
- 2 green onions, thinly sliced
- 1 can mandarin orange segments, drained
- 1 can sliced water chestnuts, drained
- 1 container (6 oz) lemon fat-free yogurt
- 2 tbs reduced-sodium soy sauce
- Mixed salad greens

Directions

- In large bowl, mix chicken, grapes, celery, onions, orange segment s and water chestnuts.
- In small bowl, mix yogurt and soy sauce.
- Pour over chicken mixture; toss until Combined
- Cover and refrigerate at least 2 hours or until chilled.
- Serve on salad greens

Nutrition Facts

Calories per Serving: 210 cal Fat: 3g Protein: 23g Carbohydrates: 22g

702. TURKEY ENCHILADA

Preparation 480 Minutes
Serves 10 Persons

Ingredients

- 1 (14.5 oz.) can diced tomatoes
- 2 cups chicken broth
- 1/2 cup all-purpose flour
- 1/3 cup chili powder

- 2 tsps ground cumin
- 1 garlic clove
- 1 tsp salt
- 1 tsp oregano
- 4 turkey breast halves, skinless, boneless
- 1 pinch cayenne pepper, if desired

Directions

- Add cayenne pepper, salt, oregano, cumin, garlic, flour, chili powder, tomatoes and chicken broth into a high-speed electric blender.
- Process mixture until a smooth consistency is reached.
- Add turkey breast into a slow cooker pot and top with the sauce mixture until wholly covered.
- Secure slow cooker lid and cook on high for 4-6 hours, or on 8-9 hours on low.
- Remove turkey, shred with 2 forks, return into the sauce and stir until incorporated.

Nutrition Facts

Calories per Serving: 93 cal Fat: 2g Protein: 10g Carbohydrates: 8g

703. TASTY FIESTA TURKEY

Preparation 50 Minutes

Serves 6 Persons

Ingredients

- 1 1/2 tbsps chili powder
- 3 cups water
- 3/4 cup mild salsa
- 1/4 cup parsley, chopped
- 1 cup onion, chopped
- 3/4 cup (diced) red pepper
- 6 turkey breast halves
- 3 cups instant brown rice
- 1 cup (frozen) corn kernels

Directions

- Coat a 10" skillet with cooking spray and place over med-heat.
- Add red pepper and turkey into the hot skillet and cook until turkey is well cooked and browned.
- Add onions into the skillet and cook for 30 seconds.
- Add salsa, corn, chili powder, rice and water into the skillet and simmer until the rice is well cooked, for 10 minutes.
- Serve rice with turkey and garnish with chopped parsley.

Nutrition Facts

Calories per Serving: 284 cal Fat: 4g Protein: 31g Carbohydrates: 30g

704. ZETSY LIME TURKEY

Preparation 60 Minutes

Serves 4 Persons

Ingredients

- 2 tbsps white vinegar
- 1/2 cup lime juice 1 tsp paprika
- 3 tbsps oregano, dried
- 1/2 (chopped) medium onion
- 1/4 tsp ground black pepper
- 4 turkey breast halves, skinless, boneless
- 1/2 cup lemon zest, thinly sliced

Directions

- Add lime zest, onion, pepper, paprika, oregano, vinegar and lime juice into a bowl and stir until well combined.
- Add turkey into a fairly big baking dish and top with lime juice sauce until wholly coated.
- Place aluminum foil over dish until covered and transfer into a refrigerator for 4 hours or more.
- Heat up oven to 375ºF.
- Transfer the baking dish with the aluminum foil cover into the preheated oven.
- Bake turkey for 30 minutes, remove foil cover and bake until turkey juices run clear and marinade starts to boil, for 15 minutes.
- Remove turkey and let sit until cool for 5 minutes.
- Serve and enjoy.

Nutrition Facts

Calories per Serving: 150 cal Fat: 3g Protein: 23g Carbohydrates: 8g

705. WALNUT TURKEY MEATBALL IN TOMATO SAUCE

Preparation 70 Minutes

Serves 4 Persons

Ingredients

- Pomodoro sauce
- 2 tablespoons olive oil
- 1 large sweet onion, chopped
- 3 garlic cloves, minced
- 16 plum tomatoes, cored and chopped
- 1 tablespoon dried thyme
- 1 tablespoon dried winter savory
- Salt and freshly ground black pepper
- Meatball
- 1 pound ground turkey
- 2 eggs, beaten
- ½ small onion, minced
- 2 cloves garlic, chopped
- ½ cup whole-wheat panko
- ½ cup grated Parmesan
- ¼ cup walnuts, pulsed in a blender
- 3 tablespoons chopped fresh oregano leaves
- 1½ teaspoons ground cumin

Directions

- Heat the olive oil in a large pot over medium heat.
- Add the onion and cook, stirring occasionally, until softened, 4–5 minutes.
- Add the garlic and cook 2–3 minutes more.
- Add the chopped tomatoes, thyme, savory, and salt and pepper and cover. Cook, stirring occasionally, until broken down and chunky, 45 minutes to 1 hour.
- Meanwhile, put all the meatball ingredients in a large bowl and mix gently with your hands to combine.
- Scoop up about 2 tablespoons of the mixture, shape into a ball, and arrange on a tray or baking sheet.
- Repeat with the remaining mixture; you should have about 12 meatballs.
- Heat a large pan, sprayed lightly with oil, over medium heat.
- Working in batches, arrange the meatballs in the pan without crowding and cook, gently rotating them from time to time, until browned on all sides.
- Ladle some of the tomato sauce into the pan.
- Remove meatballs and sauce from pan and repeat with the others; it will take two or three batches to complete all the meatballs.

Nutrition Facts

Calories per Serving: 390 cal Fat: 18g Protein: 40g Carbohydrates: 22g

706. BALSAMIC AND GARLIC CHICKEN THIGHS

Preparation 35 Minutes

Serves 6 Persons

Ingredients

- Chicken thighs (boneless) - 12 medium
- Olive oil - 1/4 cup
- Balsamic vinegar - 1/4 cup
- Garlic (minced) - 6 cloves
- Italian seasoning - 1 teaspoon
- Sea salt - 1 teaspoon
- Black pepper - ¼ teaspoon

Directions

- Take a large glass mixing bowl and add in the balsamic vinegar, olive oil, minced garlic, salt, pepper and Italian seasoning. Whisk well to combine.
- Add in the chicken and toss until the chicken thighs are well coated with the marinade.
- Place the marinated chicken in the refrigerator and let it sit for around 2 hours. Flip halfway to ensure the chicken retains the flavor well.
- Once the chicken is almost done marinating, preheat the oven by bringing the temperature up to 425 degrees Fahrenheit.
- Take a large baking sheet and line it with a parchment paper sheet.
- Place the chicken on the lined baking sheet. Make sure you arrange the chicken pieces in a single layer and leave some space between the pieces.
- .Place the baking sheet into the preheated oven and bake for around 20 minutes. Cook in batches if necessary.

Nutrition Facts

Calories per Serving: 364 cal Fat: 18g Protein: 43g Carbohydrates: 3g

707. SAUTEES CHICKEN WITH TEXAS SPICE RUB

Preparation 25 Minutes

Serves 4 Persons

Ingredients

- ½ teaspoon kosher salt
- ½ teaspoon chili powder
- ¼ teaspoon ground cumin
- ⅛ teaspoon freshly ground pepper
- 4 boneless skinless chicken breasts
- 2 teaspoons extra virgin olive oil
- Lime wedges

Directions

- Stir together the salt, chili powder, cumin, and pepper in a small bowl.
- Sprinkle the chicken with the spice mixture.
- Heat a large skillet over medium heat.
- Add the oil and tilt the pan to coat the bottom evenly.
- Add the chicken and cook, turning once, until the juices run clear, about 4 minutes on each side.
- Divide the chicken among 4 plates and serve at once with the lime wedges.

Nutrition Facts

Calories per Serving: 145 cal Fat: 5g Protein: 23g Carbohydrates: 1g

708. SPICY CACTUS TURKEY

Preparation 20 Minutes

Serves 2 Persons

Ingredients

- 3 (remove husks) fresh tomatillos
- 2 turkey breast halves, skinless, boneless
- 1 (16 oz.) jar canned nopales (cactus)
- 3 (seeded) fresh jalapeno peppers

Directions

- Add water into a pot over med-heat.
- Add turkey breasts into the boiling water and cook for about 10 minutes, until juices run clear and no pink remains.
- Drain water from turkey breasts and let sit until cooled.
- Shred cooled turkey breasts into thin strands. Add water into the pot and bring to boiling.
- Add cactus, jalapeno peppers and tomatillos into the boiling water and cook for about 5 minutes until veggies are softened.
- Drain water from veggies.
- Add jalapeno peppers and tomatillos into a high-speed electric blender and process until a smooth consistency is reached.
- Pour the jalapeno mixture into the shredded turkey pot and place over med- heat.
- Dice cactus and transfer into the pot with the shredded turkey.
- Simmer mixture for about 5 minutes, until heated through.

Nutrition Facts

Calories per Serving: 174 cal Fat: 3g Protein: 26g Carbohydrates: 12g

709. CHICKEN WITH GREEN CURRY SAUCE

Preparation 25 Minutes

Serves 4 Persons

Ingredients

- ¾ cup reduced-fat coconut milk
- 1 teaspoon green curry paste
- 1 teaspoon cornstarch
- 4 boneless skinless chicken breasts
- ½ teaspoon kosher salt
- 4 tbs chopped fresh cilantro, divided
- 4 teaspoons canola oil, divided
- 2 teaspoons minced fresh ginger
- ¼ cup thinly sliced scallions 1 tablespoon lime juice
- 2 teaspoons Asian fish sauce

Directions

- Whisk together the coconut milk, curry paste, and cornstarch in a small b owl until smooth. Set aside.
- Sprinkle the chicken with the salt, then with 2 tablespoons of the cilantr o, pressing to adhere.
- Heat a large skillet over medium heat.
- Add 2 teaspoons of the oil and tilt the pan to coat the bottom evenly.
- Add the chicken and cook, turning once, until the juices run clear, about 4 minutes on each side.
- Transfer to a plate and cover to keep warm.
- Increase the heat to medium-high.
- Add the remaining 2 teaspoons oil and tilt the pan to coat the bottom evenly.
- Add the ginger and cook, stirring constantly, until fragrant, 30 seconds.

- Add the coconut milk mixture and the scallions and bring to a boil.
- Cook, stirring constantly, until the sauce is slightly thickened, about
- 1 minute. Remove from the heat and stir in the remaining 2 tablespoons cilantro, the lime juice, and fish sauce.
- Add any accumulated juices from the chicken to the skil- let.
- Divide the chicken among 4 plates. Spoon the sauce evenly over the chicken and serve at once.

Nutrition Facts

Calories per Serving: 197 cal Fat: 10g Protein: 24g Carbohydrates: 4g

710. BRAISED CHICKEN WITH ORANGE

Preparation 45 Minutes

Serves 6 Persons

Ingredients

- 4 large oranges
- 2½ pounds bone- in chicken pieces, skinned
- 1½ teaspoons ground cumin, divided
- ½ teaspoon kosher salt, divided
- ¼ teaspoon freshly ground pepper
- 2 teaspoons extra virgin olive oil
- 1 small onion, thinly sliced
- 1 cup low-sodium chicken broth
- 1 tablespoon capers, rinsed and drained
- 3 tbs. chopped fresh Italian parsley

Directions

- Grate 1 tablespoon zest and squeeze 1 cup juice from the oranges and set aside.
- Sprinkle the chicken with 1 teaspoon of the cumin, ¼ teaspoon of the salt, and the pepper.
- Heat a large nonstick skillet over medium-high heat. Add the oil and tilt the pan to coat the bottom evenly.
- Add the chicken and cook, turning often, until well browned on all sides, about 8 minutes. Transfer to a plate.
- Add the onion to the skillet and cook, stirring often, until softened 5 minutes.
- Add the stock, capers, orange juice, the remaining ½ teaspoon cu min, and the remaining ¼ teaspoon salt and bring to a boil. Retur n the chicken to the skillet.
- Cover, reduce the heat to low, and simmer until the juices of the chicken run clear and the sauce is slightly thickened, about 30 minutes. Stir in the parsley. Divide the chicken evenly among 6 plates. Spoon the sauce evenly over the chicken and serve at once

Nutrition Facts

Calories per Serving: 150 cal Fat: 5g Protein: 21g Carbohydrates: 5g

711. BALSAMIC CHICJEN AND MUSHROOMS

Preparation 20 Minutes

Serves 4 Persons

Ingredients

- Chicken breasts (boneless) – 1 pound
- Olive oil – 1 tablespoon
- All-purpose flour – ¼ cup
- Margarine (without trans-fat) – 1 tbs.
- Button mushrooms (white) – 10 ounces
- Black pepper – ¼ teaspoon
- Balsamic vinegar – 1/3 cup
- Chicken broth (fat-free) – ½ cup

Directions

- Place the chicken breasts in the center of the plastic bag and use a mallet to pound them into a thin layer.
- Place the flour into a shallow dish and dredge the chicken breast in the same. Make sure both sides are evenly coated.
- .Place a nonstick pan over a medium-high flame. Pour in the olive oil and let it heat through.
- Add the chicken breasts to the pan and cook on each side for 5 minutes. Once done, transfer onto a platter lined with tissue papers.
- Wipe the pan clean and return the pan to the flame. Add the margarine and let it melt through.
- Toss the pepper and sliced mushrooms into the pan and sauté for around 5 minutes.
- Pour balsamic vinegar into the pepper and mushrooms. Boil until the liquid reduces.
- Pour in the chicken broth and let it simmer for about 2 minutes. Transfer the chicken breasts into the pan and cook for about 5 minutes.

Nutrition Facts

Calories per Serving: 240 cal Fat: 9g Protein: 27g Carbohydrates: 12g

712. LOW CARB TURKEY MEATLOAF

Preparation 60 Minutes

Serves 12 Persons

Ingredients

For the meatloaf:

- Turkey (ground) - 2 pounds
- Onion (finely chopped) - ½ large
- Garlic (minced) - 6 cloves
- Tomato sauce - 1/3 cup
- Italian seasoning - 2 teaspoon
- Sea salt - 1 ½ teaspoon
- Black pepper - ¼ teaspoon
- Almond Flour (blanched) - ½ cup
- Eggs - 2 large

For the toppings:

- Bacon - 10 slices
- Barbeque sauce (sugar-free) - ¼ cup

Directions

- Start by preheating the oven by setting the temperature to 350 degrees Fahrenheit. Prepare a baking sheet by lining it with a sheet of parchment paper.
- Take a large glass mixing bowl and add in the ground turkey, onion, garlic, tomato sauce, Italian seasoning, sea salt, pepper, blanched almond flour and eggs. Mix until well combined.
- Transfer the meatloaf mixture onto the prepared baking sheet and form a loaf-like shape measuring around 6X10 inches.
- Place the bacon slices on top of the meatloaf log by arranging them side by side. Ensure that the ends of the bacon slices are tucked under the meatloaf on both sides.
- Place the baking sheet into the oven and bake for around 30 minutes.
- Once the meatloaf is done baking, take the baking sheet out of the oven and top it with the barbeque sauce.
- 8.Return the baking sheet to the oven and let it cook for another 30 minutes.

- 9. Take the meatloaf out of the oven and let it rest for at least 10 min.
- 10. Transfer onto a serving platter and slice it into 12 equal portions with a serrated knife.

Nutrition Facts

Calories per Serving: 241 cal Fat: 17g Protein: 19g Carbohydrates: 4g

713. MARINATED CHICKEN

Preparation 25 Minutes

Serves 4 Persons

Ingredients

- ½ cup olive oil 2
- tablespoon fresh rosemary
- 1 teaspoon minced garlic Juice and zest of
- 1 lemon
- ¼ cup chopped fresh flat-leaf parsley
- Fine-grained kosher salt and freshly ground black pepper, to taste
- 4 boneless, skinless chicken breasts

Directions

- Mix all the ingredients except the chicken together in a plastic bag or bowl.
- Place the chicken in the container, and shake or stir so the marinade thoroughly coats the chicken. Refrigerate up to 24 hours.
- Heat a grill to medium heat and cook the chicken for 6 to 8 minutes a side.
- Turn only once during the cooking process.
- Serve with a Greek salad and brown rice.

Nutrition Facts

Calories per Serving: 386 cal Fat: 31g Protein: 25g Carbohydrates: 2g

714. OVEN FRIED CHICKEN LEGS

Preparation 85 Minutes

Serves 6 Persons

Ingredients

- 1 cup bread crumbs
- ¼ tsp. salt, or less 1 tsp. paprika
- 1 tsp. poultry seasoning
- ½ tsp. onion salt
- ¼ tsp. pepper 2 Tbsp. canola oil
- 12 chicken legs (thigh and drumstick), skin removed

Directions

- Mix bread crumbs, seasonings, and oil.
- Rinse chicken legs under running water and roll each leg in crumb mixture, shak- ing off excess.
- Place legs in two rows in greased 9×13-inch baking pan, alternating thick and thin side of legs.
- Bake at 350°F for 1 hour.
- Remove from oven and place in clean, hot casserole dish.
- Wrap well in newspaper for transporting to church.

Nutrition Facts

Calories per Serving: 240 cal Fat: 11g Protein: 27g Carbohydrates: 7g

715. OVEN BARBECUED CHICKEN

Preparation 80 Minutes

Serves 6 Persons

Ingredients

- 3 Tbsp. ketchup
- 2 Tbsp. Worcestershire sauce
- 2 Tbsp. vinegar
- 2 Tbsp. light soy sauce
- 3 Tbsp. brown sugar
- 1 tsp. spicy brown mustard
- 1 tsp. salt
- 1 tsp. pepper 12 boneless, skinless chicken thighs,
- 2 lbs. total

Directions

- In a mixing bowl, combine ketchup, Worcestershire sauce, vinegar soy sauce, brown sugar, mustard, salt, and pepper.
- Blend well.
- Lay chicken pieces in one layer in well-greased baking dish.
- Pour sauce over top.
- Bake at 350°F for 40 minutes.
- Turn pieces over.
- Bake 35 more minutes.

Nutrition Facts

Calories per Serving: 130 cal Fat: 6g Protein: 13g Carbohydrates: 1g

716. CHICKEN WITH FRESH HERBS

Makes 6 servings

Ingredients:

For Chicken

- 3 whole chicken breasts with bones and skin on, halved, 5 oz each half
- Salt and black pepper to taste
- 12 small sprigs oregano
- 12 basil leaves
- 12 sage leaves
- 12 thin slices fresh ginger
- 3 garlic cloves, cut into 4 slices each

For Sauce

- 1 clove garlic, minced
- 1 tsp minced fresh ginger
- 2 Tbsp butter
- 2 Tbsp olive oil
- 1 1/2 tsp Dijon mustard
- 1 Tbsp soy sauce (Kikkoman)
- 2 cups chicken stock, homemade or College Inn
- 1 tsp chopped oregano
- 1 tsp chopped basil
- 1 tsp chopped sage
- Salt and black pepper to taste

Directions:

- Wash and dry chicken breasts.
- Season with salt and pepper. Lift skin of each breast half along one edge and place 2 each of herbs, ginger, and garlic slices under skin.
- Cover with plastic wrap and refrigerate several hours. Bring to room temperature before cooking. Make Sauce Saute garlic and ginger in butter and oil briefly, until lightly browned.
- Add mustard, soy sauce, and chicken stock. Simmer until reduced by half.
- Add all other ingredients Taste and season with salt and pepper. To Finish Preheat oven to 375 F.
- Place chicken breasts in a nonstick baking pan and brush with sauce.
- Bake chicken for about 30 minutes, basting with sauce 2 or 3 times.
- Transfer breasts to warm platter, bring remaining sauce to a boil, and pour sauce over chicken.

Nutritional Info:

Carbohydrates: 1.7 g Protein: 5.2 oz

717. CHICKEN WITH MUSHROOMS IN A CHAMPAGNE CREAM SAUCE

Makes 2 servings

Ingredients:
- 2 boneless, skinless chicken breasts, 4 oz each
- Salt and black pepper to taste
- 2 Tbsp clarified butter (see Note)
- 1 tsp minced shallot
- 1/2 cup sliced mushrooms
- 1/4 cup champagne or dry sparkling wine
- 1/4 cup chicken stock, homemade or College Inn
- 2 oz heavy cream
- 1 Tbsp sliced and blanched almonds, toasted

Directions:
- Wash and dry chicken breasts.
- Pound briefly with a meat mallet to tenderize. Season with salt and pepper. Heat butter in skillet large enough to hold both breasts.
- Add chicken. Brown on one side, then turn over and brown the other side.
- Remove from pan and keep warm.
- Add shallots and mushrooms to skillet and saute until slightly browned.
- Deglaze pan with champagne, stirring to loosen pan drippings. Bring to a simmer, reduce slightly, then add chicken stock.
- Again, bring to a simmer, and reduce by half.
- Add heavy cream, stirring. Return to a simmer, reduce slightly to thicken.
- Season with salt and pepper. Pour sauce over chicken, top with toasted almonds, and serve.

Nutritional Info:
Carbohydrates: 2.78 g Protein: 4.43 oz

718. HOT ITALIAN CHICKEN

Ingredients:
- 6 boneless, skinless chicken breasts (about 3 lbs)
- 1 cup (150 g) grated Parmesan cheese
- (use the cheap stuff in the shaker for this)
- 2 tablespoons (8 g) dried parsley
- 1 tablespoon (3 g) dried oregano
- 2 teaspoons paprika
- 1 teaspoon salt
- 1/2 teaspoon pepper
- 1/2 cup (120 ml) extra-virgin olive oil
- 6 cloves garlic, minced
- 1 cup (240 ml) hot sauce

Directions:
- Cut your chicken breasts into finger-sized pieces. Set aside.
- Preheat oven to 350°F (180 °C).
- Combine cheese and spices in a bowl. Line a 9" (22.5 x 32.5 cm) baking pan with foil.
- Combine the olive oil and garlic in a bowl. Dip each chicken finger in the olive oil, roll in the cheese/seasoning mixture, and arrange on the foil-lined pan.
- Bake for 45 minutes.
- After removing from the oven, place the chicken fingers in shallow dish and pour hot sauce over chicken, thoroughly coating each piece.

719. TURKEY ROAST

Ingredients:
- 2 tablespoons (30 g) butter
- 1 small onion, diced
- 2 4-ounce (115 g) cans mushrooms, drained
- 1 cup (240 ml) heavy cream
- 2 teaspoons chicken bouillon concentrate
- 2 tablespoons (30 ml) dry sherry
- 1 teaspoon guar or xanthan (optional, but it makes the sauce thicker)
- 3/4 cup (120 g) grated Parmesan cheese
- 3 cups (675 g) cooked spaghetti squash, scraped into strings
- 3 cups (330 g) diced leftover turkey

Directions:
13. Over medium heat, melt butter in a heavy skillet, and start the onions and the mushrooms sauteing in it.
14. While that's cooking, combine the cream, bouillon concentrate, sherry, and guar, if you're using it, in a blender, and blend it for just ten seconds or so, to combine.
15. Go back and stir your veggies!
16. When the onion is limp and translucent, transfer half of the vegetables into the blender, add the Parmesan, and blend for another 20 seconds or so, to puree the vegetables.
17. Combine this cream sauce with the spaghetti squash, the rest of the vegetables and the turkey, and mix everything well.
18. Put in a 10-cup (2.4 L) casserole that you've sprayed with nonstick cooking spray.
19. Bake uncovered at 400 °F (200 °C) for 20 minutes, until bubbly.

720. TURKEY'N'EGGS

Ingredients:
- 1 pound (455 g) ground turkey
- 2 tablespoons (30 ml) olive oil
- 4 cloves garlic, crushed
- 2 teaspoons dried oregano
- 1/2 teaspoon ground cinnamon
- 1/2 teaspoon ground cloves
- 1 teaspoon pepper
- 2 tablespoons (30 ml) dry sherry
- 1 teaspoon Splenda
- 1 teaspoon salt or Vege-Sal
- 8 eggs
- 1 cup (240 g) canned diced tomatoes, drained
- 1/4 cup (40 g) minced onion

Directions:
- Start the turkey browning in the olive oil, crumbling it as you go.
- When it's mostly browned, add the garlic, oregano, cinnamon, cloves, and pepper.
- Cook it for 2 or 3 more minutes, then stir in the sherry, Splenda, and salt or Vege-Sal.
- Remove from the heat.
- Now scramble the eggs, and stir in the tomatoes and onion.
- Put the skillet back on the heat, pour the eggs over the turkey, and scramble till the eggs are set.

721. FRIED CHICKEN

Serves 4;

Ingredients:
- Nonstick cooking spray
- 10 ounces raw boneless skinless chicken breasts (fat trimmed off)
- 1/2 cup nonfat plain yogurt
- 1/2 cup bread crumbs
- 1 teaspoon garlic powder
- 1 teaspoon paprika
- 1/2 teaspoon dried thyme

Directions:

1. Preheat oven to 350°F. Prepare baking pan with nonstick cooking spray. Cut each
chicken breast into four equal pieces; marinate in yogurt for several minutes.
2. Mix together bread crumbs, garlic powder, paprika, and thyme; dredge chicken in crumb mixture.
3. Arrange on prepared pan; bake 20 minutes.
4. To give chicken a deep golden color, place pan under broiler last 5 minutes of cooking.
5. Watch closely to ensure chicken "crust" doesn't burn.

Nutritional Analysis: (per serving):
Calories: 118 Protein: 19g Carbohydrates: 5g Fat: 2g Saturated Fat: 1g Cholesterol: 44mg Sodium: 91mg Fiber: 0g

Buttermilk Ranch Chicken Salad

Serves 4; Serving Size: 1/2 recipe

Ingredients:
- 1 tablespoon real mayonnaise
- 3 tablespoons nonfat plain yogurt
- 1/2 cup nonfat cottage cheese
- 1/2 teaspoon cider vinegar
- 1 teaspoon brown sugar
- 1 teaspoon Dijon mustard
- 1/2 cup buttermilk
- 2 tablespoons dried parsley
- 1 clove garlic, minced
- 2 tablespoons grated Parmesan cheese
- 1/2 teaspoon sea salt (optional)
- 1/2 teaspoon freshly ground pepper (optional)
- 1 cup chopped cooked chicken breast
- 1/2 cup sliced cucumber
- 1/2 cup chopped celery
- 1/2 cup sliced carrots
- 4 cups salad greens
- 1/2 cup red onion slices
- Fresh parsley for garnish (optional)

Directions:
- In blender or food processor, combine mayonnaise, yogurt, cottage cheese, vinegar, brown sugar, mustard, buttermilk, parsley, garlic, cheese, salt, and pepper; process until smooth.
- Pour over the chicken, cucumber, celery, and carrots.
- Chill at least 2 hours.
- To serve, arrange 1 cup of salad greens on each of four serving plates.
- Top each salad with an equal amount of chicken salad.
- Garnish with red onion slices and fresh parsley if desired.

Nutritional Analysis: (per serving, without salt):
Calories: 147 Protein: 18g Carbohydrates: 11g Fat: 4g Saturated Fat: 1g Cholesterol: 33mg Sodium: 184mg Fiber: 2g

722. FREACH CHICKEN

Servings: 4

Ingredients:
- 2 pounds boneless chicken breasts
- 4 ounces fat-free French dressing
- 1/2 cup sugar-free apricot preserves
- 1 small envelope of onion soup mix

Directions
- Preheat the oven at 350 degrees F.
- Wash the chicken and cut into 2" pieces, and place the pieces in a small casserole dish.
- Mix the remaining ingredients and pour 1/2 of the sauce over the chicken.
- Cover and bake for 45 minutes.
- Stir in the remaining sauce and bake uncovered another 20 minutes,

Nutritional Facts (Per Servimg)
Calories: 151.0 Total Fat: 1.0 g Cholesterol: 65.0 mg

723. POULTRY TASTE-OF SUMMER CHICKEN

Servings: 6

Ingredients:
- 3/4 cup Italian fat-free salad dressing
- 3/4 cup unsweetened pineapple juice
- 3/4 cup white wine or white grape juice
- 6 boneless skinless chicken breast halves (1 1/2 pounds)

Directions
- In a large reusable plastic bag, combine the salad dressing, pineapple juice and wine or grape juice.
- Add the chicken.
- Seal bag and turn to coat; refrigerate for 8 hours or overnight.
- Drain and discard marinade.
- Grill chicken, covered, over medium heat for 6-7 minutes on each side or until juices run clear.

Nutritional Facts (Per Serving)
Calories: 140 Fat: 3 g (1 g sat) Cholesterol: 63 mg Sodium: 151 mg

724. POULTRY SKINLESS ROAST CHICKEN WITH HERBS AND SPICES

Ingredients:
- 1 whole roasting chicken, without skin
- 2 medium garlic cloves, smashed
- 1 medium shallots
- 1 pinch fresh rosemary (1 sprig)
- 1 oz parsley sprigs, 1/2 bunch
- 1 tsp ground cayenne (red pepper)

Directions
- Remove the skin from the chicken.
- Stuff the chicken with the aromatics and rub the outside of the bird with the safflower oil.
- Tuck the legs of the chicken underneath and place on a roasting rack.
- Season liberally with salt (optional) and pepper,
- cayenne, and paprika.
- Roast in a 500 degree F oven for 15 minutes.
- Turn the oven down to 350 degrees F and cook until the juices run away from the bird clear, approx 35 minutes.
- Let the bird rest and collect its juices.

221

- The chicken will have a nice rust color and be packed with flavor.

Nutritional Facts

Calories 210.6 Total Carbs 2.5g Dietary Fiber 0.9g Sugars 0.6g

725. PEPPER-LIME CHICKEN

Serving: 4

Ingredients:

- 2 1/2 lbs, Chicken breast halves (with bones)
- 1/2 teaspoon finely shredded lime peel
- 1/4 cup lime juice
- 1 Tablespoon extra-virgin olive oil
- 2 cloves garlic, minced
- 1 Tablespoon chopped fresh basil or thyme
- or 1 teaspoon dried basil or thyme, crushed
- 1/2 to 1 teaspoon cracked black pepper
- 1/4 teaspoon salt

Directions

20. If desired, skin chicken.
21. Preheat broiler.
22. Place chicken pieces, bone side up, on the unheated rack of a broiler pan.
23. Broil 4 to 5 inches from heat about 20 minutes or until lightly browned.
24. Meanwhile for glaze, in a bowl stir together lime peel, lime juice, oil, garlic, basilic, pepper and Kosher salt.
25. Bush chicken generously with glaze. Turn chicken; brush generously with glaze.
26. Discard any remaining glaze. Broil for 5 to 15 minutes more or until chicken is no longer pink.(170 degrees)

Nutritional Facts (Per Serving)

Calories: 120 Fat: 4 g (1 g Sat.) Cholesterol: 51 mg

726. TURKEY BURGER

Serving: 4

Ingredients:

- 10 oz ground turkey
- 1 oz silken tofu (2 tablespoons)
- 1/2 tsp ground cumin
- 1/4 tsp garlic powder
- 1 tsp canola oil (in spray bottle)
- 1/2 medium avocadoes , 6 slices
- 2 tbsp fat free sour cream
- 4 Lettuce, green leaf, fresh, outer leaf , about the size of a burger

Directions

- Preheat oven to 350 degrees F.
- Combine the ground turkey, tofu, cumin, and garlic in a bowl and mix well.
- Form into two patties.
- Heat a medium non-stick skillet over medium heat. Mist both sides of each burger with canola oil spray. Cook in the skillet 3-1/2 minutes.
- Transfer to a pre-heated 350 degree F oven and bake five minutes or until cooked through.
- Let stand five minutes to cool slightly. Place each burger on a piece of leaf lettuce.
- Top each burger with three slices of avocado, a tablespoon of sour cream and the remaining slices of leaf lettuce.

Nutritional Facts

Calories 355.9 Total Carbs 8.4g Dietary Fiber 2.1g Sugars 1.5g

727. CURRY CHICKEN

Servings: 2

Ingredients:

- 1/2 teaspoon mustard seeds, crushed
- 1/4 teaspoon cumin seeds, crushed
- 1 cup canned diced tomato, drained
- 1 tablespoon vegetable oil
- 1/4 teaspoon ground turmeric
- 1/4 teaspoon ground red chili
- 1/4 teaspoon salt
- 1 pound (about 1 3/4 cups) cubed cooked chicken breast
- 3/4 cup light coconut milk

Directions

- Heat a large skillet over medium heat.
- Add the mustard and cumin seeds.
- Cook 2 minutes or until seeds are fragrant, stirring frequently.
- Combine the tomato and oil in a small bowl; add to the seeds.
- Cook 1 minute, stirring constantly. Stir in the turmeric, red chili, and salt.
- Cook, stirring, for another minute.
- Add chicken and cook for 1 minute.
- Stir in coconut milk and cover.
- Simmer over low heat 10 minutes or until chicken is cooked through.
- Serve hot, spooned over warm basmati rice.

Nutritional Facts

Calories: 219 Fat: 12g Cholesterol: 71mg Total Fat 23.7g Saturated Fat 5.3g Unsaturated Fat 18.4g

728. BLACK PEPPER CITRUS CHICKEN

Yield: 4 servings

Ingredients:

- 1 tablespoon canola oil, divided
- 1 1/4 teaspoons freshly ground black pepper, divided
- 1/4 teaspoon salt
- 4 (6-ounce) skinless, boneless chicken breast halves
- 1 cup vertically sliced onion

Directions

- Heat 1 teaspoon oil in a large nonstick skillet over medium-high heat.
- Sprinkle 1/2 teaspoon pepper and salt over chicken.
- Add chicken to pan; cook 2 minutes on each side or until browned.
- Remove chicken from pan; keep warm. Add remaining
- 2 teaspoons oil to pan.
- Add onion and garlic to pan; sauté 2 minutes.
- Add wine; cook 1 minute.
- Return chicken to pan.
- Add remaining 3/4 teaspoon pepper and juices.
- Cover, reduce heat, and simmer 4 minutes or until chicken is done.
- Sprinkle with parsley.

Nutritional Facts

Calories 240(22% from fat) Fat 5.9g (sat 0.8g,mono 2.6g,poly 1.5g) Protein 39.6g Cholesterol 99mg

729. LEMON SAGE TURKEY

Servings: 2

Ingredients:
- 3 tbsp grated lemon rind
- 1/4 cup fresh lemon juice
- 3 tbsp ground thyme
- 2 tbsp sage, ground (or rubbed sage)
- 1 tbsp black pepper, cracked

Directions
- Preheat oven to 350 degrees F.
- Whisk together lemon rind and juice, thyme, sage, pepper, and salt.
- Reserve. Take out giblets and neck from turkey, save for another use or discard.
- Wash and dry turkey. Cut off any extra fat from surface of turkey.
- Beginning at the neck, insert fingers between skin and meat and gently separate.
- Tuck wing tips under turkey. Massage the lemon mixture under the skin of the turkey and on the surface.
- Add 1 can of broth to the bottom of a roasting pan.
- Arrange turkey, breast side up on a cooking spray coated rack. Move rack to roasting pan and place a meat thermometer into the thickest part of the thigh, being sure not to touch bone.
- Cook for 1 1/2 hours.
- Add another can of broth into the pan and cook another 1 1/2 hours, the meat thermometer should read 180 degrees F.
- Take turkey out of oven, cover with foil, and let rest 15 to 20 minutes. Take off skin before serving.

Nutritional Facts
Calories 265.1 Total Carbs 2g Dietary Fiber 0.7g Sugars 0.5g Total Fat 24.3g

730. ASIAN GRILLED CHICKEN BREASTS

Servings: 1 breast

Ingredients:
- 1/4 cup olive oil
- 1 tablespoon soy sauce
- 2 cloves garlic, crushed
- 1 tablespoon minced ginger
- 1 tablespoon Dijon mustard
- salt to taste
- freshly ground black pepper
- 6 skinless, boneless chicken breasts

Directions
- Mix the oil, soy sauce, garlic, ginger, mustard, salt and pepper, and brush on the chicken breasts.
- Refrigerate for at least 30 minutes or overnight.
- Preheat the grill.
- Grill the breasts for 5 to 6 minutes on each side, depending on the thickness.
- Let the chicken rest on a plate for 1 or 2 minutes before serving.

Nutritional Facts
Calories 166 Carbohydrate 0 g Fat 6 g

731. BEER CHICKEN

Yield: 8 servings

Ingredients:
- 1 chicken, 4 to 6 pounds (1 3/4 to 2314 kg)
- 3 tablespoons (12 g) Cajun seasoning
- 12 ounces (355 ml) beer
- 3 cloves garlic

Directions:
- Remove and discard the fat from inside the body cavities of the chicken.
- Remove the package of giblets and set aside for another use.
- Rinse the chicken, inside and out, under cold running water; then drain and blot dry, inside and out, with paper towels.
- Sprinkle 1 tablespoon (4 g) of the seasoning inside the body and neck cavities; then rub the rest allover the skin of the bird.
- If you wish, rub another 112-tablespoon of the seasoning between the flesh and the skin. Cover and refrigerate the chicken while you preheat the grill.
- Pop the tab on the beer can.
- Using a "church key" type of can opener, punch six or seven holes in the top of the can.
- Pour out the top inch (2 112 cm) of beer; drop the peeled garlic cloves into the holes in the can.
- Holding the chicken upright (wings at top, legs at bottom), with the opening of the body cavity down, insert the beer can into the lower cavity.
- Oil the grill grate. Stand the chicken up in the center of the hot grate, over the drip pan.
- Spread out the legs to form a sort of tripod to support the bird.
- Cover the grill and cook the chicken until fall-off-the-bone tender, about an hour, depending on size.
- Use a thermometer to check for doneness. The internal temperature should be 180°F (82°C).
- Using tongs, lift the bird to a cutting board or platter, holding a metal spatula underneath the beer can for support.

Nutritional Analysis:
25 g water; 81 calories (66% from fat, 32% from protein, 2% from carb); 6 g protein; 6 g total fat; 2 g saturated fat; 2 g

732. INJECTOR CHICKEN BREASTS

Yield: 4 servings

Ingredients:
- 1/4 cup (60 ml) low-sodium chicken broth
- 1 teaspoon Worcestershire sauce
- 1 tablespoon (15 ml) lemon juice
- 4 chicken breasts

Directions:
- Mix together broth, Worcestershire sauce, and lemon juice.
- Inject into chicken breasts.
- Grill over medium heat until done, about 15 minutes.

Nutritional Analysis:
71 g water; 81 calories (10% from fat, 87% from protein, 3% from carb); 17 g

733. CHICKEN KABOBS

Yield: 4 servings

Ingredients:
- 18 ounces (510 g) pineapple chunks
- 1 teaspoon cumin
- 1 teaspoon coriander
- I/S teaspoon garlic powder
- (continued on page 162)
- Main Dishes: Chicken and Turkey 161

- 1 tablespoon (7 g) chili powder
- 1 teaspoon cilantro
- 2 tablespoons (30 g) plain yogurt
- 10 ounces (280 g) boneless skinless chicken breasts
- 1 red bell pepper
- 1 onion
- 8 cherry tomatoes

Directions:
- Drain pineapple, reserving juice.
- In a large bowl blend together spices and yogurt.
- Add juice from pineapple and stir to mix.
- Cut the chicken into cubes and add to the mixture. Cover and refrigerate for 1 to 2 hours.
- Cut pepper and onion into cubes.
- Arrange chicken,
- pineapple, and vegetables on skewers.
- Grill over medium heat about 10 minutes, turning and basting with remaining marinade frequently.

Nutritional Analysis:
230 g water; 201 calories (15% from fat, 47% from protein, 38% from carb); 24 g protein; 3 g total fat; 1 g

734. SPANISH CHICKEN KABOBS
Yield: 6 servings
Ingredients:
- 1/3 cup (80 ml) lime juice
- 1 tablespoon (15 ml) vegetable oil
- 1 tablespoon (21 g) honey
- 6 boneless skinless chicken breasts
- 1 2 pearl onions, peeled
- 1 green bell pepper, seeded, and cut into 2-inch (5 cm) pieces
- 162 500 Low-Glycemic-Index Recipes
- 1 papaya, peeled, seeded, and cut into 2-inch (5 cm) pieces
- 11/2 cups (250 g) fresh pineapple chunks

Directions:
- Combine lime juice, vegetable oil, and honey in a shallow dish.
- Add chicken; toss gently.
- Cover and marinate in refrigerator 8 hours or overnight, stirring occasionally.
- Remove chicken from marinade.
- Alternate chicken, onion, pepper, papaya, and pineapple on 6 skewers.
- Coat grill rack with nonstick vegetable oil spray.
- Grill kabobs over medium-hot coals 15-20 minutes or until chicken is cooked through and vegetables are crisp-tender.

Yield: 6 servings
Nutritional Analysis: 264 g water; 161 calories (1g% from fat, 44% from protein, 38% from carb); 18 g Protein; 3 g total fat; 1 g

735. CHICKEN FINGERS
Yield: 5 servings
Ingredients:
- 1/3 cup (10 g) cornflake crumbs
- 1/2 cup (55 g) pecans, finely chopped
- 1 tablespoon (1.3 g) parsley flakes
- 1/8 teaspoon garlic powder
- 12 ounces (340 g) boneless skinless chicken breast halves, cut into 1 x 3-inch (21/2 x 7 1/2 cm) strips
- 2 tablespoons (30 ml) skim milk

Directions:
- In a shallow dish, combine cornflake crumbs, pecans, parsley, and garlic powder.
- Dip chicken in milk and then roll in crumb mixture.
- Place in a 15 x 10 x 1-inch (38 x 25 x 21/2 cm) baking pan.
- Bake in a 400°F (200°C, or gas mark 6). oven for 7-g minutes or until chicken is tender and no longer pink.

Nutritional Analysis:
47 g water; 213 calories (47% from fat, 46% from protein, 7% from carb); 24 g Protein; 11 g total fat; 2 g

736. JALAPENO AND BACON CHICKEN BREASTS
Servings: 6
Ingredients:
- 6 chicken breast halves, skinned
- 1 tablespoon chili powder
- salt
- 1/2 cup reduced-sodium chicken broth
- 2 tablespoons lemon juice

Directions
- Sprinkle chicken with chili powder and a little salt. Arrange chicken, bone-side down, in a 4-1/2 to 6-quart slow cooker.
- Pour chicken broth and lemon juice around chicken in cooker.
- Top with jalapeno pepper slices.
- Cover and cook on low-heat setting for 5 to 6 hours or on high-heat setting for 2-1/2 to 3 hours.
- Transfer chicken and jalapeno peppers to a serving platter, reserving cooking liquid.
- Cover chicken with foil to keep warm.
- If using low-heat setting, turn to high heat setting.
- For sauce, in a small bowl combine cornstarch and water; stir into liquid in cooker.
- Add cream cheese; whisking until combined.
- Cover and cook about 15 minutes more or until thickened.
- If desired, sprinkle chicken with bacon.

Nutritional Facts
Calories 329 Total Fat (6 g sat. fat, 11g total fat)
Cholesterol 143mg Sodium 489mg Carbohydrates 5g
Protein 49g Exchanges 7 very lean meat, 2 Fat

737. GRILLED CHICKEN SALAD
Serving: 2
Ingredients:
- 1–2 lbs boneless, skinless chicken breast
- Season salt
- Worcestershire Sauce
- Romaine lettuce
- Spinach
- Carrots
- Cucumbers
- Green onion
- Tomatoes
- Avocado

Directions

- Grill chicken over medium flame, brushing with Worcestershire and sprinkling lightly with season salt.
- When cooked thoroughly, cut into strips and set aside.
- Cut lettuce, spinach, carrots, cucumbers, tomatoes, onion, and avocados.
- Toss everything together.
- Top with strips of grilled chicken and drizzle with your favorite low-fat dressing.

Nutritional Facts
(without dressing):
Calories 206 Fat 2g Cholesterol 70mg Sodium 478mg Carbohydrates 10g Protein 27g Servings: 4

738. GREEK CHICKEN

Servings:6
Ingredients:
- 3 pounds (1.4 kg) cut-up chicken
- 2 tablespoons (30 g) butter
- 2 tablespoons (30 ml) olive oil
- 1 cup (160 g) chopped onion
- 1 cup (240 g) canned diced tomatoes
- 4 tablespoons (55 g) tomato paste
- 1/4 cup (60 ml) dry red wine
- 1 clove garlic, crushed
- 1/4 teaspoon ground allspice
- 1/2 teaspoon ground cinnamon
- 1/4 cup (60 ml) chicken broth

Directions:
- In your big, heavy skillet, brown the chicken all over in the butter and olive oil.
- When it's golden all over, remove from the pan and pour off all but about 1 tablespoon of the fat.
- In that fat, saute the onion a bit.
- When it's golden, add the tomatoes, tomato paste, wine, garlic, spices, and chicken broth.
- Stir it all together, and bring to a simmer.
- Add the chicken back to the skillet, turn the burner to lowest heat, cover, and cook for 30 minutes.
- Uncover and simmer for another 30 minutes, then serve.

739. LEMON MUSTARD HERB CHICKEN

Servings:6
Ingredients:
- 1/3 cup (80 ml) lemon juice
- 1/3 cup (80 g) spicy brown mustard
- 1 tablespoon (4 g) rubbed sage
- 1 1/2 teaspoons dried thyme
- 3 cloves garlic, crushed
- 24 ounces (680 g) boneless, skinless chicken breast
- 3 scallions

Directions:
- Mix together the lemon juice, mustard, sage, thyme and garlic.
- Put your chicken breast on a plate, and spread this mixture over both sides.
- Let it sit for ten minutes, and a little more won't hurt.
- Heat up your electric tabletop grill, and throw the chicken breast in.
- Set your oven timer for 5 minutes.
- If there's some of the lemon-mustard mixture still on the plate, use it to baste the chicken halfway through the cooking time.
- Slice up the scallions, including the crisp part of the green.
- When the timer goes off, put the chicken on a serving plate, scatter the scallions over it, and serve.

740. PINEAPPLE-ORANGE GRILLED CHICKEN BREASTS

Serves 4; Serving Size: 1/2 recipe
Ingredients:
- 6 ounces pineapple juice
- 4 ounces orange juice
- 1/2 cup cider vinegar
- 1 tablespoon chopped fresh tarragon
- 1/2 tablespoon fresh rosemary
- 1 pound boneless skinless chicken breast, cut into 4 pieces

Directions:
1. Mix pineapple juice, orange juice, vinegar, tarragon, and rosemary in large shallow dish.
2. Add raw chicken breasts to marinade; cover and refrigerate 3–4 hours. Turn pieces of chicken to cover with marinade.
3. Heat grill to medium-high; place chicken on grill. Grill approximately 7–10 minutes on each side until chicken is cooked through.

Nutritional Analysis: (per serving):
Calories: 165 Protein: 27g
Carbohydrates: 10g Fat: 2g
Saturated Fat: 0g Cholesterol: 58mg
Sodium: 75mg

741. HERBED CHICKEN AND BROWN RICE DINNER

Serves 4; Serving Size: 1/2 recipe
Ingredients:
- 1 tablespoon canola oil
- 4 (4-ounce) boneless skinless chicken breast pieces
- 1/2 teaspoon garlic powder, divided
- 1/2 teaspoon dried rosemary, divided
- 1 (10 1/2 -ounce) can low-fat reduced-sodium chicken broth
- 1/2 cup water
- 2 cups uncooked instant brown rice

Directions:
- Heat oil in large nonstick skillet on medium-high heat.
- Add chicken; sprinkle with half the garlic powder and rosemary.
- Cover and cook 4 minutes on each side or until cooked through.
- Remove chicken from skillet and set aside.
- Add broth and water to skillet; stir to deglaze pan and bring to a boil.
- Stir in rice and remaining garlic powder and rosemary.
- Top with chicken and cover; cook on low heat 5 minutes.
- Remove from heat and let stand covered 5 minutes.

Nutritional Analysis: (per serving):
Calories: 300 Protein: 33g
Carbohydrates: 26g Fat: 6g Saturated Fat: 1g Cholesterol: 75mgSodium: 112mg Fiber: 0g

742. WALNUT CHICKEN

Serves 4; Serving Size: 1/2 recipe

Ingredients:

- 1/2 pound (12 ounces) boneless skinless chicken breast
- 1 teaspoon sherry
- 1 egg white
- 2 teaspoons peanut oil
- 2 drops toasted sesame oil (optional)
- 1/2 cup ground walnuts
- Nonstick cooking spray

Directions:

1. Preheat oven to 350°F. Cut chicken into bite-sized pieces; sprinkle with sherry and set aside.
2. In a small bowl, beat egg white and oils until frothy. Fold chicken pieces into egg mixture; roll individually in walnuts.
3. Arrange chicken pieces on baking sheet treated with nonstick cooking spray. Bake 10–15 minutes or until walnuts are lightly browned and chicken juices run clear.

utritional Analysis: (per serving):

Calories: 159 Protein: 18g Carbohydrates: 1g Fat: 9g Saturated Fat: 1g Cholesterol: 44mg Sodium: 51mg

743. CHICKEN AND MUSHROOM RICE CASSEROLE

Serves 8; Serving Size: 1/2 recipe

Ingredients:

- Nonstick cooking spray
- 1 recipe Condensed Cream of Chicken Soup (see recipe in Chapter 4)
- 1 cup diced chicken breast
- 1 large onion, chopped
- 1/2 cup chopped celery
- 1 cup uncooked rice (not instant rice)
- Freshly ground black pepper to taste (optional)
- 1 teaspoon dried herbes de Provence (optional)
- 2 cups boiling water
- 2 1/2 cups chopped broccoli florets
- 1 cup sliced fresh mushrooms

Directions:

Preheat oven to 350°F.

- In 4-quart casserole dish treated with nonstick spray, combine condensed soup, chicken breast, onion, celery, rice, and seasonings; mix well.
- Pour boiling water over top; bake covered for 30 minutes.
- Stir casserole; add broccoli and mushrooms.
- Replace cover; return to oven to bake additional 20–30 minutes or until celery is tender and rice has absorbed all liquid.

Nutritional Analysis: (per serving):

Calories: 165 Protein: 9g Carbohydrates: 30g Fat: 1g saturated Fat: 0g Cholesterol: 15mg Sodium: 41mg

744. EASY CHICKEN PAPRIKASH

Serves 4; Serving Size: 1/2 recipe

Ingredients:

- 1 recipe Condensed Cream of Chicken Soup (see recipe in Chapter 4)
- 1/2 cup skim milk
- 2 teaspoons paprika
- 1/2 teaspoon ground cayenne pepper (optional)
- 1/2 pound (4 ounces) chopped cooked boneless skinless chicken
- 1 1/2 cups sliced steamed mushrooms
- 1/2 cup diced steamed onion
- 1/2 cup nonfat plain yogurt
- 4 cups cooked medium-sized egg noodles

Directions:

1. In saucepan, combine soup, skim milk, paprika, and pepper (if using); whisk until well mixed. Bring to a boil over medium heat, stirring occasionally.
2. Reduce heat to low and stir in chicken, mushrooms, and onion; cook until chicken and vegetables are heated through, about 10 minutes. Stir in yogurt.
3. To serve, put 1 cup of warm, cooked noodles on each of four plates. Top each portion with an equal amount of chicken mixture. Garnish by sprinkling with additional paprika if desired.

Nutritional Analysis:

Calories: 376 Protein: 22g Carbohydrates: 58g Fat: 6g Saturated Fat: 2g Cholesterol: 78mg Sodium: 135mg Fiber: 4g

745. CHICKEN AND BROCCOLI CASSEROLE

Serves 4; Serving Size: 1/2 recipe

Ingredients:

- Nonstick cooking spray
- 2 cups broccoli florets
- 1/2 pound (8 ounces) chopped cooked chicken
- 1/2 cup skim milk
- 1/2 cup (2 tablespoons) real mayonnaise
- 1/2 teaspoon curry powder
- 1 recipe Condensed Cream of Chicken Soup (see recipe in Chapter 4)
- 1 tablespoon lemon juice
- 1/2 cup (2 ounces) grated Cheddar cheese
- 1/2 cup bread crumbs
- 1 teaspoon melted butter
- 1 teaspoon olive oil

Directions:

1. Preheat oven to 350°F. Treat 11" × 7" casserole dish with nonstick spray.
2. Steam broccoli until tender; drain.
3. Spread out chicken on bottom of dish; cover with steamed broccoli.
4. In medium bowl, combine milk, mayonnaise, curry powder, soup, and lemon juice; pour over broccoli.
5. In small bowl, mix together cheese, bread crumbs, butter, and oil; sprinkle over top of casserole. Bake 30 minutes.

Nutritional Analysis: (per serving):

Calories: 328 Protein: 26g Carbohydrates: 20g Fat: 17g Saturated Fat: 6g Cholesterol: 67mg Sodium: 254mg Fiber: 3g

746. CHICKEN AND GREEN BEAN STOVETOP CASSEROLE

Serves 4; Serving Size: 1/2 recipe

Ingredients:

- 1 recipe Condensed Cream of Chicken Soup (see recipe in Chapter 4)
- 1/2 cup skim milk
- 2 teaspoons Homemade Worcestershire Sauce (see recipe in Chapter 6)
- 1 teaspoon real mayonnaise
- 1/2 teaspoon onion powder
- 1/2 teaspoon garlic powder

- 1/2 teaspoon ground black pepper
- 1 (4-ounce) can sliced water chestnuts, drained
- 2 1/2 cups frozen thawed green beans
- 1 cup sliced mushrooms, steamed
- 1/2 pound (8 ounces) cooked chopped chicken
- 1 1/2 cups cooked brown long-grain rice

Directions:
1. Combine soup, milk, Worcestershire, mayonnaise, onion powder, garlic powder, and pepper in a saucepan; bring to a boil.
2. Reduce heat; add water chestnuts, green beans, mushrooms, and chicken. Simmer until vegetables and chicken are heated through, about 10 minutes. Serve over rice.

Nutritional Analysis: (per serving):
Calories: 305 Protein: 23g Carbohydrates: 36g Fat: 8g Saturated Fat: 2g Cholesterol: 48mg Sodium: 101mg Fiber: 6g

747. CHICKEN PASTA WITH HERB SAUCE

Serves 4; Serving Size: 1/2 recipe
Ingredients:
- 1 recipe Condensed Cream of Chicken Soup (see recipe in Chapter 4)
- 1/2 cup skim milk
- 1/2 teaspoon Homemade Worcestershire Sauce (see recipe in Chapter 6)
- 1 teaspoon real mayonnaise
- 1/2 cup grated Parmesan cheese
- 1/2 teaspoon chili powder
- 1/2 teaspoon garlic powder
- 1/2 teaspoon dried rosemary
- 1/2 teaspoon dried thyme
- 1/2 teaspoon dried marjoram
- 1 cup sliced mushrooms, steamed
- 1/2 pound (8 ounces) chopped cooked chicken
- 4 cups cooked pasta
- Freshly ground black pepper (optional)

Directions:
1. Combine soup, milk, Worcestershire, mayonnaise, and cheese in saucepan; bring to a boil.
2. Reduce heat and add chili powder, garlic powder, rosemary, thyme, and marjoram; stir well.
3. Add mushrooms and chicken; simmer for 10 minutes until heated through.
4. Serve over pasta and top with freshly ground pepper if desired.

Nutritional Analysis: (per serving):
Calories: 393 Protein: 26g Carbohydrates: 52g Fat: 8g Saturated Fat: 2g Cholesterol: 48mg Sodium: 71mg

748. CHICKEN AND ASPARAGUS IN WHITE WINE SAUCE

Serves 4; Serving Size: 1/2 recipe
Ingredients:
- 1/2 tablespoon butter
- 1 tablespoon olive oil
- 1 teaspoon finely chopped garlic
- 1/2 cup finely chopped onion
- 4 boneless skinless chicken breast halves, pounded to 1/2" thickness
- 10 ounces asparagus spears, cut diagonally in 2" pieces
- 1/2 pound mushrooms
- 1/2 cup dry white wine
- 1/2 cup water
- 1 tablespoon chopped fresh parsley
- Salt and pepper to taste

Directions:
1. Melt butter and olive oil in a large skillet over medium heat. Add chopped garlic and onions; sauté 1–2 minutes.
2. Add chicken; cook 5 minutes or until the chicken is brown on both sides. Remove chicken and set aside.
3. Add asparagus and mushrooms to skillet; cook 2–3 minutes.
4. Return chicken to skillet; add white wine and water. Bring to a quick boil; boil 2 minutes to reduce the liquid.
5. Reduce heat; cover and simmer 3 minutes or until chicken and vegetables are tender.
6. Add chopped parsley, season with salt and pepper to taste, and serve.

Nutritional Analysis: (per serving):
Calories: 186 Protein: 21g Carbohydrates: 7g Fat: 8g Saturated Fat: 2g Cholesterol: 51mg Sodium: 57mg

749. CHICKEN KALAMATA

Serves 4; Serving Size: 1/2 recipe
Ingredients:
- 2 tablespoons olive oil
- 1 cup chopped onion
- 1 teaspoon minced garlic
- 1 1/2 cups chopped green peppers
- 1 pound boneless skinless chicken breast, cut into 4 pieces
- 2 cups diced tomatoes
- 1 teaspoon dried oregano
- 1/2 cup pitted chopped kalamata olives

Directions:
1. Heat olive oil over medium heat in large skillet. Add onions, garlic, and peppers; sauté for about 5 minutes until onions are translucent.
2. Add chicken pieces; cook for about 5 minutes each side until lightly brown.
3. Add tomatoes and oregano. Reduce heat and simmer 20 minutes.
4. Add olives; simmer an additional 10 minutes before serving.

Nutritional Analysis: (per serving):
Calories: 311 Protein: 31g Carbohydrates: 25g Fat: 11g Saturated Fat: 2g Cholesterol: 66mg Sodium: 787mg

750. ROTISSERIE CHICKEN

Yield: 8 servings
Ingredients:
- 1 teaspoon paprika
- 1 teaspoon onion powder
- 1/2 teaspoon black pepper
- 1/2 teaspoon thyme
- 1/4 teaspoon garlic powder
- 1/4 cup (85 g) honey
- 1 large roasting chicken (6 to 7 pounds or 23/4 to 3 kg)

Directions:
- Mix spices into honey.
- Brush onto chicken.
- Roast at 325°F (170°C, gas mark 3) until done, basting occasionally with pan juices.

Nutritional Analysis:

16 9 water; 71 calories (18% from fat, 30% from protein, 51% from carb); 5 g protein; 1 g total fat; 0 g

751. GRILLED ROASTING CHICKEN

Yield: 12 servings

Ingredients:

- 1 large roasting chicken, 5 to 6 pounds (2 to 23/4 kg)
- 2 tablespoons (30 ml) olive oil
- 1 teaspoon paprika
- 1 teaspoon onion powder
- 1/2 teaspoon black pepper
- 1/2 teaspoon thyme
- 1/4 teaspoon garlic powder
- 1 teaspoon liquid smoke

Directions:

- Split chicken in half along the backbone and breastbone.
- Mix together remaining ingredients and rub into both sides of chicken halves.
- Grill over indirect heat, turning occasionally, until done. (2 hours)
- Place over low heat for the last 15 minutes to brown skin.

Nutritional Analysis:

0 g water; 28g calories (6g% from fat, 30% from protein, 1% from carb); 22 g protein; 22 g total fat; 6 g saturated fat; g g monounsaturated fat; 4 g polyunsaturated fat; 1 g carb; 0 g fiber; 0 g sugar; 2 mg

752. OVEN BARBECUED CHICKEN

Yield: 4 servings

Ingredients:

- 1 whole chicken, cut into pieces
- 1/4 cup (60 ml) water
- 1/4 cup (60 ml) vinegar
- 3 tablespoons (45 ml) vegetable oil
- 1/2 cup (140 g) chili sauce, see recipe in chapter 2
- 3 tablespoons (45 ml) Worcestershire sauce
- 1 teaspoon dry mustard
- 1/2 teaspoon pepper
- 2 tablespoons (20 g) onion, chopped

Directions:

- Preheat oven to 350°F (180°C, or gas mark 4).
- Combine all ingredients except chicken in saucepan, place over heat, and simmer for 5-10 minutes.
- Place chicken in a large baking pan.
- Pour half of the barbecue sauce over chicken and bake, uncovered, for about 45-60 minutes.
- Baste with remaining barbecue sauce every 15 minutes during cooking.

Nutritional Analysis: 101 g water; 177 calories (62% from fat, 26% from protein, 12% from carb); 11 g Protein; 12 g

753. OVEN FRIED CHICKEN

Yield: 6 servings

Ingredients:

- 2 pounds (g00 g) boneless skinless chicken breast
- 3/4 cup (175 ml) olive oil
- 3 tablespoons (33 g) Dijon mustard
- 1/4 teaspoon black pepper
- 1/2 teaspoon paprika
- 1 cup (110 g) pecan, ground
- 1/2 cup (70 g) yellow cornmeal

Directions:

- Preheat the oven to 400°F (200°C, or gas mark 6).
- Pound the chicken breast halves to an even thickness.
- Pour 112 cup (120 ml) of the oil into a g x13-inch (23 x 33 cm) baking dish, and heat it in the hot oven for 10 minutes.
- Combine the remaining oil with the mustard, salt, pepper, and paprika in a shallow bowl and mix well.
- Combine the pecans and cornmeal on a sheet of wax paper.
- Dip the chicken pieces in the seasoned oil and then in the nut mixture.
- Remove the pan from the oven and place the chicken pieces in the pan.
- Bake for 10 minutes and then turn with tongs and bake for an additional 15 minutes.
- Drain on paper towels and serve immediately.

Nutritional Analysis:

121 g water; 586 calories (65% from fat, 26% from protein, g% from carb); 38 g Protein; 43 g total fat; 5 g

754. CHICKEN AND GARLIC

Makes 4 servings

Ingredients:

- 4 small chicken breasts, bone in (about 16 oz meat)
- Salt and black pepper to taste
- 1 Tbsp olive oil
- 2 shallots, chopped
- 2 stalks celery, chopped
- 12 mushrooms, quartered (about 3 oz)
- 20 whole garlic cloves
- 1 tsp thyme leaves
- 1 tsp oregano leaves
- 2 bay leaves
- 1 1/2 cups dry white wine
- 3 cups chicken stock, homemade or College Inn
- 1/4 cup chopped parsley

Directions:

Preheat oven to 350 F.

- Wash and dry chicken. Season with salt and pepper. Heat oil in roasting pan on top of stove.
- Brown chicken on all sides.
- Remove from pan and set aside. Add vegetables and garlic to pan and saute until garlic is lightly browned. Add thyme, oregano, and bay leaves.
- Add wine and bring to a simmer. Simmer 5 minutes. Add stock and return chicken to pan. Cover. Place pan in preheated oven and cook covered for 1 hour. Remove lid.
- Cook about 20 minutes more, or until sauce is thickened. Remove from oven.
- Transfer chicken to a platter. Add parsley to sauce. If sauce is desired consistency, taste for seasoning and add salt and pepper to taste.
- Otherwise, reduce sauce by cooking on stove, then taste and season.
- Pour sauce over chicken and serve.

Nutritional Info:

Carbohydrates: 4.8 g Protein: 4.43 OZ

755. CHICKEN AND VERMICELLI, LOW-CARBED

Makes 8 servings

Ingredients:
- 1/2 medium head cabbage
- 1/4 pound fresh mushrooms, sliced, or
- 7 cup spinach, chopped
- 2 tablespoons butter
- 2 cups sour cream
- 4 eggs
- 1/2 teaspoon seasoning salt
- 1/8 teaspoon pepper optional
- 1 1/2 pounds chicken, cooked and cut into bite-sized pieces
- Cooking oil spray
- Topping ingredients:
- 1 cup pecan pieces, chopped
- 2 tablespoons butter, melted
- 1/2 teaspoon seasoning salt
- 1/2 cup Parmesan cheese, freshly grated

Directions:
- Prepare the cabbage "noodles": Cut the cabbage away from the core. Slice it into 1/2"-wide strips. You should end up with 8 to 10 cups of cabbage strips.
- Place them into a 5-quart pot with a lid. Add about 1" water to the bottom of the pot, cover it, and cook the cabbage for about 8 minutes, until it is just getting tender.
- Drain it and let it rest in the colander while you prepare the rest of the meal.
- While the cabbage is cooking, cook the mushrooms in the butter in a frying pan over medium heat until they are cooked through, about 5 minutes.
- Set them aside to cool. In a large mixing bowl, combine the sour cream, eggs, seasoning salt, and pepper until they are well mixed.
- Add the cooled mushrooms and chicken, stirring well. Set this aside. Place the cooked cabbage into the bottom of a 9" x 13" baking pan that has been sprayed with cooking oil spray.
- Pour the sauce over the top of the cabbage, stirring just enough to coat it evenly, making sure the chicken and mushrooms are evenly distributed throughout Smooth the top with the back of a spoon.
- Combine the topping ingredients, except for the cheese, in a small dish. Sprinkle them over the top of the chicken-and-cabbage mixture.
- Sprinkle the cheese over that. Bake the casserole in a 375 F oven for about 30 minutes, or until the center is set.

Nutritional Info:

Carbohydrates: 9 g Fiber: 3 g Protein: 18 g Fat: 33 g Calories: 396

756. CHICKEN WINGS IN PEANUT SAUCE

Servings:6

Ingredients:
- 4 lb split chicken wings, wing tips removed
- 2 Tbsp vegetable oil
- 1 Tbsp finely grated fresh ginger
- 1 garlic dove, minced
- 1/4 cup smooth natural peanut butter
- 1 Tbsp freshly squeezed lime juice
- 2 tsp fish sauce
- 2 tsp soy sauce
- 1 tsp each Splenda and Canadian Sugar Twin or 4 tsp. (20 ml) Splenda
- sea salt
- 1/4 tsp Dried chile flakes

Directions:
- Preheat the oven to 500 F (260 C).
- In a large bowl, toss together the wings, oil, ginger, and garlic. Spread out on 1 or 2 non-stick, rimmed baking sheets in a single layer.
- Bake for 25 minutes. Remove from the oven and turn on the broiler.
- In a clean bowl large enough to hold the wings, combine the peanut butter, lime juice, fish sauce, soysauce,
- sweetener, salt, and chile flakes to taste.
- Mix until smooth. Add the wings, discarding the pan juices, and toss well to coat with the sauce.
- Spread the wings on the baking sheet in a single layer. Broil 4 to 6 inches (10 to 15 cm) from the heat for 4 to 5 minutes on each side or until nicely browned and crispy.

Nutritional Info:

Carbohydrates: 3.1 g Fiber: 0.9 g Protein: 63.9 g Fat: 53.4 g Calories: 760

757. LEMON BAKED CHICKEN

Servings:4

Ingredients:
- 4 lemons
- 4 skinless boneless chicken breasts
- 2 Tbs butter
- 1/2 c flour
- 1/2 tsp pepper
- 1 tsp salt

Directions
- Squeeze 1/2 c juice from lemons, marinate chicken in juice and refrigerate, at least an hour and up to 12 hours.
- Heat oven to 350 and butter a roasting pan.
- Melt butter, then combine flour, salt and pepper.
- Roll chicken in flour mix and set in roasting pan. Drizzle with melted butter and cook in pre-heated oven until well browned, 50-55 min.

Nutritional Facts

Cal. 534 Protein 50g Sodium 695g Carb 10g Servings: 4

758. DELICIOUS CHICKEN NUGGETS

Preparation time: 10 minutes
Cooking time: 15 minutes
Servings: 2

Ingredients:
- ½ cup coconut flour
- 1 egg
- 2 tbsp. garlic powder
- 2 chicken breasts, cubed
- Salt and black pepper to the taste
- ½ cup ghee

Directions:
- In a bowl, mix garlic powder with coconut flour, salt and pepper and stir.
- In another bowl, whisk egg well.
- Dip chicken breast cubes in egg mix, then in flour mix.
- Heat up a pan with the ghee over medium heat, drop chicken nuggets and cook them for 5 minutes on each side.

- Transfer to paper towels, drain grease and then serve them with some tasty ketchup on the side.

Nutrition: cal.60, fat 3, fiber 0.2, carbs 3, protein 4

759. CHICKEN WINGS AND TASTY MINT CHUTNEY

Preparation time: 20 minutes
Cooking time: 25 minutes
Servings: 6

Ingredients:
- 18 chicken wings, cut in halves
- 1 tbsp. turmeric
- 1 tbsp. cumin, ground
- 1 tbsp. ginger, grated
- 1 tbsp. coriander, ground
- 1 tbsp. paprika
- A pinch of cayenne pepper
- Salt and black pepper to the taste
- 2 tbsp. olive oil
- *For the chutney:*
- Juice of ½ lime
- 1 cup mint leaves
- 1 small ginger piece, chopped
- ¾ cup cilantro
- 1 tbsp. olive oil
- 1 tbsp. water
- Salt and black pepper to the taste
- 1 Serrano pepper

Directions:
- In a bowl, mix 1 tbsp. ginger with cumin, coriander, paprika, turmeric, salt, pepper, cayenne and 2 tbsp. oil and stir well.
- Add chicken wings pieces to this mix, toss to coat well and keep in the fridge for 20 minutes.
- Heat up your grill over high heat, add marinated wings, cook for 25 minutes, turning them from time to time and transfer to a bowl.
- In your blender, mix mint with cilantro, 1 small ginger pieces, juice from ½ lime, 1 tbsp. olive oil, salt, pepper, water and Serrano pepper and blend very well.
- Serve your chicken wings with this sauce on the side.

Nutrition:
cal.100, fat 5, fiber 1, carbs 1, protein 9

760. CHICKEN CHOWDER WITH YOGURT AND TOMATO

Preparation Time: 35 minutes
Servings 6

Ingredients:
- 3 deboned and chopped chicken drumsticks
- 2 tbsp.s coconut oil
- 1/2 tsp. freshly ground mixed peppercorns
- 1/2 tsp. sea salt
- 1/2 cup thinly sliced celery
- 2 chopped shallots
- 2 cloves roughly chopped garlic
- 1 deveined and minced fresh jalapeno
- 2 cups water
- 2 cups homemade sugar-free tomato bisque
- 1/2 cup Greek-style yogurt
- 1 bay leaf
- 1 tbsp. flax seed meal
- Garden Chervil

Directions:
- Put the coconut oil in a large pan and melt over a medium heat. Brown the chicken for around 6 minutes while stirring every now and then. Season with pepper and salt to taste. Take the meat off the heat and keep warm.
- Sauté the garlic, jalapeno, shallots and celery in what is left of the oil until they are fragrant and tender.
- Put a little of the tomato bisque in the pan to scrape and stir the brown bits. Then add the water and the rest of the tomato bisque.
- Add the bay leaf and chicken and simmer on a low-medium heat for 25 minutes.
- Then put in the yogurt and flax seeds and cook on a low heat until the dish is hot. Put into individual bowls and sprinkle with fresh garden chervil.

Nutrition:
Calories 238 Protein 36g ;Fat 15.5g ; Carbs 6.1g ;Sugars 4.8g

761. COUNTRY ROOT VEGETABLE AND CHICKEN

Preparation Time: 25 minutes | **Servings** 4

Ingredients:
- 1 chopped parsnip
- 1/2 cup chopped turnip
- I chopped carrot
- 1 tsp. minced garlic
- 1 tbsp. olive oil
- Pepper and salt to taste
- 2 boneless chicken breasts, cut into cubes
- 1 cup heavy cream
- 4 cups water
- 1 cup full-fat milk
- 1 whole egg
- 2 bouillon cubes
- 4 tbsp.s roughly chopped fresh chives

Directions:
- Put the oil in a large pot and heat over a medium heat. Sauté the garlic until it is fragrant. Add the carrot, parsnip and turnip and cook until they are soft.
- Mix in the cubed chicken and cook for 3-4 minutes or until it isn't pink anymore. Stir every now and then and add the pepper and salt.
- Pour in the heavy cream, milk and water. Crumble the bouillon cubes into the pan and bring to the boil.
- Once it has reached boiling point, bring the heat down to low-medium.
- Simmer for 20 minutes and then put in the beaten egg. Cook for a further minute.
- Take the pan from the heat and serve on individual plates. Garnish with chopped chives.

Nutrition:
Calories 342 ; Protein 22.4g , Fat 25.2g ; Carbs6.3g ; Sugars 3.4g

762. ZESTY CAULIFLOWER SALAD WITH CHICKEN DRUMSTICKS

Preparation Time: 20 minutes
Servings 2

Ingredients:
- 2 chicken drumsticks
- 1/2 head of cauliflower
- 2 tsp.s butter
- Ground black pepper and sea salt to taste
- 1 tsp. Hungarian paprika
- 1 finely minced red onion

- 2 tbsp.s dry white wine
- 1 tsp. Dijon mustard
- 1/2 cup mayonnaise
- 1/2 cup Colby cheese grated
- 2 tbsp.s fresh Italian parsley for serving

Directions:

- In a large pot boil the cauliflower until it is soft. Cut into little florets and put in a bowl.
- On a medium-high heat warm the butter in a pan. Put in the salt, pepper, Hungarian paprika and the chicken.
- Turn the chicken drumsticks over now and then and cook for 7 to 8 minutes.
- While this is cooking, mix the red onion, wine, mustard and mayonnaise together. Put this mixture in the bowl with the cauliflower and mix. Sprinkle the grated cheese on top.
- Serve the warm chicken drumsticks with the salad. Scatter the parsley on top.

Nutrition:
Calories 444 ;Protein 36g Fat 20.6d ; Carbs 5.7g ; Sugars 3.2g

763. CHICKEN BREASTS WITH PARMESAN AND PEPPERS

Preparation Time: 30 minutes
Servings 4

Ingredients:

- 1/4 tsp. ground black pepper
- 1 tsp. salt
- 1 pound butterflied chicken breasts
- 2 tsp.s vegetable oil
- 1/3 cup freshly grated Parmigiano-Reggiano cheese
- 1/3 cup crushed pork rinds
- 1 minced garlic clove
- 1 tsp. fresh or dried dill
- 1 garlic clove, minced
- 3 bell peppers, cut into quarters lengthwise

Directions:

- Put your oven on at 420 degrees F. Cover the sides and bottom of a baking pan with a sheet of foil.
- Put the chicken breast on the baking pan and season with pepper and salt to taste.
- Mix together the garlic clove, vegetable oil, cheese, pork rinds and dill.
- Plunge each chicken breast into this mixture and put the chicken back in the pan.
- Add the quartered bell peppers to the baking pan surrounding the chicken.
- Cook until juices run clear. This should take 20 minutes. Serve hot.

Nutrition: Calories 367 Protein 16.9 g, Fat 43g ; Carbs 6g ;Sugars 6g.

764. SPAGHETTI SQUASH AND CHICKEN SAUSAGE

Preparation Time: 15 minutes
Servings 4

Ingredients:

- 1/2 pounds sliced cheddar & bacon chicken sausages
- 2 tsp.s tallow
- 1 deveined and minced banana pepper
- ½ cup finely chopped yellow onions
- 1 tsp. kosher salt
- 8 ounces spaghetti squash
- 1 tsp. minced garlic
- 1/4 tsp. freshly ground black pepper
- 2/3 cup whipped cream
- 1/4 cup chicken broth

Directions:

- Put a pan over a moderate heat and melt the tallow. Cook the sausages for
- around 8 minutes. Take them out of the pan and keep warm.
- Cook the pepper, garlic and onions in the remaining fat.
- Put in the pepper, salt, chicken broth and the squash. Bring to the boil and allow to thicken.
- 4. Pour in the whipped cream and simmer until completely heated. Serve with the warm sausages. Bon appétit!

Nutrition:
Calories 447 Protein 21.3g ; Fat 37.3g ; Carbs2.8g ; Protein 21.3g ; Sugars 1.6g

765. CASHEW-BASIL PESTO COVERED CHICKEN WINGS

Preparation Time: 35 minutes
Servings 4

Ingredients:

- 1 pound skinless chicken wings
- 1 cup scallions
- Ground black pepper and salt to taste
- 1 tsp. cayenne pepper
- **For the Cashew-Basil Pesto:**
- 1/2 cup cashews
- 2 minced garlic cloves
- 1/2 cup olive oil
- 1/2 cup fresh basil leaves
- 1/2 cup Romano cheese

Directions:

- Set your oven to 392 degrees F. Rub cayenne pepper, black pepper and salt
- into the chicken wings.
- Lightly grease a baking dish and put the chicken wings in. Sprinkle the scallions around the wings.
- Roast for half an hour, turning the baking dish once.
- Blitz the cheese, cashews, garlic and basil n a food processor. Slowly, but constantly pour in the oil. Season with sea salt.
- Put the chicken wings on a plate. Decorate with the cashew-basil pesto and roasted scallions. Bon appétit!

Nutrition:
Calories 580 Protein 44.8g, Fat 38.7g ;Carbs 5g ;Sugars 1.5g .

766. CHICKEN BREASTS FROM THE MEDITERRANEAN

Preparation Time: 40 minutes
Servings 8

Ingredients:

- 4 boneless and skinless chicken breasts
- 1/2 tsp. dried basil
- 2 pressed garlic cloves
- 1 tsp. dried oregano
- 1 sprig rosemary
- 2 sprigs thyme
- Ground pepper and salt to taste
- 1/2 cups chicken stock
- 2 tbsp.s peanut oil
- 1 deveined and thinly sliced bell pepper
- 10 pitted Kalamata olives

Directions:

- Preheat the peanut oil over a medium-high heat. Rub the chicken breast with the garlic, basil, oregano, rosemary, thyme, pepper and salt.
- Fry the chicken for 4 to 6 minutes until it is brown.
- Put in the chicken stock, the bell pepper and the Kalamata olives. Bring to the boil and then turn the heat down to medium-low. Partially cover the pan and simmer for half an hour.

Nutrition:

Calories 306 ;Protein 31.7g ;Fat 17.8g ;Carbs 3.1g ;Protein 31.7g ;Sugars 1.3g

767. ROAST TURKEY AND AN AVOCADO SAUCE

Preparation Time: 1 hour 40 minutes | Servings 4

Ingredients:

- 1 1/2 tbsp.s olive oil
- 2 big turkey legs
- 1 tbsp. poultry seasoning

For the Sauce:

- 1 small pitted and mashed avocado
- 1 ounce mascarpone cheese
- 1 ounce full-fat sour cream
- 1/3 tsp. sea salt
- 1 tsp. fresh lemon juice
- 2 tbsp.s finely chopped fresh cilantro

Directions:

- Put your oven on to 345 degrees F. Drizzle the turkey legs with the olive oil
- and scatter the poultry seasoning over the legs.
- Put the turkey legs on a baking sheet and roast for around 45 minutes. Then
- turn the legs over and cook for 50 minutes.
- While the turkey legs are cooking, make the sauce. Whisk together the
- avocado, mascarpone cheese, sour cream, salt, lemon juice and the cilantro. Put it into the refrigerator.
- When the turkey is cooked, cut the meat off the bones. Serve with the avocado sauce on the side.

Nutrition:

Calories 362 Protein 22.3g, Fat 34.9g ;Carbs 5.6g ;Sugars 0.3g

768. GORGONZOLA PANNA COTTA WITH CHICKEN

Preparation Time: 20 minutes + chilling time

Servings 4

Ingredients:

- 2 boneless and skinless chicken breasts
- 1 tbsp. olive oil
- 2 gelatin sheets
- 3 tbsp.s water
- 3/4 cup heavy cream
- 2 tsp.s granular Swerve
- 1 cup gorgonzola dolce, crumbled
- 1/2 tsp. whole black peppercorns
- 1/2 tsp. ground bay leaf
- Salt and cayenne pepper, to taste

Directions:

- In a heavy-bottomed skillet heat the olive oil over a medium-high heat. Fry
- the chicken breasts until they are brown; about 5 to 6 minutes each side.
- The day before soften the gelatin sheets by soaking them in cold water for
- about 3 to 4 minutes. Place in a pan; add the cheese, water, Swerve and
- cream.
- Sprinkle in the spices. Stir and simmer over a low heat for a few minutes and
- then pour into 4 individual ramekins.
- Put the ramekins in the refrigerator overnight. Then run a thin knife around
- the edge of the panna cotta. Turn over each ramekin onto individual plates.
- Serve the panna cotta with the fried chicken breasts.

Nutrition:

Calories 483 Protein 35.2 g, Fat 38.5g ;Carbs 1.5g ;Protein 38.5g ;Sugars 0.8g

769. MEDITERRANEAN CHICKEN IN A HERB SAUCE

Preparation Time: 50 minutes

Servings 6

Ingredients:

- 1 1/2 pounds skinless chicken legs
- 2 tbsp.s ghee
- 1/2 cup dry sherry
- 2 minced garlic cloves
- 1/2 cup chopped scallions
- 2 chopped thyme sprigs
- 1 chopped rosemary sprig
- 1 tbsp. chopped fresh basil
- 1 tbsp. chopped fresh oregano
- 1 cup heavy cream
- 1/2 tsp. crushed mixed peppercorns
- 1/2 tsp. salt

Directions:

- Put the oven on at 400 degrees F.
- Preheat a pan and melt the ghee over a medium heat. Brown the chicken legs for approximately 6 to 8 minutes.
- Stir in the thyme, rosemary, basil, oregano, garlic, scallions, and sherry.
- Lightly grease a casserole dish and put the chicken mixture in. Put the lid on.
- Bake until a meat thermometer says 165 degrees F. This takes around 35
- minutes. Take the chicken out of the casserole dish.
- Mix the cooking juices with the crushed peppercorns, salt and heavy cream.
- Simmer for 2 minutes or until the sauce is thick. Pour the sauce over the chicken and serve. Bon appétit!

Nutrition: Calories 333 Protein 33.5g ;Fat 20.2g ;Carbs 2g ;Sugars 0.3g

770. CHICKEN MEATBALLS

Preparation time: 10 minutes

Cooking time: 15 minutes

Servings: 3

Ingredients:

- 1 pound chicken meat, ground
- Salt and black pepper to the taste
- 2 tbsp. ranch dressing
- ½ cup almond flour
- ¼ cup cheddar cheese, grated
- 1 tbsp. dry ranch seasoning
- ¼ cup hot sauce+ some more for serving
- 1 egg

Directions:

- In a bowl, mix chicken meat with salt, pepper, ranch dressing, flour, dry ranch seasoning, cheddar cheese, hot sauce and the egg and Stir very well.
- Shape 9 meatballs, place them all on a lined baking sheet and bake at 500 degrees F for 15 minutes.

- Serve chicken meatballs with hot sauce on the side.

Nutrition:
cal.156, fat 11, fiber 1, carbs 2, protein 12

771. TASTY GRILLED CHICKEN WINGS

Preparation time: 2 hours and 10 minutes
Cooking time: 15 minutes
Servings: 5

Ingredients:
- 2 pounds wings
- Juice from 1 lime
- 1 handful cilantro, chopped
- 2 garlic cloves, minced
- 1 jalapeno pepper, chopped
- 3 tbsp. coconut oil
- Salt and black pepper to the taste
- Lime wedges for serving
- Ranch dip for serving

Directions:
- In a bowl, mix lime juice with cilantro, garlic, jalapeno, coconut oil, salt and pepper and whisk well.
- Add chicken wings, toss to coat and keep in the fridge for 2 hours.
- Place chicken wings on your preheated grill over medium high heat and cook for 7 minutes on each side. Serve these amazing chicken wings with ranch did and lime wedges on the side.

Nutrition:
cal.132, fat 5, fiber 1, carbs 4, protein 12

772. BAKED CHICKEN

Preparation time: 10 minutes
Cooking time: 20 minutes
Servings: 4

Ingredients:
- 4 bacon strips
- 4 chicken breasts
- 3 green onions, chopped
- 4 ounces ranch dressing
- 1 ounce coconut aminos
- 2 tbsp. coconut oil
- 4 ounces cheddar cheese, grated

Directions:
- Heat up a pan with the oil over high heat, add chicken breasts, cook for 7 minutes, flip and cook for 7 more minutes.
- Meanwhile, heat up another pan over medium high heat, add bacon, cook until it's crispy, transfer to paper towels, drain grease and crumble.
- Transfer chicken breast to a baking dish, add coconut aminos, crumbled bacon, cheese and green onions on top, introduce in your oven, set on broiler and cook at a high temperature for 5 minutes more.
- Divide between plates and serve hot.

Nutrition:
cal.450, fat 24, fiber 0, carbs 3, protein 60

773. TASTE-OF SUMMER CHICKEN

Servings: 6

Ingredients:
- 3/4 cup Italian fat-free salad dressing
- 3/4 cup unsweetened pineapple juice
- 3/4 cup white wine or white grape juice
- 6 boneless skinless chicken breast halves(1 1/2 pounds)

Directions
- In a large reusable plastic bag, combine the salad dressing, pineapple juice and wine or grape juice.
- Add the chicken. Seal bag and turn to coat; refrigerate for 8 hours or overnight.
- Drain and discard marinade.
- Grill chicken, covered, over medium heat for 6-7 minutes on each side or until juices run clear.

Nutritional Facts
Calories: 140 Fat: 3 g (1 g sat) Cholesterol: 63 mg Sodium: 151 mg Carbohydrates: 3 g Fiber: trace Protein: 23 g Diabetic Exchange: 3 lean meat

774. PARMESAN CHICKEN STRIPS

Servings: 10

Ingredients:
- 8 ounces boneless skinless chicken breasts
- 1/4 cup (1 ounce) grated fat-free Parmesan cheese
- 1/4 teaspoon chili powder or Hungarian paprika. or to taste
- 1/2 teaspoon oregano
- 1/2 teaspoon basil
- 1/8 teaspoon garlic powder
- Salt and freshly ground pepper to taste
- 1 egg, beaten

Directions
- Preheat the oven to 350 degrees.
- Cut the chicken into 1-inch strips. Mix the cheese, chili powder, oregano, basil, garlic powder. salt and pepper in a shallow dish.
- Dip the chicken in the egg and coat with the cheese mixture.
- Arrange the coated chicken strips on a baking sheet sprayed with nonstick cooking spray.
- Bake for 18 to 20 minutes or until the chicken is cooked through and light brown, turning once.
- Serve with fat-free ranch salad dressing, if desired.

Nutritional Facts
Calories 38 Cholesterol 34 mg Carbohydrate 1.9g

775. ITALIAN GRILLED CHICKEN

Servings: 6

Ingredients:
- 6 chicken breasts
- 1/4 cup olive oil
- 3 cloves garlic, crushed
- Fresh ground black pepper
- 1/4 cup fresh basil leaf, chopped
- 1/4 cup melted butter
- 3 sprigs fresh rosemary
- 1 Tbsp Parmesan cheese

Directions
- To grill, skin chicken breasts and rub in pepper to taste.
- Blend basil, olive oil, butter, garlic and Parmesan cheese at low speed using an electric blender, chopper or processor till smooth.
- Baste chicken lightly with mixture.
- Grill over medium coals basting during cooking time with basil sauce.

- During this time add the rosemary branches to coals for added smoke flavor.
- Do this 2 or 3 times.
- Grill 10 minutes each side depending on barbecue temperature.
- Garnish with fresh basil and serve this grilled chicken recipe with rice or Italian pasta.

Nutrition Facts

Calories 403 Calories from Fat 273 (67%) Total Fat 30.3g 46% Saturated Fat 10.1g 50% Carbohydrate 0.9g

776. GRILLED TURKEY BREAST WITH BASIL & MOZZARELLA

Servings: 4

Ingredients:

- Olive oil for coating
- 1 package Honeysuckle White® Turkey Breast
- 4 slices mozzarella cheese
- 1 small bunch fresh basil leaves
- Salt and freshly ground pepper, 1/8 tsp cayenne pepper
- 1 large clove garlic, minced
- 1/4 cup salted butter, at room temperature

Directions

- Prepare your gas or charcoal grill for medium-high direct heat grilling. Oil the grill rack.
- Butterfly the turkey breasts using a long, thin, sharp knife:
- Cut each turkey tenderloin horizontally into the thickest part, to within 1/2-inch of the other side (so that it can be opened like a book) then cut each in two.
- Do the following with each breast: Open the tenderloin like a book and place between sheets of plastic wrap. Pound lightly, using a meat mallet, to even out the thickness. Remove the top sheet of wrap.
- Place 1 slice of cheese and a few basil leaves on one half of the breast.
- Sprinkle with salt and pepper and close the breast. Coat with a little olive oil, and sprinkle both sides with salt and pepper.

- In a small bowl, combine the remaining 3 ingredients with a fork and mix well.
- Form into a log in waxed paper and refrigerate until ready for use.
- Grill turkey breasts for 3 to 5 minutes on each side, or until no longer pink in the center.
- Top each breast with a pat of the garlic butter.

Nutrition Facts

Serving Size 6.9oz/194.6g Calories per serving 350 Calories from Fat 163 Carbohydrate 1.2g

777. CHICKEN SHAWARMA

Ingredients:

Marinade for chicken:

- Chicken breast pieces 150 gram
- Curd/Yogurt- 50gms
- Chili powder 1 and a 1/2 tsp.
- Cumin powder: 1/2 tsp.
- Cinnamon powder: 1/4 tsp.
- Cardamom powder: 1/4 tsp.
- Zatar (Middle Eastern spice: will be available in Nature's Basket): 1 tsp.
- A pinch of nutmeg

Directions:

- Crushed ginger and one pod of garlic.
- Marinating is the key. Mix all of this in the chicken and coat it well and let it sit for 2-3 hours.
- Either grilled if you have that option or cook in a pan with some ghee/ coconut oil. Don't over cook it. The piece will still be succulent if tossed properly.
- Sauce:
- 80 ml fresh mixed with a dash of olive oil and chopped fennel leaves. Add salt to taste, mix well.
- Refrigerate the same.

Nutritional Facts:

Protein: 36.3 g Fats: 3.5 g Carbs: 2.3 g

778. CHICKEN LAAL MIRCH

Ingredients:

- Boneless chicken: 200 gm.
- Red chili, Ginger, garlic and jeera paste: 2 tsp
- Salt to taste

- Dash of lime/lemon juice
- Curd/Yogurt: 1 tsp.
- Chicken masala: 1 tsp.
- Melted butter: 1 tsp.

Directions:

- Marinate the chicken with all the ingredients and keep for 4-5 hours in fridge or less.
- Grill for 20 minutes.
- You can marinade and grill directly also, but the longer you keep the chicken marinated, the more flavorful it will be.

Nutritional Facts:

Fat: 10 g Protein: 50 g Carbs: 2.7 g

779. GHEE ROASTED CHICKEN

Ingredients:

- For Chili paste:
- 4-5 dry green chilies
- 1tbsp. coriander seeds
- 2 tbsp. cumin seeds
- 1 tbsp. fennel seeds
- 1 tbsp. peppercorn
- For Marinade:
- Chicken: 150 grams
- Chili paste (the one mentioned above)
- Turmeric: ¼ tsp.
- Salt to taste
- Yogurt: 30 gm. (2 tbsp.)

Directions:

- Dry roast these ingredients and then transfer to a blender.
- Add 1 inch ginger, 2-3 cloves of garlic, 1tsp. lemon juice and ½ onion and blend it to a smooth paste.
- Mix the chicken and the marinade ingredients and refrigerate for minimum 1-2 hrs.
- In a pan, add 15 gm. ghee and add the chicken with all the marinade.
- Roast/cook the chicken till cooked through.
- Serve on a bed of green veggies and sprinkle some lemon juice on top.

Nutritional Facts:

Fat: 17.9 g Protein: 35.6 g Carbs: 4.4 g

780. CHICKEN SHEEKH KABAB

Ingredients:

- Minced Chicken: 200 grams
- Egg: 1
- Salt to taste
- Coriander and cumin powder: 1/2 tsp. each
- Garam Masala: 1 tsp.
- Black pepper: 1/2 tsp.
- Red Chili powder: 1 tsp.
- Onions: 30 grams, finely chopped
- Ginger Garlic paste: 1 tbsp.
- Melted butter: 5 grams
- A handful of finely chopped coriander.

Directions:

- In a bowl, add all the Ingredients except the egg. Mix very well.
- Now in a small bowl, lightly beat one egg. Pour only half of it into the chicken mixture. Mix well. If the mixture is sticky, don't add the remaining egg.
- Now cover the bowl and keep it in fridge for 1-2 hours, to help the chicken mixture firm up.
- When ready to cook, take the mixture out and let it come down to room temp. You can cook it in a pan or oven/grill.
- Pre heat oven in the grill mode at 200 C. Give a sausage like shape to the mixture around a wooden/steel skewers (if you have it). Grease the baking tray with
- some butter and place the kababs on it. Bake for about 20 minutes, flipping it in between.
- If making in a pan, add some butter and make sausage like shapes. Cook it in the pan until all sides are browned and the kabab is cooked through.

Nutritional Facts:

Fat: 13.2 g Protein: 44.8 g Carbs: 4 g

781. GRILLED CHICKEN & GARLIC PARSLEY LEMON SAUCE

Ingredients:

- Boneless Chicken Breast Fillet: 150 gm.
- Butter: 10 gm.
- Garlic: 2 pods, thinly sliced
- Cheese Slice: 1
- Water: 2-3 spoons
- Fresh Parsley: A handful, chopped
- Pepper and Salt to taste
- Paprika powder to taste
- Lemon Juice: 1 tbsp.

Directions:

- Rub the chicken with some salt, pepper and paprika powder. Rub 5 gm. melted butter on the chicken and grill until it's cooked through.
- Heat some butter in a pan. Once hot, add the sliced garlic and sauté for a few seconds.
- Then add the cheese slice and stir quickly till it melts. Pour in 2-3 spoons of water so the cheese doesn't stick to the pan.
- Then add the chopped parsley, pepper powder, salt, and the lemon juice. Mix well and turn off the heat.
- Pour this over the grilled chicken and enjoy.

Nutritional Facts:

Fat: 16 g Protein: 40.6 g Carbs: 1 g

782. SLOW COOKER BALSAMIC CHICKEN

Serving Size: 10 servings

Overall Time: 4 hours and 15 minutes

Ingredients:

- Chicken breasts (3 lbs. Boneless and skinless)
- Diced tomatoes (2 cans, 14.5 oz.)
- Medium onion (1 medium, thinly sliced)
- Garlic (4 cloves)
- Balsamic vinegar (½ cup; for gluten-free use white balsamic vinegar)
- Olive oil (1 tbsp.)
- Dried oregano (1 tsp,)
- Dried basil (1 tsp.)
- Dried rosemary (1 tsp.)
- Thyme (½ tsp.)
- Ground black pepper to taste
- Salt to taste

Directions:

- Pour olive oil onto the bottom of slow cooker.,
- Place chicken breasts in slow cooker, sprinkle salt and pepper on each piece of breast.
- Place sliced onion on top of the chicken; then add in all dried herbs and cloves of garlic. Pour in balsamic vinegar and place tomatoes on top.
- Cook for 4 hours on high. Serve over pasta.

Nutritional Facts:

Calories: 190   Carbs: 5.2g

783. CHICKEN SOUP

Serving Size: 4 servings

Prep Time: 6 hours and 10 minutes

Ingredients:

- Onion (1 medium, chopped)
- Celery (3 stalks, diced)
- Carrots (3 medium, diced)
- Apple cider vinegar (1 tsp.)
- Fresh Herbs (1 tbsp. fresh)
- Chicken breasts (2 organic, bone-in, skin-on)
- Chicken thighs (2 organic, bone-in, skin-on)
- Sea salt (1 tsp.)
- Fresh ground pepper (½ tsp.)
- Filtered water (3-4 cups)

Directions:

- Arrange the ingredients in the same order listed in a suitable size crockpot; place chicken bone side down on top of the vegetables.
- Pour enough water to cover over vegetables and let it come half way up to the chicken. Cook on low pressure for 6-8 hrs.
- Take out the chicken and let it cool slightly. De-bone and take off the skin.
- Use a fork to tear meat apart and add to soup in the crockpot.
- Adjust seasonings as desired.
- Reheat and serve.

Nutritional Facts

Calories: 292   Carbs: 8g

784. CHICKEN & KALE SOUP

Serving Size: 4 servings

Prep Time: 6 hours and 5 minutes

Ingredients:

- Chicken thigh / breast (2 lbs. Skinless, boneless)
- Chicken bone broth (3 ½ cups, homemade)
- White onion (1 medium, chopped)
- Garlic (4 cloves, smashed)

- Shredded carrots (1 ½ cups, shredded)
- Kale (4 cups, chopped)
- Parsley (1 ½ tsp.)
- 1 1/2 tsp. Parsley
- Salt and pepper to taste

Directions:
- Clean and wash whole chicken thighs and place in the slow cooker.
- Lay with onions, add garlic and chicken bone broth.
- The secret to the yummy flavor of this delicious soup is in the homemade bone broth. If homemade bone broth is not available at the time of cooking the soup use bone-in chicken instead. You will get all the health benefits plus a richer taste.
- Remove bones when soup is done.
- Let the chicken, onions, garlic, and broth cook on low for about 4 to 6 hours.
- The chicken will start coming apart. Use a fork to assist in separating the chicken into chunks.
- Add carrots, parsley, kale, and pepper & salt to taste. Cook for a further hour.

Nutritional Facts:
Calories: 261 Carbs: 2g

785. DRUNKEN CHICKEN WINGS

Ingredients:
- 1 tablespoon (15 ml) fish sauce
- 1 tablespoon (6 g) grated ginger
- 2 teaspoons black pepper
- 1 teaspoon chili garlic paste
- ¼ cup (6 g) Splenda
- 2 tablespoons (30 ml) sugar-free imitation honey
- ¼ cup (60 ml) bourbon

Directions:
- Throw your wings into a large resealable plastic bag.
- Mix together everything else.
- Reserve some of the marinade for basting and pour the rest over the wings.
- Press out the air, seal the bag, and toss it in the fridge. Let your wings live it up for at least a few hours.
- When it's time to cook, light your grill; you'll want it medium-high.
- When the fire is ready pour off the marinade and arrange the wings on the grill.
- Grill for 7 to 10 minutes per side, basting often with the reserved marinade.
- Make sure you use clean utensils each time you baste to avoid cross-contamination.

Nutritional Facts:
Carbohydrate 1g, protein 9g.

786. ROAST CHICKEN WITH BALSAMIC VINEGAR

Yield: 4 servings

Ingredients:
- 1 cut up broiler-fryer
- Bay leaves
- Salt or Vege-Sal
- Pepper
- 3 to 4 tablespoons (45 to 60 ml) olive oil
- 3 to 4 tablespoons (42 to 56 g) butter
- ½ cup (60 ml) dry white wine
- 3 tablespoons (45 ml) balsamic vinegar

Directions:
- Preheat the oven to 350°F (180°C, or gas mark 4).
- Tuck a bay leaf or two under the skin of each piece of chicken.
- Sprinkle each piece with salt and pepper and arrange them in a roasting pan.
- Drizzle the chicken with olive oil and dot them with the same amount of butter.
- Roast in the oven for 1½ hours, turning each piece every 20 to 30 minutes.
- When the chicken is done, put it on a platter and pour off the fat from the pan.
- Put the pan over medium heat and pour in the wine and balsamic vinegar.
- Stir this around, dissolving the tasty brownstuff stuck to the pan to make a sauce.
- Boil this for just a minute or two, pour into a saucebot or a pitcher, and serve with the chicken.
- Discard the bay leaves before serving.

Nutrition Facts:
Carbohydrates 2g , protein 44g.

787. ORANGE-FIVE-SPICE ROASTED CHICKEN

Yield: 5 to 6 servings

Ingredients:
- 3 pounds (1.4 kg) chicken thighs
- ¼ cup (60 ml) soy sauce
- 2 tablespoons (30 ml) canola or peanut oil
- 1 tablespoon (15 ml) lemon juice
- 1 tablespoon (15 ml) white wine vinegar
- 1 tablespoon (1.5 g) Splenda
- 2 tablespoons (40 g) low-sugar orange marmalade
- 2 teaspoons five-spice powder

Directions:
- Place the chicken in a big resealable plastic bag.
- Mix together everything else.
- Reserve some of the marinade for basting and pour the rest into the bag.
- Seal the bag, pressing out the air as you go.
- Turn the bag to coat the chicken and throw it in the fridge.
- Let it sit for at least a couple of hours, and longer is fine. Preheat your oven to 375°F (190°C, or gas mark 5).
- Haul the chicken out of the fridge, pour off the marinade, and arrange the chicken in a baking pan.
- Roast your chicken for 1 hour and baste 2 or 3 times with the reserved marinade, making sure to use a clean utensil each time you baste to avoid cross contamination.

Nutritional Info:
Protein 32 g carbohydrate 3 g; fiber; 3 g

788. GREEK ROASTED CHICKEN

Yield: 5 servings

Ingredients:
- 3 to 4 pounds (1.4 to 1.8 kg) of chicken (whole, split in half, cut-up

broiler-fryer, or cut-up parts of your choice)
- ¼ cup (60 ml) lemon juice
- ½ cup (120 ml) olive oil
- ½ teaspoon salt
- ¼ teaspoon pepper

Directions:
- Wash the chicken and pat it dry with paper towels.
- Combine the lemon juice, olive oil, salt, and pepper and stir them together well.
- If you're using a whole chicken, rub it all over with some of this mixture, making sure to rub plenty inside the body cavity as well. If you're using cut-up chicken, put it in a large resealable plastic bag, pour the marinade over it, and seal the bag.
- Let the chicken marinate for at least an hour or as long as a day.
- At least 1 hour before you want to serve the chicken, pull it out of the bag. You can either grill your chicken or you can roast it in a 375°F (190°C, or gas mark 5) oven for about 1 hour. Either way, cook it until the juices run clear when it's pierced to the bone.

Nutritional Facts:
Carbohydrates 1g, protein 52g.

789. CLASSIC BARBECUED CHICKEN

Yield: 5 servings

Ingredients:
- 3 pounds (1.4 kg) cut-up chicken
- 1 cup (40 g) Classic Barbecue Rub
- ½ cup (120 ml) chicken broth
- ½ cup (120 ml) oil
- ½ cup (120 ml) Kansas City Barbecue Sauce

Directions:
- Wood chips or chunks, soaked for at least 30 min
- Get your grill going, setting it up for indirect smoking. While the grill's heating, sprinkle the chicken with all but a tablespoon of the rub.
- Combine the reserved rub with the chicken broth and oil to make a mop.
- When your fire is ready, place the chicken over a drip pan, add the wood chips or chunks, and close the grill.
- Let it smoke for half an hour before you start to baste it with the mop.
- Then mop it every time you add more chips or chunks, using a clean utensil each time you baste.
- Smoke the chicken for about 90 minutes or until an instant-read thermometer registers 180°F (85°C).
- When the chicken is just about done, baste the skin side with the Kansas City Barbecue Sauce and move it over the fire, skin-side down, for 5 minutes or so.
- Baste the other side with the sauce using a clean utensil, turn it over, and give it another 5 minutes over the fire.
- Boil the remainder of the sauce and serve with the chicken.

Nutritional Info
Carbohydrate 9g fiber 1g, protein 35g.

790. KOREAN BARBECUED CHICKEN

Yield: 4 servings

Ingredients:
- 2 pounds (910 g) chicken pieces
- 2 tablespoons (33 g) chili garlic paste
- 3 tablespoons (45 ml) dry sherry
- 1 tablespoon (15 ml) soy sauce
- 4 cloves garlic, crushed
- 1½ tablespoons (23 ml) toasted sesame oil
- 1 tablespoon (6 g) grated ginger
- 2 scallions, minced
- 2 teaspoons black pepper
- 1 tablespoon (1.5 g) Splenda

Directions:
- Put the chicken in a large resealable plastic bag. Mix together everything else.
- Reserve some marinade for basting and pour the rest over the chicken.
- Press out the air, seal the bag, and toss it in the fridge. Let your chicken marinate for several hours.
- When it's time to cook, fire up the grill. You'll want it at medium to medium-high.
- When the grill is ready for cooking, remove the chicken from the bag and pour off the marinade.
- Cook the chicken skin-side up for about 12 to 15 minutes, keeping the grill closed except when basting. Turn it skin-side down and let it grill for 7 to 9 minutes, again with the grill closed.
- Turn it skin-side up again and let it grill until the juices run clear when pierced to the bone and an instant-read thermometer registers 180°F (85°C).
- Baste several times with the reserved marinade while cooking, making sure to use a clean utensil each time you baste.
- Discard remaining marinade and serve chicken.

Nutritional Info:
carbohydrate 1 g protein 30g

791. CHICKEN WITH BACON, CREAM, AND THYME

Makes 4 servings
Per serving.

Ingredients:
- 4-8 oz boneless chicken breast halves with skin
- Sea salt and freshly ground black pepper
- 8 bacon slices
- 8 small fresh thyme sprigs
- 1 Tbsp vegetable oil
- 1/2 cup chicken stock or water
- 1 cup whipping cream
- 1 garlic dove, minced

Directions:
- Preheat the oven to 350 F (175 C).
- Lightly season the chicken with salt and pepper. Wrap 2 bacon slices around each breast, forming an x in the middle of the skin side.
- Tuck 2 thyme sprigs per breast behind the bacon.
- Heat the oil in an ovenproof frying pan over medium-high heat.
- Place the chicken breasts, bacon side down, in the pan and cook until the bacon and chicken skin are browned.
- Turn over and cook until the other side is browned.
- Drain off the fat and add the stock or water, cream, and garlic.
- Bring to a boil. Transfer the pan to the oven. Bake for 15 to 20 minutes, or until the cream has thickened.

- Season to taste with salt and pepper. Let sit a few minutes before serving.

Nutritional Info:
Carbohydrates: 2.1 g Fiber: 0 g Protein: 43.7 g Fat: 41.7 g Calories: 565

792. CINNAMON-SPICED LEMON CHICKEN

Makes 4 servings

Ingredients:
- 8 large bone-in chicken thighs with skin
- Sea salt and freshly ground black pepper
- 1 tsp ground cinnamon
- 1 tsp ground cumin
- 1 tsp sweet or hot paprika
- 1/4 cup freshly squeezed lemon juice
- 2 Tbsp extra-virgin olive oil
- 2 Tbsp unsalted butter, cut into small pieces

Directions:
- Preheat the oven to 400 F (200 C).
- With a sharp knife, slash the thighs once or twice on each side.
- Place in a large bowl and season liberally with salt and pepper.
- In a small bowl, mix the cinnamon, cumin, paprika, lemon juice, and oil.
- Add to the chicken and toss to coat. Place the thighs in a single layer in a baking dish. Dot with the butter.
- Bake for 30 minutes, basting occasionally with the butter. Turn on the broiler.
- Broil 4 o 6 inches (10 to 15 cm) from the heat until golden brown. Serve with the pan juices.

Nutritional Info:
Carbohydrates: 2.3 g Fiber: 0.6 g Protein: 31.3 g Fat: 32.3 g Calories: 429

793. CHUNKY CHICKEN STEW

Makes 6 Servings

Ingredients:
- 1-3 1/2 pound chicken cut up
- 1 medium turnip
- 1 large carrot optional
- 2 large stalks celery
- 1 medium onion
- 1 teaspoon seasoning salt
- 1/2 teaspoon lemon pepper
- 1/2 tablespoon parsley flakes
- 2 cups water or Rich Stock (page 254)
- 3/4 cup sour cream
- 2 eggs

Directions:
- Place the chicken into a large pot with a lid.
- Cut all of the veggies up into 3/4" to 1" chunks.
- Place them in the pot with the chicken and season them with the seasoning salt, lemon pepper, and parsley.
- Add the water to the pot and cover it.
- Bring it to a boil over medium heat; then reduce the heat to simmering.
- Simmer the chicken and veggies over medium-low heat for about 1 hour 15 minutes total.
- Remove the pot from the heat. In a small bowl, stir together the sour cream and the eggs. Pour them into the stew and serve immediately.

Nutritional Info:
Carbohydrates: 5 g Fiber: 4 g Protein: 25 g Fat: 27 gCalories: 364

794. SKINLESS ROAST CHICKEN WITH HERBS AND SPICES

Ingredients:
- 1 whole roasting chicken, without skin
- 2 medium garlic cloves, smashed
- 1 medium shallots
- 1 pinch fresh rosemary (1 sprig)
- 1 oz parsley sprigs, 1/2 bunch
- 1 tsp ground cayenne (red pepper)

Directions
- Remove the skin from the chicken.
- Stuff the chicken with the aromatics and rub the outside of the bird with the safflower oil.
- Tuck the legs of the chicken underneath and place on a roasting rack.
- Season liberally with salt (optional) and pepper, cayenne, and paprika.
- Roast in a 500 degree F oven for 15 minutes.
- Turn the oven down to 350 degrees F and cook until the juices run away from the bird clear, approx 35 minutes.
- Let the bird rest and collect its juices.
- The chicken will have a nice rust colour and be packed with flavor.

Nutritional Facts:
Calories 210.6 Total Carbs 2.5g Dietary Fiber 0.9g Sugars 0.6g

795. PEPPER-LIME CHICKEN

Ingredients:
- 2 1/2 lbs, Chicken breast halves (with bones)
- 1/2 teaspoon finely shredded lime peel
- 1/4 cup lime juice
- 1 Tablespoon extra-virgin olive oil
- 2 cloves garlic, minced
- 1 Tablespoon chopped fresh basil or thyme
- or 1 teaspoon dried basil or thyme, crushed
- 1/2 to 1 teaspoon cracked black pepper
- 1/4 teaspoon salt

Directions
- If desired, skin chicken.
- Preheat broiler. Place chicken pieces, bone side up, on the unheated rack of a broiler pan.
- Broil 4 to 5 inches from heat about 20 minutes or until lightly browned.
- Meanwhile for glaze, in a bowl stir together lime peel, lime juice, oil, garlic, basil, pepper and Kosher salt.
- Bush chicken generously with glaze. Turn chicken; brush generously with glaze.
- Discard any remaining glaze.
- Broil for 5 to 15 minutes more or until chicken is no loner pink.(170 degrees)

Nutritional Facts
Calories: 120 Fat: 4 g (1 g Sat.) Cholesterol: 51 mg

796. ORANGE-TANGERINE CHICKEN

Yield: 5 servings

Ingredients:
- 1 3½ to 4-pound (1.6 to 1.8 kg)
- whole roasting chicken

- 1 teaspoon salt or Vege-Sal
- 1 teaspoon Splenda
- 1 drop blackstrap molasses
- 1 teaspoon chili powder
- 3 tablespoons (60 g) low-sugar
- orange marmalade
- 1 12-ounce (360-ml) can tangerine Diet-Rite soda
- 2 to 3 teaspoons oil
- 1 teaspoon spicy brown mustard

Directions:

- Prepare your grill for indirect cooking if you have a gas grill, light only one side; if you're using charcoal, pile the briquettes on one side of the grill and light.
- Remove the neck and giblets from the chicken. Rinse the chicken and pat it dry with paper towels.
- In a small bowl combine the salt or Vege-Sal, Splenda, molasses, and chili powder.
- Spoon out half the mixture (1½ teaspoons) into a bowl and reserve; rub the rest inside the cavity of your chicken. Stir the low-sugar orange marmalade into the reserved seasoning mixture.
- Open the can of tangerine soda and pour out 2/3 cup (160 ml). Put ¼ cup (60 ml) of the soda you poured off into the marmalade/seasoning mixture and stir it in—you can drink the remainder of the soda you poured off or throw it away.
- Now, using a church-key-type can opener, punch several more holes around the top of the can.
- Spray the can with nonstick cooking spray and set it in a shallow baking pan.
- Carefully place the chicken down over the can, fitting the can up into the cavity of the chicken.
- Rub the chicken with the oil. Okay, you're ready to cook!
- Make sure you have a drip pan in place.
- 1Set the chicken, standing upright on its soda can on the side of the grill not over the fire and spread the drumsticks out a bit, making a tripod effect.
- 1Close the grill and cook the chicken at 250°F (130°C) or so for 75 to 90 minutes or until the juices run clear when it's pricked to the bone.
- 1You can also use a meat thermometer—it should register 180°F (85°C). while the chicken is roasting, add the mustard to the marmalade/soda/seasoning mixture and stir the whole thing up.
- 1Use this mixture to baste the chicken during the last 20 minutes or so of roasting.
- 1When the chicken is done, carefully remove it from the grill—barbecue gloves come in handy here or use heavy hot pads and tongs.
- 1Twist the can to remove it from the chicken and discard.
- 1Let the chicken stand for 5 minutes before carving. In the meantime, heat any leftover basting sauce to boiling—and serve as a sauce with the chicken.

Nutritional Facts

Carbohydrate 5g protein 40g.

797. CHICKEN PHILLY CHEESE STEAK SANDWICH

Prep Time: 10 minutes   Cook Time: 15 minutes

Serves: 2

Ingredients:

- 2 teaspoon of oil
- ¾ lb of boneless & skinless chicken breast, sliced thinly
- 1 clove of minced garlic
- ½ teaspoon of ground paprika
- 6 oz mushrooms, sliced thinly
- 1 tablespoon of unsalted butter
- ½ green pepper, sliced thinly
- ½ large onion, sliced thinly
- ½ teaspoon of ground black pepper
- 4 oz of sliced provolone cheese
- 1 teaspoon of salt
- 2 hoagie sandwich rolls
- Mayo, optional

Directions:

- Heat oil in a skillet over medium heat. Add chicken, sauté until cooked and browned. Remove from heat and set aside.
- Melt the butter in the same skillet; add mushroom, onions, pepper and sauté for a few minutes until desired doneness.
- Next stir in minced garlic, seasonings and chicken, cook until the garlic is fragrant.
- Add cheese and cook covered for a few minutes until the cheese melts, remove from heat and set aside.
- Toast the buns, spread with mayo and fill with cheese steak mixture, enjoy!

Nutritional Facts

Calories: 669kcal Carbohydrates: 41g Protein: 71g Fat: 24g Saturated Fat: 11g Cholesterol: 184mg

798. CHICKEN WITH LEMON GARLIC SAUCE

4 – Servings

Ingredients:

- Chopped parsley, 2 tbsp.
- Olive oil, 1 tbsp.
- Heavy cream, .24 c
- Chicken broth, 1 c
- Lemon juice, 2 tbsp.
- Minced garlic, 1 tbsp.
- Salted butter, 2 tbsp.
- Diced shallots, .33 c
- Red pepper flakes, .5 tsp.
- Salt
- Pepper
- Boneless skinless chicken breasts, 4

Directions:

- Pound the chicken to half inch thickness. Sprinkle the chicken with pepper and salt.
- Mix together the red pepper flakes, garlic, lemon juice, and chicken broth.
- Place your oven rack to the lower third and place it at 37
- Place oil in a pan and place in the chicken. Let it cook for two to three minutes on each side. The chicken doesn't have to be fully cooked at this point. Set in aside.
- Lower the heat and add in the shallots with the chicken broth mixture. Deglaze the pan.
- The heat up a bit and allow the sauce to simmer within 10 – 15 mins. See to it that there's about a third of a cup of sauce left.

- Once thickened, take it off the heat and stir in the butter until completely melted. Whisk in the heavy cream. Set it back on the heat, but make sure it doesn't boil.
- Add the chicken back in and coat it with the sauce. Slid it in the oven and cook for five to eight minutes, or until the chicken has cooked through.
- Top with the parsley.

Nutrition Facts:

Calories: 302 Fats: 16.1 grams Proteins: 33.9 grams Carbohydrates: 4.6 grams

799. GREEK MARINATED CHICKEN

Prep Time: 5 minutes
Cook Time: 30 minutes
Total Time: 35 minutes
Servings: 8 people

Ingredients:

- ounce tube of plain Greek Yogurt, (I use Chobani)
- 2 Tablespoons extra virgin olive oil (if you have flavored olive oil, use it!)
- 6 cloves fresh garlic, minced
- Half Tablespoon dried oregano
- 1 lemon, (juice and zest)
- 1/2 teaspoon salt
- 1/4 teaspoon pepper
- 1/4 cup fresh chopped parsley
- 4 lbs boneless and skinless chicken thighs and drumsticks

Directions

- To make the marinade, combine the yogurt, olive oil, minced garlic, oregano, lemon juice, parsley, salt, and pepper in a bowl. Stir well.
- Use a cheese grater or zester to scrape a thin layer of lemon zest from half the lemon. Add lemon zest to the bowl of marinade ingredients.
- Grab a gallon-sized Ziplock bag and add the chicken pieces and marinade to the bag. Move the chicken around to ensure each piece is well coated.
- Refrigerate the chicken in the marinade for at least 1 hour. I like to marinate mine overnight! The longer the marinade, the more flavorful!
- After marinating, you can choose to grill the chicken or bake in the oven. If you bake in the oven, preheat the oven to 350 and bake for the breasts for 30 minutes. If you are making thighs and drumsticks, I like to cook them for 35-40 minutes to ensure done.
- If you choose to grill the chicken, grill for a total of 30-35 minutes or until the juices run clear and the chicken is done all the way through. Your chicken regardless of the cut needs to reach an internal temperature of 165 degrees Fahrenheit before it is considered done.
- Top with freshly grated lemon zest and serve.

Nutrition Facts:

Calories: 301kcal | Protein: 43g | Fat: 12g | Saturated Fat: 2g | Cholesterol: 215mg | Sodium: 347mg | Potassium: 555mg | Vitamin A: 55IU | Calcium: 20mg | Iron: 1.8mg

800. CHICKEN PICCATA

Prep Time: 10 Minutes
Cook Time: 20 Minutes
Total Time: 30 Minutes

Ingredients:

- 4 boneless skinless chicken breast halves
- salt and black pepper, to taste
- 1/3 cup flour, (I used gluten-free flour)
- 4 Tbsp butter
- 4 Tbsp olive oil
- 1/2 cup chicken stock or dry white wine
- 2 Tbsp lemon juice
- 2 Tbsp shallots, chopped
- 3 cloves garlic, minced
- 2 Tbsp drained capers
- 2 Tbsp chopped fresh parsley

Directions

- Place each chicken breast between a plastic wrap and lightly pound it to 1/4-inch thickness.
- Season both sides of chicken breasts with salt and black pepper. Place flour in a shallow dish, and dip chicken breasts into flour to coat, shake off excess.
- Heat 2 Tbsp butter and 2 Tbsp olive oil in a large skillet over medium-high heat.
- Add chicken (in batches if necessary) to the skillet and cook until golden and cooked through, about 3 minutes per side.
- Transfer chicken to a platter; cover with foil to keep warm.
- Add the remaining 2 Tbsp olive oil, chicken stock (or white wine), lemon juice, shallots, and minced garlic to the skillet.
- Boil until the sauce thickens slightly, about 2 minutes. Stir in capers and the remaining 2 Tbsp butter.
- Plate the chicken and pour the lemon piccata sauce over the chicken. Sprinkle with parsley.

Nutrition Facts:

Calories: 410kcal | Carbohydrates: 10g | Protein: 38g | Fat: 23g | Saturated Fat: 9g | Cholesterol: 139mg | Sodium: 429mg | Potassium: 702mg | Vitamin A: 565IU | Vitamin C: 8.6mg | Calcium: 19mg | Iron: 1.4mg

801. BAKED CHICKEN CORDON BLEU

Prep Time:10 Mins
Cook Time:25 Mins
Total Time:35 Mins
Yield:6 Servings

Ingredients:

- Cooking spray
- 12 thin-sliced, 36 oz total skinless boneless chicken breasts, 3 oz each
- Salt and fresh cracked pepper
- 1 large egg
- 2 large egg whites
- 1 tbsp water
- 1/2 cup seasoned breadcrumbs
- 1/4 cup grated parmesan cheese
- 5 oz 6 slices thinly sliced lean deli ham, sliced in half
- 6 slices 4.4 oz sargento reduced-fat swiss cheese, cut in half

Directions:

- Preheat oven to 450°F. Spray a large non-stick baking sheet with cooking spray.
- Wash and dry the chicken cutlets; lightly pound the chicken to make thinner and lightly season with salt and black pepper.

- Lay the chicken on a working surface and place a slice of ham on top of the chicken, then the cheese and roll, setting them aside seam side down.
- In a medium bowl, whisk eggs and egg whites along with water to make an egg wash.
- In another medium bowl, combine breadcrumbs and parmesan cheese.
- Dip the chicken into the egg wash, then into the breadcrumbs.
- Place chicken onto the baking sheet seam side down. Spray the top of the chicken with more cooking spray and bake for about 25 minutes.

Nutrition Facts: Facts

Calories: 378kcal, Carbohydrates: 8g, Protein: 55g, Fat: 10g, Sodium: 813mg, Fiber: 0.5g, Sugar: 1g

802. PERFECT GRILLED CHICKEN BREASTS

Prep time: 2 minutes
Cook time: 20 minutes
Additional time: 10 minutes

Ingredients:

- 6 chicken breasts
- 12 oz Italian dressing
- 1 tbsp garlic powder
- 3 tbsp soy sauce
- 1 tsp salt
- 1 tsp black pepper

Directions

- Put chicken breasts in a large zip bag and cover with Italian dressing, garlic powder, and soy sauce.
- Gently squeeze the air out of the bag.
- Shake the bag so all the chicken is covered with a dressing.
- Place the bag in a bowl and refrigerate overnight.
- Pre-heat and clean grill- rubbing ½ an onion on the hot grill cleans and flavors the grates.
- Remove chicken from the bag with marinade.
- Season with salt and pepper.
- Cook chicken on medium-high heat until 165 internal temperature, about 15 minutes.
- Enjoy when hot, or refrigerate and use for s sack-lunch.

Nutrition Facts: Facts

Calories345 Total Fat16g Saturated Fat3g Trans Fat 0g UnsaturatedFat12g Cholesterol102mg Sodium1480mg Carbohydrates 7g Fiber 0g Sugar 6g Protein 38g

803. HEALTHY CHICKEN PICCATA

Prep Time: 30 Minutes
Cook Time: 25 Minutes
Total Time: 30 Minutes
Yield: 4 Servings

Ingredients:

- 1 lemon
- 1 pound boneless skinless chicken breasts
- ¼ cup all-purpose flour
- ½ teaspoon salt
- ½ teaspoon ground pepper
- 1 tablespoon plus 4 teaspoons extra-virgin olive oil, divided
- 1 large sweet onion, sliced
- 1 clove garlic, minced
- 1 cup reduced-sodium chicken broth
- ¼ cup dry white wine
- 4 teaspoons drained capers
- ¼ cup chopped parsley

Directions

- Prepare Lemon And Chicken: Cut lemon in half. Juice half of it, and cut the remaining half into thin slices. Cut chicken breasts into 8 thin cutlets.
- Dredge Chicken: Whisk flour, salt, and pepper in a shallow dish or pie plate.
- Dredge chicken in the flour mixture, turning to coat. Discard 2 teaspoons dredging flour and reserve the rest to thicken the sauce in step
- Brown Chicken: Heat 2 teaspoons oil in a large non-stick skillet over medium-high heat.
- Add half the chicken and cook until the bottom is browned, 2 to 4 minutes. Turn over and continue cooking until browned on the bottom, 2 to 3 minutes.
- Set aside on a plate.
- Repeat with 2 teaspoons oil and the remaining 4 pieces of dredged chicken, adjusting the heat to medium-low to prevent the chicken from burning.

Transfer the second batch of chicken to the plate.
- Cook Onions And Garlic: Wipe out the skillet with a clean paper towel.
- Add the remaining 1 tablespoon oil and place the skillet over medium-high heat.
- Add onion, and cook, stirring often until soft and browned 5 to 7 minutes.
- Add garlic, and cook, stirring constantly until the garlic is fragrant and just starting to brown, 30 to 90 seconds.
- Make Sauce: Sprinkle the remaining dredging flour over the onion mixture and stir to coat.
- Stir in broth, white wine, capers, lemon slices, and the lemon juice, increase heat to high and bring to a simmer, stirring constantly.
- Finish Dish: Add the chicken and any accumulated juices from the plate to the skillet and turn to coat in the sauce.
- Bring to a simmer while turning the chicken in the sauce until the sauce is thickened, and the chicken is completely cooked through and hot, 3 to 4 minutes. Stir in parsley, remove from the heat and serve.

Nutrition Facts

Calories: 264 Sugar: 2 G Sodium: 550 Mg Fat: 9 G Saturated Fat: 1 G Carbohydrates: 14 G Fiber: 1 G Protein: 28 G

804. CHICKEN, SHRIMP AND STEAK SKEWERS WITH SOFRITO

Preparation Time: 25 Minutes
Marinating Time: 24 Hours
Cooking Time: 15 Minutes

Ingredients

- 1 1/4 pounds skinless chicken thigh meat, cut into 20 one-ounce segments
- 1 1/4 pounds lean skirt steak, fat removed, cut into 10 two-ounce segments
- 20 large shrimp
- 1 onion, chopped
- 1/4 red bell pepper, chopped
- 1/4 yellow bell pepper, chopped
- 1/4 green bell pepper, chopped
- 3 sweet chilies, chopped

- 2 cloves garlic, minced
- 1/2 cup fresh cilantro leaves
- 1 tablespoon vegetable oil
- 1 green pepper
- 1 red onion
- 1 medium papaya (optional)

Directions
Sofrito:

- Place chicken pieces, steak pieces, and shrimp in a shallow dish. Place all sofrito ingredients in an electric blender. Blend into a coarse puree. Pour entire contents of blender over chicken, steak, and shrimp. Cover and marinate for 24 hours in the refrigerator.
- When ready to grill skewers, slice green pepper into 20 strips, cut the red onion into 20 wedges, and peel papaya and cut into 20 cubes.
- To assemble skewers, place 2 pieces of chicken, 1 piece of steak, 2 shrimp, 2 strips of green pepper, 2 wedges of red onion, and 2 cubes of papaya on each skewer, alternating for color and variety.
- Discard any remaining sofrito. Place the skewers on a hot grill and cook thoroughly, turning to heat evenly, for approximately 15 minutes until chicken and beef are cooked through. (If desired, you may instead broil skewers using the oven broiler.)
- Serve immediately.

Nutrition Facts
Carbohydrates: 8g| Protein: 26g| Fat: 9g| Saturated Fat: 3g| Sodium: 115mg| Fiber: 2g

805. CHICKEN JAMBALAYA

Preparation Time: 1 Hour

Ingredients
- 2 tablespoons vegetable oil
- 2 onions, chopped
- 1 green pepper, chopped
- 2 cloves garlic, minced
- 2 cups cubed, cooked chicken
- 1 cup uncooked rice
- 1 bay leaf, crumbled
- 1/2 teaspoon thyme
- 1/2 teaspoon salt-free Creole seasoning
- 3–4 drops hot pepper sauce
- 1 can (16 ounces) tomatoes
- 1/2 cup unsalted chicken broth

Directions
- Heat vegetable oil in a large pot, then sauté onions, green pepper, and garlic until tender.
- Add chicken and rice, stirring until well coated with oil.
- Add bay leaf, thyme, Creole seasoning, hot pepper sauce, tomatoes, and broth.
- Cover and simmer until rice is tender and liquid is absorbed about 30–40 minutes.

Nutrition Facts
Carbohydrates: 33g| Protein: 16g| Fat: 10g| Saturated Fat: 2g| Sodium: 60mg| Fiber: 2g

806. CHICKEN WITH BEAN THREAD AND RICE NOODLES

Preparation Time: 25 Minutes
Cooking Time: 20 Minutes

Ingredients
- 4 ounces bean threads
- 1 tablespoon oil
- 3 garlic cloves, chopped
- 1 large onion, chopped
- 1/4 cup soy sauce
- 2 1/2 cups low-sodium chicken broth
- 8 ounces rice noodles
- 4 stalks celery, thinly sliced
- 3 medium carrots, thinly sliced
- 1/2 cup sliced fresh mushrooms
- 3 cups cooked diced chicken breast
- Pepper to taste

Directions
- Soak bean threads in warm water until soft, about 10 minutes.
- Drain and cut into small pieces; pat dry.
- Place oil in a large nonstick skillet over medium heat. Add garlic and sauté for 1 minute.
- Add onion and soy sauce.
- Cover and simmer for 10 minutes.
- Add chicken broth and bean threads and bring to a boil.
- Meanwhile, soak rice noodles in warm water just until soft, about 3 minutes.
- Drain. Add rice noodles, celery, carrots, and mushrooms to the onion mixture. Increase heat to medium-high and cook, stirring occasionally, until broth evaporates, about 5–8 minutes.
- Add chicken and pepper. Stir to combine. Serve warm.

Nutrition Facts
- Carbohydrates: 29g| Protein: 19g| Fat: 4g| Saturated Fat: 1g| Sodium: 596mg| Fiber: 2g

807. CHICKEN FLORENTINE PIZZA FOR DIABETICS

Preparation Time: 15 Minutes
Baking Time: 10–12 Minutes

Ingredients
- 10-ounce, precooked thin pizza crust (such as Boboli)
- 1 packet (1.6 ounces) Knorr Alfredo pasta sauce mix
- 1 cup skim milk
- Half a 10-ounce package frozen chopped spinach, thawed and well-drained
- 4 ounces diced, fully cooked chicken breast (try thawed, frozen diced chicken breast for convenience)
- 3/4 cup shredded part-skim mozzarella cheese
- 2 tablespoons grated Parmesan cheese
- 1/8–1/4 teaspoon red pepper flakes

Directions
- Preheat oven to 400°F. Place pizza crust on a baking sheet or baking stone and set aside. In a saucepan, whisk together Alfredo sauce mix and milk until blended.
- Stirring constantly, cook over medium-high heat until thickened (about 1–2 minutes).
- Spread Alfredo sauce evenly over pizza crust.
- Top evenly with spinach and chicken, then mozzarella and Parmesan cheeses.
- Sprinkle with red pepper flakes and bake 10–12 minutes, or until cheese is melted and bubbly.

Nutrition Facts

- Carbohydrates: 30g| Protein: 18g| Fat: 8g| Saturated Fat: 3g| Sodium: 788mg| Fiber: 2g

808. CILANTRO POLLO ENCHILADAS

Preparation Time: 30 Minutes
Baking Time: 20 Minutes

Ingredients

- 4 skinless, boneless chicken breast halves, cooked and shredded
- 1 cup fat-free sour cream
- 1 1/2 cups shredded, low-fat Cheddar cheese
- 4 green onions, chopped
- 1 teaspoon ground cumin
- 1/4 cup chopped fresh cilantro
- 1/2 teaspoon pepper
- 12 6-inch corn tortillas
- 8 ounces fresh salsa

Directions

- Preheat oven to 350°F.
- In a large bowl, combine shredded chicken, fat-free sour cream, cheese, green onions, cumin, cilantro, and pepper.
- Mix well. Place a large spoonful of chicken mixture on each corn tortilla, roll it up, and place it seam-side-down in a 9" x 13" baking dish.
- Cover with fresh salsa. Bake at 350°F for about 20 minutes or until bubbly and heated through.

Nutrition Facts

Carbohydrates: 41g| Protein: 31g| Fat: 5g| Saturated Fat: 2g| Sodium: 401mg| Fiber: 4g

809. INDIAN BROILED CHICKEN

Preparation Time: 10 Minutes
Marinating Time: At Least 6 Hours
Cooking Time: 10–15 Minutes

Ingredients

- 1 cup plain, nonfat yogurt
- 1 tablespoon finely minced or grated ginger root
- 2 large cloves garlic, peeled and minced
- 1 tablespoon paprika
- 1 teaspoon coriander
- 1 teaspoon cumin
- 1 teaspoon ground black pepper
- 1/2 teaspoon cayenne pepper
- 2 pounds boneless, skinless chicken breasts (4 split breasts)

Directions

- In a small bowl, combine all ingredients except chicken.
- Place the chicken pieces in a flat dish and cover them evenly with yogurt marinade.
- Refrigerate the chicken for at least 6 hours and up to one day. Preheat the oven broiler.
- Spray a broiler rack with nonstick cooking spray.
- Place coated chicken pieces on the broiler rack, broiling 10–15 minutes per side until juices run clear when pierced with a fork.

Nutrition Information

Carbohydrates: 3g| Protein: 26g| Fat: 4g| Saturated Fat: 1g| Sodium: 79mg| Fiber: <1 g

810. PENNY-WISE CHICKEN POT PIE

Preparation Time: 25 Minutes
Baking Time: 30 Minutes

Ingredients

Filling:

- 3 tablespoons reduced-calorie stick margarine
- 1/3 cup all-purpose flour
- 1/2 teaspoon salt
- 1/8 teaspoon garlic powder
- 1/8 teaspoon black pepper
- 1/2 teaspoon dried parsley
- 1/4 teaspoon dried thyme
- 2 cups water
- 3/4 cup skim milk
- 2 cubes reduced-sodium chicken bouillon
- 1 can (15 ounces) mixed vegetables, drained (such as Veg-All)
- 1 small onion, finely diced
- 2 cups (about 10 ounces) shredded, cooked chicken breast
- Cooking spray

Topping:

- 2 cups baking mix
- 2/3 cup skim milk

Directions

- Preheat oven to 400°F. Melt margarine in a large saucepan over medium heat.
- Stir in flour, salt, garlic powder, pepper, parsley, and thyme; a thick paste will form.
- Whisk in water and 3/4 cup milk; add bouillon cubes.
- Continue to stir with wire whisk until mixture thickens slightly.
- Add mixed vegetables, onion, and chicken; stir to combine.
- Spoon into a 2-quart casserole coated with cooking spray and set aside.
- In a mixing bowl, combine baking mix and 2/3 cup milk and stir until a soft, sticky dough forms.
- Drop dough by rounded tablespoonfuls on top of the chicken mixture.
- Bake uncovered for 30 minutes or until topping is golden and filling is bubbly.

Nutrition Information

Carbohydrates: 26g| Protein: 12g| Fat: 7g| Saturated Fat: 2g| Sodium: 660mg| Fiber: 3g

811. EASY CHEESY VEGETABLE CASSEROLE

Preparation Time: 20 Minutes
Baking Time: 30 Minutes

Ingredients

- 1 1/2 cups water
- 4 medium white or yellow potatoes, peeled and sliced 1/2-inch thick
- 1 cup bite-size raw cauliflower florets
- 1 cup bite-size raw broccoli florets
- 4 medium carrots, peeled and sliced into 1/4-inch coins
- 1 medium onion, chopped
- 2 cups frozen, cut green beans
- Nonstick cooking spray
- 1 can (10 3/4 ounces) reduced-fat, reduced-sodium cream of chicken soup
- 1/2 cup skim milk
- 1 cup shredded reduced-fat Cheddar cheese

Directions

- Bring water to a boil in a large pot over high heat.

- Add the potatoes and cook, covered, for 5 minutes.
- Add the cauliflower, broccoli, carrots, onion, and frozen green beans. Return water to a boil, cover, and cook 10 to 12 minutes until vegetables are tender.
- Drain. Spray a 2-quart baking dish with cooking spray. Add cooked vegetables. Combine the canned soup and milk.
- Pour soup mixture over the vegetables, mixing gently.
- Preheat oven to 350°F.
- Cover and bake casserole for 20 to 25 minutes.
- Uncover and sprinkle with cheese.
- Bake 3 to 4 minutes longer, until cheese melts.

Nutrition Facts

- Carbohydrates: 27g| Protein: 9g| Fat: 5g| Saturated Fat: 3g| Sodium: 475 mg, Fiber 5g, Calcium: 214mg

812. QUICK CHICKEN NOODLE SOUP

Preparation Time: 5 Minutes
Cooking Time: 20 Minutes.

Ingredients

- 2 cans (14.5 ounces each) 50% less sodium, fat-free chicken broth
- 3 cups water
- 1 1/2 teaspoons salt-free herb seasoning (such as Spice Islands Salt-Free Original Seasoning or Mrs. Dash)
- 2 teaspoons instant minced onions
- 2 cups uncooked, cholesterol-free egg noodles
- 1 can (10 ounces) 96% fat-free chunk chicken in water
- 1 can (15 ounces) no-salt-added mixed vegetables, drained
- Black pepper to taste

Directions

- Place broth, water, salt-free seasoning, and instant minced onions in a 2-quart pan and bring to a boil over high heat.
- Reduce heat to medium and add noodles; cook until tender (approximately 6–8 minutes).
- Drain and flake chicken; stir into soup along with vegetables. Season with black pepper to taste. Heat through.

Nutrition Facts

- Carbohydrates: 10g| Protein: 10g| Fat: 1g| Saturated Fat: <1 g| Sodium: 284m| Fiber: 2g

813. DIABETIC CHICKEN NOODLE SOUP RECIPE

Preparation Time: 45 Minutes

Ingredients

- 2 (8 ounces each) boneless, skinless chicken breasts
- 6 cups water
- 1 can (14 1/2 ounces) fat-free, 1/3 less-sodium chicken broth
- 1/3 cup finely diced carrot
- 1 cup diced onion (approximately 1/2 large onion)
- 1/2 cup finely diced celery
- 1 teaspoon dried parsley
- 1 teaspoon garlic powder
- 1/2 teaspoon poultry seasoning
- 1/2 teaspoon salt
- 1/8 teaspoon black pepper
- 4 ounces dry angel hair pasta (break noodles in half)

Directions

- Place chicken, water, broth, carrot, onion, and celery in a one-gallon pot and bring to a boil.
- Cook until the chicken is no longer pink (about 15 minutes).
- Remove chicken and skim any fat from broth (or refrigerate broth for 2 to 3 hours and then skim fat).
- Dice chicken into bite-size pieces.
- Return chicken to the skimmed broth along with all remaining ingredients.
- Place over high heat and return to a boil.
- Reduce heat to medium-high and boil gently until pasta is cooked (3 to 5 minutes).
- Serve right away; the pasta will continue to absorb liquid if the soup is left simmering.

Nutrition Facts

Carbohydrates: 10g| Protein: 21g| Fat: 3g| Saturated Fat: 1g| Sodium: 276mg| Fiber: <1g

814. OVEN "FRIED" CHICKEN FOR DIABETICS

Preparation Time: 15 Minutes
Baking Time: 20–25 Minutes

Ingredients

- 1/3 cup dry unseasoned bread crumbs
- 2 teaspoons sesame seeds
- 1 1/2 tablespoons grated Parmesan cheese
- 1/4 cup fat-free mayonnaise (not salad dressing mayonnaise)
- 1/4 teaspoon salt
- 1/8 teaspoon garlic powder
- 2 dashes of cayenne pepper
- 1/4 teaspoon poultry seasoning
- 4 (4 ounces each) boneless, skinless chicken breast halves
- Cooking spray

Directions

- Preheat oven to 425°F.
- Place bread crumbs, sesame seeds, and Parmesan cheese in a large zip-top bag and shake gently to combine.
- In a small bowl, whisk together mayonnaise, salt, garlic powder, cayenne pepper, and poultry seasoning.
- Using a pastry brush, coat both sides of each piece of chicken with the mayonnaise mixture.
- Place chicken, one piece at a time, into the bread crumb mixture in the zip-top bag, seal and shake to coat chicken well.
- Transfer chicken to a foil-lined baking sheet coated with cooking spray.
- Spray chicken evenly with cooking spray.
- Bake for 20 to 25 minutes or until juices run clear and chicken is no longer pink in the center.

Nutrition Facts

Carbohydrates: 9g| Protein: 37g| Fat: 6g| Saturated Fat: 2g| Sodium: 446 mg| Fiber: 1g

815. ALOHA CHICKEN

Preparation Time: 15 Minutes

Cooking Time: Approximately 45 Minutes.

Ingredients

- 1 can (15 1/4 ounces) pineapple tidbits in juice, drained, with juice reserved
- 1/4 cup honey
- 1/4 cup red wine vinegar
- 1/8 teaspoon black pepper
- 1 pound boneless, skinless chicken tenderloins (alternately, 2-inch-wide strips of boneless, skinless chicken breast can be used)
- Cooking spray
- 1/4 cup chopped onion
- 1/4 cup finely chopped red bell pepper
- 1/4 cup finely chopped green bell pepper

Directions

- Preheat oven to 350°F.
- Combine 1/4 cup of reserved pineapple juice (discard remainder), honey, vinegar, and black pepper in a small bowl; whisk well and set aside.
- Place chicken in an 8" x 8" baking pan coated with cooking spray.
- Top evenly with pineapple tidbits, onion, and peppers.
- Pour juice mixture over.
- Bake uncovered until chicken is cooked through and vegetables are tender for about 45 minutes.

Nutrition Facts

- Carbohydrates: 29g| Protein: 21g| Fat: 1g| Saturated Fat: <1g| Sodium: 69mg| Fiber: 1g

816. TWO-MINUTE TURKEY WRAP

Preparation Time: 2 Minutes

Ingredients

- 1 (8-inch) flour tortilla (use flavored tortilla if desired)
- 1 teaspoon horseradish sauce (not pure horseradish)
- 3 ounces deli-sliced turkey breast
- 1 slice (2/3 ounce) fat-free American cheese
- 1/4 cup alfalfa sprouts

Directions

- Spread tortilla lightly with horseradish sauce.
- Lay turkey over tortilla.
- Place cheese in the center of the tortilla over the turkey, then top with sprouts.
- Fold in about an inch on the top and bottom of the tortilla, then roll up the tortilla from left to right.
- Serve immediately or wrap tightly in plastic wrap and refrigerate for future use.

Nutrition Facts

Carbohydrates: 27g| Protein: 36g| Fat: 5g| Saturated Fat: 1g| Sodium: 414mg| Fiber: 1g

817. DIABETIC CHICKEN, BROCCOLI, AND RICE BAKE RECIPE

Preparation Time: 15 Minutes

Baking Time: 25–30 Minutes

Ingredients

- Cooking spray
- 1 package (10 ounces) frozen, chopped broccoli, thawed
- 1 cup cooked white rice (warm slightly if using leftover rice)
- 2 cups (about 8 ounces) diced cooked chicken breast
- 1 can (10 3/4 ounces) Campbell's Healthy Request cream of chicken soup
- 1/4 cup reduced-fat mayonnaise
- 1/4 cup skim milk
- 1/8 teaspoon curry powder
- 1 teaspoon dill
- 1/2 teaspoon lemon juice
- 1 tablespoon fine, dry bread crumbs
- Paprika

Directions

- Preheat oven to 350°F. Coat an 8" x 8" pan with cooking spray.
- Layer broccoli at bottom of the pan.
- Top evenly with rice and then chicken. In a large bowl, whisk together soup, mayonnaise, milk, curry powder, dill, and lemon juice; mix well.
- Pour evenly over the chicken. Sprinkle top of casserole with bread crumbs and paprika.
- Spray cooking spray over bread crumbs (to help them crisp during baking).
- Bake uncovered for 25–30 minutes, or until bubbly.
- This recipe freezes well.

Nutrition Facts

Carbohydrates: 20g| Protein: 23g| Fat: 8g| Saturated Fat: 2 g| Sodium: 382mg| Fiber: 2g

818. BOW TIES WITH CHICKEN AND MUSHROOM SAUCE

Preparation Time: 25 Minutes

Ingredients

- 2 cups (about 5 ounces) uncooked bow tie pasta
- 1 can (10 3/4 ounces) reduced-fat, reduced-sodium cream of mushroom soup (such as Campbell's Healthy Request)
- 3/4 cup skim milk
- 1 can (4 ounces) sliced mushrooms, drained
- 1/8 teaspoon black pepper
- 1/8 teaspoon garlic powder
- 1 can (5 ounces) chunk white chicken, drained and flaked
- Dash cayenne pepper

Directions

- Bring a saucepan of water to a boil, add pasta, and cook al dente, about 11 minutes.
- Meanwhile, in a separate pan, stir together soup, milk, mushrooms, black pepper, garlic powder, chicken, and cayenne pepper.
- Bring to a simmer over medium-low heat and heat through.
- Pour sauce over drained pasta and toss to coat.

Nutrition Facts

Carbohydrates: 32g| Protein: 9g| Fat: 3g| Saturated Fat: 1g| Sodium: 460mg| Fiber: 2g

819. CURRIED CHICKEN SALAD

Preparation Time: 25 Minutes
Chilling Time: 1 Hour

Ingredients

- 3 cups diced cooked chicken breast
- 1 carrot, grated
- 1 onion, finely chopped
- 2 celery stalks, chopped
- 1/2 cup raisins
- 3 tablespoons lemon juice
- 2 teaspoons curry powder
- 1 tablespoon honey
- 1/4 cup light mayonnaise
- 1 small head of romaine lettuce, washed and dried
- 2 tomatoes, cored and sliced into wedges
- 1 cup julienned radish

Directions

- In a large bowl, combine chicken, carrot, onion, celery, and raisins.
- In a separate small bowl, combine lemon juice, curry, honey, and mayonnaise.
- Stir curry mixture into chicken mixture, blending well. Chill for 1 hour.
- To serve, line plates with romaine lettuce leaves, mound chicken salad on the lettuce, and garnish the sides with tomato wedges and julienned radish.
- Serve immediately.

Nutrition Facts

Carbohydrates: 21g| Protein: 23g| Fat: 6g| Saturated Fat: 1g| Sodium: 156mg| Fiber: 3g

820. ROSEMARY CHICKEN ORZO

Preparation Time: 40 Minutes

Ingredients

- Cooking spray
- 8 ounces fully cooked boneless, skinless chicken breast strips (such as frozen Tyson's Fully Cooked Chicken Breast Strips)
- 2 cloves (or teaspoons) minced garlic
- 1 3/4 cups dry orzo pasta
- 1 (14-ounce) can fat-free, 1/3less-sodium chicken broth
- 1/2 cup water
- 1/2 teaspoon dried rosemary
- 1/2 teaspoon salt
- 1 medium zucchini (approximately 6–7 inches long), cut lengthwise into fourths, then crosswise into 1/4-inch-thick slices
- 4 Roma tomatoes, seeded and chopped (approximately 2 1/2 cups)
- 1 small onion, coarsely chopped (approximately 1 cup)
- 8 ounces fresh mushrooms, quartered

Directions

- Coat a large nonstick skillet with cooking spray and warm over medium-high heat.
- Add chicken, garlic, orzo, and broth; cover and bring to a boil. Reduce heat to medium-low and simmer 8–9 minutes, or until most of the liquid is absorbed. Stir occasionally to prevent sticking.
- Stir in remaining ingredients and return to a simmer (if mixture becomes too dry, add water to prevent sticking).
- Simmer 5–7 minutes, or until pasta is tender and vegetables are crisp-tender.

Nutrition Facts

Carbohydrates: 35g| Protein: 13g| Fat: 4g| Saturated Fat: <1g| Sodium: 238mg| Fiber: 3g

821. SKILLET CHICKEN PICCATA

Preparation Time: 5 Minutes
Cooking Time: 20 Minutes

Ingredients

- 4 four-ounce boneless, skinless chicken breasts
- 1 cup plus 1 tablespoon all-purpose flour
- Nonstick cooking spray
- Black pepper
- 2 teaspoons extra-virgin olive oil
- 1 tablespoon light margarine
- 1/2 teaspoon minced garlic
- 1 cup fat-free, low-sodium chicken broth
- 3 tablespoons fresh lemon juice
- 1/4 cup thawed and drained frozen green peas
- 1/4 cup chopped green onion

Directions

- Using a meat mallet, pound chicken breasts to a uniform thickness.
- Spread 1 cup flour on a dinner plate or shallow dish and dredge chicken pieces in flour. Spray a large skillet with nonstick cooking spray and heat to medium-high.
- Brown floured chicken pieces on both sides (about 2–3 minutes per side), then remove from skillet to a clean plate.
- Sprinkle chicken with black pepper.
- Lower heat under skillet to medium, and add olive oil, margarine, and garlic to skillet.
- When margarine has melted, sprinkle 1 tablespoon flour over the mixture and stir into a roux (pastelike mixture).
- Slowly add chicken broth to skillet, stirring constantly with a whisk or spoon.
- Continue stirring until sauce thickens, then mix in lemon juice. Return chicken to skillet, spooning some of the sauce over the chicken.
- Cover skillet and cook an additional 7–10 minutes over medium heat until sauce bubbles and chicken is cooked through.
- Add peas and green onion to the pan and cook 2 minutes more, then serve.

Nutrition Facts

Carbohydrates: 3g| Protein: 29g| Fat: 7g| Saturated Fat: 2g| Cholesterol: 78g| Sodium: 692mg| Fiber: 1g

822. PESTO CHICKEN SALAD

Preparation Time: 20 Minutes
Cooking Time: 10 Minutes

Ingredients

- 4 ounces boneless, skinless chicken breast
- Nonstick cooking spray
- 1 tablespoon prepared pesto
- 2 cups spring mix type lettuce, washed and patted dry
- 1 small cucumber, peeled and diced
- 1 cup fresh broccoli florets, coarsely chopped
- 6 baby carrots, sliced in half
- 10 grape tomatoes
- 2 tablespoons shredded Parmesan cheese

- 1/4 cup fat-free balsamic vinaigrette dressing

Directions

- Heat a small skillet over medium heat.
- Cut chicken breast into bite-size pieces.
- Spray a nonstick skillet with cooking spray and add chicken.
- Turn pieces frequently and add additional spray if needed to prevent sticking.
- When chicken is cooked through (about 5–7 minutes), add pesto and stir well to coat each piece.
- Remove chicken from pan and allow to cool.
- On each of two salad or dinner plates, spread a cup of lettuce, followed by a layer of cucumber, then broccoli.
- Add half the cooled chicken to each, then place carrots and tomatoes around the mound in a decorative pattern.
- Sprinkle 1 tablespoon of Parmesan cheese and drizzle 2 tablespoons of dressing onto each salad.

Nutrition Facts

Carbohydrates: 19g| Protein: 19g| Fat: 7g| Saturated Fat: 3g| Cholesterol: 45mg| Sodium: 493mg| Fiber: 4g

823. HOISIN CHICKEN WITH ORANGE SAUCE

Preparation Time: 45 Minutes, Including Cooking The Rice

Cooking Time: 15–20 Minutes

Ingredients

- 1 pound boneless, skinless chicken tenderloins or breasts
- 1 tablespoon canola oil
- Juice of 1 medium orange
- 2 tablespoons hoisin sauce
- 2 teaspoons sesame seeds
- 2 cups broccoli florets cut into bite-size pieces
- 2 medium oranges, peeled, with seeds removed, divided into sections, and sections cut in half
- 2 cups cooked brown rice

Directions

- Cut chicken into bite-size pieces. Heat oil in a large skillet over medium heat.
- Add chicken pieces and brown on both sides.
- When chicken is lightly browned but not cooked through, add orange juice and hoisin sauce to skillet. Cook 2 minutes.
- Add sesame seeds and broccoli pieces. Cover and cook for a few minutes until broccoli has turned bright green. Add the orange segments, and mix well. Cook for about 1 minute more to heat orange; do not overcook. Serve mixture on brown rice.

Nutrition Facts

- Carbohydrates: 40g| Protein: 20g| Fat: 7g| Saturated Fat: 1g| Cholesterol: 55mg| Sodium: 531mg| Fiber: 5g

824. SPICY APRICOT GLAZED CHICKEN

Preparation Time: 5 Minutes

Cooking Time: 25 Minutes

Ingredients

- Nonstick cooking spray
- 2 four-ounce boneless, skinless chicken breasts
- 1/2 teaspoon grated fresh ginger
- 2 tablespoons Smuckers Simply Fruit Apricot Spreadable Fruit
- 1 tablespoon rice wine vinegar
- 1/2 teaspoon crushed red pepper flakes
- 1 teaspoon extra-virgin olive oil
- Black pepper

Directions

- Preheat oven to 375°F.
- Spray a small baking sheet with nonstick cooking spray.
- Place the chicken breasts on the sheet.
- Combine the ginger, apricot spread, vinegar, pepper flakes, and olive oil in a small bowl with a fork or small whisk.
- Using a pastry brush or small spoon, spread the mixture evenly on the tops of the chicken breasts.
- Place in the oven, and bake for approximately 25 minutes until chicken is cooked through.
- Sprinkle with black pepper before serving.

Nutrition Facts

Carbohydrates: 19g| Protein: 19g| Fat: 7g| Saturated Fat: 3g| Cholesterol: 45mg| Sodium: 493mg| Fiber: 4g

Bayou Chicken

Preparation Time: 15 Minutes

Cooking Time: 30 Minutes

Ingredients

- 1 tablespoon extra-virgin olive oil
- 1/2 pound boneless, skinless chicken breast
- 1 cup chopped onion
- 1/2 cup chopped celery
- 1/2 pound Healthy One's Skinless Smoked Sausage
- 1 cup canned navy (or pinto) beans, rinsed
- 1 can (14.5 ounces) low-sodium diced tomatoes
- 1 can (14 ounces) fat-free, low-sodium chicken broth
- 1 cup uncooked brown rice
- 1/2 teaspoon thyme
- 1/4 teaspoon chopped garlic
- 1/4 teaspoon black pepper
- 1/4 cup chopped fresh parsley
- Hot sauce (to taste)

Directions

- In a large skillet, heat olive oil over medium heat.
- Cut chicken breast into bite-size pieces.
- Add chicken, onions, and celery to the skillet.
- Stirring frequently, cook just until chicken is white on all sides and onions and celery have softened. Slice sausage into thin slices and add to skillet; cook 1 minute more.
- Add beans, tomatoes, chicken broth, rice, thyme, garlic, and pepper, stirring well.
- Bring to a boil, while stirring, over medium heat, then reduce heat to low and cover.
- Simmer for approximately 20 minutes until rice is tender and has absorbed most of the liquid.

- Just before serving, stir in chopped parsley and a few drops of hot sauce.

Nutrition Facts

Carbohydrates: 60g| Protein: 26g| Fat: 6g| Saturated Fat: 4g| Cholesterol: 42mg| Sodium: 553mg| Fiber: 12g

825. "THINK THIN" CHICKEN GRAVY

Preparation Time: 1 Minute

Cooking Time: 10 Minutes

Ingredients

- 1 tablespoon reduced-calorie margarine
- 2 tablespoons plus 2 teaspoons all-purpose flour
- 1 can (14 ounces) 99% fat-free, low-sodium chicken broth
- 1/4 teaspoon black pepper
- 1/4 teaspoon onion powder

Directions

- In a small saucepan, melt margarine over medium heat.
- Sprinkle flour in, using a whisk to combine to form a paste. Slowly add chicken broth, whisking continuously.
- Add black pepper and onion powder, and continue whisking until heated through.
- Gravy will be moderately thick.

Nutrition Facts

Carbohydrates: 2g| Protein: 1g| Fat: 2g|Sodium: 192mg

826. CHICKEN DINNER SALAD WITH GREEN ONION DRESSING

Preparation Time: 10 Minutes

Cooking Time: 30 Minutes To Cook Chicken

Ingredients

- 4 cooked chicken breasts (3 ounces each), boneless, skinless
- 4 cups iceberg lettuce, washed and torn into bite-size pieces
- 4 small tomatoes (about 3 1/2 inches in diameter) or 24 grape tomatoes
- 1 large cucumber (about 8 inches), sliced thinly
- 1 cup grated carrot
- 4 ounces green onions
- 1/4 cup canola oil or extra-virgin olive oil
- 1/3 cup red wine vinegar
- 1 teaspoon Worcestershire sauce
- 1 teaspoon dry mustard
- 2 packets Splenda
- 2 tablespoons water
- 1/4 teaspoon black pepper
- 2 dashes salt
- 1/4 cup fresh cilantro leaves (optional)

Directions

Dressing:

- Cut chicken into bite-size cubes and set aside.
- Place 1 cup torn iceberg lettuce on each of four salad plates.
- Quarter each tomato and place quarters around each plate, or place 6 grape tomatoes on each plate.
- Distribute cucumber slices evenly between tomato slices on each plate.
- Top with grated carrots (1/4 cup per plate) and chicken.
- Trim the roots and 2 inches from the tops of the green onions.
- In a blender or food processor, combine all dressing ingredients and blend thoroughly until well mixed.
- Pour approximately 1/4 cup dressing over each salad. Top with cilantro if desired.

Nutrition Facts

Carbohydrates: 12g| Protein: 18g| Fat: 15g| Saturated Fat: 2g| Cholesterol: 56mg| Sodium: 411mg| Fiber: 3g

827. CARIBBEAN CHICKEN SALAD

Preparation Time: 25 Minutes

Ingredients

- 3 cups diced, cooked chicken breast (approximately 1 1/4 pounds)
- 1 can (8 ounces) crushed pineapple canned in juice, drained well
- 1/4 cup finely diced celery
- 1/2 cup toasted walnut pieces
- 3/4 cup fat-free mayonnaise (not salad dressing style mayonnaise)
- 1 tablespoon lime juice
- 1 teaspoon poppy seeds
- 1/4 teaspoon coarse ground black pepper
- 1 ripe medium mango, peeled, seeded, and diced into bite-size pieces

Directions

- Combine chicken, pineapple, celery, and walnuts in a bowl.
- In a separate bowl, whisk together mayonnaise, lime juice, poppy seeds, and pepper.
- Spoon over the chicken mixture and toss gently to coat. Gently toss in mango.
- Refrigerate until serving time.

Nutrition Facts

Carbohydrates: 13g| Protein: 24g| Fat: 6g| Saturated Fat: 1g| Sodium: 219mg| Fiber: 1g

828. LIME GRILLED CHICKEN RECIPE FOR DIABETICS

Preparation Time: 15 Minutes

Ingredients

- 1/4 cup fresh-squeezed lime juice (the juice of approximately 2–3 small limes; do not use lime juice concentrate)
- 2 teaspoons corn oil
- 2 tablespoons chopped, fresh cilantro leaves
- 1 clove (or 1 teaspoon) minced garlic
- 1/2 teaspoon chili powder
- 2 four-ounce boneless, skinless chicken breast cutlets(alternatively, pound chicken breasts to 1/4-inch thickness with a meat mallet)
- 2 teaspoons grated lime peel

Directions

- In a small bowl, whisk together lime juice, oil, cilantro, garlic, and chili powder.
- Pour into a large, zip-top bag. Add chicken cutlets and shake to coat well.
- Marinate at least 6–8 hours (or overnight) in the refrigerator, gently shaking the bag 2 or 3 times during marinating to recoat the chicken.
- Preheat grill to medium-high heat. Place chicken on grill rack and grill until juices run clear when meat is pierced with a fork, about 15 minutes.
- Discard remaining marinade.
- Sprinkle cooked chicken with lime peel.

- Chicken is tasty topped with salsa and served over rice, wrapped in warm flour tortillas, or sliced over salad greens.

Nutrition Facts

Carbohydrates: 5g| Protein: 27g| Fat: 3g| Saturated Fat: 1g| Sodium: 77mg| Fiber: 1g

829. TERIYAKI CHICKEN DRUMMIES

Total Time: 1 Hour 30 Minutes

Ingredients

- 1 bottle (10 ounces) low-sodium teriyaki sauce, divided
- 4 cloves garlic, crushed
- 1/4 teaspoon black pepper
- 3 pounds chicken drummettes (about 24 pieces total)
- 1 tablespoon toasted sesame seeds

Directions

- Reserve 1/4 cup teriyaki sauce; set aside.
- Combine remaining teriyaki sauce, garlic, and pepper in a shallow baking dish.
- Add drummettes; marinate in the refrigerator for 30 minutes, turning once.
- Preheat oven to 400°F. Spray baking sheet with nonstick cooking spray. Remove drummettes from dish; discard marinade.
- Place drummettes, skin side up, on a prepared baking sheet.
- Bake for 30 minutes or until golden brown.
- Immediately remove drummettes to the large bowl.
- Add reserved 1/4 cup teriyaki sauce; toss to coat evenly. Sprinkle with sesame seeds.

Nutrition Facts

Carbohydrates: 2g| Protein: 12g| Fat: 10g| Saturated Fat: 2g| Cholesterol: 40mg| Sodium: 300mg

830. SPAGHETTI SQUASH WITH CHUNKY TOMATO SAUCE

Total Time: 30 Minutes

Ingredients

- 1 tablespoon extra virgin olive oil
- 2 cups (6 ounces) sliced baby Bella mushrooms
- 1/2 cup diced onion
- 1/2 cup diced green bell pepper
- 1 can (about 14 ounces) no-salt-added diced tomatoes
- 1/2 cup no-salt-added pasta sauce
- 1/3 cup water
- 1/2 teaspoon dried oregano
- 1/4 teaspoon salt (optional)
- 1/8 teaspoon black pepper
- 4 (3-ounce) cooked chicken sausage links, cut into pieces
- 1 spaghetti squash (about 4 pounds)
- 2 tablespoons chopped fresh Italian parsley

Directions

- Cut spaghetti squash lengthwise in half. Remove seeds. Place squash in 12×8-inch microwavable dish. Cover with vented plastic wrap. Microwave on high for 9 minutes or until squash separates easily into strands when tested with a fork. Cut each squash half lengthwise in half; separate strands with a fork.
- Heat oil in a large skillet over medium-high heat. Add mushrooms, onion, and bell pepper; cook and stir for 7 minutes or until vegetables are tender.
- Stir tomatoes, pasta sauce, water, oregano, salt, if desired, and black pepper into skillet. Cover bring to a simmer; reduce heat and simmer 5 minutes. Stir sausage pieces into the sauce.
- Divide squash evenly among 4 plates. Spoon sauce over squash; sprinkle with parsley.

Nutrition Facts

Carbohydrates: 23g| Protein: 21g| Fat: 12g| Saturated Fat: 3g| Cholesterol: 73mg| Sodium: 549mg| Fiber: 7g

831. DIABETIC LEMON CHICKEN RECIPE

Preparation Time: 5 Minutes
Cooking Time: 30 Minutes

Ingredients

- Nonstick cooking spray
- 1 pound boneless, skinless chicken breast (4 pieces)
- 1 tablespoon olive oil
- 1 large lemon
- 1/2 teaspoon onion powder
- 1/2 teaspoon white pepper
- 1 1/2 teaspoons oregano

Directions

- Preheat oven to 375°F. Tear off a piece of aluminum foil that's large enough to wrap up all four pieces of chicken.
- Spray the aluminum foil with nonstick cooking spray (on one side only), and lay the chicken breasts on the sprayed foil.
- Drizzle with olive oil. Grate 1 tablespoon of lemon zest and set aside.
- Juice the lemon, removing the seeds.
- Pour lemon juice over the chicken, then sprinkle the chicken with lemon zest, onion powder, white pepper, and oregano.
- Fold the aluminum foil over the chicken and roll the edges of the foil together to make a sealed packet.
- Place packet on a jelly roll pan or in a large, shallow casserole dish.
- Bake 30 minutes.
- Remove from oven and carefully open foil, using tongs to remove chicken to a serving plate.

Nutrition Facts

Carbohydrates: 3g| Protein: 30g| Fat: 7g| Saturated Fat: 2g| Cholesterol: 96mg| Sodium: 347mg

832. BASIL CHICKEN BITES

Preparation time: 5 minutes
Cooking time: 14 minutes

Ingredients

- 1 pound chicken breast tenderloins
- 1 1/2 teaspoons dried basil
- 1/4 teaspoon black pepper
- 1/8 teaspoon salt (optional)
- 1/4 teaspoon garlic powder
- 1 tablespoon extra-virgin olive oil

Directions

- Cut tenderloins into bite-size pieces, about 2 inches long.
- Place pieces in a plastic bag along with basil, pepper, salt, and garlic powder.

- Shake well to coat. Heat olive oil in a large skillet over medium heat. Add chicken.
- Sauté over medium heat, turning frequently, until chicken is cooked through, about 10–12 minutes.

Nutrition Facts

Protein: 24g| Fat: 8g| Saturated Fat: 2g| Cholesterol: 90mg| Sodium: 341mg with salt| 50mg without salt,

833. LOW-SODIUM HERB ROASTED CHICKEN RECIPE

Preparation Time: 20 Minutes
Cooking Time: 90 Minutes To 2 Hours, 15 Minutes.

Ingredients

- 1 six- to seven-pound oven roaster (Note: Kosher chickens and chickens labeled "basted" or "self basted" have sodium added.)
- 2 tablespoons olive oil
- Carrots (optional)
- 2 teaspoons garlic powder
- 1 teaspoon black pepper
- 1 1/2 teaspoons ground thyme
- 3/4 teaspoon ground sage
- 3/4 teaspoon marjoram
- 3/4 teaspoon ground rosemary
- 1/4 teaspoon nutmeg
- 1 1/2 teaspoons thyme leaves
- 1 1/2 teaspoons rosemary leaves
- 1 lemon

Directions

- Remove neck and giblets from, then rinse and pat dry chicken.
- Rub olive oil on inside and outside of the chicken, then place breast-side up in a shallow roasting pan, on a rack or a "bed" of carrots, if desired.
- Mix all dry ingredients in a small bowl and rub on chicken (inside and out).
- Slice the lemon and squeeze the juice onto the chicken (inside and out).
- Place lemon rinds inside the chicken and around legs and wings.
- Roast uncovered at 350°F until a thermometer inserted into the breast meat registers 165°F.
- Depending on the size of the bird, this will take between 90 minutes and 2 hours, 15 minutes.

Nutrition Facts

Protein: 21g/17g| Fat: 10g/16g| Saturated Fat: 3g/5g| Cholesterol: 85mg/110mg| Sodium: 45mg/55mg

834. EASY SOUTH-OF-THE-BORDER GRILLED CHICKEN FOR DIABETICS

Preparation Time: 5 Minutes
Cooking Time: 20 Minutes.

Ingredients

- 1/2 cup reduced-fat sour cream
- 2 teaspoons lemon juice
- 1 packet taco seasoning (If watching sodium, look for reduced-sodium taco seasoning.)
- 4 small skinless, boneless, chicken breasts

Directions

- In a medium bowl, mix sour cream, lemon juice, and taco seasoning with a wire whisk.
- Rinse chicken breasts and pat dry. Dip chicken breasts in sour cream mixture and coat evenly.
- Grill breasts for about 10 minutes on each side or until done.
- Serve. If a grill is not available, you can also sauté the chicken breasts on the stovetop in a skillet coated with nonstick cooking spray over medium to medium-low heat.

Nutrition Facts

Carbohydrates: 5g| Protein: 26g| Fat: 7g| Saturated Fat: 3.5g| Cholesterol: 74mg| Sodium: 639mg

835. SLOW-COOKED SOUTHWESTERN CHICKEN CHILI

Preparation time: 25 minutes

Ingredients

- 1 1/2 medium onions, chopped
- 3 medium plum tomatoes, chopped
- 2 cloves garlic, minced
- 2 cups fat-free, low-sodium chicken broth
- 2 cups shredded, cooked chicken breast
- 1 can (15 ounces) kidney beans with liquid
- 1 can (15 ounces) sweet corn with liquid
- 1 small can (6 ounces) tomato paste
- 2 teaspoons chili powder
- 1 teaspoon cumin
- 1 teaspoon dried oregano
- 1/2 cup chopped cilantro (optional)

Directions

- In a slow cooker or Crock-Pot, add all ingredients except cilantro, combine well, and turn on high setting for two hours.
- Reduce to low setting and cook for additional 5 hours, stirring occasionally, until vegetables are tender.
- Ladle into soup bowls and garnish each serving with 2 tablespoons of chopped cilantro (optional).
- Serve immediately.

Nutrition Facts

Carbohydrates: 16g| Protein: 24g| Fat: 2g| Sodium: 79mg| Fiber: 4g

836. ASIAN RAINBOW CHICKEN SALAD

Preparation Time: 25 Minutes

Ingredients

- 2 cups chopped cooked chicken (light meat)
- 4 cups napa cabbage, shredded coarsely
- 1 cup red cabbage, shredded coarsely
- 3/4 cup sliced mushrooms
- 1 cup shredded carrots
- 3 tablespoons chopped fresh cilantro
- 1 cup sliced cucumbers
- 1 cup sliced green onions
- 1 cup canned mandarin oranges, drained
- 2 tablespoons chopped, unsalted peanuts
- 2 tablespoons peanut oil
- 4 tablespoons rice vinegar
- 3/4 teaspoon black pepper
- 1 teaspoon light soy sauce
- 1 clove garlic, minced
- 1 teaspoon Dijon mustard
- 1 1/2 teaspoons honey

Directions

- In a large salad bowl, add chicken, shredded napa cabbage, shredded red cabbage, sliced mushrooms, shredded

carrots, fresh cilantro, sliced cucumbers, sliced green onions, mandarin oranges, and chopped peanuts.
- In a small mixing bowl, whisk together peanut oil, rice vinegar, black pepper, light soy sauce, minced garlic, mustard, and honey.
- Add dressing to salad and toss to distribute all ingredients.
- Serve immediately.

Nutrition Information

Carbohydrates: 11g| Protein: 16g| Fat: 8g| Saturated Fat: 2g| Sodium: 120mg| Fiber: 3g

837. MOROCCAN LEMON CHICKEN WITH OLIVES

Preparation Time: 20 Minutes
Cooking Time: 1 Hour

Ingredients

- 1 tablespoon olive oil
- 6 skinless, boneless chicken breasts (approximately 4 ounces per breast)
- 1 large onion, chopped
- 2 cloves garlic, minced
- 2 sticks whole cinnamon
- 2 teaspoons ground cumin
- 2 teaspoons ground turmeric
- 1/2 teaspoon freshly ground black pepper
- 2 lemons
- 2 small plum tomatoes, chopped
- 1 cup water
- 18 large green olives

Directions

- Heat olive oil in a large pan. Place chicken breasts in hot oil and cook on all sides until slightly browned on the surface.
- Remove from pan and set aside. To the pan add onion, garlic, cinnamon sticks, cumin, turmeric, and black pepper.
- Cook about 5 minutes, stirring, until onion is cooked. Return chicken to pan and cover.
- Squeeze the juice of two lemons, reserving lemon peels.
- Add lemon juice to the pan. Slice lemon peels into strips and add to the pan with chopped tomatoes, water, and olives.
- Cover the pan and bring contents to a boil, then reduce heat to low and allow the mixture to simmer for about 45 minutes, until chicken is tender, occasionally lifting the lid to stir the mixture and check that liquid available in the pot is adequate to avoid burning.
- When chicken is done, arrange contents on a platter, discarding cinnamon sticks. Serve immediately. (This dish is excellent served with couscous.)

Nutrition Facts

Carbohydrates: 4g| Protein: 28g| Fat: 5g| Saturated Fat: 1g| Sodium: 194mg| Fiber: 1g

838. WHOLE-GRAIN ROTINI WITH ASPARAGUS AND CHICKEN

Preparation Time: 15 Minutes
Cooking Time: 18 Minutes

Ingredients

- 1 large red bell pepper
- 8 ounces whole-grain rotini pasta
- 2 tablespoons extra-virgin olive oil
- 1 pound fresh asparagus, ends trimmed, cut into 2–2 1/2-inch pieces
- 1 pound cooked chicken breast (skinless and boneless), cut into bite-size pieces
- 1 teaspoon minced garlic
- 1/2 pound fresh mushrooms, sliced
- 1 1/4 cups fat-free low-sodium chicken broth
- 1 1/2 teaspoons fresh thyme
- 1/4 cup grated Romano cheese
- Black pepper to taste

Directions

- Cut bell pepper into approximately 2 1/2-inch pieces and arrange pieces on a broiler-safe pan. Place in the broiler, and broil until flesh is soft and skin has some browning.
- Remove and let cool. Once cool, cut into strips.
- Bring at least 2 quarts of water to a boil, add rotini, and cook for about 8–10 minutes.
- Drain and reserve in a bowl. Heat olive oil in a large nonstick skillet on medium heat.
- Add asparagus and sauté for 2 minutes.
- Add chicken breast and garlic and stir constantly for about 1 minute more to heat (if sticking occurs, add 2 tablespoons of the chicken broth rather than more oil).
- Quickly add mushrooms, red pepper, chicken broth, and thyme.
- Heat until just about boiling then quickly add reserved pasta and combine with a slotted spoon or spatula.
- Carefully transfer the mixture into a large pasta or serving dish and top with Romano cheese and black pepper.

Nutrition Facts

Carbohydrates: 50g| Protein: 35g| Fat: 12g| Saturated Fat: 3g| Cholesterol: 80mg| Sodium: 690mg| Fiber: 8g

839. CHICKEN WITH SPINACH AND ARTICHOKES

Total Time: 45-50 Minutes

Ingredients

- 1 cup frozen chopped spinach, thawed and well-drained
- 4 canned artichoke hearts, drained and chopped
- 1/4 cup plus 2 tablespoons grated Parmesan cheese, divided
- 1/4 cup frozen chopped onions, thawed and well-drained
- 1/4 cup fat-free mayonnaise
- 1/2 teaspoon minced garlic
- 1/8 teaspoon black pepper
- 1 cup chopped cooked chicken pieces

Directions

- Preheat oven to 375°F. Coat 1-quart casserole with nonstick cooking spray.
- Combine spinach, artichoke hearts, 2 tablespoons cheese, onions, mayonnaise, garlic, and pepper in a medium bowl.
- Place chicken in prepared casserole; top evenly with spinach mixture.
- Top with remaining 1/4 cup cheese.
- Bake 30 minutes or until cheese is browned.

Nutrition Facts

Carbohydrates: 19g| Protein: 37g| Fat: 11g| Saturated Fat: 4g| Cholesterol: 89mg| Sodium: 797mg| Fiber: 8g

840. GRILLED BUFFALO CHICKEN TENDERS

Total Time: 50 Minutes

Ingredients

- 2 skinless chicken breast cutlets (about 4 ounces each)
- 6 tablespoons Walden Farms Calorie Free Thick 'N Spicy BBQ Sauce, divided
- 1/4 cup Walden Farms Calorie Free Bleu Cheese Salad Dressing
- 1 dash hot sauce (optional)

Directions

- Cut chicken into "tender" size pieces. Marinate chicken in Walden Farms
- Calorie Free Thick 'N Spicy BBQ sauce for at least 30 minutes.
- Prepare grill for direct grilling. Brush off excess BBQ Sauce, then place chicken on the grill.
- Stir dash hot sauce, if using, into remaining Walden Farms Calorie Free Thick 'N Spicy BBQ Sauce and baste the chicken as it grills.
- Grill chicken until cooked through and juices run clear.
- Serve with Walden Farms Calorie Free Bleu Cheese Salad Dressing for dipping.

Nutrition Facts

Protein: 36g| Fat: 4g| Saturated Fat: 1.5g| Cholesterol: 65 mg| Sodium: 490mg

841. CHOPPED ROASTED CHICKEN SALAD

Total Time: 1 Hour

Ingredients

- 2 cloves garlic, minced
- 1 teaspoon dried basil
- 1 teaspoon balsamic vinegar
- 1/4 teaspoon red pepper flakes
- 2 bone-in skin-on chicken breasts
- 6 cups chopped romaine lettuce
- 2 cups chopped baby arugula
- 1/2 cup quartered red or yellow grape tomatoes
- 1/2 cup chopped drained artichoke hearts
- 1/2 cup chopped roasted red peppers
- 1/2 cup canned cannellini beans, rinsed and drained
- 1/2 cup low-fat balsamic vinaigrette dressing

Directions

- Preheat oven to 400°F. Place a wire rack on a rimmed baking sheet.
- Combine lettuce, arugula, tomatoes, artichoke hearts, roasted peppers, beans, and remaining chicken in a large serving bowl. Serve with dressing.
- Combine garlic, basil, vinegar, and red pepper flakes in a small bowl.
- Carefully spread half of the garlic mixture under the skin of each chicken breast.
- Place chicken on wire rack. Roast 45 minutes or until no longer pink in the center.
- Remove skin; let stand until cool enough to handle.
- Chop chicken; reserve 1/2 cup for Chicken Caprese Panini or another use.

Nutrition Facts

Carbohydrates: 15g| Protein: 29g| Fat: 9g| Saturated Fat: 1g| Cholesterol: 76mg| Sodium: 728mg| Fiber: 4g

842. PROVENÇAL LEMON AND OLIVE CHICKEN

Total Time: 3-6 Hour

Ingredients

- 2 cups chopped onion
- 2 pounds skinless chicken thighs
- 1 medium lemon, thinly sliced and seeded
- 1/2 cup pitted green olives
- 1 tablespoon white vinegar or olive brine
- 2 teaspoons herbes de Provence
- 1 bay leaf
- 1/2 teaspoon salt
- 1/8 teaspoon black pepper
- 1 cup fat-free reduced-sodium chicken broth
- 1/2 cup minced fresh parsley

Directions

- Place onions in the slow cooker.
- Arrange chicken thighs and lemon slices over onion.
- Add olives, vinegar, herbes de Provence, bay leaf, salt, and pepper. Pour in broth.
- Cover; cook on LOW 5 to 6 hours or on HIGH 3 to 3 1/2 hours or until chicken is tender.
- Remove and discard bay leaf. Stir in parsley before serving.

Nutrition Facts

Carbohydrates: 5g| Protein: 18g| Fat: 10g| Saturated Fat: 3g| Cholesterol: 75mg| Sodium: 400mg| Fiber: 1g

843. CHICKEN AND SWEET POTATO CHILI FOR DIABETICS

Total Time: 30 Minutes

Ingredients

- 1 to 2 sweet potatoes, peeled and cut into 1/2-inch chunks
- 2 teaspoons canola oil
- 1 cup chopped onion
- 3/4 pound boneless skinless chicken breasts or chicken tenders, cut into 3/4-inch chunks
- 3 cloves garlic, minced
- 2 teaspoons chili powder
- 1 can (14 1/2 ounces) diced fire-roasted tomatoes, undrained
- 1 can (16 ounces) no-salt-added kidney beans or pinto beans, drained
- 1/2 cup chipotle or jalapeño salsa

Directions

- Place sweet potatoes in a large saucepan and add enough water to cover.
- Bring to a boil. Reduce heat; simmer for 5 minutes or until almost tender.
- Drain sweet potatoes; set aside. Heat oil in a large saucepan over medium heat.
- Add onion; cook and stir for 5 minutes.
- Add chicken, garlic, and chili powder; cook 3 minutes, stirring frequently.
- Add tomatoes, beans, salsa, and sweet potatoes; bring to a boil over high heat.
- Reduce heat; simmer uncovered 10 minutes or until chicken is cooked through.

Nutrition Facts

Carbohydrates: 34g| Protein: 27g| Fat: 1g| Saturated Fat: 1g| Cholesterol: 49mg| Sodium: 496mg| Fiber: 7g

844. EASY CHICKEN, SPINACH, AND WILD RICE SOUP

Total Time: 20 Minutes

Ingredients

- 1 can (about 14 ounces) reduced-sodium chicken broth
- 1 3/4 cups chopped carrots
- 2 cans (10 3/4 ounces each) reduced-fat reduced-sodium condensed cream of chicken soup, undiluted
- 2 cups cooked wild rice
- 1 teaspoon dried thyme
- 1/4 teaspoon dried sage
- 1/4 teaspoon black pepper
- 2 cups coarsely chopped baby spinach
- 1 1/2 cups chopped cooked chicken
- 1/2 cup fat-free half-and-half or fat-free (skim) milk

Directions

- Bring broth to a boil in a large saucepan over medium-high heat. Add carrots; cook 10 minutes.
- Add soup, rice, thyme, sage, and pepper to the saucepan; bring to a boil.
- Stir in spinach, chicken, and half-and-half; cook and stir 2 minutes or until heated through.

Nutrition Facts

Carbohydrates: 28g| Protein: 22g| Fat: 7g| Saturated Fat: 2g| Cholesterol: 62mg| Sodium: 624mg| Fiber: 3g

845. VEGETABLE-CHICKEN NOODLE SOUP

Total Time: 35 Minutes

Ingredients

- 1 cup chopped celery
- 1/2 cup thinly sliced leek (white part only)
- 1/2 cup chopped carrot
- 1/2 cup chopped turnip
- 6 cups fat-free reduced-sodium chicken broth, divided
- 1 tablespoon minced fresh parsley
- 1 1/2 teaspoons fresh thyme or 1/2 teaspoon dried thyme
- 1 teaspoon minced fresh rosemary leaves or 1/4 teaspoon dried rosemary
- 1 teaspoon balsamic vinegar
- 1/4 teaspoon black pepper
- 2 ounces uncooked yolk-free wide noodles
- 1 cup boneless skinless chicken breast, cooked and diced

Directions

- Combine celery, leek, carrot, turnip, and 1/3 cup chicken broth in a large saucepan. Cover; cook over medium heat 12 to 15 minutes or until vegetables are tender, stirring occasionally.
- Stir in remaining 5 2/3 cups broth, parsley, thyme, rosemary, vinegar, and pepper; bring to a boil. Add noodles; cook until noodles are tender.
- Stir in chicken. Reduce heat to medium; simmer until heated through.

Nutrition Facts

Carbohydrates: 12g| Protein: 10g| Fat: 2g| Saturated Fat: 1g| Cholesterol: 18mg| Sodium: 73mg| Fiber: 1g

846. CHICKEN NUGGETS WITH BARBECUE DIPPING SAUCE

Total Time: 30-40 Minutes

Ingredients

- 1 pound boneless skinless chicken breasts
- 1/4 cup all-purpose flour
- 1/4 teaspoon salt
- Dash black pepper
- 2 cups crushed reduced-fat baked cheese crackers
- 1 teaspoon dried oregano
- 1 egg white
- 1 tablespoon water
- 3 tablespoons barbecue sauce
- 2 tablespoons no-sugar-added peach or apricot fruit spread

Directions

- Preheat oven to 400°F. Cut chicken into 40 (1-inch) pieces.
- Place flour, salt, and pepper in a large resealable food storage bag. Combine cracker crumbs and oregano in a shallow bowl. Whisk together egg white and water in a small bowl.
- Place 6 to 8 chicken pieces in bag with flour mixture; seal bag. Shake until chicken is well coated. Remove chicken from bag; shake off excess flour. Coat all sides of chicken pieces with egg white mixture. Roll in crumb mixture. Place in shallow baking pan. Repeat with remaining chicken pieces. Bake 10 to 13 minutes or until golden brown.
- Meanwhile, combine barbecue sauce and jam in a small saucepan; cook and stir over low heat until heated through. Serve chicken nuggets with dipping sauce.

Nutrition Facts

Carbohydrates: 16g| Protein: 14g| Fat: 4g| Saturated Fat: 1g| Cholesterol: 61mg| Sodium: 313mg| Fiber: 1g

847. PROSCIUTTO, ASPARAGUS, AND CHICKEN PIZZA

Total Time: 30 Minutes

Ingredients

- 1 package (10 ounces) prepared whole-wheat pizza crust
- 1/2 cup pizza sauce
- 4 asparagus spears, cut into 1-inch pieces, microwaved for 1 minute
- 1/2 cup chopped prosciutto
- 1/2 cup chopped red onion
- 1 cup shredded cooked chicken breast
- 1/2 cup finely shredded part-skim mozzarella cheese

Directions

- Heat oven to 450°F. Place pizza crust on a baking sheet.
- Spread pizza sauce on crust and arrange prosciutto, onion, and chicken on top.
- Sprinkle evenly with cheese.
- Bake 10 to 12 minutes or until cheese is melted and crust edges are brown.

Nutrition Facts

- Carbohydrates: 27g| Protein: 9g| Fat: 5g| Saturated Fat: 3g| Sodium: 475mg| Fiber: 5g| Calcium: 214mg

848. ASPARAGUS AND CHEDDAR STUFFED CHICKEN BREASTS FOR DIABETICS

Total Time: 50-60 Minutes

Ingredients

- 20 asparagus spears (about 2 bunches)
- 2 cups fat-free reduced-sodium chicken broth
- 1 medium red bell pepper, chopped
- 1/2 teaspoon roasted crushed garlic
- 1 teaspoon dried parsley
- 1/4 teaspoon black pepper
- 4 boneless skinless chicken breasts (about 1/4 pound each)
- 4 tablespoons shredded reduced-fat Cheddar cheese
- 4 tablespoons corn relish (optional)

Directions

- Snap woody stem ends off asparagus and discard.
- Cut off asparagus tips about 4 inches long; set aside. Slice asparagus stalks and combine with broth, red pepper, garlic, parsley, and black pepper in a saucepan. Cook over medium-high heat for 25 minutes, stirring occasionally.
- While vegetables cook, place each chicken breast half between plastic wrap, and pound with a rolling pin until approximately 1/4 inch thick.
- Preheat electric indoor grill with lid.
- Lay 5 asparagus tips across one end of each pounded breast. Top each with 1 tablespoon cheese and fold in half.
- Place stuffed breasts on the grill and cook with lid closed for 6 minutes.
- Spoon vegetable sauce onto serving plates and top with cooked breast. Garnish with corn relish, if desired.
- **Gelatin Salad:** If desired, serve with Gelatin Salad.
- Mix 4 cups ready-to-use shredded cabbage, 1 cup mandarin orange segments, and 1/2 cup fat-free vinaigrette in a medium bowl.
- Divide mixture evenly among 4 salad plates.
- Remove orange gelatin from 4 ready-to-use, sugar-free gelatin dessert cups and slice gelatin with an egg slicer or knife. Top each salad with gelatin slices.
- Garnish each serving with 1/2 tablespoon dried cranberries. Refrigerate until ready to serve.

Nutrition Facts

Carbohydrates: 5g| Protein: 33g| Fat: 4g| Saturated Fat: 2g| Cholesterol: 83mg| Sodium: 317mg| Fiber: 2g

849. CREAMY BAKED CHICKEN WITH ARTICHOKES AND MUSHROOMS

Total Time: 50-60 Minutes

Ingredients

- 6 boneless skinless chicken breasts (about 4 ounces each)
- 1 1/2 teaspoons paprika
- 1 1/2 teaspoons dried thyme
- 1/2 teaspoon salt
- 1/2 teaspoon black pepper
- 1 can (14 ounces) artichokes packed in water, drained
- 1 tablespoon butter
- 1 package (8 ounces) sliced cremini mushrooms
- 2 tablespoons all-purpose flour
- 3/4 cup low-sodium chicken broth
- 1/2 cup fat-free half-and-half

Directions

- Preheat oven to 375°F.
- Place chicken in a 13X9-inch baking dish. Combine paprika, thyme, salt, and pepper in a small bowl; mix well. Reserve 1 teaspoon seasoning mixture; set aside. Sprinkle the remaining seasoning mixture evenly over the chicken. Cut artichokes in half; arrange around chicken.
- Melt butter in a large saucepan over medium heat.
- Add mushrooms and reserved 1 teaspoon seasoning mixture; cook and stir 5 minutes or until tender. Sprinkle flour over mushrooms; cook and stir for 1 minute.
- Stir in broth; simmer for 3 minutes or until thickened.
- Stir in half-and-half; cook 1 minute. Pour evenly over chicken and artichokes.
- Bake 30 minutes or until no longer pink.

Nutrition Facts

Carbohydrates: 14g| Protein: 29g| Fat: 6g| Saturated Fat: 2g| Cholesterol: 79mg| Sodium: 425mg| Fiber: 7g

850. GRILLED CHICKEN ADOBO

Total Time: 5 Hours

Ingredients

- 1/2 cup chopped onion
- 1/3 cup lime juice
- 6 cloves garlic, coarsely chopped
- 1 teaspoon ground cumin
- 1 teaspoon dried oregano
- 1/2 teaspoon dried thyme
- 1/4 teaspoon ground red pepper
- 6 boneless skinless chicken breasts (about 1/4 pound each)
- 3 tablespoons chopped fresh cilantro (optional)

Directions

- Combine onion, lime juice, and garlic in a food processor.
- Process until onion is finely minced.
- Transfer to large resealable food storage bag.
- Add cumin, oregano, thyme, and red pepper; knead bag until blended. Place chicken in bag; press out air and seal.
- Turn to coat chicken with marinade. Refrigerate 30 minutes or up to 4 hours, turning occasionally.
- Spray grid with nonstick cooking spray. Prepare grill for direct cooking.
- Remove chicken from marinade; discard marinade. Place chicken on the grid.
- Grill 5 to 7 minutes on each side over medium heat, or until chicken is no longer pink in center.
- Transfer to clean serving platter and garnish with cilantro, if desired.

Nutrition Facts

Carbohydrates: 1g| Protein: 25g| Fat: 3g| Saturated Fat: 1g| Cholesterol: 69mg| Sodium: 61mg| Fiber: 1g

851. QUICK ORANGE CHICKEN

Total Time: 20 Minutes

Ingredients

- 2 tablespoons frozen orange juice concentrate
- 1 tablespoon no-sugar-added orange marmalade
- 1 teaspoon Dijon mustard
- 1/4 teaspoon salt
- 4 boneless skinless chicken breast halves (about 1 pound)
- 1/2 cup fresh orange sections
- 2 tablespoons chopped fresh parsley

Directions

- For the sauce, combine juice concentrate, marmalade, mustard, and salt in the 8-inch shallow microwavable dish until juice concentrate is thawed.
- Add chicken, coating both sides with sauce. Arrange chicken around the edge of the dish without overlapping. Cover with vented plastic wrap.
- Microwave on high for 3 minutes; turn chicken over.
- Microwave on medium-high (70%) for 4 minutes, or until chicken is no longer pink in center.
- Remove chicken to a serving plate. Microwave remaining sauce on high for 2 to 3 minutes, or until slightly thickened.
- To serve, spoon sauce over chicken; top with orange sections and parsley.

Nutrition Facts

Carbohydrates: 8g| Protein: 27g| Fat: 1g| Saturated Fat: 1g| Cholesterol: 66mg| Sodium: 234mg| Fiber: 1g

852. FAJITA-SEASONED GRILLED CHICKEN

Total Time: 20 Minutes

Ingredients

- 2 boneless skinless chicken breasts (about 4 ounces each)
- 1 bunch green onions, ends trimmed
- 1 tablespoon olive oil
- 2 teaspoons fajita seasoning mix

Directions

- Prepare grill for direct cooking.
- Brush chicken and green onions with oil. Sprinkle both sides of chicken breasts with seasoning mix.
- Grill chicken and onions for 6 to 8 minutes or until chicken is no longer pink in the center.
- Serve chicken with onions.

Nutrition Facts

Carbohydrates: 8g| Protein: 19g| Fat: 8g| Saturated Fat: 1g| Cholesterol: 43mg| Sodium: 186mg| Fiber: 2g

853. GRILLED CHICKEN WITH CORN AND BLACK BEAN SALSA

Total Time: 30 Minutes

Ingredients

- 1/2 cup corn
- 1/2 cup finely chopped red bell pepper
- 1/2 (15-ounce) can black beans, rinsed and drained
- 1/2 ripe medium avocado, diced
- 1/4 cup chopped fresh cilantro
- 2 tablespoons fresh lime juice
- 1 tablespoon chopped sliced pickled jalapeño pepper
- 1/2 teaspoon salt, divided
- 1 teaspoon black pepper
- 1/2 teaspoon chili powder
- 4 boneless skinless chicken breasts (4 ounces each), pounded to 1/2-inch thickness
- Nonstick cooking spray

Directions

- Combine corn, bell pepper, beans, avocado, cilantro, lime juice, jalapeño, and 1/4 teaspoon salt in a medium bowl.
- Set aside.
- Combine black pepper, remaining 1/4 teaspoon salt, and chili powder in a small bowl; sprinkle over chicken.
- Coat grill pan with cooking spray.
- Cook chicken over medium-high heat 4 minutes per side or until no longer pink in center.
- Serve chicken topped with half of the salsa; refrigerate remaining salsa for another use.

Nutrition Facts

Carbohydrates: 16g| Protein: 30g| Fat: 7g| Saturated Fat: 1g| Cholesterol: 60mg| Sodium: 425mg| Fiber: 5g

854. ASIAN CHICKEN

Total Time: 2 Hour

Ingredients

- 3 pounds boneless skinless chicken breasts
- 1/2 cup reduced-sodium soy sauce
- 1/4 cup fresh lemon juice
- 1 tablespoon honey
- 2 teaspoons sesame oil
- 1 teaspoon dry mustard
- 1 teaspoon grated fresh ginger or 1/2 teaspoon powdered ginger
- 1 teaspoon minced garlic
- 1/4 teaspoon red pepper flakes

Directions

- Place soy sauce, juice, honey, oil, mustard, ginger, garlic, and red pepper flakes in a gallon-size resealable food storage bag.
- Add chicken. Seal bag. Turn to coat evenly.
- Place bag in pan. Chill in refrigerator 1 hour or overnight.
- Preheat oven to 350°F. Line roasting pan with foil. Remove chicken from bag and place in pan. (Discard unused marinade.)
- Bake chicken breasts for 30 minutes or until no longer pink in the center.

Nutrition Facts

Carbohydrates: 4g| Protein: 32g| Fat: 3g| Saturated Fat: 1g| Cholesterol: 78mg| Sodium: 475mg| Fiber: 1g

855. LEMON PEPPER CHICKEN WINGS

Total Time: 60 Minutes

Ingredients

- Large baking sheet, lined with foil, with a wire rack set on top
- 2 pounds free-range chicken wings
- 2 tablespoons grated lemon zest
- 2 tablespoons freshly squeezed lemon juice
- 1 tablespoon freshly ground black pepper
- 1 teaspoon sea salt

Directions

- Preheat oven to 375°F (190°C).
- Pat chicken dry with paper towels, removing as much moisture as you can.
- Arrange on the wire rack over the prepared baking sheet, leaving space in between, if possible.
- Roast in preheated oven for 30 to 35 minutes, flipping them over halfway through until juices run clear when chicken is pierced.
- Meanwhile, in a large bowl, combine lemon zest, lemon juice, pepper, and salt.
- Add wings to the lemon sauce and toss until evenly coated. Serve hot.

Nutrition Facts

Carbohydrates: 2g| Protein: 27g| Fat: 20g| Fiber: 1g

856. GRILLED MARINATED CHICKEN

Total Time: 4 Hour

Ingredients

- 8 whole chicken legs (thighs and drumsticks attached) (about 3 1/2 pounds)
- 6 ounces frozen lemonade concentrate, thawed
- 2 tablespoons white wine vinegar
- 1 tablespoon grated lemon peel
- 2 cloves garlic, minced

Directions

- Remove skin and all visible fat from the chicken.
- Place chicken in a 13×9-inch glass baking dish. Combine remaining ingredients in a small bowl; blend well.
- Pour over chicken; turn to coat. Cover; refrigerate for 3 hours or overnight, turning occasionally.
- To prevent sticking, spray the grid with nonstick cooking spray. Prepare coals for grilling.
- Place chicken on grill 4 inches from medium-hot coals.
- Grill 20 to 30 minutes or until cooked through (165°F), turning occasionally.
- Garnish as desired.

Nutrition Facts

Protein: 22g| Fat: 7g| Saturated Fat: 2g| Cholesterol: 77mg| Sodium: 75mg| Fiber: 1g

857. BARLEY AND SAUSAGE GUMBO

Total Time: 6 Hour

Ingredients

- 1 small onion, chopped
- 1 large green bell pepper, chopped
- 1 cup frozen sliced okra
- 1 medium stalk celery, chopped
- 1 clove garlic, minced
- 1 cup reduced-sodium chicken broth
- 1 cup no-salt-added tomato purée
- 1/4 cup uncooked pearl barley
- 1 teaspoon dried oregano
- 1/4 teaspoon salt (optional)
- 1/8 teaspoon red pepper flakes
- 2 low-fat chicken andouille sausages (3 ounces each), sliced 1/2 inch thick

Directions

- Place onion, bell pepper, okra, celery, and garlic in the slow cooker.
- Add chicken broth, tomato purée, barley, oregano, salt, if desired, and red pepper flakes; stir.
- Add sliced sausages. Cover; cook on LOW 5 to 6 hours. Let stand 5 minutes before serving.

Nutrition Facts

Carbohydrates: 24g| Protein: 12g| Fat: 5g| Saturated Fat: 1g| Cholesterol: 31mg| Sodium: 363mg| Fiber: 6g

858. "PAPPARDELLE" OF CHICKEN WITH WINTER PESTO

Preparation time: 15 minutes
Cooking time: 15 minutes.

Ingredients

- 2 quarts water
- Olive oil cooking spray
- 6 garlic cloves, chopped
- Dash of cinnamon
- Dash of paprika
- Crushed red pepper flakes
- 1 cup fresh basil leaves
- 1 small onion, thinly sliced
- 8 cups finely chopped escarole
- 4 cups unsalted chicken stock (such as Kitchen Basics)
- Salt
- 12 ounces skinless, boneless chicken breast, sliced lengthwise into strips 1/8 inches thick
- 1 ounce Parmigiano-Reggiano cheese, finely grated on a Microplane grater

Directions

- Bring 2 quarts of water to a simmer in a medium pot; you will be using this to poach the chicken strips.
- Lightly coat a medium skillet with olive oil cooking spray and place over medium-high heat.
- Add the garlic and cook until golden brown. Add the cinnamon, paprika, red pepper flakes, basil leaves, and onion.
- Cook until the onion has softened, about 2 minutes.
- Add the escarole and cook until it has wilted and softened, another 2 minutes.
- Add the stock, bring to a simmer, cover, and cook until tender, about 5 minutes.
- Add a pinch of salt to the now-simmering water.
- Turn off the heat and add the chicken and stir so that all the strips are separated. Cook just until the strips have turned white; they will be half-cooked.
- Using a slotted spoon, transfer the strips to a plate to cool.
- Check the escarole mixture; you want to cook it until most of the stock has evaporated and it looks like thick soup or sauce, then turn off the heat. Stir in half the cheese and season with salt to taste.
- Add the chicken strips, toss them to coat with the mixture, and continue to cook until the chicken strips have cooked through about 90 seconds.
- Spoon the mixture onto four plates, dividing it equally; top with the remaining cheese, and serve.

Nutrition Facts

Carbohydrates: 8.25g| Protein: 28.5g| Fat: 3g| Sodium: 267mg| Fiber: 2.5g

PLANT BASET DIABETIC RECIPES

859. BANANA LOTION PIE CHIA PUDDING

Ingredients

- 1/4 cup chia seeds
- 1/2 cup full-fat coconut milk
- 1/2 cup almond milk (I take advantage of homemade almond milk)
- 1 tbsp agave (maple syrup works too)
- 1 tsp cinnamon
- 1 banana, mashed
- 1 banana, chopped (to top)
- coconut flakes (to best)

Directions:

- Mix the chia seeds, milk almond, agave, cinnamon and mashed banana collectively in a bowl. Whisk until nicely Mixed.
- Make sure the bowl is covered and put it inside the fridge for one hour to firm up
- Plate the chia puddings into 2 cups and topped with cut bananas and coconut chips
-

Nutrition Facts:

Calories: 350 Sugar: 19g Fat: 17g
Saturated Fat: 4g Carbohydrates: 37g
Fibre: 12g Protein: 5g

860. CHICKPEA FLOUR SCRAMBLE

Ingredients:

- 60g of chickpea flour or use 1/2 cup + 2 Tbsp more besan/gram flour
- 125ml water
- 1 tbsp Nutritional yeast
- 1 tbsp flaxseed meal
- 0.5 tsp of baking powder
- 0.25 tsp salt
- 1/4 tsp of turmeric
- 1/4 tsp or less paprika
- 1/8 tsp Kala namak Indian sulphur dark salt for the eggy flavour
- generous dash of dark pepper

VEGGIES:

- 1 tsp oil divided
- One clove of garlic
- 1/4 cup (40 g) chopped onions
- 2 tbsp all of asparagus natural bell pepper, zucchini or even other veggies.
- 1/2 (0.5) natural chile
- 2 tbsp chopped crimson bell pepper or tomato
- cilantro and dark pepper for garnish

Directions:

- Blend all the components below chickpea flour batter and maintain aside. You may also make use of lentil batter from my lentil frittata.
- Heat 1/2 tsp essential oil in a skillet over moderate heat. Add onion and garlic and make until translucent. 3 mins.
- Add vegetables,
- Add in the crimson bell pepper or even tomato and mix inside. You now can add in a few spices or blends or some cut greens if you want.
- Cook for just two 2 minutes roughly until the edges begin to set. Scramble up the combination and continue steadily to cook. The mixture is sure to get messy and doughy. Scrape underneath and allow it to cook undisturbed for just two 2 mins roughly before scrambling once again. Continue to cook before edges begin to dry out — total 4 to 5 minutes based on your stove and pan.
- Allow the doughy mixture to sit down off warmth for 1-2 minutes. After that break right into smaller chunks. Sprinkle black pepper generously — function over multigrain toast or in tacos or burritos.

Nutrition Facts:

Fat: 6g Sodium: 355mg Potassium: 575mg Carbohydrates: 25 Fiber: 6g
Sugar: 5g Protein: 10g Vitamin A: 545IU
Vitamin C: 16mg Calcium: 81mg Iron: 2.5mg

861. CARROT CAKE OVERNIGHT OATS

Ingredients:

- ⅓ cup rolled oats
- 1 tablespoon ground flaxseed
- ¼ tsp ground cinnamon
- ⅛ tsp ground nutmeg
- based on sweetness preferred)
- ¼ cup raw shredded carrot
- 2 tablespoons chopped new pineapple
- 1 tablespoon shredded unsweetened coconut (and also a little additional for garnishing)
- 1 tablespoon raisins (optional)
- 1 tablespoon chopped walnuts or pecans (optional)
- ¼ tsp pure vanilla extract
- ½ mug unsweetened almond milk

Directions:

- In a bowl mix all INGREDIENTS and mix well.
- Cover and invest the refrigerator overnight.
- In the early morning, stir the mixture, and add 1-2 tablespoons of almond milk or water.
- Heat inside the microwave or even on the stovetop.)
- Garnish with shredded coconut, nuts, and a drizzle of pure maple syrup!
- Enjoy!

Nutrition Facts:

Calories: 242 kcal Fat: 9g
Carbohydrates: 35g Sugar: 6g
Fiber: 8g Protein: 7g

862. FRUIT-FILLED PROTEIN-PACKED OVER NIGHT QUINOA & OATS

Ingredients

- ¼ cup huge flaked gluten free of charge rolled oats
- ¼ cup cooked quinoa
- But this is simply not dairy-free)
- ¾ glass unsweetened almond milk
- Several drops of liquid stevia or even 1 tsp real honey, maple syrup, or even agave)
- ¼ banana, mashed
- 1 tablespoon ground flaxseed
- ¼ cup raspberries
- ¼ cup blueberries
- ¼ cup diced peaches
- 1 tsp cinnamon
- Optional Toppings: toasted coconut, butter almond, almonds, seeds, dried fruits, fruits, etc.

Directions:

- In a moderate bowl mix oats, quinoa, ground flax, and stevia and stir to mix.
- Add mashed banana, berries,
- Pour inside almond milk, and blend INGREDIENTS together.
- Invest the fridge and keep overnight.
- In the morning, eliminate from the fridge, heat on the stove top or in the microwave, or enjoy cold!
- If you discover the combination is too thick each morning just add some more almond milk!
- Get innovative with toppings... include nut butter, nuts, seeds, even more fruit, coconut, etc!

Nutrition Facts:

Calories: 290 kcal Fat: 6g Carbohydrates: 41g Sugar: 11g Fiber: 11g Protein: 19g

863. COCONUT RICE PUDDING

Ingredients

- 1 can lighting coconut milk
- 12 cardamom pods (may sub 1/2 tsp ground cardamom)
- 1/2 tsp cinnamon
- 1/4 tsp vanilla extract
- 2 tbsp maple syrup
- 1/2 cups cooked rice (I utilized jasmine rice)
- 2 tsp orange zest

Directions:

- Put the cardamom pods and coconut milk in a little pot on medium-high heat. Let bubble for just one minute,
- Using a spoon, take away the cardamom pods.
- Add the vanilla , cinnamon extract and maple syrup and stir until mixed.
- Following, add the rice and permit simmer on medium-low warmth for 10 minutes before rice becomes good and creamy.
- Stir inside the orange zest.
- Shredded coconut, or any toppings you like!

Nutrition Facts:

Calories: 293 Sugar: 6g Fat: 6g Saturated Fat: 2g Carbohydrates: 53g Fiber: 1g Protein: 5g

864. SUPER GREEN AVOCADO SMOOTHIE

Ingredients

- 1 banana
- 1/2 avocado
- 1 cup baby spinach
- 1/2 cup simple coconut yogurt
- 1/2 lemon, juice
- 1 cup water

Directions:

- Slice and peel banana, and put into a new blender. Reduce avocado in two, scoop out the meats with a spoon and increase blender.
- Add also a mug or a couple of baby spinach, 1/2 mug yogurt (we utilized coconut yogurt) and fruit juice of half of a lemon. Pour in regards to a cup of drinking water (more if you would like a thinner smoothie).
- Blend until smooth, pour into eyeglasses or jars and function with a new sprinkle of chia seeds and blueberries.

Nutrition Facts:

Calories: 167 Total fat: 6g Saturated fat: 1g Trans fat: 0g Unsaturated fat: 4g Cholesterol: 1mg Sodium: 53mg Carbohydrates: 28g Fiber: 4g Sugar: 18g Protein: 4g

865. SUNBUTTER BAKED OATMEAL CUPS

Ingredients

- 1/2 cup (120g) unsweetened applesauce*
- 1/2 cup (125g) No Sugar Added SunButter
- 1/2 cup (120g) non-dairy milk
- 1/4 cup (35g) coconut sugar
- 1/2 (cup (150g) rolled oats
- 1/4 cup (30g) hemp seeds**
- 2 tbsp (20g) chia seeds
- 1 tsp cinnamon
- 1/4 tsp salt
- Toppings of preference: nuts, seeds, jam, etc.

Directions:

- Spray/grease a 12 glass muffin pan with coconut essential oil.
- Whisk the applesauce together, coconut sugars, SunButter, and milk.
- Include the oats, and salt. Mix to combine.
-
- Add toppings of preference and press inside lightly.
- Enjoy!
- Keep leftovers inside the fridge within an airtight container for a week, or freeze for storage longer.

Nutrition Facts:

Calories: 153 Sugar: 5g Fat: 8g Saturated Fat: 0g Carbohydrates: 15g Fiber: 3g

866. AVOCADO EGG SALAD

Ingredients

- 2 avocados
- 8 eggs
- a small number of dill
- a small number of parsley
- juice of 1 lemon
- a pinch of salt
- a drizzle of essential olive oil (as needed)

Directions:

- Hard boil the eggs. Protect the eggs with drinking water in a saucepan. change heat off, Operate under cool water and crack off the shells. Slice the eggs into small parts.
- Pulp the avocados. Pulp the avocados in a bowl with the back of a huge wooden spoon until mostly smooth.
- Mix and serve. Herbs, lemon fruit juice, salt, and essential olive oil if you want it. Serve immediately at space temperature, or chill and assist cold.

Nutrition Facts:

Calories: 265 Total Fat: 19.9g Cholesterol: 297.6mg Sodium: 234.5mg Total Carbohydrate: 11.4g SOLUBLE FIBER: 7.2g Sugars: 3.6g Protein: 13g Vitamin A: 151µg Vitamin C: 31.7mg

867. BLUEBERRY FRENCH TOAST WITH BANANA MOUSSE

Ingredients

For the Toast

- ¼ cup milk almond

- ½ tablespoon flour
- ½ tbsp maple syrup
- ½ tbsp Nutritional yeast
- 1 slice sandwich bread (toasted)
- 1 dash sea salt
- ½ tbsp vanilla extract

For the Topping

- 1 moderate banana (blend until easy)
- ½ cup blueberries

Directions:

- Dip the bread in to the batter from each sides until its soaked full with it, it is most effective if the breads is a little dry.
- Heat up a large skillet and fry the toast from both sides until golden brown, approx. 1-2 moments on each part on medium heat.
- Serve with banana lotion and fresh blueberries.

Nutrition Facts:

Calories: 287 Protein: 8g Fat: 4g Carbs: 62g Fiber: 7g Sugar: 27g Vitamin A: 209.16IU

868. BLUEBERRY PANCAKES

Ingredients

For the dry

- ½ tsp baking powder
- ½ tsp baking soda
- ½ tsp sea salt
- ½ cup wheat flour
- For the wet INGREDIENTS
- ⅔ cup milk almond
- ½ cup aquafaba
- ¼ cup frozen blueberries
- ½ tsp lime (fruit juice and zest)
- ½ cup maple syrup
- ½ tbsp sunflower oil
- ½ tsp vanilla extract

For the topping

- ¼ cup blueberries (washed)
- ½ tbsp maple syrup
- For the frying oil
- ½ tbsp sunflower oil

Directions:

- Use a huge bowl and combine the dry INGREDIENTS.
- Add the wet components except the blueberries in order to a blender and mix and soon you see bubbles.
- Combine the wet and dry elements with the blueberries and reserve.
- Add a little of the frying oil to the pan and heat it up.
-
- When the oil is very warm, add the batter and fry the pancake for 2-3 minutes from every relative side.
- Serve the pancakes immediately or keep them heated in the oven and soon you finished the complete batch.
- Enjoy!

Nutrition Facts:

Calories: 482 Total Fat: 13g Sodium: 817.107mg Total Carbohydrate: 82g Dietry Fiber: 4g Sugars: 26g Protein: 9g Vitamin A 179.94IU Calcium: 349.76mg

869. BURRITO WITH SWEET POTATO

Ingredients

For the beans

- ½ tsp black pepper (floor)
- ¼ cup cooked black coffee beans (rinsed)
- ½ tsp dried smoked paprika
- ½ tsp ground cumin
- ½ tsp olive oil
- ¼ medium onion (chopped)
- ¼ medium reddish colored bell pepper (chopped)
- ½ tsp sea salt
- 1 tsp tomato paste
- For the avocado tomato mix
- ¼ avocado (dice into little pieces)
- ½ cup refreshing coriander (thinly sliced)
- ½ tsp lime (juiced)
- ¼ moderate tomato (dice into little pieces)
- For the kale
- ½ oz kale (stems eliminated and chopped)

For the sweet potato

- 3 oz nice potato (skin taken out and chopped)
- For the tortilla
- 2 tortillas whole wheat grains tortilla

Directions:

- Heat up the essential oil in a new pot and fry the onion until golden dark brown for approximately 5 minutes.
- Add all of those other INGREDIENTS for the coffee beans and simmer for approximately 5 more mins until hot, stir occasionally.
- Boil the sweet potato until soften for about 3-5 minutes based on size, be sure you don't overcook it.
- Work with a bowl and include the substances for the avocado tomato blend and set aside.
- To put together the burrito add lovely potato, kale, coffee beans and avocado tomato combine to 1 tortilla wrap.
- Fold inside the sides of the tortilla on the filling and roll when you tuck the edges.
- Heat up a new pan and roast each burrito until golden dark brown from each side for approximately 2-5 minutes.
- Function 2 burritos for every serving, it is possible to cut them in two if you like, enjoy!

Nutrition Facts:

Calories: 521 Protein: 16g Fat: 18g Carbs: 77g Fiber: 20g Sugar: 10g

870. APPLE CINNAMON BAKED OATMEAL

Ingredients

- 1½ cups fat-free of charge milk or even soy milk
- ½ cup packed brown sugar
- ½ cup egg alternative or egg whites
- 1 tablespoon melted margarine
- ½ teaspoon cinnamon
- 2 cups rolled oats (not instant)
- 1 teaspoon baking powder
- 1½ cups chopped apples

Directions:

- In a little bowl blend the milk, brown sugars, egg substitute/whites, cinnamon and margarine.
- Pour the wet combination in to the bowl with the oats; include the apples and mix to combine.

- Spoon the mixture right into a 8-by-8-in. pan coated with cooking food spray and bake for 30 to 40 a few minutes, until top is company and a toothpick happens clean in the guts.

Nutrition Facts:

Calories: 160 Total fat: 3g Saturated fat: < 1g Sodium: 80mg Total Carbohydrate: 30g FIBER: 3g

Sugars: 18g Protein 4g Vitamin A: 248 IU Vitamin C: 1.5 mg Calcium: 56mg.

871. CHAI SMOOTHIE BOWL

Ingredients

For the chai tea

- 1 cup milk almond
- ½ tbsp black peppercorn
- 1 stick cinnamon stick
- ½ tbsp cloves whole
- ½ inch new ginger (thinly sliced)
- ½ tbsp natural cardamom pods (cracked)
- 1 tbsp loose leaf black tea
- 1 tsp star anise
- ½ cup of water

For the smoothie

- 1 medium banana
- 1 oz unflavoured sun warrior protein powder
- For the topping
- ½ moderate banana (thinly sliced)
- 1 tablespoon dried goji berries
- 2 tablespoons granola

Directions:

- Add all of the INGREDIENTS concerning the chai tea to the pot and simmer regarding 10 minutes.
- Stress the chai tea and invite it to cool off to space temperature before you place it into the fridge.
- Use the fantastic chai tea and include it alongside the smoothie components to a blender and mix until smooth.
- For helping add the smoothie to a bowl and sprinkle with the topping, enjoy!

Nutrition Facts:

Calories: 410 Protein: 32g Fat: 9g Carbs: 60g Fiber: 9g Sugar: 27g

872. TEMPEH AVOCADO SANDWICH WITH HUMMUS

Ingredients

- ½ avocado (sliced)
- 1 dash dark pepper (ground)
- ¼ mug cherry tomatoes (washed and reduce in half)
- ½ tsp extra virgin essential olive oil
- 4 tbsps hummus
- 2 medium iceberg lettuce (washed and sliced)
- 1 dash sea salt
- 2½ oz tempeh (thinly sliced)
- 2 slices wholegrain sandwich bread (toasted)

Directions:

- Add the hummus to each slice of toast and best along with the sandwich ingredients, enjoy!

Nutrition Facts:

Calories: 582 Protein: 28g Fat: 32g Carbs: 53g Fiber: 13g Sugar: 6g

873. BANANA PROTEINS SMOOTHIE BOWL WITH HEMP AND CACAO

Ingredients

For the smoothie bowl

- 1 cup almond milk
- 1 moderate banana (frozen optional)
- 1 cup ice
- 1 oz unflavoured sun warrior protein powder

For the topping

- 1 tablespoon cacao powder
- 1 tablespoon dried goji berries
- 2 tablespoons granola
- 1 tbsp hemp hearts

Directions:

- Include the smoothie bowl elements to the blender and mix until smooth.
- Add it to the bowl and sprinkle along with the toppings, enjoy!

Nutrition Facts:

Calories: 405 Protein: 35g Fat: 14g Carbs: 46g Fiber: 8g Sugar: 20g

874. BLUEBERRY HEMP PEAR PORRIDGE

Ingredients

- 1 cup almond milk
- ½ cup blueberries
- ½ tbsp hemp seeds
- ½ medium pear (sliced)
- ½ cup porridge oats

Directions:

- Add the almond milk and porridge oats in order to a saucepan, bring in order to the boil and simmer intended for 5 minutes.
- Add the porridge in order to bowls, garnish along with the rest of the INGREDIENTS and serve very hot.

Nutrition Facts:

Calories: 463 Protein: 17g Fat: 11g Carbs: 78g Fiber: 13g Sugar: 16g

875. VANILLA BREAKFAST MILLET WITH APPLE

Ingredients

For the millet

- 1 cup almond milk
- 2 dates (pitted and thinly sliced)
- ½ cup millet (washed)
- 1 dash sea salt
- ½ tsp turmeric powder
- ½ oz unflavoured sun warrior proteins powder
- ½ tbsp vanilla extract

For the apple

- ½ medium apple company (washed and chopped)
- ½ tsp sunflower oil
- For the topping
- 1 tbsp hemp hearts
- ½ tbsp maple syrup

Directions:

- Work with a saucepan and include almond milk, vanilla extract, millet and dates, simmer and sometimes stir for approximately 10 minutes.
-
- Take the millet of heat and mix in the proteins powder, salt and turmeric and add it to the bowl.
- Add the sprinkle and apples with the topping, enjoy!

Nutrition Facts:

Calories: 405 Fat: 11g Carbs: 57g Fiber: 7g Sugar: 25g Protein: 21g

876. MATCHA SMOOTHIE BOWL WITH BANANA MILK

Ingredients

- 1 medium banana (chopped)
- 2 tablespoons dried goji berries
- 4 tbsps fresh mint (washed and stems removed)
- ½ tsp matcha green tea extract powder
- 1 persimmon fruit (chopped)
- 1 tsp sesame seeds
- 1 cup of water

Directions:

- Add banana, ice, drinking water, matcha powder and 1/2 of the mint results into the blender and blend until smooth.
- Add the smoothie in order to the bowl and sprinkle all of those other INGREDIENTS at the top, enjoy!

Nutrition Facts:

Calories: 289 Fat: 2g Protein: 5g Carbs: 69g Fiber: 12g Sugar: 41g

877. TACOS

Ingredients

For the tofu

- ½ tsp black pepper (floor)
- ½ tablespoon extra virgin essential olive oil
- 3 oz strong tofu (crumbled)
- ½ tsp ground cumin
- ½ tbsp Nutritional yeast
- ½ tsp sea salt
- ½ tsp turmeric powder

For the topping

- ½ avocado (thinly sliced)
- 1 tbsp refreshing cilantro (thinly sliced)
- ¼ lime (juiced)
- ¼ medium reddish onion (thinly sliced)
- ¼ moderate tomato (thinly sliced)

For the beans

- ¼ cup cooked black coffee beans (rinsed)
- ½ tsp dried smoked paprika
- ½ tablespoon extra virgin essential olive oil
- ¼ medium onion (sliced)
- ½ tsp sea salt
- ½ cup nice corn kernels (rinsed)

For the taco

- 3 tortillas corn tortilla

Directions:

- Add all of those other INGREDIENTS for the coffee beans, stir well and change the taste.
- Work with a frying pan and warmth up the essential oil for the tofu, add the tofu and stir fry for approximately 5 minutes.
- Add all of those other tofu ingredients, mix everything well and modify taste.
- Warmth up the corn tortillas inside the microwave for two mere seconds and wrap them inside a damp papers towel in order to avoid that they will dry.
- For helping the breakfast taco put coffee beans and tofu and sprinkle with the toppings and put avocado slices, enjoy!

Nutrition Facts:

Calories: 544 Protein: 20g Sugar: 6g Carbs: 69g Fiber: 18g Fat: 25g

878. CONGEE WITH SMOKED VEGETABLES AND TOFU

Ingredients

For the congee

- ¼ cup of rice
- ½ tsp sea salt
- 1½ cups water
- For the stir fry
- ½ moderate carrot (diced into little pieces)
- ½ inch clean ginger (minced)
- 1 clove garlic (minced)
- ⅓ oz radish (diced into little pieces)
- 3 oz smoked strong tofu (diced into little pieces)
- ½ cup spinach (washed)
- ¼ tablespoon toasted sesame oil
- ¼ moderate zucchini (diced into little pieces)

For the topping

- ½ tsp roasted sesame seeds
- ½ moderate scallion (thinly sliced)
- ½ tbsp soy sauce

Directions:

- Work with a rice cooker or just simmer the congee substances for an hour and soon you have a new sloppy rice soup.
- Use a wok or a large frying pan and heat up the oil.
- Include the tofu, carrot, radish, zucchini and ginger and roast them for approximately 10 minutes.
- Add the garlic and fry for approximately 1-3 more minutes.

Nutrition Facts:

Calories: 299 Protein: 12g Fiber: 3g Sugar: 4g Fat: 6g Carbs: 48g

879. SCRAMBLED EGGS

Ingredients

For the tofu egg

- ½ tsp black pepper (surface)
- ½ tsp dark salt (Kala namak)
- 4½ oz strong tofu (crumbled)
- ½ tsp ground cumin
- ½ tbsp Nutritional yeast
- ½ tsp paprika powder
- ½ tsp turmeric powder
- ½ tbsp water

For the vegetables

- ½ glass cherry tomatoes (quartered)
- ½ tablespoon extra virgin essential olive oil
- ½ medium reddish coloured onion (thinly sliced)
- ½ mug shiitake mushrooms (washed and cut)
- ½ tbsp soy sauce
- For the topping
- ½ moderate scallion (thinly sliced)

For the refried beans

- ½ tsp chilli powder
- ½ cup cooked black beans
- ½ cup cooked kidney beans
- ½ tsp dried smoked paprika
- ½ tablespoon extra virgin essential olive oil
- ½ tsp ground cumin
- 1 tsp maple syrup

- ½ medium crimson onion (thinly sliced)
- ½ tsp sea salt
- ½ tbsp tomato paste
- ¼ cup of water
- 1 tsp white wines vinegar

Directions:

- Heat up the essential olive oil and fry the onion for approximately 2-5 minutes.
- Add the soy sauce in order to the sliced mushrooms and blend well.
- Use a huge bowl and combine the components for the tofu egg.
- Add the tofu egg and cherry tomatoes and mix fry for 5-10 minutes.
- Adjust taste before helping and sprinkle the scallions at the top.

Nutrition Facts:

Calories: 561 Protein: 34g Fiber: 22g Sugar: 14g Fat: 21g Carbs: 69g

880. AMARANTH POWER PUBS WITH HEMP SEEDS

Ingredients

For the dry ingredients

- ½ tsp allspice
- ½ cup amaranth popped
- ½ tsp cinnamon ground
- ½ cup dried goji berries
- ½ cup hemp seeds
- 1 dash sea salt
- ½ cup sunflower seeds
- ½ glass walnut halves (chopped)

For the wet ingredients

- ½ medium apple (grated)
- ½ cup date
- ½ cup dried apricots
- ½ cup additional virgin coconut oil
- ½ tbsp vanilla extract

Directions:

- Add the batter in order to the baking dish and bake for approximately 20-25 minutes.
- Let the energy bars completely cool off before a person slice them.

Nutrition Facts:

Calories: 189 Protein: 5g Fiber: 3g Sugar: 8g Fat: 12g Carbs: 18g

881. OMELETTE WITH MUSHROOM

Ingredients

For the omelette

- ¼ cup aquafaba
- ½ tsp dark salt (Kala namak)
- ½ cup chickpea flour
- ¼ tablespoon corn starch
- 3 oz extra company tofu
- 1 tbsp Nutritional yeast
- ½ tsp olive oil
- ½ tsp turmeric powder

For the garnish

- One moderate scallion (thinly sliced)
- ½ moderate tomato (washed and sliced)
- For the mushroom
- 1 oz button mushroom (sliced)
- ½ tsp dried smoked paprika
- ½ tsp olive oil
- ½ tbsp soy sauce

Directions:

- Add all of the omelette elements except the essential oil to the blender and mix until smooth, include a little more aquafaba in case the mixture doesn't mix properly or mix it in batches.
- Heat up the essential oil for the mushrooms and mix fry the mushrooms for approximately five minutes until slightly golden dark brown, cook max. 2 servings in the pan every time.
- Increase it to the mushrooms and present it an excellent stir.
- Add the vegan omelette mixture in order to the mushrooms and fry to get 5-8 minutes on moderate until golden brown.
- Use a following pan and temperature up the essential oil for the omelette simply change the pan and rapidly add the omelette another pan to fry another side.
- Serve the omelette with tomato slices privately and sprinkle with scallions, enjoy!

Nutrition Facts:

Calories: 205 Protein: 17g Fiber: 6g Sugar: 6g Fat: 10g Carbs: 22g

882. AQUAFABA GRANOLA WITH DATES (OIL-FREE)

Ingredients

For the granola

- ½ cup almonds (crushed)
- ½ cup aquafaba
- ½ cup date (pitted)
- ½ cup flaxseed
- ½ cup jumbo rolled oats
- ½ cup pumpkin seeds
- 1 dash sea salt
- For the almond milk
- 1 cup almond milk

Directions:

- Mix the granola substances alongside with Aquafaba.
- Disperse everything on a baking tray covered with baking document and bake for approximately thirty minutes until golden brown.
- Based on the oven the time can vary greatly between 25-35 minutes, it's really vital that you keep a close vision so that it doesn't get burned.
- Enjoy!

Nutrition Facts:

Calories: 383 Protein: 16g Fiber: 9g Sugar: 6g Fat: 22g Carbs: 35g

883. PROTEIN MUFFINS

Ingredients

For the muffin

- 1 tsp baking powder
- 1 tsp dark salt (Kala namak)
- ¼ cup chickpeas
- 1 dash dried smoked paprika (optional)
- 1 tsp garlic powder
- 3 tbsps Nutritional yeast
- 12 oz silken tofu
- 1 tsp turmeric powder

For the vegetables

- ½ mug mushroom (thinly sliced)
- 1 tsp olive oil
- 1 moderate shallot (thinly sliced)
- 1½ oz tomato (diced)

Directions:

- Heat up the essential oil in a new skillet and sautee the veggies for approximately 5 minutes.

- Work with a bowl and mash the chickpeas with a fork, mix with all of those other INGREDIENTS until smooth, include tomatoes, mushrooms and onions last.
- Work with a muffin tin protected with suitable paper or perhaps a ramekin.
- Allow muffins completely cool off to firm, enjoy!

Nutrition Facts:

Calories: 146 Total Body fat: 8g Carbohydrate: 15g Proteins: 14g Sugars: 3g

884. SPICY BUFFALO CHICKPEA WRAPS

Ingredients

DRESSING + SALAD

- 1/3 cup hummus (or store-bought)
- 1/2 - 2 Tbsp maple syrup (plus much more to taste)
- 1 little lemon, juiced (1 small lemon yields ~2 Tbsp or 30 ml)
- 1-2 Tbsp warm water (to thin)
- big stems removed, roughly cut)

BUFFALO CHICKPEAS

- Drained and dried // ~ 1/4 cups per can when drained)
- 1 Tbsp coconut oil (or sub grape seed or essential olive oil)
- 4 Tbsp hot sauce* (divided // I used Louisiana's Pure Crystal Hot Sauce)
- 1/4 tsp garlic powder (or sub 1 minced garlic clove per 1/4 tsp powder)
- 1 pinch sea salt

FOR SERVING

- 3-4 vegan-pleasant flour tortillas, pita, or flatbread
- Diced (optional)
- Diced (optional)
- Thinly sliced (optional)

Directions:

- Make the dressing with the addition of hummus, maple syrup, and lemon juice to a new combining bowl and whisking to mix. Add warm water until solid but pourable.
- Taste and change flavor as needed, adding romaine lettuce or even kale, and toss. Reserve.
- To make chickpeas, put drained, dried chickpeas to another blending bowl. Add essential coconut oil, 3 Tbsp boiling sauce (amount as the initial recipe is written // modify if altering batch dimension), garlic powder,
- Heat an iron or cast-iron skillet over moderate heat. Once hot, add sauté and chickpeas for 3-5 minutes, mashing several chickpeas softly with a spoon to generate texture (see photo).
- Stir to mix. Set aside.
- To assemble, best each wrap with a new generous part of the dressed romaine salad, and top with 1/4 mug buffalo chickpeas and a fresh sprinkle of diced tomatoes, avocado, and/or onion (optional).
- Serve immediately. Store leftovers separately in the fridge around 3 days, though best when new. You can benefit from the buffalo chickpeas cold, room heat, or heated up.

Nutrition Facts:

Calories: 254 Fat: 6.4G Fiber: 5.7g Sugar: 5.1G

885. CHICKPEA SUNFLOWER SANDWICH

Ingredients

SANDWICH

- 15- ounce can easily chickpeas (rinsed and drained)
- cut back on added salt)
- Nutty flavor)
- Use half just as much mustard)
- 1 Tbsp maple syrup (or sub agave or honey or even vegan)
- 1/4 cup chopped red onion
- 2 Tbsp refreshing dill* (finely chopped)
- 1 healthy pinch each salt and pepper (to taste)
- 4 pieces rustic bread (lightly toasted // gluten-free for GF eaters)
- Sliced avocado, onion, and or lettuce (optional // for serving)

GARLIC HERB SAUCE optional

- 1/4 cup hummus
- 1/2 moderate lemon, juiced (1/2 lemon yields ~ 1 Tbsp)
- 3/4 - 1 tsp dried dill*
- 2 cloves garlic (minced)
- Water or even unsweetened almond milk (to thin)
- Sea salt to flavor (optional // I didn't want any)

Directions:

- Prepare garlic herb sauce and reserve.
- Add chickpeas to the mixing bowl and lightly mash with the fork for texture. Add sunflower seeds then, mayo, mustard, maple syrup, reddish onion, dill, salt, and pepper and blend with a spoon. Taste and adapt seasonings as needed.
- Toast bread (if desired) and prepare any sandwich toppings you wish (tomato, onion, lettuce).
- Scoop a healthy level of filling onto 2 of the bits of bread, add desired sauce and toppings, and top with some other two slices of a loaf of bread.
- Sunflower-chickpea mixture could keep covered in the fridge for a few days, making it ideal for quick weekday lunches!

Nutrition Facts:

Calories: 532 Fat: 30g Saturated body fat: 4g Sodium: 1144mg Potassium: 584mg Carbohydrates: 52g Fiber: 14g Sugars: 8g Protein: 17g Supplement A: 34IU Supplement C: 5mg Calcium: 119mg Iron: 4mg

886. RAINBOW "RAW-MAINE" TACO BOATS

Ingredients

LETTUCE

- 1 head romaine lettuce (organic when possible // sectioned off into individual leaves // huge bottom stems removed)

FILLING

- 1/2 cup beet hummus or simple hummus (keep this recipe natural with sprouted hummus)
- 1 cup halved cherry tomatoes
- 1/2 cup alfalfa sprouts
- 1 cup finely shredded carrots (I utilized my mandolin with the medium-tooth blade)
- 3/4 cup sliced red cabbage
- 1 moderate ripe avocado (cubed)

- 1 Tbsp hemp seeds (optional)

SAUCE

- 1/3 cup tahini (to help keep this recipe natural, use natural untoasted tahini)
- 2 Tbsp lemon juice
- 1 Tbsp maple syrup
- 1 pinch sea salt (optional)
- Water (to thin)

Directions:

- If making hummus, To help keep this recipe natural, use a natural, sprouted hummus dip (bought at most food markets).
- Prepare sauce with the addition of tahini, lemon juice, maple syrup, and salt to a little mixing bowl and whisk to combine. Then add drinking water 1 Tbsp (15 ml) at the same time until a pourable dressing will be formed. Taste and change taste as needed, adding even more salt for overall flavor, lemon for acidity, or maple syrup for sweetness. Transfer to a helping vessel or ramekin or reserve.
- Top with tomatoes then, sprouts,
- Either drizzle with tahini sauce or serve privately. Best when fresh. Shop leftover tacos in the fridge around 3 days (make sure to add lime or lemon fruit juice to avocado to help significantly it from switching). Tahini sauce could keep for 4-5 days.

Nutrition Facts:

Calories: 314 Fat: 23.2G Fiber: 9.3g Sugar: 6.2g Protein: 8g

887. QUINOA GADO-GADO BOWL

Ingredients

GADO-GADO

- 1/2 cup whitened or red quinoa (very well rinsed and drained)
- 1 cup of water
- 1 cup greens beans (trimmed)
- 1/2 medium red bell pepper (thinly sliced)
- 3/4 cup mung bean sprouts
- 2/3 cup shredded red cabbage
- 2 whole carrots (thinly sliced with a knife or mandolin)

SPICY PEANUT SAUCE

- Cashew butter, or sun butter)
- 1 Tbsp gluten-free of charge tamari (or soy sauce or even GF)
- 2-3 Tbsp maple syrup (to taste)
- 3 Tbsp lime juice
- 1 tsp chili garlic sauce (more to flavor // 1 Thai reddish colored chili, minced // or 1/4 tsp crimson pepper flake // amounts as original recipe is created)
- 3-4 Tbsp drinking water (to thin)

FOR SERVING optional

- Cilantro
- Lime wedges
- Red pepper flake

Directions:

- Heat a little saucepan over medium warmth and add rinsed, stirring regularly, to eliminate excess liquid and put in a nutty taste to the quinoa. Adding water, stir, and provide to a minimal boil. Then reduce temperature to a simmer, cover, and make for about 18-20 moments or until all liquid is usually absorbed and quinoa will be tender. Remove lid, and tripped heat.
- While quinoa is cooking food, cover, and make until only tender - about 4 mins.
- Once steamed, add natural beans to a plate of ice drinking water to "shock" them (cease them from cooking). Reserve.
- Make peanut sauce with the addition of peanut butter, tamari, and chili garlic sauce/Thai chili/red pepper flake to a little mixing bowl and whisk to combine. Then add drinking water 1 Tbsp (15 ml) at the same time until a semi-heavy, but the pourable sauce will be formed.
- Taste and modify flavor while needed, adding a lot more tamari for saltiness, lime fruit juice for acidity, or even chili garlic sauce/Thai chili/crimson pepper flake for high temperature! You want this to become a stability of tangy, sweet, salty, and spicy. Therefore you shouldn't be shy with the seasonings!
- To function, crimson bell pepper, and carrots. Role with peanut sauce and any extra toppings (optional), such as for example cilantro,
- Store leftovers separately inside the refrigerator around 4-5 times (peanut sauce maintains for 1+ week). Greatest when fresh.

Nutrition Facts:

Calories: 527 Fat: 23.1G Fiber: 10.9g Sugar: 20.2G

888. VEGAN "BLT" SANDWICH

Ingredients

- 2 slices Vegan Sandwich Bread (or store-bought)
- 5-6 slices Eggplant Bacon (or 1/4 cup Coconut Bacon // quantity as the initial recipe is written)
- 2 Tbsp Vegan Aquafaba Hummus or Mayo
- 1/4 medium red or white onion (thinly sliced)
- 1/2 medium ripe tomato (thinly sliced)
- 2 leaves green lettuce

Directions:

- Toast bread (optional). For the time being, heat skillet over moderate heat. Once hot, include eggplant bacon (if making use of coconut bacon, After that flip and make for another 1-2 a few minutes on the other hand until warmed through. Remove from warmth and set aside.
- To assemble a sandwich, Then best one item with Eggplant or Coconut Bacon, onion, top with another little bit of bread, slice (optional), and revel in.
- It could be made in advance (up to a few hrs), but best when fresh.

Nutrition Facts:

Calories: 253 Fat: 9.8G Sugar: 5.8g Protein: 10.8

889. GREEK GODDESS BOWL

Ingredients

CHICKPEAS

- Drained and dried very well on a towel)
- 1 Tbsp essential oil (coconut or avocado are usually best // omit if staying away from oil)

- 1 Tbsp Shawarma Spice Blend (or comparable spices you have readily available)
- Omit)
- 1/4 tsp ocean salt
- BOWL
- 3/4 cup Vegan Tzatziki
- 1 batch Crimson Pepper Hemp Tabbouleh (or sub chopped parsley)
- 1/2 cup natural or kalamata olives (pitted and halved/chopped)
- 1/2 cup cherry tomatoes (halved)
- 1 moderate cucumber (thinly sliced)
- 1 modest carrot (optional // sliced thinly on a diagonal into "chips")

FOR SERVING optional
- Vegan Naan or Flatbread
- Traditional Vegan Falafel
- Garlic Dill Sauce
- Tahini Dressing

Directions:
- Put washed, shawarma Spice Mix, maple syrup, toss to mix.
- Bake for 20-23 moments or before chickpeas is somewhat crispy and golden brownish. Remove from oven and reserve.
- Tabbouleh (or even parsley), Best with prepared chickpeas and garnish with new lemon juice.
- This bowl is tasty as is,
- Best when fresh, nevertheless, you can shop leftovers (separately) around 3-4 days inside the refrigerator.

Nutrition Facts:
Calories: 519 Fat: 34.8G Fiber: 13.3g Sugar: 19.4g Protein: 12g

890. CURRIED CAULIFLOWER, GRAPE, AND LENTIL SALAD

Ingredients
CAULIFLOWER
- 1 head cauliflower (split into florets)
- 1/2 Tbsp melted the coconut oil (or water)
- 1/2 Tbsp curry powder (or store-bought)
- 1/4 tsp ocean salt
- Natural CURRY TAHINI DRESSING*
- 4 1/2 Tbsp natural curry paste (or store-purchased, though fresh is most beneficial)
- 2 Tbsp tahini
- 2 Tbsp lemon juice
- 1 Tbsp maple syrup
- 1 Pinch each salt and black pepper
- Water to thin

SALAD
- Kale, spinach (or even other green of preference)
- 1 cup prepared lentils (rinsed and drained)
- 1 cup red or natural grapes (halved)
- Fresh cilantro (optional)

Directions:
- Collection a baking sheet (or even more as required) with parchment papers.
- Increase cauliflower to a mixing bowl and toss along with coconut oil (or drinking water), curry powder, and sea salt. Transfer to a baking sheet and roast cauliflower for 20-25 mins or until golden dark brown and tender.
- Prepare to dress with the addition of natural curry paste, tahini, salt, and pepper to a mixing bowl and whisk to mix. If needed, slim with drinking water until pourable.
- Taste and adapt flavor like needed, adding more environment-friendly curry paste for a new stronger curry taste, tahini for higher thickness, lemon fruit juice for acidity, or even maple syrup for sweetness.
- Assemble salad with the addition of lettuce to a heaping platter or bowl. Best with lentils,
- Best served fresh. Store dressing separately for 1 week.

Nutrition Facts:
6G Fiber: 9.8g Sugar: 12.8G

891. ABUNDANCE KALE SALAD WITH SAVORY TAHINI DRESSING

Ingredients
ROASTED VEGETABLES
- 1 moderate zucchini (sliced in 1/4-inch rounds)
- 1 medium lovely potato (sliced in 1/4-inch rounds)
- 1 cup reddish cabbage (shredded)
- 1 Tbsp melted the coconut oil (or sub drinking water or use our way for oil-free vegetables)
- 1 Pinch sea salt
- 1/2 tsp DIY curry powder (or store-bought)

DRESSING
- 1/3 cup tahini
- 1/2 tsp garlic powder (plus much more to taste)
- 1 Tbsp coconut aminos (plus much more to flavor or sub tamari or soy sauce)
- because the feeling is more extreme)
- 1 big clove garlic (minced)
- ~1/4 cup water (to thin)

SALAD
- Romaine, mixed greens, etc.)
- 4 little radishes (thinly sliced)
- 3 Tbsp hemp seeds
- 1 ripe avocado (cubed)
- 2 Tbsp lemon apple or juice cider vinegar

TOPPINGS optional / choose your favorites
- 1 batch Crispy Baked Chickpeas
- 2 cups cooked quinoa* (We cooked my quinoa with curry powder // omit to help keep grain-free)
- DIY Kimchi (or even store-bought)

Directions:
- If helping with quinoa or crispy chickpeas, prepare at the moment (follow links / see information for PREPARATION). Otherwise, check out step 2.
- Preheat oven to 375 degrees F (190 C) and arrange zucchini, cabbage, and sweet potatoes about the baking sheet (a number of as needed). Drizzle with essential coconut oil (or sub-oil-free choices), ocean salt, and curry powder and toss to mix — roast for 20 a few minutes or until tender and somewhat golden brown.
- For the time being, prepare the dressing with the addition of tahini, taste, and change seasonings as

needed, including even more garlic powder for garlic taste or salt for saltiness. Reserve.
- Assemble salad with the addition of greens, and avocado to a big mixing bowl. Include the lemon fruit juice (or apple company cider vinegar) and lightly toss to combine.
- Add roasted veggies and any desired toppings (quinoa) and assist with dressing.
- Best when fresh, though leftovers keep well saved in the refrigerator up to 3 days. Dressing kept separately will keep for 7 days. Chickpeas should be collected independently at room temperature to maintain crispiness.

Nutrition Facts:

Calories: 410 Fat: 30.6G Fiber: 8.7g Sugar: 3.5g Protein: 12g

892. LOADED KALE SALAD

Ingredients

QUINOA
- 3/4 cups (138 g) quinoa*, well rinsed
- 1/2 cups (360 ml) water

VEGETABLES
- 4 huge carrots* (halved + roughly cut)
- 1 entire beet* (thinly sliced)
- 2 Tbsp drinking water (or sub avocado or melted coconut essential oil)
- 1 pinch sea salt
- 1/2 tsp curry powder (optional)

DRESSING
- 1/3 cup tahini
- 2-3 Tbsp lemon juice*
- 1-2 Tbsp maple syrup (based on preferred sweetness*)
- 1 pinch sea salt
- 1/4 cup Drinking water (to thin)
- SALAD
- 8 cups kale (torn or approximately chopped // or sub other green)
- 1/2 cup cut cherry tomatoes
- 1 ripe avocado cubed
- 1/4 cup hemp seeds (optional)
- 1/2 cup sprouts of preference (optional // I used broccoli)

Directions:

- Heat a little pot over medium temperature and add rinsed, stirring often. Then add drinking water and bring it to a minimal boil. Once boiling, reduce high heat to a simmer, cover-up, once prepared, remove the lid, and reserve.
- Add drinking water (or essential oil) and seasonings of preference and toss to coating.
- For the time being, prepare the dressing with the addition of tahini, and salt to a little combining bowl and whisk to mix. Taste and modify taste as needed, adding even more lemon fruit juice for acidity, see information for a savory version.
- Arrange kale on a new serving platter or even bowl and best with tomatoes, avocado, cooked quinoa, and any desired toppings, such as for example hemp seeds or even sprouts. Serve with dressing privately, or toss to mix.
- Store leftovers (preserve dressing individual for best results) inside the refrigerator around 3 days. The dressing could keep nicely covered in the fridge around 1 week.

893. PORTOBELLO POT ROAST

Ingredients

- 120mls red or white wine , I think red is most effective
- 4 big portobello mushrooms sliced into 3/4-inch pieces
- 1 large onion sliced
- 2 cloves garlic pressed
- 3 tablespoons flour if sensitive to gluten use gluten-free flour
- 1 teaspoon rubbed sage
- 1 teaspoon dried basil
- If you use all the broth it will finish up with thin gravy like in my video. I personally would instead use less and also have a thicker sauce. Generally about 500 MLS complete.
- Four large potatoes quartered
- 4 huge carrots cut into 3-inch pieces
- Salt and freshly floor black pepper or even lemon pepper to flavor
- or 1 tablespoon of soy tamari or sauce
- 4 sprigs fresh thyme
- 1 sprig fresh rosemary

Directions:

- Preheat the oven to 350 degrees F (for slow cooker PREPARATION observe recipe notes)
- In a large saucepan (or a sizable stovetop to oven just like a Dutch Oven, Permit them to prepare through, and brownish a bit-you'll have to exercise them around and to switch them-and then eliminate from the pan and reserve.
- Mix the flour, sage, and basil together in a little bowl. Stir in 1/4 glass of the broth to produce a paste and pour the mixture into the same pan you use for the mushrooms and onions. While stirring continuously over medium heat, very slowly add the rest of the broth to ensure that you create a gravy or sauce.
- Once the mixture just begins to boil, turn the heat off and increase any additional seasonings you like, such dried natural herbs and black pepper.
- Include the potatoes, carrots, pepper and salt, and Worcestershire sauce in order to the gravy combination.
- If more liquid is required to keep the vegetables carefully from blow-drying, add more broth.
- Include the mushrooms and onions in order to blend and ladle into a big ceramic or cup pot or even casserole dish with the lid, layering within the sprigs associated with rosemary and thyme.
- Place the top on and placed it into the oven and bake for one hour. Eliminate from the oven and work hot.

Nutrition Facts:

Calorie consumption: 199kcal
Carbohydrates: 39.4g Protein: 6.1g
Fat: 0.8g Sodium: 578mg Fiber: 5.7g
Glucose: 8.7g Vitamin A: 10650IU
Vitamin C: 42.1mg Calcium: 70mg
Iron: 2.3mg

894. TUNA SALAD

Ingredients

- 2 cans garbanzo coffee beans (chickpeas), (3 cups) rinsed and drained
- 2 Tablespoons mayonnaise (vegan)
- 1 Tablespoon prepared yellowish mustard

- 2 Tablespoons nice pickle relish
- 1 Tablespoon jarred capers, chopped
- 1/2 cup celery, chopped

Directions:

- In a moderate bowl, (or work with a meals processor and the pulse functionality.)
- Add all of those other ingredients in order to the pot and combine it until combined.
- Serve immediately or even refrigerate until prepared to serve.

Nutrition Facts:

Calorie consumption: 207kcal Carbohydrates: 27g Protein: 9g Fat: 7g Sodium: 670mg Potassium: 287mg Fiber: 8g Sugar: 1g Vitamin A new: 145IU Supplement C: 0.5mg Calcium: 67mg Iron: 2.3mg

895. NO-BAKE CINNAMON APPLE POWER BARS

Ingredients

- soak them in water for 10-15 minutes then drain well first
- ½ mug 125g cashew butter
- 85 ml | ⅓ cup brown rice syrup
- 1 teaspoon vanilla extract
- ¼ teaspoon salt
- 1 teaspoon cinnamon
- ¼ glass 0r 4 tablespoons surface flax seed
- 80 ¾ or g cup chopped dried apple.
- 55 g or 1½ cup puffed rice
- (Make sure to use gluten-free of charge oats if necessary.

Directions:

- Put the dates in a food processor chip and process until actually finely chopped and beginning to ball up. If you don't possess a food processor, you can cut them actually finely instead.
- In a little pan, place the dates, vanilla, cinnamon, and salt.
- The dates won't melt; nevertheless, you will be able to smush them up and mix everything well.
- While that's happening, but the flax, dried apple company, puffed rice, and oats to a huge bowl. Stir well.

- Pour inside the warm mix from the pan. It will not be runny and can still be very thick. Make sure to scrape the pan out properly rather than leave any behind.
- Stir everything together until all of the dry components are coated. It does take a little arm power. Make sure to scrape into the bottom part of the bowl, and that means you don't miss any dried out bits.
- Spoon into the prepared tin and push down effectively all over, so it is flat and compacted.
- Devote the fridge to create for at the very least 3 - 4 hours.
- When set, cut into squares or pubs.

Nutrition Facts:

Calorie consumption: 240kcal Carbohydrates: 41g Protein: 5g Fat: 8g Sodium: 77mg Fiber: 4g Sugar: 20g

896. BLUEBERRY BRAN MUFFINS

Ingredients

- 230g or 1.5 cups spelled flour
- 60g or 1 cup wheat bran
- ½ or 50g cup rolled oats
- ½ or 80g cup coconut sugar
- 2 tablespoons terrain flax seed
- 2 teaspoons baking powder
- 1 teaspoon baking soda
- 1/2 teaspoon salt
- 312mls or 1¼ cups nondairy milk
- 140g or ½ cup unsweetened apple company sauce
- 1 tablespoon apple company cider vinegar or lemon juice
- 148g or 1 cup refreshing or frozen blueberries

Directions:

- Preheat oven to 400°F and collection muffin trays
- Add all the dry ingredients in order to a sizable bowl (except blueberries)
- Add all the wet ingredients to some other bowl or even jug and mix them together well.
- Pour the wet ingredients into the dry INGREDIENTS and stir until just combined. Do not over blend as this may affect the muffins' completed texture.

- Add the blueberries and stir until equally distributed.
- Spoon carefully into the muffin liners and bake for about 20 minutes or even until a toothpick and choose / skewer could be inserted into the middle and turn out almost clean.

Nutrition Facts:

Calorie consumption: 177kcal Carbohydrates: 40.7g Fat: 1.7g Sodium: 179.4mg Fiber: 4.8g Sugars: 19g Vitamin A: 100IU Vitamin C: 1.7mg Calcium: 90mg Iron: 1.8mg

897. WHITE BEAN AND ARTICHOKE VEGAN SANDWICH FILLING

Ingredients

- In case you have entire cashew nuts or halves after that 75g could be more than half of a cup - for precision, you need to weigh them.
- 1 clove garlic
- 1 teaspoon rosemary fresh
- ¼ teaspoon salt plus a little more to taste at the end
- ¼ teaspoon black pepper plus a little more to feel at the end
- finely grated zest of a lemon
- 90 MLS nondairy milk 6 tablespoons
- or cooked fresh types chopped roughly
- 270 g prepared white beans around 1¼ cups
- ¼ glass hulled sunflower seeds roasted

Directions:

- If you don't have an extremely high powered blender, soak the cashew nuts in boiling drinking water for quarter-hour then drain them before proceeding.
- Include the cashew nuts, garlic, lemon zest, and milk to a blender or even food processor and mix until completely smooth.
- In a bowl,
- Pour on the dressing and stir nicely; thus, everything is coated.
- Taste and add a lot more seasoning. I loved extra dark pepper in mine.

Nutrition Facts:

Calorie consumption: 110kcal
Carbohydrates: 14g Protein: 6g Fat: 4g
Sodium: 134mg Fiber: 4g Sugar: 1g

898. CHEESE AND ONION CRISPY ROASTED CHICKPEAS

Ingredients

- 2 cups 1540 ml can cooked chickpeas
- 2 tablespoons aquafaba liquid from the may consist of chickpeas
- 3 tablespoons onion powder
- 1/2 teaspoon garlic powder
- 3 tablespoons Nutritional yeast
- ½ teaspoon salt

Directions:

- Preheat oven to 400°F
- Pour chickpeas onto the baking tray and bake for thirty minutes.
- Remove from the oven and carefully pour right into a bowl.
- Add the stir and aquafaba well.
- Add another INGREDIENTS and make sure all of the chickpeas are coated.
- Bake for ten minutes.
- Remove from oven and stir all of them around a bit.
- Put back the oven then change the oven off.
- Leave inside the oven until it really is entirely cold without starting the door. I make them at night and depart them in the oven overnight.
- Remove from the oven and store within an airtight container. I came across they keep much better in cup jars than they perform in plastic containers..

Nutrition Facts:

Calorie consumption: 78kcal
Carbohydrates: 14g Protein: 5g Fat: 1g
Sodium: 286mg Fiber: 3g Sugar: 2g

899. SEEDY POWER COOKIES

Ingredients

- 1 medium banana
- 8 Medjool dates
- ½ mug walnuts or pecan nuts or perhaps a mixture of both, for a nut-free of charge version, just change the nuts with any seeds or a combination of even more seeds and much more dried fruit. Simply keep carefully the quantity the same.
- ½ cup ground flax seed
- ½ cup pumpkin seeds
- ½ cup raisins may sub for any additional dried fruits of an identical size
- ¼ goji berries may sub for any various other dried fruits of an equal size
- 3 tablespoons hemp hearts
- 2 tablespoons cacao nibs may sub for chocolate chips
- 1 cup shredded coconut I used unsweetened nevertheless, you can use sweetened in the event that's all you have
- A drop of drinking water if needed

Directions:

- Preheat oven to 300°F
- Add the dates and banana to the blender or food processor chip Process/blend until the puree.
- Scrape out there and into a big bowl.
- Add all some other INGREDIENTS and mix well to mix. Its an extremely stiff mixture. Therefore, it is really a little complicated.
- If the combination is a little dry out, you can include a drop or even two drinking water to take it together.
- Put on a new cookie sheet and drive straight down with the palm of one's hands to flatten into cookie designs. They must be about ½ an inch solid.
- Because they are shaped into cookies, regardless of what technique you use,
- Bake at 300°F for about 25 minutes or even until beginning to color around the edges.
- Cool on a new cooling tray.

Nutrition Facts:

Calorie consumption: 235kcal
Carbohydrates: 26g Protein: 5g Fat: 12g Saturated Body fat: 5g Sodium: 36mg Potassium: 151mg Fiber: 5g Sugar: 17g Supplement A: 600IU Supplement C: 2.5mg Calcium: 50mg Iron: 1.6mg

900. MINT CHOCOLATE TRUFFLE LARABAR BITES

Ingredients

- 130g or 10 significant Medjool dates, pitted
- 200g or 1½ cups raw almonds
- 180g or 1 cup chocolate chips, I utilized semi-sweet dark ones
- ¼ or 20g cup cocoa powder
- ¼ or 28g cup coconut flour
- ¼ - ½ teaspoon peppermint extract, (start at the low finish of the scale after that taste once it's combined together. In the event that you would choose it just a little stronger after that add even more but perform it very gradually)
- 2 tablespoons water

Directions:

- Include the dates, chocolate chips, coconut flour, and cocoa and process once again until well combined.
- Add the peppermint water and extract/oil.
- Process until good combined and balling up.
- Taste a little bit and add a lot more peppermint if required. Process again to mix if you do,
- You may make them whatever size you like. Mine was how big are walnuts.

Nutrition Facts:

Calorie consumption: 80kcal
Carbohydrates: 10g Protein: 2g Fat: 5g
Sodium: 2mg Potassium: 73mg Fiber: 2g Sugar: 6g

901. TRI COLORED BACKYARD PASTA SALAD

Ingredients

- 1 pound box of tri-colored pasta
- 2 large handfuls of extremely greens I bought a massive bag of natural mixed baby kale, spinach, and chard - finely cut
- 2 glasses of yellow cherry tomatoes - sliced
- 1/4 cup of fresh basil - chopped finely
- Dressing:
- 1/2 cup of white wine vinegar
- 3 tablespoons of lemon juice
- 1 teaspoon of additional virgin olive oil
- 1 teaspoon of dried Italian seasoning
- 1/2 teaspoon of ground sea salt
- Ground dark pepper to taste

Directions:
- Dressing:
- Whisk the vinegar, lemon fruit juice, essential olive oil, Italian seasoning,
- Pasta salad:
- Cook the pasta based on the PREPARATION upon the pasta, drain and devote a large bowl. Place the finely chopped very greens, basil, tomatoes, and dressing on the pasta and toss until mixed. Refrigerate within a limited air container. It could be eaten hot or chilly.

Nutrition Facts:
3Mg Calcium: 62mg

902. CHIPOTLE TOMATO RICE ENERGY BOWL

Ingredients
Chipotle Tomato Rice:
- 1 tablespoon olive oil
- 1 small onion, diced
- 2 cloves garlic, minced
- 1 ½ cups moderate grain brown rice, uncooked
- 15-ounce can crushed tomatoes
- 3 cups of water
- 1 veggie broth bouillon cube
- ½ teaspoon chipotle seasoning or powder
- ½ teaspoon salt (optional)

Toppings:
- 2 cups kale, chopped
- 15-ounce can black beans, rinsed, drained
- 1 cup frozen lovely corn, thawed
- 1 cup cherry tomatoes, halved
- 1 little avocado, sliced into 8 slices
- 1 bell pepper (orange, yellow, red, or natural), thinly sliced
- ¼ cup pumpkin seeds
- ½ glass vegan ranch dressing (may choose Southwest or Chipotle taste)*

Directions:
- To create Chipotle Tomato Rice:
- Place essential olive oil in a moderate pot and heat.
- Sauté garlic and onion in oil for 9 minutes.
- Add dark brown rice and toast it for just two 2 minutes, stirring.
- Add more crushed tomatoes,
- Stir well, cover up with a new lid, and provide to a new simmer. Cook over moderate heat about one hour, until liquid will be absorbed and grains are usually tender. May include additional water to displace water dropped to evaporation as required.
- To create Chipotle Tomato Rice Strength Bowls:
- Place one-4th of the rice (a new scant 1 mug each) into 4 person serving bowls (or food prep containers). Note: Might serve rice hot, comfortable, as desired.
- Top each plate of rice with ½ glass chopped kale; 1/3 mug black beans; ¼ glass corn; ¼ mug cherry tomatoes;
- Serve immediately.

Nutrition Facts:
Calories: 415 Glucose: 3 g Sodium: 237 mg Body fat: 14 g Saturated Body fat: 2 g Carbohydrates: 64 g Fiber: 15 g Protein: 15 g

903. GREEN GODDESS BUDDHA BOWL

Ingredients
Buddha Bowl:
- 2 cups cooked whole grain sorghum, cooled
- 15.5-ounce may white beans (we.e., Good Northern, cannellini)
- 1 bunch clean asparagus, trimmed, sliced
- 4 cups packed child arugula leaves
- 1 medium avocado, sliced
- 1 medium cucumber, sliced
- ¼ cup pumpkin seeds

Green Goddess Dressing:
- E., soy, almond, coconut)
- 1/4 huge ripe avocado, peeled, sliced
- 1/4 cup diced cucumber, with peel
- 3 tablespoons chopped new herbs (i.e., dill, cilantro)
- 1 stalk green onion, green and white parts, diced
- 1 small garlic clove
- Pinch white pepper
- 2 tablespoons lemon juice, squeezed freshly

Directions:
- To create Buddha Bowls (makes 4):
- Cook whole grain sorghum to create 2 cups, in accordance with package PREPARATION, and amazing, draining any staying liquid.
- Rinse and drain whitened beans and reserve.
- Blanch asparagus by food Preparations it in boiling drinking water for 3-4 moments, until tender, but brilliant green; set aside.
- Arrange 1 glass arugula leaves at the bottom of every large, individual helping bowl (4).
- ½ mug prepared, cooled sorghum;
- Serve immediately.
- To create Green Goddess Dressing:
- Place all of the dressing INGREDIENTS into the container of a little blender and process until smooth.
- Makes 1/2 glass (4 servings).

Nutrition Facts:
MEAL: 1 bowl Calories: 393 Sugars: 4 g Sodium: 20 mg Body fat: 9 g Saturated Body fat: 1 g Carbohydrates: 69 g Fiber: 18 g Proteins: 18 g Cholesterol: 0 mg

904. PISTACHIO TURMERIC RICE ENERGY BOW

Ingredients
Turmeric Rice:
- 1 tablespoon extra virgin essential olive oil
- 1 cup brownish rice, uncooked
- 1 tablespoon grated refreshing ginger
- 2 cloves garlic, minced
- 2 teaspoons turmeric
- ½ teaspoon freshly ground dark pepper
- 2 cups of water
- 1 cube vegetable bullion
- 1 teaspoon agave syrup
- ½ lemon, juiced

Toppings:
- 1 cup canned chickpeas, rinsed, drained
- 1 cup pistachios, shelled
- ½ cup dried cranberries

- 1 avocado, sliced
- 1 cup fresh spinach
- Extra virgin essential olive oil (if desired)

Directions:

- TO GET READY Turmeric Rice: Heat essential olive oil in a new medium pot. Include rice, ginger, garlic, turmeric, and dark pepper and sauté for just two 2 minutes.
- Add water, veggie bullion, stir well, cover-up, until just tender, however, not mushy.
- Mix in lemon fruit juice and get rid of heat.
- Or 4 for little servings). Pistachios and spinach. Best with a drizzle of additional virgin essential olive oil if desired.

Nutrition Facts:

Calories: 442 Glucose: 14 g Sodium: 122 mg Body fat: 24 g Saturated Body fat: 3 g Carbohydrates: 49 g Fiber: 11 g Protein: 13 g

905. MEDITERRANEAN EDAMAME QUINOA BOWL

Ingredients

Salad Bowl:

- 2 cups packed loosely, fresh greens (we.e., infant kale, arugula, romaine)
- ½ mug frozen shelled edamame, thawed
- ½ cup cherry tomatoes, halved
- ½ cup cooked quinoa
- 10 Kalamata olives, pitted, whole
- 1 little Persian cucumber, with peel, sliced
- ¼ cup sliced red onions
- 2 tablespoons pinenuts
- Mediterranean Vinaigrette:
- 1 tablespoon extra virgin essential olive oil
- 1 ½ tablespoon burgundy or merlot wine vinegar
- 1 little clove garlic, minced
- Pinch sea salt (optional)
- Pinch black pepper
- Pinch smoked red paprika
- ½ teaspoon dried oregano

Directions:

- Fill one big,
- Arrange the following along with the greens: edamame, prepared quinoa, Kalamata olives, sliced red-colored onions, and pinenuts.
- To help make the vinaigrette, whisk olive oil together, Burgandy or merlot wine vinegar, garlic, ocean salt (optional), dark pepper, crimson paprika, and oregano.
- Drizzle the dressing on the salad bowl, evenly.
- Makes one large, person-sized serving. On the other hand, assemble all components in a moderate salad bowl to offer 4 small meals.

Nutrition Facts:

Calories: 516 Sugars: 8 g Sodium: 303 mg Body fat: 34 g Saturated Body fat: 3 g Carbohydrates: 44 g Fiber: 10 g Protein: 16 g

906. NOURISH LENTIL BOWL

Ingredients

Lentils:

- 7 cups (about 1 lb dried) cooked French natural lentils (see information below to create lentils from scratch)
- Roasted Winter Vegetables:
- 3 cups chopped, such as for example butternut or acorn)
- 1 red or whitened onion, sliced
- 2 cups mushrooms, sliced
- 2 garlic cloves
- 2 tablespoons extra-virgin essential olive oil
- 1 tablespoon balsamic vinegar
- such as for example oregano, thyme, and rosemary)

Toppings:

- 1 cup pomegranate seeds (from 1 big pomegranate)
- ¾ cup pecans

Directions:

- Prepare lentils (see PREPARATION below if you would like to cook from scratch) or use ready, seasoned lentils (refrigerated or canned, packaged). Reserve.
- On a sizable baking sheet, arrange chopped squash evenly, onions, mushrooms, in a little dish, mix essential olive oil, vinegar, if desired).
- To prepared Nourish Lentil Bowls, divide lentils among 6 individual helping bowls (1 heaping glass each). Divide roasted veggies among each dish (about 1 cup each). Best with pomegranate seeds (about 3 tablespoons each) and pecans (2 tablespoons each). Optional: Might garnish with greens, such as, for example, arugula, basil, or spinach).

Nutrition Facts:

Calories: 482 Glucose: 10 g Sodium: 260 mg Body fat: 15 g Saturated Body fat: 2 g Carbohydrates: 66 g Fiber: 27 g Protein: 23 g

907. EDAMAME MASALA DARK BROWN BASMATI RICE BOWL

Ingredients

- 1/2 cups brown basmati rice, uncooked
- 3 cups of water
- 1 ½ tablespoon vegetable oil
- 1 onion, diced
- 1 small (or 1/2 large) natural chili, finely diced
- 1 tablespoon grated clean ginger
- 4 cloves minced fresh garlic
- 1 tablespoon ground cumin
- 2 teaspoons ground coriander
- ½ teaspoon ground mustard
- 1 teaspoon ground turmeric
- ½ teaspoon ocean salt (optional)
- ½ teaspoon black pepper
- 1 28-ounce can diced tomatoes, with liquid
- ½ cup finely chopped new cilantro (reserve some for garnish)
- 12-ounce bag frozen shelled edamame
- 2 teaspoons garam masala
- 1 lemon, juiced

Directions:

- Cook basmati rice inside water, in accordance with package PREPARATION, until tender.
- Meanwhile, heat oil inside a new larges skillet and increase onion, chilies, ginger, and dark pepper, stirring regularly.
- Insert canned tomatoes,

- Add edamame and cilantro, stirring well to mix.
- Cover with a new lid and make for 20-25 mins, until thickened.
- Combine garam masala,
- Serve over dark brown basmati rice.

Nutrition Facts:

Calories: 331 Sugars: 3 g Sodium: 181 mg Body fat: 8 g Saturated Body fat: 1 g Carbohydrates: 58 g Fiber: 7 g Protein: 12 g

908. EGG SALAD SANDWICH

Ingredients

- 3 ounces super-strong tofu in vacuum cleaner packaging*
- 1 Tablespoon sliced natural onion or minced yellowish onion
- 2 teaspoons shelled pumpkin sunflower or seeds
- 1 Tablespoon vegan mayonnaise + additional for slathering (Vegenaise is the best.)
- 1/4 teaspoon stoneground mustard
- 1/8 teaspoon black salt kala namak
- Grind dark pepper to taste
- Tiniest pinch turmeric for color (optional)
- 2 slices sandwich bread

Directions:

- Crumble the tofu right into a moderate-sized bowl together with your fingers. Add the sliced natural or minced onion, pumpkin seeds,
- Combine all the INGREDIENTS with a new fork, mashing a few of the tofu. You need it to involve some texture still. So don't create a puree,
- Taste for just about any adjustments and put a lot more mayo, stoneground mustard, dark salt, or pepper that you may like.
- Slather mayonnaise on 2 slices of a sandwich loaf of bread, and fill up with the tofu mixture.

Nutrition Facts:

Calorie consumption: 347kcal Carbohydrates: 32g Protein: 15g Fat: 17g Saturated Body fat: 2g

909. EASY GRILLABLE VEGGIE BURGERS

Ingredients

- 1 cup cooked brownish rice*
- 1 cup natural walnuts (or sub breads crumbs)
- 1/2 Tbsp avocado oil (plus much more for cooking)
- 1/2 moderate white onion (finely diced // 1/2 onion yields ~3/4 cup)
- 1 Tbsp each chili powder, cumin powder, and smoked paprika
- 1/2 tsp each sea salt and dark pepper (plus much more for coating burgers)
- 1 Tbsp coconut sugars (or sub natural brown or muscovado glucose)
- Drained and patted dried out)
- Use gluten-free of charge bread crumbs)
- 3-4 Tbsp vegan BBQ sauce

Directions:

- Heat skillet over moderate heat. Once hot, include natural walnuts and toast for 5-7 minutes, stirring regularly, until fragrant and golden dark brown. Let cool and shift onto the next phase.
- For the time being, heat exactly the same skillet over moderate heat. Once very hot, add onion and oil. Season with a little of salt and pepper and sauté for 3-4 minutes, or until onion will be fragrant, smooth, and translucent. Remove from warmth and set aside.
- Once walnuts are usually cooled, pepper and coconut sugars and blend until an excellent meal (see picture) is achieved. Reserve.
- To a large combining bowl, add drained, dried black coffee beans and mash nicely with a fork, leaving just a few whole beans (see photograph).
- Following add cooked rice, panko loaf of bread crumbs, BBQ sauce, if dried out, if as well wet, add even more panko bread crumbs. Flavor and change seasonings as needed.
- For much larger burgers, To greatly help type the patties, collection your 1/2 or 1/4 measuring mug with plastic material wrap and pack with burger mixture. Press right down to pack firmly, then raise out by the plastic material wrap's edge, and somewhat flatten with hands to create a 3/4-in . thick patty. Set on a baking plate or even sheet for grilling.
- If grilling, heat the grill at the moment and brush the grill surface area with oil to help ease cooking. Otherwise, heat exactly the same skillet you used previously to medium heat.
- As soon as skillet is hot, put sufficient oil to lightly coating underneath of your skillet, adding your burgers - just as much as will comfortably easily fit into the pan. Otherwise, flip gently then. They aren't as company as meat burgers,
- Remove burgers from temperature to let great slightly, and prepare any toppings/sides at the moment (such as for example grilling/toasting your buns).

Nutrition Facts:

Calories: 314 Fat: 15.9g Saturated excess fat: 1.6g Polyunsaturated fat: 10.19g Monounsaturated extra fat: 3.19g Sodium: 550mg Potassium: 395mg Carbohydrates: 36.5g Fiber: 8.4g Sugars: 5.4g Protein: 9.4g Vitamin A: 975IU Vitamin C: 2.36mg Calcium: 76.95mg Iron: 3.25mg

910. MAC 'N' CHEESE

Ingredients

- 1 mind roasted garlic (observe PREPARATION for method)
- 10-12 ounces gluten-free penne* (I really like Bionaturae penne bought at Whole Foods)
- 4 Tbsp olive or grape seed oil
- 4 cloves garlic, minced (4 cloves yield 2 Tbsp)
- 4 1/2 Tbsp arrowroot starch*
- 2 cups unsweetened simple almond milk (plus much more as needed)
- ~1/4 tsp each sea salt and pepper (to taste)
- 5 Tbsp Nutritional yeast (plus much more to taste)
- 1/2 cup vegan parmesan cheese (plus much more for serving)

Directions:

- To roast garlic, drizzle the very best with a little of essential oil, a sprinkle of salt and wrap in foil.
- Place on oven rack and roast for 45 minutes - one hour, depending on dimension of garlic. You'll understand it's done once the garlic is quite fragrant and the light bulb is golden brownish. Remove from oven, unwrap slightly, and let cool.
- At the 40-moment mark, once boiling, add pasta and stir to avoid noodles from sticking. Cook in accordance with package PREPARATION (generally about 8-10 moments). Once cooked fully, drain and aside set.
- In the meantime, start preparing sauce. Warmth a big, oven-safe skillet over moderate heat. Once warm, add essential oil and minced new garlic. Or until lighting golden brown. Immediately include arrowroot starch and whisk - prepare for 1 minute.
- Add almond milk while whisking slowly, then cook for just two 2 minutes more than medium heat, stirring often. The sauce will probably look just a little clumpy - that's Okay! We're likely to blend it.
- Transfer mixture to a new blender, combined with the roasted garlic. Simply drive up from the bottom and the softened cloves should arrive right out - therefore gratifying (and delicious).
- Next add pepper and salt, Nutritional yeast, and vegan parmesan cheese and blend about higher until creamy and easy, scraping disadvantages as needed.
- Salt
- Since it warms back up, it will thicken and obtain super cheesy (see image). Leave it as will be. To thin slightly, add almond milk 1 Tbsp at the same time until desired consistency will be achieved. Switch off heat if it begins bubbling too aggressively.
- Add prepared, Broil pasta on higher for 1-2 mins (optional), or until golden dark brown (see photo). Watch carefully as it could burn quickly.
- Serve immediately.
- Leftovers keep covered inside the refrigerator for 3 days, though ideal when fresh.

Nutrition Facts:

Calories: 523 Fat: 23.6G Sugar: 1.9g Protein: 13.5g

911. MOROCCAN LENTIL-STUFFED EGGPLANT

Ingredients

EGGPLANT

- 4 small eggplants
- Sub water)
- 1 pinch sea salt

LENTILS

- 1 batch Moroccan-Spiced Lentils
- 1 3/4 cups crushed tomatoes (crushed are usually best for taste and texture // can sub diced or puréed tomatoes)
- 1/4 tsp each sea salt and black pepper (plus much more to taste)
- 1/2 tsp smoked paprika (plus much more to taste)

TOPPING

- 1/2 Tbsp vegan parmesan cheese
- 1/2 Tbsp gluten-free panko breads crumbs (I love Ian's brand panko loaf of bread crumbs)

FOR SERVING optional

- Fresh cut parsley or cilantro
- White or brownish rice or cauliflower rice

Directions:

- Crushed tomatoes, salt, and paprika.
- Heat over moderate heat until bubbling. After that reduce high temperature to simmer and make for five minutes more.
- Taste and modify flavor as needed, including even more salt and pepper for general taste or paprika for smokiness.
- See information if thinly slicing and rolling the eggplant. Otherwise, work with a knife to slice an angled divot out from the center of one's eggplants.
- Then work with a spoon to scrape out a hollow center.
- Leave sufficient eggplant flesh so it is sturdy enough to carry the lentils (notice photo). (Conserve leftover eggplant to create things such as Eggplant Curry,)
- Heat a big rimmed skillet over moderate heat. Once sizzling, Cook using one side for 4-5 a few minutes or until somewhat charred. Then flip the eggplant over on the other hand, cover, and make for 4-5 moments more. You are considering the eggplant to become softened and browned externally.
- After the eggplant is cooked, There must be plenty to fill up the eggplant plus some overflow, which may be spooned into the dish. Top with vegan parmesan cheese and panko breads crumbs.
- Bake uncovered for 30-35 minutes or before eggplant is soft and browned and the lentils are usually bubbling. The bread crumbs ought to be browned.
- Greatest when fresh, though leftovers preserve covered in the fridge around 4 days or inside the freezer around 1 month.

Nutrition Facts:

Calories: 429 Fat: 9.8G Fiber: 33.4G

912. GARLIC AND WHITE WINE PASTA WITH BRUSSELS SPROUTS

Ingredients

BRUSSELS SPROUTS

- 16 ounces Brussels Sprouts (halved)
- 1-2 Tbsp essential olive oil
- 1 pinch each sea salt + black pepper

SAUCE + PASTA

- 3 Tbsp essential olive oil or vegan butter
- 4 large cloves garlic, cut (yields ~3 Tbsp as original recipe is created)
- 1/3 cup dry whitened wine (Pinot Grigio, are usually best)
- 4 Tbsp arrowroot starch (or cornstarch)
- 1 3/4 glass unsweetened plain almond milk
- 4 Tbsp Nutritional yeast
- Sea salt + dark pepper to taste
- 1/4 cup vegan parmesan cheese (plus much more for serving)

- 10 ounces vegan, gluten-free pasta* (brown rice pastas are plentiful - or this penne from Bionaturae)

FOR SERVING (optional)
- Garlic bread*
- Simple green salad*

Directions:
- As needed, drizzle with oil, and time of year generously with salt and pepper and toss. Arrange in one layer and reserve.
- Reserve while preparing sauce.
- Heat a huge rimmed skillet over moderate heat. Once popular, add garlic and oil. Sauté for three minutes or until fragrant and incredibly slightly golden brown, adding wine (see photo). Be cautious - it could flame, but only briefly. Mix and sauté for 2-4 minutes, or until the wines has decreased by about half.
- Add whisk and arrowroot, adding almond milk and whisk. At this point, it'll be very clumpy - that is normal. Transfer to a higher velocity blender and add dietary yeast, salt + pepper, and vegan parmesan cheese. Blend on higher until creamy and clean.
- Taste and adapt flavor while needed, adding a lot more vegan parmesan or even Nutritional yeast for cheesiness, or salt and pepper for more overall taste.
- Transfer sauce back again to the skillet and warm more than medium-low warmth until bubbly even though whisking. of which point it is possible to lower heat to reduced and simmer until pasta will be cooked. If it appears too thick, slim with almond milk. If as well thin, increase temperature to medium to motivate thickening.
- Around this time, therefore i did that final.
- Once cooked serve with staying Brussels sprouts and extra vegan parmesan cheese for taste. I also like a little of red pepper flake, but that is optional.
- Greatest when fresh, though leftovers hold well in the fridge for 2-3 times.

Nutrition Facts:
Calories: 509 Fat: 18.4G Fiber: 7.7g Sugar: 2.3G

913. KALE SALAD WITH SAVORY TAHINI DRESSING

Ingredients

ROASTED VEGETABLES
- 1 moderate zucchini (sliced in 1/4-inch rounds)
- 1 medium nice potato (sliced in 1/4-inch rounds)
- 1 cup reddish cabbage (shredded)
- 1 Tbsp melted coconut oil (or sub drinking water or use our way for oil-free vegetables)
- 1 Pinch sea salt
- 1/2 tsp DIY curry powder (or store-bought)

DRESSING
- 1/3 cup tahini
- 1/2 tsp garlic powder (plus much more to taste)
- 1 Tbsp coconut aminos (plus much more to flavor or sub tamari or soy sauce)
- because the flavor is more extreme)
- 1 big clove garlic (minced)
- ~1/4 cup water (to thin)

SALAD
- Romaine, mixed greens, etc.)
- 4 little radishes (thinly sliced)
- 3 Tbsp hemp seeds
- 1 ripe avocado (cubed)
- 2 Tbsp lemon apple or juice cider vinegar
- TOPPINGS optional / choose your favorites
- 1 batch Crispy Baked Chickpeas
- 2 cups cooked quinoa* (We cooked my quinoa with curry powder // omit to help keep grain-free)
- DIY Kimchi (or even store-bought)

Directions:
- If helping with quinoa or crispy chickpeas, prepare at the moment (follow links / see information for PREPARATION). Otherwise, check out step 2.
- Preheat oven to 375 degrees F (190 C) and arrange zucchini, cabbage, and sweet potatoes in baking sheet (a number of as needed). Drizzle with coconut essential oil (or sub oil-free choices), ocean salt, and curry powder and toss to mix. Roast for 20 mins or until tender and somewhat golden brown.
- For the time being, prepare dressing with the addition of tahini, taste and change seasonings as needed, incorporating even more garlic powder for garlic taste, or salt for saltiness. Reserve.
- Assemble salad with the addition of greens, and avocado to a sizable mixing bowl. Include the lemon fruit juice (or apple company cider vinegar) and softly toss to combine.
- Add roasted veggies and any desired toppings (quinoa,) and function with dressing.
- Best when fresh, though leftovers keep well saved in the refrigerator up to 3 days. Dressing kept separately will keep for 7 days. Chickpeas should be saved separately at room temperature to maintain crispiness.

Nutrition Facts:
Calories: 410 Fat: 30.6G Fiber: 8.7g Sugar: 3.5g Protein: 12g

914. BUTTERNUT SQUASH VEGGIE PIZZA

Ingredients

SAUCE
- 3 cups butternut squash (cubed*)
- 3 cloves garlic (whole // skin removed)
- 2 Tbsp essential olive oil (divided)
- 1 pinch sea salt + black pepper
- 1 Tbsp maple syrup

PIZZA
- 1/2 cups broccolini (chopped // huge stems removed)
- 1/2 cup reddish colored onion (chopped)
- 1/2 cup prepared chickpeas (rinsed and thoroughly dried // optional)
- 1 pinch sea salt + black pepper
- 1 tsp dried oregano
- 6 ounces store-bought pizza dough (I REALLY LIKE Trader Joe's Garlic and

Herb or WHOLE WHEAT GRAINS // or this gluten-free recipe)
- 1 cup Butternut Squash Sauce (recipe above)
- 1/2 cup vegan parmesan store-bought or cheese vegan mozzarella cheese*

FOR SERVING optional
- Vegan parmesan cheese
- Red pepper flakes

Directions:
- Toss to mix.
- Move squash and garlic to a new blender or meals processor with remaining essential olive oil (1 Tbsp as initial recipe is written // modify if altering batch dimension) and maple syrup. Purée until smooth and creamy, adding more essential olive oil or perhaps a touch of drinking water if it's too solid. The consistency ought to be creamy and spreadable (not really pourable).
- Taste and adapt seasonings as needed. Reserve.
- Heat a big skillet over medium high temperature. Once hot, broccolini, pepper and salt, and oregano. Stirring frequently. Reserve.
- Roll out there pizza dough into a straight circle and move to a parchment-lined circular baking sheet (or even similarly-shaped object).
- Top with ~ 1 mug sauce (you should have leftover sauce, that you can reserve for some other pizzas // amount as initial recipe is written // change if altering batch dimension), vegetables, and chickpeas.
- Exchange pizza to the oven, bake for 13-18 a few minutes, or until crust edges are usually golden brown.
- Dried oregano, and crimson pepper flakes (optional). Though greatest when fresh.

Nutrition Facts:
Calories: 171 Fat: 6.2G Sugar: 4.1g Protein: 6.2g

915. YELLOW COCONUT CURRY WITH MANGO

Ingredients
CURRY
- 1/2 Tbsp coconut essential oil (or avocado or grape seed essential oil)
- 1 medium shallot, minced
- 2 Tbsp minced refreshing ginger
- 2 cloves minced garlic (2 cloves yield ~1 Tbsp)
- 1 Thai red-colored chili (or serrano pepper // stem removed and thinly sliced with seeds)
- 1 cup chopped crimson cabbage (optional)
- 3 Tbsp reddish curry paste*
- 2 14-ounce cans gentle coconut milk (sub 1 can of full body fat per 2 cans lighting for additional creamy texture)
- 3 Tbsp coconut glucose (plus much more to taste)
- 1/4 tsp ocean salt (plus much more to taste)
- 2-3 tsp tamari (or soy sauce or even gluten-free)
- 1 tsp ground turmeric
- 1 reddish bell pepper (seeds and stem taken out // cut into bite-sizing pieces)
- 1/4 cup natural peas (optional // frozen or fresh)
- 2 ripe mangos
- 1/4 cup roasted cashews (salted is most beneficial)
- 1 medium lemon, juiced

FOR SERVING optional
- Lemon wedges
- Thai (or normal) basil, or clean cilantro, for serving
- Dark brown rice* or coconut quinoa
- Steamed broccoli

Directions:
- Heat a huge cast iron or metal skillet with a high rim over medium heat. Once scorching, add coconut essential oil, shallot, ginger, garlic, Put in a pinch of ocean salt and sauté for 2-3 minutes, stirring frequently.
- Put cabbage (optional) and crimson curry paste and mix, and cook for just two 2 minutes more.
- Include coconut milk, coconut sugars, sea salt, tamari,
- Once simmering, A simmer is wanted by you, not a boil, that ought to be around reduced to medium-low heat.
- Cook for 5-10 moments, stirring occasionally,
- At this time also taste and modify the flavor of the broth as needed. I added even more coconut glucose for sweetness, tamari and ocean salt for saltiness, and turmeric for earthiness.
- Add mango,
- Serve over rice or even coconut quinoa, or even steamed broccoli (broccoli getting the best). This dish will get elevated with the help of more lemon fruit juice and Thai or normal basil.

Nutrition Facts:
Calories: 400 Fat: 23.9G Fiber: 4.2G

916. BAKED QUINOA DARK BEAN FALAFEL

Ingredients
- 1 cup prepared and cooled quinoa (make certain it's prepared and completely cooled before making use of)
- 15-ounce can dark beans (rinsed, drained, dried)
- 1/4 cup pumpkin seeds (raw or roasted)
- 5 cloves garlic (pores and skin removed and crushed)
- 1/2 tsp ocean salt, plus much more to taste
- 1 tsp ground cumin
- 1/2 tsp floor coriander
- 2 Tbsp tomato paste
- 2 Tbsp coconut aminos
- 1 chipotle pepper in adobo sauce (omit for much less spicy falafel)
- 1 tsp dietary yeast (optional)

Directions:
- Add rinsed, bake for quarter-hour or until coffee beans show up cracked and feel dried out to touch (see coffee beans in food processor picture).
- Add cooked/cooled quinoa then, salt, and dietary yeast (optional). Mix to mix

until a textured dough types (you're not searching for a purée).
- Taste and adapt flavor like needed, adobo sauce for warmth, cumin for smokiness, or even salt for overall taste.
- Bake for a quarter-hour.
- These falafel are tasty with hummus, Attempt garnishing with chili garlic sauce for additional heat. Or take pleasure in as is!
- Store leftovers covered inside the refrigerator around 3-4 days. To freeze, Adding to a freezer-secure container and freeze around one month.

Nutrition Facts:

Calories: 60 Fat: 1.9G Fiber: 1.8g Sugar: 0.9G

917. KALE SALAD WITH CRISPY CHICKPEAS

Ingredients

- 10 ounces kale (loosely chopped or torn // ~6 cups as original recipe is written)

CHICKPEAS

- Drained and thoroughly dried)
- 1/2 Tbsp olive, avocado or grape seed, oil
- 2 1/2 - 3 Tbsp tandoori masala spice mix* (see information for DIY blend)
- DRESSING
- 1 head garlic
- 1/4 cup tahini
- 2 Tbsp essential olive oil + more for roasting garlic
- 2 medium lemons* (juiced)
- 1-2 Tbsp maple syrup (or honey or even vegan)
- 1 pinch each salt + pepper
- Warm water (to thin)

Directions:

- Add drained chickpeas to a mixing bowl and toss with essential oil and seasonings.
- Increase garlic cloves and seasoned chickpeas to a baking sheet. Drizzle garlic with a little of olive or grape seed essential oil. Bake for 20-23 minutes or before chickpeas are somewhat crispy and golden dark brown and the garlic will be fragrant and somewhat browned. Remove from oven and reserve.
- Squeeze garlic out there of skins / peel away skins and increase a combining bowl. Add all remaining dressing INGREDIENTS and whisk to combine vigorously, smashing the garlic with the whisk. Flavor and change seasonings as desired, including more lemon for lighting and maple syrup for sweetness. Set aside.
- Put kale to a sizable mixing bowl. Before incorporating dressing, Adding just as much dressing as preferred (some could be leftover) and blend with a spoon.
- Top with serve and chickpeas. Best when fresh, though leftovers retain in the fridge for a few days.

Nutrition Facts:

Calories: 669 Fat: 44.2g Saturated fats: 5.9g Sodium: 138mg Potassium: 1123mg Carbohydrates: 59.8g Fiber: 16.5g Glucose: 15.5g Proteins: 20.2g Vitamin A: 14200IU Vitamin C: 283.8mg Calcium: 440mg Iron: 6.7mg

918. LENTIL SALAD WITH CURD CHEESE

Ingredients

- 35 g lentils, dry product
- 125 ml vegetable broth
- 1 medium-sized tomato (s)
- 1/4 clove of garlic
- 1/2 medium onion (s)
- 1 shot of lemon juice
- 1 tablespoon of olive oil
- salt
- pepper
- 1 tsp parsley
- 100 g herb curd

Directions:

- Cook the lentils in vegetable broth according to the package PREPARATION so that they still have a bite. Tip: Red lentils only need around 10 minutes!
- Dice the tomato, finely chop the garlic and onion.
- Mix lemon juice, olive oil, salt, pepper, onions and garlic into a dressing and then mix with the lentils and tomato. Chop parsley and sprinkle over it.
- Eat herb curd as a dip.

Nutrition Facts:

Calories (kcal): 378 Fat: 21g Protein: 18g Carbohydrates: 25g

919. BULGUR HACK CHILI

Ingredients

- 1.5 tbsp olive oil
- 1 medium onion (s)
- 3 cloves of garlic
- 1 medium-sized bell pepper
- 1 pod of chilli (serrano)
- 1.5 tsp cumin (ground)
- 1 tsp chili powder
- 0.5 tsp oregano (dried)
- 500 g ground beef
- 70 g bulgur
- 400 g tomato (chunks)
- 200 g kidney beans, canned
- 1 tsp salt
- 1 tbsp sour cream
- lime slices

Directions:

- Heat the oil in a large saucepan or roaster.
- Meanwhile, roughly chop the onion and cut the garlic into thin slices. Dice the paprika and halve serrano chilies.
- Put everything in the pot and stir-fry for 10 minutes until the onion is golden brown and the chillies are tender.
- Add spices and sauté for 1 minute.
- Chop and sweat for 3 minutes until it's no longer pink. Stir the raw bulgur into the mixture.
- Mash the beans lightly, add tomato, salt and 150 milliliters of water to the pan, then bring to a simmer.
- Let it simmer under the lid for 30 minutes. Season with salt, pepper, serve with sour cream and slices of lime.

Nutrition Facts:

Calories (kcal): 442 Fat: 24g Protein: 32g Carbohydrates: 27g

920. LIME PRAWNS ON WILD RICE

INGREDIENTS

- 150 g Swiss chard (alternatively: spinach)
- 150 g zucchini
- salt

- pepper
- 50 g brown rice, raw
- 150 g shrimp
- 1 tablespoon of olive oil
- 2 tsp coriander (fresh, chopped)
- 2 sprinkles of lime juice

Directions:

- Prepare the rice according to the package PREPARATION. Fry the shrimp in hot oil for 3 to 4 minutes on both sides until they turn pink.
- Wash the chard (or spinach) and zucchini, cut and add to the prawns in the pan. Then season with salt and pepper.
- Mix shrimp and vegetables with rice, season with coriander, lime juice, salt and pepper, and serve.

Nutrition Facts:

Calories (kcal): 482 Fat: 17g Protein: 39g Carbohydrates: 44g

921. SWEET POTATO CURRY WITH PUMPKIN

Ingredients

- 1/2 medium onion (s)
- 1 clove of garlic
- 1-2 pods of chilli
- 1 tbsp coconut oil
- 1 tsp garam masala
- 1/2 tsp turmeric
- 1/2 tsp cumin
- 200 g tomato (s) (peeled)
- 250 g butternut squash
- 250 g sweet potato (s)
- 200 ml coconut milk
- 1 shot of water
- 1/2 can of chickpeas, can
- 2 sprigs of coriander

Directions:

- Finely chop the onion and garlic, core the chili peppers and chop them as well.
- Heat the coconut oil in a large saucepan at high speed. Braise the onions, garlic and chilli until translucent. Add Garam Masala, turmeric, cumin and curry and continue to fry.
- Add the peeled tomatoes and chop them roughly with a wooden spoon.
- Peel and core the pumpkin, peel the sweet potatoes and cut them into equal pieces.
- Switch the hob down to medium heat and add the vegetables to the pan. Add coconut milk and enough water to cover everything. Simmer for 30 to 40 minutes until the vegetables are cooked but still firm to the bite.
- Drain and rinse the chickpeas. Add to the curry and simmer for 10 minutes until the mixture thickens a little. Then arrange with the coriander branches.

Nutrition Facts:

Calories (kcal): 596 Fat: 32g Protein: 12g Carbohydrates: 61g

922. PASTA WITH CHICKPEA SAUCE

Ingredients

- 1 medium onion (s)
- 2 tablespoons of olive oil
- 1 can of chickpeas, can
- 250 ml vegetable broth
- 1 tbsp tomato paste
- Herbs
- salt
- pepper
- 200 g raw pasta (e.g. spaghetti)

Directions:

- Chop the onion and sauté in olive oil in a saucepan.
- Add chickpeas, vegetable stock, tomato paste and Italian herbs.
- Cook on medium heat for 5 minutes, season with salt and pepper.
- Cook and serve the pasta according to the package preparation.

Nutrition Facts:

Calories (kcal): 638 Fat: 19g Protein: 22g Carbohydrates: 91g

923. SPICY TOFU WITH QUINOA AND AVOCADO SALAD

Ingredients

- 40 g quinoa
- 75 g smoked tofu
- 1/2 medium bell pepper (red)
- 1/2 medium avocado (s)
- 2 sprigs of coriander
- 1 tbsp lime juice
- 1 pinch of salt
- 1 pinch of pepper

Directions:

- Cook the quinoa according to the package PREPARATION.
- Dice tofu, bell pepper and avocado and put in a bowl. Chop the coriander and mix everything. Season with lime juice, salt and pepper. Mix in the quinoa.

Nutrition Facts:

Calories (kcal): 547 Fat: 38g Protein: 24g Carbohydrates: 30g

924. CHILI WITHOUT CARNE

Ingredients

- 1 medium-sized onion (s) (large)
- 1 medium-sized carrot (s)
- 2 cloves of garlic
- 2 tablespoons vegetable oil
- 1 medium-sized bell pepper (red)
- 1 tsp turmeric
- 1 tsp oregano
- 1 tsp chilli flakes
- 1 tbsp tomato paste
- 1 can of chopped tomatoes (can)
- 400 g canned lentils
- 1/2 can of kidney beans, canned
- 1 pinch of salt
- 1 pinch of pepper
- 2 pods of jalapeños
- 50 g gouda (grated)

Directions:

- Cut the onion, grate the carrot and press the garlic.
- Heat vegetable oil in a large saucepan at a low setting and add the onion, carrot and garlic. Let sweat without lid for 15 minutes, turning, over low heat.
- Meanwhile, dice the peppers.
- Now put the spices in the pot and heat for another minute.
- Raise the heat to medium heat, add the peppers and tomato paste and heat with stirring for another minute.
- Add chopped tomatoes, fill the can with water and pour this into the pot as well. Bring the chilli to a boil, then reduce the heat again and simmer at low temperature for 25 minutes until the mixture thickens.

- Finally, stir lentils and kidney beans into the chilli. Heat for another 5 minutes and then season to taste with salt and pepper. Cut the jalapeños into slices and garnish the chilli with it and with the grated cheese.

Nutrition Facts:

Calories (kcal): 536 Fat: 25g Protein: 25g Carbohydrates: 50g

925. TEXMEX SALAD

Ingredients

- 125 g chicken breast
- 1 tsp olive oil
- salt
- pepper
- 100 g romaine lettuce
- 1/2 medium bell pepper (yellow)
- 1 medium-sized tomato (s)
- 50 g black beans
- 1 tbsp salsa
- 2 tbsp guacamole

Directions:

- Cut the chicken breast very finely or turn it through the wolf.
- Put the oil in a pan, season the meat with salt and pepper and fry.
- Cut the lettuce, bell pepper and tomato into small pieces, drain the beans and put everything in a bowl where it is mixed with the meat.
- Salsa and guacamole as a side dish.

Nutrition Facts:

Calories (kcal): 442 Fat: 15g Protein: 43g Carbohydrates: 34g

926. POBLANO AND PORTOBELLO FAJITAS

Ingredients

- 1 Tbsp olive or coconut oil
- 1 whole poblano pepper (seeds removed and thinly sliced)
- 2 medium bell peppers (seeds removed and thinly sliced)
- 1 whole jalapeño (seeds removed and thinly sliced)
- 1 medium yellow or white onion (cut into thin rounds)
- 2 large portobello mushrooms* (stems removed // wiped clean and thinly sliced)
- 2 medium ripe avocados
- 1 Tbsp lime juice (juice of 1/2 lime as original recipe is written)
- Sea salt, cumin, & garlic powder
- 1 tsp A1 steak sauce
- 6 small flour or corn tortillas
- Fresh red onion, hot sauce, cilantro, salsa (optional)

Directions:

- Heat a large skillet and a medium skillet over medium-high heat. Once hot add a dash of olive or coconut oil to the large skillet, then the onion and peppers. Season generously with salt, cumin and garlic powder.
- Cook until softened and slightly caramelized, stirring often. Set aside and cover to keep warm.
- At the same time, add a dash of oil to the medium pan. Then add the mushrooms. Season with a bit of salt and once softened and brown (see photo), add a dash of A1 (vegan-friendly) for more flavor (optional). Remove from heat, set aside and cover.
- Prepare guacamole by adding avocados to a bowl then adding lime juice and a generous pinch of salt. Fresh cilantro and onion are optional.
- Warm tortillas in the microwave or oven and you're ready to go. Serve tortillas with peppers and onions, mushrooms, guacamole, and any other toppings you desire such as salsa, hot sauce, and cheese or sour cream (for non-vegan).

Nutrition Facts:

Calories: 362 Fat: 20.4g Saturated fat: 2.9g Sodium: 38.2mg Potassium: 1046.7mg Carbohydrates: 42.4g Calcium: 70mg Iron: 2mg

927. STUFFED PEPPERS WITH QUINOA

Ingredients

- 168 g quinoa or rice - washed hot
- 500 ml vegetable broth - alternatively water, however, loses its taste
- 4 large - yellow, orange or red peppers, cut lengthways, core casing removed
- 15 ml of frying and baking oil
- 1 red onion - finely chopped
- 38 g tomato paste
- 150 g mushrooms - halved and sliced
- 400 g canned tomatoes or passata
- 265 g black beans - drained and washed well
- ½ teaspoon of garlic granules
- 1 tsp cumin
- 2 tsp Italian herbs *
- 1 Bird eye chilli or another chilli powder to taste.
- Salt at will
- Black pepper at will

For gratinating:

- Vegan processed cheese
- Vegan parmesan

Directions:

- Put the quinoa and vegetable stock in a saucepan and bring to a boil. As soon as it boils, turn back the heat a little and let simmer for 20 minutes. Now there should be no more liquid, and the quinoa should be nice and fluffy.
- Preheat the oven to 190 degrees and prepare a large baking dish.
- Place the halved peppers in the baking dish with the open surface facing up.
- Heat a large pan with the frying oil for the filling. Fry the onion until translucent. Add tomato paste and mushrooms.
- Add tomato pieces and beans. Season with garlic, cumin, Italian herbs, chilli, salt and pepper and stir well until everything has combined.
- Stir in the quinoa. Season to taste and season as needed.
- Use a spoon to fill the halves of the paprika. Fill up well and press down again and again.
- (optional) pour vegan processed cheese over it.
- **Important!** Pour some water (about 50m onto the bottom of the baking dish, so nothing can burn).
- Put in the oven and bake for 45 minutes.
- Remove from the oven, let cool briefly and serve.
- Keeps covered in the fridge for 2-3 days. Reheat in the steam cooker or 20 minutes in the oven at 175 degrees.

Nutrition Facts:
Calories 372 Sodium 613mg Carbohydrates 65g Sugar 12g Protein 16g

928. COLORFUL QUINOA SALAD WITH POMEGRANATE

Ingredients

- 30 g quinoa
- 1 dash of lime juice
- 2 sprigs of mint
- 1 handful of arugula
- 2 tbsp pomegranate seeds
- 1 tablespoon of olive oil
- salt
- pepper
- 1 tbsp pine nuts

Directions:

- Preparations Colorful quinoa salad with pomegranatePrepare quinoa according to package PREPARATION.
- Crumble the feta, then add to the quinoa together with lime juice and chopped mint.
- Fold in the arugula, add the pomegranate seeds and season the salad with olive oil, salt and pepper.
- Roast pine nuts fat-free in a pan and top salad.

Nutrition Facts:

Calories (kcal): 333 Fat: 23g Protein: 8g Carbohydrates: 25g

929. SALAD WITH SMOKED TOFU

Ingredients

- 80 g smoked tofu
- 1 clove of garlic
- 1 piece (s) of ginger
- 1 pinch of chilli flakes
- 1/2 tbsp rapeseed oil
- 50 g glass noodles
- 1 medium carrot (s)
- 2 medium spring onion (s)
- 1/4 medium mango
- 3 sprigs of coriander
- salt
- Pepper

Directions:

- Preparations of glass noodle salad with smoked tofuCut the tofu into 1 cm cubes. Dice the garlic and ginger finely, roughly chop the peanuts.
- Heat the oil in the pan, fry the tofu in it for about 3 minutes. Add garlic and ginger, season with chilli flakes, then deglaze with soy sauce. Take the pan off the stove.
- Prepare glass noodles according to package PREPARATION, then drain.
- In the meantime, grate the carrot cut the spring onion into rings and mango into fine strips, chop the coriander.
- Mix glass noodles with tofu and vegetables, season with salt and pepper. Sprinkle the salad with peanuts. The salad tastes lukewarm or cold.

Nutrition Facts:

Calories (kcal): 436 Fat: 15g Protein: 18g Carbohydrates: 58g

930. EGGPLANT CAVIAR WITH BASIL PISTOU

Ingredients

- 450 g eggplant (s)
- 150 ml of olive oil
- 2 medium-sized lemon (s) (organic)
- 6 medium-sized olive (s) (Kalamato)
- 1 sprig of parsley
- 1 pinch of salt
- 1 pinch of pepper
- 1 clove of garlic
- 190 g basil

Directions:

- Preparations of eggplant caviar with basil pistouDice the eggplant and briefly fry in 1/3 of the oil until the vegetables soften. Let rest for 1 hour.
- Squeeze lemons and grate the zest of 1 lemon.
- Roast pine nuts, chop olives and chop the parsley. Mix 5 tablespoons of lemon juice, lemon peel, parsley, olives, pine nuts, salt and pepper with the eggplant cubes.
- Squeeze the garlic, mix with the basil leaves and the remaining lemon juice. Stir in the rest of the olive oil and season to taste.
- Place the eggplant vegetables in the middle of the plate on the basil sauce.

Nutrition Facts:

Calories (kcal): 800 Fat: 79g Protein: 7g Carbohydrates: 15g

931. POTATO CURRY WITH PUMPKIN

Ingredients

- 1/2 medium onion (s)
- 1 clove of garlic
- 1-2 pods of chilli
- 1 tbsp coconut oil
- 1 tsp garam masala
- 1/2 tsp turmeric
- 1/2 tsp cumin
- 200 g tomato (s) (peeled)
- 250 g butternut squash
- 250 g sweet potato (s)
- 200 ml coconut milk
- 1 shot of water
- 1/2 can of chickpeas, can
- 2 sprigs of coriander

Directions:

- Preparations of sweet potato curry with pumpkinFinely chop the onion and garlic, core the chili peppers and chop them as well.
- Heat the coconut oil in a large saucepan at high speed. Braise the onions, garlic and chilli until translucent. Add Garam Masala, turmeric, cumin and curry and continue to fry.
- Add the peeled tomatoes and chop them roughly with a wooden spoon.
- Peel and core the pumpkin, peel the sweet potatoes and cut them into equal pieces.
- Switch the hob down to medium heat and add the vegetables to the pan. Add coconut milk and enough water to cover everything. Simmer for 30 to 40 minutes until the vegetables are cooked but still firm to the bite.
- Drain and rinse the chickpeas. Add to the curry and simmer for 10 minutes until the mixture thickens a little. Then arrange with the coriander branches.

Nutrition Facts:

Calories (kcal): 596 Fat: 32g Protein: 12g Carbohydrates: 61g

932. TOASTED CHARD WITH MACADAMIA CHEESE

Ingredients

- 125 g macadamia nuts
- 2 tsp vegan probiotic powder
- 1 medium shallot (s)
- salt
- 200 g Swiss chard (with different colored stems)
- 2 tablespoons of olive oil
- 1 tbsp sherry vinegar
- 1/2 tbsp rapeseed oil
- 1/2 medium grapefruit
- 1 tbsp hazelnuts
- Sprouts (for decoration)

Directions:

- Prepare "cheese" two days in advance: cover the nuts with water and soak them for 24 hours.
- Pour macadamias through a sieve to catch the water. Mix the probiotic powder with the water until it becomes frothy.
- Puree the mixture with the nuts to a smooth mass. Leave covered for 18 to 48 hours.
- The longer you wait, the more flavorful the cheese will be. Then put the mass in a cheese cloth and drain in the fridge.
- Chop the shallot finely and add to the cheese with a little salt.
- Wash the chard and swirl in olive oil. Cover with aluminum foil and roast at 185 degrees for 2 hours.
- Peel the leaves, peel the chard stalks, dice and put in the fridge.
- Mix the sherry vinegar and rapeseed oil, season to taste and pour over the chard.
- Arrange with macadamia cheese, grapefruit, hazelnuts and sprouts.

Nutrition Facts:

Calories (kcal): 699 Fat: 66g Protein: 10g Carbohydrates: 16g

933. COUSCOUS SALAD WITH SOY DIP

Ingredients

- 50 g raw couscous
- 2 medium sized tomato (s)
- 1 medium spring onion (s)
- 1 tbsp parsley (chopped)
- 1 tbsp mint (chopped)
- 1 tbsp lemon juice
- 1 tablespoon of olive oil
- salt
- pepper
- 150 g soy yogurt (natural)

Directions:

- Preparations of couscous salad with soy dipCook the couscous according to the package PREPARATION and then let it cool a little.
- Dice the tomatoes and spring onions and mix in a small bowl with parsley, mint, lemon juice and olive oil.
- Then stir the whole thing under the couscous and season with salt and pepper.
- Now spice up the soy yogurt with a dash of lemon juice and reserve.
- Instead of soy yogurt, you can of course, also use normal, natural yogurt or quark. Then the dish is no longer vegan.

Nutrition Facts:

Calories (kcal): 415 Fat: 18g Protein: 16g Carbohydrates: 45g

934. SWEET DESSERT TARTE FLAMBÉE

Ingredients

For the dough:

- 1/2 cube of yeast, fresh
- 130 ml of water
- 250 g buckwheat flour
- 2 Tablespoons of sugar
- 1 Tsp salt
- 3 Tablespoons of olive oil

For covering:

- 3 peach
- 3 EL Mandelmus
- 2 EL agave nectar
- 40 g almond, chopped
- mint leaf

Directions:

- Crumble the yeast and dissolve in 50 milliliters of lukewarm water. Put the flour in a bowl and press a hollow in the middle. Mix the yeast mixture with the sugar and some flour from the edge of the trough, then let the batter rise for about ten minutes.
- Add remaining dough INGREDIENTS and knead into a smooth dough that no longer sticks to your hands. If necessary, add a little flour or water for a smooth consistency during kneading. Shape the dough into a ball and leave covered in a warm place for 45 minutes.
- In the meantime, remove the peach pulp from the core and cut into fine slices.
- Preheat the oven to 210 degrees (top / bottom heat). Knead the dough again after letting it rise and divide it into two portions. Roll out each dough portion thinly on a piece of baking paper. Brush the flatbread with almond butter. Place peach slices on the dough flat like tiles, drizzle with agave syrup and sprinkle with chopped almonds. Bake crispy bread on the middle shelf within 15 minutes. Serve half a flame cake sprinkled with mint leaves.

Nutrition Facts:

calories 470kcal carbohydrates 69g fat 82g Protein 8g

935. NO BAKE PROTEIN ENERGY BALL

Ingredients

- 2 cups rolled oats, gluten free if needed
- ½ cup pumpkin seeds
- 1 cup hemp seeds
- ½ cup cacao nibs
- 1 cup pecans, any nut works or leave out for nut free
- ½ cups goji berries
- 2 ½ cups dates
- 1 teaspoon vanilla extract
- pinch sea salt
- ½ - ¾ cup water
- ½ cup unsweetened shredded coconut

Directions:

- Place oats, pumpkin seeds, hemp seeds, cacao nibs, and pecans in a large bowl.
- Place goji berries in a small bowl and fill with warm water.
- Allow to soak for 5 minutes or until they soften a bit.

- Once slightly soft, drain water and place berries into the bowl with the rest of the ingredients.
- Place dates, vanilla extract, salt and water in a food processor. Mix until partially smooth and partially chunky. This is similar to my date paste recipe but not as smooth and has a tad less water.
- Put into the bowl with the rest of the ingredients. Using your hands, mix everything together well until you get a dough like consistency.

Nutrition Facts:

Calories 225 Carbohydrates 27g Protein 6g Sugar 13g Fat 11g

936. FUDGE BROWNIES

Ingredients

- 3/4 cup gluten-free quick oats
- 1/4 cup water
- 3/4 cup cooked or canned black beans
- 1 medium yellow squash (~200g)
- 1.5 tsp baking powder
- 1/4 cup cocoa powder
- 3/4 cup granulated erythritol
- 1/4 tsp salt
- 1 tsp natural butter flavor
- 1 tsp vanilla extract
- 1/2 tsp liquid stevia

Directions:

- 1. Preheat oven to 350F, spray 8×8 baking pan with non-stick cooking spray, an set aside.
- 2. Add oats to blender and process until flour-like consistency is reached.
- 3. Add in remaining INGREDIENTS, and blend until smooth.
- 4. Pour into prepared baking dish, and bake for 30 minutes or until a toothpick inserted into the center comes out clean.
- 5. Once brownies have cooled, dust with powdered erythritol if desired.

Nutrition Facts:

Calories 59 Protein 3g Fat 1g Sodium 75mg Potassium 126mg

937. POMEGRANATE MASGHATI DESSERT

Ingredients

- 3 cups no-sugar-added pomegranate juice, divided (see Tip)
- 6 tablespoons cornstarch
- ⅓ cup sugar, plus more as needed
- 1 tablespoon rose water (optional)
- ¼ cup pomegranate seeds, plus more for garnish
- Chopped or slivered raw pistachios, for garnish
- Ground dried rose petals, for garnish

Directions:

- Set aside a 9- to 10-inch, 1- to 2-inch-deep serving dish (a regular pie plate works). Whisk 1 cup pomegranate juice with cornstarch in a small bowl until completely smooth, without any lumps; set aside.
- Combine sugar and the remaining 2 cups pomegranate juice in a medium saucepan.
- Bring to a simmer (little bubbles start to appear on the sides) over medium-high heat; cook, stirring, until the sugar dissolves, about 5 minutes.
- Whisk the cornstarch mixture and add it to the saucepan. Reduce the heat to medium-low and start stirring immediately.
- Continue to stir until it starts to set, 2 to 5 minutes. Don't go anywhere during this process know the mixture is ready when it lightly coats the back of a spoon. At the very last moment, add rose water and pomegranate seeds; stir to combine and remove from the heat.
- Immediately pour the masghati into the serving dish and smooth the top.
- Set aside to cool to room temperature, then refrigerate, uncovered, to fully set and chill, 6 to 8 hours.
- Once chilled, garnish with pomegranate seeds, pistachios and rose petals, if desired, and serve cold.

Nutrition Facts:

149 calories 0.1 g total fat 37.2 g carbohydrates 0.4 g fiber 29 g sugar 0.6 g protein

938. VANILLA CUPCAKES

Ingredients

- 1 1/4 cups white whole wheat flour OR 3/4 cup almond meal plus 3/4 cup coconut flour
- 3/4 cup erythritol or sugar
- 1 tsp baking soda
- 1/2 tsp salt
- 1 cup almond milk
- 1 tablespoon vanilla extract
- 1/3 cup applesauce
- 1 tsp distilled white or apple cider vinegar
- 2 tablespoons unsweetened cocoa powder

Directions:

- Preheat oven to 350°F. Line a 12 cup muffin tin with cupcake liners and set aside.
- In a large bowl, combine the flour, erythritol or sugar, baking soda, and salt. Add in the almond milk, vanilla extract, applesauce, and vinegar until the batter is uniform and no pockets of flour remain. Take care not to over stir. Scoop 1/2 cup of the batter into another bowl and set aside.
- Evenly distribute the batter into the cupcake liners. The trick to doing this is using an ice cream scoop. It makes the process very neat and keeps the cupcakes the same size so they bake evenly. Bake in the oven at 350°F for about 25 minutes, or until a toothpick inserted into the center comes out clean. Allow to cool before frosting.
- Meanwhile, add 2 tablespoons of unsweetened cocoa powder and 1 tablespoon almond milk to the reserved 1/2 cup batter and stir until combined. Chill in the fridge until the cupcakes are completely cool. Spread the frosting over the cooled cupcakes and devour.

Nutrition Facts:

Calories: 50 cal Fat: 0.5 grams g

939. CHOCOLATE FUDGE TRUFFLES

Ingredients

- 1½ cups Homemade Vegan Sweetened Condensed Milk
- 2 tsp Vanilla Creme-Flavored Stevia Extract
- 168g (1¼ cups, lightly packed) Chocolate Brown Rice Protein Powder
- 20g (¼ cup) Unsweetened Dutch Processed Cocoa Powder
- ⅛ tsp Salt

Directions:

- In a large bowl, whisk together the condensed milk and stevia extract.
- Add in the protein powder, cocoa powder, and salt. Whisk together until completely combined (mixture should thicken like frosting). Cover and refrigerate the mixture for 5+ hours (mixture should firm up).
- Line a cookie sheet with parchment paper.
- Use a cookie scoop (for the food service peeps, I used the #40 1½ tbs purple disher) to portion the fudge onto the cookie sheet. Refrigerate uncovered for 30 minutes to an hour.
- Roll the scoops between your palms to form balls, then place back in the fridge for another 30 minutes to an hour. Serve and enjoy!

Nutrition

Calories 100 Carbohydrates 4g protein 12g Fat 5g Sugar 0.5g

940. CHOCOLATE AVOCADO COOKIES

Ingredients

- 2 ¼ cup white whole wheat flour OR 2 3/4 cup almond meal plus 1/4 cup coconut flour
- 1/2 teaspoon salt
- 1 teaspoon baking soda
- 1/2 cup granulated sugar or erythritol
- 1/2 cup brown sugar OR 1/2 cup erythritol plus 1 teaspoon of molasses
- 1/2 cup unsweetened cocoa powder
- 1/4 cup mashed avocado
- 1/4 cup unsweetened almond milk
- 2 teaspoons vanilla extract
- 2 eggs or 1 Tablespoon egg replacer plus ¼ cup water
- chocolate chips

Directions:

- Preheat oven to 350°F. Line a baking sheet with parchment paper or a silicone mat and set aside.
- Add the flour, salt, baking soda, cane sugar or erythritol, brown sugar or erythritol plus molasses, and unsweetened cocoa powder into the bowl of stand mixer. Alternately, you can add the INGREDIENTS to a large mixing bowl and stir by hand. Using the paddle attachment, stir the dry INGREDIENTS on low speed. Add in the mashed avocado, unsweetened almond milk, vanilla extract, and eggs or egg replacer and continue to stir until combined but not overworked. The dough will be a bit crumbly, but that's okay. Just use your hands to squish it all together. Stir in the chocolate by hand.
- Using a 1/2 tablespoon measure, scoop the dough into balls and place on the baking sheet two inches apart. Press down into cookie shapes. Bake in the oven at 350°F for about 12 minutes. Let cool on wire racks. Stored in a ziplock bag in the refrigerator, these cookies should last at least a week. Devour.

Nutrition Facts:

Calories: 30 cal Fat: 0.5 grams g

941. AVOCADO CHOCOLATE MOUSSE

Ingredients

- 1¼ cups unsweetened almond milk or canned coconut milk
- 1 pound dairy-free dark chocolate, preferably 60% cacao, coarsely chopped
- 4 small ripe avocados—pitted, peeled and chopped
- ¼ cup agave syrup
- 1 tablespoon finely grated orange zest
- 2 tablespoons puffed quinoa
- 2 teaspoons Maldon sea salt
- 2 teaspoons Aleppo pepper flakes
- 1 tablespoon extra-virgin olive oil

Directions:

- 1. In a small saucepan, heat the almond or coconut milk over medium-high heat until it registers 175°F on an instant-read thermometer. Remove from the heat and stir in the chopped chocolate until melted; let cool to room temperature.
- 2. In the bowl of a blender, combine the avocados, agave, orange zest and cooled chocolate mixture; blend on high speed until smooth.
- 3. To serve, divide the mousse among four bowls. Sprinkle evenly with the puffed quinoa, sea salt and Aleppo pepper, and drizzle with the olive oil.

Nutrition facts:

596 calories 42g fat 92g carbs 26g protein 12g sugars

942. GOLDEN MYLK CHEESECAK

Ingredients

Almond Crust

- 1 tablespoon flax meal
- 1½ cups whole almonds
- 3 tablespoons coconut oil
- 2 tablespoons agave

Golden Milk Cheesecake Filling

- 16 ounces vegan cream cheese, at room temperature
- 1½ cups vegan powdered sugar
- ¾ cup coconut milk
- 1 teaspoon ground turmeric, plus more for finishing
- ½ teaspoon ground ginger
- ½ teaspoon ground cinnamon
- Pinch black pepper
- Toasted coconut flakes, for finishing

Directions:

- Preheat the oven to 375°F. Place a 9-inch springform pan on a baking sheet.
- In a medium bowl, mix together 3 tablespoons water and the flax meal.
- In the bowl of a food processor, pulse the almonds until they're finely chopped. Transfer to the bowl with the flax mixture and mix in the coconut oil, agave and egg white until well combined.
- Press the mixture into the base and halfway up the sides of the springform pan. Bake until the crust is lightly golden, 12 to 14 minutes. Cool completely.
- Wipe out the bowl of the food processor. Add the cream cheese,

vegan powdered sugar, coconut milk, turmeric, ginger, cinnamon and black pepper to the food processor and puree until smooth.

• Pour the filling into the crust and transfer to the refrigerator. Chill until the filling is set, 2 to 3 hours. Leave the cheesecake chilled until you're ready to serve.

• To serve, dust with turmeric and serve with toasted coconut flakes.

Nutrition Facts:

Almond Crust

172 calories 15g fat 8g carbs 5g protein 4g sugars

Golden Mylk Cheesecake Filling

236 calories 17g fat 23g carbs 3g protein 19g sugar

943. PEANUT BUTTER MUDSLIDE ICE CREAM

Ingredients

- 1 cup dark chocolate chips
- 3 cans coconut cream, divided
- 1/4 cup peanut butter
- 1/2 cup granulated sugar
- 2 teaspoons vanilla extract
- 1/4 teaspoon salt
- 1/4 cup graham cracker crumbs

Directions:

• In a blender, combine all but 1/2 cup of the coconut cream with peanut butter, sugar, vanilla extract, and salt until smooth. Remove and place into fridge for at least 2 hours.

•

• Once chilled, begin to assemble your ice cream. In a small saucepan, heat 1/2 cup of the coconut cream over low heat until scalding. Remove from heat, add in chocolate chips, and allow to sit for 5 minutes. After 5 minutes, stir to combine. Chocolate chips should be fully melted by this point! Allow to cool to room temperature while you churn your ice cream base.

• Place coconut cream mixture into an ice cream maker and churn according to manufacturers PREPARATION.

• Scoop half of ice cream into freezer-safe container, then spoon in half of ganache mixture and half of graham cracker crumbs. Top with remaining half of ice cream and remaining half of ganache and graham cracker crumbs. Swirl with a knife, then place in freezer for at least 8 hours, preferably overnight.

944. LEMON CAKE

Ingredients

bark

- 2½ cups of nuts
- 1 cup of boneless dates
- 2 tablespoons of maple syrup or agave

To Fill

- 3 cups of prepared cauliflower rice (without salt and pepper)
- 3 avocados, halved and boneless
- 1½ cups of crushed pineapple
- ¾ cup of maple syrup or agave

Zest and juice of 1 lemon

- ½ teaspoon of pure vanilla extract
- ½ teaspoon of lemon extract
- A pinch of cinnamon

Additive

- 1½ cups of natural coconut yogurt (or other milk-free yogurt)
- 1 teaspoon of pure vanilla extract
- 3 tablespoons of maple syrup or agave

Directions:

• Place the outer ring of a 9-inch springform pan on a parchment-lined baking sheet.

• CRUST: In the bowl of a food processor, pulse the pecans until they are finely ground. Add the dates and maple syrup, and pulse until the mixture comes together, about 1 minute.

• Transfer the mixture to the prepared springform ring and press it into an even layer. Wipe out the bowl of the food processor.

• FILLING: In the food processor, combine the cauliflower rice with the avocados, pineapple, maple syrup, lemon zest and lemon juice. Process until the mixture is very smooth.

• Add the vanilla extract, lemon extract and cinnamon; pulse to combine. Pour the mixture into the prepared pan on top of the crust. Transfer to the freezer and freeze until very firm (at least 5 hours and up to overnight).

• Remove the cake from the freezer and let rest at room temperature for 15 to 20 minutes. Remove the outer ring from the cake.

• TOPPING: In a medium bowl, whisk the yogurt with the vanilla extract and maple syrup to combine. Pour onto the cake and spread into an even layer.

945. BROWNIES

Ingredients

• 2 cups tightly packed dates, pitted (measured after pitting // make sure they're fresh! If dry, soak in warm water 10 minutes, drain, then add to processor)

• 1/4 cup warm water

• 1/2 cup salted peanut butter* (if unsalted, add a healthy pinch of salt to the batter)

• 2 Tbsp melted coconut oil* (if avoiding coconut oil, see notes)

• 1/3 cup cacao or unsweetened cocoa powder

• 1/3 cup dairy-free dark chocolate chips (*optional* // we like Enjoy Life)

• 1/2 cup roughly chopped raw walnuts (*optional* // or other nut of choice)

Directions:

• Preheat oven to 350 degrees F (176 C) and line a standard loaf pan (or similar size pan) with parchment paper. Set aside.

• Add dates to food processor and blend until small bits or a ball forms. If your food processor has a difficult time processing the dates, ensure there are no pits in the dates *and* that your dates are fresh and sticky. If too dry they can have a difficult time blending. (It may also be an issue of food processor strength if it has a hard time blending.)

• Once blended, separate the dates into chunks using a spoon. Then add hot water and blend until a sticky date paste forms. Scrape down sides as needed.

• Add peanut butter, coconut oil, and cacao powder and pulse until a sticky batter forms. It should be tacky and thick (scrape down sides as needed). Lastly add chocolate chips and walnuts (optional) and pulse to incorporate.

• Transfer batter to lined loaf pan and spread into an even layer. For a smooth top, lay some parchment paper on top and use a flat-bottomed object (like a drinking glass) to press into an even layer.

• Bake on the center rack for 15 minutes - the edges should be slightly dry. Remove from oven and let cool in the pan for 10 minutes. Then carefully lift out of the pan using the edges of the parchment paper and let cool on a plate or cooling rack for at least 20 minutes before slicing. The longer they cool, the firmer they will become.

• Enjoy warm or cooled. Store leftovers covered at room temperature up to 3 days, in the refrigerator up to 5-6 days, or in the freezer up to 1 month (let thaw before enjoying).

Nutrition Facts:

Calories: 215 Fat: 8.1g Carbohydrates: 36.7g Fiber: 3.9g Sugar: 30.4g Protein: 3.6g

946. SEA SALT BUTTERSCOTCH TART

Ingredients

Shortbread Crust

• ½ cup granulated sugar
• ¼ cup virgin coconut oil, at room temperature, or softened butter
• 1 teaspoon pure vanilla extract
• 2 cups almond meal flour
• ½ teaspoon salt

Filling

• ⅔ cup packed light brown sugar or coconut sugar
• ⅔ cup canned coconut cream
• ½ cup coconut oil or butter
• 1 teaspoon kosher salt
• Flaked sea salt, as needed
• 1 Granny Smith apple, sliced (optional)

Directions:

• Preheat the oven to 375 ° F and place a 9-inch or 4-by-14-inch cake pan nearby.

• BARK: In a bowl with a hand mixer or a food processor with a paddle, stir the granulated sugar, coconut oil and vanilla until they are foamy. Mix almond flour and salt. Then press the mixture evenly over the bottom and sides of the cake pan.

• Place the entire cake pan in the freezer for 10 minutes to harden, then bake in the oven until the edge is golden and the center is crispy (15 minutes). Remove from the oven and let cool.

• FILLING: Mix the brown sugar, coconut cream, coconut oil and salt in a saucepan.

• Bring to the boil and cook over medium heat for about 25 minutes

• Dip the tip of a fork in the boiling sugar and then in the ice water; If the sugar sticks between the forks without dissolving, the filling is done.

• Pour it into the cooled crust, sprinkle it with sea salt, place the apple slices on it as desired and let it cool and harden before cutting and serving.

Nutrition Facts:

431 calories 33g fat 32g carbs 6g protein 27g sugars

947. SIMPLE BECHAMEL SAUCE

Ingredients

• 3 tablespoons vegan butter
• 2 tablespoons flour
• 2 cups unheated milk
• Season the salt and pepper
• A pinch of nutmeg (optional)

Directions:

• Melt the butter in a saucepan over medium heat. Add the flour and beat until thick and bubbly but not browned (approximately 2 minutes).

• Pour the warm milk into the pan and continue stirring until the sauce has thickened (approximately 3 minutes).

• Add salt, pepper and nutmeg to the pan and stir.

• Use it immediately or, if done beforehand, put wax paper over the sauce until ready to use.

Nutrition Facts:

Calories: 128 Carbohydrates: 9 g Fat: 10 g Protein: 1 g Sodium: 168 mg

948. MOZZARELLA AND CASHEW CHEESE SAUCE

Ingredients

• 1 1/2 cups of raw cashews (soaked for at least 4 hours)
• 1 cup of water
• 2 tablespoons lemon juice
• 2 tablespoons cornstarch

Directions:

• Soak the cashews for at least 4 hours or overnight.

• Put all the INGREDIENTS in the blender and stir until smooth.

• Pour over pizza or nachos and bake. The cornstarch makes the sauce slightly firm when baked and creates a beautifully baked crust.

• It lasts only about three days in the fridge, but can be kept in the freezer for about a month. You just need to be completely defrosted before using it.

949. SPICY CHEESE SAUCE

Ingredients

• 1 cup raw cashews (soaked for at least 3 hours) or raw sunflower seeds (also soaked)
• 1 clove garlic
• 1/2 cup Nutritional yeast
• 1/3 cup of water
• 2TB Extra virgin olive oil
• 1/2 teaspoon paprika
• 1/4 tsp Chipotle pepper powder
• 1/2 teaspoon sea salt (more to taste)
• 1 teaspoon Cumin (more to taste)

Directions:

• Put all the INGREDIENTS in a powerful blender.

• Mix everything smooth and creamy.

• Adjust the spices to taste and add more water to obtain the desired consistency.

950. GREEN CHEESE SAUCE AND NACHO CHILE

Ingredients

• 1 cup raw cashews, soaked in 2 cups of water for 2-4 hours, drain and rinse
• 1/4 cup roasted red pepper, diced (glass is fine)

- 1/4 cup green chilies, diced (cans are fine)
- 2 tablespoons yeast flakes
- 2 teaspoons lemon juice
- 1 cup of water
- 1/4 teaspoon cayenne pepper
- 1/2 teaspoon sea salt

Directions:

- Combine drained cashews, red peppers, green peppers, yeast flakes, lemon juice, water, cayenne pepper and sea salt in a blender or food processor.
- Mix until smooth and occasionally scrape the sides to make sure everything is well mixed.

951. HOMEMADE WORCESTERSHIRE SAUCE

Ingredients

- 1 cup apple cider vinegar
- 1/3 cup dark molasses
- 1/4 cup tamari
- 1/4 cup of water
- 3 tablespoons lemon juice
- 1 1/2 tablespoons salt
- 1/2 tablespoon dried mustard powder
- 1 teaspoon onion powder
- 3/4 teaspoon ground ginger
- 1/2 teaspoon black pepper
- 1/4 teaspoon garlic powder
- 1/4 teaspoon cayenne pepper
- 1/4 teaspoon ground cinnamon
- 1/8 teaspoon ground cloves or allspice
- 1/8 teaspoon ground cardamom

Directions:

- Mix all the INGREDIENTS in a blender.
- Pour the mixture into a medium size saucepan and boil.
- Remove from heat and pour into a sterile beer glass or a clean 12.7 oz beer bottle or cider with a tight lid or lid. Store in the fridge. let it remain that way for a long time!

Nutrition Facts:

Total calories: 428 Total arbohydrates: 115 g Total Fat: 1g Total protein: 4 g Total Sodium: 11435 g Total Sugar: 58 g

952. TZATZIKI

Ingredients

- 1 cup of natural vegan yogurt
- 1/4 cucumber (grated)
- 1 tablespoon of fresh dill
- 1 teaspoon of lemon peel
- 1 tablespoon of Nutritional yeast
- 1 tsp black pepper
- 1 teaspoon of salt
- 1 chopped clove of garlic
- 1 tablespoon of olive oil
- 1 tablespoon of lemon juice

Directions:

- Mix all INGREDIENTS in a medium bowl.
- Stir together.
- Place on a serving plate, cover well and refrigerate up to 1 hour before serving.

Nutrition Facts:

Total calories: 301 Total carbohydrates: 28 g Total fat: 19 g Total protein: 8 g Total sodium: 64 mg Total sugar: 13 g

953. SPICY MUSTARD

Ingredients

- ½ cup of vegan mayonnaise
- 1 heaping tablespoon of Dijon mustard
- 3 heaping tablespoons of brown rice syrup (agave would work too)
- 1 teaspoon of red wine vinegar
- ¼ teaspoon of cayenne pepper
- ⅛ teaspoon of chili powder

Directions:

- Mix and mix all INGREDIENTS in a small bowl. Save up to 1 week (maybe more time, but I haven't tried it).
- Try adding more INGREDIENTS to your liking.

954. FISH SAUCE

Ingredients

- 1/2 cup grated wakame (see notes)
- 2 cups of filtered water
- 2 large cloves of garlic, crushed
- 1 teaspoon of whole peppercorns
- 1/3 cup of dark soy sauce with mushroom flavor, normal soy sauce or gluten-free tamari
- 1 teaspoon of Genmai Miso (it's quite salty, so optional)

Directions:

- Combine the wakame, garlic, peppercorns and water in a large pan and cook.
- Lower the heat and simmer for about twenty minutes. Strain and return the liquid to the pot.
- Add the soy sauce, cook again and cook until the mixture is almost salty and unbearable.
- Remove from the heat and add miso.
- Transfer to a bottle and keep in the fridge.
- Use one by one to replace fish sauce in vegan recipes.

Nutrition Facts:

Total calories: 183 Total carbohydrates: 43 g Total fat: 0 g Total protein: 5 g Total sugar: 20 g

955. CREAMY CUCUMBER HERB

Ingredients

- 3 ounces of cashew nuts, soaked in water for 2 hours
- 2 1/2 ounces of cucumber, peeled and chopped
- 1/4 cup of unsweetened milk
- 1/2 ounce chopped shallot
- 1/2 lemon juice
- 1 small clove of garlic, peeled
- 1 teaspoon of apple cider vinegar
- 1/2 teaspoon of salt
- 1/4 tsp garlic powder
- A pinch of ground black pepper
- 1 tablespoon of finely chopped fresh dill
- 1 tablespoon of finely chopped fresh parsley
- 1 tablespoon of finely chopped fresh chives

Directions:

- Add all the INGREDIENTS except herbs in a small blender and mix to a creamy and smooth consistency.
- Add the herbs and mix well.

Nutrition Facts:
Total calories: 482 Total carbohydrates: 27 g Total fat: 38 g Total protein: 15 g Total sodium: 54 mg Total sugar: 6 g

956. HARISSA

Ingredients
- 1/4 cup of dried red cayenne pepper
- 20 soft red peppers like Byadgi or Wide Chili (also dried)
- 1 1/2 tablespoons of cumin
- 1 teaspoon of coriander seeds
- 4 cloves of garlic
- 1 teaspoon of salt
- 3 tablespoons of olive oil
- 1/4 cup fresh coriander
- 1 tablespoon of chopped mint (optional)

Directions:
- Soak the chillies with 1/2 cup of warm water for 15 minutes. Drain and keep water.
- Meanwhile, roasted cumin and coriander. Grind the powder in a coffee grinder.
- Put the paprika, ground spices, garlic, salt and olive oil in a blender with a little water and cut into a paste.
- Add the chopped coriander and mint and press several times. Use a little more water if necessary.
- Store the mixture in the refrigerator then use as needed.

Nutrition Facts:
Total calories: 531 Total carbohydrates: 21 g Total fat: 49 g Total protein: 7 g Total sodium: 2188 g Total sugar: 3 g

957. CHEESE PASTE

Ingredients
- 1/2 cup chopped red peppers
- 2 tbsp water
- 2 tbsp Nutritional yeast
- 2 tbsp freshly squeezed lemon juice
- 3/4 teaspoon Himalayan crystal salt or sea salt
- 1/4 tsp paprika powder
- 1/4 teaspoon smoked paprika powder
- 1/4 teaspoon turmeric powder
- 2 large pinches of cayenne
- 1 cup finely ground cashews

Directions:
- Combine red peppers, water, yeast, lemon juice, salt, paprika powder, smoked paprika, turmeric powder, cayenne pepper and finely ground cashews in a blender.
- Mix until smooth.

Nutrition Facts:
Total calories: 624 Total carbohydrates: 42 g Total Fat: 44g Total protein: 25 g Total Sodium: 1606g Total Sugar: 10 g

958. TOASTED BANANA CARAMEL SAUCE

Ingredients
- 2 large ripe bananas
- 1/4 cup coconut sugar (use 1/2 cup if your bananas are not overripe or if you like sweeter things)
- 2 tbsp brown rice syrup
- 1/2 cup milk without milk
- 1 tsp pure vanilla extract
- 1/4 teaspoon salt

Directions
- Put all ingredients in a blender or food processor and beat for a few seconds until smooth.
- Pour the mixture into a pan and bring to a boil.
- Reduce heat and simmer for 20 minutes, stirring constantly. It may be necessary to adjust the heat as it boils.

Nutrition Facts:
Calories 69 Sodium 85mg Potassium 113mg Carbohydrates 18g 1g fiber

959. ROASTED RED PEPPER HUMMUS

Ingredients
- 15.5 oz canned chickpeas (washed and drained)
- 1 clove of garlic
- 2 tbsp tahini
- 1/2 teaspoon cumin powder
- 2 tbsp lemon juice
- 1/2 teaspoon of sea salt
- 1/2 roasted red pepper (I used it in a jar instead of roasting mine)
- 2-3 tablespoons of water (if necessary to dilute) (you can also use extra virgin olive oil if desired)

Nutrition Facts
- With the food processor running, put the garlic clove and process until minced.
- Turn off the processor, scrape the sides and add chickpeas, tahini, cumin, lemon juice, salt and roasted red pepper.
- If you want to tune a little, drizzle a few tablespoons of water (or oil if desired) on top of the food processor while it is running.
- Use as a pasta for sandwiches or as a sauce for vegetables, crackers or chips. Yum!

Nutrition Facts:
Calories 109 Fats 3g Sodium 132mg Potassium 146mg Carbohydrates 14g 3g fibre 1g sugar 5g protein Iron 1.3mg

960. QUESO

Ingredients
- 1 1/2 cups pumpkin (peeled and sown before dicing - or you can buy a pack of pre-sliced pumpkin)
- 1/2 cup raw cashew nuts
- 1 tbsp fresh lemon juice
- 1/2 teaspoon smoked paprika
- 2 tbsp Nutritional yeast
- 1/2 teaspoon salt
- 1/2 teaspoon saffron
- 3-4 tablespoons non-dairy milk (or water)
- 1/4 cup of your favorite salsa (I like Trader Joe's Salsa Authentica)
- 1 tin of 4.5 oz diced green peppers

INSTRUCTIONS
- Add the diced squash and cashews in a pan and cover with water for at least 1 inch.
- Bring to a boil, lower the heat to med and cook for about 20 minutes until the pumpkin is tender.
- When the pumpkin/cashews are ready, drain and pour into a high-speed blender.
- Add lemon juice, smoked paprika, Nutritional yeast, salt and turmeric. Mix until completely smooth by adding non-

dairy milk (or water) 1 tbsp at a time to move things around if necessary. You will need to use the tamper to push the ingredients to the bottom. Do not do too thin! Use just enough liquid to mix everything. I used about 3-4 tablespoons.

- When completely smooth, pour the mixture into a pan (you can use the same one you used for pumpkin/cashews) and mix in the parsley and chopped green peppers. * Gently heat the queso over medium heat until thickened and bubbling. * *
- Serve immediately with Tortilla Chips.

Nutrition Facts:

Calories 68 3g5 Fats Potassium 97mg Carbohydrates 8g 1g fiber 2g sugar 3g protein

961. SUN-DRENCHED TOMATO SPREAD

Ingredients

- 1 cup raw yarn
- 1 cup sun-dried tomatoes (not oil-packed!)
- 1/2 cup water
- 2 garlic cloves
- 2 green onions
- 4-5 large fresh basil leaves
- Juice of 1/2 lemon
- 1/2 tsp salt
- Pepper pepper

INSTRUCTIONS

- Soak the cucumber and sun-dried tomatoes in hot water for 30 minutes. Rinse and rinse.
- Place the licorice and sun-dried tomatoes in a food processor that fits into the S blade. Start the puree, then pour 1/2 cup into the water. Pour the puree over the sides of the bowl until smooth.
- Add remaining ingredients and puree until smooth.
- Get into the fridge.

Nutrition Facts:

Calories 53 Fat 3G Saturated fat 1 g Carbohydrates 5 g Fiber 1 g Sugar 2 g Protein 2g Calcium 40 mg 1.3mg of iron

962. MIXED HERBS WITH ALMONDS AND PEPITA PESTO

Ingredients

- 1 cup wrapped fresh basil leaves
- 1 cup wrapped arugula
- 2 cloves garlic (grated)
- 1/2 cup raw pepita
- 1/4 cup raw almonds
- 1/4 cup fresh lemon juice
- 2 tbsp virgin olive oil
- 1/2 tsp salt (or to taste)
- 1/8 teaspoon pepper (or to taste)
- 2-3 tbsp of thin water

INSTRUCTIONS

- Place all INGREDIENTS except olive oil and water in a food processor.
- Processing Before combining, split sides as needed.
- Sprinkle olive oil on top while the machine is still running. This should work smoothly.
- Add Water 1 Ch. Simultaneously process after each addition and scroll through the pages as needed until you reach the desired consistency.

Nutrition Facts:

Calories 157 Fat 13 g 2 Potassium 140 g Carbohydrates 7 g Fiber 3G1 Sugar 1 g Protein 4g 1.3mg of iron

963. SPICY MARINARA SAUCE

Ingredients

- 1/2 sweet onion (dough)
- 1/4 cup vegetable broth (or water) (extra 1-2 tbsp, if needed)
- 3 garlic cloves (minced)
- 1 / 4-1 / 2 tsp crushed red pepper flakes
- 28 ounces canned crushed tomatoes
- 1/2 tsp salt (or to taste)
- 2 tsp dried basil
- 1 tsp dried oregano
- 1 teaspoon balsamic vinegar

Directions:

- Dried onions in vegetable broth (or water) for 4-5 minutes until softened. If the onion starts to stick, add an additional 1-2 tbsp vegetable broth (or water).
- Add grated garlic and red pepper flakes and sauce for 1 minute.
- Add the crushed tomatoes, salt, basil, oregano and balsamic vinegar. Boil for 20 minutes on low heat.
- Using a blender, blend the sauce until smooth (or desired consistency). Alternatively, you can carefully slice the sauce into a blender, puree.
- Taste and adjust seasoning as needed.
- Enjoy pasta and zadon, or bread baking vinegar.

Nutrition Facts:

Calories 42 Sodium 282 mg Potassium 333 mg Carbohydrates 10 g Fiber 2 g Sugar 1 g Protein 2g 4% Iron 1.8 mg

964. DILUTED BANANA CARAMEL SAUCE

Ingredients

- 2 large very ripe bananas
- 1/4 cup coconut sugar (use 1/2 cup if your banana is not too ripe or you like sweet sides)
- 2 tbsp brown rice syrup
- 1/2 cup milk milk
- 1 teaspoon pure vanilla extract
- 1/4 tsp salt

Directions:

- Put all INGREDIENTS in a blender or food processor and puree for a few seconds until smooth.
- Pour the mixture into the baking sheet and bring to a boil.
- Reduce heat and simmer for about 20 minutes, stirring frequently.

Nutrion Facts

Calories 69 Sodium 85 mg Potassium 113 mg Carbohydrates 18 g Fiber 1 g Sugar 12 gr Calcium 20 mg

965. MAPLE WALNUT VEGAN CREAM CHEESE

Ingredients

- 1 1/2 cup raw yarn (soaked in water for several hours or overnight)
- 1/4 cup dairy free plain yogurt (I used tasty coconut downstairs)
- 4 tbsp pure maple syrup
- 2 tbsp fresh lemon juice
- 1/2 tsp salt (I used Himalayan pink salt)

- 1/4 cup finely chopped walnuts *

Directions:

- Make sure your kelps have been soaked in water for at least 3-4 hours or overnight. The longer the better.
- In a food processor bowl, clean the soaked licorice, yogurt, maple syrup, lemon juice and salt. Rinse sides as needed so that all INGREDIENTS are incorporated. Continue cleaning until the mixture is silky smooth.
- Transfer the mixture to a small bowl. Sprinkle with chopped walnuts. Store in refrigerator.

Nutrition Facts:

Calories 122 Fat 8g Sodium 100mg4% Carbohydrates 9 g Sugar 6 g Protein 4g8 Calcium 20 mg Iron 1.1mg

SNACKS

966. CUCUMBER SANDWICH BITES

Preparation Time: 5 minutes
Cooking Time: 0 minutes
Servings: 12
Ingredients:

- One cucumber, sliced
- Eight slices of whole wheat bread
- Two tablespoons cream cheese, soft
- One tablespoon chive, chopped
- ¼ cup avocado, peeled, pitted, and mashed
- One teaspoon mustard
- Salt and black pepper to the taste

Directions:

1. Spread the mashed avocado on each bread slice.
2. Also, spread the rest of the ingredients except the cucumber slices.
3. Divide the cucumber slices into the bread slices.
4. Cut each slice in thirds, arrange on a platter and serve.

Nutrition:

Calories: 187 Fat: 12.4g Fiber: 2.1g Carbohydrates: 4.5g Protein: 8.2g

967. SUMMER SQUASH RIBBONS WITH LEMON AND RICOTTA

Preparation Time: 20 minutes
Cooking Time: 0 minutes
Servings: 4
Ingredients:

- Two medium zucchini or yellow squash
- ½ cup ricotta cheese
- Two tablespoons fresh mint, chopped, plus additional mint leaves for garnish
- Two tablespoons fresh parsley, chopped
- Zest of ½ lemon
- Two teaspoons lemon juice
- ½ teaspoon kosher salt
- ¼ teaspoon freshly ground black pepper
- One tablespoon extra-virgin olive oil

Directions:

1. Using a vegetable peeler, make ribbons by peeling the summer squash lengthwise. The squash ribbons will resemble the wide pasta, pappardelle.
2. In a bowl, mix the ricotta cheese, mint, parsley, lemon zest, lemon juice, salt, and black pepper.
3. Place mounds of the squash ribbons evenly on four plates, then dollop the ricotta mixture on top. Sprinkle with the olive oil, then garnish with the mint leaves.

Nutrition:

Calories: 90 Total Fat: 6g Cholesterol: 10mg Total Carbohydrates: 5g Fiber: 1g

968. GREEN BEANS WITH PINE NUTS AND GARLIC

Preparation Time: 10 minutes
Cooking Time: 20 minutes
Servings: 4 to 6
Ingredients:

- 1-pound green beans, trimmed
- One head garlic (10 to 12 cloves), smashed
- Two tablespoons extra-virgin olive oil
- ½ teaspoon kosher salt
- ¼ teaspoon red pepper flakes
- One tablespoon white wine vinegar
- ¼ cup pine nuts, toasted

Directions:

1. Preheat the oven to 425°F.
2. In a large bowl, blend the green beans, garlic, olive oil, salt, and red pepper flakes and mix—put it in a single layer on the baking sheet. Roast for 10 minutes, stir, and roast for another 10 minutes, or until golden brown.
3. Mix the cooked green beans with the vinegar and top with the pine nuts.

Nutrition:

Calories: 165 Total Fat: 13g Total Carbohydrates: 12g Fiber: 4g Sugars: 4g Protein: 4g

969. CUCUMBERS WITH FETA, MINT, AND SUMAC

Preparation Time: 15 minutes
Cooking Time: 0 minutes
Servings: 4
Ingredients:

- One tablespoon extra-virgin olive oil
- One tablespoon lemon juice
- Two teaspoons ground sumac
- ½ teaspoon kosher salt
- Two hothouse or English cucumbers, diced
- ¼ cup crumbled feta cheese
- One tablespoon fresh mint, chopped
- One tablespoon fresh parsley, chopped
- 1/8 teaspoon red pepper flakes

Directions:

1. In a bowl, whisk together the lemon juice, olive oil, sumac, and salt. Add the cucumber and feta cheese and toss well.
2. Transfer to a serving dish and sprinkle with mint, parsley, and red pepper flakes.

Nutrition:

Calories: 85 Total Fat: 6g Cholesterol: 8mg Total Carbohydrates: 8g Fiber: 1g Protein: 4g

970. CHERRY TOMATO BRUSCHETTA

Preparation Time: 15 minutes
Servings: 4
Ingredients:

- 8 ounces assorted cherry tomatoes, halved
- 1/3 cup fresh herbs, chopped (such as basil, parsley, tarragon,
- dill)
- One tablespoon extra-virgin olive oil
- ¼ teaspoon kosher salt
- 1/8 teaspoon freshly ground black pepper
- ¼ cup ricotta cheese
- Four slices whole-wheat bread, toasted

Directions:

1. Combine the tomatoes, herbs, olive oil, salt, and black pepper in a medium bowl and mix gently.

2. Spread one tablespoon of ricotta cheese onto each slice of toast—spoon one-quarter of the tomato mixture onto each bruschetta. If desired, garnish with more herbs.

Nutrition:

Calories: 100 Total Fat: 6g Cholesterol: 5mg Total Carbohydrates: 10g Fiber: 2g Protein: 4g

971. ROASTED ROSEMARY OLIVES

Preparation Time: 5 minutes
Cooking Time: 25 minutes
Servings: 4
Ingredients:

- 1 cup mixed variety olives, pitted and rinsed
- Two tablespoons lemon juice
- One tablespoon extra-virgin olive oil
- Six garlic cloves, peeled
- Four rosemary sprigs

Directions:

1. Preheat the oven to 400°F.

2. Combine the olive oil, olives, lemon juice, and garlic in a medium bowl and mix.

3. Spread in a single layer on the prepared baking sheet. Sprinkle on the rosemary—roast for 25 minutes, tossing halfway through.

4. Take away the rosemary leaves from the stem and place them in a serving bowl. Add the olives and mix before serving.

Nutrition:

Calories: 100 Total Fat: 9g Cholesterol: 0mg Total Carbohydrates: 4g

972. SPICED MAPLE NUTS

Preparation Time: 5 minutes
Cooking Time: 10 minutes **Servings:** 2
Ingredients:

- 2 cups raw walnuts or pecans
- One teaspoon extra-virgin olive oil
- One teaspoon ground sumac
- ½ teaspoon pure maple syrup
- ¼ teaspoon kosher salt
- ¼ teaspoon ground ginger
- 2 to 4 rosemary sprigs

Directions:

1. Preheat the oven to 350°F.

2. In a bowl, combine the nuts, olive oil, sumac, maple syrup, salt, ginger, mix. Spread in a sole layer on the prepared baking sheet. Add the rosemary. Roast for 8 to 10 minutes, or wait until golden and fragrant.

3. Remove the rosemary leaves from the stems and place them in a serving bowl. Add the nuts and toss to combine before serving.

Nutrition:

Calories: 175 Total Fat: 18g Cholesterol: 0mg Total Carbohydrates: 4g Protein: 3g

973. FIGS WITH MASCARPONE AND HONEY

Preparation Time: 5 minutes
Cooking Time: 5 minutes
Servings: 4
Ingredients:

- 1/3 cup walnuts, chopped
- Eight fresh figs halved
- ¼ cup mascarpone cheese
- One tablespoon honey
- ¼ teaspoon flaked sea salt

Directions:

1. In a frypan with medium heat, toast the walnuts, often stirring, for 3 to 5 minutes.

2. Arrange the figs cut-side up on a plate or platter. Using your finger, create a small depression in each fig's cut side and fill with mascarpone cheese. Sprinkle with a bit of the walnut, drizzle with the honey, and add a tiny pinch of sea salt.

Nutrition:

Calories: 200 Total Fat: 13g Cholesterol: 18mg Total Carbohydrates: 24g Protein: 3g

974. PISTACHIO-STUFFED DATES

Preparation Time: 10 minutes
Cooking Time: 0 minutes
Servings: 4
Ingredients:

- ½ cup unsalted pistachios shelled
- ¼ teaspoon kosher salt
- 8 Medjool dates, pitted

Directions:

1. In a food processor, add the salt and pistachios. Process until combined to chunky nut butter, 3 to 5 minutes.

2. Split open the dates and spoon the pistachio nut butter into each half.

Nutrition:

Calories: 220 Total Fat: 7g Cholesterol: 0mg Total Carbohydrates: 41g Protein: 4g

975. PORTABLE PACKED PICNIC PIECES

Preparation Time: 10 minutes
Cooking Time: 0 minutes
Servings: 1
Ingredients:

- 1-slice of whole-wheat bread, cut into bite-size pieces
- 10-pcs cherry tomatoes
- ¼-oz. aged cheese, sliced
- 6-pcs oil-cured olives

Directions:

1. Pack each of the ingredients in a portable container to serve you while snacking on the go.

Nutrition:

Calories: 197 Total Fats: 9g Fiber: 4g Carbohydrates: 22g Protein: 7g

976. MEDITERRANEAN PICNIC SNACK

Total Time: 10 min
Serves 2
Ingredients
- Crusty whole-wheat bread – 1 slice
- Cherry tomatoes – 10
- Oil-cured olives – 6
- Sliced aged cheese – ¼ ounce

Instructions
- Combine the bread pieces, cheese, tomatoes and olives into a portable container.
- Serve and enjoy.

Nutrition Information:
Calories per serving: 197; Carbohydrates: 22g; Protein: 7g; Fat: 9g; Sugar: 0g; Sodium: 454mg; Fiber: 1g

977. TOMATO AND BASIL FINGER SANDWICHES

Total Time: 15 min
Serves 4
Ingredients
- Whole-wheat bread – 4 slices
- Mayonnaise – 8 teaspoons
- Tomato thick slices – 4
- Freshly ground pepper – 1/8 teaspoon
- Salt – 1/8 teaspoon
- Sliced fresh basil – 4 teaspoons

Instructions
- Cut bread into rounds that are larger than tomato and then spread each with mayonnaise.
- Top it with tomatoes, basil, salt and pepper.

Nutrition Information:
Calories per serving: 85; Carbohydrates: 13g; Protein: 3g; Fat: 3g; Sugar: 2g; Sodium: 324mg; Fiber: 1g

978. GREEK YOGHURT WITH STRAWBERRIES

Total Time: 10 min
Serves 2
Ingredients
- Nonfat plain Greek yoghurt – ½ cup
- Sliced fresh strawberries – ½ cup

Instructions
1. Place yoghurt in a bowl and then top with the strawberries.

Nutrition Information:
Calories per serving: 80; Carbohydrates: 7g; Protein: 12g; Fat: 1g; Sugar: 4g; Sodium: 130mg; Fiber: 2g

979. HERBED OLIVES

Total Time: 20 min
Serves 4
Ingredients
- Favorite olives – 3 cups
- Olive oils – 2 teaspoons
- Dried oregano – 1/8 teaspoon
- Dried basil – 1/8 teaspoon
- Crushed clove garlic – 1
- Freshly ground pepper to taste

Instructions
- Toss the olives, basil, garlic, oregano and pepper into a medium bowl.

Nutrition Information:
Calories per serving: 47; Carbohydrates: 1g; Protein: 0g; Fat: 5g; Sugar: 0g; Sodium: 224mg; Fiber: 1g

980. BACON-WRAPPED CHICKEN TENDERS

Total Time: 25 min
Serves 4
Ingredients
- Chicken breast tenderloins – 1 lb
- Bacon slices – 8
- Cheddar cheese – 4 slices

Instructions
- Fill a bowl with water and then add salt. Add the chicken breasts and then allow to stay in the water for 10 minutes.
- Get the oven preheated to 4500F and then line baking sheet with parchment paper.
- Remove chicken from the water and then pat to dry. Place a piece of cheese over each chicken piece and wrap together in bacon slice.
- Place the wrapped chicken on a baking sheet with the cheese side up.
- Repeat with the remaining cheese, chicken and bacon. Bake for 16 minutes or until the chicken is well cooked.
- Place it under a broiler for a few minutes until bacon is crisp.
- Serve and enjoy.

Nutrition Information:
Calories per serving: 301; Carbohydrates: 1g; Protein: 25g; Fat: 17g; Sugar: 0g; Sodium: 210mg;

981. SWEET AND SPICY MEAT BALLS

Total Time: 30 min
Serves 6
Ingredients
- Cooked meatballs – 16 oz
- Crushed red pepper – ½ tablespoon
- Cayenne pepper – ½ teaspoon
- Grape jelly – 12 ounce
- Water – 1 cup
- Chopped green onions for garnish

Instructions
- Add the cooked meatballs into the pot. In a bowl, mix the grape jelly, chili sauce, spices and water and then combine.
- Pour the mixture into the pot and stir. Cover and lock the lid.
- Set to cook on high pressure for 10 minutes and then quick release pressure once ready.
- Let the meatballs cool. After that, serve and garnish with green onions.

Nutrition Information:
Calories 330; Fat 16g; protein 7g ; Net carbs 12g; Fiber 1g; Sugar 2g; Sodium 539mg

982. GARLIC BREAD

Total Time: 1 hr
Serves 4
Ingredients
- Egg white – 3 pieces
- Apple cider vinegar – 2 teaspoons
- Sea salt – 1 teaspoon
- Almond flour - 300ml
- Ground psyllium husk powder – 5 tablespoons
- Baking powder - 2 teaspoons
- Boiling water - 300 ml
- Garlic Butter
- Butter - 110g
- Garlic clove -   1pc
- Fresh parsley chopped – 2 teaspoons
- Salt

Instructions

- Set the oven at 350F while mixing the dry ingredients in a bowl.
- Let the water boil. Add vinegar and egg whites to the bowl and then whisk or stir with a manual mixer for 30 seconds, ensuring that you do not over mix.
- Using your hands, make 10 pieces rolling them into hot dog buns. Create enough space on the baking sheet to enable expansion.
- Place in the oven on lower rack and leave to bake for 50 minutes.
- Prepare garlic butter as the bread is baking by mixing all ingredients together and then place in the fridge.
- Remove the buns from the oven and let them cool. Remove the garlic butter from the fridge and set aside.
- Slice the buns in halves and spread the garlic butter on each side and then proceed to bake the bread for 10 minutes.

Nutrition Information:

Calories per serving: 53; Carbohydrates: 5g; Protein: 2g; Fat: 4g; Sugar: 0g; Sodium:98mg; Fiber: 0g

983. CHOCOLATE BISCUITS

Total Time: 25 min

Serves 8

Ingredients

- Whole almonds – 2 cups
- Chia seeds – 2 tablespoons
- Unsweetened shredded coconut – ¼ cup
- Egg – 1
- Coconut oil – 1 cup
- Cacao powder – ¼ cup
- Stevia – 3 tablespoons
- Salt – ¼ teaspoon
- Baking soda – 1 teaspoon

Instructions

- Get the oven preheated to 3500F.
- Blend whole almonds and chia seeds into a fairly fine mixture.
- Have all the ingredients mixed together.
- Place the mixture on aluminum foil and then refrigerate for about 30 minutes.
- Cut the dough into thin biscotti shapes and then bake for about 12 minutes.
- You can enjoy while warm or let it cool and dry further.

Nutrition Information:

Calories 80; Fat 5g; protein 1g; Net carbs 13g; Fiber 0g; Sugar 1g; Sodium 0g

984. WHIPPED COCONUT CREAM WITH BERRIES

Total time – 15 min

Serves 1

Ingredients

- Unsweetened full fat coconut milk – 1 can
- Berries of choice
- Dark chocolate (Optional)

Instructions

- Let coconut milk stay in the fridge overnight for about 12 hours.
- Scoop the thick part and leave water.
- Whip with a mixer for about 3 minutes.
- Mix in the berries.
- Top the cream with chocolate shavings.
- Serve and enjoy.

Nutrition Information:

Calories 100; Fat 12g; protein 2g; Net carbs 8g; Fiber 0g; Sugar 2g; Sodium 400mg

985. SOUS VIDE EGG BITES

Total Time: 450 min | Serves 4

Ingredients

- Large eggs – 4
- Strips of cooked bacon – 4
- Cheddar cheese – ¾ cup
- Heavy cream – ¼ cup
- Cottage cheese – ½ cup

Instructions

- Set the oven to 3500F.
- Crack eggs into a blender. Add cottage cheese and a half cup of cheddar cheese. Pulse until well mixed.
- Spray the glass bowls with cooking spray and then pour ½ cup of the mixture into bowls. Top it up with the remaining shredded cheese and bacon.
- Place the bowls into a baking dish. Fill the baking dish with water.
- Bake for 35 minutes or until the mixture becomes solid.

Nutrition Information:

Calories 120; Fat 9g; protein 3g; Net carbs 9g; Fiber 0g; Sugar 2g; Sodium 0mg

986. PEPPERONI CHIPS

Total Time: 20 min

Serves 4

Ingredients

- Pepperoni – 4 oz

Instructions

- Turn the oven to broil and then line the baking sheet with parchment paper.

Instructions

- Place pepperoni slices in a single layer. Bake for 2 minutes and watch as they brown in the edges.
- Remove from the oven. Transfer to a tray and allow to cool for 10 minutes.
- Serve and enjoy.

Nutrition Information:

Calories per serving: 96; Carbohydrates: 1g; Protein: 6g; Fat: 8g; Sugar: 0g; Sodium:48mg; Fiber: 0g

987. CHEDDAR BASIL BITES

Total Time 50 min

Serves 24

Ingredients

- Heavy whipping cream – 2 tablespoons
- Butter – 6 tablespoons
- Shredded cheddar cheese – 1cup
- Coconut flour – ¼ cup
- Grated parmesan cheese – ¼ cup
- Fresh basil – 2 tablespoon

Instructions

- Get the oven preheated to 3250F and then line two baking sheets with parchment paper.
- Place butter in a medium bowl. Add heavy cream and combine.
- Add parmesan cheese, cheddar cheese and coconut flour and then combine using a spatula.
- Fold in basil and use your hand to incorporate the mixture.

- Place parchment paper over the counter and then roll the mixture out to about ¼ inch thick. Use a cookie cutter to cut the 24 pieces of crackers. After that, place the crackers on the baking dish.
- Bake for 15 minutes and check towards the end to ensure you don't overcook them.

Nutrition Information:

Calories per serving: 58; Carbohydrates: 0.5g; Protein: 2g; Fat: 5g; Sugar: 0g; Sodium:78mg; Fiber: 0g

988. ZUCCHINI CHIPS

Total Time: 25min
Serves 4
Ingredients

- Organic zucchini – 1 pound
- Olive oil – 1/3 cup
- Unrefined sea salt to taste

Instructions

- Trim the ends of zucchini and then thinly slice them.
- Oil a microwave safe plate with olive oil and then place zucchini slices. Spray with olive oil and unrefined sea salt to taste.
- Cook for 10 minutes uncovered. Check the chips. Cook for more minutes until crispy.
- Allow to cool and then serve with dressings and dips of your choice.

Nutrition Information:

Calories 290; Fat 27g; protein 4g; Net carbs 7g; Fiber 1g; Sugar 1g; Sodium 210mg

989. EASY ALMOND BUTTER FAT BOMBS

Total Time: 10 min
Serves 6
Ingredients

- Almond butter – ¼ cup
- Unrefined coconut oil – ¼ cup
- Cacao powder – 2 tablespoons
- Erythritol – ¼ cup

Instructions

- Mix almond butter and coconut together in a bowl. Microwave for about 45 minutes and then stir until smooth.
- Stir in cacao powder and erythritol and then pour into silicone molds.
- Refrigerate until firm.

Nutrition Information:

Calories per serving: 189; Carbohydrates: 3g; Protein: 3g; Fat: 19g; Sugar: 0g; Sodium:220mg; Fiber: 2g

990. GREEK ORANGE HONEY CAKE WITH PISTACHIOS

Total Time: 30 min
Serves 6
Ingredients

- Large eggs – 5
- Low fat Greek yoghurt – 1 cup
- Granulated sugar – 2 cups
- Ground almonds – 5 tablespoons
- Zest of lemon – 1
- All-purpose flour – 1 ¼ cup
- Course semolina – 1 cup
- Baking powder – 2 teaspoons
- Virgin olive oil -3/4 cup
- Shaved almonds for topping (optional)
- Honey Pistachio Syrup
- Shelled salted pistachios – 1 ¼ cup
- Honey – 1 ¼ cup
- Orange juice – 2
- Lemon juice – 1

Instructions

- Get the oven preheated to 3500F. Grease the baking dish with butter and dust with flour and then shake the pan to evenly coat it with flour.
- Place ingredients for the cake into a mixing bowl and then whisk to combine. Pour butter into the prepared baking pan and then spread the mixture evenly using a spatula.
- Bake in the oven for 30 minutes or until golden and cooked through. Remove from the oven once ready. Set aside to cool.
- Once the cake has cooled, prepare the honey syrup by toasting pistachio into a non-stick pan and then place over medium heat.
- Stir in honey once it begins to smell and then add orange and lemon juice. Bring to a boil for about 2 minutes or until syrupy.
- Stab some holes into the cake to create holes. Pour honey pistachio syrup over the cake evenly.
- Sprinkle the shaved almonds as desired.
- Cut the cake to squares. Serve and enjoy.

Nutrition information:

Calories per serving: 352; Carbohydrates: 58g; Protein: 8g; Fat: 10g; Sugar: 32g; Sodium:30mg; Fiber: 3g

991. AVOCADO CHIPS

Total Time: 30 min
Serves 4
Ingredients

- Large ripe avocado – 1
- Freshly grated parmesan – ¾ cup
- Lemon juice – 1 teaspoon
- Garlic powder – ½ teaspoon
- Kosher salt
- Italian seasoning – ½ teaspoon
- Freshly ground black pepper

Instructions

- Get the oven preheated to 3250F and then line the baking dish with parchment paper.
- In a bowl, mash avocado and then stir in parmesan, lemon juice, garlic powder, salt, pepper and Italian seasoning.
- Place scoops of the mixture on the baking sheet and leave space of 3" apart between each scoop.
- Place in the oven and bake until crisp and golden or for 15 minutes.
- Remove from the oven and then allow to cool.
- Serve while at room temperature.

Nutrition Information:

Calories per serving: 160; Carbohydrates: 17g; Protein: 2g; Fat: 3g; Sugar: 0g; Sodium: 12mg; Fiber: 3g

992. PEPPERONI PIZZA MOZZARELLA CRISPS

Total Time: 15 min
Serves 4
Ingredients

- Shredded mozzarella cheese – ½ cup
- Diced pepperoni
- Garlic powder – 1 teaspoon

Instructions

- Get the oven preheated to 3500F and then line the cookie sheet in parchment paper.
- Place mozzarella onto the parchment paper and spread it slightly in a circle.
- Sprinkle mozzarella with garlic powder and basil and then top with pieces of chopped pepperoni.
- Place in the oven and allow to bake for 6 minutes or until the edges of the cheese turn golden brown.
- Remove from the oven. Allow to cool.
- Enjoy with your preferred dip.

Nutrition information:
Calories per serving: 158; Carbohydrates: 18g; Protein: 20g; Fat: 18g; Sugar: 0g; Sodium:420mg; Fiber: 0g

993. PARMESAN CRISPS

Total Time: 20 min
Serves 2
Ingredients

- Grated parmesan cheese – 8 tablespoons
- Provolone cheese – 2 slices
- Medium jalapeno – 1

Instructions

- On a parchment paper, place eight mounds of parmesan cheese an inch apart from one another.
- Slice the jalapeno and then lay on the parchment paper. Bake at 4250F for about 5 minutes.
- Remove from the oven. Allow to cool and then lay each one onto a mound of parmesan as you slightly press it down.
- Split each of the provolone slice into pieces and then place over jalapeno and parmesan.
- Let it bake for 5 more minutes. After that, remove and allow to cool.

Nutrition Information:
Calories per serving: 162; Carbohydrates: 1.5g; Protein: 14g; Fat: 10g; Sugar: 1g

994. TOASTED SPICY ALMONDS

Total Time: 1 hr 10 min
Serves 6
Ingredients

- Almonds – 4 cups
- Butter – 2 tablespoons
- Ground cinnamon – 1 teaspoon
- Vanilla extract – 1 tablespoon
- Egg whites – 2
- Salt - 1 teaspoon

Instructions

- Get the oven preheated to 4500F.
- Add all ingredients apart from almonds into a bowl and then stir until well combined.
- Add almonds to the mixture and then combine until well coated.
- Transfer the mixture into a baking pan. Allow to bake for about 10 minutes as you stir occasionally.
- Remove from the oven once ready. Allow to cool before serving.

Nutrition information:
Calories per serving: 350; Carbohydrates: 9g; Protein: 11g; Fat: 7g; Sugar: 0g; Sodium:356mg; Fiber: 5g

995. TOMATO BASIL SKEWERS

Total Time: 20 min
Serves 4
Ingredients

- Fresh mozzarella balls – 16
- Fresh basil leaves – 16
- Cherry tomatoes – 16
- Olive oil to drizzle
- Salt and freshly ground pepper

Instructions

- Thread mozzarella, tomatoes and basil on a small skewer and then drizzle with oil and sprinkle with salt and pepper.

Nutrition information:
Calories per serving: 46; Carbohydrates: 1g; Protein: 3g; Fat: 3g; Sugar: 0g; Sodium:217mg; Fiber: 1g

996. COLD FETA OLIVE SPREAD

Preparation Time: 24 hours
Ingredients:

- cup olives, pitted, sliced ¼ cup feta, diced
- 1 tbsp extra-virgin olive oil
- 1 clove garlic, crushed
- 1 tsp chopped rosemary
- Juice and zest of half a whole lemon
- Pinch of ground pepper and crushed red pepper

Directions:

- Combine all ingredients in a bowl with lid. Mix well.
- Cover and refrigerate for up to 24 hours.
- Serve as toppings for your choice of crackers or baguette for snacks.

Nutrition information:
Per 2 tbsp serving: 73 calories, 7g total fat, 2g sat, 4g monosaturated, 6g cholesterol, 263mg

997. FUN PICNIC SNACK

Preparation Time: 5 minutes
Ingredients:

- slices whole-wheat bread
- 12 pcs. olives, cured in oil
- 20 pcs. cherry tomatoes
- ½ cup aged cheese, cubed

Directions:
1. Arrange all ingredients on your favourite platter and serve.

Nutrition information:
201 calories, 11g total fat, 3.5g sat, 1g monosaturated, 8g cholesterol, 693mg sodium, 23g total carbohydrates

998. CREAMY BLUEBERRY

Preparation Time: 2 hours and 5 minutes
Ingredients:

- cup reduced-fat cream cheese ¼ cup low-fat plain Greek yogurt 1 cup fresh blueberries
- 1 tsp freshly grated lemon zest
- 1 tsp honey

Directions:
- In a medium bowl, break up cream cheese using a fork. Add yogurt and honey.
- Using an electric mixer, beat at high speed until mixture is creamy. Stir in lemon zest.

Nutrition information:
156 calories, 7g total fat, 4g sat, 0g monosaturated, 22g cholesterol, 151mg

999. CHERRIES IN RICOTTA

Preparation Time: 5 minutes

Ingredients:
- 1 ½ cups cherries, pitted
- ¼ cup part-skim ricotta
- 2 tbsp toasted slivered almonds

Directions:
- In a bowl, place cherries and microwave until warm.
- Top with ricotta and almonds.

Nutrition information:
Per serving: 133 calories.

MEDITERRANEAN SPINACH CAKES

Preparation Time: 10 minutes
Cooking Time: 20 minutes

Ingredients:
- ¾ cup fresh spinach
- cup finely shredded Parmesan cheese
6 ¼ cup low-fat cottage cheese
- 1 egg, beaten
- ½ a clove garlic, minced Salt and pepper

Directions:
- Preheat oven to 400 degrees F.
- In a food processor, pulse spinach until finely chopped then place in a bowl. Add in cottage cheese, Parmesan, garlic, egg, salt and pepper. Mix well.
- Spray muffin cooking pan with a healthy cooking spray (olive oil is great). Add in spinach mixture.
- Bake for 20 minutes. Let it stand for 5 minutes. Place muffins in a serving plate. Sprinkle with parmesan if desired.
- Serve.

Nutrition information:
Per 2 serving: 141 calories, 8g total fat, 4g sat, 3g monosaturated, 123g cholesterol

1000. CREAMY LENTIL CAKES

Preparation time: 10 minutes
Cooking time: 10 minutes

Ingredients:
- 1 cup cooked lentils
- 1 whole egg and 1 egg white
- ¼ cup breadcrumbs
- 4 tbsp reduced fat sour cream
- 1 tbsp olive oil
- 1 jalapeno, minced
- 1 clove garlic, minced
- 2 tbsp diced carrot
- 1 tbsp chopped cilantro
- Juice of 1 lime
- 1 tbsp and 1 tsp cumin
- salt

Directions:
- Heat olive oil in a skillet, sauté onion, jalapeno, garlic and carrots for about 3-4 minutes. Switch off heat.
- In a bowl, combine cooked lentils and sautéed mixture. Add eggs, breadcrumbs, cumin and chopped cilantro. Combine thoroughly.
- Form patties from the mixture and fry in the skillet for 2 minutes on each side on medium high heat. Place aside.
- In a small bowl, combine sour cream, lime juice and 1 tsp cumin.
- Arrange the lentil cakes on a bed of spinach and top with the sour cream dressing. Serve and enjoy.

Nutrition information:
Calories per serving: 86; Carbohydrates: 1g; Protein: 3g; Fat: 3g;

1001. ROASTED SQUASH WRAP

Preparation time: 15 minutes
Cooking time: 30 minutes

Ingredients:
- 4 wedges Kabocha squash, about 2cm thick each ½ cup cubed cucumber
- Half a whole avocado, mashed
- 4 leaves Swiss chard
- 1 tbsp olive oil
- Salt and pepper to taste

Directions:
- Preheat oven to 425 degrees F.
- Slice squash into wedges and toss with oil and sprinkle with pepper and salt. Place in a baking tray and bake for 15 minutes. Flip each squash and cook for another 15 minutes. Place aside.
- Lay collard flat, place a squash wedge in the middle and smear an avocado on top of the squash, sprinkle with salt and pepper and top with cucumber slices. Roll and serve.

Nutrition information:
Calories per serving: 66; Carbohydrates: 2g; Protein: 1g; Fat: 3g;

1002. OLIVE FETA-HONEY CAKES

Preparation time: 5 minutes
Cooking time: 25 minutes

Ingredients:
- cup ground almonds
- cup feta cheese
- cup sugar
- 1 tbsp honey
- 3 tbsp extra virgin olive oil
- cup flour
- tsp baking powder ¼ cup olives, halved 2 tbsp brown sugar

Directions:
- Preheat oven to 347 degrees F.
- In a mixer, process cheese, honey and sugar until a smooth texture is achieved. Pour in the olive oil.
- In another bowl, combine flour, baking powder and almonds. Combine with the cheese mixture.
- Divide batter among greased cake molds and top each with olive oil and brown sugar. Bake for 25 minutes. Serve.

Nutrition information:
Calories per serving: 46; Carbohydrates: 1g; Protein: 3g; Fat: 3g; Sugar: 0g; Sodium:217mg; Fiber: 1g

1003. HAZELNUT COOKIES

Preparation time: 10 minutes
Cooking time: 30 minutes

Ingredients:
- cup and 2 tbsp sugar 2 egg whites
- 1 cup toasted hazelnuts, skinned Pinch of salt
- tsp vanilla extract

Directions:
- Preheat oven to 325 degrees Fahrenheit with a rack close to the oven's centre. Prepare a parchment paper lined baking sheet.
- In a food processor, pulse nuts and sugar until finely ground and scrape into a large bowl.
- Using an electric mixer, beat egg whites and salt in a bowl on high speed until stiff peaks form.
- Using a rubber spatula, gently fold egg whites into nut mixture. Add vanilla and mix until combined.
- Pour batter using tablespoon with 2 inches apart on the prepared baking sheets.
- Bake until golden brown switching the pans back to front and top to bottom halfway for 30 minutes. Let it cool for 5 minutes before serving.

Nutrition information:
Per cookie serving: 88 calories, 5g total fat, 0g sat, 4g monosaturated, 0g cholesterol, 46mg sodium, 10g total carbohydrates, 1g dietary fibre, 61mg potassium, 2g protein

1004. FETA-OLIVE CAKES

Preparation time: 15 minutes
Cooking time: 25 minutes

Ingredients:
- 6 tbsp powdered sugar
- 3 tbsp ground almonds
- ½ cup all purpose flour
- cup extra virgin olive oil 2 tbsp crumbled feta cheese 1 tbsp honey
- ½ tsp baking powder
- cup pitted Kalamata olives, halved 1 tbsp sugar

Directions:
- Preheat oven to 350 degrees Fahrenheit.
- In a mixer, process cheese, sugar and honey until smooth. Add olive oil.
- In a bowl, combine flour, ground almonds and baking powder. Combine to the cheese mixture while mixing.
- Pour batter into greased muffin pans and top with half an olive.
- Sprinkle top with brown sugar and bake for 25 minutes until lightly brown.

Nutrition information:
Calories per serving: 76; Carbohydrates: 5g; Protein: 1g; Fat: 3g;

1005. ROOT VEGETABLE PAVE

Total Time Prep: 40 min. **Bake:** 1-3/4 hours + standing

Ingredients
- 3 medium russet potatoes, peeled
- 2 large carrots
- 2 medium turnips, peeled
- 1 large onion, halved
- 1 medium fennel bulb, fronds reserved
- 1/2 cup all-purpose flour
- 1 cup heavy whipping cream
- 1 tablespoon minced fresh thyme, plus more for topping
- 1 tablespoon minced fresh rosemary
- 1/2 teaspoon salt
- 1/2 teaspoon pepper, plus more for topping
- 1 cup shredded Asiago cheese, divided

How To Make It
- Preheat oven to 350°. With a mandoline or vegetable peeler, cut the first 5 ingredients into very thin slices. Transfer to a large bowl; toss with flour. Stir in the cream, thyme, 1 tablespoon rosemary, salt and pepper.
- Place half of the vegetable mixture into a greased 9-in. springform pan. Sprinkle with 1/2 cup cheese. Top with remaining vegetable mixture. Place pan on a baking sheet and cover with a double thickness of foil.
- Bake until vegetables are tender and easily pierced with a knife, 1-3/4 to 2 hours.
- Remove from oven and top foil with large canned goods as weights. Let stand 1 hour. Remove cans, foil and rim from pan before cutting. Top with remaining cheese.
- Add reserved fennel fronds and, as desired, additional fresh thyme and pepper. Refrigerate leftovers.

Nutritional Information
1 slice: 248 calories, 15g fat (9g saturated fat), 46mg cholesterol, 216mg sodium, 23g carbohydrate

1006. SPINACH AND ARTICHOKE PIZZA

Total Time Prep: 25 min.
Bake: 20 min.

Ingredients
- 1-1/2 to 1-3/4 cups white whole wheat flour
- 1-1/2 teaspoons baking powder
- 1/4 teaspoon salt
- 1/4 teaspoon each dried basil, oregano and parsley flakes
- 3/4 cup beer or nonalcoholic beer

TOPPINGS:
- 1-1/2 teaspoons olive oil
- 1 garlic clove, minced
- 2 cups shredded Italian cheese blend
- 2 cups fresh baby spinach
- 1 can (14 ounces) water-packed quartered artichoke hearts, drained and coarsely chopped
- 2 medium tomatoes, seeded and coarsely chopped
- 2 tablespoons thinly sliced fresh basil

How To Make It
- Preheat oven to 425°. In a large bowl, whisk 1-1/2 cups flour, baking powder, salt and dried herbs until blended. Add beer, stirring just until moistened.
- Turn dough onto a well-floured surface; knead gently 6-8 times, adding more flour if needed. Press dough to fit a greased 12-in. pizza pan.
- Pinch edge to form a rim. Bake until edge is lightly browned, about 8 minutes.
- Mix oil and garlic; spread over crust. Sprinkle with 1/2 cup cheese; layer with spinach, artichoke hearts and tomatoes.
- Sprinkle with remaining cheese.
- Bake until crust is golden and cheese is melted, 8-10 minutes. Sprinkle with fresh basil.

Nutritional Information

1 slice: 290 calories, 10g fat (6g saturated fat), 27mg cholesterol, 654mg

1007. BREADSTICK PIZZA

Prep: 25 min. **Bake:** 20 min.

Ingredients

- 2 tubes (11 ounces each) refrigerated breadsticks
- 1/2 pound sliced fresh mushrooms
- 2 medium green peppers, chopped
- 1 medium onion, chopped
- 1-1/2 teaspoons Italian seasoning, divided
- 4 teaspoons olive oil, divided
- 1-1/2 cups shredded cheddar cheese, divided
- 5 ounces Canadian bacon, chopped
- 1-1/2 cups shredded part-skim mozzarella cheese
- Marinara sauce

How To Make It

- Unroll breadsticks into a greased 15x10x1-in. baking pan.
- Press onto the bottom and up the sides of pan; pinch seams to seal. Bake at 350° until set, 6-8 minutes.
- Meanwhile, in a large skillet, saute the mushrooms, peppers, onion and 1 teaspoon Italian seasoning in 2 teaspoons oil until crisp-tender; drain.
- Brush crust with remaining oil. Sprinkle with 3/4 cup cheddar cheese; top with vegetable mixture and Canadian bacon.
- Combine mozzarella cheese and remaining cheddar cheese; sprinkle over top. Sprinkle with remaining Italian seasoning.
- Bake until cheese is melted and crust is golden brown, 20-25 minutes.
- Serve with marinara sauce.
- Freeze option: Bake crust as directed, add toppings and cool.
- Securely wrap and freeze unbaked pizza.
- To use, unwrap pizza; bake as directed, increasing time as necessary.

Nutritional Information

1 piece (calculated without marinara sauce): 267 calories, 11g fat (6g saturated fat), 27mg cholesterol, 638mg sodium, 29g carbohydrate (5g sugars, 2g fiber), 13g protein

1008. SUMMER DESSERT PIZZA

Total Time

Prep: 35 min. + chilling **Bake:** 15 min. + cooling

Ingredients

- 1/4 cup butter, softened
- 1/2 cup sugar
- 1 large egg
- 1/4 teaspoon vanilla extract
- 1/4 teaspoon lemon extract
- 1-1/4 cups all-purpose flour
- 1/4 teaspoon baking powder
- 1/4 teaspoon baking soda
- 1/4 teaspoon salt

GLAZE:

- 1/4 cup sugar
- 2 teaspoons cornstarch
- 1/4 cup water
- 1/4 cup orange juice
- TOPPING:
- 4 ounces cream cheese, softened
- 1/4 cup confectioners' sugar
- 1 cup whipped topping
- 1 firm banana, sliced
- 1 cup sliced fresh strawberries
- 1 can (8 ounces) mandarin oranges, drained
- 2 kiwifruit, peeled and thinly sliced
- 1/3 cup fresh blueberries

How To Make It

- In a small bowl, cream butter and sugar until light and fluffy. Beat in egg and extracts. Combine flour, baking powder, baking soda and salt; add to creamed mixture and beat well. Cover and refrigerate for 30 minutes.
- Press dough into a greased 12- to 14-in. pizza pan. Bake at 350° for 12-14 minutes or until light golden brown. Cool completely on a wire rack.
- For glaze, combine sugar and cornstarch in a small saucepan. Stir in the water and orange juice until smooth. Bring to a boil; cook and stir for 1-2 minutes or until thickened. Cool to room temperature, about 30 minutes.
- For topping, in a small bowl, beat cream cheese and confectioners' sugar until smooth. Add whipped topping; mix well. Spread over crust. Arrange fruit on top. Brush glaze over fruit. Store in the refrigerator.
- Test Kitchen Tips
- Use premade sugar cookie dough to save a bit of time.
- If you're in a pinch, orange marmalade works in place of the glaze.

Nutritional Information

1 piece: 176 calories, 7g fat (4g saturated fat), 29mg cholesterol, 118mg sodium, 27g carbohydrate (17g sugars, 1g fiber), 2g protein.

1009. PATRIOTIC TACO SALAD

Total Time Prep: 10 min. **Cook:** 20 min.

Ingredients

- 1 pound ground beef
- 1 medium onion, chopped
- 1-1/2 cups water
- 1 can (6 ounces) tomato paste
- 1 envelope taco seasoning
- 6 cups tortilla or corn chips
- 4 to 5 cups shredded lettuce
- 9 to 10 pitted large olives, sliced lengthwise
- 2 cups Kerrygold shredded cheddar cheese
- 2 cups cherry tomatoes, halved

How To Make It

- In a large skillet, cook beef and onion over medium heat until meat is no longer pink; drain. Stir in the water, tomato paste and taco seasoning. Bring to a boil. Reduce heat; simmer, uncovered, for 20 minutes.
- Place chips in an ungreased 13x9-in. dish. Spread beef mixture evenly over the top. Cover with lettuce. For each star, arrange five olive slices together in the upper left corner. To form stripes, add cheese and tomatoes in alternating rows. Serve immediately.
- Editor's Note: If you wish to prepare this salad in advance, omit the layer of chips and serve them with the salad.

Nutritional Information

1 cup: 357 calories, 20g fat (9g saturated fat), 63mg cholesterol, 747mg sodium, 24g carbohydrate (4g sugars, 2g fiber), 20g protein.

1010. KALE BRUSCHETTA

Ready In: 25 minutes

Ingredients

- 1 bunch kale
- 1 loaf fresh 100% whole-grain bread, sliced
- ½ cup Cannellini Bean Sauce
- 1 cup grape tomatoes, halved
- balsamic glaze

How To Make It

- Place the kale leaves in a large pot of boiling water. Cover and cook until tender, about 5 minutes. Drain in a colander, then squeeze out any extra liquid with your hands (you don't want soggy bread).
- Toast 8 pieces of bread, and place them on a handsome serving platter.
- Spread a tablespoon of the Cannellini Bean Sauce on the toasted bread, then cover with a layer of kale and top with a scattering of grape tomatoes. Drizzle generously with the balsamic glaze, and grab one for yourself before they all disappear.

1011. CARAMELIZED ONION & PEPPER VEGAN QUESADILLAS

Prep-time: 2 hours 15 minutes
Cook Time: 15 minutes

Ingredients

- ¾ cup raw cashews, soaked for 2 hours
- ½ cup nutritional yeast flakes
- 1 lime, juiced
- ½ tablespoon stoneground mustard, no-salt added
- ½ cup water
- 1 yellow onion, sliced thin
- 1 red bell pepper, sliced thin
- 1 yellow bell pepper, sliced thin
- 1½ tablespoons ground cumin
- 1½ teaspoon chili powder
- 8 100% corn tortillas, no salt or oil added
- 2 cups fresh spinach, loosely packed

How to Make It

- Make the cheese sauce: Add the cashews, nutritional yeast, lime, stoneground mustard and water to a blender. Blend until it the sauce is creamy. Set it aside.
- Make the onion-pepper filling: Place a sauté pan over medium heat. Add the sliced onion and bell pepper. Stir in the cumin and chili powder. Cover and cook for 5 minutes, stirring occasionally so the veggies don't stick to the bottom of the pan. Then stir in a tablespoon of water and continue cooking uncovered. When the water evaporates stir in another tablespoon of water, continuing to sauté until the onions are caramelized.
- Turn the heat to low. Pour the cheese sauce into the onion and peppers. Stir well and then cover with a lid so the mixture doesn't dry out.
- Make the first quesadilla: Place a non-stick pan over medium heat. Let it heat for 5 minutes. Then place one of the tortillas into the pan. Set a timer, letting the first side toast for 2 minutes and then flip. Set the timer for another 2 minutes. As you wait, carefully scoop about ¼ of the filling onto the tortilla and spread it evenly, forming a single layer of peppers and onions. Layer ½ cup of spinach across the onions and peppers. Place the second tortilla on top of the spinach.
- Once the timer goes off or the bottom side is toasted, use a large spatula to carefully flip the entire quesadilla. Toast the second tortilla for 2-3 minutes.
- When the quesadilla is done transfer it to a plate. Repeat this process with the remaining filling to make a total of 4 quesadillas. Note that subsequent quesadillas may require less cooking time because the pan will be hotter. You may want to turn the heat down slightly after the first couple. Slice the quesadillas into triangular pieces and serve.
- Chef's Note: Soaking the cashews softens them so they become creamy when blended. If you're using a high-powered blender such as a vitamix, the nuts do not need to be soaked.

1012. WAFFLED FALAFEL

Prep Time: 20 minutes

Ingredients:

- 2 Large Egg Whites
- 2 cans of Garbanzo Beans
- 1 1/2 tablespoons of All Purpose Flour
- 1/4 cup of Chopped Fresh Parsley
- 1 Chopped Medium Onion
- 1/4 cup of Chopped Fresh Cilantro
- 3 Cloves of Roasted Garlic
- 1/4 teaspoon of Cayenne Pepper
- 2 teaspoons of Ground Cumin
- 1 teaspoon of Ground Coriander
- 1/4 teaspoon of Ground Black Pepper
- 1 3/4 teaspoons of Salt
- Pinch of Ground Cardamom
- Cooking Spray

Directions:

1. Preheat your waffle iron. Spray inside of your iron with your cooking spray.

2. Process your garbanzo beans in your food processor until they are coarsely chopped.

3. Add in your egg whites, cilantro, onion, parsley, cumin, flour, coriander, garlic, salt, black pepper, cayenne pepper, and ground cardamom to your garbanzo beans.

4. Pulse in your food processor until your batter resembles a coarse meal. Scrap down the sides while pulsing.

5. Pour your batter into your bowl and stir it with your fork.

6. Spoon 1/4 cup of batter onto each section of your waffle iron. Cook until they are evenly browned. Should take approximately 5 minutes. Repeat the process with your batter until it has all been used.

Nutrition information:

Calories per serving: 66; Carbohydrates: 2g; Protein: 1g; Fat: 3g;

1013. ARTICHOKES ALLA ROMANA (SERVES 8)

Prep Time: 40 minutes

Ingredients:

- 4 Large Artichokes
- 1/3 cup of Grated Parmesan Cheese

- 2 cups of Fresh Whole-Wheat Breadcrumbs
- 2 tablespoons of Finely Chopped Flat-Leaf Parsley
- 1 cup + 3 tablespoons of Vegetable Stock
- 1 tablespoon of Olive Oil
- 2 Halved Lemons
- 1 tablespoon of Grated Lemon Zest
- 3 cloves of Finely Chopped Garlic
- 1 teaspoon of Chopped Fresh Oregano
- 1 cup of Dry White Wine
- 1 tablespoon of Minced Shallot
- 1/4 teaspoon of Ground Black Pepper

Directions:

1. Preheat your oven to 400 degrees.
2. In your bowl, combine your olive oil and breadcrumbs. Toss well to coat. Spread your crumbs in your shallow baking pan and put in your oven, stirring once halfway through, until your crumbs are lightly golden. Should take approximately 10 minutes. Set to the side to cool.
3. Working with 1 artichoke at a time, snap off any of their tough outer leaves and trim their stem flush with their base. Cut off the top 1/3 of the leaves using a serrated knife, and trim off any of the remaining thorns with your scissors.
4. Rub the cut edges with your lemon half to prevent discoloration. Separate the inner leaves and pull out any small leaves from the center.
5. Using your melon baller or spoon, scoop out the fuzzy choke, then squeeze some of your lemon juice into the cavity. Trim all your remaining artichokes in the same exact manner.
6. In your large-sized bowl, toss your breadcrumbs with your Parmesan, garlic, pepper, lemon zest, and parsley. Add your 3 tablespoons of vegetable stock, 1 tablespoon at a time, using just enough for your stuffing to begin sticking together in smaller clumps.
7. Using 2/3 of your stuffing, mound it slightly in the center of your artichokes. Then, starting at the bottom, spread the leaves open and spoon a rounded teaspoon of your stuffing near the base of each leaf. (The artichokes can be prepared to this point hours ahead and kept refrigerated.)
8. In your Dutch oven with a tight fit lid, combine your 1 cup of vegetable stock, shallot, oregano, and wine. Bring to a boil, then reduce your heat to low.
9. Arrange your artichokes, stem end down, in the liquid in a single layer. Cover and simmer until all your outer leaves are tender. Should take approximately 45 minutes (add more water if necessary).
10. Transfer your artichokes to your rack and allow it to cool slightly. Cut each of your artichokes into quarters.

Nutrition information:

Calories per serving: 46; Carbohydrates: 5g; Protein: 2g; Fat: 4g;

1014. MEDITERRANEAN WRAP

Ingredients

- 1 red onion, sliced
- 1 zucchini, sliced
- 1 eggplant, sliced
- ¼ pound fresh mushrooms, sliced
- 1 red bell pepper, sliced
- 1 tablespoon olive oil
- salt and ground black pepper to taste
- 4 whole grain tortillas
- ¼ cup goat cheese
- ¼ cup basil pesto
- 1 large avocado, sliced

Directions

- Place the onion, zucchini, eggplant, mushrooms, and bell pepper into a large container with a tight fitting lid. Drizzle the olive oil over the vegetables and season with salt and pepper. Close the lid and shake to coat.
- Heat a grill pan or skillet over medium heat. Place the seasoned vegetables on the preheated pan, stir and cook until tender, about 10 minutes.
- Spread each tortilla with 1 tablespoon goat cheese and 1 tablespoon pesto. Divide the sliced avocado among the tortillas and top with the mixed veggies. Fold in the bottom of each tortilla and roll each up into a snug wrap.

Nutrition Facts

Per Serving: 436 calories; protein 14.6g; carbohydrates 48.4g; fat 26.3g; cholesterol 16.2mg; sodium 433.3mg

1015. SNACK CRACKERS

Prep Time: 65 minutes

Ingredients:

- 1 (1 ounce) package ranch dressing mix
- 1 teaspoon garlic powder
- ½ teaspoon dried dill weed
- ½ cup vegetable oil
- 1 (12 ounce) package oyster crackers

Directions

- Mix together ranch dressing mix, garlic powder, dill and vegetable oil.
- Add crackers and mix gently until the crackers are coated with the mixture.
- Stir every 10 minutes for 1 hour. Store in an airtight jar.

Nutrition Facts

Per Serving: 217 calories; protein 2.3g; carbohydrates 19.6g; fat 14.2g; sodium 699.1mg. Full Nutrition

1016. FURIKAKE SNACK MIX

Prep Time: 65 minutes

Ingredients

- Decrease Serving
- 20
- Increase Serving
- Adjust
- Original recipe yields 20 servings
- Ingredient Checklist
- ½ cup butter
- ½ cup white sugar
- ½ cup corn oil
- ½ cup light corn syrup (such as Karo®)
- 2 (12 ounce) packages crispy corn and rice cereal (such as Crispix®)
- 1 (1.9 ounce) container aji nori furikake (seasoned seaweed and sesame rice topping)

Directions

- Preheat oven to 225 degrees F (110 degrees C).
- Melt the butter and sugar together in a small sauce pan over low heat. Remove from heat, then stir in the corn oil and corn syrup. Place the cereal on a

large baking sheet. Pour the butter mixture over the cereal, then sprinkle the furikake while tossing the cereal to coat.
- Bake in the preheated oven until the cereal is dry, stirring every 15 minutes to keep cereal from browning too quickly. Allow to cool, then store in an airtight container.

Nutrition Facts
Per Serving: 274 calories; protein 2.5g; carbohydrates 43g; fat 10.7g; cholesterol 12.2mg; sodium 393mg.

1017. APPLE CHEESECAKE SNACK BARS

Time Prep: 30 minutes
Ingredients
- 1 teaspoon butter, or as needed
- Crust:
- 1 ½ cups graham cracker crumbs, or more as needed
- ⅓ cup butter, melted
- Filling:
- 2 (8 ounce) packages cream cheese, at room temperature
- ½ cup white sugar
- 2 large eggs
- 1 teaspoon vanilla extract
- 3 Granny Smith apples - peeled, cored, and diced
- 2 tablespoons white sugar
- ½ teaspoon ground cinnamon
- ¼ teaspoon ground nutmeg
- ¼ teaspoon ground allspice

Streusel:
- ½ cup brown sugar
- ½ cup all-purpose flour
- 1 tablespoon finely chopped walnuts, or to taste (Optional)
- ¼ teaspoon ground cinnamon
- ¼ cup butter, cut into small pieces

Directions:
- Preheat the oven to 350 degrees F (175 degrees C). Lightly butter a 9x13-inch baking pan.
- Mix graham cracker crumbs and melted butter together in a bowl until crumbly, adding more crumbs if mixture is too wet. Press crust into the prepared baking pan.
- Bake in the preheated oven until golden and set, 7 to 8 minutes. Remove from the oven and set aside.
- Beat cream cheese and 1/2 cup sugar using an electric mixer in a large bowl until smooth. Add eggs, one at a time, beating after each addition. Beat in vanilla extract on low speed until mixture is blended. Pour filling over warm crust.
- Stir apples, 2 tablespoons sugar, cinnamon, nutmeg, and allspice together in a separate bowl; spoon evenly over filling.
- Mix brown sugar, flour, walnuts, and cinnamon for streusel together in a bowl. Mix or cut butter into walnut mixture using your fingers or a knife until crumbly. Sprinkle over apple layer.
- Bake in the preheated oven until cheese filling is set, 30 to 35 minutes.
- Remove from the oven and let cool completely, about 30 minutes. Cut into small squares and refrigerate until ready to serve

Nutrition Facts
Per Serving: 192 calories; protein 2.7g; carbohydrates 18.6g; fat 12.3g; cholesterol 48.3mg; sodium 127.4mg

1018. FRESH PARFAIT

Preparation time: 10 minutes
Cooking time: 0 minutes
Servings: 6
Ingredients:
- 4 cups non-fat yogurt
- 3 tablespoons stevia
- 2 tablespoons lime juice
- 2 teaspoons lime zest, grated
- 4 grapefruits, peeled and chopped
- 1 tablespoon mint, chopped

Directions:
1. In a bowl, combine the yogurt with the stevia, lime
juice, lime zest and mint and stir
2. Divide the grapefruits into small cups, add the yogurt
mix in each and serve.
Nutrition: calories 200, fat 3, fiber 4, carbs 15, protein 10

1019. SPICED CARROT RAISIN BREAD

Serves 18
Ingredients
- 1 1/2 cup whole-wheat pastry flour
- 1/2 teaspoon baking soda
- 1 1/2 teaspoons baking powder
- 1/2 teaspoon salt
- 1 tablespoon cinnamon
- 1/2 teaspoon nutmeg
- 1/4 teaspoon cloves
- 1/4 teaspoon paprika or cayenne
- 1 tablespoon grated lemon zest
- 1/4 cup ground flaxseed
- 2 eggs
- 1/2 cup brown sugar
- 1/4 cup honey
- 1/2 cup unsweetened applesauce
- 1/4 cup olive oil
- 3/4 teaspoon almond extract
- 2 cups shredded carrots (about 4 carrots)
- 2/3 cup raisins

Directions
- Combine dry Ingredients. In a different bowl, combine wet Ingredients. Add carrots and raisins. Mix wet to dry ingredients until moist. Pour into a greased bread pan. Bake at 375 for about an hour.

Nutritional analysis per serving
Serving size: 1 (1/2-inch thick) slice
Calories 136 Sodium 150 mg Total fat 4 g Total carbohydrates 22 g Saturated fat 0.5 g Dietary fiber 2 g Trans fat 0 g Sugars 8 g Monounsaturated fat 2.5 g Protein 3 g Cholesterol 21 mg

1020. PUMPKIN BARS

Preparation time: 10 minutes
Cooking time: 15 minutes
Servings: 14
Ingredients:
- 2 ½ and cupsalmond flour
- ½ teaspoon baking sbla
- 1 tablespoon flax seed
- 3 tablespoons water
- ½ cup pumpkin flesh mashed
- ¼ cup coconut sugar
- 2 tablespoons coconut butter
- 1 teaspoon vanilla extract

Directions:

1. In a bowl, mix flax seed with water and stir.
2. In another bowl, mix flour with, baking soda, flax meal, pumpkin, coconut sugar, coconut butter and vanilla, stir well, spread on a baking sheet, press well, bake in the oven at 350 degrees F for 15 minutes, leave aside to cool down, cut into bars and serve.

Nutrition:

calories 210, fat 2, fiber 4, carbs 7, protein 8

1021. EASY PEAR CRISP

Makes 6 Servings
Ingredients
- Canola oil in a pump sprayer
- 5 ripe, juicy pears, such as Comice or Anjou, peeled, cored, and cut into
- ½-inch pieces
- 2 tablespoons amber agave nectar or grade B maple syrup
- 1 tablespoon fresh lemon juice
- 2 teaspoons cornstarch
- ½ teaspoon freshly grated nutmeg
- 1 cup Make It Your Way Granola

Directions

27. Preheat the oven to 350°F. Lightly spray an 11 × 8½-inch baking dish with the oil.
28. Mix the pears, agave, lemon juice, cornstarch, and nutmeg in the baking dish.
29. Bake, stirring after 15 minutes, until the pears are tender and have given off their juices, about 30 minutes.
30. Remove from the oven and sprinkle the granola over the pear mixture.
31. Return to the oven and bake just to heat the granola, about 5 minutes.
32. Remove from the oven and let stand for 5 to 10 minutes at room temperature.
33. Spoon into dessert bowls and serve warm.

Nutritional Analysis Per Serving

(1 serving) 201 calories, 4 g protein, 38 g carbohydrates, 5 g fat, 6 g fiber, 0 mg cholesterol, 7 mg sodium, 292 mg potassium. Food groups: 1 whole grain, 1 fruit.

1022. ROASTED PINEAPPLE WITH MAPLE GLAZE

Makes 4 Servings
Ingredients
- 1 ripe pineapple
- Canola oil in a pump sprayer
- ¼ cup grade B maple syrup (see "Maple Syrup," here)
- 1 tablespoon unsalted butter, melted

Directions

- Preheat the oven to 425°F.
- Using a large, sharp knife, cut the pineapple in quarters lengthwise. Cut each quarter lengthwise to yield 8 wedges. Reserve 4 of the wedges for another use.
- Working with 1 pineapple wedge at a time, use a paring knife to cut the flesh from the rind in one piece. Cut the flesh vertically into 5 large chunks, keeping them nestled in the rind.
- Arrange the pineapple wedges in a baking dish and spray lightly with oil.
- Roast until just beginning to brown, about 15 minutes. Whisk together the maple syrup and butter in a small bowl.
- Brush the mixture over the pineapple and bake until the pineapple is glazed, about 5 minutes more.
- Transfer to four wide dishes, drizzle with the liquid from the baking dish, and serve hot.

Nutritional Analysis Per Serving

(1 serving) 138 calories, 1 g protein, 29 g carbohydrates, 3 g fat, 2 g fiber, 8 mg cholesterol, 4 mg sodium, 171 mg potassium. Food groups: 2 fruits.

1023. CARAMELIZED ONIONS AND BELL PEPPERS

Servings: 4
Ingredients:
- 2 red bell peppers, cut into strips
- 2 red onions, sliced thin
- 1 tablespoon olive oil
- 1 teaspoon butter, unsalted
- 1/4 red wine
- Pinch of salt
- Freshly ground black pepper, to taste
- 1/4 teaspoon dried basil

Directions:

1. Heat oil and butter in skillet over medium heat. Add peppers and onion and sauté, stirring, for 2 minutes.
2. Reduce heat to medium-low and continue to cook until onions and peppers soften, about 4-5 minutes.
3. Add red wine and continue to cook until wine has reduced by half, about 15-20 minutes.
4. Season with salt, pepper, and basil.

Nutritional analysis per serving

Calories: 95 Sodium: 110 mg Protein: 9 g Carbs: 9.5 g Fat: 5 g

1024. SWEET POTATO CASSEROLE

Servings: 8
Ingredients:
- 2 1/4 cups sweet potatoes, peeled, cooked, and mashed
- 1/4 cup butter, melted
- 2 tablespoons low-fat milk
- 1/4 cup honey
- 1/4 teaspoon vanilla
- 1 egg, beaten
- 1/4 cup brown sugar
- 1/4 cup all-purpose flour
- 3 tablespoons butter
- 1/2 cup chopped pecans

Directions:

1. Preheat oven to 350 degrees F. Spray a 8 x 11 inch baking pan with cooking spray
2. In a large bowl, mix together sweet potatoes, melted butter, milk, honey, vanilla, and egg.
3. In a small bowl, mix together brown sugar and flour. Cut in 3 tablespoons butter until mixture is crumbly. Add pecans and stir.
4. Sprinkle pecan mixture over sweet potatoes.
5. Bank in oven for 25 minutes or until golden brown.

Nutritional analysis per serving
Calories: 310 Sodium: 105 mg Protein: 3.2 g Carbs: 36 g Fat: 13 g

1025. KALE CHIPS

Servings: 6

Ingredients
- 1 large bunch kale
- 1 tablespoon olive oil
- 1/4 teaspoon sea salt

Directions
1. Preheat oven to 350 degrees. Line cookie sheet with parchment paper.
2. Cut stems from kale. Wash and thoroughly dry kale leaves.
3. Spread kale out on baking sheet in single layer. Drizzle with olive oil and season with salt.
4. Bake until edges are browned, about 10-12 minutes.

Nutritional analysis per serving
Calories: 110 Sodium: 210 mg Protein: 5 g Carbs: 16 g Fat: 5 g

1026. MICROWAVE-BAKED STUFFED APPLES

Servings: 4

Ingredients:
- 4 large apples
- 1/4 cup coconut flakes
- 1/4 cup dried cranberries or apricots
- 2 teaspoons orange zest, grated
- 1/2 cup orange juice
- 2 tablespoons brown sugar

Directions:
1. Cut top off apple and hollow out center with knife or apple corer. Arrange apples in a microwave-safe dish.
2. In a bowl, combine coconut, cranberries, and orange zest. Divide evenly and fill centers of apples.
3. In a bowl, mix orange juice and brown sugar. Pour over apples. Cover with microwave-safe plastic wrap and microwave on high for 7-8 minutes or until apples are tender.
4. Serve warm.

Nutritional analysis per serving
Calories: 190 Sodium: 275 mg Protein: 1 g Carbs: 46 g Fat: 2 g

1027. CARROT AND VANILLA CAKE COOKIES

Servings: 24 cookies

Ingredients
- 1/4 cup packed light-brown sugar
- 1/4 cup sugar
- 1/4 cup oil
- 1/4 cup applesauce or fruit puree
- 1 eggs
- 1/2 teaspoon vanilla
- 1/2 cup flour
- 1/2 cup whole wheat flour
- 1/2 teaspoon baking soda
- 1/2 teaspoon baking powder
- 1/8 teaspoon salt
- 1/2 teaspoon ground cinnamon
- 1/4 teaspoon ground nutmeg
- 1/4 teaspoon ground ginger
- 1 cups old-fashioned rolled oats (raw)
- 3/4 cup finely grated carrots (about 2 carrots)
- 1/2 cup raisins or golden raisins

Directions:
1. Preheat oven to 350 degrees F.
2. Mix together sugars, oil, applesauce, egg, and vanilla.
3. In a separate bowl, mix together all dry Ingredients.
4. Add dry Ingredients into wet Ingredients. Mix until just blended. Stir in carrots and raisins.
5. Drop by teaspoonful on parchment-lined cookie sheet.
6. Bake 12-14 minutes or until golden brown.

Nutritional Information (per cookie)
Calories: 80 Sodium: 55 mg Protein: 1 g Carbs: 13 g Fat: 3 g

1028. OATMEAL WALNUT CHOCOLATE CHIP COOKIES

Servings: 24 cookies

Ingredients:
- 1 cup rolled oats (not quick-cooking)
- 1/4 cup all-purpose flour
- 1/4 cup whole-wheat pastry flour
- 1/2 teaspoon ground cinnamon
- 1/4 teaspoon baking soda
- 1/4 teaspoon salt
- 1/4 cup tahini (sesame seed paste)
- 4 tablespoons cold unsalted butter, cut into pieces
- 1/3 cup granulated sugar
- 1/3 cup packed light brown sugar
- 1 large egg
- 1/2 tablespoon vanilla extract
- 1/2 cup semisweet or bittersweet chocolate chips
- 1/4 cup chopped walnuts

Directions:
1. Preheat oven to 350 degrees F. Line 2 cookie sheets with parchment paper.
2. Mix together oats, flour, cinnamon, baking soda, and salt in bowl.
3. In another large bowl, whisk together tahini, butter, sugar, brown sugar, egg, and vanilla until smooth.
4. Add in oat mixture and mix until just moistened.
5. Stir in chocolate chips and walnuts.
6. Place tablespoon-size portions of batter on cookie sheets, allowing space between.
7. Bake for about 14-16 minutes or until cookies are golden brown.

Nutritional Information (per cookie)
Calories: 110 Sodium: 45 mg Protein: 2 g Carbs: 15 g Fat: 5 g

1029. AVOCADO DETOX SMOOTHIE

Serves: 2

Preparation time: 10 minutes

Ingredients:
- ½ avocado, peeled and roughly chopped
- 1 banana, peeled and chopped
- Handful baby spinach, torn
- 1 tbsp powdered stevia
- 1 tsp turmeric, ground
- 1 tbsp flaxseed, ground
- 1 tbsp goji berries

Preparation:

34. Peel the avocado and cut in half.
35. Remove the pit and chop one half into small pieces. Wrap the other half in a plastic foil and refrigerate for later.

36. Peel the banana and cut into thin slices. Set aside.
37. Rinse the spinach thoroughly under cold running water using a colander. Chop into small pieces and set aside.
38. Now, combine avocado, banana, spinach, turmeric, flaxseed, and goji berries in a blender. Process until well combined.
39. Transfer to a serving glass and add few ice cubes.
40. Serve immediately.

Nutrition information per serving: Calories: 221, Protein: 3.1g, Total Carbs: 28.6g, Dietary Fibers: 7.5g, Total Fat: 11.8g

1030. SWEET PUMPKIN PUDDING

Serves: 4
Preparation time: 15 minutes
Cooking time: 15 minutes
Ingredients:
- 1 lb pumpkin, peeled and chopped into bite-sized pieces
- 2 tbsp honey
- ½ cup cornstarch
- 4 cups pumpkin juice, unsweetened
- 1 tsp cinnamon, ground
- 3 cloves, freshly ground

Preparation:
- Peel and prepare the pumpkin. Scrape out seeds and chop into bite-sized pieces. Set aside.
- In a small bowl, combine pumpkin juice, honey, orange juice, cinnamon, and cornstarch.
- Place the pumpkin chops in a large pot and pour the pumpkin juice mixture.
- Stir well and then finally add cloves.
- Stir until well incorporated and heat up until almost boiling.
- Reduce the heat to low and cook for about 15 minutes, or until the mixture thickens.
- Remove from the heat and transfer to the bowls immediately.
- Set aside to cool completely and then refrigerate for 15 minutes before serving, or simply chill overnight.

Nutrition information per serving: Calories: 232, Protein: 2.7g, Total Carbs: 56g, Dietary Fibers: 4.6g, Total Fat: 0.9g

1031. BEET SPINACH SALAD

Serves: 3
Preparation time: 15-20 minutes
Cooking time: 40 minutes
Ingredients:
- 2 medium-sized beet, trimmed and sliced
- 1 cup fresh spinach, chopped
- 2 spring onions, finely chopped
- 1 small green apple, cored and chopped
- 3 tbsp olive oil
- 2 tbsp fresh lime juice
- 1 tbsp honey, raw
- 1 tsp apple cider vinegar
- 1 tsp salt

Preparation:
- Wash the beets and trim off the green parts. Set aside.
- Wash the spinach thoroughly and drain. Cut into small pieces and set aside.
- Wash the apple and cut lengthwise in half. Remove the core and cut into bite-sized pieces and set aside.
- Wash the onions and cut into small pieces. Set aside.
- In a small bowl, combine olive oil, lime juice, honey, vinegar, and salt. Stir until well incorporated and set aside to allow flavors to meld.
- Place the beets in a deep pot. Pour enough water to cover and cook for about 40 minutes, or until tender. Remove the skin and slice. Set aside.
- In a large salad bowl, combine beets, spinach, spring onions, and apple.
- Stir well until combined and drizzle with previously prepared dressing.
- Give it a good final stir and serve immediately.

Nutrition information per serving: Calories: 215, Protein: 1.8g, Total Carbs: 23.8g, Dietary Fibers: 3.6g, Total Fat: 14.3g

1032. GRILLED AVOCADO IN CURRY SAUCE

Serves: 2
Preparation time: 15 minutes
Cooking time: 25-30 minutes
Ingredients:
- 1 large avocado, chopped
- ¼ cup water
- 1 tbsp curry, ground
- 2 tbsp olive oil
- 1 tsp soy sauce
- 1 tsp fresh parsley, finely chopped
- ¼ tsp red pepper flakes
- ¼ tsp sea salt

Preparation:
- Peel the avocado and cut lengthwise in half. Remove the pit and cut the remaining avocado into small chunks. Set aside.
- Heat up the olive oil in a large saucepan over a medium-high temperature.
- In a small bowl, combine ground curry, soy sauce, parsley, red pepper and sea salt.
- Add water and cook for about 5 minutes, stirring occasionally.
- Add chopped avocado, stir well and cook for 3 more minutes, or until all the liquid evaporates.
- Turn off the heat and cover. Let it stand for about 15-20 minutes before serving.

Nutrition information per serving: Calories: 338, Protein: 2.5g, Total Carbs: 10.8g, Dietary Fibers: 7.9g, Total Fat: 34.1g

1033. BROCCOLI CAULIFLOWER PUREE

Serves: 2
Preparation time: 10-15 minutes
Cooking time: 15-20 minutes
Ingredients:
- 2 cups fresh broccoli chopped
- 2 cups fresh cauliflower, chopped
- ½ cup skim milk
- ½ tsp salt
- ½ tsp Italian seasoning

- ¼ tsp cumin, ground
- 1 tbsp fresh parsley, finely chopped
- 1 tbsp olive oil
- 1 tsp dry mint, ground

Preparation:

- Wash and roughly chop the cauliflower.
- Place it in a deep pot and add a pinch of salt. Cook for about 15-20 minutes.
- When done, drain and transfer it to a food processor. Set aside.
- Wash the broccoli and chop into bite-sized pieces.
- Add it to the food processor along with milk, salt, Italian seasoning, cumin, parsley, and mint.
- Gradually add olive oil and blend until nicely pureed.
- Serve with some fresh carrots and celery.

Nutrition information per serving: Calories: 138, Protein: 6.1g, Total Carbs: 12.7g, Dietary Fibers: 4.6g, Total Fat: 7.5g

1034. CAPRESE SNACK

Prep Time: 10 minutes

Ingredients:

- 2 tablespoon of green pesto
- 8 ounce of fresh cherry tomatoes
- 8 ounce of mozzarella, mini cheese balls
- Fresh basil
- Salt and pepper

Instructions:

1. Cut the tomatoes and mozzarella balls in half and transfer to a mixing bowl
2. Add pesto, basil, salt and pepper and stir until well combined.
3. Taste to adjust seasoning.

Nutrition per Serving

Calories: 270kcal | Carbohydrates: 15.5g | Protein: 14.9g | Fat: 13.6 g | Saturated Fat: 7.5g

RECIPES A TO Z

Recipe	Page
"Pappardelle" Of Chicken With Winter Pesto	251
"Think Thin" Chicken Gravy	243
15 Minute Low-Carb Oatmeal	33
3-Alarm Chili	47
5 Layer Salad	70
5-Way Chili	53
Abundance Kale Salad With Savory Tahini Dressing	260
Acorn Squash Nests	34
Air Fryer "Roasted" Asparagus	95
Air Fryer Baked Potatoes	98
Air Fryer Chimichangas	96
Air Fryer Coconut Shrimp	98
Air Fryer Lemon Pepper Shrimp	97
Air Fryer Meatloaf	98
Air Fryer Potstickers	97
Air Fryer Recipes	93
Air Fryer Rib-Eye Steak	98
Air Fryer Roast Vegetables	95
Air Fryer Vegetables	94
Air Fryer Vegetables	94
Air Fryer Vegetables	96
Air Fryer Veggies	95
Air-Fried Shrimp	96
Airfried Vegetables	94
Air-Fryer Roasted Veggies	93
All-In-One Burger Stew	57
Almond Crusted Fish Fillets	192
Aloha Chicken	240
Amaranth Power Pubs With Hemp Seeds	257
Ambrosia Salad Recipe	68
Angelic Cupcakes	87
Angelic Macaroons	87
Apple And Oatmeal Cookie Crumble	89
Apple Butter Rolls	88
Apple Cinnamon Baked Oatmeal	255
Apple Cinnamon Grill	87
Apple Pecan Spice Squares	89
Apple-Cheddar Scones	89
Apple-Walnut Salad With Blue Cheese-Honey Vinaigrette	76
Apricot Brisket	149
Aquafaba Granola With Dates (Oil-Free)	258
Artichoke And Leek Soup	55
Artichoke Sandwich Spread	106
Arugula Salad With Sun-Dried Tomato Vinaigrette	71
Asian Chicken	251
Asian Fish	197
Asian Rainbow Chicken Salad	246
Asian Soup With Shredded Chicken And Rice	48
Asian Vegetable And Soba Noodle Salad	78
Asparagus And Cheddar Stuffed Chicken Breasts For Diabetics	249
Asparagus And Edamame Salad	201
Asparagus Bake	199
Asparagus Chef Salad	208
Asparagus Frittata	44
Asparagus Pepper Stir-Fry	200
Asparagus With Mustard Vinaigrette	105
Asparagus With Pine Nuts And Pimento	208
Asparagus With Scallops	163
Asparagus-Berry Salad	62
Avocado And Blueberry Fruit Salad	72
Avocado And Goat Cheese Toast	43
Avocado Chocolate Mousse	277
Avocado Egg Salad	254
Avocado Ice Cream	92
Ayurvedic Digestive Tea	155
Bacon & Egg Muffins	33
Bacon Breakfast Enchiladas	35
Baked Oatmeal	31
Baked Plantain For Diabetics	99
Baked Quinoa Dark Bean Falafel	270
Baked Stuffed Onions With Spinach Feta	206
Balanced Blood Sugar Smoothie	153
Balsamic And Garlic Chicken Thighs	212

Balsamic Beef, Mushrooms, And Onions	143
Balsamic Brussels Sprouts	203
Balsamic Chicjen And Mushrooms	213
Balsamic-Basil Sliced Tomatoes	107
Banana Lotion Pie Chia Pudding	252
Banana Proteins Smoothie Bowl With Hemp And Cacao	255
Banana Raspberry Refresher	156
Banana Split Ice Cream Pie	83
Banana-Berry Smoothie Recipe For Diabetics	155
Barbecued Shrimp Over Tropical Rice	190
Barley And Sausage Gumbo	251
Basil And Sausage Frittata	25
Basil Chicken Bites	245
Basmati Rice Pilaf	101
Beef And Broccoli Stir-Fry	121
Beef And Broccoli Stroganoff	148
Beef Meatballs On Bok Choy Nests	151
Beef Pork And Lamb	108
Beef Stew (Low-Carb)	56
Beef With Cabbage And Carrots	145
Beefy Barley Mushroom Soup	150
Beets With Horseradish Cream	83
Berry Delicious Smoothie Pack	154
Berry French Toast Stratas	26
Black Bean And Rice Recipe For Diabetics	107
Black Bean And Vegetable Enchiladas	102
Black Beans And Rice	105
Black Pepper And Coffee Steak	122
Blackberry Ginger Overnight Bulgar	29
Blackberry Lemonade	156
Blackberry Pulled Pork Shoulder	116
Blackened Shrimp With Tomatoes And Red Onion	189
Blueberry Bliss	86
Blueberry Bran Muffins	262
Blueberry Cupcakes With Cream Cheese Frosting	83
Blueberry French Toast With Banana Mousse	254
Blueberry Hemp Pear Porridge	255
Blueberry Pancakes	254
Black Pepper Citrus Chicken	218
Bleu Burger	134
Boo-Tiful Bean Dip	160
Bountiful Harvest Vegetable Salad	73
Bow Ties With Chicken And Mushroom Sauce	241
Braise Chicken With Wild Mushroom	210
Braised Chicken With Orange	213
Breakfast Burrito	29
Breakfast Burrito Casserole	40
Breakfast Casserole With Sausage And Cheese	27
Breakfast Cup Omelettes	35
Breakfast Quesadilla	33
Broccoli & Potato Chowder	60
Broccoli And Squash Medley	199
Broccoli Cauliflower Puree	297
Broccoli Rabe Saute	203
Broccoli With Asian Tofu	209
Broiled Dijon Burgers	123
Brown Rice, Asparagus, And Tomato Salad	76
Browned Butter Spritz Cookies	92
Brownies	278
Breadstick Pizza	291
Breakfast Casserole	130
Bubbly Taco Salad Bowls Recipe	67
Buckwheat Apple Muffins	37
Bulgur Hack Chili	271
Bulgur, Grape, And Kale Salad	200
Burrito With Sweet Potato	254
Butternut Bisque	61
Butternut Squash And Millet Soup	59
Butternut Squash Soup	52
Butternut Squash Veggie Pizza	269
Buttered Salmon With Creole Seasonings	166
Bacon And Salmon Bake	179
Bacon-Wrapped Chicken Tenders	285
Baked Bread Crumb–Crusted Fish With Lemon	172
Baked Chicken	228
Baked Chicken Cordon Bleu	236
Baked Fish	184
Baked Orange Roughy With Spicy Plum Sauce	174
Baked Red Snapper Almandine	172
Baked Snapper With Orange-Rice Dressing	173

Item	Page
Barbecued Sea-Bass	169
Barley-Spinach-Fish Bake	171
Basil-Lime Shrimp	165
Beef & Broccoli	124
Beef & Pumpkin Stew	110
Beef & Pumpkin Stew	131
Beef Fillet With Port	127
Beef Gravy Supreme	124
Beef Pecan	124
Beef Stroganoff	120
Beef Stew	121
Beef Stew With Pumpkin	125
Beef Tips In Crockpot	130
Beer Chicken	218
Beet Spinach Salad	297
Cajun Air Fryer Salmon	97
Cajun Stew	57
Caldo De Res	146
Cantaloupe Cooler	156
Caprese Salad	72
Caramelized Onions And Bell Peppers	295
Caribbean Chicken Salad	243
Carrot And Vanilla Cake Cookies	296
Carrot Cake Overnight Oats	252
Cauliflower Almond Soup	57
Cauliflower Pilaf	87
Chai Smoothie Bowl	255
Char-Grilled Fish Kebabs With Pesto Potatoes	185
Cheddar Stuffed Beef Burger	144
Cheese And Onion Crispy Roasted Chickpeas	263
Cheese Bread Cups	26
Cheese Paste	281
Cheese Souffle' Casserole	32
Cheeseburgers	150
Cheesy Artichoke Dip	157
Cheesy Party Bake	160
Chef Lala'S Goodness Platter	146
Cherry Tomato Bruschetta	283
Chicken And Cantaloupe Salad With Toasted Pecans	75
Chicken And Spinach Salad	74
Chicken And Sweet Potato Chili For Diabetics	248
Chicken Barley Soup	57
Chicken Dinner Salad With Green Onion Dressing	243
Chicken Florentine Pizza For Diabetics	238
Chicken Jambalaya	237
Chicken Marinade For Grilling	158
Chicken Nuggets With Barbecue Dipping Sauce	248
Chicken Salad Stuffed Avocado	205
Chicken Stir-Fry	210
Chicken With Bean Thread And Rice Noodles	237
Chicken With Green Curry Sauce	213
Chicken With Spinach And Artichokes	247
Chicken, Shrimp And Steak Skewers With Sofrito	237
Chickpea Flour Scramble	252
Chickpea Sunflower Sandwich	258
Chicken & Kale Soup	231
Chicken Breasts From The Mediterranean	227
Chicken Breasts With Parmesan And Peppers	226
Chicken Chowder With Yogurt And Tomato	225
Chicken Fingers	219
Chicken Kabobs	219
Chicken Kalamata	223
Chicken Laal Mirch	230
Chicken Marsala	210
Chicken Meatballs	228
Chicken Philly Cheese Steak Sandwich	234
Chicken Pasta With Herb Sauce	222
Chicken Shawarma	229
Chicken Sheekh Kabab	230
Chicken Soup	231
Chicken Wings In Peanut Sauce	224
Chicken Wings And Tasty Mint Chutney	225
Chicken With Bacon, Cream, And Thyme	233
Chicken With Fresh Herbs	215
Chicken With Lemon Garlic Sauce	235
Chicken With Mushrooms In A Champagne Cream Sauce	215
Chicken And Broccoli Casserole	222
Chicken And Green Bean Stovetop Casserole	222
Chicken And Garlic	224
Chicken And Mushroom Rice Casserole	221

Chicken And Vermicelli, Low-Carbed	224
Chicken And Asparagus In White Wine Sauce	222
Chilaquiles Casserole	44
Chili Beef	126
Chili Without Carne	272
Chili-Bacon Scallops	182
Chinese Steamed Fish	177
Chipotle Spicy Fish Tacos	162
Chipotle Tomato Rice Energy Bowl	264
Chipotle Cheeseburgers	112
Chipotle Cheeseburgers	135
Chocolate Avocado Cookies	277
Chocolate Avocado Smoothie	156
Chocolate Chip Frozen Yogurt	88
Chocolate Cinnamon Cake	85
Chocolate Clusters	86
Chocolate Fudge Truffles	277
Chocolate Hazelnut Coffee	156
Chocolate Mint Sandwich Cookies	84
Chocolate Mocha Pudding	90
Chocolate Pancake With Strawberries	27
Chocolate Peanut Butter & Banana Smoothie Pack	154
Chocolate-Baked Grapefruit	85
Chocolate Biscuits	286
Chopped Chicken Salad	158
Chopped Roasted Chicken Salad	247
Chunky Chicken Stew	233
Chunky Strawberry Salad With Poppyseed Dressing	66
Cheddar Basil Bites	286
Cherries In Ricotta	289
Cheesy Salmon Casserole	179
Cheese Casserole	126
Cheeseburger Casserole	125
Cheesesteak Lettuce Cups	111
Chicken Piccata	235
Chicken Salad	68
Cilantro Pollo Enchiladas	238
Cinnemon Apple Saute'	81
Cinnamon-Spiced Lemon Chicken	233
Clam Spaghetti	161
Classic Beef Stew	148
Classic Gumbo	194
Classic Barbecued Chicken	232
Classic Meatloaf	114
Cobb Salad	69
Coconut Pie	80
Coconut Rice Pudding	253
Cod Gratin	161
Cod Nuggets	31
Cold Feta Olive Spread	288
Cold Herb Soup	51
Cold Peach Soup	52
Colorful Quinoa Salad With Pomegranate	273
Colorful Vegetable Casserole	99
Congee With Smoked Vegetables And Tofu	256
Cool Wheat Berry Salad	77
Corn And Tomato Polenta	208
Corn Eggs And Popato Bake	31
Corny Zucchini Medley	106
Corned Beef Brisket	119
Cottage Cheese Breakfast Bowl (Keto, Low Carb, Diabetic Friendly)	36
Country Root Vegetable And Chicken	226
Country-Style Collard Greens	103
Couscous Salad With Soy Dip	274
Couscous With Vegetables	208
Crab Soup	194
Cranberry-Glazed Pork Chops	147
Cranberry-Nut Spread	160
Creamed Peas And Mushrooms	199
Creamy Baked Chicken With Artichokes And Mushrooms	249
Creamy Cucumber Herb	280
Creamy Quinoa With Peachs	26
Creamy Yellow Squash Soup	59
Crispy Brussel Sprouts Quinoa Salad Recipe	65
Crock-Pot Vegetable Soup	143
Crunchy "Fried" Catfish Fillets	174
Crunchy Vegetable Salad With Chipotle-Ranch Dressing	80
Crunchy Vegetable Salad	63

Crustless Asparagus And Tomato Quiche	46
Crustless Spinach Quiche	45
Crustless Caprese Quiche	25
Crusted Salmon	161
Crab Cakes With Sesame Crust	171
Creamy Apple Cinnamon Steal-Cut Oatmeal	27
Creamed Spinach	198
Creamy Blueberry	288
Creamy Lentil Cakes	289
Creamy Shrimp Pie With Rice Crust	171
Creamy Chopped Cauliflower Salad	64
Cucumber Buttermilk Soup	55
Cucumber Mango Salad	70
Cucumber Salad	69
Cucumber Sandwich Bites	283
Cucumber Yogurt Dressing	78
Cucumbers With Feta, Mint, And Sumac	283
Cumin-Crusted Fish Fillets	186
Curried Cauliflower, Grape, And Lentil Salad	260
Curried Chicken Salad	241
Curried Lima Bean Aperitif Soup	55
Curry Chicken	218
Caprese Snack	298
Caramelized Onion & Pepper Vegan Quesadillas	292
Cashew-Basil Pesto Covered Chicken Wings	227
Dessert Recipes	80
Deviled Eggs	32
Diabetes-Friendly Chocolate Chia Smoothie Recipe	153
Diabetes-Friendly Sourdough French Toast	35
Diabetic Beef And Artichoke Casserole Recipe	145
Diabetic Braised Lamb With Carrots	140
Diabetic Breakfast Egg Cups	43
Diabetic Chicken Noodle Soup Recipe	239
Diabetic Chicken, Broccoli, And Rice Bake Recipe	240
Diabetic Fish And Seafood Recipes	161
Diabetic Lemon Chicken Recipe	245
Diabetic Macaroon	92
Diabetic Poultry (Chicken) Recipes	210
Diabetic Sauces, Dips, And Dressing	157
Diabetic Spiced Baked Apples Recipe	92
Diabetic Stuffed Peppers Recipe	102
Diabetic Summer Squash Side Dish Recipe	105
Diabetic Vegetarian And Vegan Recipes	198
Dijon Salmon With Green Bean Pilaf	177
Dill Green Beans	104
Dilled Salmon Pasta With Asparagus	187
Dilly Tuna Salad	167
Diluted Banana Caramel Sauce	282
Dirty Rice	150
Dragon Fruit Smoothie Bowl	152
Drunken Chicken Wings	231
Delicious Chicken Nuggets	225
Deviled Crab	170
Easy Cheesy Vegetable Casserole	239
Easy Chicken, Spinach, And Wild Rice Soup	248
Easy Cream Of Tomato Soup	49
Easy Diabetic Breakfast: Mixed Berry Parfait	38
Easy Grillable Veggie Burgers	266
Easy Low Carb Baked Fish	185
Easy Pear Crisp	295
Easy South-Of-The-Border Grilled Chicken For Diabetics	245
Easy Sugar-Free Breakfast Sausage	41
Easy-As-Pie Holiday Soup	60
Edamame Masala Dark Brown Basmati Rice Bowl	266
Egg And Avocado Toasts	43
Egg Salad Sandwich	266
Eggnog Sandwich Cookies	85
Eggplant Caviar With Basil Pistou	273
Eggs A La Shrimp	26
Eggs With Tomatoes, Olives And Feta	29
Ensenada Shrimp Tostadas	198
Estofado De Bistec Con Papas	152
Exotic Amaretto Maroon Carrots	103
Easy Meatloaf	114
Fajita-Seasoned Grilled Chicken	250
Fall Harvest Coleslaw	80
Fast 'N' Fiery Grilled Catfish	197
Fat-Free Honey Mustard Sauce	157
Fennel Wheat Berry Salad	75
Fettuccine And Vegetable Salad	147

Recipe	Page
Fiesta Fish Tacos	193
Figs With Mascarpone And Honey	284
Fillet Steak With Deep-Fried Onions	126
Fish Amandine	176
Fish Creole	195
Fish Cakes	170
Fish Fillet Crusted With Cumin	162
Fish Pie	178
Fish Pie	184
Fish Sauce	280
Fish With Chinese Ginger Scallion Sauce	196
Fish And Asparagus With Tarragon Mustard Sauce	181
Florentine Fish Roll-Ups	192
Flourless Chocolate Cake	93
Freach Chicken	217
Fresh Asparagus Topped With Sunny-Side-Up Eggs	202
Fresh Garlic Shrimp Linguine	191
Fresh Parfait	294
Fresh Peas With Mint	201
Fried Brown Rice For Diabetics	100
Fried Chicken	216
Frozen Berry Ice Cream	88
Fruit & Nut Quinoa	83
Fruit Cake Oatmeal	32
Fruit Salad With Creamy Banana Dressing	75
Fruit Soup	51
Fruit-Filled Protein-Packed Over Night Quinoa & Oats	253
Fruity Oat Bars	82
Fresh Tomato And Clam Sauce With Whole-Grain Linguine	168
Fresh Peach Salad Recipe With Basil	68
Fudge Brownies	275
Fudgy Brownies	81
Fun Picnic Snack	288
Furikake Snack Mix	293
Fall Harvest Coleslaw	63
Feta-Olive Cakes	290
Feta-Spinach Salmon Roast	169
Garden Pasta Salad	76
Garlic And Lime Beef Roast With Cilantro Pesto	123
Garlic And White Wine Pasta With Brussels Sprouts	268
Garlic Grilled Beef Brochettes	151
Garlic Roasted Rib	120
Garlic Snow Peas With Cilantro	205
Garlicky Mustard Lamb Chops	141
German-Style Potato Salad	79
Ghee Roasted Chicken	230
Ginger, Orange, And Sesame Dressing	72
Ginger-Caraway Carrots	105
Gingered Snow Peas	108
Ginger Mustard Fish	181
Gingerbread Biscuits	82
Girl Chef'S Grilled Lobster	188
Glazed Ham Balls	118
Glazed Plum Pastry	89
Glazed Carrots	199
Gluten-Free Banana Bread	43
Glazed, Grilled Salmon	166
Golden Mylk Cheesecak	277
Gorgonzola Panna Cotta With Chicken	227
Grape Tomato Salad With White Beans And Cucumber	73
Greek Christmas Bread	100
Greek Festival Fish	192
Greek Goddess Bowl	260
Greek Navy Bean And Vegetable Soup	55
Greek Shrimp	194
Greek Steak Wraps	120
Green Bean And Red Pepper Sauté	106
Green Bean, Walnut, And Blue Cheese Pasta Salad	77
Green Beans And Red Onion Salad	208
Green Beans With Mushrooms	206
Green Beans With Pine Nuts And Garlic	283
Green Cheese Sauce And Nacho Chile	279
Green Goddess Buddha Bowl	264
Green Smoothie	154
Greens And Broccoli Salad With Poppy Vinaigrette	72
Greens And Pear With Maple-Mustard Dressing	74
Grillades Of Pork	143
Grilled Buffalo Chicken Tenders	247
Grilled Chicken Adobo	250

Grilled Chicken With Corn And Black Bean Salsa	250
Grilled Lamb Chops	118
Grilled Lamb Chops With Garlic And Herbs	135
Grilled Lamb Loin Chops With Corn On The Cob And Grilled Romaine	135
Grilled Marinated Chicken	251
Grilled Pork Chops With Cherry Sauce	142
Grilled Romaine And Asparagus Salad	79
Grilled Salmon	185
Grilled Sea Scallops With A Watermelon Three-Way & Dandelion Greens	188
Grilled Steak And Black Bean Tacos	145
Grilled Steak With Sweet Pepper Salsa	122
Grilled Chicken & Garlic Parsley Lemon Sauce	230
Grilled Chicken Salad	220
Grilled Flank Steak With Cumin Aioli	128
Grilled Glazed Salmon	181
Grilled Haddock With Peach-Mango Salsa	168
Grilled Roasting Chicken	223
Grilled Salmon With Roasted Peppers	172
Grilled Tuna With Honey Mustard	174
Grilled Turkey Breast With Basil & Mozzarella	229
Grilled Avocado In Curry Sauce	297
Greek Chicken	220
Greek Marinated Chicken	235
Greek Orzo Pasta Salad With Lemon Vinaigrette	66
Greek Orange Honey Cake With Pistachios	287
Greek Roasted Chicken	232
Greek Roasted Fish With Vegetables	182
Greek Yoghurt With Strawberries	285
Grilled Leg Of Lamb Steaks	114
Grilled Romaine And Asparagus Salad	63
Garlic Bread	285
Garlicy Peppered Creole Salmon Fillets	183
Halibut With Vegetables	162
Ham And Broccoli Frittata	38
Ham And Pineapple Salad For One	77
Harissa	281
Harvest Salad	65
Hash Brown Breakfast Casserole For Diabetics	151
Healthy Breakfast Skillet	36
Healthy Sugar-Free Granola	37
Hearty Butternut Squash Soup	50
Hearty Meatball Soup	115
Hearty Pot Roast	119
Herb And Parmesan Crusted Fish	162
Herb Roasted Chicken	211
Herb-Crusted Rack Of Lamb	140
Hippie Breakfast Porridge	39
Hoisin Chicken With Orange Sauce	242
Hold-The-Mayo Coleslaw	79
Holiday Stuffed Beef Tenderloin	145
Homemade Pesto Sauce: Nut Free	158
Homemade Worcestershire Sauce	280
Honey Spiced Lamb Casserole	138
Honeydew Agua Fresca	155
Honey-Soy Broiled Salmon	169
Hot Italian Chicken	215
Hot Shrimp With Cool Salsa	191
Hamburgers	128
Hazelnut Cookies	290
Healthy Shakshuka	30
Herbed Chicken And Brown Rice Dinner	221
Herbed Olives	285
Herby Mediterranean Fish With Wilted Greens & Mushrooms	183
Healthy Chicken Piccata	236
Ice Cream Cake	88
In-A-Wink Guacamole Dip	160
Indian Broiled Chicken	238
Indian Red Curry	133
Indonesian Pork Tenderloin	117
Injector Chicken Breasts	219
Instant Refried Beans Recipe For Diabetics	104
Italian Pasta Soup With Fennel	59
Italian Pork Chops	116
Italian Style Pork Chops	108
Italian-Style Caponata	159
Italian Grilled Chicken	229
Jalapeño Cheeseburgers	149
Johnnycakes And Pumpkin Butter	34
Juicy Lamb Burgers	139

Entry	Page
Jumbletti	143
Jalapeno And Bacon Chicken Breasts	220
Kale Chips	296
Kale Salad With Crispy Chickpeas	270
Kale Salad With Savory Tahini Dressing	268
Keto Cherry Chocolate Brownies	93
Keto Ranch Dressing	157
Kiwi Vanilla Yogurt Smoothie	152
Korean-Style Beef And Pasta	144
Korean Barbecued Chicken	232
Kale Bruschetta	292
Keema	129
Lamb And Vegetable Stew	141
Lamb Chops Curry	118
Lamb Gyros	137
Lamb Kebabs With Verdant Salsa	141
Lamb Shanks With Barley, Garden Peas, And Mint	137
Lamb, Sweet Potato, And Almond Slow-Cooked Curry	139
Layered Mexican Salad	71
Lemon Asparagus And Carrots	206
Lemon Cake	278
Lemon Chiffon Topped With Berries	80
Lemon Pepper Chicken Wings	251
Lemon-Pepper-Glazed Veggie Toss	102
Lentil Salad With Curd Cheese	270
Lettuce Salad With Hot Bacon Dressing	62
Lighter Lamb Hotpot	137
Lime Grilled Chicken Recipe For Diabetics	244
Lime Prawns On Wild Rice	271
Loaded Kale Salad	261
Louisiana Broiled Catfish	197
Low Carb Bbq Sauce	157
Low Carb Breakfast Burritos	36
Low Carb Diabetic Breakfast Smoothie	154
Low Carb Hamburger Helper	136
Low Carb Turkey Meatloaf	214
Low Carb Cabbage Rolls	124
Low-Carb Breakfast Scramble	41
Low-Carb Steak Breakfast Hash	34
Low-Carb Beef Stroganoff	133
Low-Carb Parsley Mashed Cauliflower With Fish Cutlets	184
Low-Carb Stroganoff Stew	129
Lower Carb Strawberry Smoothie	153
Low-Sodium Herb Roasted Chicken Recipe	245
Lumpia In The Air Fryer	97
Luscious Lentils	103
Luscious Lobster Salad	78
Lemon Baked Chicken	225
Lemon Mustard Herb Chicken	220
Lemon Sage Turkey	218
Leek And Pork Stir Fry	115
Mac 'N' Cheese	267
Main-Dish Mediterranean Salad	75
Make-Ahead Mashed Potatoes	101
Mandarin Chicken Salad	211
Maple And Apple Pork Chops	142
Maple And Cinnamon Peaches	82
Maple And Sage Pork Chops	141
Maple Walnut Vegan Cream Cheese	282
Marinated Air Fryer Vegetables	94
Marinated Asparagus, Tomato, And Hearts Of Palm	207
Marinated Chicken	214
Matcha Smoothie Bowl With Banana Milk	256
Mediterranean Breakfast Egg Muffins	28
Mediterranean Breakfast Quinoa	30
Mediterranean Breakfast Sandwich	29
Mediterranean Chicken Stew	56
Mediterranean Edamame Quinoa Bowl	265
Mediterranean Frittata	30
Mediterranean Omelette	28
Mediterranean Roasted Pepper Dip	159
Mediterranean Toast	28
Mediterranean Tuna Cups	164
Merlot Marinated Beef Kebeb	121
Mexican-Style Steak And Eggs Breakfast	40
Microwave Lima Bean Casserole	99
Microwave-Baked Stuffed Apples	296
Mini Marinated Beef Skewers	149
Mint Chocolate Truffle Larabar Bites	263
Mint-Green Tea Coolers	155

Miso Soup	51
Mixed Berry Snack Cake	81
Mixed Greens With Cranberries, Bacon, And Walnuts	45
Mixed Herbs With Almonds And Pepita Pesto	282
Mocha Crinkle Cookies	85
Mom'S Chicken Soup With Egg White Matzo Balls	49
Moroccan Lamb Stew	140
Moroccan Lemon Chicken With Olives	246
Moroccan Lentil & Vegetable Soup For Diabetics	60
Moroccan Lentil-Stuffed Eggplant	267
Moroccan Lamb Stew With Apricots	113
Morroccan Carrot Salad	70
Moussaka	136
Mozzarella And Cashew Cheese Sauce	279
Mushroom & Chicken Skillet	61
Mushroom And Walnut Meat Loaf	119
Mushroom Barley Soup	54
Mushroom Scrambled Eggs	45
Mushroom Surprise	39
Makes 8 Cakes	166
Mandarin Beef Saute	129
Marvelous Meatballs	109
Marvelous Meatballs	129
Mediterranean Chicken In A Herb Sauce	228
Mediterranean Picnic Snack	284
Mediterranean Spinach Cakes	289
Mediterranean Wrap	293
Melon, Tomato & Onion Salad With Goat Cheese	64
Messican Salad	69
Meatball Soup	109
Meatball Soup	130
Meatloaf	134
Mixed Green Salad With Grapefruit & Cranberries	64
Moqueca	183
New England Clam Chowder	58
Nightshade-Free Taco Meat	130
No Bake Protein Energy Ball	275
No-Bake Cinnamon Apple Power Bars	262
Nourish Lentil Bowl	265
Oat Risotto With Chorizo	38
Oatmeal Recipe For Diabetic Children	36
Oatmeal Walnut Chocolate Chip Cookies	296
Olive Feta-Honey Cakes	289
Omelette With Mushroom	257
Orange And Apricot Chiffon Cake	90
Orange Cupcakes With Orange-Ginger Frosting	91
Orange Spice Coffee Mix	156
Orzo Stuffed Peppers	102
Orange Cinnamon Beef Stew	109
Orange Cinnamon Beef Stew	131
Orange-Five-Spice Roasted Chicken	232
Orange-Tangerine Chicken	234
Oven "Fried" Chicken For Diabetics	240
Oven Barbecued Chicken	214
Oven Fried Chicken Legs	214
Overnight Oats	34
Oven Barbecued Chicken	223
Oven Fried Chicken	223
Pancakes	28
Pancakes – Diabetic Friendly	40
Pancakes With Berries And Whipped Cream	30
Parmesan And Asparagus Frittata	31
Parmesan Spinach Dip	159
Parmesan-Crusted Halibut With Spicy Brussels Sprouts	203
Parsley, Pear, And Walnut Salad	79
Parsley, Pear, And Walnut Salad	63
Pasta E Fagioli (Pasta And Bean Soup)	51
Pasta With Chickpea Sauce	271
Peach Smoothie (Diabetic)	153
Peanut Butter Mudslide Ice Cream	278
Pear And Cranberry Salad	74
Penny-Wise Chicken Pot Pie	238
Peppered Shrimp Skewers	193
Pesto Chicken Salad	242
Pesto Pasta With Scallops	191
Philly Cheesesteak Lettuce Cups	132
Pineapple Kale Smoothie	153
Pineapple-Orange Grilled Chicken Breasts	221
Pistachio Turmeric Rice Energy Bow	265
Pistachio-Stuffed Dates	284

Pie With Mushrooms, Smoked Cheddar, Bacon, And Sour Cream	110
Pie With Mushrooms, Smoked Cheddar, Bacon, And Sour Cream	131
Plant Baset Diabetic Recipes	252
Poblano And Portobello Fajitas	272
Polish Chilled Fish In Horseradish Sauce	99
Pomegranate Masghati Dessert	275
Pork And Cabbage	118
Pork Chops With Apple Stuffing	117
Pork Chops With Onion Gravy	116
Pork Loin Chopstopped With Peach Salsa	108
Pork Stir-Fry	149
Portabello Mushroom Stroganoff	201
Portobello Pot Roast	261
Portable Packed Picnic Pieces	284
Potato Curry With Pumpkin	273
Potato, Broccoli, And Fennel Salad	202
Poultry Skinless Roast Chicken With Herbs And Spices	217
Poultry Taste-Of Summer Chicken	217
Power Granola	42
Primavera Fish Fillets	196
Prosciutto, Asparagus, And Chicken Pizza	249
Protein Muffins	258
Provençal Lemon And Olive Chicken	247
Pumpkin Apple Protein Bars	42
Pumpkin Bars	294
Pumpkin Custard	86
Pumpkin Spice Mini Donuts	84
Parmesan Chicken Strips	229
Parmesan Crisps	288
Parmesan Crusted Catfish	168
Patriotic Taco Salad	291
Pepper-Lime Chicken	217
Pepper-Lime Chicken	234
Pepperoni Chips	286
Pepperoni Pizza Mozzarella Crisps	287
Perfect Grilled Chicken Breasts	236
Peach Salmon	179
Potato Salad	62
Queso	281
Quick' ' N Healthy Taco Salad	71
Quick Broccoli Soup	61
Quick Chicken Noodle Soup	239
Quick Orange Chicken	250
Quick Rainbow Tortellini Vegetable Salad	78
Quinoa Gado-Gado Bowl	259
Rainbow "Raw-Maine" Taco Boats	259
Raisin-Apricot Loaf Cake Mix	90
Red Pepper Soup	52
Rib Of Beef	126
Rich-Tasting Red Clam Sauce	101
Roasted Air Fryer Vegetables	95
Roasted Asparagus	208
Roasted Beet And Carrot Salad	204
Roasted Eggplant With Spiced Lamb	138
Roasted Leg Lamb	117
Roasted Pineapple With Maple Glaze	295
Roasted Red Pepper Hummus	281
Roasted Sea Bass	164
Roasted Stuffed Portobello Mushrooms With Spinach-Cilantro Pesto	207
Roasted Winter Vegetable Blend	108
Romaine, Red Onion, And Fennel Salad With Tart Lime Dressing	209
Rosemary Chicken Orzo	241
Rotisserie Chicken	223
Roast Beef Melt	128
Roast Chicken With Balsamic Vinegar	231
Roast Turkey And An Avocado Sauce	227
Roasted Rosemary Olives	284
Roasted Squash Wrap	289
Red Hot Sirloin	128
Roast Leg Of Lamb	112
Roasted Lamb Breast	113
Root Vegetable Pave	290
Salad Recipes	62
Salad With Smoked Tofu	273
Salmon & Asparagus With Lemon-Garlic Butter Sauce	176
Salmon & Shrimp Pasta	186

Salmon With Cilantro-Lime Salsa	187
Santa Fe Grilled Vegetable Salad	71
Sautéed Shrimp Recipe For Diabetics	193
Sauteed Spinach	209
Sauteed Spinach With Garlic	206
Sautees Chicken With Texas Spice Rub	212
Savory Bread Dressing	101
Scallop And Artichoke Heart Casserole	190
Scrambled Eggs	257
Scallops And Shrimp With White Bean Sauce	175
Sea Salt Butterscotch Tart	279
Seafood Kabobs	196
Seafood Kabobs Hawaiian	196
Seafood Sausage Gumbo	186
Seasoned Brussels Sprouts	106
Seedy Power Cookies	263
Sesame Beef Stir-Fry	123
Sesame Date And Almond Balls	82
Sesame Sugar Snap Peas	203
Sesame Tuna Steak	163
Sesame-Crusted Swordfish	197
Shakshouka Mediterranean Breakfast	27
Shepherd'S Pie – Diabetic Friendly	139
Shredded Beef For Tacos	122
Shrimp & Caper Vermicelli	190
Shrimp And Beet Smörgåsor	195
Shrimp And Watermelon Ceviche	191
Shrimp Caprese Pasta	189
Shrimp Creole	163
Shrimp In Brandy Cream	165
Shrimp In Curried Coconut Milk	165
Shrimp Microwave Casserole	173
Shrimp Po'Boy	195
Shrimp Stewed In Curry Butter	164
Side Dish Recipes	99
Simple Bechamel Sauce	279
Simple Grilled Lamb Chops	112
Simple Spiced Tea Mix For Diabetics	155
Sirloin Steak Antipasto Salad	74
Sirloin Steak Strips	111
Sirloin Steak Strips	133
Sizzlin' Catfish	197
Skillet Chicken Piccata	241
Skillet Barbecued Salmon	179
Skinless Roast Chicken With Herbs And Spices	233
Slightly Italiano Meat Loaf	110
Slightly Italiano Meat Loaf	132
Slow Cooker Breakfast Casserole	44
Slow Cooker Chicken Noodle Soup	46
Slow Cooker Chipotle Beef Stew	122
Slow Cooker Pork Tenderloin	116
Slow Cooker Balsamic Chicken	230
Slow Cooker Corned Beef And Cabbage	111
Slow Cooker Corned Beef And Cabbage	133
Slow Cooker Lamb Chops	113
Slow-Cooked Roast Leg Of Lamb	136
Slow-Cooked Southwestern Chicken Chili	246
Slow-Roasted Salmon	170
Smoked Sausage Pita Pockets	147
Smoked Mussels And Pasta	175
Smoked Shrimp And Cheese Quesadillas	171
Smoothie Breakfast Bowl	41
Smoothies Recipes	152
Smopky Pork Chops And Tomatoes	117
Smothered Burgers	124
Snacks	283
Snack Crackers	293
Soothing Cucumber Mint Soup	209
Soups And Stew	46
Sour Cream Mashed Potatoes	199
Sous Vide Egg Bites	286
Southern Crab Cakes With Rémoulade Dipping Sauce	189
South-Of-The-Border Bean Dip	159
Southwest Breakfast Quiche	42
Southwest White Bean Stew	58
Spaghetti Squash With Chunky Tomato Sauce	244
Spanish Chicken Kabobs	219
Spanish Potato Omelet	44
Spiced Carrot Raisin Bread	294
Spiced Citrus Tea	155

Spiced Maple Nuts	284
Spicy "Fried" Fish Fillet	168
Spicy Apricot Glazed Chicken	242
Spicy Black Bean Burritos	105
Spicy Buffalo Chickpea Wraps	258
Spicy Beef Roast	112
Spicy Beef Roast	133
Spicy Cactus Turkey	213
Spicy Cheese Sauce	279
Spicy Fish Tacos	192
Spicy Guacamole	158
Spicy Marinara Sauce	282
Spicy Mustard	280
Spicy Pork Chop Supper	151
Spicy Shrimp Appetizers	193
Spicy Tofu With Quinoa And Avocado Salad	271
Spicy Tortilla Soup	48
Spinach & Bacon Egg Cups	32
Spinach Almond Casserole	100
Spinach And Parmesan Egg Bites	46
Spinach Salad With Beets	77
Spinach Salad With Pomegranate Vinaigrette	76
Spinach Salad With Seared Bok Choy, Ginger, And Cilantro	204
Spinach Saute With Mushrooms	207
Spinach Smoothie (Low-Carb & Gluten-Free)	153
Spinach Vegetable Kugel	206
Spinach With Garlic, Raisins, And Peanuts	203
Spinach, Crab, And Artichoke Dip	189
Spinach, Feta, And Grape Tomato Omelet	204
Splenda Four Ingredient Peanut Butter Cookies	86
Spring Vegetable Soup With Scallion And Dill-Flecked Matzo Balls	50
Springtime Dip	160
Springtime Panzanella	73
Spaghetti Squash And Chicken Sausage	226
Squash And Apple Soup	54
Squash And Corn	107
Steak And Mushroom Soup	48
Stir-Fried Snow Peas	106
Stir-Fried Ginger Scallops With Vegetables	175
Stir-Fry Beef And Spaghetti	148
Stir-Fryed Beef & Zucchini With Pesto	119
Stuffed Eggplant	144
Stuffed Peppers With Quinoa	272
Stuffed Pork Tenderloin	142
Stuffed Pork Tenderloin With Collard Greens	142
Stuffed Cabbage Rolls	111
Stuffed Cabbage Rolls	132
Stuffed Eggplant	198
Steak With Mustard Sauce	127
Sugar Snap Peas And Carrots	207
Sugar-Free French Toast	39
Summer Fruit Smoothie	42
Summer Squash Ribbons With Lemon And Ricotta	283
Summer Strawberry Orange Cups	86
Summer Dessert Pizza	291
Sunbutter Baked Oatmeal Cups	253
Sun-Drenched Tomato Spread	282
Sun-Dried Tomato Pesto Dip	160
Sun-Dried Tomato Seasoned Salmon	187
Super Green Avocado Smoothie	253
Sweet And Smoky Baked Eggs	41
Sweet Dessert Tarte Flambée	274
Sweet Potato Casserole	295
Sweet Potato Casserole	200
Sweet Potato Curry With Pumpkin	271
Sweet Potato Minestrone	59
Swordfish Veracruz	177
Sweet Onion–Baked Yellowtail Snapper	174
Sweet Pumpkin Pudding	297
Sweet And Spicy Meat Balls	285
Saigon Shrimp	164
Salmon Cakes	180
Salmon Casserole	173
Salmon Hash	173
Salmon In Citrus Vinaigrette	166
Salmon In Ginger Cream	165
Salmon Patties	170
Salmon Teriyaki	167
Salmon With Lemon Lime Butter	180

Salmon Pinwheels	176
Salisbury Steak	115
Sesame Shrimp And Asparagus	168
Sea Bass With Tapenade Cream Sauce	182
Spinach & Warm Mushroom Salad	64
Spinach And Artichoke Pizza	290
Spicy Salad Recipe	69
Tacos	256
Tangerine Panna Cotta	81
Tangy Onion Dip	161
Tangy Spinach Dip	159
Tangy Steamed Green Bean Salad	107
Tarragon Seafood Pasta Salad	187
Tasty Breakfast Oats	25
Tasty Fiesta Turkey	211
Tasty Souffle'	30
Tempeh Avocado Sandwich With Hummus	255
Teriyaki Chicken Drummies	244
Texmex Salad	272
The Ultimate Green Smoothie Recipe	152
The Best Macaroni Salad Recipe	68
The Ultimate Wedge Salad Recipe	65
Tilapia Fillet With Fruity Salsa	164
Tilapia	178
Toasted Banana Caramel Sauce	281
Toasted Chard With Macadamia Cheese	274
Tofu Berry Smoothie	156
Tomato And Veggie Gazpacho	200
Tomato Caprese Salad	62
Tomato-Basil Soup	52
Tomato Basil Skewers	288
Tomato And Basil Finger Sandwiches	285
Toasted Spicy Almonds	288
Tri Colored Backyard Pasta Salad	264
Triple-Quick Shrimp And Pasta	194
Tropical Green Shake	155
Tropical Paradise Green Smoothie Pack	154
Trout And Ghee Sauce	185
Trout And Special Sauce	178
Truite Au Bleu	182
Traditional Stovetop Tuna-Noodle Casserole	170
Tuna Bake With Cheese Swirls	163
Tuna Macaroni Salad	70
Tuna Salad	262
Tuna Casserole	167
Tuna Steaks	176
Tuna And Spinach Bake	180
Turkey Gravy For Diabetics	101
Turkey Minestrone	49
Turkey Enchilada	211
Turkey Burger	217
Turkey Roast	215
Turkey'N'Eggs	216
Turmeric Lamb Chops With Crispy Potatoes And Broccoli	138
Two-Minute Turkey Wrap	240
Tzatziki	280
Taco Meat	109
Tangerine-Beef Stir-Fry	132
Tasty Grilled Chicken Wings	228
Taste-Of Summer Chicken	228
Teriyaki Kabobs	134
Upma	39
Vanilla Breakfast Millet With Apple	256
Vanilla Cupcakes	275
Vegan "Blt" Sandwich	260
Vegetable Pancake	Healthy Breakfast	Diabetic Diet	37
Vegetable Soup	47
Vegetable Soup With Shirataki And Edamame	201
Vegetable-Chicken Noodle Soup	248
Vegetarian Chili With Brown Rice	60
Vietnamese Pho	205
Walnut Turkey Meatball In Tomato Sauce	212
Warm Shrimp, Artichoke, And Parmesan Salad	191
Watercress Soup	54
Where'S-The-Beef Bean Burgers	104
Whipped Coconut Cream With Berries	286
White Bean And Artichoke Vegan Sandwich Filling	263
White Chili	53
Whole-Grain Rotini With Asparagus And Chicken	246

Winter Fruit And Spinach Salad	77
Waffled Falafel	292
Walnut Chicken	221
Wild Rice Salad With Blueberries And Herbs	66
Yellow Coconut Curry With Mango	269
Yogurt Lime Tartlets	91
Zesty Broccoli Salad	103
Zesty Vegetarian Chili	58
Zetsy Lime Turkey	211
Zucchini And Tomato Frittata	28
Zucchini Chips	287
Zucchini Ribbon Salad	73
Zesty Cauliflower Salad With Chicken Drumsticks	226
Aioli Fish Bake	181
Apple Cheesecake Snack Bars	294
Artichokes Alla Romana (Serves 8)	292
Asian Grilled Chicken Breasts	218
A-Taste-Of-Italy Baked Fish	172
Avocado Chips	287
Avocado Detox Smoothie	296
Egg Salad	62
Eggs Florentine With Yogurt Salsa	25
Extra-Crispy Fish With Lemon-Dill Dip	167
Easy Chicken Paprikash	221
Easy Salmon Or Tuna Patties	180
Easy Tuna Casserole	169
Easy Almond Butter Fat Bombs	287

Printed in Great Britain
by Amazon